Teaching for Diversity and Social Justice

For over 30 years, *Teaching for Diversity and Social Justice* has been the definitive sourcebook of theoretical foundations, pedagogical and design frameworks, and curricular models for social justice teaching practice. Thoroughly revised and updated, this fourth edition continues in the tradition of its predecessors to cover the most relevant issues and controversies in social justice education (SJE) in a practical, hands-on format. Filled with ready-to-apply activities and discussion questions, this book provides educators and facilitators with an accessible pedagogical approach to issues of oppression in classrooms and workshops. The revised edition also focuses on providing students and participants with the tools needed to apply their learning about these issues. This fourth edition includes new and revised material for each of the core chapters in the book complemented by fully developed online teaching designs, including over 150 downloadables, activities, and handouts on the book's companion website.

A classic for educators across disciplines and contexts, *Teaching for Diversity and Social Justice* presents a thoughtful, well-constructed, and inclusive foundation for engaging people in the complex and often daunting problems of discrimination and inequality in American society.

Maurianne Adams was Professor Emerita in the Social Justice in Education Program at the University of Massachusetts Amherst, U.S.

Lee Anne Bell is Professor Emerita at Barnard College, Columbia University, U.S.

Diane J. Goodman has been an educator and consultant on diversity, equity, inclusion, and social justice issues for over three decades.

Davey Shlasko is the founder and director of Think Again Training & Consulting and Adjunct Associate Professor at Smith College School for Social Work.

Rachel R. Briggs is Lecturer in the Department of Communication at University of Massachusetts Amherst, U.S., and is an independent social justice educator.

Romina Pacheco is Director of Diversity, Equity, Inclusion, and Belonging at The Windward School, U.S.

Teaching for Diversity and Social Justice

Fourth Edition

Edited by

Maurianne Adams, Lee Anne Bell,
Diane J. Goodman and Davey Shlasko
with Rachel R. Briggs and Romina Pacheco

Routledge
Taylor & Francis Group

NEW YORK AND LONDON

Cover image: Pavel_R / Getty Images

Fourth edition published 2023
by Routledge
605 Third Avenue, New York, NY 10158

and by Routledge
4 Park Square, Milton Park, Abingdon, Oxon, OX14 4RN

Routledge is an imprint of the Taylor & Francis Group, an informa business

First edition published by Routledge 1997

Third edition published by Routledge 2016

Library of Congress Cataloging-in-Publication Data
Names: Adams, Maurianne, editor. | Bell, Lee Anne, 1949– editor. |
    Goodman, Diane, editor. | Shlasko, Davey, editor.
Title: Teaching for diversity and social justice / Edited by Maurianne Adams,
    Lee Anne Bell, Diane J. Goodman and Davey Shlasko with Rachel Briggs
    and Romina Pacheco.
Description: Fourth edition. | New York, NY : Routledge, 2023. |
    Includes bibliographical references and index.
Identifiers: LCCN 2022010343 (print) | LCCN 2022010344 (ebook) |
    ISBN 9780367437831 (hardback) | ISBN 9780367431204 (paperback) |
    ISBN 9781003005759 (ebook)
Subjects: LCSH: Critical pedagogy—United States. | Social justice—Study
    and teaching—United States. | Multicultural education—United States. |
    Teachers—Training of—United States.
Classification: LCC LC196.5.U6 T43 2023 (print) | LCC LC196.5.U6 (ebook) |
    DDC 370.11/5—dc23
LC record available at https://lccn.loc.gov/2022010343
LC ebook record available at https://lccn.loc.gov/2022010344

ISBN: 978-0-367-43783-1 (hbk)
ISBN: 978-0-367-43120-4 (pbk)
ISBN: 978-1-003-00575-9 (ebk)

DOI: 10.4324/9781003005759

Typeset in Swiss 721 and Classical Garamond
by Apex CoVantage, LLC

Visit the Companion Website at: www.routledge.com/cw/adams

Dedication

In Memoriam
Maurianne Adams
May 30, 1938–October 6, 2020

Contents

Preface

Teaching for Diversity and Social Justice: Fourth Edition offers a unified framework for helping people understand and critically analyze multiple forms of oppression in the United States. Our approach to social justice education (SJE) includes both an *interdisciplinary conceptual framework* for analyzing multiple forms of oppression and *a set of interactive, experiential pedagogical principles* to help learners understand the meaning of social difference and oppression, both in social systems and in their personal lives. In an increasingly abrasive and polarized U.S. society, we believe that SJE can play a valuable role in helping people develop a more thoughtful understanding of diversity and group interaction, better prepare to critically evaluate inequitable social patterns and institutions, and find ways to work in coalition with diverse others to create more socially just and inclusive relationships, practices, and social structures.

As social justice educators, our goal is to engage people in becoming aware of and analyzing oppressive socio-political processes and reflecting on their own position(s) and responsibilities in relation to various forms of oppression. We want to help people consider the consequences of socialization into these inequitable systems and think proactively about alternative actions given this analysis.

We believe that traditional lecture-and-listen methods will not stimulate the active involvement necessary to reach social justice goals. In our courses and workshops, we draw upon participatory pedagogies for engaging participants with new and challenging information, and we are intentional about sequence, design, and facilitation so that participants reflect on their own experiences in ways that we hope foster new awareness, critique, self-assessment, and conscious choices about the actions they take in the world.

Our approach to social justice is necessarily collaborative. This collaborative approach is reflected in how we have written this book. Some chapters are co-authored, and some are single-authored, but all have been read by a number of us and reflect major areas of agreement in our approach to SJE. For these reasons, we use the terms "our" and "we" throughout the book to reflect the broad area of consensus among the community of social justice educators who have produced this volume. As SJE continues to gain currency and visibility, we hope that practitioners, researchers, and activists acknowledge and build upon each other's work in ways that can better prepare all of us to engage the problems we face as a society in committed, sustained, and radically creative ways.

STRUCTURE AND CHANGES IN THIS FOURTH EDITION

In the years that we have been working on the fourth edition, we have experienced the Trump presidency and its aftermath of right-wing extremism and assaults on democracy, as well as racial uprisings and the Black Lives Matter movement, and we are still living in a COVID-19 pandemic. Along with many others, we have struggled with how to analyze and write about profound social events as they are occurring and to do so through a pandemic that has created upheavals in our lives. We have also dealt with the death of our beloved friend, colleague, mentor, and social justice education pioneer, Maurianne Adams. Maurianne was a co-editor and contributor to the first edition of *Teaching for Diversity and Social Justice* and remained a co-editor and contributor through all subsequent editions (including this one).

We have learned a great deal since the publication of earlier editions of *Teaching for Diversity and Social Justice (TDSJ)* in 1997, 2007, and 2016 and would like to note here the most significant changes in the fourth edition. These changes come from suggestions from users of the book and other social justice educators.

- All chapters have been reconceptualized and updated, in particular the chapter on social justice education online
- We have a stronger focus on intersectionality within each of the ism chapters
- The website is more user friendly and searchable
- A ★ has been added in the margin of the text to indicate that there is corresponding material on the website

In Part 1: Theoretical Foundations and Principles of Practice, Chapters 1–3 lay out the theories, foundations, and frameworks upon which our approach to SJE is based, including the principles of pedagogy and design and facilitation that shape our practice as social justice educators. Part 2: Teaching Diversity and Social Justice describes our approach to teaching five isms or clusters of isms (Chapters 4–11).

As in the previous edition, the detailed curriculum designs for each ism chapter (Chapters 4–11) are on the companion website for the book. Instructors and facilitators often need rapid access to downloadable designs, activities, and handouts. The website materials flesh out the design presented in each chapter and support instructors and facilitators in teaching effectively about the particular issue the chapter describes. *We therefore strongly recommend that educators carefully read the chapter before using the website materials in classes and workshops.* Activities are now searchable by purpose of activity (e.g. icebreakers) as well as by topic (e.g. institutional racism). Each chapter also has a glossary of key terms and additional resources. We are uneasy about people using our designs and activities out of context and request that users not share website activities and handouts with people who have not purchased the text to read and understand the theoretical and conceptual frameworks, historical themes, and pedagogical principles that stand behind these materials.

A consequence of our decision to move curricular materials online was space for more in-depth information in each ism chapter. The information we now offer in these chapters makes it possible for instructors and facilitators to assign them as background reading for students and workshop participants. The new and revised material in each ism chapter includes:

- An explanation of our SJE approach and rationale
- Key terms and definitions
- Central issues and historical legacies for understanding the background of each ism
- Contemporary manifestations of the ism and its intersections with other isms and identities
- Examples of individual and collective action that can challenge the ism and foster greater social justice

In response to the lack of historical knowledge we find among many students and workshop participants, we have been more deliberate in this edition about the historical underpinnings in which contemporary oppression is rooted. History operates as a core construct for discerning how each ism is connected to actions in the past that endure in the present but have come to be taken as given. Understanding these historical legacies is essential for making sense of the maintenance and reproduction of oppression in contemporary life and provides inspiration and examples of resistance and activism that can encourage students and participants to consider ways to take action in the present.

We have asked the authors to foreground intersectionality. All the chapters provide examples where the focus ism intersects with other isms, both in the overall system of oppression and in the complex lives of individuals who hold multiple, intersecting identities. While we continue to find it pedagogically useful to foreground one ism at a time, as in previous editions, here we offer examples of intersections to illustrate the kaleidoscopic and simultaneous nature of multiple forms of oppression as they play out in the lives of individuals and institutions. Each curriculum design acknowledges ways in which different issues overlap and intersect in real-life experiences, policies, and practices. More than ever, seeing the intersections is necessary for understanding how location in systems of oppression affects people in similar and different ways. Understanding the intersections also helps focus interventions that challenge oppression in all its forms.

We recognize that U.S. manifestations of oppression are embedded in a globalized economy and its multiple transnational diasporas. It no longer makes sense, if it ever did, to think of U.S.-based issues as separate from their transnational roots or repercussions. The multinational, multiethnic, multicultural, and diasporic dimensions of the topics we teach and their ripple effects on how oppressions play out, and the diversity of the participants in our classes and workshops, make the systematic study of oppression ever more complex.

OVERVIEW OF THE BOOK

In Part 1: Theoretical Foundations and Principles of Practice, Chapter 1: Theoretical Foundations for Social Justice Education describes our theoretical framework for understanding oppression and our vision for social justice, based upon lessons for change drawn from social justice movements, organizational and community advocacy and change projects, and individuals who work for social justice in their daily lives. Chapter 2: Pedagogical Foundations for Social Justice Education grounds our pedagogy by summarizing the activist and academic roots of SJE pedagogy and suggests pedagogical elements to guide classroom or workshop teaching and learning. Chapter 3: Design and Facilitation describes the principles of design and facilitation and the specific facilitation issues that arise in social justice teaching with practical strategies to address them.

In Part 2: Teaching Diversity and Social Justice, Chapter 4: Core Concepts for Teaching Social Justice Education serves as a bridge between the first three foundational chapters and the following ism chapters that apply the theory and principles to specific isms. This bridging chapter focuses upon the core concepts that need to be in all SJE practice and illustrates ways of "getting started" through a curriculum design for teaching foundational core concepts and processes. This curriculum can be used as a stand-alone introduction to core concepts of SJE or to introduce the SJE approach to one or more specific isms. We strongly encourage users to draw upon Chapter 4 and incorporate these core concepts and elements into their own teaching as they adapt the specific ism designs that follow

Chapter 5: Racism, White Supremacy, and Finding Justice for All examines the ways that racism operates differently for different communities of color, including immigrants who are incorporated into the U.S. racial structure when they arrive. This chapter also analyzes the cumulative impact of white advantage and the corresponding cumulative disadvantage for People of Color that compounds racism over time, illustrated with examples from the major interlocking institutions in our society. The chapter identifies examples of institutional and community work for racial justice.

Chapter 6: Sexism, Heterosexism, and Trans* Oppression takes an integrative approach that analyzes these three forms of oppression within a single analytic framework. It challenges binary understandings of sex, gender, and sexuality and looks at these interrelated identity concepts in relationship to sexism, heterosexism, and transgender oppression. To supplement the integrated design, the chapter website offers updated designs and activities for teaching each of these issues separately.

Chapter 7: Classism includes an analysis of the historical legacies and contemporary manifestations of class and classism. It focuses on the historical background for classism, the intersections of classism with other forms of oppression, and the reproduction of advantages and disadvantages that accumulate from the intersections of class with race, gender, age, and other forms of oppression.

Chapter 8: Religious Oppression uses the lens of Christian hegemony to explore the long history of Christian advantage and the equally long history of disadvantages for different minority religious groups in the U.S. It provides an analysis of historical U.S. and global conflicts in which religion intersects with class and other forms of oppression, and it proposes new emphases in the U.S. on religious pluralism as a route to religious justice.

Chapter 9: Ableism and Disability Justice describes the historical legacies as well as the current manifestations of the construction of a broad continuum of disabilities, including cognitive, physical, and psychological disabilities, and disabling chronic illness. The chapter explores assumptions about what constitutes a "normal" body and mind, how the physical and social environments construct disability, and how ableism is embedded in U.S. language, institutional policies, architecture, and the overall culture.

Chapter 10: Youth and Elder Oppression looks at the way both youth and elders are oppressed in a society that holds very narrow ideas about human capacity defined by age. The SJE approach to the oppression of youth and elders draws upon theories of colonialism as a way of understanding modern formulations of childhood. The challenges posed by this approach to youth and elder oppression are addressed by detailed facilitation notes.

Chapter 11: Social Justice Education Online considers the challenges and possibilities for adapting a social justice design for an online environment. The chapter highlights general design and pedagogical issues for online courses that reflect our social justice content and processes. The chapter provides a list of asynchronous and synchronous activities for online SJE. By focusing on the rationale for the pedagogical choices in each of these activities, readers will understand a process-based approach that can be applied to their own context with the tools and resources available to them.

Chapter 12: Critical Self-Knowledge for Social Justice Educators concludes the book with a discussion of what instructors and facilitators need to know about themselves in order to teach about social justice issues and interact thoughtfully, sensitively, and effectively with students and participants. It explores the importance of self-reflection and self-awareness and the ongoing process of exploration and growth that are critical to sustaining a commitment to SJE.

TERMINOLOGY

Ism is a shorthand term we use to refer to manifestations of oppression that are described in Chapters 4–11 of this volume. As in previous editions, we highlight the ways in which historical and contemporary hierarchies of advantage and disadvantage not only divide and rank social identity groups but also name them in ways that convey privileged and sub-ordinated social identities and social positions. We consider these socio-politically potent either/or categorizing processes for entire groups of peoples to be a major hallmark of oppression. At the same time, we recognize that people engage in a continuous struggle to challenge, redefine, and invent anew more meaningful ways to name and describe their lived experiences in the world—and often do so by claiming identities and terminology that stand in opposition to categorizing boxes and dualisms. The binary of dominant and subor-dinated categories cannot contain the much richer and messier terrain of lived experience that is always in tension with the constraints of oppression and the experience of simultane-ous privilege and disadvantage in the multiple identities people hold. We recognize that it is problematic to use any single set of terms to convey the complexity of human beings whose identities are derived in part from multiple social identity groups, within the phenomenon of oppression and also within the context of their cultural communities. We no longer use the terms "oppressor" and "oppressed," for example, to refer to specific advantaged or disadvantaged identity groups because these terms too often arouse objections as being too broad from participants who cannot reconcile themselves as oppressors when they feel personally quite powerless or who resist being defined as oppressed as a denial of agency.

On the other hand, we struggle to find language that doesn't trivialize the power and harm of the oppressive systems we want to expose. After wrestling with various terms, we have decided to primarily use the following: "advantaged," "privileged," and "dominant" to describe groups with greater access to social power and "disadvantaged," "marginal-ized," and "subordinated" for groups who are blocked from access to social power. We think these terms, while far from perfect, focus on the structured roles and outcomes of an oppressive system, and we hope to create an invitational rather than confrontational approach that highlights the function of unequal roles in a system rather than attributes of individual people.

As noted prior, resistance to being categorized plays out in opposition to the binaries of oppression and in new ways of naming social identity groups. In the years between edi-tions, we have witnessed the ways that language is in flux, evolving as terms are redefined by communities seeking justice. Thus, keeping up with and respecting the language that groups use to self-name is an important aspect of social justice. How to name groups is always changing, contested, and imperfect.

Generally, in the context of the United States, we refer to the original inhabitants of North America as Indigenous and Native American, though American Indian is a legally recognized term. In other countries and contexts, people may prefer other terms such as First Nation Peoples, Aboriginal, or Inuit. Whenever possible people should be identified by specific nations, peoples, or tribal designations such as Cherokee, Kiowa, or Lakota (Horse, 2012).

We use BIPOC (Black, Indigenous, and People of Color) or POC (People of Color) to refer collectively to peoples who have been racially oppressed in the U.S. BIPOC is a more recent term coined by Black people used to highlight the different histories and experiences of Black (African American) and Indigenous peoples and their oppressions as foundational to the racial infrastructure in the U.S. (BIPOC project; Plaid, 2021). We recognize that some people find the term confusing and are concerned that it obscures the experiences of other People of Color (Latinx people and Asian Americans) and impedes solidarity (Plaid, 2021). As with other groups, it is always preferable to refer to the specific racial/ethnic identities.

We follow an emerging consensus by capitalizing and not hyphenating specific eth-nicities that are derived from geographical areas (African American, American Indian or

Native American, Asian American). We choose to capitalize Black but do not capitalize white because Black represents a shared culture and history in a way that white does not (Coleman, 2020). Latinx is a relatively recent term used to refer to people from Latin America and intended to make Latino/a inclusive of men, women, transgender, nonbinary, and gender-fluid people. Some Latino/a/x people prefer Latine since it is more consistent with the Spanish language (Cuervo, 2016).

We use LGBTQ+ to refer to people who are lesbian, gay, bisexual, trans*, and queer and the myriad other ways people name their gender and sexuality beyond the normative categories (i.e. cisgender and heterosexual). We encourage the use of inclusive gender language, such as "everyone" rather than "men and women" and "they" as a gender-neutral singular pronoun for generic persons and for people who ask to be referred to as "they/them." We also recommend that facilitators invite participants to share their gender pronouns (Shlasko, 2017). The ism chapters include this in their workshop/class introductions. It is important in creating a respectful and inclusive environment to call people by the names and pronouns they would like.

Our guiding principle is to adopt language preferred by people from oppressed groups to name themselves. We also note the reclaiming by marginalized communities of previously negative terms such as "queer," "crip," or the noun "Jew" (as distinct from the adjective "Jewish"). We know that naming is a necessarily fluid and sometimes contradictory and confusing process as people/groups insist on defining themselves rather than acquiescing to names imposed by others; we also know that members of marginalized groups may reclaim negative terms among themselves but hear those terms from outsiders as offensive and inappropriate.

Not all of our contributors agree on uniform terminology, and readers will notice the use of different terms in various chapters. Authors of each curriculum design address other considerations of language usage in their respective chapters. Social justice educators need to remain sensitive and alert to changes in language, terminology preferred by specific communities, and outsider/insider language. We encourage readers to recognize that such terms will continue to evolve and change and to appreciate the significance of the power to name oneself as an important aspect of group identity and resistance.

OTHER CONSIDERATIONS

We continue to be disappointed by the citation practices of libraries, reviewers, booksellers, and scholars who fully name the first author only, as in "Adams et al. (2007)." This practice does not acknowledge and may even discourage collaborative work, since academic rewards and professional visibility tend to accrue to first authors, often presumed senior or primary. We have struggled with the question of how to represent the participation of all members of a collaborative team such that both academic rewards and professional visibility are credited equally to all whose ideas, creativity, and writing contribute to the final product.

Any line of names, however arranged, suggests a ranking order. We regret that we have found no successful alternative to the convention of alphabetical order in listing editors and contributors. However, we place a statement at the beginning of each chapter honoring the nature and value of our collaborative work with a request that people who cite us include the names of all authors. We have, in all cases, acknowledged in full citations all the co-authors of the published work we reference in this book. We consider "et al." an insult to co-authorship.

We have received feedback from hundreds of people throughout this country and internationally who use and find *TDSJ* a valuable resource. We are gratified to know that our book has been used successfully in many different settings—academic departments, student affairs, adult formal and non-formal education, workplace diversity and staff development programs, diversity curricula for general education, upper-level high school courses, faith organizations, grassroots organizing, and activist organizations.

Given the challenges to social justice in the world today and the difficulties overcome by dynamically evolving social justice movements around the world, we expect that the theory, language, and practice of SJE will continue to evolve as it has since earlier editions of *TDSJ*. We hope we have articulated some of these new developments in the current edition and that our curriculum will inspire new generations of educators and activists in the cause of social justice. We look forward to a continuing dialogue with those who use this book and to the inspiration they give to our ongoing work for social justice.

References

Coleman, N. (2020, June 5). *Why we're capitalizing Black*. Retrieved from https://www.nytimes.com/2020/07/05/insider/capitalized-black.html

Cuervo, A. (2016). Latinx: A Brief Guidebook. Retrieved from https://www.eachmindmatters.org/wp-content/uploads/2017/11/Latinx_A_Brief_Guidebook.pdf10

Horse, P. G. (2012). Twenty-first century Native American consciousness: A thematic model of Indian identity. In C. L. Wijeyesinghe & B. W. Jackson (Eds.), *New perspectives on racial identity development: Integrating emerging frameworks* (2nd ed., pp. 108–120). New York: New York University Press.

Plaid, M. D. (2021, April 9). *Newsweek*. Retrieved from https://www.newsweek.com/bipoc-isnt-doing-what-you-think-its-doing-opinion-1582494

Shlasko, D., Crath, R., Ao, J., Cochran, N., & Thorn, R. (2017). *Pronoun introductions in class*. Retrieved from https://ssw.smith.edu/student-life/resources-and-support-students/trans-gender-non conforming-resources/pronoun

Acknowledgements

This book reflects collaboration among several generations of faculty and graduate students in the Social Justice Education program at the University of Massachusetts Amherst, and the various editions reflect changes in the landscape of diversity and social justice that we have presented in classes, workshops, conferences, activism, and everyday life. The development of the theory and practice described in this volume has truly been a collaborative, multigenerational, and ongoing endeavor.

Many of the new features in this fourth edition were suggested by anonymous users of earlier editions who took the time to fill out detailed questionnaires about how they use the book in their classes and their suggestions for changes. Their input has helped make this a better edition. Each of the new editions of this book rests on the shoulders of those who went before.

This volume benefits from the thoughtful designs offered in earlier editions that provided a foundation for new directions developed by new teams of authors in the current edition. In particular, we want to thank Bailey Jackson and Rita Hardiman for their vision of SJE expressed in earlier editions. Their work continues to inspire and prepare social justice educators.

The ideas and designs in this book were developed through a collaborative process that included many people over several years, most of whom were connected to the early work that resulted in the creation, under the leadership of Bailey W. Jackson, of the Social Justice Education Program at UMASS/Amherst. For their contribution to earlier editions we want to recognize Steven Botkin, Katja Hahn D'Errico, Andrea D. Dominique, Pat Griffin, Rita Hardiman, Bobbi Harro, Bailey W. Jackson, JoAnne Jones, Khyati Y. Joshi, Tanya Kachwaha, Betsy Leondar-Wright, Linda S. Marchesani, Linda McCarthy, Mary McClintock, Donna Mellen, Benjamin J. Ostiguy, Madeline L. Peters, Kathleen J. Phillips, Laura Rauscher, Rosemarie A. Roberts, Tom Schiff, Steve Shapiro, Robin M. Smith, Beverly Daniel Tatum, Sharon Washington, Gerald Weinstein, Charmaine L. Wijeyesinghe and Felice Yeskel.

We continue to learn and be inspired by graduate students in the Social Justice Education program at the University of Massachusetts Amherst School of Education who teach the courses and workshops described here and SJE graduates who are co-authors in this edition. Their creativity, resourcefulness, and passion for teaching contributed greatly to this book and sustained us in our ongoing learning about forms of oppression and approaches to SJE. Many of our colleagues and students took time, under tight deadlines, to provide thoughtful feedback to early drafts of these chapters. Some of them provided new material for chapter websites, and we name them in those specific acknowledgements. We want to thank our authors in this new edition for rising to the challenge of incorporating substantial new material into the chapters and preparing detailed activities, handouts, and resources for the website. In most cases, we have read, reviewed, and helped revise each other's work. It takes a village—a generous community of activists, educators, and scholars.

We are fortunate to work with an amazing editor in Matthew Freiberg, who has supported us in re-envisioning this new edition and creating the companion website and for Jessica Cooke for stepping up to assist us through the editorial process. We also thank Merrill Jacobs for helping us design a website that is user-friendly and easy to navigate and Marie Louise Roberts for expert copyediting. It is a rare and great gift to have such thorough, supportive, and attentive editors.

Finally, the experience of collaborating as an editorial and writing team has been a stimulating and rewarding experience. Our energizing conversations about the work before us have challenged and stretched our understanding of SJE as we worked on this edition. We have also been excited to work with new authors, some of whom were once our students and are now our colleagues. It is a joy and a fulfillment to see the work of social justice educators grow, stretch, and influence.

Each of us has critical people in our lives and at our home institutions without whose support (personal, professional, financial) the time and commitment we put into this book would not have been possible. It would overwhelm our readers to try to list them here. They know who they are, and they have our heartfelt appreciation.

PART I

THEORETICAL FOUNDATIONS AND PRINCIPLES OF PRACTICE

1

Theoretical Foundations for Social Justice Education

Lee Anne Bell

WHAT IS SOCIAL JUSTICE?

Social justice is both a goal and a process. The *goal* of social justice is full and equitable participation of people from all social identity groups in a society that is mutually shaped to meet their needs. The *process* for attaining the goal of social justice should also be democratic and participatory, respectful of human diversity and group differences, and inclusive and affirming of human agency and capacity for working collaboratively with others to create change for our collective well-being. Domination cannot be ended through coercive tactics that recreate domination in new forms. Thus, a "power with" vs. "power over" (Kreisberg, 1992) paradigm is necessary for enacting social justice goals. Forming coalitions and working collaboratively with diverse others is an essential part of social justice.

Our *vision* for social justice is a world in which the distribution of resources is equitable and ecologically sustainable and all members are physically and psychologically safe and secure, recognized, and treated with respect. We envision a world in which individuals have equitable access to resources, opportunities, and social power and are both able to develop their full capacities and capable of interacting democratically with others. Social justice involves social actors who have a sense of their own agency as well as a sense of social responsibility toward and with others, their society, the environment, and the broader world in which we live. These are conditions we not only wish for ourselves but for all people in our interdependent global community.

WHAT IS JUSTICE?

Philosophers and others have long debated the question: What constitutes justice? Our definition of social justice draws on theories that describe justice as a fair and equitable *distribution of resources* (Rawls, 1999) with the imperative to address those who are least advantaged (Rawls, 2001). We also draw on theories that affirm the importance of fair and equitable *social processes* (Young, 2011), including recognition and respect for marginalized or subjugated cultures and groups (Young, 1990). We see these two aspects as intertwining, acknowledging that social justice must address *both* resources and recognition. Resources include fair distribution of social, political, and symbolic, as well as economic, assets. Recognition and respect for all individuals and groups requires full inclusion and participation in decision-making and the power to shape the institutions, policies, and processes that affect their lives.

Diversity and *social justice* are distinct though interconnected terms. *Diversity* refers to differences among social groups such as ethnic heritage, class, age, gender, sexuality, ability, religion, and nationality. These differences are reflected in historical experiences, language, cultural practices, and traditions that should be affirmed and respected. Concrete and genuine knowledge of different groups and their histories, experiences, ways of making meaning, and values is important to the social justice goal of recognition and respect.

DOI: 10.4324/9781003005759-2

Social justice refers to constructing society in accordance with principles of equity, recognition, and inclusion. It involves eliminating the *oppression* created when differences are sorted and ranked in a hierarchy that unequally confers power, social and economic advantages, and institutional and cultural validity to social groups based on their location in that hierarchy (Adams, 2014; Johnson, 2005). Social justice requires confronting the ideological frameworks, historical legacies, and institutional patterns and practices that structure social relations unequally so that some groups are advantaged at the expense of other groups that are marginalized. This requires attention to how different forms of oppression intersect both structurally and in the lives of individuals who are situated within distinctive matrices of oppression.

We underscore Audre Lorde's assertion that there is no hierarchy of oppression (1983) and further believe that to eradicate one form of oppression ultimately means elimination of all its forms. We further highlight the value of intersectionality for shedding light on how single axis thinking can undermine efforts for social justice (Cho, Crenshaw, & McCall, 2013). In our view, diversity and social justice are inextricably bound together. Without truly valuing diversity in all its variety, we cannot effectively address issues of injustice. Without addressing intersecting issues of injustice in all its forms, we cannot truly value diversity.

WHAT IS SOCIAL JUSTICE EDUCATION?

The approach to social justice education presented in this book includes both an *interdisciplinary conceptual framework* for analyzing multiple forms of oppression and their intersections, as well as *a set of interactive, experiential pedagogical principles and practices*. We use the term *oppression* to connote the pervasive nature of social inequality that is woven throughout social institutions as well as embedded within individual consciousness. The conceptual framework and pedagogical approach to social justice education provide tools for examining how oppression operates in the social system and its institutions, as well as in the personal lives of individuals from diverse communities.

The goal of social justice education is to enable individuals and groups to develop the critical analytical tools necessary to understand the structural features of oppression and their own socialization within oppressive systems as well as the skills to effect democratic change. Social justice education aims to help participants develop awareness, knowledge, and processes to examine issues of justice/injustice in their personal lives, communities, institutions, and the broader society. It also aims to connect analysis to action—to help participants develop a sense of agency and commitment, as well as skills and tools, for working with others to interrupt and change oppressive patterns and behaviors in themselves and in the institutions and communities of which they are a part.

Working for social justice in a society and world steeped in oppression is no simple feat. For this reason, we need clarity in how we define and analyze forms of oppression in order to discern how they overlap and operate at individual, institutional, cultural, and structural levels, historically and in the present. We hope the theoretical framework presented here— the pedagogical processes presented in Chapter 2; the facilitation and design information in Chapter 3; teaching core concepts and introductory design presented in Chapter 4; the historical information, concepts, and manifestations explored in Chapters 5–11; and the need for self-knowledge as social justice educators in Chapter 12—will help readers make sense of the many forms oppression takes, how to teach and learn about various isms,[1] and ways to act more effectively against oppressive circumstances as these arise in different contexts.

WHY THEORY?

Articulating the theoretical sources of our approach to social justice education serves several important purposes. First, theory enables social justice educators to think clearly about our intentions and the means we use to actualize them in educational settings. It provides a framework for making choices about what we do and how and for distinguishing among different approaches. For example, our embrace of Freirean theory informs our focus on helping people understand links between their own experience and the world (reading the word and the world). Our understanding of socialization and learning processes guides our recognition that information alone is not sufficient and that experiential pedagogy can engage learners in active exploration of how oppression works in their own lives as well as in social systems of which they are a part.

Second, at its best, the interaction of theory and practice (praxis) provides a framework for questioning and challenging what we do and why so that we remain open to new approaches as we encounter co-optation, resistance, insufficient knowledge, and changing social conditions. Ideally, we will keep coming back to and refining our praxis as we learn from our experiences and engagement with others, emerging knowledge about various forms of oppression, and participation in social justice movements. Thoughtful reflection can help us stay attuned to the myriad ways oppression can either seduce our participation in its support or inspire us to further learning and activism to challenge it.

Finally, theory has the potential to help us stay conscious of our position as historically, geographically situated subjects—able to learn from the past as we try to meet current conditions, in the specific contexts in which we live, in more effective and imaginative ways. As we become more aware of our interconnected world, we see more clearly how issues of oppression we confront in the U.S. are linked to both our own geographical and historical context and to conditions of others around the world, as the spread of the #MeToo, Indigenous rights, environmental justice, LGBTQ+ (lesbian, gay, bisexual, transgender, queer), and Black Lives Matter movements so clearly illustrate.

UNDERSTANDING OPPRESSION AS INTERSECTIONAL

Oppression is the term we use to describe the interlocking forces that create and sustain injustice. In this book, we focus on how oppression is manifested through racism, classism, sexism, heterosexism, transgender oppression, religious oppression, ableism, and youth and elder oppression, as well as through the overlapping systems and institutions that render these forms of injustice interdependent and mutually reinforcing. *Intersectionality* is a term that describes how the features of oppression connect at both the structural/systemic and individual/interpersonal levels and across the various manifestations described in this book. Each form of oppression or ism has historical/social legacies and current manifestations that distinguish it from other forms of oppression or isms. We believe that learning about the legacies and historical trajectories of different isms enables us to develop a deeper understanding of the particular ism under examination. Chapters 5–10 provide such a focus. At the same time, we recognize that forms of oppression co-constitute as interlocking systems that overlap and reinforce each other (Combahee River Collective Statement, 2015; Crenshaw, 2003; Hill-Collins, 2000; Nash, 2019). Thus, Chapters 5–10 also illustrate how the specific ism that is the chapter's focus intersects with isms highlighted in other chapters.

Focusing on a specific form of oppression provides valuable information for understanding its particular historical trajectory and contemporary manifestations as well as actions to challenge it. For example, an in-depth look at racism in U.S. history reveals how a system of racial categorization and hierarchy developed as the rationale for dispossession and enslavement. This system was used to incorporate and sort other groups such as immigrants from Europe, who were racialized and ranked as white/non-white. That such categories are created for the purpose of maintaining dominance is evidenced by the shifting racialization of southern Europeans into the white group as numbers of immigrants from other parts of the world increased.

Zooming out to focus on the broader pattern of interlocking systems yields important knowledge about general features of oppression that cut across different manifestations to discern how they mutually reinforce each other. For example, systems of racism and ableism are mutually reinforcing systems that employed a process of dehumanization that justified institutionalization in prisons or mental hospitals as well as cruel medical experiments. If we take an intersectional perspective, we can trace how these origins continue to shape the way racially minoritized students and students with disabilities are similarly sorted and disciplined in classrooms and schools today. Examining the intersections of racism with homophobia and cisnormativity shows the different ways racism, homophobia, and transphobia shape institutions such as prisons and the differential impacts on People of Color with diverse sexual and gender identities in those institutions.

Attending to the intersections where different forms of oppression meet in the lives of particular individuals shows the important ways that social location mediates experiences of oppression. For example, a focus on Black women that looks only at the impact of racism ignores their experiences as women, while focusing only on sexism obscures their experiences as Black persons. Furthermore, these are not simply additive (race + gender) but depend on multiple other locations (class, age, physical ability, immigration status, etc.) that mutually shape how oppression operates across systems to impact their lives (Crenshaw, 1991; Hill-Collins, 2019).

An intersectional approach provides vital information for understanding how particular problems affect different populations so as to tailor interventions to be most effective. For example, intersectional analysis of an issue such as gender violence reveals the distinctive problems and obstacles experienced by differently situated women (poor, disabled, elderly, lesbian, bisexual, transgender, multiply marginalized) who experience gender violence. Their different locations in the system of sexism intersect with other isms to shape their particular experiences, and recognizing these specificities can help tailor interventions to most effectively address their situation (Cho, 2013). For example, while shelters for victims of gender violence provide effective support for many cisgender women, the intersecting impacts of racism, classism, and transphobia often mean trans* women, particularly trans* women of color, are forced onto the streets to face the added vulnerability to violence that accompanies homelessness (Bridges, 2019).

Social location also mediates privilege/structural advantage, both at the systemic level and in the lives of individuals. Systemic racism interacts with sexism, classism, and other isms in ways that mutually reinforce the advantages of dominant groups. For example, attending to how white individuals are situated within intersecting isms can reveal the differential ways the advantages of whiteness are experienced that looking at race alone may ignore. A white man who has the added systemic advantages of being upper middle class, non-disabled, middle aged, and/or Christian will experience white advantage differently than a white woman who is poor, disabled, lesbian, and/or elderly. Both still reap advantages of whiteness, but for the former, these advantages are amplified many times over by class, gender, and other advantages.

Attention to overlapping systems of oppression can also reveal the differential impacts of oppression across communities and generations. While the COVID pandemic created risks for everyone, not everyone faced the same level of risk. The pandemic intensified the unequal impacts of the virus for communities already marginalized by long-standing patterns of injustice in terms of housing, food, education, employment, and protection from violence. People already living in crowded housing could not maintain social distance in the same way as other families could. Those who could not work from home or were essential workers (disproportionately working-class people and Black and Latinx[2] workers) were more likely to be exposed to the virus, as were elderly people in nursing homes. Those with access to the internet and technology (more likely to be middle and upper class and white) were able to deal with closed schools and online education more easily than others and were more likely to have space for work and schooling at home (or the ability to escape to a country home) and the financial resources to weather loss of income during that period.

From our perspective, no single form of oppression is the base for all others; all are connected in a system that makes them possible. In our approach, we argue for the explanatory and political value of identifying the particular histories, geographies, and characteristics of specific forms of oppression, without ignoring the intersections across isms at the systemic level and in the lives of individuals and groups. Focusing on one facet of a prism does not remove it from its broader context but provides a way to highlight and focus in order to ground deeper learning and more thoughtful, targeted action.

DYNAMICS OF OPPRESSION

Oppression is often defined through such terms as *domination, coercion, cruelty, tyranny, subjugation, persecution, harassment,* and *repression.* These terms describe important overt features of oppression but do not capture the more subtle and covert aspects of how oppression is normalized in everyday life. Also often missing are terms that describe the other side of the coin: how some groups benefit from the domination and repression of other groups and the advantages and privileges gained, as well as the costs of systems of domination that ultimately cost the entire society.

In the following we define and discuss both overt and subtle features that characterize oppression. These features are illustrated with examples that show how they interlock with one another to sustain an overall system that produces inequalities across race, class, gender, sexuality, nationality, ethnicity, ability, and age. While presented as separate aspects, qualities, or characteristics, they in fact interconnect and mutually reinforce one another in ways that are not as simple to tease apart as a list of discrete terms or qualities might suggest. Rather, they should be understood as constituent parts of a dynamic process. In order to work against oppression effectively, we need to discern how these features weave together to shape our experiences with and perspectives on our social world.

HIERARCHICAL

One dynamic feature of oppression is the division of humanity into categories that are positioned in unequal, hierarchical relationships to one another, locking in advantage to some groups at the expense of others. In the United States (as well as other parts of the world), humans are sorted and ranked by race, class, gender, sexuality, age, religion, ability, and other social markers that regulate access to resources, participation, social respect,

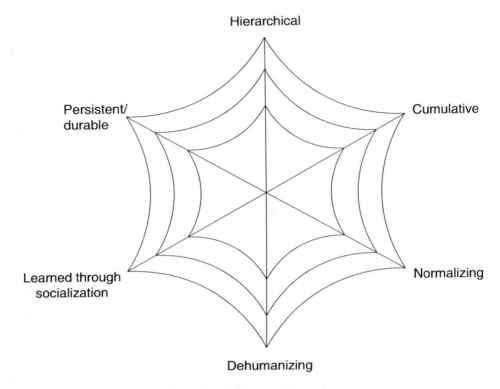

Figure 1.1 Dynamics of Oppression

and self-actualization. Like a computer operating system, categorization and hierarchy run invisibly in the background to make oppressive outcomes seem logical and inevitable.

The process of categorization and ranking of social groups is shaped by history, geography, patterns of immigration, and economic-political factors. For example, the construction of distinct racial groups was initially produced to justify the dispossession of land from the Indigenous people of the Americas and the exploitation of coerced labor from enslaved Africans brought here against their will at the founding of this nation. Immigrants from Europe and Asia were later incorporated into a racial hierarchy that positioned "white" people above all other racialized groups. Irish, Italian, and Jewish immigrants who at first were not considered white were gradually incorporated into that category. The meaning-making system of race gained force and power through its reproduction across historical eras and through institutionalized practices in law, housing, employment, schooling, government policy, and social interaction that reinforced racial hierarchy. Today, the idea of race is so taken for granted that it is difficult to see the apparatus that created it in the first place (Leonardo, 2013).

Hierarchy confers advantages, status, resources, access, and privilege to individuals/ groups positioned as *dominant* or *advantaged* in relation to individuals/groups that are positioned as *marginalized* or *disadvantaged*. It is then reproduced through ideology (beliefs about different groups of people) and structures (laws and policies) that enact the oppression. Dominant groups hold the power and authority to control the important institutions in society, determine how resources are allocated, and define what is deemed natural, good, and true. Through *cultural imperialism* dominant groups are represented as superior, more capable, and more credible—as "normal"—compared to those who are differently situated. One of the privileges of dominant group status is the luxury to see oneself as a unique individual, as simply human. A white, able-bodied, heterosexual, cis-gender man, for example, is rarely defined by those markers. If he does well at his job, he is acknowledged as a highly qualified individual. If he does poorly, the blame is attributed to him alone. That individuals in dominant groups are socialized to accept their group's socially advantaged status as normal and deserved protects them from recognizing how it has been conferred and maintained through systems of inequality.

Those at lower rungs in the hierarchy are represented as less than, inferior, and/or devi-ant. For them, social group membership trumps individuality. They are seen not merely as individuals but also defined by their social group memberships and the ascriptions the dominant society applies to their group (Cudd, 2006; Young, 1990). A Puerto Rican woman, for example, may wish to be viewed as an individual and acknowledged for her personal talents and abilities. Yet she can never fully escape the dominant society's assump-tions about her racial/ethnic group, language, and gender. If she excels in her work, she may be seen as atypical or exceptional. If she does poorly, she may be seen as representative of the limitations of her group. In either case, she rises or falls not solely on the basis of her individual qualities but always partly as a member of the social group(s) with which she is identified. Ideological beliefs about superiority and inferiority rationalize institutional arrangements that benefit the dominant group, though these are usually unspoken and often unconscious. In this way, belief systems and institutional structures become mutually reinforcing.

Whether or not individuals in a particular social group define themselves in the same way, they must deal with the stereotypes and assumptions attributed to their group. A per-son's self-defined group identity may be central, as religious identity is to a traditionally observant Jew or Muslim. Or it may be mainly background, only becoming salient in cer-tain interactional contexts, as Jewish identity may become for an assimilated Jew when confronted with antisemitism or as a Muslim identity may become for an Arab or Indian targeted by anti-Muslim prejudice (Malik, 2010). Regardless, they must struggle for indi-vidual self-definition within the burden of oppressive attributions, assumptions, and prac-tices toward their group(s). Status is always defined by the dominant group, regardless of differences among those who are so categorized. For example, the group labeled Hispanic in the United States is extremely diverse, composed of people from many different coun-tries of origin who speak various languages; are from different racial, ethnic, and socio-economic groups; and have arrived in the country under widely different conditions of immigration, colonization, or slavery over different time periods (Anzaldúa, 1987; Obdler, 1995). They may be undocumented or birthright citizens, cisgender men and women or transgender, religious or agnostic, extremely wealthy or extremely poor. In the U.S. Census, the category Hispanic includes a Spanish-speaking, upper-class white man from Cuba as well as a dark-skinned, Ki'tche'-speaking, Indigenous woman from Guatemala. The domi-nant society lumps them together in a group labeled Hispanic to which certain attributions, assumptions, and stereotypes are applied. Yet their experiences are so divergent as to have little in common at all but for the common group experience of cultural, ethnic, and lin-guistic oppression based on their categorization and location in a U.S. hierarchy. A similar process occurs for the heterogeneous group labeled Asian American that may include peo-ple who emigrate under widely divergent conditions and from many different countries, native languages, and social classes yet are lumped together under the label Asian American.

CUMULATIVE

The effects of oppression are pervasive and cumulative across time and institutions. Ideas, patterns, structures, and practices—in history, law, economic policy, social custom, and education—aggregate to rationalize and institutionalize injustice and inequality. This process creates cumulative advantage for some and cumulative disadvantage for others. The more embedded the accumulation of patterns and practices becomes, the more difficult it is to see how they were constructed in the first place; they come to be taken for granted as inevitable and unchangeable.

Critical historical analysis can reveal the relationships between particular actions, practices, policies, and laws from the past and their cumulative outcomes in the present. For example, the current situation of extreme poverty and isolation of many Indigenous communities in the U.S. can be traced to the long legacy of historical, legal, economic, and educational policies that stripped them of land, rights, cultures, religious practices, and languages (Dunbar-Ortiz, 2014). Forced relocation, conversion, mass extermination, boarding schools aimed at "removing the Indian" from the child (Fear-Segal & Rose, 2016). This history and the cumulative impact over time continues in the present, as well as across institutions and social systems. Stereotypes and misinformation purveyed through movies, textbooks, and popular culture sanitize and rationalize this history. Mainstream television, media, children's books, cartoons, and popular culture socialize others to view Indigenous people as quaint artifacts of the past who have vanished or as mascots for sports teams and wealthy casino owners (Hoffman, 2012). All these conditions combine to describe the pervasive and cumulative impact of the oppression Indigenous people face in the present as a result of a long history with racism, colonialism, religious oppression, and economic imperialism.

In the same vein, the economic, political, cultural, and social dominance of whites ties back to a long legacy of laws, policies, and practices that created cumulative advantage for whites as a group, over time and across institutions. White settlers were advantaged by receiving land taken from Indigenous people, reaping the profit of unpaid labor provided by enslaved Africans, and holding all the positions of power in the government that formed our economy and politics (Dunbar-Ortiz, 2014). Later government housing policy provided loans denied to other groups that enabled white veterans returning from war to afford houses and build equity through home ownership. This equity, in turn, enabled them to build nest eggs, afford college for their children, and support their advancement in life (Hannah-Jones, 2021; Rothstein, 2017). The compounding benefits and wealth generated over time are rendered invisible so that most white people today are unaware of their share in the cumulative benefits reaped from historical processes of dispossession and discrimination.

If one lives in a poor neighborhood in the U.S. today, they will likely go to less resourced schools; have less access to transportation, good food, and health care; have less access to opportunities for advancement; and be exposed to more environmental toxins. These disadvantages are entrenched through the historical/cumulative impacts of racism and other forms of oppression on living conditions and access to resources and opportunity (Chetty, Hendren, Kline, Saez, & Turner, 2014; Song, Massey, Rolf, Ferrie, Rothbaum & Xie, 2020). In corollary fashion, if one lives in a middle-class or upper-middle-class neighborhood, they are likely to have access to well-resourced schools; good transportation, food, and health care; a cleaner environment; and opportunities for advancement. Accumulated advantage and disadvantage consolidate in institutional policies and practices, thus entrenching privilege and disadvantage (Reeves, 2017).

Learning the history of how different groups have been treated over time is important to the work of recognizing and dismantling oppression today. Thus, each ism chapter in this book discusses historical context as key to understanding the pervasive and cumulative ways the ism has evolved and intersected with the trajectories of other isms to advantage some groups and disadvantage others.

NORMALIZING

The reproduction of oppressive dynamics comes to be assumed as natural, normal, business as usual, even by those who are disempowered. Gramsci (1971) used the term *hegemony* to explain how domination and control are maintained not only through coercion and violence but also through voluntary consent (Foucault, 1980). Power operates not only through persons or groups unilaterally imposing their will on others but through well-intentioned people acting, usually unconsciously, as agents of oppression by merely going about their daily lives. Structural injustice is thus produced and reproduced by "thousands or millions of persons usually acting within institutional rules and according to practices that most people regard as morally acceptable" (Young, 2011, p. 4). In such a system, responsibility for oppression often cannot be isolated to individual or institutional agents but is more indirect, collective, and cumulative. For example, U.S. society is structured so that millions of children go hungry each day while the rest of us consume far more than we need. Yet any consistent awareness of this fact is quickly erased by a normality organized to explain gross economic disparities as the unfortunate but inevitable result of a meritocracy where some groups simply don't work hard enough and thus deserve their fate.

Hegemony is maintained through discourse—ideas, texts, theories, language, and ideology—and networks of social and political control that Foucault (1980) called "regimes of truth." Regimes of truth legitimize what can be said, who has the authority to speak and be heard, and what is sanctioned as true (Kreisberg, 1992). For example, until women began speaking out about spousal abuse, a husband's authority to physically control his wife often went unchallenged, rendered invisible through the language of family privacy and presumptions of sexual consent in marriage. Indeed, the last state to repeal exemptions for marital rape was Delaware in 1999 (Bennice & Resick, 2003). Until the #MeToo movement, women who spoke up about sexual harassment and rape were often accused of exaggerating or misunderstanding male behavior.

The processes and effects of oppression are often woven so effectively into the social fabric that they are taken for granted, making it difficult to step outside the system to discern how oppression operates—like fish trying to understand the water in which they swim. The marginalization and exclusion of people with physical disabilities, for example, does not require overt discrimination against them (although this also happens). Business as usual is sufficient to prevent change. Barriers to access go unnoticed by those who can walk up stairs, reach elevator buttons and telephones, use furniture and tools that fit their bodies and functional needs, and generally move in a world designed to facilitate their passage. Without challenge to this status quo, it seems perfectly natural and fair to those whose access is unaffected (at the moment, since they may ultimately discover the privilege is fleeting once they experience pregnancy, accident, illness, aging, or future disability).

Hegemony is reinforced through language, ideology, and cultural/material practices. For example, despite rhetoric that the United States is a secular nation, Christian symbols, holidays, and rituals are routinely integrated into public affairs and institutions. Other religious and spiritual traditions held by large numbers of Americans, including Jews, Muslims, Hindus, Sikhs, and Indigenous people (not to mention people who have no religious affiliation), are invisible or marginalized—so much so that when members of these groups protest, they are often viewed as challenging the American (i.e., Christian) way of life (Kruse, 2015). In a similar vein, the material and other advantages of whites as a group are normalized, baked into the system (Roithmayr, 2014). As a group, whites earn more money and accumulate more assets than African Americans, Native Americans, and Latinx people; hold the majority of positions of power and influence; and command the controlling institutions in society (Demos, 2015; Oliver & Shapiro, 2006). White-dominated institutions restrict the life expectancy, infant mortality, income, housing, employment, and educational opportunities of people in these groups while enhancing opportunities for white people (Smelser, Wilson, & Mitchell, 2001). The dominant white group all too seldom recognizes how they have benefited from segregated schools and neighborhoods, social networks, and institutional policies and procedures that lock their advantages in place (Hannah-Jones, 2021). Unfortunately for all, the wealth disparities that have been cemented into our economic system are undermining economic opportunity for most Americans, with negative consequences for the whole society (Case & Deaton, 2021; Williams, 2017).

DEHUMANIZING

Another dynamic of oppression is reflected in dehumanizing language and images of groups defined as "Other" that deny their full humanness, legitimize symbolic violence and exclusion, and often lead to mistreatment and actual violence. For example, labeling Indigenous people and enslaved Africans as "savages" by colonizers who wanted their land and free labor preceded and legitimized dispossession, genocide, and enslavement. Descriptions of Jews as "vermin" were used by Nazis in Germany to justify extermination camps. Referring to Mexican and Central American people as "animals" or an "infestation" rationalized Trump administration policies that separated children from their parents and put them in cages at the U.S.-Mexico border. Language thus plays a critical symbolic and strategic role in justifying mistreatment, brutality, and violence that would otherwise not be tolerated by human beings toward our own species (Smith, 2011). This is one reason why words, beliefs, and symbols matter, not merely for the purpose of civility but because of the potential they hold for leading down the path to atrocity.

U.S. history is replete with examples of physical, emotional, and sexual mistreatment toward groups deemed "Other" and the language, institutional policies, practices, and beliefs that perpetuate and condone such treatment. Dehumanizing language has led to arguments against extending full human rights to women and Black people to vote, or to LGBTQ+ people to marry or serve in the military, or for disabled people to have access to employment and educational opportunities. In the most extreme cases, dehumanization has led to massacre, starvation, lynching, rape, murder, medical experimentation, forced sterilization, institutionalization, and incarceration.

People from marginalized groups sometimes use violence to retaliate or resist, but such examples typically represent acts of violence that are not systemic and institutionalized. For example, instances where enslaved people rebelled to get free from the brutality of plantation life and killed white people in the process are insignificant in the face of overwhelming violence directed by whites to instill fear and ward off future uprisings (Sharples, 2020).

Dehumanization also harms those who enable or remain silent in the face of mistreatment and violence toward others and ultimately leads to the degradation of society as a whole. We are all vulnerable to an insidious process of dehumanization when society comes to accept it as a normal state of affairs until challenged to be accountable. Oppression is dehumanizing for everyone, even those who benefit from it. Black Lives Matter has acted as a rehumanizing movement by revealing the dehumanization of systemic police violence and brutality against Black human beings that has largely been condoned by white society. By demanding accountability and change, Black Lives Matter, #SayHerName, and #MeToo are rehumanizing movements that demand recognition of and accountability to the humanity of victims who otherwise are rendered faceless.

LEARNED THROUGH SOCIALIZATION

Oppression is not inevitable or natural. Members of a society internalize social norms and beliefs to make meaning of their experiences, as well as to fit in and survive. Through this process of socialization, an unjust status quo comes to be accepted and replicated both by those who benefit as well as by those who suffer from oppressive systems. Attribution and internalization become reciprocal and mutually reinforcing processes. To varying degrees, poor people and affluent people alike internalize the stereotype that people who are poor deserve and are responsible for their poverty and that those who accumulate wealth work hard and deserve their wealth. Assumptions that youth are irresponsible and incapable of serious commitments, or that elders are slow and less vital than middle-aged people in their "prime," are taken as true by people of all ages. Conditions of oppression in everyday life are reinforced when we accept systems of domination without question or challenge. As eloquently put by Audre Lorde, "the true focus of revolutionary change is to see the piece of the oppressor inside us" (1984, p. 123), recognizing that both those who are advantaged and those who are penalized play a role in maintaining oppression.

When members of penalized groups accept and incorporate negative attributions of their group by the dominant society, they collude in supporting the system of oppression (David, 2014; Memmi, 1965; Miller, 1976; Phillips & Lowery, 2018). For example, through internalized sexism many women accept the belief that men are more capable in politics and business and women more naturally suited to housework and childcare. They may unquestioningly adopt assumptions about female limitations and negative stereotypes of women as weak, overemotional, and irrational. Other women may consciously reject such stereotypes but go along with male dominance as a means of survival because to challenge it may mean risking jobs, relationships, or physical security. Internalized subordination exacts a psychic toll, generating feelings of powerlessness, inferiority, and even self-hatred (Pheterson, 1990).

Through internalized domination, individuals in the advantaged group learn to look at themselves, others, and the broader society through a distorted lens in which the structural privileges they enjoy and the cultural practices of their group are taken to be universal and deserved (Jost, Banaji, & Nosek, 2004; Piff, 2014). Internalized domination has psychic consequences as well, including false feelings of superiority, entitlement, self-consciousness, guilt, fear, projection, and denial (Amico, 2016; Frankenberg, 1993; McIntosh, 2020; Pharr, 1988).

Individuals in both dominant and subordinated groups can devalue or turn on members of their own group who challenge the status quo (Bivens, 2005). Such "horizontal hostility" (Freire, 1970; White & Langer, 1999) blocks solidarity and prevents organizing for change. For example, "respectable" gay people may reinforce a narrow range of what is acceptable, helping to maintain systems of heterosexism and transgender oppression that prevent solidarity and working together to demand recognition and respect for all (Bly & Wooten, 2012). People from dominant groups can also prevent others from their group from challenging oppression. White people can label other whites who speak up against racist practices as "troublemakers," "extremists," or "bleeding hearts." Pressure against rocking the boat keeps people from challenging inequality and discrimination so that by simply doing nothing and going along with business as usual, we perpetuate an unequal status quo.

Internalized subordination and domination can be unlearned, however, through critically examining and challenging oppressive attitudes and assumptions that have been internalized and working with others to imagine and enact new ways of being. Harro (2008) created the Cycle of Socialization to trace the way individuals learn and internalize their roles through interaction with family, school, media, and other institutions in society. She then developed a counter-model called the Cycle of Liberation to illustrate how individuals can come to consciousness about ways they have been socialized into roles in the system and how they can take action to challenge and change oppressive relationships and actions (Harro, 2008). Love calls this developing a liberatory consciousness (2018). (See Chapters 4–11 for how these concepts are used in social justice education.)

PERSISTENT/DURABLE

A final feature of oppression is its persistence and ability to shape-shift into new forms to endure and override challenges against it. For example, while the 1960s civil rights movement was successful in combating legalized segregation (de jure), the system evolved new ways to segregate and discriminate in practice (de facto). Schools continue to be segregated through property taxes, district boundaries, and school "choice" programs that reproduce segregation despite policies following *Brown v. Board of Education* (Ewing, 2020). By law, people from all racialized groups have the right to vote, yet in 2021 the Supreme Court weakened enforcement of the Voting Rights Act by eliminating Section II, and state laws are making it much more difficult for People of Color to vote (and many of all races who are young, disabled, or elderly) through restrictive voter ID requirements, purging registered voters from voting rolls, shutting early voting sites in Black and Indigenous communities, and removing drop-off boxes for mail-in ballots, to name a few (Anderson, 2019). In 2021, the Supreme Court upheld new voting restrictions in Arizona that a lower court had ruled discriminated against minority voters, even while acknowledging that these restrictions would have a disproportionate effect on Black, Latinx, and Native American voters. Justice Alito argued the percentage affected would be "too small" to outweigh the state's interest in protecting against voter fraud, something that has been proven to be exceedingly rare (Brennan Center, 2021).

Haney-Lopez (2014) used the term *dog whistle* to describe coded or suggestive language that appeals to one group on issues likely to provoke controversy without attracting negative opposition from other groups. After the civil rights movement and mainstream society adopted the language of color-blindness, politicians began to use coded language to invoke racist images, without overtly naming race, in order to appeal to white voters who would hear that racial dog whistle with approval. During the 2016 presidential campaign, candidates Donald Trump and Jeb Bush used the term *anchor babies* to refer to children born in the U.S. of noncitizen women. Without explicitly mentioning race, they portrayed these children and their mothers, as well as Latinx people in general, as a menace (Bridges, 2019). Dog whistle politics has often been successful in getting white voters to work against their own self-interest to support policies that in fact favor the wealthiest few (Goodman, 2011; Haney-Lopez, 2019). For example, the deliberate use by right-wing politicians of the term *Obamacare* to refer to the Affordable Care Act (ACA) was intended to stir racial anxiety (and cover elite class interests in suppressing government programs that distribute resources downward) without directly mentioning race. In many cases, white voters and many Latinx voters were enlisted against the ACA by invoking a stereotype that government help is merely a sop to "undeserving" minorities and should be resisted by upstanding citizens. The success of this coded racial appeal in states that rejected the ACA meant that large numbers of white people in those states ended up without needed health care (Metzl, 2019).

The success of coded rhetoric is one example of the durability of oppression and its ability to shape-shift to maintain itself in the face of changing conditions. Such persistence and durability must be met by equally persistent and sturdy resistance from those who seek social justice. The long history of activism in this country demonstrates how movements for equality have persisted by adapting to changing conditions with a fierce unwillingness to give up on ideals of equality and democracy. This tenacity was exemplified most recently by activist groups who organized to encourage voting in the face of voter suppression efforts in Georgia and throughout the country.

WITH CONSEQUENCES FOR ALL

Like the miner's canary, "the distress of those who are racially [and otherwise] marginalized is the first sign of a danger that threatens us all" (Guinier & Torres, 2002, p. 11). Though the consequences of oppression fall unevenly on those positioned at the bottom, oppression has consequences for everyone. Thus, a goal of social justice education is to engage all people in recognizing the terrible social, political, and moral costs of maintaining systems of oppression (Goodman, 2011). Heather McGhee traces the legacies of racism and white supremacy that created zero-sum politics and policies that ultimately make everyone worse off through divide and conquer tactics that exploited working class people of all races (2021). Metzl (2019), in his book *Dying of Whiteness*, illustrates how racial resentment has fueled pro-gun laws in Missouri, resistance to the ACA in Tennessee, and cuts to schools and social services in Kansas, with consequent costs to white people in terms of increasing deaths by gun suicide, falling life expectancies, and rising school dropout rates that ultimately affect the whole society.

When millions of Americans are homeless and hungry, all of us pay a social and moral price. The cost of enjoying plenty while others starve is the inability to claim that our society is democratic and just and that we are decent people. Just as important, it also prevents us from developing a clear view of underlying structural problems in political and economic systems that ultimately make all people vulnerable to a changing international economy that disregards national boundaries or allegiances. The productive and creative contributions of people who are shut out of the system are lost to everyone. Rising violence and division make it increasingly difficult for anyone to feel safe. Reduced social supports, limited affordable housing, and scarcities of food and potable water loom as a possible future for all who are not independently wealthy, particularly as people reach old age. The current global pandemic and climate crisis highlight the inequalities and injustices in systems of health care, housing, labor, and other areas that fall more heavily on those at the bottom but also reveal our linked fates in the face of these challenges that cannot be overcome without addressing inequality.

ACTING FOR SOCIAL JUSTICE

A commitment to social justice requires a moral and ethical attitude toward equality and possibility and a belief in the capacity of people to transform their world. Oppression is never complete; it is always open to challenge, as is evident in past and ongoing movements for justice that have made inroads against it. Just as we are socialized into oppression, we can consciously unlearn its habits and proactively work with others to imagine, practice, and enact more just and equitable possibilities for living together on this planet.

Since social *in*justice is based on the historical, institutional, and systemic patterns outlined in the first section of this chapter, and not simply a matter of individual bias or misunderstanding, education alone cannot dismantle it. However, the consciousness, knowledge, skills, and commitments developed through social justice education can lay a foundation for working effectively with others in organized action directed at institutional and societal change.

This section identifies action strategies to challenge oppressive norms and systems. These include examples of direct action such as boycotts and civil disobedience, legislative action, the creation of alternative structures, organizational change, and community organizing, to name a few. The section also refers to individual and small-group skills and practices provided in Chapters 5–11 that can be seen as a prerequisite to effective action in broader arenas. Together these strategies provide a body of work that we can build upon in and with the communities of which we are a part to guide our evolving social justice learning and practice in the present.

DEVELOP INTERSECTIONAL CRITICAL CONSCIOUSNESS

Freire used the term *conscientização*, or *critical consciousness*, to describe the process by which oppressed people become aware of the political and social patterns that enforce their oppression, rather than accept their condition as fate (1970). The term *critical* connotes the cultivation of in-depth understanding of our social and political world to expose contradictions, what Freire called "generative themes," that undergird oppression (Ibid).

In our era, people often feel fatalistic in the face of neoliberal economic and social policies that foster competitive individualism and undermine commitment to the public good. Such policies have underwritten an increasing concentration of power in the hands of wealthy elites, distorting not only the economy but democracy itself (Konczal, 2021; Osnos, 2021). Where neoliberalism de-contextualizes individuals and puts them in competition with one another, critical consciousness takes context as essential and views institutions and individuals as interdependent. It locates the source of problems in systems that pit people against one another rather than in individuals who don't behave or choose correctly. Critical consciousness develops through joining with others to expose injustice, identify solutions to common problems, and reclaim agency and the power to act for change.

Adding *intersectional* to critical consciousness goes further by purposefully looking across forms of oppression (racism, classism, ableism, etc.) to identify how injustice operates differentially in the lives of individuals and groups situated at unequal locations within/across institutions/systems. The Black Lives Matter (BLM) movement, for example, centers the leadership of women, and queer and trans*, People of Color, in order to broaden understanding of the ways racism operates in the lives of differently positioned Black people and other People of Color, to reveal how racism operates in conjunction with sexism, homophobia, and transgender oppression (Khan-Cullors, 2018). An intersectional framework that works across hierarchies makes possible more thoughtful analysis and collaborative action to disrupt cross-cutting systems of oppression (Hill-Collins, 2020; Roberts & Jesudason, 2013).

The #SayHerName campaign, for example, organized to end the silence around how police violence impacts Black women, girls, and transgender and gender-nonconforming people, as well as Black men (Crenshaw, 2015; Langley, 2021; Ritchie, 2017). This broader focus contributed to a wholesale rethinking of policing and public safety in cities that have or are considering restructuring how local budgets and law enforcement are deployed. They are reinvesting in community programs such as housing, alleviating chronic homelessness, protecting victims of family violence (Austin), addressing the impact of violence and trauma on the community (Baltimore), hiring street outreach workers to de-escalate conflicts before they turn violent (Minneapolis), dealing with mental health and substance abuse (San Francisco), and expanding tiny house villages, employment, and services for unhoused people (Seattle), as well as other services directed at diverse populations. Such changes are likely to make life better for everyone in those cities.

Intersectional analysis—the kind we see ongoing in BLM/#SayHerName as well as in #MeToo campaigns and the Standing Rock and fossil fuel divestment and Sunrise environmental movements—illustrates the power of looking across isms to understand and confront oppressive systems. Each of these movements provide examples of intersectional critical consciousness at work in their base building and recruitment and their multidimensional framing of problems to be inclusive of diverse communities. For example, the Sunrise Movement has attended to the impact of proposals for climate action on communities of color and people with disabilities, understanding that environmental racism and the impact of proposed policies and actions on diverse communities must be taken into account. In doing so, they contribute to more thoughtful and creative planning to address environmental problems in ways that benefit all people in a community.

Critical intersectional consciousness can germinate in spaces where people from diverse locations learn about the impact of oppression on various groups in our society, over time and in the present, and experiment with alternative ways of acting in and on the world to challenge oppression. Meetings/classes, clubs/organizations, online and face-to-face networks, community action projects, and public protests are all contexts for bringing people together to reflect on the problems they face, identify the causes, and generate possibilities for democratic change. Chapters 5–11 invite students/participants to develop intersectional critical consciousness and a critique of injustice and practice skills for working with others to imagine more just alternatives. Role-playing scenarios, and creating and assessing action plans with feedback and support from peers, help participants develop confidence, clarity, and commitment to act on their beliefs. This is good preparation for participating effectively in broader institutional and social change efforts.

UNDERSTAND POWER DYNAMICS, USE LEVERS OF POWER IN CREATIVE WAYS

Whose interests does an oppressive status quo serve? Who benefits and who pays? Such questions get at the heart of how unfair advantage entrenches in purportedly fair and neutral systems to congeal into "the way things are." Asking critical questions can crack open the veneer of inequitable arrangements portrayed as unchangeable and help people discern the powerful interests that lock them in place. For example, the 2008 market collapse was due in large part to predatory lending in low-income communities of color and caused widespread misery across the country. Government bailout of banks at risk of foreclosing, but not homeowners who in many cases lost their only assets, spurred public recognition of the role of money in politics and the decreasing power of ordinary people to affect government policies (Osnos, 2021). The Occupy movement coined the slogan "We are the 99%" to harness the potential power of the majority to challenge the domination of money in politics and wealth inequality. Occupy began to change the way people understood their role in the economy and inaugurated a decade of labor unrest that most visibly led to the successful fight to raise the minimum wage. Those who participated in Occupy went on to become involved in other movements. "The same people who were in Occupy Wall Street were in Black Lives Matter, the People's Climate March, the Sunrise Movement. Some of the top activists of this generation got their start at Occupy" (Levitin, 2021).

Community power building is another approach to addressing the sense of powerlessness people feel. Like the methods of Freire (1970) and Alinsky (1971), it identifies those most impacted by structural oppression as the experts in naming the problems a community faces. This approach defines power as "the process of creating politically active constituencies out of people with problems by focusing on their strengths and the solutions embedded in their experience" (Sen, 2003, p. 47). An example is the New Georgia Project, which initiated a conversation about power in underserved communities by engaging them in discussing their concerns and hopes. Combined with a non-partisan effort to engage them in civic conversations, voter registration drives, and political decision-making, the approach exposed entrenched power in the state and would have led to the election of Stacy Abrams had not gerrymandering and voter suppression tactics narrowly succeeded (Abrams, 2020). Groups like Take Action Minnesota and Kentuckians for the Commonwealth likewise focus on building people-centered power to create structural change based on the unique needs and desires of their respective communities (see Equity Research Institute, 2020).

Social justice advocacy organizes people to use their collective power to influence public attitudes, policies, and laws aimed at creating a more just society. Organized social justice advocacy works on policy and legislative reform and in areas such as health care, immigration, the criminal justice system, education, and other areas at both national and local levels. Examples abound and include such organizations as the Equal Justice Initiative (ending mass incarceration and injustice in the legal system), Fair Fight (securing voting rights for all), the National Fair Housing Alliance (addressing housing discrimination), and the Poor People's Campaign (fighting for economic justice), to name a few. Individual advocacy can also be effective on many levels: for example, volunteering in one's local community and donating to support local organizations, voting and encouraging others to do so, and supporting products and services that align with one's values and boycotting those that do not.

Another form of using power creatively is through re-envisioning and creating new structures and institutions that enact social justice values. Restorative justice programs have been used as alternatives to the dehumanization of systems like prisons and schools that rely on punishment. For example, restorative practices in schools, as an alternative to punitive discipline, create safe and respectful spaces where students who are harmed and those responsible for the harm come together to engage in facilitated dialogue to find solutions that support the humanity of everyone involved (Thorsborne, Riestenberg, & McCluskey, 2019; Wadhwa, 2013). Another example of using power creatively is through mutual aid, where members of a community come together to meet each other's needs, working alongside social movement demands for transformative change (Lowrey, 2021; Mutual Aid Hub, n.d.; Spade, 2020).

Chapters 4–11 help participants learn about individuals and groups that have organized in the past and present to use their power for change. Attention to spheres of influence helps them identify places in their own personal, family, and community lives where they have power to influence change and then design action plans for doing so. The habits of analysis and planning action help participants develop a sense of agency and the power to act on problems they see in their lives. Social justice education thus provides a foundation for joining with democratic efforts beyond the classroom or workshop.

USE COUNTER-STORYTELLING TO IMAGINE AND ENACT JUSTICE

Counter-storytelling is a method derived from Critical Race Theory (Bridges, 2019; Delgado, 2017) to identify and critique mainstream/stock stories that rationalize oppression. On an individual and interpersonal level, counter-storytelling moves people to look beyond parochial views of the world and question narratives that normalize unjust patterns and practices. Hidden and suppressed stories of/by groups that have struggled to get ahead in the face of structural obstacles to their advancement, as well as stories of those in dominant groups who resist unearned advantage and work for equality, can inspire ideas and strategies for action in the present (Bell, 2020).

The historical record has benefited immeasurably from counternarratives unearthed by contemporary historians that center the experiences of Indigenous people, poor and working-class people, immigrants from various ethnic and religious backgrounds, African Americans, Latinx, Asian Americans, LGBTQ+ people, women, people with disabilities, and youth and elders of all groups. A more inclusive and accurate history challenges national myths of unblemished democracy and meritocracy and shows the many ways groups have resisted injustice and worked to make the country live up to its democratic promise. Historical counternarratives highlight, for example, the coalitions of diverse groups that organized to abolish slavery, extend suffrage to women, create unions to improve working conditions for laborers, end child labor, challenge anti-immigrant policies, fight for Indigenous sovereignty, and advocate for gay/lesbian and transgender rights. They provide evidence as well as hope that oppressive circumstances can change through the efforts of human actors.

Counter-storytelling values the experiences and perspectives of those who have been marginalized as critical for defining problems and designing change within institutions and society. Journalists and others have historically used this method to expose institutional inequities that need to be addressed. For example, Henning (2021), a defense lawyer and children's advocate, uses powerful personal stories from and about her young clients to illustrate how Black boys and Black girls are victimized by the criminal justice system, bring attention to systemic racism and youth oppression, and identify necessary policy and institutional changes.

Nonprofit, business, educational, and community organizations utilize storytelling to discover the needs and concerns of their members and clients, particularly those from disenfranchised and marginalized groups. They use these stories as a basis for defining a social justice mission that takes everyone into account, developing equitable practices for realizing the mission, and enlisting regular feedback from those they serve so as to update policies and practices as needed. Multicultural organizational development (MCOD) provides a counter-model to traditional ways of defining organizational success and places the creation of diverse and equitable institutions that value the contributions of all at the center of the process (Jackson, 2014; Marchesani & Jackson, 2005). Schools and communities use storytelling in youth empowerment and participatory action research projects to engage young people, especially from groups that have been marginalized, as experts in analyzing problems in their communities, designing proposals, and leading projects for change (Bell, Roberts, Irani, & Murphy, 2008; Fox & Fine, 2013; Ortega-Williams, Wernick, DeBower, & Brathwaite, 2020; Racial Justice Storytelling Kit, 2020).

Storytelling is also useful for helping individuals examine their own development within an oppressive society. When groups of people get together to study the impact of oppression in their lives through sharing stories, they begin to create a new consciousness, pride, and power. Levins Morales argues that sharing stories helps us understand how injustice affects us personally and this understanding becomes the basis for transformation, both personal and political (2019). Storytelling has helped individuals discover within groups that they were not alone in experiencing oppression, and to embrace pride and solidarity, and demand rights (for example, feminist consciousness-raising, Black Power and pride, LGBTQ+, and disability rights movements). Sharing stories is also used as part of intergroup dialogues (Zuniga, Lopez, & Ford, 2014), study circles (EverydayDemocracy.org), interfaith dialogues (NCCJ.org), community building that involves every group in a community (Essential Partners.org), and other efforts to break down barriers and build cross-group understanding, shared vision, and collaborative action for change.

Chapters 4–11 access and reflect upon counter-stories through readings, films, panels, and discussions that vividly portray the lived experiences, struggles, and aspirations of those who have been marginalized and oppressed. Participants share their own stories of socialization and identify the multiple levels on which oppression affects their lives and interactions with others who are positioned differently. Additionally, they identify and practice new attitudes and behaviors in a supportive context, in essence creating new stories that align with their desire for a more just world.

CREATE INCLUSIVE SOCIAL JUSTICE COMMUNITY

To counter the division and dehumanization oppression generates, we who work for social justice need to value and nurture community and connection across race, class, gender, sexuality, ability, age, and religion so that we never lose sight of our common humanity. Indeed, community and connection may be our greatest strength for resisting the dehumanizing imperatives of oppression and creating solidarity.

> Solidarity is not a matter of altruism. Solidarity comes from the inability to tolerate the affront to our own integrity of passive or active collaboration in the oppression of others, and from the deep recognition that, like it or not, our liberation is bound up with that of every other being on the planet, and that politically, spiritually, in our heart of hearts we know anything else is unaffordable.
>
> (Levins Morales, 2019, p. 37)

Ross uses the term "calling in" to describe a culture of openness to working through inevitable misunderstanding and conflict when diverse individuals and groups come together to challenge oppression. She argues for working in ways that invite conversation and compassion (2017). At its founding, BLM articulated a mission to create "an inclusive and spacious movement" to address racism in a way that "affirms the lives of Black queer and trans folks, disabled folks, undocumented folks, folks with records, women, and all Black lives along the gender spectrum" (BLM website; Ransby, 2018). The letter nominating BLM for the 2021 Nobel Peace Prize stated,

> Awarding the peace prize to Black Lives Matter, as the strongest global force against racial injustice, will send a powerful message that peace is founded on equality, solidarity and human rights, and that all countries must respect those basic principles.
>
> (Belham, 2021)

These principles inspired an outpouring of people from all racial groups and walks of life to join the protests against police brutality across the U.S. and around the world. BLM cofounder Alicia Garza reflects this principle in noting, "We have to reach beyond the choir and take seriously the task of organizing the unorganized—the people who don't already speak the same language, the people who don't eat, sleep and breathe social justice" (2020, p. 216).

One of the challenges of "reaching beyond the choir" is creating a framework for addressing inevitable mistakes, miscommunication, and misunderstanding while holding members accountable to shared goals. No one would argue against the importance of calling out politicians and others in positions of power as an important strategy for social movements to call attention to problems and demand change. After all, cancel culture originated in Black queer communities as a term to describe calling people in positions of power to account (Clark, 2020). But the concept can be misused to police individual behavior within communities, what Ross calls punching across rather than punching up, in ways that ultimately undermine solidarity. Organizer Phillip Agnew of Black Men Build describes the approach as: Come as you are, grow as you go. In the same spirit, Ross asks us to hold people accountable while also opening doors to those who are not schooled in particular political cultures, languages, and norms (Ross & Bond, 2019) (see also Brown, 2020).

One way to develop accountability is through listening to the voices of those at the margins and following their lead. Varshini Prakash, co-founder of the Sunrise Movement in the U.S., notes that those closest to the pain can speak toward the solutions with the greatest clarity and thus are essential to movements for change. The disability rights movement slogan, "Nothing about us without us" (Charleton, 1998), affirms the principle that no decisions should be made without the full participation of those affected. Unless people from subordinated groups are central to defining, framing, developing, and leading responses to inequities and social problems, the same power dynamics we wish to change are likely to be reproduced, and the solutions are more likely to fail. Just as youth need to be involved with issues that affect their lives in schools and the community, people who are poor need to name the issues and help set the agenda for addressing poverty-related concerns.

Social justice organizing is stronger when both those who benefit and those who are *dis*advantaged are able to work together in a sustained way to create change. The term *ally* is often used to convey the position of those in the dominant group who work in coalition with oppressed others, as in white people being allies to People of Color, but we believe people from all social groups and positions can be allies. Allyship entails being in solidarity with people from oppressed groups and recognizing that dismantling oppression serves our shared liberation. Allyship also requires humility, a willingness to listen and learn, and a commitment to do the work without expectation of reward or recognition (Goodman, 2011). A strong and embracing community can support participants in the process of envisioning how to dismantle oppression and create liberatory institutions, communities, and relationships (Love, 2018).

Chapters 4–11 explicitly attend to creation of a supportive learning community where participants can examine how they have been socialized in ways they did not choose and that supports their capacity to make new, conscious choices to take different actions in the present. Participants are encouraged to be compassionate toward themselves and others as they develop awareness, skills, and knowledge to effectively work for social justice.

CONCLUSION

Counteracting the durability and resilience of oppression requires persistence and resilience on our part as we work to transform anger at injustice into action for change. This is a lifelong process of speaking out to name injustices, joining others in taking stands against it, and participating in communities of support where we gain inspiration and renewal. There is evidence that many of today's youth activists have taken these requirements to heart as they develop lifetime commitments and attend to building communities of support that can sustain them over the long haul (Connor, 2020; Garza, 2020).

There is evidence that social justice thinkers and activists today have a greater awareness of the global context of their work, an ability to create more enduring cross-group coalitions because of their attention to intersectionality, and a realization of the need for enduring communities of play, imagination, and love (Shepard, 2011). We evolve our understanding of oppression as circumstances change, and we continually experiment with new strategies and ways to live out our visions of what a just society could be. This process ultimately becomes an affirming and authentic way to live.

As historical circumstances change and emerging social movements take up issues of oppression in the United States and throughout the world, new definitions and understandings will continue to evolve. Through highlighting the historical and contextual nature of this process, we hope to avoid the danger of reifying systems of oppression as static or treating individuals as one-dimensional and unchanging. History illustrates both how tenacious and variable systems of oppression are and how dynamic and creative we must continue to be to rise to the challenges they pose. The concepts and processes we present in this text are continuously evolving. We hope the work presented in this fourth edition will contribute to an ongoing dialogue about social justice education theory and practice in ways that can have positive impacts on our world.

Notes

1 We use the term *isms* as shorthand for referring to the forms of oppression we address in this book: racism, classism, sexism, heterosexism, trans* oppression, ableism, religious oppression, and youth and elder oppression.
2 Latinx is a gender neutral and nonbinary alternative to Latino/a.

References

Abrams, S. (2020). *Our time is now: Power, purpose, and the fight for a fair America*. New York: Henry Holt & Co.

Adams, M. (2014). Social justice and education. In M. Reisch (Ed.), *Routledge international handbook of social justice* (pp. 249–268). London: Routledge.

Alinsky, S. D. (1971). *Rules for radicals*. New York: Random House.

Amico, R. (2016). *Exploring white privilege*. New York: Routledge.

Anderson, C. (2019). *One person, no vote: How voter suppression is destroying our democracy*. Bloomsbury.

Anzaldúa, G. (1987). *Borderlands/la frontera: The new mestiza*. San Francisco: Aunt Lute Books.

Bell, L. A. (2020). *Storytelling for social justice: Connecting narrative and the arts in antiracist teaching* (2nd ed.). New York: Routledge.

Bell, L. A., Roberts, R. A., Irani, K., & Murphy, B. (2008). *The storytelling project curriculum*. Retrieved from http://www.columbia.edu/itc/barnard/education/stp/stp_curriculum.pdf

Belham, M. (2021, Jan). *Black Lives Matter Movement nominated for Nobel Peace Prize*. https://www.theguardian.com/world/2021/jan/29/black-lives-matter-nobel-peace-prize-petter-eide-norweigan-mp

Bennice, J., & Resick, P. (2003). Marital rape: History, research, and practice. *Trauma, Violence & Abuse, 4*(3), 228–246. Retrieved from http://www.jstor.org/stable/26636357

Bivens, D. (2005). What is internalized racism? In M. Potapchuk, S. Liederman, D. Bivens, & B. Major (Eds.), *Flipping the script: White privilege and community building* (pp. 43–51). Silver Spring, MD: MP Associates, Inc. and Conshohocken, PA: Center for Assessment and Policy Development (CAPD). Retrieved from http://www.capd.org/pubfiles/pub-2005–01–01.pdf

Bly, L., & Wooten, K. (2012). *Make your own history: Documenting feminist and queer activism in the 21st century*. Los Angeles: Litwin Books.

Brennan Center. (2021). Retrieved from https://www.brennancenter.org/our-work/analysis-opinion/supreme-court-clearly-wont-protect-voting-rights-congress-can

Bridges, K. (2019). *Critical race theory: A primer*. St Paul, MN: Foundations Press.

Brown, A. M. (2020). *We Will Not Cancel Us and Other Dreams of Transformative Justice*. Chico, CA: AK Press.

Case, A., & Deaton, A. (2021). *Deaths of despair and the future of capitalism*. NJ: Princeton University Press.

Charleton, J. I. (1998). *Nothing about us without us: Disability oppression and empowerment*. Berkeley: University of California Press.

Chetty, R., Hendren, N., Kline, P., Saez, E., & Turner, M. (2014). Is the United States still a land of opportunity? Recent trends in intergenerational mobility. *American Economic Review: Papers and Proceedings, 104*(5), 141–147.

Cho, S. (2013). Post-intersectionality. The curious reception of intersectionality in legal scholarship. *Du Bois Review, 10*(2), 385–404.

Cho, S., Crenshaw, K. W., & McCall, L. (2013). Toward a field of intersectionality studies: Theory, applications and praxis. *Signs: Journal of Women and Culture in Society, 38*(4), 785–810.

Clark, M. (2020). Drag them: A brief etymology of so-called "cancel culture". *Communication and the Public, 5*(3–4), 88–92. doi:10.1177/2057047320961562

Combahee River Collective Statement (2015). United States. [Web Archive] Retrieved from the Library of Congress, https://www.loc.gov/item/lcwaN0028151/

Connor, J. O. (2020). *The new student activists: The rise of neo-activism on college campuses.* Baltimore: Johns Hopkins University Press.

Crenshaw, K. W. (1991). Mapping the margins: Intersectionality, identity politics, and violence against women of color. *Stanford Law Review, 43*(6), 1241–1299.

Crenshaw, K. W. (2003). Traffic at the crossroads: Multiple oppressions. In R. Morgan (Ed.), *Sisterhood is forever: The women's anthology for a new millennium* (pp. 43–57). New York: Washington Square Press.

Crenshaw, K. W., & Ritchie, A. J. (2015). *Say her name: Resisting police brutality against black women.* New York: African American Policy Forum.

Cudd, A. (2006). *Analyzing oppression.* New York: Oxford University Press.

David, E. J. R. (2014). *Internalized oppression: The psychology of marginalized groups.* New York: Springer.

Delgado, R. (2017). *Critical race theory: An introduction.* New York: New York University Press.

Demos (2015). *The racial wealth gap: Why policy matters.* Retrieved from http://www.demos.org/publication/racial-wealth-gap-why-policy-matters

Dubai-Ortiz, R. (2021). *Not a nation of immigrants: Settler Colonialism, White Supremacy, and a History of Erasure and Exclusion.* Boston: Beacon Press.

Dunbar-Ortiz, R. (2014). *An Indigenous peoples' history of the United States.* Boston: Beacon Press.

Equity Research Institute (2020). https://dornsife.usc.edu/ERI

Ewing, E. L. (2020). *Ghosts in the schoolyard.* Chicago: University of Chicago Press.

Fear-Segal, J., & Rose, S. D. (2016). *Carlisle Indian Industrial School: Indigenous Histories, Memories, and Reclamations.* University of Nebraska Press.

Foucault, M. (1980). *The history of sexuality.* New York: Vintage Books.

Fox, M., & Fine, M. (2013). Accountable to whom: A critical science counter-story about a city that stopped caring for its youth. *Children and Society, 27*(4), 321–335.

Frankenberg, R. (1993). *The social construction of Whiteness: White women, race matters.* Minneapolis: University of Minnesota Press.

Freire, P. (1970). *Pedagogy of the oppressed.* New York: Seabury.

Garza, A. (2020). *The purpose of power: How we come together when we fall apart.* New York: One World.

Goodman, D. (2011). *Promoting diversity and social justice: Educating people from privileged groups.* New York: Routledge.

Gramsci, A. (1971). *Selections from the prison notebooks of Antonio Gramsci.* New York: International Publishers.

Guinier, L., & Torres, G. (2002). *The miner's canary: Enlisting race, resisting power, transforming democracy.* Cambridge, MA: Harvard University Press.

Haney-Lopez, I. (2014). *Dog whistle politics: How coded racial appeals have reinvented racism and wrecked the middle class.* New York: Oxford University Press.

Haney-Lopez, I. (2019). *Merge left: Fusing race and class, winning elections, and saving America.* New York: New Press.

Hannah-Jones, N. (2021). *The 1619 Project: A new origin story.* New York: The New York Times Co.

Harro, B. (2008). Updated version of the cycle of liberation. In M. Adams, W. J. Blumenfeld, R. Castenada, H. W. Hackman, M. L. Peters, & X. Zuniga (Eds.), *Readings for diversity and social justice* (pp. 463–469). New York: Routledge.

Henning, K. (2021). *The rage of innocence: How America criminalizes Black youth.* New York: Pantheon.

Hill-Collins, P. (2019). *Intersectionality as critical social theory.* Durham: Duke University Press.

Hill-Collins, P. (2000). *Black feminist thought: Knowledge, consciousness and the politics of empowerment.* New York: Routledge.

Hill-Collins, P. (2020). Intersectionality, Black Youth and Political Activism. In *The Oxford Handbook of Global South Youth Studies*, Edited by Sharlene Swartz, Adam Cooper, Clarence M. Batan, and Laura Kropff Causa, Online Publication Date: Dec 2020 DOI: 10.1093/oxfordhb/9780190930028.013.9

Hoffman, E. D. (Ed.). (2012). *American Indians and popular culture*. Santa Barbara: Praeger.

Jackson, B. W. (2014). Theory and practice of Multicultural Organizational Development, pp. 175–192. In B. Jones & M. Brazzel (Eds.), *The NTL Handbook on Organization Development and Change*. New York: Wiley.

Johnson, A. (2005). *Privilege, power and difference*. New York: McGraw-Hill.

Jost, J. T., Banaji, M. R., & Nosek, B. A. (2004). A decade of system justification theory: Accumulated evidence of conscious and unconscious bolstering of the status quo. *Political Psychology, 25*, 881–919.

Khan-Cullors, P. (2018). *When they call you a terrorist: A Black Lives Matter memoir*. New York: St. Martin's Press.

Konczal, M. (2021). *Freedom from the market: America's fight to liberate itself from the grip of the invisible hand*. New York: Free Press.

Kreisberg, S. (1992). *Transforming power: Domination, empowerment, and education*. Albany, NY: State University of New York Press.

Kruse, K. M. (2015). *One nation under God: How corporate America invented Christian America*. New York: Basic Books.

Langley, N. A. (2021). #SeeHerName: Using intersectionality and storytelling to bring visibility to Black women in employment discrimination and police brutality. *DePaul Journal for Social Justice, 114*(2–4). Retrieved from https://via.library.depaul.edu/jsj/vol14/iss2/4

Leonardo, Z. (2013). *Race frameworks: A multidimensional theory of racism and education*. New York: Teachers College Press.

Levins Morales, A. (2019). *Medicine stories: Essays for radicals*. Durham, NC: Duke University Press.

Levitin, M. (2021). How occupy Wall Street reshaped America. *The Atlantic Magazine*. Retrieved from https://www.theatlantic.com/ideas/archive/2021/09/how-occupy-wall-street-reshaped-america/620064/

Lorde, A. (1983). There is no hierarchy of oppression. *Homophobia and Education*. New York: Council on Interracial Books for Children.

Lorde, A. (1984). *Sister outsider*. Trumansburg, New York: Crossing Press.

Love, B. J. (2018). Developing a liberatory consciousness. In M. Adams, W. J. Blumenfeld, C. J. Catalano, K. S. DeJong, H. W. Hackman, L. E. Hopkins, B. J. Love, M. L. Peters, D. Shlasko & X. Zuniga (Eds.), *Readings for diversity and social justice* (4th ed., 610–615). New York: Routledge.

Lowrey, A. (2021). The Americans who knitted their own safety net. *The Atlantic Magazine*. Retrieved from https://www.theatlantic.com/ideas/archive/2021/03/americans-who-knitted-their-own-safety-net/618377/

Malik, M. (2010). *Anti-Muslim prejudice: Past and present*. New York: Routledge.

Marchesani, L., & Jackson, B. W. (2005). Transforming Higher Education Institutions Using Multicultural Organizational Development: A Case Study of a Large Northeastern University. In M. L. Ouellett (Ed.), *Teaching Inclusively: Essays on Course, Department and Institutional Change Initiatives*. Stillwater, OK: New Forms Press.

McGhee, H. C. (2021). *The sum of us: What racism costs everyone and how we can prosper together*. New York: One World Press.

McIntosh, P. (2020). *On privilege, fraudulence and teaching as learning: Selected essays 1981–2019*. New York: Routledge.

Memmi, A. (1965). *The colonizer and the colonized*. Boston: Beacon Press.

Metzl, J. 2019). *Dying of whiteness: How the politics of racial resentment is killing America's heartland*. New York: Basic Books.

Miller, J. B. (1976). *Toward a new psychology of women*. Boston: Beacon Press.

Mutual Aid Hub. (n.d.). Retrieved from https://www.mutualaidhub.org/

Nash, J. C. (2019). *Black feminism reimagined: After intersectionality*, Durham: Duke University Press.

Oboler, S. (1995). *Ethnic labels, Latino lives*. Minneapolis: University of Minnesota Press.

Oliver, M. L., & Shapiro, T. M. (2006). *Black wealth, white wealth* (2nd ed.). New York: Routledge.

Ortega-Williams, A., Wernick, L. J., DeBower, J., & Brathwaite, B. (2020). Finding relief in action: The intersection of youth-led community organizing and mental health in Brooklyn, New York City. *Youth & Society, 52*(4), 618–638. doi:10.1177/0044118X18758542

Osnos, E. (2021). *Wildland: The making of America's fury*. New York: Farrar, Strauss & Giroux.

Pharr, S. (1988). *Homophobia: A weapon of sexism*. Inverness, CA: Chardon Press.

Pheterson, G. (1990). Alliances between women: Overcoming internalized oppression and internalized domination. In L. Albrecht and R. Brewer (Eds.), *Bridges of power: Women's multicultural alliances* (pp. 34–48). Philadelphia: New Society Publishers.

Phillips, L. T., & Lowery, B. S. (2018). Herd invisibility: The psychology of racial privilege. *Current Directions in Psychological Science, 27*(3), 156–162. doi:10.1177/0963721417753600

Piff, P. K. (2014). Wealth and the inflated self: Class, entitlement, and narcissism. *Personality and Social Psychology Bulletin, 40*(1), 34–43.

Racial Justice Storytelling Kit. (2020). Retrieved from http://www.purpose.com/wp-content/uploads/2020/12/Racial-Justice-Story-Studio-Toolkit.pdf

Ransby, B. (2018). *Making all Black lives matter: Reimagining freedom in the twenty-first century*. Oakland, CA: University of California Press.

Rawls, J. (1999). *A theory of justice*. Cambridge, MA: Harvard University Press.

Rawls, J. (2001). *Justice as fairness: A restatement*. Cambridge, MA: Harvard University Press.

Reeves, R. V. (2017). *Dream hoarders*. Washington, DC: Brookings Institution.

Ritchie, A. J. (2017). *Invisible No More: Police violence against black women and women of color*. Boston: Beacon.

Roberts, D., & Jesudason, S. (2013). Movement intersectionality: The case of race, gender, disability, and genetic technologies. *Du Bois Review, 10*(2), 313–328.

Roithmayr, D. (2014). *Reproducing racism: How everyday choices lock in white advantage*. New York: NYU Press.

Ross, L. J. (2017). Reproductive justice as intersectional feminist activism. *Souls, 19*(3), 286–314.

Ross. L. J. & Bond, T. M. (2019). Calling In Rather Than Calling Out: When #MeToo Meets Reproductive Justice. https://rewirenewsgroup.com/article/2019/04/05/calling-in-rather-than-calling-out-when-metoo-meets-reproductive-justice/

Rothstein, R. (2017). *The color of law: A forgotten history of how our government segregated America*. New York: Liveright.

Sen, R. (2003). *Stir it up: Lessons in community organizing and advocacy*. San Francisco: Jossey-Bass.

Sharples, J. T. (2020). *The world that fear made: Slave revolts and conspiracy scares in early America*. Philadelphia: University of Pennsylvania Press.

Shepard, B. H. (2011). Play, creativity, and social movements: If I can't dance, it's not my revolution. New York: Routledge.

Smelser, N. J., Wilson, W. J., & Mitchell, F. (Eds., National Research Council). (2001). *America becoming: Racial trends and their consequences* (Vol. 1). Washington, DC: National Academies Press.

Smith, D. L. (2011). *Less than human: Why we demean, enslave and exterminate others*. New York: St. Martin Press.

Song, X., Massey, C. G., Rolf, K. A., Ferrie, J. P., Rothbaum, J. L., & Xie, Y. (2020). Long-term decline in intergenerational mobility in the United States since the 1850s. *Proceedings of the National Academy of Sciences of the United States of America, 117*(1), 251–258. doi:10.1073/pnas.1905094116

Spade, D. (2020). *Mutual aid: Building solidarity during this crisis (and the next)*. Verso.

Thorsborne, M., Riestenberg, N., & McCluskey, G. (Eds.). (2019). *Getting more out of restorative practice in schools: Practical approaches to improve school wellbeing and strengthen community engagement*. Philadelphia: Jessica Kingsley Pubs.

Wadhwa, A. (2013). *Race, discipline, and critical restorative justice in two urban high schools* (thesis), Harvard Graduate School of Education, Cambridge.

White, J. B., & Langer, E. J. (1999). Horizontal hostility: Relations between similar minority groups. *Journal of Social Issues, 25*(3), 537–559.

Williams, R. B. (2017). *The privileges of wealth: Rising inequality and the growing racial divide*. New York: Routledge.

Young, I. M. (1990). *Justice and the politics of difference*. Princeton, NJ: Princeton University Press.

Young, I. M. (2011). *Responsibility for justice*. New York: Oxford University Press.

Zuniga, X., Lopez, G. E., & Ford, K. A. (Eds.). (2014). *Intergroup dialogue: Engaging difference, social identities and social justice*. New York: Routledge.

Pedagogical Foundations for Social Justice Education

*Maurianne Adams, Rachel R. Briggs, and Davey Shlasko**

In this chapter, we describe our approach to social justice teaching, the theoretical and intellectual traditions that social justice education pedagogy draws upon, and the pedagogical elements that guide our practice. Here our focus is on the principles guiding how we teach and why we teach in the ways we do, as distinct from what we teach, even though we know that these are inseparable in practice. We define pedagogy as an applied philosophy of teaching and learning. Pedagogy is not only about how we teach but also about why we teach and why we teach in the ways we do. This approach is in keeping with the tradition of critical pedagogy where the term "pedagogy" conveys a holistic sense of the entire educational enterprise that is in need of critique and change, including curriculum content; teaching practices; relationships among students, teachers, administration, and various other stakeholders; and the broader institutional, social, and political contexts within which we are teaching (Apple, Au, & Gandin, 2009; Darder, Baltodano, & Torres, 2008; Sandoval, 2000; Shor, 1987).

As social justice educators, we think of our pedagogy as praxis informed by the interaction of theory, reflection, and action. In the spirit of Freire's *Pedagogy of the Oppressed* (1970), we use the term "praxis" to describe the integration of learning goals with pedagogical processes that together encourage reflection and action to create change. In this chapter we foreground pedagogy while never losing sight of the inextricable connection to content.

This chapter draws upon and is in dialogue with the *Teaching for Diversity and Social Justice (TDSJ)* third edition of this chapter, written by Maurianne Adams (Adams, Bell, & Griffin, 1997, 2007, 2016; see also Adams, 2014). The current authors' task of revising this chapter draws upon our own training in a program in which Maurianne Adams was a faculty member and a teacher and mentor to the authors. Her ideas are foundational to our social justice work, and in this chapter, we continue the legacy of evolving the social justice education (SJE) pedagogy she passed down to us.

This chapter begins with our definition of and goals for SJE pedagogy. Next, we review the historical foundations of SJE pedagogy and track how these ideas have been taken up and applied within social justice education communities of practice. Finally, we outline and explain five major elements of social justice pedagogy.

WHAT IS SOCIAL JUSTICE EDUCATION PEDAGOGY?

SJE pedagogy is a set of principles and practices that guide our continually evolving thinking about how to do teaching and learning about oppression and social justice issues. The priority of social justice educators is to affirm, model, and sustain socially just learning environments for all participants. Through this modeling, we offer hope that equitable relations and social structures can be achieved in the broader society, and through building the skills to create and sustain these socially just classrooms, we help students learn and practice

DOI: 10.4324/9781003005759-3

skills applicable to broader contexts in which we are working for social justice goals. Thus, the pedagogical choices we make as social justice educators are as important as the content we teach so that *what* participants are learning and *how* they are learning are congruent.

As social justice educators, our goal is to create the kind of socially just relationships, communities, institutions, and society that we want to live in. Thus, our pedagogies need to model the equity, fairness, inclusiveness, reciprocity, and justice for which we are striving. Because we are educators as well as social justice activists, we think of formal and informal education settings as key sites to embody and model the goals of social justice and to enact processes toward those goals. We hope to provide learning communities where we can, together, develop and practice cross-group understanding, empathy, and collaboration; conduct a critical analysis of our interpersonal interactions, social institutions, culture, and society; practice skills and build coalitions that enable taking action to challenge injustice; and together imagine the better world to which we aspire. Social justice education pedagogy is a pedagogy that is experiential, participant centered, inclusive, collaborative, and democratic. It addresses social identity and social position, explores contradictions from the social world, engages emotions as well as thought, and addresses the reproduction of systemic inequalities of advantage and disadvantage in group processes.

Our approach to education contrasts with what Freire (1970) terms "banking education," a pedagogy dominated by experts with authority who pour knowledge into the empty heads of novices expected to listen passively and receive pre-digested information. A social justice pedagogy must necessarily differ from pedagogies of banking education to challenge the visible as well as hidden influences of curriculum and facilitate the skills and knowledge that can challenge injustice and create change. In an anti-banking approach to learning, "the students—no longer docile listeners—are now critical co-investigators in dialogue with the teacher" (Freire, 1970, p. 62).

When the first edition of *TDSJ* was published, the banking model was widely accepted in U.S. formal education while social justice pedagogy was marginal. We spent as much time explaining what SJE pedagogy *is not* as what it *is*, and we had to justify its legitimacy to an academic audience. Now some aspects of SJE practice are widely used and accepted in the field of education, and "social justice" has become an oft-used term in some educational settings and educational research. Even still, many of us work in institutional contexts that are structurally opposed to social justice, where it is all too easy to do things in the expected, oppressive ways. Too often we see social justice teaching practices used in ways that mis-align with the underlying pedagogy. For example, an activity about diversity of social identities might be taken out of context and facilitated in a way that reinforces existing power imbalances without acknowledging or seeking to counter these power imbalances. The work of social justice education includes ongoing unlearning of bad habits and defaults and continual re-grounding in our pedagogical principles so that we can continue to adjust our practices to suit the overall purpose of building social justice through education.

We see SJE as a necessary tool in broader movements for justice but not as a movement in itself. We know that social injustice is not merely a matter of individual mis/understanding, and so education alone cannot dismantle it. To achieve justice, SJE must occur alongside other tools, such as community organizing, policy advocacy, direct services, and mutual aid. We see SJE as engaged with and accountable to the social justice movements in our contexts.

HISTORICAL LEGACIES

Social justice pedagogy is a living tradition that draws on theoretical and activist foundations that span many decades and several continents and combines these disparate traditions into a unique set of understandings and practices. The foundations of our (the authors') social justice pedagogies are deeply woven into how we were both trained in the Social Justice Education program at University of Massachusetts Amherst. The foundations of social justice pedagogy draw on intellectual traditions including critical pedagogy, activist movements, social psychology, and group process theory. Building upon these foundations, social justice pedagogy is also a continually evolving set of practices within a community of educators—practices that are ever changing in response to our changing world. We do social justice education in a community of practitioners who are continually re-theorizing and circulating new ideas, experiences, tools, and frameworks. We are interacting with and in many cases actively involved in social justice movements, which both draw on and inform our pedagogy and practices. Our pedagogy evolves in part to meet movements' current needs for raising awareness and disseminating understanding, analysis, and skills.

In this section of the chapter, we lay out the theoretical and activist foundations of social justice pedagogy as they were historically conceptualized. We attempt to make the lineages of our pedagogy transparent, to acknowledge the traditions that social justice pedagogy builds on, and to enable readers who wish to learn more to follow those threads. Other chapters in this volume may not mention these foundations often, but once familiar with them, you will recognize their footprints in every chapter and curriculum in this book.

FREIRE AND COMMUNITY-BASED EDUCATION

Pedagogy of the Oppressed (Freire, 1970) is a book whose integration of vision, theory, analysis, and practice has had an incalculable influence on generations of social justice educators and activists. During the 1940s through the early 1960s, Freire used a dialogic- and inquiry-based model to teach literacy to impoverished workers in his native Brazil. Although teaching basic reading and writing skills, the project was explicitly political in intent as well as content. Literacy was a requirement for voting in Brazil at the time, so to learn to read was also to gain the political power of voting. In Freirean pedagogy, instructors and facilitators identify and organize resources and initiate dialogue so that, through dialogue, the participants move to the center of their own learning and develop critical consciousness. Curricular materials were drawn from the everyday lives and concerns of his participants and were thus immediately recognizable and meaningful to them. His approach elicited "generative themes" from participants that reflected their specific experiences of oppression as well as possibilities for concrete action (Au, 2009; Shor, 1987).

In the late 1960s and 1970s, while exiled from Brazil, Freire brought his work to Chile, Guinea-Bissau, and Mozambique and spent a year as a visiting professor at Harvard. Freirean theory and pedagogy was influential in Indigenous, literacy-based, popular, participatory, labor organizing, and/grassroots and anti-colonial movements throughout the Americas and globally (Brookfield & Holst, 2011; Zajda, Majhanovich, Rust, & Sabina, 2006). It is impossible to overestimate Freire's impact on the formal and informal multicultural and critical education reform movements during the closing decades of the 20th century.

ACTIVIST MOVEMENTS

During those same decades, activists similarly used consciousness raising as a community-based political education tool to organize for collective power and social change. The Black civil rights movement in the U.S., anti-colonial movements in Africa (Sherif & Sherif, 1970), labor organizing and other poor people's organizing in the U.S. (e.g. Horton, Kohl, & Kohl, 1990), and the feminist movement in the U.S. (Evans, 1980) all drew on similar methods to Freire's. Mississippi Freedom Schools challenged segregation, conceived of education as a pathway to freedom for students, and became an entry point into the civil rights movement for a multitude of young people through social critique and other civil rights organizing strategies (Hale, 2016). Consciousness raising offers simple structures for participants to reflect on their own experiences, learn from the similar and different experiences within the group, and make connections between individual concerns and collective ones. Through consciousness raising, subordinated peoples reflected on their experiences of daily inequities and were led by these insights toward analyses that theorized and directed action against their oppression (Kaba & Shine, 2017; Sarachild, 1975; Sherif & Sherif, 1970). In some cases, consciousness-raising groups also became sites of experimentation with different group norms and processes and opportunities to practice ways of being together that could create equity in and beyond the movement.

SOCIAL PSYCHOLOGY AND GROUP DYNAMICS

Simultaneously with the social movements of the mid-20th century, social psychologists and education scholars were looking to address related issues in the realm of academic teaching. Concerned with developing teaching frameworks to support the success of racially integrated education after *Brown v. Board of Education*, they built on Dewey's (1909/1975) earlier work on democratic and experiential education as a means of engaging students with real-world social issues. There is a direct through line from the work of Dewey to Allport's classic *The Nature of Prejudice* (1954/1979), in which Allport delineated the norms, in-group and out-group social categories, and manifestations of prejudice that poisoned the possibilities for the pluralistic, democratic education envisioned by Dewey. Allport's still-illuminating analysis has shaped subsequent anti-racism and intergroup thinking and practice (Dovidio, Glick, & Rudman, 2005). His insights about racism, stereotypes, discrimination, and the conditions needed for positive intergroup relations have been elaborated and used by generations of anti-racist educators in developing guidelines for effective anti-racist learning communities.

Lewin's (1948) research on group dynamics also contributes to our understanding of the interaction between group and individual learning in social justice education (Benne, 1964; Bradford, Gibb, & Benne, 1964). His team developed simulations and role-plays in a set of procedures called "laboratory training" that provided opportunities for members of interracial groups to "get into the shoes of the other" (Lippitt, 1949). Structured, facilitated group feedback enabled participants to achieve "in the moment" insight into themselves and each other in groups of diverse individuals. Much of what we now know about socially mixed group dynamics and the role of group norms and guidelines in establishing a positive learning community for SJE derives from these sources.

More recently, the pedagogical tools associated with Lewin and Allport have been tested in structured intergroup dialogues and classes to assess the conditions that govern effective intergroup contact and cross-group interpersonal communication (Pettigrew & Tropp, 2006). These tools have been widely used in educational and community settings to build cross-group relationships and to practice cross-group communication skills (Dovidio, Glick, & Rudman, 2005; Engberg, 2004; Stephan & Vogt, 2004). The intergroup pedagogies have benefited from research that links outcomes in awareness and critical thinking about injustice to a range of social justice pedagogical tools (Gurin, Nagda, & Zúñiga, 2013; Zúñiga, Lopez, & Ford, 2012).

Social justice educators draw on theories of intergroup relations to understand how participants work through the contradictions to previous ways of thinking that they encounter in intergroup settings and design pedagogical tools that will engage contradictions productively. Social justice educators have drawn on developmental and social psychology to understand processes of personal meaning-making and change and to help participants develop a broader and more inclusive worldview (Adams, Perry-Jenkins, & Tropp, 2014; Cole, 1996; Kegan, 1982; Rogoff, 2003). In particular, theories of racial/social identity development help us understand the processes by which people come to understand themselves in various ways as members of a social identity group (Wijeyesinghe & Jackson, 2012; Helms, 1995, 1997, 2003), and we can use this understanding to craft learning opportunities suited to participants at different stages of development. Cognitive development models likewise help us conceptualize how people move through different ways of thinking and different degrees of complexity (e.g. Baxter-Magolda, 1992; Belenky, Clinchy, Goldberger, & Tarule, 1986).

LIBERATORY PEDAGOGIES IN FORMAL EDUCATION

It is striking that the keystone works in the social psychology of intergroup relations came to such similar conclusions as the movement-based consciousness-raising and political education work of the same era. Community wisdom is not always easy to cite, yet it no doubt influenced the work of scholars like Dewey, Allport, and Lewin. In more recent decades, the cross-fertilization between scholars of education and activist community educators has continued, including in the work of some well-known public intellectuals like bell hooks (1994, 2003), as well as many contributors who may never be cited in the academic literature. In Mariame Kaba and Jacqui Shine's 2017 reprint of a set of consciousness-raising guidelines from 1975, they note that there is no author listed for that original document (although authors are listed for some shorter addenda included in it). The document may have been produced collaboratively, or the author(s) may have felt that individual credit was not in the spirit of the work. Yet the document exists, and we can study it as easily as we can study the publications of the famous white men in the field. Non-academic publications and unpublished sources like pamphlets, zines, binders of workshop materials, and more recently blog posts and other dynamic web content provide vital and underrecognized foundations for our work in social justice education.

Ideas and techniques from feminist groups were formalized in academia under the rubric of feminist pedagogy (e.g. Maher & Tetreault, 2001; Weiler, 1988, 2001). The evolution of feminist pedagogy has reflected many of the productive conflicts within feminist movements. Black, Latina, and Indigenous feminist scholars have critiqued white feminist pedagogy for lack of intersectional analysis—and Freire's work for lack of feminist analysis—and formulated feminist pedagogies centering women of color that are not only feminist but also anti-racist, decolonial, and abolitionist (e.g. Omolade, 1987, 1993; hooks, 1994; Grande, 2003; Henry, 2005; Bernal, Burciaga, & Carmona, 2017; Love, 2019). Trans scholars have expanded upon feminist methods to reflect the realities of trans educators and students, opening up new possibilities in feminist pedagogy and epistemology whose implications go far beyond trans inclusion (e.g. Enke, 2012; Barcelos, 2019; Malatino, 2015; Nicolazzo, 2021). There is a movement for Indigenous and decolonizing pedagogy that emerges from Indigenous community practices (e.g. Wildcat, McDonald, Irlbacher-Fox, & Coulthard, 2014) and is often in conversation with feminist pedagogies (e.g. Grande, 2003) as well as Freirean and other critical pedagogies (e.g. Tejeda, Espinoza, & Gutierrez, 2003; Zembylas, 2018). The interplay between movement practices and scholarly explorations continues to expand and hone our understanding of liberatory pedagogies.

Mindfulness and Arts-Based Practices

In the last few decades, more social justice educators have begun (re)incorporating tools from healing traditions into their educational practice. Mindfulness practices derived from

Buddhist tradition, although often secularized and disconnected from the Buddhist context, are often used to support critical reflection and self-awareness (e.g. Ríos, 2019). Somatic practices from body-based psychotherapy and related mind/body practices can help people engage with the individual and collective trauma that comes from systems of oppression (e.g. Haines, 2019). From the art therapy world, expressive arts techniques can support students' social identity development and critical reflection (e.g. Barbera, 2011). Each of these healing practices seek to engage participants' creativity, spiritual insights, and/or the body and nervous system to support understanding, connection, and change.

Although the same practices can be used as part of psychotherapy, using these tools does not mean we are providing therapy. Rather, these bodies of knowledge add to and clarify practices around engaging emotions in learning that have always been part of SJE. They also serve as an important counterbalance to some unspoken assumptions of mainstream education that disregard the body, spirit, and emotions as irrelevant to learning. The dismissal of the body from formal education spaces is unhelpful for all learners and has particular impact for those whose bodies differ from the standard white, abled, cisgender male norm. While SJE has long critiqued the ways in which education excludes non-normative bodies, creative and mind-body practices offer us something to do about it beyond naming it.

Social justice pedagogy draws together these many disparate and complementary threads of theory and practice and combines them into a cohesive set of principles and practices. In the rest of the chapter, we outline five key elements of social justice pedagogy, explain why they are important, and provide examples of how they play out in practice. Chapter 3: Design and Facilitation provides more detail on how to implement these practices in workshops and classrooms.

THE PEDAGOGICAL ELEMENTS THAT INFORM SJE PRACTICE

Whether we are novice or seasoned social justice educators, each classroom or workshop experience feels "new" because of the mix of participants and the unknown dynamics and issues that may arise. Time and again, as educators, we go back to the drawing board as we consider the challenges and opportunities of SJE. We continue to enlarge our repertoire of pedagogical resources and facilitation skills, hoping to become more effective social justice practitioners. Our pedagogy is strengthened through apprenticeship and mentorship, collaboration and experimentation, as well as through ongoing reading and reflection on scholarship and activism. While the authors cited previously have been invaluable, learning "how to do" is a matter of ongoing experimentation and practice. Nonetheless, a set of pedagogical elements affords a helpful guide, and we ask that the following elements be considered in that spirit.

Although the five pedagogical elements[1] appear as a list, they should be understood as *concurrent, not sequential, approaches and processes.* It is only the linear format of writing principles one at a time that makes them *seem* sequential. In reality, these processes are likely to be happening simultaneously, although some approaches may be introduced earlier or later in the life of a learning community. Also, these elements are not mutually exclusive categories. You may notice some overlap among them, as well as some ways in which this chapter overlaps with Chapter 3: Design and Facilitation. The elements of social justice pedagogy are as follows:

Element 1: Consider the roles of facilitators and participants in the learning community
Element 2: Foster an inclusive learning community

Element 3: Center an analysis of systems of oppression and how they operate in society and in the classroom

Element 4: Define goals, learning objectives, and evaluation mechanisms for SJE

Element 5: Utilize collaborative and active learning

Each element is discussed in more detail in the following.

ELEMENT 1: CONSIDER THE ROLES OF FACILITATORS AND PARTICIPANTS IN THE LEARNING COMMUNITY

The first element addresses the roles of facilitators and participants in the learning community. For the purpose of this chapter, we intentionally use the term "facilitator" (rather than teacher, instructor, professor, educator, etc.) when discussing social justice education pedagogy. Even though we may also hold these other roles, we call ourselves facilitators because the heart of the work is about the people involved. The grammar of the verb "facilitate" shows us a lot about the nature of SJE teaching and learning. Whereas the transitive verb "teach" can be followed by both topics and learners (Susan teaches math; Susan teaches Johnny), "facilitate" always refers to human processes. One does not facilitate math; one facilitates groups of learners. Therefore, it is helpful for a social justice educator to learn as much as possible about the people involved when embarking on a facilitation process. This includes knowing our students/participants, ourselves, and our co-facilitators (see Chapter 12: Critical Self-Knowledge for an in-depth exploration of this topic).

Why We Need to Know Our Participants

As Freire reminds us and the developmental literature illustrates, facilitators need to start from "where" participants are—in their social identities and awareness of issues, in their ways of knowing, in their openness and interest in SJE issues:

> The educator needs to know that . . . [y]ou never get *there* by starting from *there*, you get *there* by starting from some *here*. . . . This means, ultimately, that the educator must not be ignorant of, underestimate, or reject the "knowledge of living experience" with which [participants] come to school.
>
> (Freire, 1994, p. 58)

A journey where the facilitator starts from the participants' "here" to achieve some mutually agreed upon "there" recurs in Freire's pedagogical dialogue with Myles Horton, *We Make the Road by Walking* (1990). The "we" is as important as any other word in that aphorism—it is the participants as much as the facilitators who create the ultimate structure and trajectory of a learning experience.

Participants' social identities and other characteristics affect the attitudes they bring to a session, how ready they are for particular topics or activities, how they will be able to interact with each other, and what they might require from us as facilitators. Knowing our students helps us choose appropriate activities and gives us an idea of the knowledge and experiences that our students will bring and in what areas they might have misinformation or inexperience. It can also help us anticipate particular forms of resistance that are likely to come up and plan for how we can most fruitfully address them. Our knowledge of participants can inform decisions about sequencing of topics, small-group formation, conversation structures, and even content.

However, we should be careful not to oversimplify or stereotype what we know about our students/participants, particularly based on social identities. We can make educated guesses about what people are *likely* to know, feel, say, or do, yet we must also be prepared to encounter our students/participants as whole, complex, and idiosyncratic individuals who may or may not confirm our educated guesses about them.

What We Need to Know about Our Students/Participants

As social justice educators, we need to understand what brings participants to the social justice education setting and what implicit and explicit power dynamics exist in the group. Participant motivation, experience, and previous relationships shape the group process and affect how participants are able to learn together. A history of conflict or competition in a group can undermine the trust and vulnerability that can make SJE workshops so powerful, while existing positive relationships can provide a foundation for mutual investment in each other's learning. Understanding participants' motivations, whether personal, academic, and/or professional, enables us to make the content more personally relevant and to help participants understand how a session's goals align with their own. Power relationships among participants (such as supervisor/supervisee) not only affect the group dynamic and possibilities for trust but also can have consequences beyond the workshop itself. We must address such dynamics as much as possible so that participants can make informed decisions about their vulnerability and boundaries without fear of retaliation or negative impact on their work relationships. Power dynamics related to social identities are also important and are discussed in the following as well as in Chapter 3: Design and Facilitation.

For many of our students/participants, this will not be their first experience with something like diversity education or social justice education (even if it was not what we mean by social justice education). It is helpful to know what their previous experiences have been like for them—whether they've found them a waste of time, or profoundly useful, or retraumatizing, or some combination. More specifically, it is helpful to understand what participants already know, what misinformation they might have, and what ideas might be new and/or challenging for them. No matter which identities or experiences have shaped it, knowing what we can about participants' current understandings of social justice issues allows us to design processes and content to help individual participants and the group take the specific next steps needed in their learning, rather than taking a one-size-fits-all approach.

Social justice educators also need to know students' learning styles and their access needs. Learning styles and preferences for different learning modalities (e.g. visual vs. auditory, imaginative vs. analytic, abstract vs. concrete) are a matter of individual difference but also may be related to cultural differences (Brooks-Harris & Stock-Ward, 1999). There may also be preferences for and against particular learning styles built into an organizational culture. Knowing about the teaching and learning norms participants are accustomed to within a school or organization can tell us a lot about how they are likely to encounter activities that differ from those norms.

Access needs include needs related to mobility, energy levels, sensory impairments, and so on. This is not only relevant to those with documented disabilities and accommodations; actually, everyone has access needs, it's just that some needs are already met by default while others are not (see Chapter 9: Ableism). We use the principles of Universal Design for Learning (Meyer, Rose, & Gordon, 2014) to make our default accessible to the widest possible range of students, but truly universal access is not possible (see Chapter 3: Design and Facilitation and Chapter 9: Ableism). The more we know about participants' needs, the more accurately we can design a session that works for them.

How We Learn about Our Students/Participants

Like everything else in social justice education, how we gather information about our students/participants can be as important pedagogically as what information we gather. We might use a pre-training survey, a verbal activity on the first day of class, a personal reflection paper, intake interviews, or other tools. Regardless of the specific method, it's important that we approach this pre-assessment with care for participants' safety and privacy, respect for their self-knowledge, and attention to the relationship building that is happening through the pre-assessment process.

The manner in which we gather information about students/participants and the way in which we explain it can set the tone for our teaching/learning relationship even before the group has convened. As well as learning about them, it's a way for us to demonstrate trustworthiness, respect, and collaboration. For example, any time we ask people for personal information or reflections, we should be transparent about why we want the information, what we will use it for, and who will have access to it. By asking participants about their previous learning and their learning needs, we are demonstrating that we respect their knowledge of themselves. By using that information to tailor a learning experience for them, we are demonstrating our commitment to their learning and our trustworthiness as facilitators.

What We Need to Know about Ourselves

As important as knowing about our participants is our own self-knowledge. When we facilitate a social justice learning experience, we are engaging with the participants and content both in our role (as teacher, trainer, etc.) and also as ourselves, with all our human complexities. Some of us who have been trained in a banking model of education may be tempted to think of a teacher as separate from their material. This is not the case, though. Knowledge is not objective, and our interactions with content change the meanings for us and for students/participants (Britzman, 2012). For us this is not a detriment but rather an inevitable feature of teaching/learning relationships. Engaging with these dynamics consciously rather than just letting them happen enables us to facilitate with personal and professional integrity and to more fully understand our impact on participants and each other (for more, see Chapter 12: Critical Self-Knowledge).

Social Identities

Like with participants, our social identities form a major part of who we are and the meanings we carry with us when we enter a learning environment. Our level of awareness and analysis of our own social group memberships adds another layer of complexity. Adept facilitation requires having a reasonably accurate assessment about which part of our identities and experiences we have processed and feel settled with and where we have gaps in our understanding or identity-related traumas that are unhealed. This doesn't mean we can only facilitate learning about topics where we have "perfect" awareness; indeed, being openly a "work in progress" can set a powerful example for students engaging in similar learning. Identifying our relative levels of readiness around different identities and isms can inform our decisions about our own vulnerability and risks we might take in facilitation as much as knowing our participants' readiness informs what we might ask of them.

In addition to affecting our relationship with the content, our social identities are central to the power dynamics in the learning environment. For example, participants may be more likely to believe or agree with facilitators who are white men while challenging the expertise or competence of those who are women of color. Or participants may fetishize the expertise of experience and excessively defer to a facilitator based on a marginalized identity rather than engaging with the material critically. It may be easiest to consider how our most salient identities show up in our facilitation, but those we are less aware of are equally important. A thought experiment can be useful here: asking ourselves, "Which of my identities might be most salient *to my students*?" For example, a facilitator who is white and queer, teaching about heterosexism, might often be aware of their queerness in relation to the topics of conversation. But their whiteness is also relevant, and even if it's not salient to the facilitator, it may be extremely salient to students of color in a way that shapes the teaching and learning relationship. The facilitator may need to work to incorporate whiteness into their understanding of and decisions about how they "show up" as a facilitator.

Disrupting the Student/Teacher Power Relationship

Social justice pedagogy embraces the Freirean notion of disrupting the teacher as the ultimate authority figure. Although we usually take the lead in providing a structure and content, we try to develop and support participants' leadership in steering their own learning experiences. At the same time, we must acknowledge the real power our position affords, both formal (like the power to grade students' work) and informal (like the immense influence we are likely to have on the thinking of participants socialized in a banking system of education). The way to change the power relationship of teacher over student is not to ignore it but to make it explicit and to communicate clearly about what that power relationship is, even if it's not what you would ideally want it to be.

Our power as instructors/facilitators/teachers combines with social identities in complex ways. For example, because of how expertise and authority are associated with whiteness and maleness, a Black woman who holds her power as instructor in a particular way—such as by insisting students address her as doctor or professor—is doing something very different for the group dynamic than a white man who does the same. By challenging a rigid teacher-over-student power dynamic, we are not encouraging facilitators to give up all their positional power. Rather, we encourage facilitators to think carefully about what their power is doing in the learning environment, in terms of social identities as well as positional power, and to use it strategically in order to foster the kind of learning experience they are aiming for.

One way that facilitators can appropriately disrupt default power dynamics is by modeling appropriate disclosure and speaking from the expertise of our lived experiences as well as acquired or academic expertise. By offering this honest yet crafted vulnerability, we create an environment in which students can feel safer to bring their experiences into the conversation as well. Our personal stories should create space for, rather than drown out, participants' stories. At the same time, we must take care not to tokenize ourselves. Although we speak from experience related to our social identities, we don't speak for an entire social identity group.

Sometimes, facilitating learning about an injustice that has impacted us personally can be a healing experience. But the power granted by our role, even when we seek to disrupt that power, confers an obligation to put participants' needs ahead of our own. This is particularly relevant when we choose to share personal stories as part of our facilitation. The stories should be selected and tailored to support participants' learning. If they support our own process as well, that's a happy side effect, but it's not our main goal. Telling personal stories shouldn't *harm* us, however, by retraumatizing or tokenizing or by making us more vulnerable than feels safe. For many teachers trained in more banking styles of education, self-disclosure may be new terrain. We encourage all facilitators to use disclosure planfully, with careful consideration of the desired and likely impacts on participants and yourself.

Similarly, social justice educators often speak of how we often learn something new from each new group of participants/students. In this way we are both part of the participants' learning community and separate from it. To hold our power responsibly means prioritizing participants' learning above our own and being careful not to exploit their energy for our own learning. At the same time, being open to learning from/with the group, and acknowledging to them that we are learning, can help disrupt the teacher/student power dynamic and empower participants as meaning-makers and creators of collective knowledge.

Co-facilitation

Our social justice pedagogy encourages co-facilitation in most situations—particularly a co-facilitation team who differ in their social identities most salient to the course. For example, a seminar on racism and anti-racism should usually be facilitated by two or more people with different racial identities than each other. Beyond knowing ourselves as individuals, we must get to know each other so that we can know ourselves as a team and collaboratively craft our co-facilitation dynamic to meet our goals for the learning environment. A co-facilitation relationship can be an opportunity to model collaboration, allyship, and accountability across identities. It also allows us to lean on each other's strengths and support each other's personal and professional development. Chapter 12: Critical Self-Knowledge includes an exploration of co-facilitation dynamics and approaches to building and utilizing co-facilitation relationships.

ELEMENT 2: FOSTER AN INCLUSIVE LEARNING COMMUNITY

One core principle of social justice education is that learning happens in community. SJE requires *practicing* social justice while learning about it, and that can only happen in a group. This runs counter to the mainstream of U.S. education, which is infused with individualism and often competition. For example, in mainstream education students are expected to demonstrate their knowledge by giving correct answers in class; in SJE we are more likely to encourage open-ended discussion about differing understandings, with the quality of the communication being valued as highly as the conclusions students may come to.

Our understanding of the importance of an inclusive learning community draws on the traditions of consciousness raising (Sherif & Sherif, 1970; Sarachild, 1975; Evans, 1980; Horton, Kohl, & Kohl, 1990; Kaba & Shine, 2017), feminist pedagogy (Weiler, 1988, 2001; Maher & Tetreault, 2001; hooks, 1994), and popular education (Freire, 1970, 1994; Anyon, 2009) described earlier in this chapter. These methods share an assumption that we learn together as a group not only to gain knowledge or understanding, but also to build a sense of group solidarity.

Building real relationships deepens the possibilities for learning and is also a valued outcome in itself. As such, hooks builds on the idea of the frameworks of consciousness raising and popular education when she talks about "teaching community" and "democratic education" (1994, 2003). In hooks's democratic education, the practice of engaging emotion and treating students as whole people, not separate from the course content or from the world beyond the classroom, creates space for an intimate learning community that values difference. hooks's formulation of democratic education also draws on earlier work by Allport (1954/1979), Dewey (1909/1975), and Lewin (1948), who looked at active, experiential group learning processes articulated within a social-psychological framework and directed to educational reform and anti-discrimination education. Like hooks, these educators wanted to provide an education that would prepare students to participate in a diverse, democratic society. The relationships built within the learning community can sustain learners through discussions on difficult topics and through difficult interactions with educational institutions. Students who learn in community are also often learning *for* community—not for their own individual academic achievement but in order to better serve the communities of which they are part (hooks, 2003).

Facilitating effective learning in community requires understanding group dynamics. When facilitators can recognize patterns in group dynamics, we can better create a situation in which students successfully cooperate in a diverse group. This experience can serve as a rehearsal for similarly inclusive, democratic participation beyond the classroom. Sometimes we make the group process an explicit part of the content by naming group dynamics that we notice and helping participants to decide together how they want to shape their learning community. Similarly, we can build in opportunities for participants to provide feedback to us and/or to the group about how their learning experience is going, making them active co-creators of the learning community and modeling accountable leadership. The group dynamics literature provides many useful ideas about experiential activities for learning in the "here and now," facilitated through process observation and feedback (Bradford, Gibb, & Benne, 1964; Pfeiffer & Jones, 1972–80). Theories such as Tuckman's (1965) stages of group development—Forming, Norming, Storming, and Performing—offer perspectives on how groups evolve that alert facilitators to the opportunities as well as pitfalls at various stages in a group's evolution.

Because they occur in groups, SJE experiences are sometimes emotionally, intellectual, and relationally intense. An SJE experience can be thought of as a "pressure cooker" toward complexity, metacognition, and reflection upon one's own experiences and emotions. Individual learners' developmental processes (identity development, cognitive development, and social/emotional development) rub up against each other's and at times against the group's momentum. Conflict and contradictions among group members can generate a productive friction that accelerates learning out of social necessity—students learn quickly and complexly because the relationships they're developing with each other demand it. At the same time, we don't want this productive discomfort to cross the line into harmful or retraumatizing group experiences. Establishing trusting relationships makes it possible to turn up the pressure without exploding the process.

Some of the traditions we draw on—political organizing, consciousness raising, and Freire's work—presuppose a sense of "groupness"; they are designed for people who are already living together as a community and/or working together as a group toward a common goal. In the social justice education designs in this book, we work to intentionally create a learning community with a diverse group of learners who may be new to each other. Often, we bring together participants from different social and cultural backgrounds, who bring different points of view, whose life experiences differ, and who seem at times to inhabit entirely different social and intellectual universes. The differences as well as the commonalities among participants from different social identities and social positions offer powerful opportunities for interactive and collaborative learning. To foster such learning community, we as the facilitators should make ample time and opportunities for students and facilitators to get to know each other and share space in a way that builds connections among group members.

Getting Started

How the class or workshop begins and the tone that is established at the outset sets the stage for the rest of the learning experience. Thus, SJE pays special attention to how an inclusive environment is established and how participants are welcomed into the environment and engaged actively in shaping the norms and guidelines for the learning community. When a course begins, it's important to greet the participants, structure their greeting of each other, and begin to get to know each other. We encourage facilitators to reflect on how their own personal style might fit their greeting. For example, more outgoing facilitators might individually and verbally greet participants as they enter the room. More introverted facilitators might put a greeting on the board. Having snacks and coffee or tea is often a good way to help create an atmosphere for participants to get to know each other. Facilitators should not assume that students have a particular set of social skills for making these connections. Giving explicit instructions and modeling behaviors—such as putting written instructions on a whiteboard or newsprint that asks participants to visit the snack table and then visiting it yourself and chatting with students—all work to set the tone in a classroom.

Entrance activities such as icebreakers and introduction activities also help ease any anxieties participants may be coming in with and provide structure for those who may not build relationships on their own. Providing ample opportunity to practice each other's names also supports group development and helps participants feel included. When facilitating an already-formed group, such as in a workplace setting, we should still work to establish a tone for our relationship with them, understanding that existing group dynamics will also be at play.

Early among the tone-setting activities, participants need to know what to expect of an "SJE approach." Instructors/facilitators should present some succinct, engaging, personalized remarks about what SJE is, the characteristics of the SJE approach they are using, the assumptions they make, what they hope the participants will achieve, and why they believe that a learning community needs to be inclusive and participatory. These remarks set a tone of transparency as facilitators explicitly describe their approach and assumptions about SJE. Participants also need to know what to expect in a practical sense—when the breaks will be, where the bathrooms are, etc. Facilitators can make explicit connections between these logistical details and our pedagogy—*why* it's important to consider people's different needs around pacing, breaks, and bathrooms, for example—and even if it's only implicit, providing this information demonstrates our care for participants' needs.

Explicitly Creating Norms and Guidelines

Part of establishing a learning community is creating explicit norms, guidelines, or group agreements. These guidelines not only give participants a sense of what to expect but also provide a tool to use throughout the group's time together to monitor and sustain the learning environment. Guidelines provide reminders in difficult moments, such as when participants are feeling misunderstood or when a few people are monopolizing the group's attention, that the participants have committed to an inclusive and respectful learning community.

There are many ways to go about establishing guidelines, which vary in how participatory they are. There is immense value in generating guidelines in a "bottom-up" way, with participants taking mutual responsibility for articulating their needs and commitments in the group. At the same time, facilitators should have in mind some guidelines that they know to be important for the kind of learning they want to foster and introduce those if the group doesn't generate them independently. Facilitators also need to keep in mind the responsibility that comes with their power position and can exercise that power to correct unintentional bias that participants may bring to the process of generating guidelines. For example, a group in which white, professional-class cultural norms are dominant may propose guidelines such as "no interruptions" or "don't hurt people's feelings" that would be oppressive to marginalized group members.

Meeting a Variety of Learning Needs

Among the differences participants bring to the learning community are differences in strengths, abilities, and learning styles. Some of these differences may be considered learning disabilities, others may be related to culture and educational background, and others are idiosyncratic individual differences. All these differences in learning needs should be taken seriously, and we should seek to design a learning experience that can work well for the widest possible range of learners.

Insistence on a narrow range of learning styles is one way that oppression plays out in educational systems. For instance, rigid age norms in schooling, such as the idea that all children should be able to read with equal facility at the same age, are fundamentally ableist in that they perpetuate the assumption that some bodies/minds are okay and others are not. Similarly, the emphasis on certain styles of learning, such as reading linear, fact-based texts, privilege white, professional-class cultures while devaluing cultures in which learning is more often hands-on or story-based.

To create a more inclusive learning community, we need to design learning experiences that work for participants who learn through hands-on practice or through narrative, as well as through facts and linear logic. We also need to design experiences that work for people whose reading, writing, and other academic skills are not typical for their age or education level. This is not only because it is the right and just thing to do but because it makes social justice education more effective. In social justice education, we want participants to engage with the "real world" and their roles in it—and in the real world, people learn and think in a variety of ways both across and within differences of ability, culture, and so on.

In most schools and universities students with documented disabilities have the opportunity to request accommodations to meet their specific learning needs. Educators should take these accommodations seriously and make every effort to implement them. But accommodations are an individualist solution to a structural problem. The more we design experiences to work for a wide range of needs, the fewer participants will need individual accommodations. The framework of Universal Design for Learning (UDL) offers a set of practices for designing and facilitating learning experiences that invite multiple ways of engaging and account for a variety of possible learning needs. The Universal Design for ★ Social Justice Education handout offers more detail about implementing UDL (also see Chapter 3: Design and Facilitation).

To begin thinking about different learning needs, it may be helpful to review various models of learning styles, such as Kolb's framework (1981, 1984), whose practical application is explored in Brooks-Harris and Stock-Ward's (1999) *Workshops: Designing and Facilitating Experiential Learning*. When considering these learning-style models, we encourage educators to think of them not as absolute "types" or inherent traits but as patterns that may emerge from someone's individual development, past educational experiences, culture, and any number of other factors. Our learning styles are not limitations or destinies but useful prompts for reflection on patterns or preferences in our own learning, our students' learning, and our teaching.

ELEMENT 3: CENTER AN ANALYSIS OF SYSTEMS OF OPPRESSION AND HOW THEY OPERATE IN SOCIETY AND IN THE CLASSROOM

A pedagogy of social justice education necessarily includes an analysis of systems of oppression, including how these systems operate in the classroom, community group, organization, and society more broadly. An analysis of systems of oppression goes beyond awareness of inequality to examine how it operates, how it developed historically, and who benefits. Theories of oppression and social justice issues become not just abstract ideas but ways to understand oneself, others, and the world in order to create change.

For Freire, pedagogy was an instrument to awaken oppressed peoples from their subordinated status into a consciousness of their oppression, with the expectation that once awakened, they would take actions to effect change. In a similar vein, we work with participants and students to use the workshop and classroom settings as a way to make connections between their personal experiences and systems of oppression, to equip them to work toward social justice goals. We also recognize that oppression operates through education in a multitude of ways, including through the "hidden curriculum" in which the status quo is perpetuated through the very norms and traditions of teaching and learning. Thus, we are committed to developing a pedagogy that practices social justice while teaching about social justice, both explicitly and through the hidden curriculum.

All Education Is Political: The Hidden Curriculum

One major tenet of social justice education is that all education is political. To be "neutral" is to support the status quo. Most U.S. formal schooling supports the status quo through both the "explicit" curriculum (the content that is taught) and the "hidden" curriculum (the values, policies, procedures, and pedagogies through which teaching takes place) (Beyer & Apple, 1998; Margolis, 2001; Nieto & Bode, 2008). Similarly, workplace trainings, embedded in the organizational norms and assumptions of the workplace and the field, are more often than not designed to reinforce those norms and serve the institution more than the participants. Even community-based workshops that explicitly challenge the status quo may also unintentionally reinforce it in norms and expectations that go unexamined.

Implicit curriculum also happens at an institutional level. In an academic context, instructors do not have control over what content is considered canon within their institution or field, even though they can often make decisions for their own classes. In workplace trainings, trainers cannot dictate which skills, behaviors, and roles are valued and well compensated in an industry. In order to influence what is valued in an institution and field, including whether social justice education gets funding and/or is even "allowed" to take place, it is important for social justice educators to be involved at the policy and political levels.

Addressing the hidden curriculum means that we need to change both the content of courses and how we teach. For example, syllabi that include "canonical" texts in a discipline will often be skewed toward authors who are white men, but the social identities of these authors rarely get named as such. When a syllabus centers materials by authors of color (or women, or women of color, or any non-dominant group), that focus is notable and often explicitly named. A similar pattern applies to many training contexts outside academia where topics like "leadership skills" are often framed around a few key sources written by white men or are explicitly named as "alternative" models to that default. The status quo of what is considered the canon is one way the hidden curriculum can operate. As social justice educators, we must actively work against this type of hidden curriculum.

Another example is the traditional classroom arrangement in which the students sit in orderly rows, facing the teacher who talks at the students, "giving" them information—also common in professional training settings. This arrangement implicitly values the type of person who is able to learn in this structure and reinforces hierarchies of age, rank, and educational status. To value diverse needs and engage in active learning practices (which we detail in the following in Element 5) is another way in which we resist the hidden curriculum of various settings.

Connecting Personal Experience with Understanding of Systems

Social justice education needs a pedagogy that creates learning communities where members share and learn from each other's experiences, reflect on their own and other's experiences to make sense of larger structural systems of advantage and disadvantage, and create new meanings for themselves.

In SJE classrooms and workshops, participants learn to reflect upon their own multiple, simultaneous social identities and statuses and to examine how these connect with larger systems of oppression. They also explore how institutional and cultural dynamics impact them as members of particular social groups. Participants come to understand how these dynamics or concepts are not some abstraction but part of their own realities. These approaches share a lot with consciousness-raising traditions; participants developing a critical understanding of the conditions of their own lives is both a goal and a method.

An important goal of SJE pedagogy is that participants understand the interactions among individual beliefs and behavior, institutional policies and practice, and cultural and social structures that advantage some groups while disadvantaging others. People experience all three levels simultaneously but often recognize only one at a time. It is important that participants have the opportunity to practice thinking across levels so that they become skillful at recognizing such multilayered examples in everyday life. Without a theory of oppression based on an understanding of institutional and cultural reproductions of oppression, individual experiences and stories do not "add up" to something more. In SJE, much of the new meaning-making for participants takes place in the coordination of the personal and the structural, and such coordination may feel like a stretch for participants of any age or educational background.

Similarly, people experience their multiple identities simultaneously, so it's important to support participants in developing and understanding how their multiple identities relate to multiple systems of oppression in complex ways. While this is important for all participants' learning, it is especially crucial for those whose salient identities complicate the topic at hand. For instance, an approach to classism that doesn't fully integrate the intersection of race will tend to fall flat for participants of color and can often reproduce racist dynamics that cause harm; likewise, an approach to racism that doesn't fully integrate the intersection of class will tend to be confusing and often harmful for economically poor white participants. When our approach is not intersectional, it is implicitly for only the *most* privileged people in a given group (e.g. white people who are also wealthy; class-privileged people who are also white), thus reproducing some kinds of oppression while trying to work against another.

A theoretical intersectional *analysis*—the idea that systems of oppression are entangled and mutually co-constituting and that our multiple identities and roles in these systems are inextricable—has been part of SJE for a long time (Crenshaw, 1991; Collins, 1998). But intersectional *pedagogy*—integrating intersectional analysis into our methods and curriculum—has lagged behind. Often, we focus on one identity or ism at a time, which can serve important learning purposes but can also be overwhelming and does not necessarily lend itself to more detailed explorations of particular manifestations of oppression. Focusing solely on one ism can also potentially contradict our intersectional analysis (Shlasko, 2015). Activities that are designed to demonstrate the functioning of one ism produce a unidimensional understanding, and intersections are treated as footnotes or asides rather than as central to how oppression operates. Even when the explicit curriculum talks about intersectionality, the implicit curriculum is dominated by the non-intersectional structure of activities, courses, and organizations. One way an SJE pedagogy can approach this dilemma is to continually bring in different lenses, examining issues from one angle and then another.

Social justice education comprises an analysis of oppression that is both outside and inside the classroom or workshop at one and the same moment. Oppression is "outside" in that the information about historical and contemporary manifestations of oppression that we learn about, as well as resistance and actions taken for social justice, exist "out there" in the world. At the same time, the system of oppression is inevitably "in here"—in the learning community—providing opportunities for instructors and peers to note how oppression is reproduced in the group. Learning about systems of oppression helps participants recognize and understand dynamics that may occur within the learning community; likewise, through reflecting on group dynamics, we help participants analyze social relations of power and privilege. Observations about patterns like who speaks and for how long, who gets interrupted, whose views are listened to or dismissed, how people's body language and emotional expressiveness gets interpreted, and who tends to sit next to whom all become windows into an understanding of intergroup relations and societal power dynamics. The process provides a real-time illustration of the content, and participants know that they are part of the systems they are learning about.

The coordination of personal, individual experience with larger structural and societal reference points shows the continuity of the past into the present. Just as contemporary manifestations of oppression in the outer world get reproduced inside the classroom or workshop, so too do historical legacies of injustice and oppression. Our histories are not only "out there" in the world but also "in here" in the thoughts and assumptions carried from participants' families and home communities into the shared learning community. Thus, the "outside world" comes into the learning community through the histories and experiences brought there by participants, as well as the in-the-moment interactions that illustrate broader patterns of oppression.

There are also opportunities to practice moving toward the possibilities for social justice "in here," in moments where participants become more self-aware and develop new ways of interacting and collaborating through mutual respect, equality, and inclusion. When conflict and disagreements occur, we can use those as teachable moments to explore larger-scale conflicts in society and within social justice movements. Attending to and working through conflicts in the group enables participants to develop and practice tools for analysis and skills for interacting in other settings. We recognize all settings as "real life" and resist the tendency to see classroom or workshop settings as somehow disconnected from the "real world."

ELEMENT 4: DEFINE GOALS, LEARNING OBJECTIVES, AND EVALUATION MECHANISMS FOR SOCIAL JUSTICE EDUCATION

The goal of SJE is to model social justice through our facilitation and teaching and to equip participants with knowledge and skills that they will need to become agents of social justice in their work and communities. Within that goal, our specific learning objectives may vary considerably across different educational contexts.

Types of Objectives

In SJE, we look at three kinds of objectives: content, process, and skills/action.

- **Content objectives** are often the most straightforward and familiar to those working in mainstream educational institutions. Content objectives include the information and understanding that participants will gain. Examples of content objectives are "Participants will know at least three examples of institutional-level oppression" and "Participants will understand how historical redlining contributes to present-day wealth inequality."
- **Process objectives** focus on how participants will spend their time in a session communicating, building community, learning, and practicing skills. Process objectives are less often articulated in mainstream education. Examples of process objectives include "Participants will experience listening deeply to each other" and "Participants will feel respected and supported in their learning processes."
- **Skills/action** objectives are about what participants will do, or be able to do, as a result of their participation. Examples of skills/action objectives are "Participants will be able to identify subtly coded sexism in media" and "Participants will initiate conversations with peers about microaggressions in their social circles." A training or workshop in a workplace or community organization, rather than in a classroom, may come with action goals related to the specific needs of the organization.

Content, process, and skills/action are not mutually exclusive categories. We find it useful to distinguish them to make sure we don't forget to think through the less obvious kinds of objectives. If we don't incorporate process objectives into our planning, participants will still learn something through the process, but not necessarily what we would want them to learn. Articulating process objectives is sometimes a matter of surfacing and making decisions about what would otherwise be "hidden curriculum." For instance, an implicit process objective of much mainstream education might be "students will experience a passive role in a rigid hierarchy."

We see the importance of process in participant feedback. Participants can often name a plethora of facts, ideas, and skills they learned yet say that none were as impactful as their experience in the group. Comments like "I felt included in a way I never have before" or "I learned that conversations about classism don't have to feel scary and awful" show how it is not only what people learn but how they learn it that is truly transformative. It is clear that process must be prioritized along with content when we define our learning objectives.

Skills-building objectives relate to what participants will be able to do beyond demonstrating knowledge and understanding and often include objectives related to critical thinking and communication skills. For example, we might have an objective that "participants will be able to ask and answer critical questions to identify root causes of social problems." Note how this differs from the content objective of "understand what some root causes of social problems are." In terms of communication skills, we might have an objective around being able to use a particular communication technique, such as active listening, to communicate across differences of identity and experience. Intergroup dialogue is an application of social justice pedagogy that is particularly explicit about centering objectives around communication skills (Gurin, Nagda, & Zúñiga, 2013; Zúñiga, Nagda, Chesler, & Cytron-Walker, 2007).

We may also have action objectives about what participants will *actually* do beyond the boundaries of the classroom or workshop. These are much harder to measure than the other kinds, but keeping them in mind during planning is still important. If we want participants to not only *be able to* recognize inequality in the institutions they're part of but also actually go looking for it and then organize to address it, our workshop designs should include concrete and detailed action planning.

In most school settings, participants choose their own real or potential actions with which to practice action planning. In workplace contexts, training participants might be enrolled in a training with the expectation that they will undertake a specific action, such as revising a policy or developing a program based on what they learn. Other workplace trainings have less defined outcomes, allowing participants to generate their own action ideas based on training content and aligned with the organization's mission, vision, and values. In community organizing settings, where SJE overlaps with political education, taking action is often a central goal of the learning process. A group in the early stages of planning a collective action may come together for an SJE workshop to help them build their shared understanding and skills in order to collaborate more effectively than they would otherwise be able to do.

Although concrete objectives are helpful in planning and often required by our institutions, they can also be limiting. Sometimes the ideal outcomes depend on who the participants are and what they need, which we cannot entirely predict in advance. Mindful of the principle of disrupting the teacher/student binary, we should be open to unexpected learnings emerging from the group. Scholars of queer pedagogy speak of queer interventions, in which an educator might introduce an idea or activity not to make a particular point but to see what happens (Rofes, 1998). The group can then generate new understandings, or new questions, that would not have come up if the session had been planned toward a specific, narrow objective. Other scholars refer to "enlarging the space of the possible"— not teaching an answer but expanding the range of possible answers that participants are able to imagine (Davis & Sumara, 2000; Britzman, 2012). These less directive ways of planning a learning experience can help us avoid reproducing neoliberal frameworks of learning, where the constant drive toward measurable production and progress may subtly undermine our social justice analysis.

Action as an Outcome of Social Justice Education

Social justice pedagogy assumes that knowledge alone is not enough; we are educating toward action. What kind of action, and how specifically we can set goals about action, depends to a great extent on our institutional context. In schools, and for any learning environment in which participation is not voluntary, requiring participants to take a specific kind of action toward justice is ethically problematic. Nevertheless, we can usually find ways to incorporate some form of action, or at least skill building that supports potential future action, into a session's objectives.

In semester-long courses, we often incorporate an action project as a core assignment. Participants usually work in small groups to identify a problem, design an action to address the problem, complete the action (or one step of it that can reasonably be accomplished within the course's time frame), and reflect on their experience. Their actions may be interpersonal in scale, such as initiating critical conversations with friends, or more institutional level, such as conducting a letter-writing campaign to influence institutional action. In shorter-term courses such as weekend seminars where there isn't time for a full-scale action project, we usually include an action-planning activity. Even though the action won't be completed (or even started) before the course ends, participants practice thinking through the strategies, resources, and stakeholder relationships they will need to develop in order to take action effectively. In many workplace and community-based workshops, action may not be a separate activity or assignment but rather a constant reference point, so that in every part of the workshop facilitators and participants are asking each other, "What will this mean for our action?"

Evaluation

Like everything else in social justice education, our assessment and evaluation strategies should reflect our social justice values. What and how we evaluate and assess conveys clear messages about what is valued by the instructors and/or the institution.

For the purpose of this chapter, we use "evaluation" to refer to processes that seek to judge learning on a linear scale, such as letter grades. Some of the institutional contexts in which SJE takes place, such as K–12 schools and universities, require certain types of evaluation that are often in tension with SJE pedagogy. In these settings, part of our obligation as social justice educators is to do the best we can to align our evaluation with our social justice values while enabling students to get the institution's recognition for their learning (in the form of academic credits, for example).

We use "assessment" more broadly than evaluation to mean any way of collecting information that helps us understand what is happening in a learning community. Assessment is more often qualitative compared to evaluation, although both assessment and evaluation can include qualitative and quantitative measures. The information gathered in assessment is used not to judge but rather to create opportunities for reflection and feedback, to determine what the individual participants and the group need next, and to inform facilitators' professional development and future program development.

Many of the outcomes that we value in SJE are not easy to evaluate or assess because they are internal and subjective. It is presumptuous to evaluate a participant's courage, compassion, empathy, self-awareness, curiosity, or open-mindedness, although we can sometimes assess behaviors that we assume reflect those qualities. Often, the growth that we hope to see in participants continues well beyond the scope of a single workshop or semester. A "final" evaluation catches participants at the beginning or middle of a lifelong process.

Nevertheless, we want to be able to ascertain whether our work is doing what we think it's doing—whether we are meeting our objectives. This includes individual learning objectives, such as whether participants understand the concepts we've introduced, and group-level objectives, such as whether the group can sustain dialogue while disagreeing. It also includes assessing our performance as facilitators—how skillfully we have applied the techniques and pedagogies we're using—and our success in meeting organizational objectives, such as filling a gap in the curriculum or shifting organizational culture. In order to remain accountable for our impact and be able to continually improve our practice, social justice pedagogy should include a range of evaluation and assessment strategies that center participants, respect a wide range of learning styles, and work to disrupt rather than reinforce the teacher/learner hierarchy.

Problems with Mainstream Methods of Evaluation

The evaluation processes predominant in mainstream schooling reify power structures in which some people (adults, with educational privilege, usually coded as white) are presumed to have knowledge while others (young people, People of Color, people who have not received institutional recognition of their learning in the form of a degree) are presumed to need it. This type of evaluation assumes and reinforces a rigid teacher/student hierarchy that is opposed to the goals of SJE, even if the content knowledge being evaluated is congruent with SJE. Although this book focuses on undergraduate and adult learners, the great majority of learners and facilitators have been socialized through mainstream school systems and may have internalized aspects of this approach to evaluation.

Mainstream schooling also relies heavily on evaluations that are standardized, meaning that they are normed to a population of students whose scores will fall on a bell curve. Philosophically, standardized testing is a direct descendent of eugenics. It seeks to categorize learners in order to rationalize valuing some learners over others. Such evaluations are fundamentally opposed to social justice and cannot recognize the experiential types of learning and multiple ways of knowing that we value in SJE. Even evaluation tools that are not standardized often don't measure what we want them to measure. The actual task measured by testing—for example, being able to explain a concept in writing—is almost always an abstracted substitute for the skill or knowledge we hope participants have gained—for example, being able to apply that concept to their continually evolving understanding of the world.

Assessments that are qualitative or informal also have ample room for bias. Our observations of participants' performance on assignments and/or in group interactions is informed by our own assumptions and biases and by the norms of our institutions and fields. Deciding whether someone's work is "excellent" or "competent" is not as objective a measure as it might seem. Meeting the expectations for excellence or competence often requires specific cultural capital acquired through families with intergenerational experience in higher education and/or through attending well-funded, majority-white, and majority-class-privileged schools. For example, Downey and Pribesh (2004) found that teachers more negatively interpret the behaviors of Black students as compared to white students. Unless we very intentionally integrate anti-racism and anti-oppression into evaluation practices, evaluations of any kind are likely to reproduce the oppressive systems in which they take place. Furthermore, any evaluation that seeks to measure individual accomplishments tends to reflect the neoliberal framework that focuses on individual achievement and supposedly objectively measurable outcomes, rather than on relationships and processes.

How We Conceptualize Assessment and Evaluation

A social justice approach to evaluation and assessment focuses on how information can be used to help all members of a learning community reach their individual and group goals. When we must evaluate on a linear scale, a low score should be understood not as a judgment of failure to learn but as an indicator of how much or what kinds of support that learner needs. Evaluation and assessment can be used as an opportunity for communication and collaboration. Facilitators and participants can reflect together on what is or isn't supporting them to make progress toward individual and group goals. Through the assessment process, participants may learn about how they learn and may receive feedback about their role in the learning community, which enables them to become more effective learners and community members. Thus, evaluation and assessment are teaching tools, not only tools of measurement.

Assessment and evaluation should make room for a wide range of learning styles. For example, we might evaluate participation as a core requirement of an SJE course, but only with the understanding that participation looks different for different people. Participants bring their different cultural expectations, processing speeds, and starting points to their participation. The question can't only be "Is this person participating enough?" or even "Is this person participating well?" but rather "Is this person participating in a way that supports their learning?" Depending on our goals, we might also ask whether an individual's participation is supporting the group's learning as well as their own—or, at least, not creating barriers to group learning.

Our evaluation and assessment strategies need to be participant centered, both in that they reflect the needs of the participants and in that participants are active collaborators in the process of evaluation rather than just the subjects of evaluation. Facilitators should always explain the purpose of any evaluation or assessment process in order for participants to use it effectively and to disrupt the teacher/student hierarchy. The hierarchy won't go away, especially in cases where the facilitator has authority to assign grades. While acknowledging that power relationship, we can still engage in a more collaborative evaluation and assessment process that both trusts and builds participants' capacity to honestly assess their own learning.

The more participatory the evaluation and assessment is, the more students will be able to reflect on and utilize the results to support their ongoing learning. Participatory evaluation can include having participants grade their own assignments and participation, provide feedback to peers, and engage in structured reflection activities such as reflective essays, journaling, expressive arts, one-on-one "thinking aloud" with peers, and mindful contemplation. Participatory assessment can also include group dialogue about how the learning process is going and what the group needs next. Sometimes such a dialogue emerges organically from the group process, and a skilled facilitator will recognize the information that emerges as assessment data that can be used to support the group's learning moving forward.

ELEMENT 5: UTILIZE COLLABORATIVE AND ACTIVE LEARNING

The pedagogy of SJE is a pedagogy of active learning, embedded in multiple social contexts (the content, the self in relation to others, the learning community, the institution, the whole society). Social justice education engages both the participants and the world. We aim to create a "container" in order to foster learning experiences in relative safety, but there is a constant interchange among our present learning environment, our personal histories and experiences, and the broader world. When we try out new skills during a workshop session, it is not "just practice," it is also real life—we are really doing the behaviors we are learning how to do. What we learn "in here" helps us understand and navigate the world "out there," but what's out there is always already in here, too. Our teaching methods take advantage of these inevitable complexities to materialize content as both personally relevant and socially relevant.

Meeting Participants Where They Are Both Emotionally and Cognitively

As social justice educators, we recognize that participants come to our workshops and classes from all different starting points. We often begin by inviting them to reflect on what they know already and then work to scaffold the knowledge and skills needed to engage with issues of social justice in the learning community and more broadly in the world. A scaffold is a structure that supports a building and allows builders to navigate it safely while it is under construction. Rather than assuming that students are like an empty lot just waiting to break ground, we assume they come with foundations and structures, some of which can be built upon and others that may be in need of repair or even replacement. Scaffolding learning means providing a structure to support participants as they examine their previous experiences and existing knowledges, dismantle or rebuild pieces they find flawed, and add depth, breadth, and complexity. The scaffold allows them—in fact, compels them—to connect new learning to the understanding they brought with them to the learning experience. Scaffolding provides cognitive, emotional, and relational support so that participants can do the sometimes destabilizing work of learning and unlearning, without falling apart.

Critical reflection about one's social positions and identities and critical thinking about structural inequities are SJE objectives that challenge and stretch participants, both cognitively and emotionally. Because SJE asks participants to examine their previously held beliefs, they may experience strong (often unexpected) emotions when their belief systems are contradicted by new information and perspectives that challenge what they have taken to be true. When questioning perspectives that have been shaped by family, school, or religious authorities, participants may question or resist information that challenges their entrenched worldview. They may not be prepared to use analytic frameworks when enmeshed in their own personal, emotional experiences. They may need structure, role models, and validation to support them in reaching for new awareness and working with more complex, self-reflective, and nuanced thinking skills.

Without such parallel attention to thoughts and feelings, participants cannot learn to identify or manage the influence that their emotions might have on the conclusions they reach about social justice issues. Emotional reactions can cloud thinking about issues of justice and can also be resources for new insights and understanding. We work toward developing both awareness and analysis of one's own beliefs, emotions, and actions.

Mindfulness practices are one way to support the development of critical awareness of one's own thoughts and feelings. From something as simple as starting a session with a moment of silence, to more directed meditations and somatic awareness exercises, mindfulness practices get people in the habit of noticing their own thoughts and feelings before interpreting and acting on them (e.g. Berila, 2016; Magee, 2019).

As facilitators, we not only provide information but also guide the group process, suggest frameworks for meaning-making, and confront contradictions and misunderstandings. We offer participants the resources (cognitive, emotional, and practical) they need to bring more complexity to their thinking and at times to confront long-held beliefs they have not previously examined. We observe what comes up during group discussion and encourage participants to make connections and map relationships among similar ideas. Through facilitation that attends to participants' starting places and learning processes, we create manageable steps that gradually build up to a transformative learning experience.

Active Learning

Social justice education pedagogies prioritize active engagement by the entire learning group and utilize activities designed to involve everyone. Even in activities where some participants are giving a presentation while others listen, the listeners are grappling with both the content and the relational process of the presentation. Participants apply ideas to their own lives and become active co-creators of knowledge through discussion and dialogue. They also bring their learning to explorations of their social context and try out new skills both in and beyond the "classroom."

Some of the simplest active learning activities involve physically moving around, through activities such as "Common Ground" or "Concentric Circles", or rotating through different stations to generate examples for "Five Faces" or discuss different scenarios. "Gallery Walks" also involve movement and create opportunities for participants ★ to produce work in small groups and then share it with peers. Simply moving while engaging with learning helps some learners process information more effectively, but physical movement isn't the only feature that makes these activities "active." They're also "active" in the sense that participants produce learning material for each other, rather than just receiving it from the facilitators. They take mutual responsibility for the group's learning, practicing collaboration and community while gaining information and understanding.

One specific type of active learning is experiential learning, conceptualized by Kolb (1984) as a cycle of four phases: concrete experience, reflective observation, abstract conceptualization, and active experimentation. Kolb's cycle is based on his work on learning styles (1981, 1984) and assumes that while some learners will thrive more easily in one phase of the cycle or another, the four together provide a holistic learning experience that balances reflection with action and theory with application (Anderson & Adams, 1992). With opportunities to engage in a variety of ways, the model encourages an inclusive learning environment where learners with different needs and strengths can all benefit and contribute.

The "concrete experience" part of the cycle of experiential learning can come from within or beyond the learning setting and can be more or less in the facilitators' control. Facilitators have the most control when experience comes from contrived activities designed to simulate dynamics of oppression, such as a Privilege Walk or Star Power (Mukhopadhyay, 2014; Shirts, 1969). These simulations can be powerful learning opportunities when used with very careful consideration of the group's needs. For example, we have had success with this kind of activity in a group where we knew that participants would be open to the activity's messages and the group either was relatively homogenous or had strong existing relationships. We also pay attention to differences in learning needs among participants and may strategically assign roles in a simulation so that participants are not asked to simulate an experience of oppression they already have ample experience with. With other kinds of groups, or without such detailed planning, simulations are both pedagogically and ethically questionable; they tend to provide the most learning benefit to participants who already have the most privilege, often retraumatize participants with marginalized identities, and sometimes backfire when participants distrust the outcomes because the experience is so obviously contrived (Shlasko, 2015).

Facilitators can also create opportunities for a shared experience to reflect on that are less contrived but still designed to move toward learning goals. For instance, participants in a workshop on ableism might be asked to observe access features and barriers to access in the week leading up to the workshop. That experience of observing ableism and disability justice in their everyday lives becomes the subject of reflection, abstraction (connecting the experience to broader patterns or meanings), and eventually active experimentation (taking action), such as generating ideas for advocacy. The facilitators have less control over the content that emerges, but the experience is more "real" and thus leads to more active engagement in the rest of the cycle. The cycle doesn't end with experimentation—ideally, participants' experience of taking action becomes the "concrete experience" that launches them on another round of learning.

Bringing one's experiences "into the room" is also a form of experiential learning. Activities that invite participants to share their own previous experiences are a simple way to make learning active and experiential, without the facilitator having to design the initial experience at all. Because we know that oppression is pervasive, we can usually count on some common manifestations of oppression coming up in participants' reflections on their own lives. Because it is their own real lives, they are already motivated to make sense of the experiences and take action.

Finally, the experience of participation in the learning community can itself be a seed for a cycle of experiential learning. When conflict emerges, or communication becomes confusing, or power dynamics play out, pausing to reflect and make meaning of the situation provides an opportunity to develop both understanding and skill. Participants can read an article about how often men talk over women in corporate meetings, but when their attention is drawn to the same dynamic playing out right here and now, both the theory and the implications for action can really crystallize. At the same time, participants are practicing the skill of engaging with people who are both similar and different from them, developing competencies they can use in the active experimentation phase of learning and also in many settings beyond the learning community.

Collaborative Learning

Some formal education systems are set up in explicitly competitive ways. Competition does not necessarily prohibit active learning, but along with whatever content they are learning, participants will be learning from the process to compete rather than collaborate.

An SJE pedagogy emphasizes collaboration over competition because collaboration is essential to movements for social change, and research on the psychology of bias suggests collaboration also plays a key role in particular kinds of individual change. Collaboration toward a common goal is part of what makes it possible for an intergroup experience to lead to reduced implicit bias (Pettigrew & Tropp, 2006, 2011; Staats & Patton, 2013), whereas competition can undermine this potential. Furthermore, an emphasis on collaboration helps participants learn to generate new knowledge and new solutions together, rather than only relying on an authority figure for answers.

Bearing in mind that the process is always part of the content, if we want participants to learn how to collaborate across differences (content), we should create opportunities for them to engage collaboratively within the learning community (process). The common goal toward which they are collaborating could be an action project or simply reaching their learning objectives. When participants take mutual responsibility for supporting each other's learning, they are both collaborating to learn and learning to collaborate.

Many participants have a lot of unlearning to do in terms of defaulting to a competitive approach. To focus on the needs of the group as well as their own needs, and on the group's learning as well as their own learning, contradicts most of their schooling experiences and requires repetition and practice. It is not enough to have one assignment about collaboration; rather, we should infuse it throughout the educational experience. Many of the activities often used in SJE can function in a relatively individualist way or in a much more collaborative way that provokes participants to become invested in each other's learning.

A simple kind of collaborative learning activity is one in which participants generate content for each other to learn from. For instance, participants might be assigned to read different sources and then teach back what they have learned. A gallery activity in which ★ small groups produce notes of their discussion and then learn from the other groups' notes is another example. Such activities can be made even more collaborative with the addition of a next step that asks participants to put their different pieces of content into conversation with each other to create something new, such as in the Five Faces of Classism activity (see Chapter 7: Classism). Even just sharing reactions to material in pairs can contribute ★ to collaborative learning, as participants learn from each other's reactions and come to care about each other's learning experiences. The more that participants are taking each other's learning seriously, wanting to both learn from others and support others' learning, the more collaborative their experience will be.

Any activity based on personal sharing can be collaborative because participants are learning from each other's lived experiences. When participants reflect on their own experiences and hear the experiences of others, they are able to broaden their frames of reference and increase both knowledge and empathy. There is power in learning about common experiences of oppression from the specific experiences of people with whom you have a connection. Learning from each other does not replace the resources instructors provide, especially if the group is relatively homogeneous, but contributes to and enhances the learning experience. By valuing participants' existing knowledge and experiences as "content," we shift some authority from facilitators to participants, reinforce the value of multiple perspectives, and create opportunities for relationship building among participants that can form the foundation for ongoing mutual learning.

However, personal sharing does not necessarily lead to collaborative learning. If the focus is only on gaining knowledge, these activities can be unintentionally exploitative, with the more privileged participants learning at the expense of those with less privilege. A more collaborative approach to the same kind of activity surfaces the inequalities in the group in terms of who brings what kinds of understanding and experience and who benefits most from hearing whose stories and invites the group to figure out together how best to support each other's learning needs in an equitable way. The group then learns not only from each other's knowledge and experiences but also from each other's current learning process in the context of a current, evolving relationship. Intergroup dialogue methodologies tend to emphasize this kind of relational learning.

Activities that involve experimentation and improvisation also tend to support collaboration. Applied theater activities (Boal, 1992, 2000, 2013; Schutzman & Cohen-Cruz, 1994), role-playing, and action projects of any scale can all create a more hands-on, embodied collaboration experience that more closely mirrors the kind of collaboration we hope participants will engage in beyond the learning community.

CONCLUSION

Social justice pedagogies reflect the application of theories of social justice to our understanding of learning processes and teaching practices. The theoretical foundations explored in Chapter 1: Theoretical Foundations guide and shape the pedagogical elements of social justice education. This chapter bridges our theory and practice, engaging in an example of praxis in its consideration of why we teach the way we do. Many of the explanations and examples in this chapter already point to elements of design and facilitation. The inextricable connections between content and process, inside and outside, understanding and action, and individual and group will continue to be evident as Chapter 3: Design and Facilitation gets into more detail about how to design, structure, and facilitate an SJE workshop.

Notes

* We ask that those who cite this work always acknowledge by name all of the authors listed rather than either only citing the first author or using "et al." to indicate co-authors. All collaborated on the conceptualization, development, and writing of this chapter.
1 We use the terminology of "elements" as some are framed like principles in that they're directive and others are framed as considerations for facilitators.

References

Adams, M. (2014). Social justice and education. In M. Reisch (Ed.), *The Routledge international handbook of social justice* (pp. 249–268). New York: Routledge.

Adams, M., Bell, L. A., & Griffin, P. (1997). *Teaching for diversity and social justice: A sourcebook.* London: Routledge.

Adams, M., Bell, L. A., & Griffin, P. (2007). *Teaching for diversity and social justice* (2nd ed.). London: Routledge.

Adams, M., Bell, L. A., & Griffin, P. (2016). *Teaching for diversity and social justice* (3rd ed.). London: Routledge.

Adams, M., Perry-Jenkins, M., & Tropp, L. (2014). Pedagogical tools for social justice and psychology. In C. V. Johnson, H. Friedman, J. Diaz, Z. Franco, & B. Nastasi (Eds.), *The Praeger handbook on social justice and psychology* (Vol. 2, pp. 227–248). Santa Barbara, CA: Praeger.

Allport, G. W. (1954/1979). *The nature of prejudice* (unabridged, 25th anniversary ed.). Reading, PA: Addison-Wesley.

Anderson, J. A., & Adams, M. (1992). Acknowledging the learning styles of diverse student populations: Implications for instructional design. In L. A. B. Border & N. V. N. Chism (Eds.), *Teaching for diversity: New directions for teaching and learning* (Vol. 49, pp. 19–34). San Francisco: Jossey-Bass.

Anyon, J. (2009). Critical pedagogy is not enough: Social justice education, political participation, and the politicization of students. In M. W. Apple, W. Au, & I. A. Grandin (Eds.), *The Routledge international handbook of critical education* (pp. 389–393). New York: Routledge.

Apple, M. W., Au, W., & Gandin, L. A. (2009). *The Routledge international handbook of critical education*. New York: Routledge.

Au, W. (2009). Fighting with the text: Contextualizing and reconceptualizing Freire's critical pedagogy. In M. W. Apple, W. Au, & I. A. Grandin (Eds.), *The Routledge international handbook of critical education* (pp. 221–231). New York: Routledge.

Barbera, L. E. (2011). *The Expressive Arts in Teacher Education: Cultivating Social Justice Leadership*. LAP LAMBERT.

Barcelos, C. A. (2019). Transfeminist pedagogy and the women's health classroom. *Feminist Formations, 31*(3), 1–24.

Baxter-Magolda, M. B. (1992). *Knowing and reasoning in college: Gender-related patterns in students' intellectual development*. San Francisco: Jossey-Bass.

Belenky, M. F., Clinchy, M. B., Goldberger, N. R., & Tarule, J. M. (1986). *Women's ways of knowing: The development of self, voice, and mind*. New York: Basic Books.

Benne, K. D. (1964). History of the T-group in the laboratory setting. In L. P. Bradford, J. R. Gibb, & K. D. Benne (Eds.), *T-group theory and laboratory method: Innovation in re-education* (pp. 80–136). New York: John Wiley.

Berila, B. (2016). *Integrating mindfulness into anti-oppression pedagogy*. New York: Routledge.

Bernal, D. D., Burciaga, R., & Carmona, J. F. (Eds.). (2017). *Chicana/Latina testimonios as pedagogical, methodological, and activist approaches to social justice*. London: Routledge.

Beyer, L. E., & Apple, M. W. (Eds.). (1998). *The curriculum: Problems, politics, and possibilities* (2nd ed.). Albany, NY: State University of New York Press.

Boal, A. (1992). *Games for actors and non-actors*. London: Routledge.

Boal, A. (2000). *Theater of the Oppressed*. Pluto Press.

Boal, A. (2013). *The rainbow of desire: The Boal method of theatre and therapy*. London: Routledge.

Bradford, L. P., Gibb, J. R., & Benne, K. D. (Eds.). (1964). *T-group theory and laboratory method: Innovation in re-education*. New York: John Wiley.

Britzman, D. (2012). Queer pedagogy and its strange techniques. *Counterpoints, 367*, 292–308.

Brookfield, S. D., & Holst, J. D. (2011). *Radicalizing learning: Adult education for a just world*. San Francisco: Jossey-Bass.

Brooks-Harris, J., & Stock-Ward, S. (1999). *Workshops: Designing and Facilitating Experiential Learning*. Sage.

Cole, M. (1996). *Cultural psychology: A once and future discipline*. Cambridge, MA: Harvard University Press.

Collins, P. H. (1998). It's all in the family: Intersections of gender, race, and nation. *Hypatia, 13*(3), 62–82.

Crenshaw, K. W. (1991). Mapping the margins: Intersectionality, identity politics, and violence against women of color. *Stanford Law Review, 43*(6), 1241.

Darder, A., Baltodano, M. P., & Torres, R. D. (Eds.). (2008). *The critical pedagogy reader* (2nd ed.). New York: Routledge.

Davis, B., & Sumara, D. (2000). Another queer theory: Reading complexity theory as a moral and ethical imperative. In S. Talburt & S. R. Steinberg (Eds.), Thinking queer: Sexuality, culture, and education (pp. Dewey, J. (1909/1975). *Moral principle in education*. Carbondale, IL: Southern Illinois Press.

Dewey, J. (1909/1975). *Moral principle in education*. Carbondale, IL: Southern Illinois Press.

Dovidio, J. F., Glick, P., & Rudman, L. A. (Eds.). (2005). *On the nature of prejudice: Fifty years after Allport*. Malden, MA: Blackwell.

Downey, D. B., & Pribesh, S. (2004). When race matters: Teachers' evaluations of students' classroom behavior. *Sociology of Education*, 77, 267–282.

Engberg, M. E. (2004). Improving intergroup relations in higher education: A critical examination of the influence of educational interventions on racial bias. *Review of Educational Research, 74*(4), 473–524.

Enke, F. (Ed.). (2012). *Transfeminist perspectives in and beyond transgender and gender studies.* Temple University Press.

Evans, S. (1980). *Personal politics: The roots of women's liberation in the civil rights movement and the new left.* New York: Random House.

Freire, P. (1970). *Pedagogy of the oppressed.* New York: Herder & Herder.

Freire, P. (1994). *Pedagogy of hope: Reliving pedagogy of the oppressed.* New York: Continuum.

Grande, S. (2003). Whitestream feminism and the colonialist project: A review of contemporary feminist pedagogy and praxis. *Educational Theory, 53*(3), 329–346. https://doi.org/10.1111/j.1741-5446.2003.00329.x

Gurin, P., Nagda, B. A., & Zúñiga, X. (2013). *Dialogue across difference: Practice, theory, and research on intergroup dialogue.* Russell Sage Foundation.

Haines, S. K. (2019). *The Politics of Trauma: Somatics, Healing and Social Justice.* North Atlantic Books.

Hale, J. (2016). *The freedom schools: Student activists in the Mississippi civil rights movement.* Columbia University Press.

Helms, J. E. (1995). An update of Helms's white and people of color racial identity models. In J. G. Ponterotto, J. M. Casas, L. A. Suzuki, & C. M. Alexander (Eds.), *Handbook of multicultural counseling* (pp. 181–198). Thousand Oaks, CA: Sage.

Helms, J. E. (1997). Toward a model of White racial identity development. *College student development and academic life: Psychological, intellectual, social and moral issues*, 49–66.

Helms, J. E. (2003). Racial identity and racial socialization as aspects of adolescents' identity development. *Handbook of Applied Developmental Science: Promoting Positive Child, Adolescent, and Family Development Through Research, Policies, and Programs*, 1, 143–163.

Henry, A. (2005). Black feminist pedagogy: Critiques and contributions. *Counterpoints*, 237, 89–105.

hooks, b. (1994). *Teaching to Transgress: Education as the Practice of Freedom.* London: Routledge.

hooks, b. (2003). *Teaching Community: A Pedagogy of Hope.* London: Routledge.

Horton, M., & Freire, P. (1990). *We make the road by walking: Conversations on education and social change.* Philadelphia: Temple University Press.

Horton, M., Kohl, J., & Kohl, H. (1990). *The long haul* (Vol. 84). New York: Doubleday.

Kaba, M., & Shine, J. (2017). *Trying to make the personal political: Feminism and consciousness raising. A reprint of: Consciousness-Raising Guidelines (1975).* Half Letter Press.

Kegan, R. (1982). *The evolving self.* Cambridge, MA: Harvard University Press.

Kolb, D. A. (1981). Learning styles and disciplinary differences. In A. W. Chickering (Ed.), *The modern American college: Responding to the new realities of diverse students and a changing society.* San Francisco: Jossey-Bass.

Kolb, D. A. (1984). *Experiential learning: Experience as the source of learning and development.* Englewood Cliffs, NJ: Prentice Hall.

Lewin, K. (1948). *Resolving social conflicts: Selected papers on group dynamics.* New York: Harper & Row.

Lippitt, R. (1949). *Training in community relations.* New York: Harper & Row.

Love, B. L. (2019). *We want to do more than survive: Abolitionist teaching and the pursuit of educational freedom.* Boston: Beacon Press.

Magee, R. V. (2019). *The inner work of racial justice: Healing ourselves and transforming our communities through mindfulness.* New York: Tarcher/Perigree.

Maher, F. A., & Tetreault, M. K. T. (2001). *The feminist classroom: Dynamics of gender, race, and privilege.* Rowman & Littlefield Publishers.

Malatino, H. (2015). Pedagogies of becoming: Trans inclusivity and the crafting of being. *Transgender Studies Quarterly*, 2(3), 395–410.

Margolis, E. (Ed.) (2001). *The hidden curriculum in higher education.* New York: Routledge.

Meyer, A., Rose, D. H., & Gordon, D. (Editor). (2014). *Universal design for learning: Theory and practice.* CAST Professional Publishing, an imprint of CAST, Inc.

Mukhopadhyay, C. (2014). Starpower: Experiencing a Stratified Society. Retrieved from https://www.sjsu.edu/people/carol.mukhopadhyay/race/Starpower-Activity-2014.pdf

Nicolazzo, Z. (2021). Imagining a trans* epistemology: What liberation thinks like in postsecondary education. *Urban Education*, 56(3), 511–536.

Nieto, S., & Bode, P. (2008). *Affirming diversity: The sociopolitical context of multicultural education* (5th ed.). Boston: Pearson.

Omolade, B. (1987). A Black feminist pedagogy. *Women's Studies Quarterly*, *15*(3–4), 32–39.

Omolade, B. (1993). A Black feminist pedagogy. *Women's Studies Quarterly*, *21*(3–4), 31–38.

Pettigrew, T. F., & Tropp, L. R. (2006). A meta-analytic test of intergroup contact theory. *Journal of Personality and Social Psychology*, *90*(5), 751–783.

Pettigrew, T. F., & Tropp, L. R. (2011). *When Groups Meet: The Dynamics of Intergroup Contact*. Philadelphia, PA: Psychology Press.

Pfeiffer, J. W., & Jones, J. E. (Eds.). (1972–1980). *A handbook of structured experiences for human relations training* (Vols. I-VII). San Diego, CA: University Associates.

Ríos, R. (2019). *Mindful Practice for Social Justice: A Guide for Educators and Professional Learning Communities*. London: Routledge.

Rofes, E. (1998, April). *Transgression and the situated body: Gender, sex, and the gay male teacher*. Paper presented at the Annual Meeting of the American Educational Research Association, San Diego, CA.

Rogoff, B. (2003). *The cultural nature of human development*. New York: Oxford University Press.

Sandoval, C. (2000). *Methodology of the oppressed*. Minneapolis: University of Minnesota Press.

Sarachild, K. (1975). Consciousness-raising: A radical weapon. In Redstockings (Ed.), *Feminist revolution* (pp. 144–150). New York: Random House.

Schutzman, M., & Cohen-Cruz, J. (Eds.). (1994). *Playing Boal: Theatre, therapy, activism*. New York: Routledge.

Shirts, R. G. (1969). *Starpower*. La Jolla CA: Behavioral Sciences Institute

Shlasko, D. (2015). Using the five faces of oppression to teach about interlocking systems of oppression. *Equity & Excellence in Education*, *48*(3), 349–360.

Sherif, M., & Sherif, C. (1970). Black unrest as a social movement toward an emerging self-identity. *Journal of Social & Behavioral Sciences*, *15*(3), 41–52.

Shor, I. (Ed.) (1987). *Freire for the classroom: A sourcebook for liberatory teaching*. Portsmouth, NH: Heinemann.

Staats, Cheryl with Patton, Charles (2013). *State of the science: Implicit bias review 2013*. Kirwan Institute for the Study of Race and Ethnicity. Retrieved from http://kirwaninstitute.osu.edu/docs/SOTS-Implicit_Bias.pdf

Stephan, W. G., & Vogt, W. P. (Eds.). (2004). *Education programs for improving intergroup relations: Theory, research, and practice*. New York: Teachers College Press.

Tejeda, C., Espinoza, M., & Gutierrez, K. (2003). Toward a decolonizing pedagogy: Social justice reconsidered. *Pedagogies of difference: Rethinking education for social change*, 9–38.

Tuckman, B. (1965). Developmental sequence in small groups. *Psychological Bulletin*, *63*(6), 384–399.

Weiler, K. (1988). *Women teaching for change: Gender, class & power*. Greenwood Publishing Group.

Weiler, K. (2001). Rereading Paulo Freire. *Feminist engagements: Reading, resisting, and revisioning male theorists in education and cultural studies*, 67–87.

Wijeyesinghe, C. L., & Jackson, B. W. (Eds.). (2012). *New perspectives on racial identity development: Integrating emerging frameworks* (2nd ed.). New York: New York University Press.

Wildcat, M., McDonald, M., Irlbacher-Fox, S., & Coulthard, G. (2014). Learning from the land: Indigenous land based pedagogy and decolonization. *Decolonization: Indigeneity, Education & Society*, *3*(3).

Zajda, J., Majhanovich, S., Rust, V., & Sabina, E. M. (Eds.). (2006). *Education and social justice*. New York: Springer.

Zembylas, M. (2018). Reinventing critical pedagogy as decolonizing pedagogy: The education of empathy. *Review of Education, Pedagogy, and Cultural Studies*, *40*(5), 404–421.

Zúñiga, X., Lopez, G. E., & Ford, K. A. (Eds.). (2012). Intergroup dialogue: Engaging differences, social identities, and social justice. *Equity & Excellence in Education*, *45*(1), 1–236.

Zúñiga, X., Nagda, B. A., Chesler, M., & Cytron-Walker, A. (2007). *Intergroup dialogue in higher education: Meaningful learning about social justice*. Wiley Subscription Services at Jossey-Bass.

3

Design and Facilitation

Lee Anne Bell and Diane J. Goodman*

Social justice education (SJE) courses and workshops do not simply convey content; they engage participants in examining social identities, power, privilege, and structural inequalities in our society and in their own lives. SJE can be cognitively challenging, emotionally charged, and personally unsettling. It can also be transformative, as participants develop greater personal awareness, expand knowledge that counters dominant narratives, and commit to making changes in themselves and their environments. Content and process are inextricably connected as we help participants develop skills to communicate and work together across differences while exploring social justice content. These capacities are both explicit and implicit in the design and facilitation of SJE. Given this complexity, social justice educators must be intentional about our curriculum choices and pedagogical approaches if we are to successfully accomplish social justice educational goals.[1]

INITIAL CONSIDERATIONS

As designers and facilitators of SJE, our general goals for learning encompass content, process, and skills including personal awareness, acquisition of knowledge, and skills for working with others to create change. These goals are grounded in our understanding of social justice and oppression outlined in Chapter 1: Theoretical Foundations and the elements of pedagogy outlined in Chapter 2: Pedagogical Foundations:

1. Consider the roles of facilitators and participants in the learning community
2. Foster an inclusive learning community
3. Include an analysis of systems of oppression and how they operate in society and in the classroom or workshop
4. Identify goals, learning objectives, and assessment processes for SJE
5. Utilize collaborative and active learning

We encourage readers to read these two chapters as a preface for the design and facilitation issues we discuss in this chapter. SJE facilitators always consider both general pedagogical principles as well as specific goals appropriate for a given group, workshop, session, or course.

While our approach typically foregrounds one ism at a time, we always keep in mind that systemic inequities intersect on both structural and personal levels and mutually inform and reinforce each other in various contexts (see Chapter 1: Theoretical Foundations). We also are mindful that participants are personally situated within matrices of oppression that differentially affect their connections to the topic under discussion and should inform our planning and facilitation. Finally, we want to be aware that our own intersecting social identities and positionality as instructors/facilitators will impact our responses to students/

DOI: 10.4324/9781003005759-4

participants and course/workshop material and plan for this as well. (We discuss this further in Chapter 12: Critical Self-Knowledge.)

DIFFERENTIATING DESIGN AND FACILITATION

Design includes all the planning, assessment, and evaluation activities that facilitators/instructors engage in prior to, during, and after meeting with participants. Design includes establishing goals for learning, setting an agenda for the course or workshop, selecting reading and other course materials, planning activities, and organizing small- and large-group procedures for engaging participants actively. In traditional academic courses, design also includes constructing syllabi, exams, and other assessments. *Facilitation* refers to the leadership strategies and skills that we draw upon to actively engage participants in learning, mediate interactions within the group, and guide interpersonal and group dynamics as part of the learning process. *Both* aspects are key to social justice teaching and are complementary and interconnected.

Careful design and facilitation create a learning community or holding environment within which active and engaged learning can take place. As *designers*, we want to think through our goals and purposefully organize materials, activities, and sequencing at every stage in the process. As *facilitators*, we want to model effective communication skills and respect for differences. We also want to encourage ways of interacting that are inclusive, respectful, honest, and courageous and support people to challenge injustice in our relationships and the institutional systems of which we are a part.

Although, in practice, design and facilitation are integrally related, for the sake of clarity we focus first on design and then on facilitation. In the facilitation section, we also link to design considerations at different phases of a course or workshop. We hope readers will see the interconnections between the two sections as they use these design and facilitation guidelines to develop their own social justice practice.

START WITH CLEAR GOALS AND LEARNING OUTCOMES

We previously highlighted some general goals for social justice education. Each workshop/class or educational series also needs specific goals and learning outcomes to guide the design of every session. We often see educators start with an activity they prefer or content they think is important. Yet we cannot be certain about activities/content we should include if we do not have a clear sense of what we want to accomplish and what we want participants to know and do by the end of the workshop/class. Being clear about desired outcomes helps us define our priorities and focus and informs our choices about what to include and what we inevitably won't be able to include. Once we have clear goals and learning outcomes, we can continually check as we design to ensure that activities are, in fact, aligned with our learning outcomes and effectively addressing the intended content areas.

UNIVERSAL DESIGN FOR LEARNING

Universal Design for Learning (UDL) is a useful planning model for making social justice education courses accessible to a broad spectrum of participants with and without disabilities (Burgstahler & Cory, 2008). Universal design focuses on making products, environments, and communication usable by all people, to the greatest extent possible (Burgstahler, 2012). The Universal Design model to enhance architectural accessibility in the physical environment was adapted for UDL. Initially proposed as a means for including students with disabilities in the general-education classroom, UDL is now better understood as a general-education initiative that improves outcomes for all learners, just as ramps and automatic doors for building entrances, books on tape, and auditory signals at traffic lights are useful to everyone (Ralabate, 2011).

Three core principles of UDL are providing 1) multiple means of representation, 2) multiple means of action and expression, and 3) multiple means of engagement (Meyer, Rose, & Gordon, 2014). For example, *multiple means of representation* include providing the same information through different modalities and providing multiple entry points to a lesson and pathways through content. *Multiple means of action and expression* can include providing learners with choices of ways to demonstrate knowledge and providing alternative means for response. *Multiple means of engagement* entails varying activities and sources of information so they can be personalized and contextualized to learners' lives (CAST, 2018). Instructors/facilitators using UDL principles routinely ensure the following in their course/workshop planning: wheelchair-accessible spaces, accessible and gender-neutral toilet facilities, instructional materials in a variety of formats (e.g., large print, audio, closed-captioned), materials provided in advance so people have flexible time and can use adaptive technology on their own devices, adaptable activities in class (e.g., stand up or raise hand), and choices and flexibility in time for students/participants to complete tests and assignments. Making sure that all aspects of the learning environment are accessible to all participants is essential (Burgstahler & Cory, 2008).

The range of potential disabilities may make it impossible to pre-plan for all of them, but UDL principles call on facilitators to plan for as many variations in abilities as possible. As a routine aspect of pre-assessment, facilitators should ask participants in each class/workshop about their specific learning needs, either before the course begins or at the first group meeting. By incorporating these principles in course planning, instructors are far better prepared to provide appropriate accommodations when needed. Additionally, such efforts send a proactive message about the instructor's commitment to providing an inclusive environment where every participant is welcome and supported to excel.

DIMENSIONS FOR DESIGN: AN INTERACTIVE MODEL

Well-designed curriculum sets the stage for easier and more effective facilitation. Marchesani and Adams (1992) identify four dimensions to consider for addressing diversity and equity in a classroom or workshop: 1) *instructor*, 2) *students*, 3) *curriculum*, and 4) *pedagogy*. Briefly, the four dimensions address these questions: Who are we as instructors? Who are our students? What do we teach? and How do we teach it? We have adapted these four dimensions and added two more—5) *classroom/workshop climate and group dynamics* and 6) *micro and macro context*—that affect and are affected by all other dimensions: How do the climate and interactions in the classroom affect learning? and How does the broader context and issues in society have implications for the topics and issues we are addressing?

Among other contributions, the model shown in Figure 3.1 reminds instructors/facilitators of the multilayered and interacting facets in the design and teaching of social justice courses and workshops. Each dimension offers a point of entry for considering how a course or workshop may be shaped, facilitated, and improved.

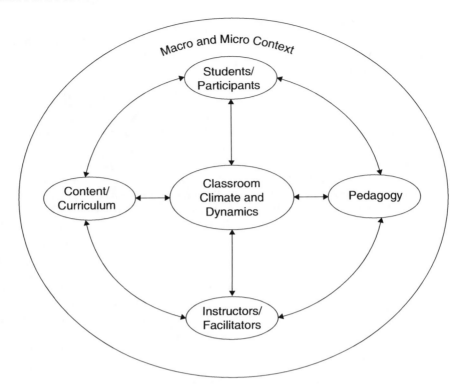

Figure 3.1 Six Dimensions of Diversity and Equity in the Learning Environment
Source: Adapted from Marchesani and Adams (1992)

CONTENT/CURRICULUM—WHAT WE TEACH

This dimension addresses choices instructors/facilitators make about what content, perspectives, and voices to include in the learning experience. Three broad goals for social justice education courses are to increase personal awareness, expand knowledge, and encourage action. The relative emphasis we place on each of these goals will vary with the specific learning goals for a particular workshop or course. For example, with novice groups, it may be useful to focus on developing personal awareness and knowledge of social justice content and to select curriculum materials that provide information and help participants reflect on their own experiences in relation to that content; with an experienced group, it may be more useful to focus on how to apply and take action on what participants have learned and to select curriculum materials and content that serve that goal.

ESTABLISH CLEAR LEARNING OUTCOMES

It is essential to define clear and realistic learning outcomes for the whole course or workshop, for each module/session, and for the individual activities we use. Curriculum content should be driven by our goals for learning, not by activities. Establishing clear learning outcomes offers benefits for both participants and facilitators. Facilitators will be better organized and prepared to communicate what is most important to learn and why and our expectations for how participants will demonstrate successful progress toward these learning goals.

Three questions for developing learning outcome goals can be helpful (Fink, 2013). 1) *What do you want learners/participants to know?* addresses cognitive learning goals and communicates what is most important for participants to have learned by the end of the course or workshop. 2) *What do you want learners to be able to do?* addresses kinesthetic learning goals and communicates the skills in which participants are expected to demonstrate proficiency by the end of the course/workshop. 3) *What critical perspectives do we want learners to understand and practice using?* addresses the particular dispositions (sometimes referred to as habits of mind) of social justice education. For example, instructors/facilitators may want participants to develop and demonstrate dispositions of critical self-reflection and the ability to use a social justice/equity lens to analyze situations thoughtfully.

Clear, realistic, and flexible learning outcomes help facilitators make decisions more effectively in the moment and as the course unfolds to assess whether or not the group is on track. Sometimes facilitators need to adapt learning goals based on what they learn in the process of working with participants. Having clarified beforehand the priorities related to content, skills, and values, instructors can more easily distinguish what comments, questions, and activities are most central to student learning and which are not. This helps facilitators assess if a question or activity, albeit interesting or fun, may at best be optional or at worst a digression or distraction from what is most important and central to the course or workshop focus.

CHOOSE ACTIVITIES AND MATERIALS

Clearly defined learning outcomes can help facilitators identify instructional materials and activities that best match the needs of the group. As instructors decide on materials, it is useful to consider such questions as: Who is included? What is included? How is it included? From whose perspective? and Using what sources? For example, in a course that addresses Lesbian, Gay, Bisexual, Queer, plus others (LGBTQ+) issues, we need to ensure that there are a range of LGBTQ+ experiences included (e.g. across race, class, gender, age), that we are using materials written and produced by diverse groups of LGBTQ+ individuals, and that the portrayal of LGBTQ+ people reflects strength, resilience, and resistance, rather than simply victimhood. We should always avoid content that presents people from disadvantaged groups in tokenized, stereotypical ways and should seek materials that reflect the diversity of experiences within a social identity group. In making such choices, we benefit from being mindful of how our own social identities, knowledge base, and values influence our decisions about what to include or not.

PARTICIPANTS—WHO WE TEACH

This dimension addresses the importance of getting to know the participants in our classes and workshops. Factors to consider include the multiple social identities, interests, expectations, needs, prior experiences, lived realities, and learning preferences that they bring to the course. Knowing about our students will help us develop appropriate learning goals and activities and anticipate and plan for their engagement, reactions, and interactions in the course or workshop.

ATTEND TO MULTIPLE SOCIAL IDENTITIES AND POSITIONALITY

Knowing the various social identities and positionality within matrices of domination and marginalization that participants bring to the learning community is important for numerous reasons. Social identities shape participants' lived experiences and relationship to the issue being explored. Those who have multiple marginalized identities often bring a different worldview and different needs to the learning space than participants with a single or no marginalized identity. In a sexism course, knowing that participants are multiracial with a mix of sexual identities, for example, can help us anticipate and provide ways to explore how they encounter sexism differently through their diverse experiences with heterosexism and racism (among other forms of oppression). We can also can be attuned to possible feelings of isolation or hypervisibility depending on the makeup of the group or the organization in which the class/workshop is being offered—for example, one of the few Latinx students or staff in a course/workshop in a predominantly white class, institution, or community setting could feel this way.

While we should not assume we know *how* participants' social identities shape their knowledge, experiences, and perspective, we can recognize that identities *do* inform the way they relate to the issues. Facilitators can anticipate dynamics between and among people with various privileged and marginalized identities and design accordingly. Some design strategies that can tailor to the specific needs of individuals and groups include: explicit class agreements that address power dynamics and different styles of communication, caucus/affinity groups where participants from the same (self-chosen) identity group can share experiences with each other, experiential activities that actively engage participants in sharing and listening to diverse perspectives, process questions that include various degrees of complexity, and choices of readings and assignments tailored to the particular group makeup.

RECOGNIZE THE INFLUENCE OF SOCIAL IDENTITY DEVELOPMENT

Social identity development helps us understand how individuals enter our courses or workshops with different levels of awareness of their own social identities in relation to larger social structures of privilege and oppression (Hardiman & Jackson, 1997). Participants in earlier phases of identity development may have done little critical thinking about their social identities and are more likely to accept the ideology and values of the dominant culture. Participants in other phases of identity development may be more conscious of their social identities and more focused on resisting the dominant paradigm and challenging systems they see as oppressive.

Attending to where participants are in their individual social identity development allows us to understand how participants from the same social identity group may have very different reactions to the same content. For example, an affluent Black student who grew up in a predominantly white community or in a family where little attention was paid to race and a Black student who grew up in predominantly Black community or in a family that was active in civil rights might have different perspectives on protests, sit-ins, and civil disobedience by other Black students on campus. While social identity development theory is not a precise diagnostic tool, it can help us anticipate dynamics among participants at similar and different points in their process, consider how to meet their diverse learning needs, and facilitate group dynamics more skillfully.

ATTEND TO THE INTERESTS AND MOTIVATIONS OF PARTICIPANTS

Each participant brings to the course or workshop a unique combination of work and life experiences. Insight into participants' personal and professional interests and motivations can help us shape learning activities, supplemental materials, and group experiences to be as relevant as possible to their lives and future goals. For example, are participants graduate or undergraduate students, community members, activists, service providers, or administrators? Are they experienced with or brand new to social justice content? Is the course/workshop required or voluntary? Such information can help guide pedagogical choices. If the course includes participants with a range of experiences and interests, we might use caucuses or work groups based on majors, career orientations, or job roles to connect to participant interests and help them apply learning.

ASSESS PREVIOUS EXPERIENCES AND COMFORT WITH SOCIAL JUSTICE ISSUES

Participants generally will have had varying opportunities to develop personal awareness and think critically about social justice issues. For some, this is their first time exploring these topics and learning in a diverse group. Others may have grown up in families, lived in communities, or been part of organizations where they experienced discussing controversial topics and are comfortable talking about this subject matter. There may be students who have had very positive (even transformative) experiences in social justice courses or workshops, while others may have had very negative prior experiences. Some participants may be used to being in an academic setting and debating views, while others may be less familiar with formal educational environments.

Participants do not always expect to be engaged actively or experientially. Consequently, an activity may feel more risky and emotionally challenging to some participants than to others. Particular pedagogical strategies can allow for different levels of self-disclosure, such as ensuring that there is time for personal reflection or sharing in pairs before asking people to contribute to a whole-group discussion. Recognizing differences in readiness and experience can help us design learning experiences that foster participation by everyone while providing levels of challenge that promote learning for all.

RECOGNIZE RELATIONSHIPS AMONG PARTICIPANTS

Another aspect to consider in designing classes/workshops are the organizational levels and types of relationships among participants. Past, present, and future relationships of participants can directly affect current group dynamics. Differences in power, placement in an organizational hierarchy, or level of educational attainment can lead participants to have varying degrees of confidence that it is safe enough to be open about their experiences, engage in large-group discussions, or participate in personally revealing learning activities. For example, participants from the same department or work setting who hold different statuses may have concerns about whether what they say and do will be used against them by supervisors or higher-ranking colleagues or coworkers. Feelings of vulnerability may make it seem too risky to be direct and honest about feelings, experiences, and perceptions in front of other participants. Individuals in high-level positions may not want to appear ignorant or vulnerable in front of those they supervise.

It is important to understand the relationships that participants bring into the room with them. Are they strangers or an ongoing work group? Do some participants directly supervise others? Have the participants had prior experiences with each other that may have already built trust or called it into question? Knowing something about the participants' prior experiences with each other helps us plan accordingly. There may be a greater need to include writing exercises, such as brief response exercises or journaling, or more paired discussions in which participants select their own partner. Caucus/affinity groups—homogeneous groups organized around particular identities, such as white and People of Color/multiracial caucus groups to discuss racism, or staff and supervisors—offer an excellent opportunity to aggregate insights and perspectives that individuals may feel too vulnerable to offer personally in a mixed group. Caucus groups typically report back key points in an anonymous way to the larger group so the group as a whole can learn from these insights.

CONSIDER INDIVIDUAL LEARNING NEEDS

By knowing about participants, we can better anticipate and design learning experiences that will accommodate individual learning needs, not just those that fit the dominant culture norms such as being able bodied, neurotypical, middle class, a native English speaker, or extroverted. For example, in addition to people who are disabled, neurodivergent, and have learning differences; international participants for whom English is not a first language; people who are taking care of young children or other family members; students who are working full-time or may be struggling financially; and participants who identify as introverts may require that we are flexible and can ensure an equitable learning experience for all. Universal Design for Learning, as well as various forms of accommodations and choices, can help ensure the learning experience is inclusive for everyone.

INSTRUCTORS/FACILITATORS—WHO WE ARE

This dimension acknowledges that we bring ourselves—our life experiences, intersecting social identities, cultural styles, preferred teaching approaches, personalities, knowledge bases, and biases—into our teaching spaces (see Chapter 12: Critical Self-Knowledge). As educators of social justice, it is especially important that we explore how we are shaped by our intersecting social identities and consequent positionality and how this affects our experiences in the classroom or workshop. Conscious attention to our own growth and development is essential ongoing work and can benefit by considering such questions as these:

- What social justice related topics am I most and least comfortable teaching?
- Which learners am I most/least effective educating?
- How do my social identities and positionality affect my teaching/facilitating?
- What behaviors or issues cause me to react strongly or emotionally in the classroom/workshop?
- How do I ensure that I am continuing my own process of development as a social justice educator and staying current on the topics I teach?

By examining our competencies and areas for further growth, we can design classes and workshops that match our skills and styles and can be conscious of the areas where we will need to grow and develop further to be most effective in our role as instructors/facilitators. (Chapter 12: Critical Self-Knowledge provides a thorough discussion of these issues.)

PEDAGOGY—HOW WE TEACH

This dimension addresses how facilitators engage with participants, with the content, and with co-facilitators (if teaching with others) to promote learning. Social justice and diversity courses/workshops can be transformative experiences. However, such growth comes only after confronting and critically analyzing previously held concepts, theories, and beliefs. The process of addressing what may well have been limited or missing information, unconscious bias, and the feelings attached to such positions is both an affective (emotional) and cognitive process. How instructors model self-reflection, critical analysis, and openness to feelings and ideas is as much a part of the growth experience for students/participants as the theoretical content. The degree to which this is done successfully determines whether an inclusive teaching and learning environment will be created and sustained.

USE A RANGE OF PEDAGOGICAL STRATEGIES AND APPROACHES

Like our students/participants, we too have learning style preferences, and unless we make conscious choices, we may fall into teaching in ways that reflect our own learning-style preferences rather than meeting the needs of the group. To be most effective, educators need to utilize a range of pedagogical strategies that meet the needs of a range of learners as well as to help learners stretch and expand their repertoire. (See Chapter 2: Pedagogical Foundations for a fuller discussion of pedagogical approaches.)

One useful model identifies three domains of learning: cognitive (intellectual), affective (social-emotional), and kinesthetic (skills and behaviors) (Bloom & Krathwohl, 1956). Research on this model has shown that learning happens and is most sustained when learners are appropriately engaged across all three domains simultaneously (Anderson & Krathwohl, 2000). *Cognitive learning* may be exemplified by listening to a lecture, reading new material, or learning new theories and definitions. An example of *socio-emotional learning* might be to ask participants to connect with someone whose experiences and perspectives differ from their own and engage in a dialogue about their thoughts and feelings in relation to the topic under discussion. *Kinesthetic learning* can be seen in experiential activities that enact and explore the dynamics of oppression, such as using role-playing to explore different perspectives and using music and art to express learning. Kinesthetic activities can be invaluable in helping learners synthesize and integrate skills, practice new behaviors, and process emotions.

Another model encourages connecting with learners through concrete experience, reflective observation, abstract conceptualization, and active experimentation (Kolb, 2015). Simulations and speak-outs, for example, engage participants in a direct and concrete manner (*concrete experience*). The processing questions that follow an activity, film, or lecture utilize *reflective observation*. Conceptual models such as the Five Faces of Oppression or Cycle of Socialization employ *abstract conceptualization*. Action projects that ask participants to apply learning to their particular contexts exemplify *active experimentation*. (See Chapter 2: Pedagogical Foundations for more detail.)

Increasingly, educators are considering trauma-informed pedagogies, mindfulness and other contemplative practices, and somatic approaches (Berila, 2016; Herr-Perrin, 2021; Magee, 2019; Menakem, 2017; Varghese, Quiros, & Burger, 2018). These modalities broaden traditional strategies and can allow for a more embodied approach, while recognizing the impact of previous experiences and trauma.

CLASSROOM CLIMATE AND DYNAMICS

Classroom/workshop climate and dynamics are central in social justice education and are shaped by and interact with the other dimensions described prior. How we design and facilitate affects whether participants feel that the space is welcoming and inclusive and how much they will be willing to authentically engage and take risks. Students frequently experience microaggressions and other forms of bias, avoid controversial content that may lead to conflict, and are concerned about a "callout culture" (Ross, 2019, 2020) that can be highly judgmental and makes it hard to take risks and make mistakes. Essential to effective social justice education is creating a strong learning community. Important considerations in climate and classroom dynamics include:

- Do all participants feel heard and respected?
- Do participants see us as trustworthy and knowledgeable facilitators/teachers?
- Are participants able to engage with each other in ways that support learning?
- Are there norms and skills for addressing microaggressions, conflicts, and divergent perspectives?
- Do the content and the pedagogy feel relevant and culturally inclusive?

The better we are at creating and sustaining an inclusive climate—by designing and implementing structures and activities that enable participants to engage honestly and thoughtfully with course material and each other—the more likely that participants will be open to express and explore unexamined beliefs and values, address inequities as they manifest in the classroom, and engage honestly with intellectually and emotionally challenging social justice content. (See Chapter 12: Critical Self-Knowledge for further discussion of these issues.)

CONTEXT: HOW DOES THE BROADER MACRO AND MICRO CONTEXT AFFECT THE OTHER FACTORS OUTLINED PRIOR?

The broader cultural, social, and political context also affects learning. On the macro level, COVID-19, Black Lives Matter, Me Too and other current issues have had a profound effect on university campuses, organizations and businesses, and the broader community. Pervasive examples in the media and in real life of racist incidents and police shootings are likely to affect the questions and concerns participants bring into the classroom or workshop. The Black Lives Matters protests in response to repeated killings of Black people have heightened feelings for many Black people and People of Color that are likely to spill into the classroom. Likewise, gun violence and harassment directed at Asian Americans may raise issues of safety for Asian American participants and the need for understanding the history of anti-Asian stereotypes and discrimination. Campus or national protests may raise questions for participants who seek information to help them understand or who desire help in figuring out how to respond effectively. Thus, it is important to pay attention to and plan for ways to address the broader context when designing course/workshop content and to be prepared for how broader issues will affect classroom climate and interaction. What recent or current local or broader societal issues might be impacting people's emotional states, topics of interest, and group dynamics?

We also need to consider the micro context since program, department, institutional, community, and/or discipline-specific expectations may shape learning outcome goals. Curricular goals in many pre-professional programs (nursing, social work, engineering, and teacher education) often reflect both institutional and national professional accreditation guidelines and may be expected to address specific learning outcomes established by their national accrediting bodies. Grassroots and community organizations and various types of workplaces may have a different set of expectations and goals than university settings.

How we teach particular content and the specific activities we choose also depend on the physical (or virtual) environment and the timing of the class or workshop. It is helpful to consider:

- How well does the space lend itself to different kinds of groupings, experiential activities, and use of educational technology?
- What challenges to access, sight lines, and mobility does the physical structure present?
- How might time of day affect participants' energy levels and the session?
- What activities or events immediately precede or follow the session that may affect participants' engagement? For example, is the session right before lunch or following another long class?

STRUCTURING ACTIVITIES

Activities comprise the core of social justice courses and workshops. Structuring activities with these dimensions in mind requires careful thought about objectives, timing and sequencing, materials and procedures, and processing and evaluation. The following steps provide a useful way to carefully plan and structure activities.

STEP 1: IDENTIFY KEY CONCEPTS, LEARNING OBJECTIVES, AND EVALUATION CRITERIA

Social justice educators need to identify the main ideas they want to address. Key concepts introduce new information or conceptual frames for participants to use in examining course content, issues raised in discussion, and their own experiences. In an ableism class, for example, participants may be introduced to the concept of stereotyping by exploring stereotypes of people with disabilities and examining the roots of these stereotypes historically and in their own socialization. Social justice educators need to set clear learning objectives for each of the activities in order to establish criteria for determining whether or not we have been successful in meeting our goals. Being intentional about the purpose of a particular activity can also help us facilitate it effectively so that participants draw the expected learnings from that activity.

STEP 2: ESTABLISH HOW LEARNERS WILL DEMONSTRATE PROGRESS

How will participants demonstrate successful progress toward the key learning goals by the end of the course or workshop? They will value a clear explanation of what is expected of them and how their progress will be assessed. If, for example, we are teaching a course for credit, students can benefit from knowing the required assignments, seeing models of exemplary work, and having a rubric that describes levels of success. In other settings, participants can develop action plans to demonstrate what they have learned.

STEP 3: SELECT/DESIGN LEARNING ACTIVITIES AND ALLOT TIME FOR EACH ACTIVITY

Each learning activity is a structured interaction with one or more key concepts. Examples of activities include: role-plays, case studies, simulations, brainstorming, interactive lecture, video, small- or large-group discussions, worksheets, or writing prompts. Activities are generally designed to engage participants with the issues experientially, cognitively, and/or emotionally and provide ways for them to interact with the content, each other, and with us as instructors at different points in the course. Some questions that can help guide the selection of activities include:

- What is the composition of this particular group of participants?
- What range of prior knowledge and experiences might they bring to this activity?
- How does this activity align with and advance progress toward one or more key learning goals?
- How does this activity fit with what participants have just been doing and with what they will be asked to do next?

It can be easy to underestimate how long it will take to complete and then debrief an activity sufficiently, especially for facilitators who are new to experiential learning or to a specific activity. If too little time is allocated for processing and synthesizing the learning outcomes that the activity is designed to promote, participants will be left to make sense of activities on their own without the benefit of facilitator guidance and the perspectives of other participants. Anticipating and allocating sufficient time for the full activity, including processing the activity and addressing questions or concerns that may emerge from the group, is essential.

While there are no firm rules about timing, we suggest that facilitators initially plan for about three times the amount of time the actual exercise or activity takes to debrief that activity. It is helpful to provide participants with estimated time frames for each activity while noting that these can be modified if needed. Leading thoughtful and probing discussions after an activity is at the heart of facilitation in social justice education courses and can often make the difference between high-quality and superficial learning.

STEP 4: ORGANIZE DIRECTIONS AND PROCEDURES FOR EACH ACTIVITY AND GATHER EQUIPMENT AND MATERIALS NEEDED

When introducing an activity, it is important to communicate what the learning objectives are, how they fit into the overall curriculum or workshop, why this activity is relevant to their learning, and what is expected of them as participants. It is also important to assemble ahead of time the materials participants may need (e.g., directions, handouts, newsprint, videos, scissors, masking tape, index cards, sticky notes, and supplemental resources) in order to complete activities. Additionally, make sure to set up and test technology beforehand. In online sessions, be sure to have links, videos, folders, and other collaborative spaces set up in advance.

STEP 5: DEVELOP PROCESSING FORMAT AND QUESTIONS FOR EACH ACTIVITY

Processing refers to the systematic and guided reflection that follows an activity. The steps involved in processing often include time for individual reflection and analysis. The goal of processing is to help participants build on prior knowledge, reflect on their learning, construct personal meaning, identify questions and contradictions, and consolidate new learning. Processing also helps facilitators assess how well participants are making sense of an activity and key learnings.

For example, before discussing an activity, a brief writing prompt can be used to give participants the opportunity to first reflect individually on how they felt about the activity and what they learned. This strategy can be particularly valuable for those who are shy or prefer time for reflection before engaging with others. Processing provides important opportunities for participants to deepen analysis of the activity and the meanings they draw from it. Discussions can take place in pairs, small groups, the whole group, or caucuses/affinity groups, depending on the activity. These opportunities allow participants to clear up points of confusion, share observations, and receive feedback from the facilitator and other participants. In such discussions, it is important to normalize respect for the expression of divergent perspectives while also encouraging students to challenge their own and others' thinking.

Personal reflection and sharing with others match the learning style modes of *concrete experience and reflective observation*. Next, facilitators can shift the dialogue toward *abstract analysis* of the issues raised by inviting participants to discuss how the activity illustrates particular dynamics of oppression. We ask them to identify questions, contradictions, or insights raised by the activity and discuss connections to other concepts. For example, following a role-play about sexual harassment, we might ask participants: How did the actions of men and women in this role-play reflect gender socialization? In what ways are the power dynamics in this situation similar to other forms of oppression? And how might the experiences of women from different racial groups compare in this situation? Participants can also be asked how they might apply the learnings from this and other activities to their lives (*application*).

STEP 6: SEQUENCE LEARNING ACTIVITIES

Careful sequencing enables us to introduce concepts and activities in an incremental way that builds upon participants' prior awareness and learning at different phases of the course/workshop (Brooks-Harris & Stock-Ward, 1999; Weinstein, 1988). Intentionally scaffolding what we address allows students to increasingly engage with more challenging material and experiences. We consider several factors in selecting and sequencing activities so that the overall flow of the course makes sense to participants.

Lower to Higher Risk

Learners need to feel safe enough to express and examine deeply held feelings, confusions, experiences, beliefs, and assumptions about oppression issues. Lower-risk activities in the beginning of a social justice education course are designed to help participants get acquainted, develop a sense of group cohesion, practice interaction guidelines that support honest engagement and learning, and acquire some basic concepts and information before moving to activities that require more risky disclosure of feelings and perspectives. Moving from individual reflection to discussions in pairs or small groups before engaging in whole-group discussions is also a way to progressively increase the level of risk and build in support as discussions proceed.

Concrete to Abstract (or Abstract to Concrete)

This sequencing principle reflects our belief that participants learn best when their understanding of oppression is firmly rooted in concrete experiences and examples that provide a foundation for analysis of abstract concepts, theory, and the multiple levels on which oppression operates. For instance, in exploring the portrayal of a marginalized group in the media, participants could be asked to watch various media platforms and note the ways members of that group are portrayed (concrete). Then they could read an analysis of how that group has historically been and is currently reflected in the media and consider the sociological significance (abstract) of the way the group has been reflected in the media. It may make sense to start with the abstract and then connect it to concrete examples when there is limited time or participants are particularly interested in theory or expert opinion.

Personal to Institutional/Cultural (or Institutional/Cultural to Personal)

In most of our courses, we begin with personal content, then introduce an institutional and cultural focus. We start with a personal focus because this level is more accessible to participants for initial exploration of the topic. After examining their own experiences and socialization, they can consider new information (e.g., readings, lectures, and discussions) and conceptual frameworks that ask them to reflect critically on their assumptions and experiences and how oppression operates on institutional and cultural levels. In some cases, it might be more appropriate for a group to start with the institutional/cultural and then move to the personal if a broader perspective would be useful first.

Difference to Dominance (or Diversity to Social Justice)

This sequencing principle first focuses on helping participants describe and understand their own experiences as members of different social groups and listen to others in the group share their experiences and perspectives. The focus is on respecting, understanding, and acknowledging difference. After this exchange, the concepts of dominance, social power, and privilege are introduced to help participants understand that difference is not neutral and that social groups are valued differently, are positioned within social hierarchies, and have greater or lesser access to social and personal resources and power.

What? So what? Now what? These questions are a handy shorthand for how to sequence and organize processes as well as content. *What?* asks what knowledge and awareness we want participants to gain. *So what?* helps students understand *why* this information or awareness is important or relevant. And *Now what?* addresses the implications of what participants have learned and the next steps to be taken given this new knowledge and awareness. In some cases, starting with the *So what?* may initially engage reluctant participants.

Other considerations related to sequencing ensure that activities are varied. Instructors need to balance activities that allow participants to move about (active), such as experiential exercises and role-plays, with ones that require more sitting and listening (passive), such as lectures and movies. How students are grouped, such as individual reflection, paired sharing, and small-group and large-group activities, also needs to be rotated.

Make Adjustments as the Class or Workshop Unfolds

More times than not, the design that instructors have prepared prior to the start of the course requires adjustment once the course begins. The flexibility to make needed design adjustments based on what is happening in the moment is an essential skill. Many factors can necessitate redesigning a course/workshop. Pre-assessment information about participants may be incomplete or inaccurate, incidents in the group may require a change in design to capitalize on a spontaneous learning opportunity or "teachable moment," student expectations for the course may not match the design, or activities may take longer than the time allotted for them in the original design and instructors need to change plans as a result. Informal evaluations or feedback in the midst of the course may signal the need to alter the design. In all of these cases, it is necessary to reevaluate and decide how to make adjustments that will maintain the flow of the course while addressing the essential key concepts and learning goals.

INTEGRATING DESIGN WITH FACILITATION

In this section, we highlight facilitation and show how it is interconnected with the design considerations described prior. Once the course/workshop begins, facilitation issues come to the fore. Facilitation involves managing the group dynamics and guiding participants through activities and the learning process. There are many aspects to good facilitation that include both task and process roles. At different times, instructors may need to guide the discussion by asking questions, be a role model by demonstrating respectful communication or sharing personal stories, present information, manage interpersonal conflict, begin and end an activity, observe and name classroom dynamics, or offer conceptual analysis. One of the skills of good facilitation is being able to utilize the appropriate role and task when needed.

DESIGN AND FACILITATION AT DIFFERENT PHASES OF A CLASS/WORKSHOP: CONFIRMATION, CONTRADICTION, AND CONTINUITY

We have adapted a model from social psychologist Robert Kegan (2009) to provide a framework for designing and facilitating workshops/classes. This model describes the changing ways people make meaning of themselves, others, and the world and the environments needed to support this developmental process. The first stage, *confirmation*, highlights the need for creating a holding environment or "container" where participants can take risks and be vulnerable so as to be able to look at their own socialization and be open to learning about systemic inequities in which we are all implicated. Once a safe-enough holding environment is created, we move to the *contradiction* stage, where prior beliefs and understandings will be challenged and held up for examination. During this stage, we want to unsettle assumptions and encourage exploration, questioning, and risk-taking. The *continuity* stage addresses the need for closure and continuity beyond the course or workshop. In this stage, we want to help participants summarize what they have learned and plan for how they will apply it once they leave the course. While this progression from confirmation to contradiction to continuity describes the course/workshop overall, these stages also occur and recur throughout the course/workshop. For example, throughout the course or workshop, facilitators can help participants make connections to how they might apply information (continuity), or at particularly challenging moments in the course, facilitators may include more ways to sustain a confirming environment (e.g., group-building activities). Table 3.1 shows design issues and facilitation strategies for each facilitating environment.

PHASE ONE: CONFIRMATION

All of us, consciously or unconsciously, develop and internalize a set of beliefs about social justice issues simply through living in this society. Each of us could be said to be *embedded* in a particular way of making sense of the world. Left unchallenged, this embeddedness leads us to take for granted our worldview as given, natural, and true, as simply "the way things are." This is especially likely for members of dominant groups who are less likely to question a status quo that serves their interests. In the social justice education classroom,

Table 3.1 Facilitation and Design Issues at Different Phases

Facilitating Environment	Design Issues	Facilitation Strategies
Confirmation	• Introductions • Learning outcomes, agenda/syllabus, and expectations • Group norms for respectful interactions • Activities to develop a supportive and inclusive learning environment	• Set and model tone • Model self-disclosure • Acknowledge the significance of feelings • Address fears and concerns
Contradiction	• Content that deepens or challenges current learning about oppression • Sharing of personal stories • Opportunities for full discussion and reflection	• Ensure equitable participation and constructive group behavior/dynamics • Surface different perspectives • Challenge inaccurate information and views • Manage conflict and different perspectives • Acknowledge and manage feelings • Utilize and address silence • Address avoidance • Reduce and manage resistance • Manage facilitator reactions
Continuity	• Identify actions for social justice • Identify support • Provide closure • Evaluate class/workshop	• Discuss appropriate action • Address need for support and potential changes in relationships • Deal with immobilizing feelings

these beliefs are exposed to critical examination and questioning, unsettling the "taken for granted" worldview. Such challenge inevitably disturbs a person's equilibrium, can be experienced as threatening, and will often raise their defenses. Equally important is to ensure that students from marginalized groups feel supported and that their experiences and realities are being reflected and validated.

CORRESPONDING FACILITATING ENVIRONMENT

The way participants experience the environment of the classroom has a powerful effect on whether or not they are willing to grapple with conflicting information, cognitive dissonance, and internal disequilibrium. If the environment is perceived as too threatening, a person's defenses may become fairly rigid. They will tend to ignore challenges to their worldview and rationalize conflicting information to fit their present belief system. In other words, they may cling to their "comfort zone" and be unwilling to consider any new material or openly engage in activities that challenge what they have taken for granted as true.

However, if the environment is perceived as supportive, a participant's defenses can be more permeable. Despite the experience of internal conflict, the person may be attracted to new information and may become willing to grapple with the contradictions and discrepancies they perceive. Facilitators are always balancing the need for both challenge and support in order to maximize participant learning.

We believe facilitators must maintain an environment that is respectful and inclusive, in which participants can express their thoughts, feelings, questions, and perspectives without being personally diminished, attacked, or silenced. At the same time, facilitators should create an environment where language and behavior that is offensive or hurtful can be challenged and where participants can be helped to understand the impact of their words or behavior, even if their intent is not to be harmful. Such a climate enables participants to be more open to critically examine their worldviews and take learning risks.

Facilitators create a supportive learning/holding environment by getting to know participants and helping them get to know each other so that they develop a secure enough sense of themselves as a group that they can relax into the learning opportunity. Establishing a positive group atmosphere and developing trust can avoid some pitfalls and help facilitators more easily manage inevitable issues and conflicts that arise. For these reasons, the initial phase of a social justice education course is critically important. Our goals in this phase are to create an environment in which participants feel *confirmed* and validated *as persons* even as they may experience challenges to their belief system. We want to construct a community of learners that is supportive and trustworthy and that fosters positive interdependence, and the sense that individuals are responsible for their own learning and the impact of their behavior on each other's learning. Our hope is that in such an environment, uncomfortable and challenging issues can be raised and explored and participants can express discomfort, sadness, confusion, anger, and fear and know they will be treated with dignity and respect.

While we want all participants to feel that the class is a respectful and supportive environment in which they can actively engage, this does not mean they will never be challenged or uncomfortable. We believe that feeling uncomfortable at times is a valuable and expected part of an effective social justice education class. Such feelings of discomfort can be experienced intellectually (e.g., encountering a challenging new perspective, new information, or experience), emotionally (getting feedback from other participants about how one's behavior or attitudes affect others in the class), or physically (experiencing shortness of breath, accelerated heartbeat, or perspiring) and are important learning opportunities for all participants. This discomfort can be the basis for intellectual breakthroughs, increased personal insight, and changes in behaviors, awareness, and actions. We can remind participants that discomfort is part of an ultimately growthful and liberating process and can help them manage their discomfort.

We refer to moments of discomfort as "learning edges" and invite participants to notice and explore when they are on a learning edge rather than retreat to a comfort zone of familiar beliefs and experiences. Differentiating "safety" and "comfort," and reframing discomfort as an essential aspect of learning in social justice education, helps participants better understand their feelings and see discomfort as an opportunity to learn. In social justice education courses, such self-awareness is an explicit learning outcome goal. At the beginning of the course, facilitators can explicitly ask students to consider how they typically deal with discomfort and name strategies for how they can stay engaged when this occurs. Learning to notice the signs of being on a learning edge is a useful mechanism for realizing when we care deeply about something or experience challenges to taken-for-granted assumptions.

Some facilitators use the language of "brave spaces" to counter the notion of "safe spaces" and recognize that these conversations involve discomfort and risk-taking. We choose not to use the term "brave spaces" in recognition of the fact that people from marginalized groups have to brave an unjust world just to survive in their daily lives and should not have that burden in an educational space with dominant group people (Ahenkora, 2020). The notion of brave spaces also may undeservedly credit dominant group members with bravery simply for being willing to engage in this work.

Instead, we like the idea put forth by Ahenkora (2020) about creating accountable spaces: "To move forward, we don't need to promise safety or expect bravery. We need to embrace accountability to foster more inclusive and equitable spaces in communities and workplaces." Accountability means being responsible for oneself and one's intentions, words, and actions. It means entering a space with good intentions but understanding that aligning intent with action is the true test of commitment. This definition of accountable spaces aligns with our suggested group agreements for creating respectful and inclusive learning environments discussed in the following.

DESIGN FEATURES OF THE CONFIRMATION PHASE

To create a *confirming* environment, we want to help people break the ice and become more familiar with each other. We also want to establish and model guidelines of listening respectfully and speaking truthfully from our own experience. We often acknowledge the stereotypes and assumptions that the culture fosters about different groups and the misinformation we all receive in order to make it possible to openly examine taboo topics. Once participants experience support and realize they are not expected to have all the answers, can be confused or uninformed, and are allowed to make mistakes despite their best intentions, they may be able to relax their defenses enough to engage with classroom activities and information that question their assumptions about social reality. Some specific design components of the confirmation phase include:

1. *Introductions:* Introductions of the instructors/facilitators and participants recognize the unique identity of each person and let people know they will not be treated as anonymous but are indeed central to the course. Learning each other's names and getting to know one another helps participants start to develop a sense of community and group cohesiveness.
   * Facilitators welcome everyone and introduce themselves with their name, pronouns, and why they chose to facilitate this seminar. Facilitators explain the importance of names and pronouns as a form of recognition and intentional practice to avoid assumptions and misperceptions. The process of self-naming honors each person's ability to self-identify and eliminates unwanted assumptions about other people's identities. Finally, facilitators should point out that inviting people to share their name and pronouns serves as a reminder to cisgender people that they typically do not have to think about pronoun use or correct misperceptions of their gender identity (see Shlasko, Crath, Ao, Cochran, & Thorn, 2017).
2. *Learning outcomes, agenda/syllabus, and expectations:* Explicitly providing a structure that participants can rely upon can allay fears as to what the course will entail. Participants can be informed of expected attendance, participation, and assignments. The agenda, outcomes, and expectations can also be developed together with or adjusted to meet the needs of a particular group. Instead of a structured agenda, some facilitators prefer to provide a more general sequence or flow for the session, recognizing that flexibility is needed. These components help participants anticipate what the focus of the course will be, have some sense of what will occur, and share responsibility for following and achieving the objectives. Participants can also begin to identify and develop their own goals for learning or set intentions for the session that reflect how they want to engage or what they want to get out of the experience.
3. *Group agreements for constructive interactions:* Participants come to social justice workshops and courses with widely varying prior experiences and degrees of knowledge. We assume that all participants have internalized oppressive messages from the dominant culture and lack accurate information about many social issues. Most have had few opportunities to think critically about their social identities and systemic

inequalities or to discuss these issues with people whose lived realities and perspectives may be very different from their own.

It is useful for both facilitators and participants to anticipate and plan for the affective and cognitive dynamics that arise when people express divergent perspectives on topics about which they have strong feelings and deeply held beliefs. When possible, it can be valuable for the participants to create their own agreements so they feel more ownership of the process and address their concerns. We can add or raise questions if we feel aspects are missing. We can suggest that participants engage with "critical humility" and recognition that we all are works in progress. Participants can be encouraged to be curious and ask questions to deepen their understanding of different perspectives and experiences rather than simply countering with their own viewpoint. Creating a list of mutual expectations and guidelines for interaction, and asking the class to agree to observe them, is one convention that sets the stage for constructive interactions. (See designs in Chapters 5–11 for examples and examples on the website.) ★

In the process of developing these agreements, we can clarify with the group what is meant by different terms (e.g., "respect"), discuss differences in conflict and communication styles, and coach participants in strategies for successful intergroup dialogue. We can explicitly name the ways that power and privilege often play out in interactions among people from dominant and subordinated social groups and ask participants to develop agreements that can mitigate or interrupt such interactions in the class. For example, one guideline might be: "Consider how your own social positionality (such as your race, class, gender, sexuality, or ability status) informs your perspectives and reactions." As instructors, we can use group agreements to ensure that dynamics of power and dominance are not unintentionally recreated in our classroom discussions. We can hold students accountable for contributing to a climate in which everyone's participation is valued.

4. *Activities to develop a supportive and inclusive learning environment:* In addition to introductions, activities early in the course can be designed to establish a norm of interaction and self-disclosure. Such activities help create group cohesiveness and a sense that everyone has something to learn and contribute. Initial interactions should be lower risk so that participants can comfortably practice what for many might be a novel experience of sharing feelings and personal experiences in the context of a classroom or workshop. Pairs and small-group activities are good vehicles for this type of relationship-building. For example, in several ism chapters, the Common Ground activity is used. This activity uses a list of prompts to identify commonalities and differences among group members.

FACILITATION ISSUES AND STRATEGIES FOR THE CONFIRMATION PHASE

Participants observe both what facilitators do as well as what we say. Some of the central facilitation issues in the confirmation phase include:

1. *Set and model tone:* As facilitators, we attempt to model and support the norms we hope to establish, including risk-taking, respect, and good humor. Co-facilitators are also role models in their interactions with each other and should demonstrate respectful dialogue and an effective collaborative relationship. As participants share their views, personal experiences, feelings, and questions in the initial class activities, facilitators can affirm and validate their willingness to take risks. We can reinforce the notion that there are no "stupid" questions. Simply stating, "Thank you for sharing

that" or "I appreciate your willingness to raise that issue" conveys that we do, in fact, value their contributions.

Not only can we respond in positive ways when people take initial risks, but we can consistently model respectful interactions. This may include paying thoughtful attention to students as they speak, not talking over them, using their correct or preferred name and gender pronouns, and interrupting comments or behaviors from others that are dismissive or insulting. Additional strategies include building on students' comments, paying attention to equitable access to airtime, inviting quiet students or those who have not spoken yet to participate, and keeping activities generally on time.

Creating an atmosphere that is both serious and light helps set a friendly and supportive tone. We want to treat social justice content as the serious issue it is while incorporating activities that include humor and playfulness that can keep students engaged, release feelings, build community, and challenge the assumption that learning about oppression is simply depressing; working for justice can be joyful, too.

2. *Model vulnerability and self-disclosure:* When instructors model appropriate levels of self-disclosure—sharing things about their own identities, experiences, process of learning about oppression, challenges, and mistakes—it builds rapport with and invites students to share about themselves. It also conveys that learning/unlearning oppression is an ongoing process. Appropriate self-disclosure on the part of the facilitator should always serve the learning needs of the participants, not the personal development of the instructor.

3. *Acknowledge significance of feelings in the learning process:* Social justice education is both a cognitive and affective process in which many different feelings arise as participants grapple with perspectives and information that deepen as well as challenge their previous understanding. It is important for facilitators to acknowledge that these feelings are a natural and appropriate part of the learning process. Providing participants with some guidance for how to recognize, listen to, and learn from feelings encourages their expression in ways that help rather than hinder learning. The introduction of concepts such as "learning edge," "comfort zone," and "hot buttons," for example, provides participants with a language and a process to use in examining and making sense of feelings that arise. This can be an opportunity to clarify the difference between "safety" and "comfort." Instructors may alert students to content that might be emotionally activating.[2] Being uncomfortable is a typical and productive reaction when confronting contradictions and challenges to what we have learned in the past and is an essential part of exploring social injustice. However, facilitators also need to be sensitive to the trauma that learners may have experienced and prepared to support and provide resources for students who may need them. Mindfulness and other embodied practices can also help participants notice, learn from, and regulate emotional reactions.

4. *Address fears and concerns:* Some fears or worries may be addressed when the learning outcomes, agenda, and expectations are presented and discussed. Facilitators can speak to some of the typical concerns people have, such as worrying about being unsupported when stereotypes about one's group are made by other participants or being blamed or shamed for ignorance or being part of the privileged group. Facilitators can reiterate (and model) to participants that we will enforce the agreed-to guidelines that interrupt disrespectful, inequitable, and oppressive group dynamics. We can communicate that we don't blame people for how they were socialized or for having inaccurate information but that we hold people accountable for their words and actions and their responsibility for unlearning oppression. We can also remind participants they have the option to pass or determine the level of participation that feels appropriate for them at different points in the workshop, as they consider their own learning edge.

PHASE TWO: CONTRADICTION

If we have succeeded in creating a supportive environment, participants may feel secure enough to open up to contradictions to their old belief system and begin a process of exploration, and they may try on different ways of understanding the world and live with the inevitable discomfort. This process can be confusing, disorienting, and, at times, frightening. Participants might feel out of control, without known boundaries or familiar ground, and may experience a sense of loss or *surrender* as they literally "excavate the ground they stand on" (Barker, 1993, p. 48).

As they learn new information, they may also experience strong emotions, such as anger and resentment, about the enormity of oppression and a feeling of betrayal by those who were supposed to tell them the truth about the social world. At the same time, they may feel a sense of freedom as they consider, discard, and eventually construct new ways of making sense of the world or of conceptualizing and naming their experiences. For some, new information can put words and theory to their feelings and experiences that can be validating and empowering.

CORRESPONDING FACILITATING ENVIRONMENT

The supportive environment for the contradiction phase is one that allows participants to immerse themselves fully in whatever contradictions and conflicts arise as a consequence of engaging previously unknown ideas and exploring their own and others' feelings and experiences. The course content and process deliberately pose and explore contradictions and encourage participants to make sense of the new material they encounter. This process is akin to Freire's notion of education for critical consciousness (1970/2018).

At this point, the environment shifts. It does not overprotect or enable participants to avoid feelings of discomfort, confusion, fear, and anger. Such feelings are an inevitable and ultimately helpful part of the learning process. Through engaging with challenging information and participating in experiential activities, participants are encouraged to let go of the comfortable and familiar and explore new territory.

This phase is not only challenging for participants—intellectually and emotionally—but often the most challenging for facilitators as well, since we are creating dissonance and raising emotions through the information and experiences we provide. This phase requires skillful facilitation to process effectively. As students engage with material that is more personally challenging and possibly encounter more conflict in the classroom or workshop, facilitators can revisit some of the activities and facilitation strategies utilized in the confirmation phase to help participants stay connected to each other, the facilitator, and the material as they encounter discomforting ideas and feelings.

DESIGN FEATURES OF THE CONTRADICTION PHASE

Activities in the contradiction phase encourage participants to face the challenges posed by new information and different perspectives. Learning activities in the contradiction phase can focus on any of the core concepts identified in Chapter 4, and exemplified in the course designs in this volume, such as socialization, historical legacies, and manifestations at the individual, institutional, and societal/cultural levels; power and privilege; and allyship and advocacy. Some key design components of the contradiction phase include:

1. *Content that deepens or challenges current understanding:* There are numerous ways instructors can offer participants opportunities to deepen or challenge their current

understandings. Readings, different types of media, experiential activities, presentations, panel discussions, guest speakers, field trips, and various discussion formats are some of the ways to introduce new ideas and content.

2. *Opportunity to share personal stories/experiences:* Asking participants to share personal experiences with the content allows them to reflect on their own experiences and listen to and reflect on the experiences of others. Hearing personal stories can be very powerful in supporting learning and changing attitudes and beliefs. Personal stories make abstract concepts concrete and can promote empathy (Bell, 2020; Eisner, 2002; Greene, 2007). For instance, hearing Muslim people describe their experiences with harassment first-hand is often more evocative than solely hearing facts and statistics about bias incidents. Hearing a white person talk about coming to terms with white privilege and struggling to find responsible ways to be an ally will likely be more powerful than a list of directives. However, facilitators need to be mindful of not putting the burden on members of marginalized groups to educate, especially when the class/workshop is predominantly composed of people from dominant groups. Invited speakers, media, arts events, readings, and community engagement are some ways participants can learn about marginalized groups without relying on peer participants.

3. *Time for full discussion and reflection:* Facilitators can create a variety of structures that allow participants to grapple more deeply with the content. Caucus/affinity groups create the space for people with a similar social identity to discuss their ideas, questions, and experiences with each other without relying on or worrying about the reactions from people with a different social identity. Instructors can ask students, both during and after class, to keep a journal or respond to prompts to further their personal reflection.

Because the activities in a social justice education course are designed to raise contradictions and challenge participants to rethink their understanding of social power relationships, discussions can be intense. We can scaffold activities and content by providing ample opportunity to process or collectively reflect on and discuss reactions to the activities. Processing is an intentional and systematic way to guide discussion of a class activity so as to encourage the expression of divergent perspectives, explore contradictions, and help participants to derive cognitive as well as affective understanding from the activity.

FACILITATION ISSUES AND STRATEGIES FOR THE CONTRADICTION PHASE

The contradiction phase can pose some of the greatest challenges to facilitators, who will need a range of skills to handle the numerous dynamics that can occur and ensure a supportive environment where participants can take intellectual and emotional risks and engage deeply. Key facilitation issues typical of the contradiction phase include:

1. *Ensure equitable participation and constructive group behavior:* As the content and experiences get more challenging, and the emotional reactions become stronger, facilitators need to ensure that the class/workshop remains a constructive learning environment. This includes carefully managing the group and power dynamics so that all participants continue to be heard. For example, when one person or small group dominates discussions, or when some participants are always silent, the facilitator can ensure equitable participation in a number of ways. Consider these examples:
    - One participant has taken an active role in class discussions, contributing to every conversation. The facilitator says, "Before we hear from you again, Steve, I'd like to see if some of the people who have not spoken up would like to say something."

- The facilitator notices that a quiet participant has been trying to say something but keeps getting cut off by other, more active participants. The facilitator asks, "Maria, it looks like you've been trying to get into this discussion. What would you like to say?"
- The facilitator notices that five participants have not said anything during large-group discussions. He says, "Let's do a quick pass go around the circle. Each person share a short sentence that describes your reaction to this activity. Choose to pass if you wish."

The instructor may also use dyads to get everyone in the group talking or ask participants to respond to a brief writing prompt as a way to help them organize their thoughts and prepare to offer comments aloud.

It is particularly important for facilitators to pay attention to the power dynamics in the class. These patterns can be expressed in a variety of ways. Participants from dominant groups may dismiss or downplay the personal experiences or views of people from marginalized groups or expect them to speak for their whole group. Or individuals from dominant groups may feel intimidated and afraid they will say something wrong and be verbally attacked by individuals from the marginalized group or other members of their dominant group. While we want to encourage participation, we want to prevent any student(s) from controlling, dominating, or subverting the class to their own particular agenda.

It can be useful to have participants practice active listening, especially to hear from peers in marginalized groups, to ensure they have understood what others said before engaging in dialogue. Participants should be encouraged to ask questions to better understand others' perspectives as opposed to only asserting their own views. Instructors should be especially sensitive to comments or behaviors that silence other students. The agreed-upon norms and guidelines can be posted visibly in the room so that when a challenge emerges, the group can go back to the posted agreements, discuss the specific guideline that may be relevant, and perhaps elaborate or revise it as needed, thus becoming a living document during the life of the learning community. If agreed-upon guidelines are not referenced when participants violate them, the learning community may be affected and group members are likely to view the guidelines as fraudulent (see Bell, 2020). Consider these examples:

- A participant rolls her eyes and looks away when a man tries to challenge her belief in the fairness of affirmative action programs. The facilitator says to her, "We may not all agree, but we need to be able to disagree respectfully. We need to express our disagreement in ways that are consistent with our discussion guidelines."
- A white student interrupts a Black student who is describing an incident of racial bias by saying, "You're just playing the race card!" The instructor stops the white student and asks him to allow the other student to finish his story. During the subsequent discussion, the instructor asks the white student, "Instead of challenging his story and analysis, is there a question you could ask that might help you understand why he experienced the situation as racially biased?"
- A student reacts to another student by saying, "You're such a homophobe if you believe that!" The facilitator responds, "We agreed there will be no name calling. How else could you express your ideas without making it a personal attack?"
- An upper-middle-class student, in response to a panel presentation by working-class activists, immediately starts to discount their experiences by saying, "My parents worked hard for what they have." The instructor intervenes and asks, "Instead of negating what they said, let's first look at what was new information for you."

Instructors should highlight and affirm behaviors that positively contribute to constructive group dynamics. In the contradiction phase, it is also important to continue to validate personal risk-taking as the class goes more deeply into the subject. Instructors can support and encourage participants to take risks in exploring new perspectives, feelings, and awareness that contradict or stretch their prior understanding. They can validate participants who express confusion or ask questions that reflect their personal struggle with issues discussed in the course. And they can acknowledge and appreciate comments and behaviors when students disagree in a constructive manner, support the learning of another student, or ask thoughtful and challenging questions that advance the conversation. Consider these examples:

- "I know it was difficult to share that, and I appreciate your honesty."
- "When you asked that question, it really opened up the discussion in interesting ways. Thank you for raising that."
- "I know it's uncomfortable to look at our biases. I respect people's willingness to do this hard work."

2. *Surface different/divergent perspectives:* Instructors need to not only ensure equitable and constructive participation but elicit a variety of perspectives so that different viewpoints can be openly aired and explored. When there is limited participation, the group misses out on learning from other's experiences and perspectives, and opportunities for addressing misinformation or confusion may be lost. Instructors should allow contradictions and tensions to emerge and should resist the tendency to smooth them over or quickly relieve uncomfortable moments. Facilitators can actively solicit divergent perspectives by summarizing what has already been said and asking for other viewpoints or providing other perspectives and asking students to react (whether as part of a discussion or in writing). Instructors can ask, "What do other people think?" or "Some people believe that . . . what do you think about that?" Exposure to divergent perspectives helps participants learn to work with contradictions and have their own thinking challenged, clarified, and extended.

Facilitators can also talk about their own experiences and perspectives in ways that advance learning. Through sharing their own stories, facilitators can provide additional information, offer missing perspectives, model their own struggles with unlearning internalized domination and subordination, and make it safer for participants to share their thoughts and experiences. If facilitators tell too many personal stories or talk about their own experiences too much, participants might begin to discount the course as the facilitator's "personal agenda." Facilitators need to be clear about the purpose of such disclosure and choose carefully when to disclose their personal reactions or stories, making sure they serve an educational purpose.

It would be disingenuous to pretend that a social justice education course is neutral or objective any more than are any other courses. Participants are correct in perceiving that there is a particular perspective represented in a social justice education course. It is essential, however, that there is room for all perspectives to be heard and challenged respectfully. When facilitators or participants squelch the expression of views or experiences that are counter to the underlying beliefs guiding the course, social justice education courses are vulnerable to charges of political correctness. We assure participants that we all have prejudices, assumptions, and limited perspectives, and we encourage them to see the course as an opportunity to consciously examine these. They can then choose views based on new information and understanding, rather than allowing unexamined attitudes and beliefs to guide their thinking.

3. *Address inaccurate information and views:* As students share their views, inevitably they will express some erroneous or distorted information. Given the amount of misinformation available on social media, it is important that these inaccuracies get addressed. We want to keep people engaged yet not allow incorrect or insensitive statements to go unchallenged. How a facilitator responds to inaccurate, or in some cases offensive, statements depends on numerous factors, including the effect of the statement on individuals in the group, the timing in the overall course and specific class, the facilitator's relationship with the individual, and the group dynamics. Sometimes instructors need to directly correct misinformation or curtail offensive remarks. Often, the approach described earlier of reflecting, questioning, and adding can be helpful to respond to inaccurate beliefs.

Reflecting: One of the most effective ways to encourage participants to think more deeply and critically is to reflect back what they say. Hearing their own words can enable participants to understand the impact of their statements and to more clearly see and identify underlying assumptions. Consider this example:

- The facilitator repeats a participant's statement, "So, what you are saying is that poor and homeless people have the same opportunity for advancement as people who have more financial resources, they just need to try harder?"

In many cases, when participants hear their words reflected back to them, they can recognize faulty logic and clarify their views. In other situations, reflection alone may not be sufficient. Participants may say things that are factually incorrect and that reiterate commonly held misconceptions. Inaccurate statements need to be addressed and corrected, not simply reflected back. Instead, the facilitator can respond to erroneous beliefs by asking further questions, depersonalizing the comment and then addressing it with accurate information or directly correcting the statement.

Posing questions: Asking questions is often an effective way to challenge assumptions, solicit factual information, and redirect discussion. Rather than directly challenging participant perspectives through statements, questions can encourage participants to examine their own assumptions and values and differentiate between anecdotal/ individual experience and sociologically and historically grounded information. Questions can also help participants understand when they are repeating unexamined beliefs or perspectives. Examples include:

- "Can you say how you came to this perspective?"
- "What kinds of portrayals of Latinx people do you see in the movies and on television? How do these portrayals affect your perception of what Latinx people are like?"
- "What might be some other reasons that parents of low-income students don't come to school events besides that they are uninterested in their children's education?"

Depersonalizing the statement: A facilitator can respond to an inaccurate or stereotypical comment directly and sensitively by first depersonalizing the statement and then focusing on the accurate information or by addressing the issue as a commonly held belief. If possible, this discussion can be connected to course concepts. Consider these examples:

- "John says he believes, as do many people, that Muslims are more likely to commit acts of terrorism in the U.S. That is a common misperception based on stereotypes of Muslims as terrorists. However, the Department of Homeland Security reports that in 2020, white supremacists were most likely to commit acts of domestic terrorism in the U.S."

- After a participant says they don't notice color and treats everyone the same, "I know many people were brought up to think that being color-blind was a way to avoid being racist or biased. While that's a good intention, let's explore why that can be problematic."

Correcting: Sometimes it is useful, even essential, to directly intervene and provide accurate information. This is particularly important if the statement may be harmful or hurtful to other participants. Consider these examples:

- A student claims that women who drink at parties and get raped are just as responsible as the man for what happened. The instructor responds, "It's never a person's fault for being sexually assaulted. Our laws and policies are clear that the individuals involved need to ensure that there is consent."
- A participant asserts that they think that people with mental illness are more likely to commit violent crimes. The facilitator replies, "There is no evidence that people with psychological disabilities are more prone to violent crime; in fact, they are more likely to be the victim of crimes."

Facilitators need to decide which combinations of strategies are most appropriate considering the particulars of a given situation. There is no simple formula. Sometimes facilitators will feel stuck in the moment and unsure of how to respond to a comment that clearly needs a response. Even when uncertain about what to do, statements that are toxic to the group and learning process must not be ignored. Some options can be to acknowledge the statement and its impact and then create space to develop a response, either in the present or later on. Facilitators could state, "Many people had a strong reaction to that statement," followed by giving participants an opportunity to do a "one-minute paper"—writing their thoughts on what just happened and the effect it had—or briefly sharing reactions in pairs. If the comment occurs at the end of a class, the instructor can follow up on email or an online discussion format or note that the matter will be discussed further at the next meeting. The instructor can also bring in additional information at a following session to shed light on the issue.

4. *Manage conflict and different views:* Conflict and disagreement can be healthy and play an important role in social justice education. Many instructors cite lack of preparation or skills for effectively addressing conflict and a concomitant fear of losing control of discussions as primary obstacles to initiating discussion of social justice issues (see Chapter 12: Critical Self-Knowledge). The initial response of many instructors to potential conflict in the classroom is to shut down any disagreement, ignore the emotional and affective tone in a class, and keep a tight focus on intellectual and informational content. Our goal is to work through immediate conflicts and emotions so as to understand the individual, institutional, and cultural implications of the topic at hand. We do so by encouraging participants to consider and analyze multiple perspectives on any given topic. Important learning opportunities are missed if participants do not have the opportunity to honestly express feelings, concerns, questions, and disagreements.

There are a number of things a facilitator can do to help ensure that conflict is constructive. First is to reinforce the agreed-upon guidelines for interaction, particularly no personal attacks. In addition, the facilitator can slow down the pace of interaction, making sure each person is heard before another person speaks. Often conflict will escalate and become unproductive when people do not feel adequately understood. Facilitators can paraphrase what each person says before another person speaks or ask the next speaker to do so before adding to the conversation. They can ensure that people are not interrupted and have the opportunity to complete their thoughts. Having the recognized speaker hold a "talking stick" or another object can also be helpful. If the conflict gets centered between just a couple of people, facilitators can invite in other views or perspectives.

Facilitators can also take a break to give everyone a chance to reflect on the interactions, share their thoughts and feelings with a partner, or free-write for a few minutes, then ask people to share their reflections. Facilitators can note common ground and areas of agreement that have surfaced. They can put the issues being discussed into a broader context and relate it to the course concepts, moving it away from personal disagreements, such as, "While you are raising different ways of addressing the gaps in educational achievement, you both agree that this is an issue that needs attention. You both recognize the role parents play in this process. Let's look at what we know about educational opportunity from the reading we have done."

Toward the end of a class or workshop segment, facilitators can help participants pull thoughts together so that they are ready to make a transition to the next activity or end the class session. In summarizing a discussion, facilitators and participants can together identify themes that emerged, unresolved questions, insights gained, divergent perspectives, and other important points raised. Time to reflect enables participants to step back, summarize their learning, and develop cognitive as well as experiential understanding of the issues raised in the activity. For example, during a classism course, the facilitators might say, "From this discussion it appears that we have several different understandings of how to define social class in this group. Can we name those differences?" or "I notice a conflict in this discussion between what many of us have believed about equal opportunity in the past and what we are beginning to see about the effects of class differences on economic opportunity." We do not expect participants to end a discussion feeling that they have completely resolved their discomfort with different ideas and perspectives. Some disorientation is a sign that they are grappling with new awareness and knowledge. Facilitators can encourage them to notice discomfort, stay on their learning edge, and consider new ideas and questions rather than retreat to the comfort of more familiar perspectives.

5. *Acknowledge and manage feelings:* For many people, the expression of feelings in a classroom is an unusual experience. This is because traditional education environments have discouraged the public expression of emotions as inappropriate. Some participants (e.g., women and some ethnic and racial groups) have been penalized for showing emotions in the classroom and criticized as less rigorous thinkers, less analytical, or unable to frame an impartial argument (Rendon, 2009). As participants explore systemic inequality, feelings such as anger, guilt, sadness, and frustration inevitably arise. Facilitators can help participants recognize feelings and remind them that feelings are a common and normal part of this process. Hearing from other people with similar feelings can be validating and can make it easier for participants to accept their own reactions. Consider these examples:
   - A participant begins to cry as she recalls how a younger brother with a developmental disability was teased by classmates at school. The facilitator says, "It seems like that is still a painful memory for you. Thanks for telling us about this experience. It is a powerful reminder of how deeply name-calling can affect us. Do other people have similar memories?"

- A facilitator asks participants to go around the circle and give a one-word description of what they are feeling in reaction to an intense video about the Holocaust. The facilitator asks, "What happens when we close ourselves off from the feelings we experience when we witness injustice? How might this serve to perpetuate antisemitism and other forms of injustice?"
- Some students may feel immobilized by feelings of guilt or the fear of saying the wrong thing or revealing their prejudices. Facilitators can remind them that they are not at fault for having misinformation and can shift the focus to learning to understand cultural conditioning as a base from which to act differently. Personal sharing from the facilitators about their own learning process and the errors they have made can help students see that such feelings can be a powerful source of growth. The introduction of a conceptual model can also provide participants with a way to understand emotions in a broader theoretical context. Facilitators can refer to the cycle of socialization, identity development theory, or learning edge/comfort zone models discussed in the introductory module to help participants understand and normalize their experience (see Chapter 2: Pedagogical Foundations and Chapter 4: Core Concepts). For example:
  - A white participant is ashamed because she could not identify any African American historical figures on a short quiz. The facilitator responds, "How does the cycle of socialization we talked about earlier help us understand how we have been kept from knowing about cultures different from our own?"
  - An Asian American student who has struggled with perfectionism and thought it was her personal problem is relieved to learn about the model minority stereotype as a way to understand her experience in a broader context.

Facilitators can acknowledge that realizing the extent of the oppression may generate a range of emotions and can provide opportunities to process feelings through class activities and other constructive outlets, such as support and affinity groups. Instructors can encourage students to simply sit with their feelings, providing support and assurance that this is a normal part of the process. Models of social identity development (see Chapter 2: Pedagogical Foundations) or other descriptions of personal growth regarding social oppression can offer students a vision of how feelings and views can be transformed in a liberatory way (Goodman, 2011; Warren, 2005).

While having emotional responses is a normal part of the process, facilitators need to ensure that feelings are not inappropriately used against other participants. One common dynamic is when white women cry in response to being challenged by women of color and the attention shifts to taking care of the white women, ignoring the issues raised by the woman of color and often casting her as a bully (DiAngelo, 2018; Hamad, 2020). In other situations, expressions of passion or anger by Black and brown individuals have been read by others as aggressive and out of control. It's important that instructors and students are familiar and comfortable with different types of emotional expression.

6. *Value silence:* Facilitators and participants alike are often uncomfortable with silence in a classroom or workshop and often keep talking to fill the silence. Yet it is useful to recognize that in social justice education, silence can have many different meanings. Participants often need silence to ponder new information or insights about an issue. A brief period of silence can provide time for participants to think through their perspectives, experiences, feelings, and ideas before launching into group discussions.

This can be especially helpful for participants whose first language is not English or who need time to reflect before responding.

Differentiating productive silence from bored or fearful silence is an important facilitator skill. Signs of a fearful or uncomfortable silence include lack of eye contact among participants, yawning, physical shifting and movement in seats, or tense expressions on faces. One strategy that is helpful for bridging these moments is a brief writing assignment—asking participants to write down their feelings at that moment or turning to a neighbor to share their thoughts—to provide a way to acknowledge and clarify reactions before moving on. Another strategy is to do a quick "whip" around the circle, in which each participant in turn says one word that describes their feelings at that moment. Sometimes simply commenting on silence opens the discussion, enabling it to restart and potentially deepen individual understanding. Consider these examples:

- In response to a processing question, the group is silent and no one is making eye contact. The facilitator says, "I'm not sure what this silence means. Can anyone say what you are thinking or feeling right now?" or "Let's just sit with this silence and give all of us time to sort out our feelings. When someone feels ready to answer one of the processing questions, please do."
- An emotional exchange between Jewish and Christian students about the prevalence of antisemitism on campus leads to a long period of silence. The facilitator says, "Why don't we each take a few minutes to jot down what we are feeling right now. Then we can talk with a partner before we come back to the whole group." Or the facilitator could say, "This topic clearly generates strong feelings," thus normalizing an emotional, as well as intellectual, response to the topic.

7. *Address avoidance:* It is not uncommon for participants to shift away from a topic that makes them uncomfortable or if they feel another issue is more pressing. Sometimes facilitators can acknowledge the importance of the new topic but remind participants of the focus of the current discussion. Other times, instructors can find ways to connect the issue raised to the course focus. Facilitators can also openly name when they notice a pattern of certain topics being avoided and discuss with participants why this may be so.

In social justice education, it is common for participants to prefer to talk about their subordinated identity (or identities) rather than consider their privileged identity (or identities). In some cases, participants may want to consider only a particular subordinated identity but not another of their subordinated identities. Facilitators should recognize the interconnections among different forms of oppression and how they mutually constitute each other while not allowing students to avoid the in-depth exploration of the particular aspect of social inequality under discussion. For example, in a racism workshop, white women who try to shift the focus to their identity as women, but not their whiteness, could be asked to think about how their whiteness affects their experience of being a woman and how this differs for women of color, or they could be asked how being a woman shapes their experience of being white and having white privilege relative to white men. We can also ask about how their experience and understanding of sexism might help them understand and/or block their understanding of racism. What are some of the similarities and differences? Often, once people have had the opportunity to acknowledge the issue that is most central to them, they are more able to explore other issues. Facilitators *can* support an intersectional focus while foregrounding a particular form of oppression or social identity for the sake of learning about a specific form of oppression.

8. *Reduce and address resistance:* Resistance, an unwillingness to consider new information or perspectives, can be expressed in many ways by members of both advantaged and disadvantaged groups. Some behaviors that can indicate resistance might be: refuting every fact that is shared, attacking the facilitator as biased, dismissing other students' experiences, or simply disengaging. Having one's worldview challenged, especially one's belief in meritocracy; being asked to acknowledge unasked-for privilege; or being asked to understand how another person is discriminated against are painful and uncomfortable experiences. There are numerous strategies that can help shift resistance (Beeman, 2015; Goodman, 2011, 2015; Ouyang, 2014).

First, the facilitator should try to *assess* what is creating the resistance—i.e., what may be provoking this level of fear or anxiety. People often feel they are being told they are bad or wrong and do not feel heard. Their core beliefs or understanding of themselves and the world are being questioned. They may fear what social change would look like and mean for them. If so, facilitators can *revisit some of the activities in the confirmation phase* that foster trust and rapport among students, affirm who people are, and recognize their strengths and qualities that align with social justice (e.g., their strong work ethic, their caring for other people, or their concern for fairness). Participants can be referred back to the discussion of comfort zone and learning edge to recall how they planned to deal with defensive feelings. The facilitator can remind students that this exploration is not about personal blame but about understanding how we are part of larger systems that impact our lived realities and those of others.

Facilitators can *build on students' current knowledge*, recognizing the nuggets of truth in their perspectives, rather than suggesting that everything they believe is false. It is almost never effective to continually try to convince a student who is being resistant to accept a particular piece of information or viewpoint. Facilitators can *encourage participants to research or explore information for themselves.* For example, participants who believe that sexism is no longer a problem can be asked to research the representation of women as heads of Fortune 500 companies, on corporate boards, in the U.S. Senate, or in other major positions of power. Students can be asked to make observations that reveal power inequities or discrimination, such as how people are represented in the media or treated in stores. Materials and activities that allow participants to *examine issues from a distance* can be less threatening and raise less resistance. Case studies, vignettes, simulations, and analogies can be used to help students identify and analyze power dynamics without feeling personally implicated or attacked. Instead of focusing at an intellectual level, the facilitator can shift to a more personal level. Sometimes hearing personal stories, whether in person or through media, can help students make a more *personal or empathic connection.* Some students can make the link between their own experiences of feeling marginalized, discriminated against, or treated unfairly to relate to the oppression experienced by another group.

Participants, especially from dominant groups, may feel less threatened by changes in the status quo by discussing the ways they and all people are harmed by oppression and what alternatives might look like that could be beneficial to all. Instructors can look for ways to *heighten students' investment* in particular social justice topics or equity more generally. How might understanding oppression help them in their work or interpersonal relationships or in helping the U.S. live up to its stated values of equal opportunity for all?

Our goal as facilitators is to help participants build resilience and internal resources that enable them to think critically and tolerate ambiguity and complexity so that they can choose behaviors and attitudes that are congruent with their commitments to fairness and justice.

9. *Manage facilitator's own reactions:* Emotional reactions in the course of social justice education are a natural and human response for facilitators as well as participants. Facilitators from marginalized groups often face a greater emotional burden and challenges to authority, competence, and credibility than facilitators from dominant groups. Instructors may need to make conscious efforts not to react inappropriately to a student's remark or behavior, though it can be helpful to share the impact the behavior had. It is important that facilitators recognize their own feelings and reactions and have strategies to deal with such situations (Obear, 2016). Some options include self-talk (telling oneself to calm down, not to take it personally, to stay in the moment), reframing the situation, taking some deep breaths, letting students know the impact of their comments, and/or taking a break to collect oneself and think about what to do. A co-facilitator, especially one who holds different social identities, can be helpful in these situations because rarely are both facilitators similarly emotionally affected at the same time. The one who is not as activated can think more clearly about what leadership role to take in the moment. While it's important to have strategies in the moment, instructors also need help to develop practices and supports outside of the classroom as well in order to do this work. (See Chapter 12: Critical Self-Knowledge for more on this topic.)

PHASE THREE: CONTINUITY

Once participants have left familiar ground and explored new territory, both affectively and intellectually, they are in a position to integrate what they have learned and establish a new foundation. This balance is gradually achieved as a new set of beliefs becomes "home base" for interpreting experience and creating meaning. The past is not wholly rejected but reinterpreted and reconstructed into a new frame of reference.

CORRESPONDING FACILITATING ENVIRONMENT

The environment once again shifts to encourage the development of stability and *continuity* based on new insights and knowledge. Activities are designed to help participants articulate and confirm what they have learned and think about what this might mean for their actions beyond the course or workshop. Opportunities are provided to imagine taking new actions, the likely consequences of such actions, and the types of support that could be called upon to sustain these changes.

DESIGN ISSUES FOR CONTINUITY

During the continuity phase, participants are asked to turn their attention to how to integrate new awareness and knowledge into their lives and to bring their experience in the course to a close. Activities focus on helping participants identify actions they want to take as they further their learning and concretize their new perspectives in actions. The goal is for all students to feel a sense of agency—that they can play a role challenging inequities and fostering justice. Participants are asked to think about how to nurture and sustain their developing understanding of, and commitment to, acting against social injustice. They are encouraged to choose and develop their own action plans suited to their particular learning and comfort level. The following guidelines help in planning this phase of the course.

1. *Identify actions for continued learning and action:* Participants can map out action plans with concrete steps to successfully accomplish their goals in ways that match their personal level of interest and skill. This means acknowledging and valuing actions at all levels of risk. Actions could include reading more about issues; committing to attending lectures or arts events on social justice themes; participating in social justice discussions and actions online; objecting to biased jokes or comments in their workplace, classes, or at the family dinner table; reviewing policies and practices in their organization; or joining a social change group. Chapters 5–11 provide action-planning activities.
2. *Identify support:* Developing support for new awareness of and commitment to address social justice issues that extend beyond the workshop boundaries is essential to helping participants bridge the gap between the class and their school, work, and personal lives. Helping participants develop support groups from the class or learn about existing organizational, community, or campus groups to join provides a way for participants to nurture relationships with others who share their developing commitments.
3. *Provide closure to the class/workshop:* Instructors can help participants achieve a sense of closure by providing a way for them to summarize what they learned, appreciate other participants, and identify next steps in continuing their learning. Closing activities can take a range of formats, including closing circles where each person shares a take-away, comments on next steps they plan to take, or expresses appreciation for someone/something in the session that contributed to their learning.
4. *Solicit feedback:* Whether or not it is formally required, it is helpful to get feedback about the class or workshop. It is useful to hear what participants found helpful and solicit suggestions for improvements, both in terms of the facilitation and the class content.

FACILITATION ISSUES IN CONTINUITY PHASE

Sometimes participants are concerned about how they will continue learning about social justice issues and have support for their new interests without the structure of the class, while others are eager to go out and change the world. Participants need assistance thinking through how they can move forward in constructive ways and sustain ongoing self-education, and reflection as a lifelong process.

1. *Address immobilizing feelings:* It is not uncommon for people to be overwhelmed by the enormity of social inequality and feel powerless to make any significant change. Hopefully in our classes/workshops they will have learned about ways people have resisted oppression and engaged in actions and movements for justice. Reminding students of these efforts can reinforce that social change is often a slow process but societal changes can and do occur through the accumulation of myriad actions, big and small, that people take together. Participants can think about actions in their organizations and communities that have led to greater equity and can consider their own spheres of influence and what they might do to make an impact. Being part of groups and collective actions can mitigate feelings of disempowerment and foster a sense of being part of a larger struggle for justice.

People from marginalized groups may feel overwhelmed, helpless, confused, despairing, hopeless, and/or angry at the enormity of oppression members of their group face. We can acknowledge such feelings while also encouraging them to identify sources of power within their group and resources that can support their efforts to make change. Examples of role models from their group who have worked for justice can be a source of inspiration and encouragement as well as offer practical tools and strategies. Helping participants recognize the value of group support and affirmation from peers who share their social identities is important for developing strength and courage for facing the broader world.

People from privileged groups may feel guilty or ashamed of their social identity or unearned advantages, which may impede their work for justice. We can remind them that immobilizing guilt only serves to maintain the unjust status quo. Instead, individuals can be encouraged to consider how they can use their access to resources, personal connections, education, time, and credibility to support social justice efforts and work in solidarity with people from other groups. They can study and learn from role models in the past and present who show how people from advantaged groups can become powerful allies and change agents. Participants can connect with others from their privileged group to deal with their feelings and explore how to work collaboratively with people from their own and other social groups.

2. *Discuss appropriate action:* Participants may leave a course with much enthusiasm and desire for creating social change. It is our responsibility to help individuals think strategically about their actions so their impact matches their intentions. Assessing their competencies and areas for growth can help individuals determine what kind of activities are most appropriate for them at this time.

Some individuals take on a missionary role, trying to convert everyone they know to adopt their social justice perspective. Instructors should remind students that other people have not shared their class experience and should discuss with them how to communicate their new knowledge and excitement in respectful and effective ways and share their learnings with others without imposing or insisting that others adopt these same views. Individuals may develop a judgmental attitude, looking down on others from their social group who have not developed the same degree of social consciousness. Instructors need to work with participants to develop the respect and compassion for those from their own social identity group who have not critically examined issues of oppression. They can remind students of their own ongoing journey and of the things that were helpful to them in their learning and development that might inform how they can interact with others.

Participants from privileged groups may try to "help" or "save" people from marginalized communities. However well intentioned, this can be experienced as patronizing and disrespectful of others' cultures and competencies. Instructors should discuss how students can work in collaboration and solidarity with subordinated groups, listening to their needs, valuing their experiences, supporting their goals, and following their leadership. As people from dominant groups work for social change, there needs to be a sense of accountability to people from the marginalized group to ensure that they are acting in ways that actually are serving the larger social justice vision.

When people leave the class/workshop with a heightened awareness of social justice issues, they may find it hard to relate in the same ways to their friends and family. Participants may notice and be more offended by biased comments, jokes, and beliefs. They may find they have less in common with people currently in their social network. We can discuss with them how to find support for their new views while renegotiating current relationships and can help them explore ways to stay engaged with family members while they continue on their social justice journey. We can share ideas for how to deal with changing friendships. We can help prepare people to manage and make decisions about the relationships in their life and find what they need to continue their growth.

GENERAL FACILITATION STRATEGIES

In the previous sections, we highlight some specific facilitation skills that might be helpful at different points and in different situations in social justice education. In the following we summarize some general strategies that are important throughout a course or workshop. Developing skill with these approaches will go a long way toward having a successful social justice course or workshop, and they are worth developing for any facilitator toolkit.

SEEK UNDERSTANDING BEFORE RESPONDING

In general, before we respond, we want to make sure that individuals feel heard and that we understand them correctly. This approach allows us to develop more thoughtful and effective responses. Immediately challenging what someone says can heighten defensiveness and close people off to further discussion. Instead, facilitators can follow three steps: *reflect*, *question*, and then *add*. First, paraphrase or repeat back in your own words what you heard someone say. It allows individuals to know that they are heard, ensures that the facilitator accurately understands what participants are saying, and provides an opportunity for participants to clarify statements that may not convey their intention. For example, the instructor might say, "It sounds like you think that . . ." or "Let me be clear, you believe that . . ."

Next, ask questions to further clarify their perspective, such as: "What led you to believe that . . .?" "Can you tell me more why you think that?" and "Can you explain what you mean by that?" Then, once individuals feel heard and the instructor has greater understanding of their perspective, the facilitator can decide on the most appropriate response. Some options might be to add information or correct misinformation, open it up to the group for other thoughts, build on the comment to move onto new topics, or simply thank them for sharing their view. The point is not to do this process in every situation in a rote manner but to be mindful of being respectful and gaining clarity before replying.

GET DISTANCE AND GAIN PERSPECTIVE

Often when we are in the middle of a situation, we can get caught up in the immediate dynamics and do not see the bigger picture. Especially in complex or challenging moments, it can be useful to try to get some distance, intellectually and emotionally, and gain perspective. Warren refers to this as "getting off the dance floor and getting up on the balcony" (2005, p. 620). From the "balcony" we can better see patterns and dynamics. She encourages instructors to "listen to the song beneath the words." Distance can often help facilitators discern the underlying issues, what is really being communicated. Instructors can also gain perspective by taking a break to reflect on the classroom dynamics and closely attend to the communication and participation patterns and non-verbal behaviors to look for the deeper issues. It can also be useful for facilitators to take a few moments to breathe, refocus their attention, and talk with a co-facilitator or other colleague to process feelings and observations in the moment before reengaging.

SHARE OBSERVATIONS NON-JUDGMENTALLY

Simply stating what you notice in a neutral and non-judgmental way can bring issues to the fore and allow for their discussion in a more thoughtful way. Observations about group dynamics can help surface underlying feelings and assumptions that can promote greater learning. Participants can also be taught and encouraged to share their own observations in constructive ways. Some examples of observations might be, "When Susan shared her powerful story, no one responded. I'm wondering how people are feeling?" or "I've noticed that when I ask people to share an example of how they've experienced privilege, several people shared stories of how they've been marginalized. I'm wondering if it seems harder to think about one's privilege?"

CONSIDER TIMING, TONE, AND WORD CHOICE

Whether reflecting back what an individual says, offering a different perspective, or sharing an observation, the timing, tone, and word choice we use matter. These qualities can make the difference between sounding respectful and insightful or judgmental and disparaging. The timing of a comment can have very different impacts depending on where the group is in its group development. The following examples illustrate how facilitators can consider timing and tone in their interventions. In reference to sharing observations, initially instructors may share observations that are less threatening but help them assess the group, such as, "I notice people are very quiet. I'm wondering if people are reluctant to share their views or if people simply need a break." At a later point, facilitators might make an observation that could have a deeper impact, for example, "I notice that the spokespeople for the small group report-outs have all been men, even though men make up only a quarter of the class. I'm wondering what people make of that."

Similarly, timing may affect how an instructor responds to a comment such as, "I don't see color. I think we should just be color-blind and treat everyone the same." At the beginning of the class, the instructor might say, "Thank you for sharing your perspective. That is a sentiment many people have. Throughout the class we'll be discussing why people believe that and the impact that approach may have on creating equity." At this point, the instructor may not want to directly challenge the statement but rather may focus on encouraging people to share their views while indicating that this view will not go unexplored. Later in the course, the instructor might respond to that statement by drawing on the class material and discussions and greater class cohesiveness to examine the problems with claiming a color-blind stance.

ASSESSMENT

We conclude with assessment, although it is relevant in all phases of SJE (planning, implementation, and follow-up). An SJE approach to evaluation and assessment focuses on how information can be used to help facilitators and members of a learning community reach their individual and group goals (see Chapter 2: Pedagogical Foundations for an in-depth discussion). Facilitators and participants can work together to co-create meaningful forms of assessment that are congruent with social justice goals (McArthur, 2018). Assessments can include formative and summative evaluations, as well as formal and informal mechanisms for feedback and evaluation, of the participants, the course experience, and the facilitators.

PRE-ASSESSMENT OPTIONS

Facilitators can gather information before designing a workshop or class to become familiar with the participants and their interests and learning needs. Instructors can interview participants individually before the session, convene focus groups with representative class/workshop members, or send a brief individual survey in which participants describe their prior experiences, hopes and fears, and learning goals for the upcoming class/workshop. Having participants complete a brief questionnaire on prior knowledge and experience can provide a sense of the range of questions/information participants are likely to bring. Facilitators can also talk with individuals who are familiar with the participants or the community from which they come.

Structured activities at the beginning of the class can also provide a sense of participants' prior experiences, expectations, and views. For example, Chapter 5: Racism uses an activity called the Prevalence of Race Continuum (see activity on website). This activity asks participants to respond to a series of statements ("You speak a language other than English at home," "You have studied people who look like you in history class," "You have ever felt racial tension in a situation and were afraid to say anything about it") by moving to signs in the room that say "True for Me," "Not True For Me," and "Neutral/Don't Know." This activity is a relatively low-risk way to get into the topic of race and gives the facilitator a sense of who is in the group and their experiences with the topic of race. Curriculum adjustments can then be made based on student identities, experiences, and interests gleaned from these activities.

STUDENT/PARTICIPANT ASSESSMENT

Formative assessment methods engage participants in regular, informal feedback on what they are learning in the course or workshop. For example, facilitators can ask participants to write one or two things they learned from a session and/or questions or confusions they still have. Such information will help facilitators respond to feedback at the next session, clarify concepts, and involve participants in planning next steps. Formative assessment strategies can also be used to identify which learning activities students found successful for developing and demonstrating knowledge and skills to meet participant and course/workshop goals.

Summative assessment measures evaluate performance for uses such as assigning final grades or evaluating participation at the end of a community or workplace learning experience. Traditional summative assessment measures include quizzes, mid- or final-term exams, and final papers or projects. Summative measures for SJE might include case studies, videos, interview exercises, community service-learning projects or other small-group assignments, journals, and reflective essays, action plans, or portfolios that summarize and illustrate learning. When grades/evaluation are used, they should be based upon assigned work and clear performance criteria. In college environments, this may include questions about assigned texts and other readings, homework assignments, and completion of in-class activities; written papers that follow a sequence of reflective questions or structured guidelines; and a final essay exam, based on broad conceptual questions prepared in advance that test participants' ability to effectively utilize new concepts and knowledge (Suskie, 2004).

Course grades should derive from evaluation activities that are clearly aligned with key outcome goals and learning activities. A neutral grading or assessment scheme, based on work completed and knowledge demonstrated, rather than views or opinions, provides a fairer basis for assessment and can be reassuring to students who may be concerned about giving "politically correct" answers. Grade points and grade percentages can be set in advance for each assignment. Students may find it helpful to see models and examples of successful assignments. Our goal is for participants to demonstrate their ability to think critically, thoughtfully examine beliefs and assumptions, increase knowledge, grapple with theoretical and conceptual interconnections, recognize course concepts in real-world examples, and identify potential plans of action (Walvoord & Anderson, 2009). (For more on this see Chapter 2: Pedagogical Foundations.)

COURSE/WORKSHOP ASSESSMENT

In the same way that participants benefit from feedback, so do instructors/facilitators. Such information can help determine what works and what can be changed or improved for the future and can provide information about our strengths and areas for growth as facilitators. Like participant assessments, course assessment can be undertaken using both formative and summative strategies.

Formative course/workshop assessments: Formative assessment can be informal, asking open-ended questions such as, "What learning activities have been most effective in helping you to learn more about ableism?" "What made these activities effective?" and "How comfortable do you feel participating in class at this point?" Facilitators can draw upon anonymous feedback periodically throughout the course and use other informal check-ins with participants, especially when facilitators notice issues such as reduced participation, hostility, confusion, or boredom.

Formative evaluation can also be formal, in which instructors develop specific questions about learning activities, sequencing, reading assignments, and grading criteria and ask participants to rate these on a Likert scale. Formative evaluation has the advantage of enabling instructors to make mid-course changes in content or learning activities based on participant feedback.

Summative course/workshop assessment can use institutionally designed forms or those created to evaluate the course/workshop as a whole. End-of-semester course-based assessment strategies provide a longitudinal perspective on what curricula, learning activities, and assessment practices work well for different students. Looking at participants' feedback on a course or workshop over several semesters can help facilitators anticipate which particular topics or exercises participants tend to find most challenging, refine assignments, and pilot innovative learning activities. Such reflection can also stimulate deeper insights into how a particular module, workshop, seminar, or course links to other courses, programs, and department and institutional learning goals (e.g., general education, disciplinary majors or minors, certificate programs, etc.).

INSTRUCTOR/FACILITATOR ASSESSMENT AND PROFESSIONAL DEVELOPMENT

Instructor engagement in ongoing self-assessment can be extremely valuable for gaining a long-term perspective on our development and support teacher/facilitator critical reflection and growth. Two techniques are to keep a daily journal and create opportunities for informal debriefing and discussion with trusted colleagues. Whether teaching alone, co-facilitating, or team teaching, developing an ongoing relationship with a trusted peer provides invaluable opportunities for reflection, review, and improvement. See Ouellett and Fraser (2005) for a team interview guide and Case, Kite, and Williams (2021) for peer mentoring processes.

An all-too-human tendency can be to skim over participant evaluations and zero in on any negative comments to the exclusion of everything else. However, it is important to reflect on and integrate the full scope of feedback (Boysen, 2016). One useful strategy is to find time at the end of the course to sit down with another instructor/facilitator to go over evaluations. We can note general themes of what went well and discuss ideas for changes or improvements in the content and teaching so that we can continue successful practices and work to improve others.

A note of caution: Student/participant evaluations of teaching in social justice courses and workshops can be limiting in at least two ways. Research shows that women and People of Color often receive lower course ratings in general (Amos, 2014; Case, Kite, & Williams, 2021; Gutiérrez y Muhs, Niemann, González, & Harris, 2012; Hamermesh & Parker, 2005; Huston, 2006), and in social justice courses, this can be especially true. Participants bring biases and projections that influence how they perceive and evaluate facilitators. The complexity of facilitating social justice courses, as well as the time it may take for students to grow and develop, are often not easily captured in the time frame in which students are asked to complete course evaluations. Required courses versus those that are elective may also receive lower evaluations. Given these realities, it is particularly important to be able to discuss and reflect on feedback with trusted colleagues to help assess what is useful (see Chapter 12: Critical Self-Knowledge for further discussion).

CONCLUSION

Both design and facilitation are critical and interconnected elements of successful social justice education. A well-designed class or workshop takes into account the various dimensions of social justice education (instructor, participants, content, pedagogy, classroom climate and dynamics, and context) and provides a thoughtful and solid foundation for the course. Effective facilitation creates a supportive and respectful environment in which participants are invited to discuss and raise questions about new information and perspectives and choose new beliefs and actions based on a critical examination of their own values, skills, and knowledge base. The design and facilitation issues and strategies discussed in this chapter can assist facilitators in planning and conducting classes/workshops in which all participants, from both advantaged and marginalized groups, are engaged in a positive and productive learning experience for all.

Notes

* We ask that those who cite this work always acknowledge by name all of the authors listed rather than either only citing the first author or using "et al." to indicate co-authors. All collaborated on the conceptualization, development, and writing of this chapter.
1 We use the terms "participants"/"students" and "faculty"/"instructors"/"facilitators" interchangeably because our work is used in a variety of contexts.
2 We prefer not to use "trigger" due to its violent connotation.

References

Ahenkora, E. (2020). *Safe and brave spaces don't work (and what you can do instead)*. Retrieved from https://medium.com/@elise.k.ahen/safe-and-brave-spaces-dont-work-and-what-you-cando-instead-f265aa339aff

Amos, Y. T. (2014). To lose is to win: The effects of student evaluations in a multicultural education class on a Japanese faculty with a non-native English accent. *Understanding and Dismantling Privilege, 4*(2), 116–133. Retrieved from http://www.wpcjournal.com/article/view/12220

Anderson, L. W., & Krathwohl, D. R. (Eds.) (2000). *A taxonomy for learning, teaching, and assessing: A Revision of Bloom's taxonomy of educational objectives*. Saddle River, NJ: Pearson.

Barker, P. (1993). *Regeneration*. New York: Penguin.

Beeman, A. (2015). Teaching to convince, teaching to empower: Reflections on student resistance and self-defeat at predominantly white vs. racially diverse campuses. *Understanding and Dismantling Privilege, 5*(1). Retrieved from https://www.wpcjournal.com/article/view/12211

Bell, L. A. (2020). *Storytelling for social justice: Connecting narrative and the arts in antiracist teaching* (2nd ed.). New York: Routledge.

Berila, B. (2016). *Integrating mindfulness into anti-oppression pedagogy*. New York: Routledge.

Bloom, B. S., & Krathwohl, D. R. (1956). *Taxonomy of educational objectives: The classification of educational goals, by a committee of college and university examiners. Handbook 1: Cognitive domain*. New York: Longmans.

Boysen, G. A. (2016). Using student evaluations to improve teaching: Evidence-based recommendations. *Scholarship of Teaching and Learning in Psychology, 2*(4), 273–284. doi:10.1037/stl0000069

Brooks-Harris, J. E., & Stock-Ward, S. R. (1999). *Workshops: Designing and facilitating experiential learning*. Thousand Oaks, CA: Sage Publications.

Burgstahler, S. (2012). Universal design: Process, principles, and application. Retrieved from http://www.washington.edu/doit/Brochures/Programs/ud.html

Burgstahler, S., & Cory, R. (2008). *Universal design in higher education: From principles to practice*. Cambridge, MA: Harvard Education Press.

Case, K. A., Kite, M. E., & Williams, W. R. (2021). *Navigating difficult moments in social justice teaching*. Washington, DC: American Psychological Association.

CAST. (2018). *Universal design for learning guidelines version 2.2*. Retrieved from http://udlguidelines.cast.org

DiAngelo, R. (2018). *White fragility: Why it's so hard for white people to talk about racism*. Boston: Beacon Press.

Eisner, E. (2002). *The arts and the creation of mind*. New Haven, CT: Yale University Press.

Fink, D. (2013). *Creating significant learning experiences: An integrated approach to designing college courses*. San Francisco: Jossey-Bass.

Freire, P. (1970/2018). *Pedagogy of the Oppressed*. New York: Bloomsbury Publishing.

Goodman, D. (2011). *Promoting diversity and social justice: Educating people from privileged groups* (2nd ed.). New York: Routledge.

Goodman, D. (2015). Can you love them enough to help them learn? Reflections of a social justice educator on addressing resistance from white students to anti-racism education. *Understanding and Dismantling Privilege, 5*(1), 62–73. Retrieved from http://www.wpcjournal.com/article/view/12208

Greene, M. (2007). Imagination, oppression and culture: Creating authentic openings. In a collection of works by Maxine Greene curated by the Maxine Greene Foundation. Available at https://maxinegreene.org/uploads/library/imagination_oc.pdf

Gutiérrez y Muhs, G., Niemann, Y. F., González, C. G., & Harris, A. P. (2012). *Presumed incompetent: The intersections of race and class for women in academia*. Logan, UT: Utah State University Press.

Hamad, R. (2020). *White Tears/Brown Scars: How White feminism betrays women of color*. Catapult.

Hamermesh, D. S., & Parker, A. M. (2005). Beauty in the classroom: Instructors' pulchritude and putative pedagogical productivity. *Economics of Education Review, 24*, 369–376.

Hardiman, R., & Jackson, B. (1997). Conceptual foundations for social justice courses. In M. Adams, L. A. Bell, & P. Griffin (Eds.), *Teaching for Diversity and Social Justice: A Sourcebook*. New York: Routledge.

Herr-Perrin, A. (2021, November 15). Six tips for cultivating a trauma informed higher education classroom at the beginning of each semester. *Faculty Focus*. Retrieved from https://www.facultyfocus.com/articles/effective-classroom-management/

Huston, T. A. (2006). Race and gender bias in higher education: Could faculty course evaluations impede further progress toward parity? *Seattle Journal for Social Justice, 4*(2), Article 34.

Kegan, R. (2009). *The evolving self: Problem and process in human development.* Cambridge, MA: Harvard University Press.

Kolb, D. A. (2015). *Experiential learning: Experience as the source of learning and development.* Englewood Cliffs, NJ: Prentice Hall.

Magee, R. V. (2019). *The inner work of racial justice: Healing ourselves and transforming our communities through mindfulness.* New York: Tarcher/Perigree.

Marchesani, L., & Adams, M. (1992). Dynamics of diversity in the teaching-learning process: A faculty development model for analysis and action. In M. Adams (Ed.), *Promoting diversity in college classrooms: Innovative responses for the curriculum, faculty, and institutions* (pp. 9–19). New Directions for Teaching and Learning, No. 52. San Francisco: Jossey-Bass.

McArthur, J. (2018). *Assessment for social justice: Perspectives and practices within higher education.* London and New York: Bloomsbury Academic.

Menakem, R. (2017). *My Grandmother's Hands: Racialized Trauma and the Pathway to Healing our Hearts and Bodies.* Las Vegas, NV: Central Recovery Press.

Meyer, A., Rose, D., & Gordon, D. (2014). *Universal design for learning: Theory and practice.* Wakefield, MA: CAST Publishing.

Obear, K. (2016). *Turning the tide.* Washington, DC: Difference Press.

Ouellett, M., & Fraser, E. (2005). Teaching together: Interracial teams. In M. Ouellett (Ed.), *Teaching inclusively: Resources for course, department and institutional change in higher education.* Stillwater, OK: New Forums Press.

Ouyang, H. (2014). Transforming resistance: Strategies for teaching race in the ethnic American literature classroom. *Understanding and Dismantling Privilege, 4*(2). Retrieved from https://www.wpcjournal.com/article/view/12280

Ralabate, P. K. (2011). *Universal design for learning: Meeting the needs of all students.* American Speech-Language-Hearing Association. Retrieved from https://leader.pubs.asha.org/doi/10.1044/leader.FTR2.16102011.14

Rendon, L. (2009). *Sentipensante (sensing/thinking) pedagogy: Educating for wholeness, social justice and liberation.* Sterling, VA: Stylus Press.

Ross, L. (Aug. 17, 2019). I'm a Black Feminist: I think call out culture is toxic. *New York Times,* https://www.nytimes.com/2019/08/17/opinion/sunday/cancel-culture-call-out.html

Ross, L. (2020, November 19). *What if instead of calling people out, we called people in.* Retrieved from https://www.nytimes.com/2020/11/19/style/loretta-ross-smith-college-cancel-culture.html

Shlasko, D., Crath, R., Ao, J., Cochran, N., & Thorn, R. (2017). *Pronoun introductions in class.* Retrieved from https://ssw.smith.edu/student-life/resources-and-support-students/trans-gender-non conforming-resources/pronoun

Suskie, L. (2004). *Assessing student learning: A common sense guide.* Bolton, MA: Anker Publishing.

Varghese, R., Quiros, L., & Burger, R. (2018, March). Reflective practices for engaging in trauma-informed culturally competent supervision. *Smith College Studies in Social Work, 88*(2). doi:10.1080/00377317.2018.1439826

Walvoord, B., & Anderson, V. J. (2009). *Effective grading: A tool for learning and assessment in college* (2nd ed.). San Francisco: Jossey-Bass.

Warren, L. (2005). Strategic action in hot moments. In M. L. Ouellett (Ed.), *Teaching inclusively* (pp. 620–630). Stillwater, OK: New Forum Press.

Weinstein, G. (1988). Design elements for intergroup awareness training. *Journal for Specialists in Group Work, 13*(2), 96.

PART II

TEACHING DIVERSITY AND SOCIAL JUSTICE

4

Core Concepts for Teaching Social Justice Education

*Maurianne Adams, Rani Varghese, and Ximena Zúñiga**

This chapter offers a bridge between the chapters that frame our approach to social justice education (SJE) (Chapters 1–3, 12) and the chapters that apply those frameworks to specific manifestations of oppression (Chapters 5–11). The purpose of this chapter is to outline core components, concepts, and frameworks that can be used in an introductory SJE course or workshop as well as incorporated into ism-specific classes and workshops. We find these core concepts to be effective for introducing social justice issues to a variety of participant groups. We discuss facilitation considerations and provide learning activities for teaching or facilitating these core concepts. In addition to serving as a bridge between SJE theory and practice, this chapter can also serve as a stand-alone introduction to SJE in its own right without application to any specific ism (racism, ableism, classism, etc.).

Our approach to SJE does not prioritize white supremacy over patriarchy or another hegemonic system, but rather approaches all manifestations of oppression as having similar and distinct dynamics needing to be addressed in the interests of achieving social justice for everyone. We do not claim that these core concepts are the only way to approach SJE; even the authors in this volume think about and use these core concepts differently. In some contexts, instructors may want to help participants explore other terminology and frameworks, since they offer additional entry points and modes of analysis. Such concepts can be incorporated or set alongside the SJE approach described here and can generate fruitful discussions.

PART 1: CORE CONCEPTS OF OUR APPROACH TO SJE

Seven core concepts distinguish our approach to SJE. The core concepts are presented with examples we use in our introductory SJE courses to illustrate each concept and with links to handouts we use to help participants understand and apply the concepts. The seven core concepts are:

1. A social justice approach differs from a diversity approach.
2. Individuals are categorized into social identity groups within societal hierarchies that maintain unequal positions of advantage and disadvantage.
3. Socialization is the process by which oppression is learned, reinforced, and reproduced.
4. Historical legacies and belief systems maintain systems of oppression.
5. Systems of oppression should be analyzed at multiple levels of social organization.
6. Interlocking systems of oppression are intersectional at every level.
7. Systems of oppression can be challenged, resisted, and changed by individual and collective action.

As we present these core concepts, we look both at single social justice issues and at isms in relation to each other. At times we focus on one ism so that we can gain an understanding

DOI: 10.4324/9781003005759-6

of the distinct mechanisms or structures of each oppression. At other times, we focus on how different systems of oppression intersect with each other. We understand social justice issues as manifestations of societal oppression *and* as opportunities for everyday resistance, visioning justice, transformation, and change. This balance reflects and helps participants understand the historical legacy of the struggle for social justice, in which inequality and oppression has always existed alongside everyday resistance, transformation, and change.

CORE CONCEPT 1: A SOCIAL JUSTICE APPROACH DIFFERS FROM A DIVERSITY APPROACH

We want to make clear to participants what distinguishes our approach from other approaches to diversity, equity, and inclusion. As discussed in Chapter 1: Theoretical Foundations, our SJE approach incorporates an understanding of *both* social diversity and structural inequalities based on history, politics, and policies through which members of social identity groups experience advantages or disadvantages in systems of oppression. A diversity approach generally emphasizes cultural and linguistic differences among members of a community or organization and fosters the appreciation of differences among and within groups in a pluralistic society. For example, a diversity approach to exploring race might focus on understanding the cultural values and traditions, religious affiliations, educational experiences, families, and national and language origins for specific racial/ethnic groups, like Puerto Ricans or Mexicans, US-born African Americans, or Afro-Caribbeans. Yet this approach often does not examine the biases and daily microaggressions people from these groups encounter, the historical legacies of systemic racism, pervasive institutional discrimination, and opportunities for resisting oppression and creating social change.

In contrast, a social justice approach centers the examination of unequal social structures, supremacist ideologies, and oppressive practices by which members of dominant social groups, whether knowingly or unconsciously, perpetuate the cumulative impact of advantages for some and disadvantages for others that creates an overall structured social system described as *oppressive*.

A social justice approach is based on a vision of society organized upon principles of social justice and draws on a theory of oppression and liberation, among other theories and frameworks, to analyze the ways in which societies fall short of such a vision (see Chapter 1: Theoretical Foundations; Adams, 2014; Collins, 2019; Feagin, Vera, & Ducey, 2015; Lyiscott, 2019; Rawls, 2003; Sen, 2009; Young, 1990; Watkins & Schulman, 2008). Hence, one of the goals of SJE approach is to foster the development of an intersectional understanding of and resistance to systems of oppression, which entails an acknowledgement of one's role in the oppressive system (as a privileged and/or marginalized social group member) and a commitment to develop social justice literacy (e.g., vision, knowledge, awareness, skills) and liberatory practices. To achieve this goal, this approach relies on practices and methodologies that challenge dominant scripts and systemic inequalities while forging spaces of co-empowerment, collective action, mutual aid, healing, joy, and solidarity for the long haul.

CORE CONCEPT 2: INDIVIDUALS ARE CATEGORIZED INTO SOCIAL IDENTITY GROUPS WITHIN SOCIETAL HIERARCHIES THAT MAINTAIN UNEQUAL POSITIONS OF ADVANTAGE AND DISADVANTAGE

Central to SJE is an understanding of how individuals are categorized into social groups and placed in oppressive hierarchies. We introduce the concept of hierarchy as a hallmark of oppression to illustrate the ways in which groups are categorized in relation to other groups to create relative privilege and disadvantage.

Following Young (1990), we define *social group or social identity group* as a collective ★ of persons who have an affinity to one another based on similar experiences, practices, and ways of life. Social identity groups are a collection of people who may share similar linguistic, social, and cultural experiences within socially constructed categories of race, ethnicity, language, religion, gender, and so on. For example, social identity groups within the social category of gender may include man, woman, transgender, nonbinary, and genderqueer. Similarly, the social category of ethnicity may include Puerto Rican, Irish, Cape Verdean, Japanese, or African American (see handouts in Quadrant 1). Members of social groups ★ may have an affinity with one another because of the ways they experience their status or social location in society. Such an approach to studying social groups emerged from social movements that opposed the injustices experienced by specific groups—women; African Americans; Indigenous, Puerto Rican, and Chicano people; disabled people; and lesbian and gay people, for example. Their claims were for justice that had been historically and contemporaneously deferred or denied on the basis of their social group memberships and social identities (Young, 1990).

We find it important to clarify that our definition of social groups is distinct from other designations. Social identity groups are different from social groups derived from voluntary associations such as social clubs, political parties, sport teams, activist or grassroots organizations, etc. They are voluntary, whereas one's race or class or gender or age is not voluntary and is often lifelong. One can ignore, even deny, these identities, but they do not go away (see Young, 1990, pp. 42–48 for an illuminating discussion of these distinctions; Kirk & Okazawa-Rey, 2018).

We help participants understand that as individuals, we do not choose the meanings that are attached to our social group memberships, yet we do have some degree of agency in how we make meaning of them. For example, members of disadvantaged social groups often contest derogatory terms applied to their group by reclaiming these terms and giving them positive meaning. Hence, the embracing of "queer" by people who see themselves as outside social norms of heterosexuality and/or binary gender as an affirmative spin on a term that has been used as a negative slur (and is still negative to some people). Similarly, "Black" and "Afro-Latino" have been embraced as positive umbrella terms for communities of color who affirm their African heritage, despite specific ethnic identities they might also claim (African American or Dominican) and in contradiction to the pejorative associations attached to Blackness in the dominant culture. In addition to reclaiming terms, sometimes communities and movements seek to replace terms whose meanings are offensive, outdated, and/or inaccurate. Shifts in the words groups use to describe themselves, and that may eventually be adopted by government and other institutions, reflect new layers in the construction of social categories.

We ask that participants be aware that terminology and meanings associated with social group memberships change over time. For example, terms like "retarded," "idiot," and "feebleminded" that originated as medical diagnoses were used to stigmatize and disenfranchise people within the medical system, in legal proceedings, and in communities. Because of this oppressive history, disability advocates pushed for a shift to language that is more descriptive and less value laden, such as "people first" language—"people with intellectual disabilities" or "disabled person." In 2010, these efforts gained legal recognition in Rosa's Law, which changed the references to "mental retardation" in many federal statutes to refer instead to "intellectual disability" (Department of Education, 2017).

We have participants explore the mosaic of social group identities to which they belong, reminding them that *social identity* refers to our sense of belonging to, identification with, or assignment into a social identity group. We distinguish personal identities (specific qualities or attributes such as our individual names, personality traits, birth order, social interests, etc.) from social identities (race, class, sexuality, gender, etc.) and how these are experienced in a person's life. Some social identities are inherited from our families (such as religion, first language, or ethnicity) or from groups assigned at birth (such as sex based on primary and secondary sex characteristics). Some are relatively fixed, while others may emerge or change over time. For example, our social class may change due to economic circumstances, relocation to a different part of the country, or other life events that impact our cultural, economic, and linguistic capital. People born with no disabilities may acquire a disability through accident, illness, or aging. All of us start off as infants, later children, age into the category of adult, and likely eventually become elders. Although some social identities are considered observable, other identities are not. We may notice someone's skin color and make assumptions about their racial or ethnic identity yet be unaware of someone's experience with chronic illness or a learning disability as those identities may be invisible.

Context and location also impact our social identities. African migrants often express their shock at being defined as Black, which challenges their ethnic sense of self as Nigerian or African. Some identities may be ascribed, or attributed to an individual based on how others perceive or experience them, which may not match how someone self-identifies, such as assuming a racial/ethnic or gender identity. Identities can also be self-claimed—how an individual sees and experiences themselves. Therefore, even within the same social identity group, people may have different self-claimed social identities. For example, among people who identify as deaf, some may identify as being disabled while others may not; among light-skinned people from Latin America, some may identify as Latin@ and some may identify as white.

We may also focus on a single social identity at a time—though in actuality, we experience our social identities simultaneously. One is not separately a white person, an elder, and a woman but rather an aging white woman. How she experiences her gender is affected by her age, race, and other social identities. (See core concept 6 for more discussion of intersectionality.) At times, certain identities may be more salient, often when we feel different or disadvantaged in relation to others. For example, in a racially diverse group of women, a white woman may be more conscious of her race than her gender, while in a racially diverse group of men, she may be more conscious of her gender.

In SJE, the emphasis is on our social identities and how our feelings, experiences, and aspirations may be supported or deflected by membership in a social group that may be advantaged or disadvantaged. While we are taught that these are personal and individualized, the goal of SJE is to examine the structural causes of these experiences. We are likely to "internalize" such experiences as "personal" identity even though the sources are external.

Our social identity groups—whether ascribed or self-claimed—take on meaning in the context of larger social structures that position some social groups in advantaged position in relation to others. A central task in SJE courses is to help participants understand, explore, and compare how people are privileged and/or marginalized on the basis of both particular social group memberships and intersecting group memberships.

We engage participants in examining the advantages and disadvantages they experience based on their various social identities. Almost everyone has some identities that confer advantage (privilege) and others that confer disadvantage. People are often less aware of their advantaged identities and more aware of their disadvantaged identities. While the salience of particular identities may vary depending on context and other factors, they all matter. For example, Barack Obama is widely referred to as the first Black president of the

US. In addition to being Black, he is also male, heterosexual, and Christian; benefits from considerable financial and educational privilege as a lawyer and college professor; and is the biracial son of a white mother. His Blackness is salient in public discourse because his success as a leader contradicts many of the dominant associations with Blackness, while his privileged identities may seem unremarkable because they are shared with most other political leaders. Yet those privileged identities probably played an important role in securing voter confidence in him, even though the privileges they confer are less secure than they would be for a politician who is white. Thus, it is rarely useful to categorize someone simply as advantaged or disadvantaged; instead, we encourage participants to consider *how* someone is advantaged and/or disadvantaged by particular social group memberships and combinations of social group memberships.

We also acknowledge that oppression is not binary and people have complex identities and lived experiences that may fall along a continuum rather than on one side of an advantaged/disadvantaged dichotomy. Social justice educators acknowledge the complex identities and relationships to power that arise in these gray areas using a variety of concepts including "border identities" (Anzaldúa, 2012), adjacent or proximate identities, degrees of access to power along a continuum, and provisional or context-dependent access to power. By *border identities*, we mean identities that border but do not fully fit either category. For example, multiracial people of *mestizo* or biracial descent are often forced to straddle across group boundaries of racial categorization in unique and nuanced ways. *Adjacent identities* are identities that are next to or adjoining these categories. An example of an adjacent identity is a white parent whose intimate relationship to racism comes through their experiences of raising children of color. While they are advantaged, given that they are racially marked as white, they may have an insider or intimate view of racism and maybe even experience being targeted, given their close proximity to People of Color. Likewise, a person from a working-class family who attends an elite school and gains access to some but not all the privileges of class—such as familiarity with elite cultural norms and access to elite social networks but not financial credit or accumulated wealth—has proximity to owning-class privilege. With regard to disability, some disabled people or people with disabilities are disadvantaged by ableism across many areas of their life (work, personal relationships, health care, education, etc.), while others may experience disadvantage in a more limited way (only in health care, for example) while retaining access to some aspects of abled bodied privilege (such as being seen as competent at work).

Privileges are benefits and unearned advantages given to members of dominant groups that are denied to, and often at the expense of, people from marginalized groups. Some privileges are material—such as access to adequate health care—while others are nonmaterial—such as the ability to experience oneself as normal and central in society. The concept of *privilege* reminds us that such benefits are not earned but rather result from social advantage relative to others' disadvantage (Case, 2013; Johnson, 2018; Kimmel & Ferber, 2009; Wildman, 1996; see also Chapter 1: Theoretical Foundations). People are often unaware of privileges accorded to them because those privileges have been *normalized* to be expected. By contrast, people who are denied the same privileges are often painfully aware of them. Advantaged groups sometimes oppose social justice change efforts because they fear losing privileges that they assume to be their "rights" even though those so-called rights are not enjoyed by everyone. Some examples of privileges include:

- White men can count on being perceived as professional and their expertise as legitimate.
- Heterosexual couples, especially those who conform to norms of gender expression, can count on their relationships being seen as natural.

- Owning-class and professional middle-class young people can make decisions about which career paths to pursue without worrying about supporting themselves or their family members financially.

Additional examples of privilege can be found in each ism chapter.

CORE CONCEPT 3: SOCIALIZATION IS THE PROCESS BY WHICH OPPRESSION IS LEARNED, REINFORCED, AND REPRODUCED

We examine with participants the socialization process by which oppression is learned and internalized because we think it important to understand that we don't choose to be part of an oppressive system *and should not be blamed for what we have been socialized to believe*. Once we become aware of our socialization, however, we have a responsibility to act against it and for liberation.

As members of social identity groups, we all get systematic training on how to enact prescribed roles across categories of difference (e.g., race, gender, or class) within systems of oppression. This socialization is a lifelong process by which we inherit, internalize, and replicate the dominant norms and frameworks of our society and learn to accept them as the "way things are," the "right way," or "common sense." The socialization process is pervasive, consistent, self-perpetuating, and not easily recognizable. We may see social identity categories as essential and natural and social hierarchies that confer advantage or disadvantage as inevitable. Our socialization processes rarely point out that our norms perpetuate a worldview that justifies and maintains advantage for some and disadvantage for others. For example, whites taught to "not see color" unconsciously internalize and act upon messages about white racial superiority.

Vygotsky (1978) explains how we transform external norms, events, and processes, such as childhood, parental, educational, and other external experiences, into our intra-personal belief systems. This general principle of *internalized socialization*, as an ongoing process by which external activities and processes become reconstituted as part of an interior self, helps explain to social justice educators why individuals from dominant groups may internalize one set of messages, largely positive, about their social identity group while individuals from marginalized groups may internalize another set of messages, largely negative.

Oppression depends on the internalization and reenactment of advantaged and disadvantaged social group relationships within society. Disadvantaged social groups can live in a system of oppression that injures them or deprives them of certain rights without having the language or consciousness to name the oppression or understand their situation as an effect of oppression, rather than the natural order of things Freire (1970) and Memmi (1957, 1991) also described this as "psychological colonization," whereby disadvantaged groups internalize their oppressed condition and collude with the oppressive ideology and social system, a process Freire (1970) referred to as "playing host to the oppressor" (p. 30). Internalized oppression/inferiority and internalized domination/superiority are discussed further in the next core concept.

In this volume, we use a framework called the Cycle of Socialization (Harro, 2013a), shown in Figure 4.1, as a way to illustrate the role of individuals and institutions in socializing us into oppressive systems from childhood throughout the lifespan. The Cycle of Socialization illuminates how the lifelong process of socialization is reinforced in multiple social institutions—families, neighborhoods, schooling, workplaces—and at different levels of social organization, such as the personal, the institutional, and the societal. These distinctions across levels will be presented as a later concept.

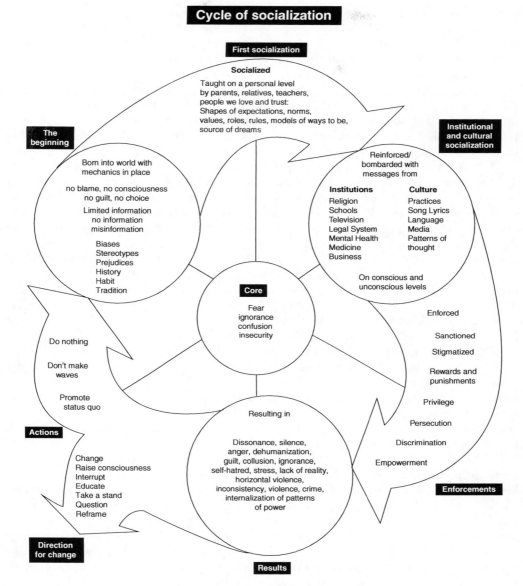

Figure 4.1 Cycle of Socialization

In our introductory courses, we go through the model, providing examples to illustrate each circle in the diagram. Our "first socialization" takes place through interactions with members of immediate and extended family, teachers, and other trusted adults. The messages we receive are usually mutually reinforcing, although sometimes contradictory (e.g., between messages received at home and at school). Such contradictions offer space to question received norms. For example, at home boys may be free to explore dress or activities that are associated with boys as well as girls while in school they may be pressured to adopt more traditional gender behaviors.

Socialization continues through cumulative encounters with social institutions, like medical systems, police, courts, banks, and workplaces, through which we learn the roles we are expected to play so as to navigate institutions successfully as a person with our social identities. Whether consciously or not, we are reminded again and again of how we are privileged and/or disadvantaged relative to others. When we are conscious of being disadvantaged, we may feel that it's not fair; if we experience advantages, we may accept them as normal and deserved. To the extent that the process is not interrupted, we transmit these norms and assumptions to the next generation, thus perpetuating the cycle. Socialization can be framed as essential for survival, of course. For example, many Black families talk about the dangers of racism early in the lives of their children.

The dominant norms and belief systems we are socialized to accept can be described as hegemonic (see Chapter 1: Theoretical Foundations). Hegemonic norms wield power because most people behave in accordance with social norms without being told or forced to do so and judge harshly those who behave otherwise. For those who benefit from the norms by virtue of their membership in privileged social groups, going along with business as usual provides unquestioned social advantages. One of the subtlest advantages is the ability to see oneself and be seen as "normal," in contrast with those considered different, strange, alien, or "other." People who are marginalized as "different" relative to the often unnamed, dominant group are excluded on the basis of that difference (Brookfield, 2005; Johnson, 2018; see also Chapter 1: Theoretical Foundations). Hegemonic norms are reinforced and sustained at all levels of society and come to feel compulsory, as if there is no safe way to behave other than the expected norm. The feeling is accompanied by tangible material rewards for conforming and punishments for diverging from the norm. The pervasive individual, cultural, and institutional reinforcement of heterosexism as the norm means that most people across identity categories go through life with a more or less conscious understanding that people who identify as heterosexual fit the norm, while those who identify as queer, bisexual, lesbian, or gay do not. Norms form part of a pervasive hegemonic system that can be enormously difficult to change, such as seeing as "normal" families outside the heterosexual two-parent norm.

Our socialization includes unconsciously or consciously learned *biases* and *prejudice* about different social groups, particularly marginalized or excluded groups in society. These stereotypes may be characterized as negative, such as the stereotype that women are too emotional and not good at science or math, or positive, such as the stereotype that Asians are good at math. Both cases are harmful in that they "essentialize" everyone in the social identity group based on partial information, misinformation, or missing information. Stereotypes are inaccurate and damaging in several ways. While a stereotype may be framed as based on something true, the information is often taken out of a historical context and exaggerated. For example, the stereotype that Jewish people are "clannish"—prefer to socialize with other Jews—does not consider the history of forced isolation of European Jewish communities in walled ghettos for many centuries. Without this context, the characterization discounts a long history of violent relocation by implying that its cultural ripple effects are mere matters of preference. Furthermore, stereotypes often target one group based on a characteristic that is shared by many other groups who aren't targeted. Continuing the previous example, in cities (where new immigrants moved to be close to acquaintances from the "old country"), there are still neighborhoods that are primarily inhabited by people of Irish, Italian, or Polish descent, and many in these groups prefer "in-marriage" rather than "intermarriage" for their children, but they are not called "clannish." The stereotype applies a value judgment to Jews, in particular, for an ethnic-centered communalism typical of many other communities.

Stereotypes both overgeneralize and ignore diversity within a group. Furthermore, they are reinforced by selective attention to behaviors that match the stereotype and ignore or rationalize behaviors that contradict it. For example, if a man of color violently attacks someone, his behavior may be interpreted as typical of his group and magnified by media attention. But if a white person commits a similar crime, the behavior is usually interpreted as an individual fault or outlier, not part of a broader pattern and not worthy of much media attention. Similarly, when Muslims plan or commit attacks, they are labeled "terrorists" and their behavior is interpreted as stemming from their religious tradition. Meanwhile, white men (who commit the majority of mass shootings in the US) are seen as individual actors, and their behavior is attributed to mental illness or a response to personal feelings of alienation rather than ascribed to their race and/or religion. The media are quick to label them "lone wolves."

There are many opportunities for challenging and rescripting socialization. Harro's Cycle of Liberation (see diagram on website) (Harro, 2013b) offers a path for individuals to become conscious of their roles in systems, build skills and knowledge to resist the norms they have learned, and disrupt the cycle on multiple levels through awareness, analysis, action, and accountability (see diagram in Quadrant 1). Organizations, such as the 100 Black Men of America, offer training to prepare Black children and adolescents for interacting with the police based on a long legacy of fatal encounters for Black people at the hands of police. Social movements can also organize resistance to oppressive norms and structures in the larger society. For example, people with disabilities work as individuals and in community to claim a sense of their own value and beauty. Those committed to disability justice may form organizations to advocate for structural and cultural changes that increase opportunities for self-determination and interdependence. Members of privileged social groups can also break out of the Cycle of Socialization by unlearning and relearning about their social identity and systemic oppression and choosing to become allies and change agents in collaboration with disadvantaged groups (Goodman, 2011; Singh, 2019).

Both the Cycle of Socialization and Cycle of Liberation suggest that someone who questions and challenges the current situations in the hope of personal or systemic change may experience risk and loss. They may feel they are damaging family relationships or sacrificing familial support, placing themself at odds with their friends or religious community, or making professional sacrifices that will have lifetime financial consequences. It is critical that social justice educators include information about sources of support, networks, organizations, or historical examples of structural change to provide encouragement, hope, and safety nets for individuals who are seeking change.

CORE CONCEPT 4: HISTORICAL LEGACIES AND BELIEF SYSTEMS MAINTAIN SYSTEMS OF OPPRESSION

We focus on helping participants understand how today's manifestations of oppression grow out of the legacy of past accumulated and persistent inequality and see that the cumulative impact of advantages for some and disadvantages for others creates an overall structured social system described as *oppressive* or as *systemic oppression*. The examination of historical legacies illustrates how different manifestations of oppression evolved over time and helps us understand how norms, ideas, and institutions that may now seem natural or inevitable actually grew out of specific historical and social processes. Examining the historical legacies of social movements can likewise help us learn from past practices and envision possibilities for change.

We center the concept of "oppression" to describe and examine the interlocking forces that create and sustain social inequality and social injustice. These social forces "press" on people and hold them down, blocking access to material resources (e.g., sustainable living wage) or symbolic resources (e.g., respectful treatment) (Johnson, 2018). Novelist William Faulkner's famous statement, "The past is never dead. It's not even past," conveys this sense of the continuity of history and why we must dig deep into the past if we are to build a better future. Johnson (2018) argues that for every social category that confers privilege (e.g., male, white, upper class, Christian, heterosexual), one or more categories are oppressed in relation to it. Like privilege, oppression results from the social relationship between privileged and oppressed social group categories that impact individuals differently as consequences of their multiple social locations. As described in Chapter 1: Theoretical Foundations, oppression is the cumulative effect of disadvantages and injustices members of targeted social groups endure "not because a tyrannical power coerces them but because of the everyday practices of a well-intentioned liberal society" (Young, 1990, p. 41). Hence, oppression is a structural phenomenon rather than the result of individual actions or policies. Its causes are deeply embedded in unquestioned norms, habits, and supremacy logics that underlie institutional rules, policies, and practices that mark and regulate everyday social life.

Although there is almost always a history of injustice behind the establishment of social categories, it is often challenging for participants to think about how social identity categories are also social constructions with tangled historical roots. The term "social construction" refers to the idea that norms, ideas, and institutions that may now seem natural or inevitable actually grew out of specific historical and social processes.

The social construction of institutions is perhaps easier to trace because we can often point to a discrete beginning. Institutions emerge in specific contexts, driven by the goals and interests of individuals and groups with the power to implement their decisions at those times. Institutions tend to perpetuate themselves and often outlive their original intentions. For example, long-term incarceration of criminals began in the late 18th century as a well-intentioned alternative to the public humiliation of whipping and hanging and was the first penal system in the Western world intended to rehabilitate as well as punish. Within less than 100 years, strong evidence showed that incarceration, especially solitary confinement, was, in fact, more damaging than rehabilitative. But by that time, other institutions had grown up around incarceration that had their own interests to protect (McLennan, 2008), and all of these institutions are more entrenched today as a result of the expansion of the prison industrial complex (Alexander, 2012; Davis, 2012). Private prisons contract with states and Immigration and Customs Enforcement (ICE) to fill prison beds for profit; unions for prison guards protect their members' job security; outside companies hire prisoners at extremely low wages; and politicians cite incarceration as proof that they are "tough on crime." Questions about whether incarceration diminishes crime, is appropriate for a particular crime, is cruel and unusual, or is racially biased bump up against established institutions and accepted ideas that perpetuate the status quo. Thus, consideration of the historical legacies of social institutions—in connection with why they were established and who now benefits—enables participants to understand how historical and cultural forces shape the manifestations of oppression we see today.

The social construction of "race" illustrates the powerful impact of a construct that was created and used to subordinate peoples with darker skin color for the purposes of enslavement, economic exploitation, and/or colonization and conquest (see Chapter 5: Racism). The fluidity and instrumental nature of racial categories is captured by the term "racialization": *the extension of racial meaning to a previously racially unclassified relationship, social practice, or group* (Omi & Winant, 2015, p. 111, italics in the original). The process of racialization helps explain how the US has racialized geographically and historically diverse migrants through a shifting color line that sorts people into a racially stratified workforce and grants or refuses them citizenship (see also Chapter 7: Classism and Chapter 8: Religious Oppression). Rather than a biological or even purely cultural fact, race is a social fact constructed through legal, economic, cultural, and other forces in the service of creating and maintaining inequality.

In our introductory SJE course, exploring social construction and historical legacies enables participants to understand that oppression inherited from the past is not immutable or inevitable. With this insight, change becomes not only possible but also plausible. The exploration of historical legacies of injustices, resistance, and social movements can also help participants see current social justice work as legitimate and feasible and can inspire them to build upon past efforts to create new openings for social justice. It also creates opportunities for participants to learn from the strategies of past movements, including what worked well and what was problematic. Participants learn that injustices rooted in historical legacies are "not their fault," although they learn that it becomes their responsibility to work toward change. Participants can learn about the importance of coalitions across differences and of intersectional analysis and action, not as buzzwords but as practical and ethical concerns that activists have grappled with over time. Hence, social oppression cannot be understood "as a closed world from which there is no exit, but as a limiting situation which [we] can transform. . . . Humans live in a world which [we] are constantly re-creating and transforming" (Freire, 1970, pp. 31, 98–99).

While hegemonic norms, ideas, and institutions are defended on the assumption that they couldn't be any other way, movements of resistance and change are often undermined by the accusation that their ideas are too new and unprecedented. Activists participating in the Occupy movement were acting in the spirit of populist and direct democratic practices that carried forward the US historical tradition of 18th-century populist rent revolts (Zinn, 2003) that bear striking resemblance to today's foreclosure resistance projects. Trans activists are told that trans issues are difficult to understand because they are so "new," although trans people have been organizing and advocating for their rights in the US since the mid-20th century and people who did not fit into their society's primary gender categories have existed throughout time and across cultures.

Historical legacies are transnational as well as US centered, and it is important to understand the interconnections among global and US instances of oppression and resistance. For example, the 20th-century Black Consciousness and anti-apartheid movements in South Africa were linked to the civil rights and racial consciousness movements in the US. Likewise, 19th- and 20th-century anti-colonial nationalist movements in Africa, Arab nations, and the Americas were inspired in part by the anti-colonial aspects of the American Revolution and the anti-monarchy ideas from the French Revolution. More recently, Black Lives Matter and #MeToo have become global movements led by grassroot organizations working to challenge multiple forms of interpersonal and police and state violence across the world.

Although the historical legacies described in this volume refer primarily to US manifestations of oppression, they provide a foundation for asking broader questions: How does racism in the US differ from racism elsewhere, and what historical forces led to those differences? How does violence against women or less powerful religious groups differ from one geographic context to another in the past and present? Especially in classes or workshops with participants who themselves or whose families migrated from outside the US, instructors and facilitators will be wise to make room for discussion of how categories, like gender, sexuality, race, and religion, are constructed differently in other places.

Therefore, social justice educators need to commit to lifelong learning to continually learn more about the socialization processes and historical legacies for marginalized and dominant groups. Gaining a complex and nuanced understanding of how dominant or hegemonic belief systems and ideological scripts interact with counterstories or abolitionist belief systems (in particular contexts) is central to this work. The complexities of socialization into historical legacies and the potential resistance to such socialization need to take into account intergenerational family traditions, educational systems, religious education, gender/sexual role expectations, class locations, neighborhoods and segregation, institutional policies and practices, unexamined social norms, and the privileging of some groups over others through dominant social or political systems. The anticipation of this knowledge constitutes a lifetime's commitment to learning about and working to address social justice issues at the personal, interpersonal, institutional, and socio-cultural level in everyday life.

CORE CONCEPT 5: SYSTEMS OF OPPRESSION SHOULD BE ANALYZED AT MULTIPLE LEVELS OF SOCIAL ORGANIZATION

To help participants understand the pervasiveness of oppression, we analyze the multiple levels upon which it operates. Manifestations of oppression can be examined (and challenged) at every level of society, from the most individual and personal to the most structural and systemic. Scholars and educators use different conceptual frameworks and language to describe, conceptualize, and examine social inequalities and hierarchies that exist in human societies. Before presenting a conceptual framework that we find particularly useful, we briefly summarize for participants a few others that also may aid in understanding this core concept.

Some scholars use multi-level conceptualizations and terms for understanding how social systems are organized and operate. For instance, Kirk and Okazawa-Rey (2018) distinguish among three levels of social organization and interaction: *micro* (individual and small-group relations that take place in families, sports clubs, and classrooms), *meso* (larger-scale groupings, such as schools, organizations, and communities), and *macro* (the overarching economic, cultural, ideological, social, and legal dimensions of social structure). Collins (1990) and other scholars refer to *multiple levels of domination* that operate along multiple axes, such as race, gender, and social class, to describe how people experience and resist oppression at the levels of personal biography, community, and social institutions. Lyiscott (2019) argues that oppression in our society can be analyzed (and resisted and transformed) at both micro (internalized and interpersonal) and macro (institutional and ideological) levels. This framework centers the ongoing tension between "oppression" and the "resistance" that can be taken at any of these levels.

Young (1990) identifies five historical and current social conditions that maintain and reproduce injustice: exploitation, marginalization, powerlessness, cultural imperialism, and violence (or the threat of violence). In order to expand how we analyze vast and deep injustices beyond economic inequality, mainly money and goods, favored by writers in the social justice tradition (Rawls, 2003), Young focuses on conditions, such as access to power, decision-making, and resources, considered "rights," such as schooling, health care, and safe neighborhoods. With this in mind, Young names what she calls the "faces" or forms of oppression experienced by marginalized groups as a way for social justice educators to analyze and explain experiences of oppression by individuals and social groups from a broader analytical perspective. Young's approach is used in several chapters of this book.

Hardiman, Jackson, and Griffin (2007) have suggested that the dynamics of an overarching cultural and societal system of inequality that is maintained and reproduced institutionally and by individuals can be envisioned as a three-dimensional "cube," as shown in Figure 4.2. It is important to note that while different analytical approaches may use similar terms, these terms may or may not be defined in the same way in different frameworks. We also acknowledge that terminology in SJE is continually evolving and that no set of

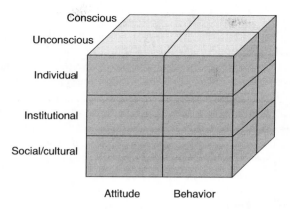

Figure 4.2 Three-Dimensional Matrix of Oppression
Source: Hardiman, Jackson, & Griffin (2007)

conceptualizations and terms will ever fully capture something as complex as the structural relations that create and maintain group inequalities.

In our introductory courses, we rely primarily on a multi-level conceptual framework that examines how social inequality is maintained and reproduced at three levels of social organization—the individual, the institutional, and the social/cultural. We recognize that these three levels are not "levels" in a literal or fixed sense because aspects of one level will always permeate and come into play in other levels. Nevertheless, we find this conceptual framework useful for drawing general distinctions among levels of social organization, for describing interactions among them, and for analyzing how oppression and resistance operate at multiple levels in our society.

This "cube" adds another set of dimensions to our three-level model. It examines the differences between *individual attitudes* and *behaviors and institutional behaviors and policies* that are both *conscious* and *unconscious*. Attitudes, behaviors, and policies, whether conscious or not, help create or perpetuate advantages or disadvantages for members of different social identity groups. This visual representation is a helpful conceptual organizer for participants to see how these levels intersect (Hardiman, Jackson, & Griffin, 2007, p. 39).

The Individual Level

At the individual level, we focus on understanding the individual attitudes, beliefs, and behaviors that maintain one or more forms of oppression, intentionally or unintentionally. These attitudes are often based on unexamined *stereotypes* or overly generalized assumptions about groups of people that are embedded in the dominant culture and that many people, consciously or unconsciously, reproduce through their behaviors. Examples of individual/interpersonal-level attitudes, based on stereotypes, and the oppressive behaviors that may result include:

- The belief that Black or Latino men are dangerous and criminal, causing women to clutch their purses when encountering men of color and drivers to close their car windows and lock their doors when they drive through a poor and/or racially marked neighborhood;
- The assumption that people with physical disabilities are helpless or useless and thus to resist hiring them.

These examples illustrate the difference between *attitudes* and *behaviors* as well as the relationship between them, but it is not always clear where the line between *conscious* or *unconscious* might fall. Someone might be conscious of their behavior but not realize it is based on an unconscious attitude. Or they may be conscious of a particular attitude without recognizing its connection to an unconscious stereotype or pattern of behavior. The research on *implicit bias*, also known as *implicit social cognition*, offers a useful analytic tool for understanding the *impact* of internalized unconscious biases that are activated involuntarily, usually outside of someone's awareness or intentional control (Kirwan Institute, 2013). Individuals (as well as institutions) often deny their *intention* to discriminate, but research demonstrates that implicit biases inform attitudes and ultimately shape behaviors and actions, including microaggressions (Banaji & Greenwald, 2013; Chugh, 2018; Kirwan Institute, 2013).

Microaggressions are commonplace, everyday interactions that intentionally or unintentionally reinforce a person's subordinated status within a system of oppression (Sue, 2010). Members of marginalized groups experience a cumulative impact from the barrage of behaviors that express stereotyped assumptions and biases from members of privileged groups (Huber & Solórzano, 2014; Sue, 2010). Recent studies underscore the biopsychosocial cumulative impact of microaggressions, for example, on Black people, including stress-related diseases and mental health, commonly referred to as racial battle fatigue (Geronimus, 1992; Geronimus, Bound, Waidmann, Colen, & Steffick, 2001; Watson, 2019; Quaye, Karikari, Carter, Okello, & Allen, 2020; Smith, Yosso, & Solórzano, 2006; Winters, 2020). For example:

- A low-income student might hear people say that poor people are lazy and responsible for their own poverty, encounter friends' assumptions that everyone has middle-class privilege, get invited to participate in a valuable extracurricular learning experience they can't afford, or hear people with similar backgrounds referred to as "white trash" or "ghetto."
- A transgender person might be addressed or referred to with pronouns that do not reflect their identity, asked what their "real" name is, stared at, asked inappropriately personal questions about their anatomy, or told that they're in the "wrong" restroom.

Internalized subordination or internalized oppression refers to ways in which members of marginalized and disadvantaged groups, through their socialization, internalize the dominant group's negative ideology about their group and accept a definition of themselves that is hurtful and limiting, causing them to think, feel, and act in ways that accept the devaluation of their group. *Internalized domination or internalized superiority* describes the behaviors, thoughts, and feelings of privileged or advantaged group members who, through their socialization, have learned to think and act in ways that express entitlement and privilege (David, 2014; Singh, 2019; Watkins & Shulman, 2008).

One further dimension of oppression that occurs primarily at the individual and interpersonal/intergroup level can be described as *horizontal oppression* in contrast to *vertical or hierarchical oppression* (Hardiman & Jackson, 1997). This term comes from the phrases "horizontal violence" and "horizontal hostility" used by Pharr (1997) to describe situations in which members of marginalized or subordinated groups misdirect their rage at members of other marginalized groups rather than at the more dangerous and powerful members of dominant groups. For example, a woman may make negative remarks about another woman's attire, or a working-poor parent may discourage a child from pursuing higher education. Horizontal oppression also works within and among advantaged groups. For example, white people may cast aspersions on white organizations or individuals that are working for racial justice, Christians may discourage other Christians from educating themselves about non-Christian religious communities, or children who do not have disabilities may tease other children for making friends with a child who does have a disability.

Horizontal and vertical manifestations of oppression can be mutually reinforcing. For example, in the early years of the US labor movement, stereotypes and hostility about subordinated racial groups and newly arrived immigrants were used to break up unionizing efforts among mill and factory workers. Vertical hostility across race was used to foment horizontal violence and exclusion in the working class.

The Institutional Level

At the institutional level, oppression is produced, maintained, and reproduced by the policies and practices of institutions, such as government agencies, business and industry, nursing homes and hospitals, banking and finance, K–12 and postsecondary education, religious organizations, and the legal system (including divorce and custody law, mechanisms of inheritance such as wills and trusts, police and criminal courts, civil fines, and prisons). The *institutional level* refers both to broad fields, such as health care, and to specific organizations, such as a sports team or a school. Institutions maintain and reproduce advantages and disadvantages by whom they employ, how they recognize and reward success, and whose transgressions they punish. The policies and practices of privilege or exclusion reflect such institutional norms.

The relationship between individual bias and institutional discrimination is complex. On one hand, institutions reinforce the socialization of individuals into systems of oppression through discriminatory policies and practices. On the other hand, individual attitudes or behaviors are often the vehicles by which a discriminatory institutional policy is carried out. For example, a career counselor in a high school at which students are tracked into separate Advanced Placement and vocational tracks may evaluate the potential for college-bound or vocational students based on implicit biases or prejudices about students' family background, neighborhood, or use of accented or vernacular English. In such cases, the counselor's implicit biases (individual level) plays out through the school's tracking system (institutional level) to produce long-term, material, and discriminatory consequences for student access to higher education and employment. Counselors who become aware of their implicit biases can choose to avoid individual-level discrimination, but in order to address the institutional level, they must work to change policies and practices as well as their own behavior.

Examples of discriminatory institutional practices and policies include:

- Dress codes for front office or sales positions that advantage people who meet dominant beauty norms and disadvantage those who do not (including people with disabilities, people perceived as gay or queer, people who wear ethnically or religiously marked attire such as head coverings, and people perceived as fat).
- Workplace schedules that institute mandatory days off for major Christian holidays, while non-Christians who want time off for their religious holidays must file a request and use vacation time or unpaid leave.

Oppressive policies and practices are often difficult to notice because they seem standard and usual. For example, many application and intake forms require people to indicate gender and provide only two options. This practice, along with the broader norm of assuming that sex and gender are binary, is so pervasive that most people whom it doesn't directly impact do not notice it. But for people who are trans and/or intersex, it means they may be required to misrepresent themselves or be excluded entirely. Institutional-level oppression can also go unnoticed because many oppressive policies seem "neutral" at first glance.

Often these policies do not state an explicit discriminatory intent, yet their impact reinforces inequality. For example, college admissions policies reward applicants for extracurricular experiences, such as volunteer activities or travel abroad, that are only available to people with significant class privilege. Such policies do not explicitly say that the college wishes to prioritize wealthy applicants, and the policies may be rationalized by seemingly reasonable explanations. Nevertheless, applicants from poor and working-class backgrounds whose need to work may prevent volunteer activity or travel are disadvantaged, and those from professional and owning-class backgrounds are advantaged by this practice.

Unofficial institutional practices, such as norms of dress, appearance, communication, group interaction, and self-presentation, are generally not apparent to people in privileged groups because they have always "fit in" with the organizational culture. For members of marginalized groups, however, the daily experiences of trying to figure out or being reminded that they don't match accepted norms contribute to the cumulative impact of oppression.

The Social-Cultural Level

Social systems and cultural norms convey messages about what is correct and expected by the larger society. In an oppressive society, the positions of privileged and advantaged groups are maintained and reproduced through networks of institutions that make up society and through unquestioned beliefs, hegemonic norms, and ideologies; advantages provided by what Feagin (2013) terms a *white dominant racial frame* or a *male dominant frame* (Chun & Feagin, 2020) as well as *compulsory heterosexuality* (Rich, 1980) support and give meaning to those systems.

For example, heterosexuality is a dominant norm. People who are heterosexual don't need to "come out" because it is the assumed default. Individuals and couples who are heterosexual (or perceived as heterosexual) can experience themselves as normal and unremarkable and encounter institutions designed to meet their needs (at least on the dimension of sexual orientation). If they want to have children through pregnancy or adoption, their fitness as parents is unlikely to be questioned. If it is necessary to make decisions for each other during medical emergencies, they can be confident that hospitals will recognize their right to do so.

Meanwhile, people who identify as lesbian, gay, bisexual, trans*, queer, plus others are continually reminded that they do not fit the norm, starting with the need for a "coming out" process of realizing and disclosing their sexual orientation. If they want to have children, many people will doubt their fitness as parents, and adoption agencies may legally reject them. In many states, the non-gestational parent still has to legally adopt their children. Legal documents, like health-care proxies and wills, may be ignored by hospitals and courts that choose not to recognize their relationship.

The pervasive cultural, institutional, and individual reinforcement of heterosexuality as the norm means that most people go through life with a more or less conscious understanding that heterosexuals fit the norm, while queer, bisexual, lesbian, and gay people do not. Norms form part of a pervasive hegemonic system that can seem enormously difficult to change. Yet, resistance to compulsory heterosexuality (and gender binary systems) occurs every day—locally, nationally, and globally. Examples of recent policy changes, such as Executive Order 14021, Guaranteeing an Educational Environment Free from Discrimination on the Basis of Sex, including Sexual Orientation or Gender Identity, and Executive Order 14031, Advancing Equity, Justice, and Opportunity for Asian Americans, Native

Hawaiians, and Pacific Islanders, demonstrate the power of transgressing and resistance at the individual level when groups coalesce to bring changes at the institutional and policy level.

For marginalized peoples, hegemonic norms and structural obstacles press on them everywhere they turn. This can be experienced as a "web of oppression" because of the interacting and overwhelming experience of disadvantage, insult, and violence expressed in multiple situations and contexts The reproduction of cultural norms, supremacy ideologies, and structural patterns adds up to a system of advantage and disadvantage that is much larger than the sum of its parts. Hegemonic norms and practices take place at a social/cultural level, although their specific manifestations are most clear at the institutional level. It can be difficult for participants in SJE courses and workshops to make meaningful distinctions between these two levels. The point is not to categorize each example as one level or the other but rather to understand that examples at the individual and institutional levels interact and reinforce each other and are upheld by broader cultural/societal patterns and structures. Examples of cultural norms and societal practices include:

- The common practice of viewing "women's" work, such as childcare, homecare, and clerical work, as well as working-class "men's" work, such as physical labor and trades, as less important and frequently as less worthy of generous remuneration.
- The culturally reinforced reluctance to vote for non-Christian politicians (including atheists) because of an assumption that only Christians can be trusted to act morally.

CORE CONCEPT 6: INTERLOCKING SYSTEMS OF OPPRESSION ARE INTERSECTIONAL AT EVERY LEVEL

Intersectionality describes the ways social identities and systems of oppressions interact, resulting in varied experiences and opportunities. We introduce intersectionality as a critical and analytical lens through which we can view and understand the world (Hulko, 2009). Intersectionality supports a complex and contextual understanding of individuals' lived experiences along multiple axes of systems of privilege and oppression based on categories such as race, gender, socio-economic class, and sexuality (Crenshaw, 2003). Social identities and social location in systems of oppression intersect to create a complex experience that is not reducible to one identity or system of oppression (Crenshaw, 2003; Hankivsky, 2014). As previously discussed, social identity group memberships do not act independently of one another, and identities do not intersect in a simply additive way, although one identity group may be situationally more salient than another at any given moment.

Furthermore, intersectionality helps us understand that individuals' social group identity experiences are also shaped by the interaction among multiple advantaged and disadvantaged social group memberships within the context of connected systems, structures of power, and institutions. These individual experiences are situated in interpersonal, group, or community dynamics and institutional and ideological structures. When examining why Black men are overrepresented in incarceration rates, it is vital to inquiry and understand how their everyday experiences interface with school systems with zero-tolerance policies in which they experience racial harm and surveillance, live in communities in which they encounter regular police searches and brutality, and enter judicial and criminal justice systems that are inequitable, resulting in differential sentencing. Thus, developing an intersectional analysis requires coordinating the examination of individuals' experiences across social identity categories with how these experiences are influenced by their social location in various systems of advantage and disadvantage rooted in historical legacies reinforced by contemporary hegemonic beliefs and unequal power relations, as discussed in core concepts 4 and 5.

The construct of intersectionality has a long history in social and intellectual movements yet is commonly recognized in academic contexts as emerging through critiques by Black, queer, working-class women in the 1970s and early 1980s who questioned the assumptions made by many white, middle-class feminists that the oppression of women was uniform and homogeneous (Beal, 1995; Combahee River Collective, 1982; Collins, 1990, 2000; Crenshaw, 1991). By placing Black women's experience at center of analysis, Collins proposed that:

> A both/and conceptual lens of the simultaneity of race, class, and gender oppression and . . . the need for a humanistic vision of community creates new possibilities for an empowering Afrocentric feminist knowledge. Many Black feminist intellectuals have long thought about the world in this way because this is the way we experience the world.
>
> (pp. 221–222)

In so doing, these scholars and activists recognized that "eradicating sexism would require a deconstruction of other structures of domination" (Nash, 2019, pp. 7–8). Crenshaw is contemporarily credited for coining the term "intersectionality." Her work highlights how individuals and groups experience the convergence of structures and systems of power and oppression, resulting in marginality (Collins, 2019), whereas other writers see intersectionality as an opportunity for gaining individual and collective empowerment. For example, "reproductive justice activists have dynamically used the concept of intersectionality as a source of empowerment to propel one of the most important shifts in reproductive politics" from a sole focus on choice (Ross, 2017, p. 286). Reproductive justice work increasingly represents a form of intersectional activism, responding to overlapping systems of oppression, such as sexism, racism/white supremacy, classism/capitalism, and historical inequality, experienced by women of color while recognizing their collective power and building solidarity, support, and connection.

Collins (2019) discusses constructs for analyzing intersectionality in academic and political practice. Three that we find helpful are relationality, social context, and complexity. *Relationality* stresses how social identities are maintained through relational processes that give meaning and influence not only to personal experience but to one's practice—as a workshop facilitator, classroom teacher, or grassroots community organizer; *social context* examines the context in which experience, awareness, and knowledge are produced and how they impact the understanding and application of intersectionality; and *complexity* speaks to dynamic and iterative processes underlying intersectional subjectivities, knowledge, and practice (Collins, 2019; Collins & Bilge, 2016). In social justice classrooms, intersectionality allows educators and students to ask both/and questions that support a simultaneous, relational, structural, and complex understanding of oppression.

The recognition that systems of power are rooted in interlocking systemic forms of oppression based on race, class, sexuality, or gender represents a paradigmatic shift. It replaces additive or binary models of oppression with intersecting axes of race, gender, social class, and other social categories that might be operating at any or all three levels of social organization—the individual, institutional, cultural/societal—each representing sites of oppression as well as potential sites for resistance, as discussed in core concepts 3, 4, and 5.

As Collins (2019) points out, the imaging of intersectionality as roads or pathways that intersect at crossings or intersections has a significant metaphorical value by "linking social structures and the ideas that reproduce them" in "the tangible, spatial relations of everyday life" (p. 27). In Collins's view, this approach enables the examination of oppressive

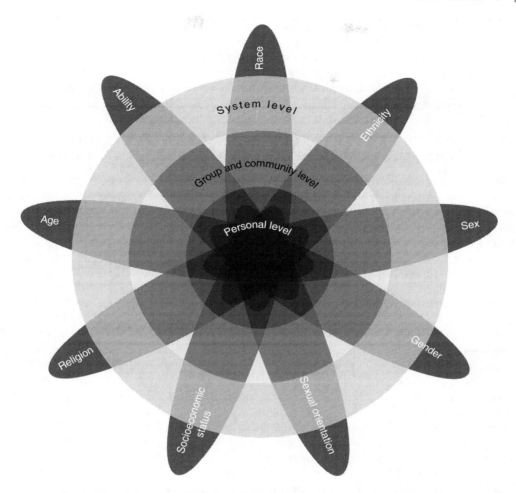

Figure 4.3 Matrix of Interlocking Systems and Levels of Oppression and Resistance

structures and relations in new and more complex and nuanced ways and helps scholars, educators, and activists to identify specific "action strategies for *how* to move forward in solving social problems and in grappling with existing puzzles" (p. 34).

But there is a limit to the generalizability of this approach if it is "centered" at the core of intersecting axes (Figure 4.3). While this "center" allows space for inquiry into multiple systems of oppression, the question remains whether the "center" implies some core identity, a "fixity or status" that "does not adequately represent the fluidity of identities" for a "self" in systems that is always in process (Holvino, 2012, p. 171).

In sum, it is important to understand individual, cultural, and institutional levels of experience and realities of intersectionality as outlined in the core concepts 1, 2, 3, 4, and 5. It is also important to recognize the relational nature of intersectional experiences. For example:

- DACA (Deferred Action for Childhood Arrivals) students are not provided federal funding although they and their families pay taxes (i.e., intersection of different systems of oppression including xenophobia, racism, and classism).

- Black girls are suspended in schools six times more often than white girls their age (i.e., intersection of youth oppression, racism, sexism, and perhaps classism).
- Working-class trans women of color who are victims of domestic violence interact with numerous systems—police and judicial courts, hospitals, and shelters—at which they may experience multiple and intersecting forms of oppression (i.e., intersection of sexism, racism, classism, gender oppression/transphobia).

CORE CONCEPT 7: SYSTEMS OF OPPRESSION CAN BE CHALLENGED, RESISTED, AND CHANGED BY INDIVIDUAL AND COLLECTIVE ACTION

One of the main aspirational goals of SJE is to support participants to recognize oppression in any situation they encounter, to engage in vision-driven practices that center intersectional critical awareness, hope, and possibility (Duncan-Andrade, 2009, Harro, 2013b; Lyiscott, 2019); and to develop the motivation, knowledge, and skills to take action (Pasque & Harris, 2013; Singh, 2019; Zúñiga, 2018). Vision-driven justice goals and practices are built into some of the core concepts addressed earlier in this chapter, such as questioning one's Cycle of Socialization in order to engage in a Cycle of Liberation that embraces deep awareness of self and others as well as collaboration with others to create change. Instead of feeling hopeless and overwhelmed by the pervasive impacts of oppression on entire groups of people, we want to support participants to take stock of their own stories of resistance to oppressive scripts, envision justice from an intersectional lens, and turn their attention to places where they can embrace opportunities for creating change, individually and in collaboration—networks and coalitions—with others (Barber, 2016; Bell, 2020; Brown, 2017; Love, 2019). Thus, we build into our SJE curriculum and pedagogy readings and activities to imagine possibility and build self- and system-based intersectional awareness, knowledge, skill, agency, and practice for change.

B.J. Love (2013) describes "developing a liberatory consciousness," and she identifies awareness, analysis, action, and accountability/allyship as key ingredients for guiding individual action. Awareness and analysis involve identifying places in which the normalization of systems of privilege and disadvantage should be questioned, resisted, and changed at all levels—social, cultural, institutional, and personal. But it is also necessary for us to translate our awareness and analysis into actions by working in collaboration with others, across and within social identity groups, in ways that make us accountable and able to re-evaluate our actions in conversation with others. This may require learning to speak up and listening to others' perspectives, practicing relational organizing skills, and identifying ways of taking action in challenging situations. Learning to question oneself and others and to resist and transform hegemonic norms and oppressive practices can take many forms. Historical accounts of past and recent people's struggles for human and civil rights provide powerful illustrations of how members of different social groups have organized for minimum wage, educational equity, immigration reform, economic equity (i.e., redistribution of wealth), and environmental justice.

One important lesson we share with participants from reading about and studying abolitionist movements and people's struggles is that we must not despair. John Lewis's (2020) letter, published the day of his funeral, urged us to consider that "ordinary people can with extraordinary vision" get into "good trouble, necessary trouble" by voting, by participating in nonviolent change, and by studying and learning the lessons of history "because humanity has been involved in this soul-wrenching, existential struggle for a very long time" (*New York Times*, July 30 A 23). Through the study of history, as Zinn (2002) reminds us, "We can find not only war but resistance to war, not only injustice but rebellion against injustice, not only selfishness but self-sacrifice, not only silence in the face of tyranny but defiance, not only callousness but compassion" (p. 4). Things do change as a result of such struggles. The study of history and sharing stories of struggle can motivate and inspire people to create and sustain change.

Individuals can learn to recognize and interrupt their own complicity in the reproduction of systems of privilege and oppression (Case, 2013; Leondar-Wright, 2014; Pittelman, 2005; Singh, 2019; Young, 2011). They can also engage in social justice literacy practices as tools of analysis and action against oppression. For instance, Lyiscott's (2019) Four I's Fugitive Framework—intrapersonal, interpersonal, institutional, and ideological literacies—invites participants to learn to read "white privilege" as it manifests at multiple levels in school practices to help them identify what they could do to question, disrupt, or transform such realities.

Certainly, "walking the talk" is one of the most challenging steps in moving from critical analysis to action planning and enactment. This requires intentional planning and critical analysis that includes understanding how various forms of privilege and oppression are connected at multiple levels in a specific context, self-awareness of one's intersecting identities and positionality, and skill sets and embodied practices for authentically communicating and collaborating across differences within and across identity groups. It takes a vision of the end goal, so one will know whether or not the desired change has been achieved. These challenging processes are addressed by a growing literature on inter-group dialogue, transformative justice, participatory action research, and intersectional coalitions (Aldana, Richards-Schuster, & Checkoway, 2016; Barber, 2016; Brown, 2017, 2021; Lakey, 2020; Leondar-Wright, 2014; Ransby, 2018; Spade, 2020; Zúñiga, Lopez, & Ford, 2014).

Scholar and community activists use a variety of terms to talk about change at individual, community, or institutional levels. *Allies* are people who work in solidarity with others toward a shared goal of change. Allies might be members of privileged groups who are ready to leverage their privilege toward change, or they might be members of marginalized groups who are actively working on behalf of their own group as well as for and with other groups. Others are *accomplices, co-conspirators, activists, advocates*, and *change agents*, all of whom are likely to be individuals working within and across social groups in networks or coalitions in schools, communities, or organizations to challenge, re-imagine, and/or transform oppressive structures (Brown, 2017, 2021; hooks, 1992, 2001; Singh, 2019). Change at the cultural and societal level calls for broad-based social movements (Leondar-Wright, 2014; Ransby, 2018).

There are countless opportunities in our personal lives, at the individual and interpersonal level, for us to question oppressive beliefs and discriminatory practices and policies and to work in collaboration with others to change them. For example:

- Anyone can interrupt offensive jokes and educate friends and colleagues in any context (locker rooms, parties, workplace) about the cumulative impact of microaggressions.
- A teacher can incorporate current social justice issues into courses not ordinarily focused on social justice content.
- A community organizer can create networks of teachers, school administrators, and service providers to create continuity of support for the children of migrant workers or homeless or incarcerated youth.
- People of all ages can make commitments to practice awareness, analysis, action, and accountability in their relationships and interactions (for additional examples see Brown, 2017; Johnson, 2018; Singh, 2019; Tatum, 2018).

While the tools for creating change at the personal and interpersonal level may include our own growing awareness, knowledge, commitments, passions, and skills for interrupting oppression and the increased capacity to leverage support for social justice actions in our own sphere of influence, these are not necessarily sufficient to challenge hegemonic forces at the institutional and cultural/ideological level. We can certainly take active roles in social movements, organizations, and institutions to change policies and practices impacting people's lives, such as police brutality, the prison industrial complex, health-care disparities, and school-to-prison pipelines, but we are likely to be more effective promoting change beyond personal and interpersonal contexts by engaging in grassroots organizing for change that is connected to local and regional social justice issues (Barber, 2016; Boggs, 2012; Brown, 2017).

Forging pathways for collective action may require understanding the role of solidarity, relational organizing, coalitions, and social movements in contributing to the most durable change making (Collins, 2019; Harro, 2013b; Pharr, 1997; Taylor, 2016). Social movement methods, such as protests, strikes, sit-ins, boycotts, mutual aid, and campaigns informing the public of specific discriminatory policies and practices, have been historically effective in advancing social justice goals. Along with historical examples, such as civil rights or women's right movements, instructors and participants should be aware of current local, regional, or national alliances and solidarity efforts forging coalitions and networks to resist supremacy ideologies and discrimination practices by either engaging in effective action toward legal, structural, and economic changes (Barber, 2016; Ransby, 2018) or creating new alternatives, such as the use of restorative practices in urban schools to combat the school-to-prison pipeline (Davis, 2019).

Not everyone who participates in SJE courses or workshops will choose to take action. Still, it is important that participants be equipped with the conceptual and practical tools and skills to recognize instances of oppression in everyday life, to consider how to intervene to change those instances, and to create plans for action that are consistent with the visions of change (Brown, 2017, 2021; Domingue & Neely, 2013; Gumbs, 2020; Spade, 2020).

For example, participants can be supported to:

- Practice listening, dialogic practices, healing-centered, and restorative justice practices and skills.
- Recognize examples of oppression and resistance in everyday life.
- Analyze current and historical examples of intra- and intergroup solidarity, collective care, and social action, particularly on the part of youth-led movements for Black Lives Matter, gun control, immigration reform, transgender rights, and environmental concerns.
- Engage in mutual aid in communities, grassroots organizing, and restorative practices in school led by youth.
- Participate in equity committees to better address the needs of marginalized groups that may include disrupting hegemonic practices and norms.

The examples listed here represent valuable methods and skills for translating core concepts into action, advancing social justice goals in one's spheres of influence, and engaging in the complex communication and decision-making needed to create transformative change at personal, institutional, and cultural levels. Supporting participants to find confidence and competence, inspiration, courage, and sustainability for the long haul is an important goal for social justice educators (Brown, 2017; Obear, 2018).

DESIGN FOR TEACHING CORE SOCIAL JUSTICE CONCEPTS

The design that follows embodies the core concepts using principles of design and facilitation from the two preceding chapters. The focus on how to teach core concepts offers a bridge from Chapter 1: Theoretical Foundations to the designs in the ism chapters that follow.

The design also draws upon the pedagogical elements offered in Chapter 2: Pedagogical Foundations. These elements are implicit in the design and include 1) consider the roles of facilitators and participants in the learning community; 2) foster an inclusive learning community; 3) center an analysis of systems of oppression and how they operate in society and in the classroom; 4) define goals, learning objectives, and evaluation mechanisms for SJE; and 5) utilize collaborative and active learning. Although SJE pedagogy, design, and facilitation—like social justice theory—have already been examined in the preceding three chapters, here we provide examples of activities that incorporate these frameworks to help instructors and facilitators get started.

Instructors/facilitators should be aware that the core concepts constitute key content areas for designing the learning process of an SJE course. The dynamics of oppression that are "out there" in the larger social world are also "in here" in learning communities. SJE is not a matter of abstract knowledge alone; it involves the lived experience of facilitators and participants in the class.

This part of the chapter offers a sample four-quadrant design. It can serve as a stand-alone course or workshop that introduces the core concepts of SJE, or it can serve as the introductory segment of a single- or multiple-ism course or workshop. However, if this design is used, its effectiveness resides in foregrounding the core concepts. Taken together, the core concepts help us analyze various manifestations of oppression in the past and present. The ism-focused chapters that follow this chapter (e.g., racism, classism), although they also present core concepts, do so in a way that is embedded in the exploration of a specific ism. Here, we focus attention on the core concepts as content. We call attention to the pedagogical and design decisions we have made so that instructors and facilitators who might want to make other choices can do so without losing sight of the core concepts that are the crux of our approach.

The general progression of the design is the following. Quadrant 1 begins by establishing a learning community with various active-learning pedagogies that enable participants to get to know each other individually. It then briefly introduces the core concepts of our SJE approach. The personal learning focus of Quadrant 2 builds on these core concepts, even though some, such as the interrelationship of "levels" (individual, institutional, cultural/societal), is not explored in depth until later. By introducing the concepts early, we help participants contextualize the personal work they will do in Quadrant 2 in developing awareness of socialization processes, social categories, social group memberships, social identities, and intersections among social identities. Quadrant 3 takes participants to the bigger picture (institutional and cultural/societal levels). The focus is on historical legacies, social construction, and analysis of current examples of oppression and intersections. Quadrant 4 focuses on "What's next?" by presenting frameworks and rubrics that participants can use to identify opportunities for change and to develop action plans.

As discussed in Chapter 3: Design and Facilitation, this design strives for a balance among different learning styles, between formal and informal learning modes, and between self-focused reflection and engagement with others. Opportunities for creating such balance will differ depending on the specific needs and contexts of each set of participants and facilitators. We offer this design for illustrative purposes only and explain (in Part 3) *how* and *why* we chose the options presented in this design, rather than suggest (incorrectly) that one size fits all. We encourage instructors and facilitators to use this design as an example of how to apply concepts of pedagogy, design, and facilitation from Chapter 2: Pedagogical Foundations and Chapter 3: Design and Facilitation and consider how best to embody those concepts in their own work.

Detailed activity descriptions, along with handouts and other materials needed to implement the design, are available on the website for this chapter. Where the design calls for a lecture presentation, we have not provided a script; rather, we assume that instructors and facilitators will use content already presented in this chapter, other chapters, and/or additional sources to prepare their lecture.[1]

OVERVIEW OF TEACHING CORE SOCIAL JUSTICE CONCEPTS QUADRANTS

Quadrant 1: Introductions, Learning Community, and SJE Approach

1. Welcome Activity
2. Introductions
3. Creating Learning Community
4. Comfort Zones, Learning Edges, and Activations
5. SJE Approach
6. Closing Activity

Quadrant 2: Cycle of Socialization and Social Identity and Positionality

1. Check-In and Opportunity to Revisit Guidelines
2. Cycle of Socialization
3. Interrupting the Cycle of Socialization: Empowerment and Advocacy
4. Personal Identity and Social Identity
5. Social Group Membership, Positionality, and Intersectionality
6. Closing Activity

Quadrant 3: Institutional Manifestations and Historical Legacies

1. Historical Overview
2. Manifestation of Oppression
3. Web of Oppression
4. Web of Resistance
5. Closing Activity

Quadrant 4: Action and Change

1. Envisioning Change
2. Frameworks for Creating Change
3. Taking Action Terminology
4. Action Continuum and Spheres of Influence
5. Action Planning
6. Affirmations

QUADRANT 1: INTRODUCTIONS, LEARNING COMMUNITY, AND SJE APPROACH

Learning Objectives [content and process outcomes]:
1. Develop a collaborative learning community based on personal and community guidelines or aspirations
2. Distinguish SJE approach from other approaches (such as diversity education)
3. Identify key elements of SJE approach to oppression and its manifestations at various levels and types, and examples of resistance and liberation

Key Concepts:
- Social justice, diversity, SJE
- Oppression as a structural phenomenon; resistance and change
- Various manifestations of oppression and resistance: levels and types; resistance and liberation
- Comfort zones, learning edges, activation

Activities and Options:

1. Welcome: We offer two options, both icebreakers in which participants get to know each other. Option A allows participants to mingle freely, while in Option B, interactions are more structured.

2. Introductions:

   Option A: In dyads, participants introduce each other using suggested prompts that focus more on personal identity (i.e., interests).

   Option B: Participants introduce themselves to the whole group by sharing something about the meaning of their names. This provides an early opportunity to begin thinking about salient social identities on a personal level.

   Option C: Common Ground (or Meet and Greet) is a more structured opportunity for sharing and highlights commonalities and differences within the group.

3. Learning community: Both options establish group norms, guidelines, or aspirations; Option A is an abbreviated version, and Option B contains more in-depth discussion based on participants' hopes and concerns.

4. Comfort zone, learning edge, and activations: This includes presentation and discussion of these concepts and their definitions, particularly as they concern the use of group guidelines/aspirations.

5. SJE approach to oppression: This includes manifestations of oppression at the personal, institutional, societal, and cultural levels. The different options focus on some or all core concepts using different conceptual organizers.

6. Closing activity: Opportunity to bring some closure to this segment before transitioning to a different topic, taking a break, or ending a session.

QUADRANT 2: CYCLE OF SOCIALIZATION AND SOCIAL IDENTITY AND POSITIONALITY

Learning Objectives:

1. Understand processes of socialization within institutional structures, including internalization and reproduction of received messages (both conceptually and personally)

2. Understand the concept of social identities and their relationship to statuses of advantage and disadvantage

3. Become aware of intersections of multiple identities and statuses

Key Concepts:

- Socialization, reproduction, internalization, and resistance
- Social categories, social group memberships, and social group identity
- Social status and position: Advantage, inclusion, social power, and privilege; disadvantage, exclusion, powerlessness, and marginalization
- Intersectionality: Intersections of multiple (different) social group identities and location

Activities and Options:

1. Check-in and opportunity to revisit learning community guidelines/aspirations.

2. Cycle of Socialization: Both options review the Cycle of Socialization model. Option A uses a lecture presentation, including visual representations of the cycle, and Option B involves participants in an activity based on the cycle.

3. Interrupting the Cycle of Socialization: Identifying experiences of advocacy or empowerment: This activity encourages participants to draw on their own experiences to share personal examples of advocacy or empowerment.

4. Personal identity and social identity:
     Option A: Instructors and facilitators can prepare their own lecture on personal and social identity by drawing upon the text in this chapter (and the PowerPoint slides provided for Quadrant 1 on Part 1 of the website for this chapter).
     Option B: An interactive activity generating examples of these two concepts with participant input.
5. Social group memberships, positionality, and intersectionality: Option A: An interactive lecture presentation on these core concepts. Option B: Participants take an individual inventory, followed by small-group exploration of situations in which they have felt advantaged or disadvantaged based on their social group memberships.
6. Closing activity: Opportunity to bring some closure to this segment before transitioning to a different topic, taking a break, or ending a session.

QUADRANT 3: INSTITUTIONAL MANIFESTATIONS AND HISTORICAL LEGACIES

Learning Objectives:
1. Develop an awareness of the multiple manifestations of oppression at different levels, individual, institutional, and cultural, and how they intersect and reinforce each other to create a hegemonic "web" of oppression
2. Understand how hegemony and the "web" of oppression impacts individuals
3. Understand concepts such as social construction and hegemony as links between historical legacies and contemporary manifestation
4. Explore current impacts of selected historical legacies and historical resistance movements
5. Understand current individual, collective, and institutional examples and efforts toward change

Key Concepts:
- Institutional manifestations of oppression
- Social construction and hegemony
- Role of historical legacies behind current institutional manifestations
- Historical and current intersections
- Historical examples and current opportunities for resistance and change

Activities and Options:
1. Historical overview: Option A is a lecture presentation noting key historical moments for each of three different isms and addressing social construction and hegemony. Option B is a group activity in which participants discuss key historical events related to different isms and generate examples of current-day manifestations.
2. Current examples of oppression: Both options ask participants to generate a variety of examples of contemporary manifestations of oppression. Option A uses the "levels and types" framework, and Option B uses the "Five Faces of Oppression" framework.
3. Web of oppression: An interactive, kinesthetic activity demonstrating how interconnections among institutional manifestations of oppression create a ubiquitous "web."
4. Web of resistance: A continuation of the web of oppression focusing on its impermanence and highlighting opportunities for change.
5. Closing activity: Opportunity to bring some closure to this segment before transitioning to a different topic, taking a break, or ending a session.

QUADRANT 4: ACTION AND CHANGE

Learning Objectives:

1. Explore some of the different pathways individuals and groups can take to envision, plan, initiate, and create change
2. Develop skills for planning for change in one's personal life, community, or workplace
3. Understand key considerations for initiating a change plan, such as individual and collective action, action continuum, and spheres of influence
4. Consider specific frameworks for creating individual and collective change
5. Plan a realistic and feasible action plan to effect change toward social justice

Key Concepts:

- Models for creating change: liberatory consciousness, Cycle of Liberation, action continuum, and spheres of influence
- Action-planning skills (identifying goals, clarifying roles, and assessing risks/challenges, social support, and resources)
- Empowerment, co-allyship, advocacy, and solidarity

Activities and Options:

1. Envisioning change: An opportunity to visualize ways of creating change in small groups and the large group.
2. Frameworks for creating change:
    Option A: Uses Love's (2013) Four Elements of Liberatory Consciousness to encourage participants to think about their own agency in systems and possibilities for liberation.
    Option B: Uses Harro's (2013b) stages of the Cycle of Liberation to structure an activity focusing on self-empowerment, building community, and transforming institutions and organizations.
3. Taking action terminology: Supports the development of a shared language for taking action and creating change.
4. Action continuum and spheres of influence: Encourages discussion about possible action steps participants can take to begin to create changes in their personal lives and the lives of their communities.
5. Action planning: Individual and small-group activity that supports participants to generate realistic action plans.
6. Affirmations: An opportunity to affirm the learning and bring closure to the four quadrants before transitioning to a different topic or ending the course/workshop.

PART 3: FACILITATION ISSUES FOR CORE SJE CONCEPTS

An intentional SJE learning community is grounded in the principles described in the preceding chapters on theory, pedagogy, facilitation, and design. Those chapters offer different entry points and judgment calls in the preparation of SJE courses and workshops. This stand-alone or introductory session on core SJE concepts involves decisions about the following questions concerning sequence and facilitation:

1. Where and how to start
2. How to build an inclusive learning community

3. How to bring participant social identities and social positions into focus
4. How to work with expressions of emotions and challenges posed by complex ideas
5. How to balance focusing on specific identities with acknowledgement and exploring intersections
6. How to provide the knowledge and skills needed to move toward taking action for change
7. How to provide closure at the conclusion of the course/workshop or how to transition from this opening segment of a longer course/workshop

WHERE AND HOW TO START

An important decision for instructors and facilitators is whether to begin with "big picture" knowledge and awareness of social systems or to start with self-knowledge and personal awareness. Factors to consider include the characteristics of the ism, the readiness of participants, and the time available. If we choose to begin with the "big picture," we start by explaining what we mean by an SJE approach. The approach taken in this design is to start with the personal by building community and engaging participants.

Therefore, we devote Quadrant 1 to welcoming, active sharing, and community-building activities that immediately get participants engaged with each other and with the topic. This establishes that the class will be interactive and that what participants bring to the class will be part of the content for discussion. We interactively establish guidelines or aspirations for the learning community and introduce the concepts of comfort zones, learning edges, and activations. Even before we introduce the SJE approach and core concepts, participants have begun to make personal connections to the content. Once this active learning environment has been established, we can make the transition to some of the "big picture" concepts of social categories, social group membership, oppression, resistance, and liberation at different levels of social organization—concepts that will be explored in greater depth in Quadrants 2, 3, and 4.

HOW TO BUILD AN INCLUSIVE LEARNING COMMUNITY

The development of an SJE learning community is an ongoing process that needs explicit and careful attention early and throughout the course or workshop. We begin with an opening (or upon-arrival) activity that serves as a meet-and-greet or icebreaker before the session starts officially. We go over the agenda, do logistical announcements, and introduce our frameworks and assumptions, all of which contribute to setting the tone as much as the attention paid to introductions and establishing norms and guidelines. This is also a good time to remind participants of the opportunity to tell instructors about any accessibility needs that have not yet been communicated.

Guidelines or group agreements generated by the participants as a way of acknowledging and addressing their hopes and concerns is one key element that should happen near the beginning. As participants propose guidelines or group agreements based on their aspirations of how they will engage, facilitators may need to pose clarifying questions about guidelines that are overly general. Often the answers to such clarifying questions reveal assumptions based on cultural, linguistic, generational, or gendered differences. For example, the indicators of listening vary across cultures/abilities, such as preferring more or less eye contact. It is important to note these differences in how our various identities and experiences impact our expectations and desires for a learning environment. Facilitators should be careful not to have too many guidelines that limit or restrict communication, honesty, and difference of expression. Once established, the guidelines or community aspirations can be used as a reference point for processing group interactions throughout the course or workshop. For example, the facilitator might periodically ask the group to revisit the guidelines to clarify expectations and ask if there are guidelines participants need to add, delete, modify, or specify further.

In co-generating guidelines, participants often mention a concern about whether the course/workshop will be a "safe" place to take risks. Similarly, many participants come into SJE courses or workshops with worries that they will "make a mistake" and "push the buttons of" ("activate") someone else.[2] Often participants are afraid that they will be personally attacked for saying something or repeating a stereotype they've heard in the popular culture that is offensive and activates other participants (Ross, 2019). Facilitators may remind participants to put their attention to inviting conversation when oppressive language shows up or mistakes are made and to stress that these are learning opportunities.

Facilitators may want to revisit the distinction between safety and comfort. Participants often find it reassuring to know that although there will be times when everyone is uncomfortable, the facilitator and the participants establish that no one will be personally attacked. The concepts of comfort zones, learning edges, and activations can help introduce the idea that discomfort is sometimes productive for learning (refer to activity and definitions in Quadrant I of website). Facilitators can note that people in dominant groups are often made to feel comfortable in mainstream contexts and may learn more from discomfort that helps them see the advantages they take for granted. They can also serve as guides to help participants understand and explore their emotional reactions (anger, annoyance, etc.) to course content, activities, and other participants' perspectives.

These discussions establish the expectation of a challenging environment in which discomfort is expected and can be a sign of growth and learning and in which efforts to stretch oneself are supported. Facilitators can assure participants that to learn and grow, they need a learning environment in which mistakes can be made, difficult questions can be asked, contradictory information and experiences can be explored, and people can find ways to support each other and draw on each other's different experiences to expand their own knowledge, awareness, and skills (Goodman, 2011; Ross, 2019; Wasserman & Doran, 1999).

Once established, the guidelines or community agreements can be used as a reference point for processing group interactions throughout the course or workshop. For example, the facilitator might periodically ask the group to revisit the guidelines to clarify expectations and ask if there are guidelines participants need to add, delete, modify, or specify further.

In addition to the specific activities that serve to build a learning community in Quadrant 1 (especially establishing guidelines), instructors or facilitators need to be mindful of how they will convene and greet the group on the first day and even before the session begins. Throughout the course, community-building and wellness need to be sustained through active facilitation of individual and group learning, sometimes including the informal interaction among participants. Community-building should be introduced intentionally and then honored and maintained with care and attention through ongoing debriefs and closures for course or workshop segments.

HOW TO BRING PARTICIPANT SOCIAL IDENTITIES AND SOCIAL POSITIONS INTO FOCUS

Our core concepts highlight the complex relationships between individuals' social identities and systemic patterns of oppression. The design provides many opportunities to notice and highlight these interconnections as they emerge in conversation. For example, we can help participants link someone's personal anecdote to larger institutional or cultural/societal patterns that the group has read or discussed, or we can ask the group for personal examples that illustrate institutional or cultural/societal patterns. The back-and-forth between personal and system examples enables participants to recognize these linkages in situations outside the classroom or workshop.

Many participants are unaware of the multiple ways in which they are implicated in the issues we are discussing. Some will strongly identify with one social group identity that feels vulnerable or marginalized, while others will deny or feel shame about their privileged social group identity. Many participants are unaware of the ways their own behaviors, communication patterns, and attitudes may reflect and reproduce some of the larger patterns of advantage and disadvantage that are discussed as course topics.

Facilitators can use the introductory activities in Quadrant 1 to assess participants' readiness and anticipate potential gaps in understanding and tensions in communication. Facilitators' observations about which concepts participants struggle with or get defensive about can inform decisions about how best to approach these concepts later when they are addressed in greater depth. For example, when participants are struggling with the concept of privilege, the facilitator might turn to activities listed among additional resources in Part 2 of the chapter website.

The value of the experiential learning approach that we use in SJE comes from the discussion ("processing") of activities in which social identities become visible and participants learn by doing. It is important to remember that the learning emerges not from the activity itself so much as from the discussion in which participants process what they noticed, how they felt, and new insights they derived about themselves, the group, and the readings under examination.

WORKING WITH EXPRESSION OF EMOTIONS AND CHALLENGES POSED BY COMPLEX IDEAS

In a stand-alone SJE course or workshop that focuses on core concepts, participant concerns are likely to emerge. Sometimes participants may have strong emotional reactions to the content or to interactions that occur in the course/workshop. (This is discussed in more depth in Chapter 3: Design and Facilitation.)

One such challenge can occur when participants express the view that some isms are more important than others and should get priority attention. Facilitators can address this by noting that all forms of oppression are damaging, that different forms of oppression have greater or lesser salience at different points in time or different contexts, and that while we may choose to center a form of oppression at times, it can be divisive to establish a hierarchy of oppression when the ultimate goal is everyone's liberation, as Audre Lorde (1996) argued.

Another participant view that can come across as resistance is that people who belong to marginalized or disadvantaged groups have an "agenda" and that people in privileged groups are to blame. Facilitators can address the notion that oppressed people may have an "agenda" by appreciating the energy and forcefulness with which oppressed people have brought social injustice to the forefront of everyone's consciousness. Changing a society in the direction of social justice takes everyone's effort, and people with privilege can use access to resources to advocate and work for change.

Defensiveness on the part of people with social advantage—or anger on the part of people who experience disadvantage—can be addressed in two ways. First, facilitators can acknowledge and validate emotions and provide opportunities to reflect on emotional reactions through free writing or pair shares. Second, facilitators can connect anger or shame about instances of oppression in the present moment to the historical legacies that shaped current realities and that none of us created. The focus on historical legacies allows participants to put aside defensiveness, resentment, or fear that they are personally being blamed in order to see how current inequities and injustices have long roots in the past. Rather than blaming past actors, we can understand the past and learn from it to create a better future. Anger and outrage are essential "fuel" to generate change. Discussion can focus on how to use one's feelings as motivation to work with others who share that outrage about injustice and oppression.

Whether or not an explicit guideline has been established about responding to activations or soft spots or hot buttons, facilitators can remind participants that everyone is there to learn. Participants who feel activated can be invited to describe their feelings so that their feelings can be validated and others can learn from the experience. The facilitator can also provide context for why certain statements might be difficult to hear. Those whose statements triggered or activated others can be asked to listen rather than defend their comments, to sit on their "learning edges" and pay attention to a different perspective. Remind participants that we are more interested in the impacts of comments than on a speaker's intention, although it is also useful to explore the (mis)information or experience that a triggering experience is based on. Encourage participants to view these exchanges as "food for thought" rather than attempts to change an individual participant's views on the spot. No one can actually listen and learn when they feel defensive or chastised.

There are many choices for facilitators to intervene when participants' hot buttons are activated in response to something they heard. These moments provide learning opportunities about the difference between intention, impact, and accountability; the consequences of microaggressions experienced by people from marginalized groups; and the defensiveness of privileged people when accused of wrongdoings they don't understand.

We approach these difficult moments with generosity, not blame, and talk about the "learning edge," or when we are out of our learning comfort zone, that all of us may experience in such moments. We may discuss and model for participants how to give feedback in thoughtful ways. We may ask participants to tell us what kind of feedback would be most useful or would help the group understand why the words or the situation was activating.

Facilitators learn when to intervene in challenging interactions. The role of the facilitator is not to protect a participant based on something they have said or done, unless there is a clear concern about safety, but to hold space and ease the way for the participant and those impacted to process the moment. As a learning community gains experience in honoring its own aspirations and guidelines, facilitators might turn to the group to ask whether there are other approaches to an idea or opinion that has been voiced. That becomes an opportunity to explore, openly, the (mis)information behind the stereotypes or socialization that led to assumptions that are now being challenged in SJE contexts.

Participants are often not aware of beliefs or misinformation until they are challenged, and they may be surprised by the strength of emotions associated with these beliefs. Participants may react to each other in ways that are not helpful in sustaining a learning community. These are some of the reasons we emphasize the importance of clear community guidelines or aspirations from the very beginning of a class or workshop, so that we can refer to them as they (inevitably) become challenged or violated.

It helps if facilitators acknowledge, upfront and early in a course or workshop, that some of the new ways of thinking are likely to challenge old ways of thinking and that information may emerge that challenges accepted stereotypes. By alerting participants in advance, they can be better prepared for the times that will happen. Facilitators might also want to explain that SJE courses and workshops will present experiences and perspectives that contradict older ways of thinking and that by working through these contradictions, participants will develop critical and reflexive thinking skills that will be helpful in other parts of their lives.

FINDING A BALANCE BETWEEN SINGLE ISM/IDENTITY FOCUS AND THE INTERSECTIONS WITH OTHER ISMS/IDENTITIES

It can be difficult to hold onto the examination of more than one ism at a time and look at the intersection among isms, yet explorations that ignore intersectionality are incomplete. In our approach, we try to find a balance by foregrounding one ism while also recognizing its interactions with other isms.

Facilitators can model making connections between SJE isms—keeping the focus on a specific oppression while showing the connections to other oppressions. When exploring a particular topic or issue through the lens of one form of oppression, participants can be asked to consider the intersecting impact of other social identities and forms of oppression. They can be asked to examine the range of experiences within a social identity group due to other intersecting social identities and look at events considering how various forms of oppression interlink to shape its occurrence. Texts or essays that illustrate intersections can also be very helpful. Facilitators can remind participants of the goals that participants will come away from these classes and workshops by focusing on one form of oppression with some depth while appreciating that social identities and social justice issues are always complicated by their intersections at all levels and in all contexts.

INCORPORATING OPPORTUNITIES FOR RESISTANCE AND ACTIONS FOR CHANGE

Our emphasis on the historical legacies behind current manifestations of oppression—as well as the historical legacies of resistance and change—creates numerous opportunities throughout a course or workshop to re-imagine the present and what is possible that will reshape or transform the future (Brown, 2017; hooks, 1992, 2001; Johnson, 2018; Lyiscott, 2019; Pasque & Harris, 2013). Opportunities for action and change are explored throughout our design, not only through a segment devoted to action planning toward the end (although the focused action-planning activities are in Quadrant 4). Current and historical examples of social action and activism are used to inspire participants and to help imagine new possibilities as well as conceptual frameworks, such as Harro's (2013b) Cycle of Liberation and Love's (2013) Developing a Liberatory Consciousness. In some cases, facilitators may wish to start a course by imagining a different world without oppression or may want to integrate action planning throughout the sequence. The sequencing of action and change is an important element of course or workshop design, as is an approach to facilitation/instruction that is hopeful and explores openings for change.

In some organizational contexts, encouraging participants to take action may be discouraged or risky. In some individual cases, participants may not intend to take action against the forms of oppression addressed in the course/workshop. In these situations, facilitators can frame the action-focused segments as opportunities to build skills in planning and collaboration that can be useful in many different family, community, and work situations. Participants' work in action planning will, therefore, be hypothetical—that is, what might you do, how might you do it, with whom might you work, and what steps might you take. In other contexts in which encouraging real action is fair game, participants may actually implement their action ideas. Collaborative action projects can be woven into the design of a course or workshop and scaffolded to build the capacity for informed action and collaboration (Zúñiga, Nagda, Chesler, & Cytron-Walker, 2007).

On the continuum from action "against inclusion and social justice" to actions "for diversity and social justice," action for positive change can take many forms—from an understanding and analysis of one's own role (usually unrecognized and unacknowledged) in the hegemonic structures that create inequality (Young, 2011) to a willingness to engage with new social movements (Anyon, 2005; Barber, 2016; Southern Poverty Law Center, 2017). Domingue and Neely (2013) encourage instructors/facilitators to frame social action as an ongoing journey, not as one or more isolated events; to act, not to react; and to challenge themselves to re-imagine what change can be. Their key suggestions include:

- Emphasize social action at the beginning of courses or workshops and maintain the focus throughout.
- Provide current historical examples of activism, especially by students and youth (see Dache, Quaye, Linder, & McGuire, 2019; Linder, Quaye, Lange, Evans, & Stewart, 2020; Wong, 2018).
- Promote opportunities for student or community leadership and hold participants accountable.
- Provide frequent, consistent support through frequent check-ins, coaching, and celebrations of victories (Domingue & Neely, 2013).

CLOSURE OR TRANSITION

Since participants' learning experiences about key concepts are often emotional, it is important to acknowledge the closure of this course or workshop. Even if this design is used as a segment of a longer course or workshop, the completion of the segment should be marked. Facilitators should communicate appreciation of the individual and collaborative efforts of the learning community and express hope that participants will build on what they have learned, develop new skills, continue to take risks, and maintain the bonds they have forged.

In those cases, in which this is the beginning of a longer class or additional workshops, facilitators can use check-ins as an opportunity to gather feedback about what participants feel worked well for them and what they would like to see changed as they continue in this learning community. Facilitators can also provide some continuity by previewing what is to come in the next phase of a course or series of workshops.

Notes

* We ask that those who cite this work always acknowledge by name all of the authors listed rather than either only citing the first author or using "et al." to indicate co-authors. All collaborated on the conceptualization, development, and writing of this chapter.
1 The companion website was edited by Itza D. Martínez, University of Massachusetts, as lead collaborator.
2 We choose not to use the word "trigger" due to its violent connotation.

References

Adams, M. (2014). Social justice and education. In M. Reisch (Ed.), *Routledge international handbook of social justice* (pp. 249–268). Routledge.

Aldana, A., Richards-Schuster, K., & Checkoway, B. (2016). Dialogic pedagogy for youth participatory action research: Facilitation of an intergroup empowerment program. *Social Work with Groups, 39,* 4. doi:10.1080/01609513.2015.1076370

Alexander, M. (2012). *The new Jim Crow: Mass incarceration in the age of color blindness*. The New Press.

Anyon, J. (2005). *Radical possibilities: Public policy, urban education, and a new social movement*. Routledge.

Anzaldúa, G. (2012). *Borderlands: La Frontera*. Aunt Lute Books.

Banaji, M. R., & Greenwald, A. G. (2013). *Blindspot: Hidden biases of good people*. Delacorte Press.

Barber, W. J. (2016). Appendix for organizers: Fourteen steps forward together. In W. J. Barber II & J. Wilson-Hartgrove (Eds.), *The third reconstruction* (pp. 127–130). Beacon Press.

Beal, F. (1995). Double jeopardy: To be Black and female. In B. Guy-Sheftall (Ed.), *Words of firefire: An anthology of African American feminist thought* (pp. 146–156). New Press.

Bell, L. A. (2020). *Storytelling for social justice: Connecting narrative and the arts in anti-racist teaching*. Routledge.

Brookfield, S. (2005). *The power of critical theory: Liberating adult learning and teaching*. Wiley.

Brown, M. A. (2017). *Emergent strategy, shaping change, changing worlds*. AK Press.

Brown, M. A. (2021). *Holding change: The way of emergent strategy facilitation and mediation*. Emergent Strategy Series No. 4. AK Press.

Boggs, G. L. (2012). *The next American revolution*. University of California Press.

Case, K. (Ed.). (2013). *Deconstructing privilege: Teaching and learning as allies in the classroom*. Routledge.

Chugh, D. (2018). *The person you mean to be: How good people fight bias*. Harper Collins.

Chun, E. B., & Feagin, J. R. (2020). *Rethinking diversity frameworks in higher education*. Routledge.

Collins, P. H. (1990). *Black feminist thought: Knowledge, consciousness, and politics of empowerment*. Unwin Hyman.

Collins, P. H. (2000). *Black feminist thought: Knowledge, consciousness and the politics of empowerment* (2nd ed.). Routledge.

Collins, P. H. (2019). *Intersectionality as critical social theory*. Duke University Press.

Collins, P. H., & Bilge, S. (2016). *Intersectionality*. Polity Press.

Combahee River Collective. (1982). A Black feminist statement. In G. T. Hull, P. B. Scott, & B. Smith (Eds.), *All the women are White, all the men are men, but some of us are brave: Black women's studies* (pp. 13–22). Feminist Press.

Crenshaw, K. W. (1991). Mapping the margins: Intersectionality, identity politics, and violence against women of color. *Stanford Law Review, 43*(6), 1241–1299.

Crenshaw, K. W. (2003). Traffic at the crossroads: Multiple oppressions. In R. Morgan (Ed.), *Sisterhood is forever: The women's anthology for a new millennium* (pp. 43–57). Washington Square Press.

Dache, A., Quaye, S. J., Linder, C., & McGuire, K. M. (Eds.). (2019). *Rise Up! Activism as education*. Michigan State University Press.

David, E. (2014). *Internalized Oppression: The Psychology of Marginalized Groups*. Springer Publishing.

Davis, A. Y. (2012). *The meaning of freedom and other difficult dialogues*. Haymarket Press.

Davis, F. E. (2019). *The little book of race and restorative justice: Black lives, healing and US social transformation*. Good Books.

Department of Education. (2017). *Rose's law, federal register*. Retrieved from https://www.federal register.gov/documents/2017/07/11/2017-14343/rosas-law

Domingue, A. D., & Neely, D. S. (2013). Why is it so hard to take action: A reflective dialogue about facilitating for social action engagement. In L. M. Landerman (Ed.), *The art of effective facilitation: Reflections from social justice educators* (pp. 231–252). Stylus Publishing.

Duncan-Andrade, J. M. R. (2009). Note to educators: Hope required when growing roses in concrete. *Harvard Educational Review, 79*(2), 181–194.

Feagin, J. (2013). *The White racial frame: Centuries of Racial framing and counter-framing*. Routledge.

Feagin, J. P., Vera, H., & Ducey, K. (2015). *Liberation sociology* (3rd ed.). Routledge.

Freire, P. (1970). *Pedagogy of the oppressed*. Herder & Herder.

Geronimus, A. T. (1992). The weathering hypothesis and the health of African-American women and infants: Evidence and speculations. *Ethnicity & Disease*, 207–221.

Geronimus, A. T., Bound, J., Waidmann, T. A., Colen, C. G., & Steffick, D. (2001). Inequality in life expectancy, functional status, and active life expectancy across selected black and white populations in the United States. *Demography, 38*, 227–251.

Goodman, D. (2011). *Promoting diversity and social justice: Educating people from privileged groups* (2nd ed.). Routledge.

Gumbs, A. P. (2020). *Undrowned: Black feminists lessons from marine mammals*. AK Press.

Hankivsky, O. (2014). *Intersectionality 101*. Vancouver, BC, Canada: The Institute for Intersectionality Research & Policy, Simon Fraser University. Retrieved from http://www.sfu.ca/iirp/documents/resources/101_Final.pdf

Hardiman, R., & Jackson, B. W. (1997). Conceptual foundations for social justice courses. In M. Adams, L. A. Bell & P. Griffin (Eds.), *Teaching for diversity and social justice* (2nd ed., pp. 26–35). Routledge.

Hardiman, R., Jackson, B. W., & Griffin, P. (2007). Conceptual foundations for social justice education. In M. Adams, L. A. Bell, & P. Griffin (Eds.), *Teaching for diversity and social justice* (2nd ed., pp. 35–66). Routledge.

Harro, B. (2013a). The cycle of socialization. In M. Adams, W. J. Blumenfeld, C. Castañeda, H. W. Hackman, M. L. Peters, & X. Zúñiga (Eds.), *Readings for diversity and social justice* (3rd ed., pp. 45–51). Routledge.

Harro, B. (2013b). The cycle of liberation. In M. Adams, W. J. Blumenfeld, C. Castañeda, H. W. Hacksman, M. L. Peters, & X. Zúñiga (Eds.), *Readings for diversity and social justice* (3rd ed., pp. 618–624). Routledge.

Holvino, E. (2012). The "simultaneity" of identities: Models and skills for the twenty-first century. In C. L. Wijeyesinghe & B. W. Jackson (Eds.), *New perspectives on racial identity development: Integrating emerging frameworks* (2nd ed., pp. 161–191). New York University Press.

hooks, b. (2001). *All about love: New visions*. Harper Collins.

hooks, b. (1992). *Teaching to transgress*. Routledge.

Huber, L. P., & Solórzano, D. G. (2014). Racial microaggressions as a tool for critical race research. *Race Ethnicity and Education, 18*(3), 297–320.

Hulko, W. (2009). The time- and context-contingent nature of intersectionality and interlocking oppressions. *Affilia: Journal of Women & Social Work, 24*(1), 44–55. doi:10.1177/0886109908326814

Johnson, A. (2018). *Privilege, power, and difference* (3rd ed.). McGraw-Hill.

Kimmel, M. S., & Ferber, A. L. (Eds.). (2009). *Privilege: A reader* (2nd ed.). Westview Press.

Kirk, G., & Okazawa-Rey, M. (2018). Identities and social locations: Who am I? Who are my people? In M. Adams, W. J. Blumenfeld, C. Castañeda, H. W. Hackman, M. L. Peters, & X. Zúñiga (Eds.), *Readings for diversity and social justice* (3rd ed., pp. 9–15). Routledge.

Kirwan Institute. (2013). *State of the science: Implicit bias review*. Columbus, OH: Ohio State Kirwan Institute for the Study of Race and Ethnicity.

Lakey, G. (2020). *Facilitating group learning: Strategies for success with diverse adult learners*. PM Press.

Leondar-Wright, B. (2014). *Missing class: Strengthening social movement groups by seeing class cultures*. Cornell University Press.

Lewis, J. (2020, July 30). Together, you can redeem the soul of our nation. Op Ed. *New York Times*, A.23.

Linder, C., Quaye, S. J., Lange, A. C., Evans, M. E., & Stewart, T. J. (2020). *Identity-based student activism: Power and oppression on college campuses*. Routledge.

Lorde, A. (1996). There is no hierarchy of oppressions. In J. Andrzejewski (Ed.), *Oppression and social justice: Critical frameworks* (5th ed., p. 51). Pearson Custom Publishing.

Love, B. J. (2013). Developing a liberatory consciousness. In M. Adams, W. J. Blumenfeld, R. Castañeda, H. W. Hackman, M. L. Peters, & X. Zúñiga (Eds.), *Readings for diversity and social justice* (3rd ed., pp. 601–605). Routledge.

Love, B. L. (2019). *We want to do more than survive. Abolitionist teaching and the pursuit of education freedom*. Beacon Press.

Lyiscott, J. (2019). *Black Appetite. White Food: Issues of Race, Voice, and Justice Within and Beyond the Classroom*. Routledge.

McLennan, R. M. (2008). *The crisis of imprisonment: Protest, politics, and the making of the American penal state, 1776–1941*. Cambridge University Press.

Memmi, A. (1957, 1991). *The colonizer and the colonized* (expanded ed.). Beacon Press.

Nash, J. (2019). *Black feminism reimagined*. Duke University Press.

Obear, K. (2018). *In it for the Long Haul: Overcoming burnout & passion fatigue as social justice agents*. Morgan James Publishing.

Omi, M., & Winant, H. (2015). *Racial formation in the United States* (3rd ed.). Routledge.

Pasque, P. A., & Harris, B. L. (2013). Moving from social justice to social agency: Keeping it messy. In K. Kline (Ed.), *Reflection in action: A guidebook for faculty and student affairs professionals* (pp. 133–151). Stylus.

Pharr, S. (1997). *Homophobia: A weapon of sexism* (expanded ed.). Chardon.

Pittelman, K. (2005). *Classified: How to stop hiding your privilege and use it for social change*. Soft Skull Press.

Quaye, S. J., Karikari, S. N., Carter, K. D., Okello, W. K., & Allen, C. (2020). "Why can't I just chill?" The visceral nature of racial fatigue. *Journal of College Student Development*, 61(5), 609–623.

Ransby, B. (2018). *Making all Black lives matter: Reimagining freedom in the 21st century*. University of California Press.

Rawls, J. (2003). *Justice as fairness: A restatement*. Harvard University Press.

Rich, A. C. (1980). Compulsory heterosexuality and lesbian existence. *Signs*, 5(4), 631–660.

Ross, L. J. (2017). Reproductive justice as intersectional feminist activism. *Souls*, 19(3), 286–314.

Ross, L. J. (2019). Speaking up without tearing down. *Teaching Tolerance*. Retrieved from https://www.tolerance.org/magazine/spring-2019/speaking-up-without-tearing-down

Sen, A. (2009). *The idea of justice*. Harvard University Press.

Singh, A. (2019). *The racial healing handbook: Practical activities to help you challenge privilege, confront systemic racism, and engage in collective healing*. New Harbinger.

Smith, W. A., Yosso, T. J., & Solórzano, D. G. (2006). Challenging racial battle fatigue on historically white campuses: A critical race examination of race-related stress. In C. A. Stanley (Ed.), *Faculty of color: Teaching in predominantly White colleges and universities* (pp. 299–327). Anker.

Southern Poverty Law Center (2017). *SPLC on campus: A guide to bystander intervention*. Retrieved from https://www.splcenter.org/sites/default/files/soc_bystander_intervention_guide_ web_final. pdf

Spade, D. (2020). *Mutual aid: Building solidarity during this crisis (and the next)*. Verso.

Sue, D. W. (2010). *Microaggressions in everyday life: Race, gender, and sexual orientation*. John Wiley & Sons.

Tatum, B. D. (2018). *Why are all the Black kids sitting together in the cafeteria? And other conversations about race*. Basic Books.

Taylor, K. Y. (2016). *From #BlackLivesMatter to Black Liberation*. Haymarket Books.

Vygotsky, L. S. (1978). *Mind in society: The development of higher psychological processes* (M. Cole, V. John-Steiner, S. Scribner, & E. Souberman, Trans.). Harvard University Press.

Wasserman, I. C., & Doran, R. F. (1999). Creating inclusive learning communities. In A. L. Cooke, M. Brazzel, A. S. Craig, & B. Greig (Eds.), *NTL reading book for human relations training* (8th ed., pp. 307–310). NTL Institute for Applied Behavioral Sciences.

Watkins, M., & Shulman, H. (2008). *Toward psychologies of liberation*. Palgrave.

Watson, K. T. (2019). *Revealing and uprooting cellular violence: Black men and the biopsychosocial impact of racial microaggressions*. [Doctoral dissertation, University of California Los Angeles]. UCLA Electronic Theses and Dissertations.

Wildman, S. M. (1996). *Privilege revealed: How invisible preference undermines America*. New York University Press.

Winters, M. (2020). *Black Fatigue: How racism erodes the body, mind and spirit*. Berrett-Koehler.

Wong, A. (2018). The Renaissance of Student Activism. In M. Adams, W. J. Blumenfeld, D. C. J. Catalano, K. S. DeJong, H. W. Hackman, L. E. Hopkins, B. J. Love, M. Peters, D. Shlasko, & X. Zúñiga (Eds.), *Readings for diversity and social justice* (4th ed., pp. 649–652). Routledge.

Young, I. M. (1990). *Justice and the politics of difference*. Princeton University Press.

Young, I. M. (2011). *Responsibility for justice*. Oxford University Press.

Zinn, H. (2002). *You can't be neutral on a moving train*. Beacon Press.

Zinn, H. (2003). *A people's history of the United States: 1492–present*. Harper-Collins.

Zúñiga, X. (2018). Chapter introduction; Selections for working for social justice: Visions and strategies for social change. In M. Adams, WJ. Blumenfeld, Catalano, C. J., DeJong, S., H. Hackman, Hopkins, L. E., Shlasko, D., M. L. Peters, & X. Zúñiga (Eds.), *Readings for diversity and social justice* (4th ed., pp. 599–652). Routledge.

Zúñiga, X., & Lee, E. Y. (2015). Adaptation of Matrix of interlocking systems and levels of oppression and resistance (Figure 4.3). Social Justice Education, University of Massachusetts, Amherst. In P. H. Collins (1990), *Black feminist thought: Knowledge, consciousness, and the politics of empowerment*. Routledge.

Zúñiga, X., Lopez, G. E., & Ford, K. (2014). *Intergroup dialogue: Engaging difference, social identity and social justice*. Routledge.

Zúñiga, X., Nagda, B. A., Chesler, M., & Cytron-Walker, A. (2007). Intergroup dialogues in higher education: Meaningful learning about social justice. *ASHE-ERIC Higher Education Report Series*, 32(4).

5

Racism, White Supremacy and Finding Justice for All

Lee Anne Bell and Michael S. Funk*

INTRODUCTION

Martin Luther King, Jr. once observed that poor white people in the South had nothing to feed their children but Jim Crow, a poignant example of the power of racism to convince economically oppressed white people to work against their own economic self-interest in exchange for the crumbs of white supremacy. Fears that any gain by Black people would mean a loss for poor whites prevented coalitions against conditions like the indentured servitude of sharecropping that impoverished them all.

Zero-sum thinking, assuming that a gain for one group inevitably means a loss for other groups, prevents people from recognizing possibilities for mutual gain. The fallacy of zero-sum thinking at the heart of racism leads all too many white people to believe their well-being is threatened when People of Color, especially Black people, get ahead, rather than recognize what they could gain by working together. McGhee vividly illustrates how this operated in the 1950s when many white communities destroyed state-of-the-art public swimming pools rather than share them with Black people, thus depriving everyone who couldn't afford a private (segregated) country club of a shining public good (2021). Zero-sum thinking undermines the possibilities of working together across racial lines to address the urgent challenges we now face as a country and prevents us from realizing the shared social benefits, or solidarity dividend (Ibid), that could be gained.

This chapter deconstructs the historical development of the zero-sum fallacy of racism; the harm it has caused not only to Indigenous, African American, Asian American, Latinx and multiracial people but also to white Americans; and the damage it has done and continues to do to this country's founding principles. Although there are many historical examples, three events in the current era make this observation increasingly relevant: the Black Lives Matter (BLM) movement, the COVID pandemic, and the voter suppression efforts that followed the refusal of an outgoing president to acknowledge the results of an election for the first time in U.S. history. We can add the escalating threats of climate change and the role that racism plays in preventing concerted action to address it.

BLM exposed in the most powerful way possible the intolerable violence and death suffered by Black Americans at the hands of police as an encapsulation of the many harms perpetrated on People of Color by a racist system. It also underscored the social costs of a society that incarcerates rather than educates so many of its Black and brown citizens, from a prison industrial complex that saps resources away from other human needs like decent housing and health care for all, to increased insecurity, violence and fear that affect everyone. In a similar way, the COVID pandemic made vividly clear the harm caused by an administration that disregarded the lives of the most vulnerable Americans, particularly Americans of color, and in so doing hurt everyone, albeit unequally. Finally, the attack on election integrity and the peaceful transfer of power emboldened voter suppression laws in many states—aimed particularly at People of Color and young people but also impacting poor and older people of all races—and violated a core principle of democracy: free and fair elections (Anderson, 2018). These three interlocking events illustrate that racism, like

DOI: 10.4324/9781003005759-7

climate change, will ultimately lead to destruction of our country if we do not address it once and for all. Only when we work together as equal citizens in our multiracial democracy can we realize the solidarity dividend that will enable us to solve the escalating economic, climate and social problems facing us today.

Fortunately, there are also examples throughout our history of people from all racialized groups working in solidarity to challenge racism and white supremacy and to envision and enact multiracial democracy. The BLM movement embodies a multiracial and international coalition of men and women, lesbian, gay, bisexual, trans and queer (LGBTQ+) people, youth and elders working to reimagine policing and build communities that provide safety and support for all. The COVID pandemic likewise prompted people from diverse communities to support one another with food, care, shelter, finances and other support and helped force the government to enact far-reaching legislation aimed at supporting middle- and working-class families and addressing child poverty. The 2020 election increased voter participation from all racial groups and illustrated the significance of having every vote count. Throughout this chapter we point to other examples of the power of multiracial coalitions to enact the ideals on which this country was founded.

OUR APPROACH

We start from the premise that race is not real but created in order to advance the interests of a few over the many. Race is a *social construction* that takes the range of physical differences within the human population and presents these as distinct and separate biological categories. While fabricated, race has a long history of using human differences to rationalize unjust socio-economic arrangements (Frederickson, 2003; Smedley & Smedley, 2011). Thus, we need to recognize not what race *is* but what race *does* to understand and challenge the purposes it was constructed to serve (Bridges, 2019; Haney-López, 2006).

We define *racism* as a pervasive system of advantage and disadvantage based on the socially constructed category of race. This system justifies discrimination, oppression, dispossession and exclusion for people from targeted racialized groups and creates and sustains systemic benefits for the group racialized as white (see glossary of terms and definitions on website.

★ A second premise is that racism is created and sustained through a racial hierarchy that divides groups against one another to maintain the power and dominance of those at the top. DuBois (1935) described whiteness as a "public and psychological wage" that gave otherwise exploited poor whites a valuable social status based on their categorization as "not-Black." Whites without material property could at least claim the psychological property of whiteness (Harris, 1993). This mentality thwarted cross-racial, cross-class solidarity throughout our history and prevented advances that would better serve People of Color as well as working- and middle-class white people (McGhee, 2021; Metzl, 2019). Racism links white supremacy and wealth supremacy to ensure that those at the top of the racial/ class hierarchy can hoard wealth and power for themselves (Brown, 2021; Haney-López, 2019). Indeed, this zero-sum mentality has led to a stagnant economy and declining middle class for the past 40 years (Tankersley, 2020).

A third premise is that it is important to understand both 1) the distinctive and shared ways that racism operates on different racialized groups, historically and in the present, as well as 2) how racism operates through intersections with other forms of oppression. The foundational frames for racism in this country are the colonization and genocide of the Indigenous people and the enslavement of Africans, which provided free land and free labor to white colonizers. We add additional lenses to discern how racism manifests in both similar and different ways for Asian Americans, Latinx people, Arab Americans and others. Further, we look at how race intersects with class, gender, sexual orientation, religion, age and other axes of difference to provide a more nuanced understanding of how racism functions in different contexts.

Finally, we contextualize racism within U.S. connections to the broader world. From the outset, the U.S. justified colonial adventures abroad through racist ideas about manifest destiny and white superiority. Wherever the U.S. expropriated natural resources and labor from other nations to support economic and/or foreign policy objectives, the negative effects on the home economic and political systems of affected countries impelled streams of migration to the U.S. (Gonzalez, 2011). The slogan among immigration activists, "We are here because you were there," illustrates this circular connection. Large numbers of people have emigrated to the United States as a result of U.S. interventions that made life in their countries of origin unsafe or not economically feasible. Current immigration policy at the U.S. border with Mexico flounders partly on the unwillingness to address the impact of U.S. drug and economic policies on neighboring countries that rebound to affect this country as well.

KEY CONCEPTS

Racism is pervasive because it is enacted on multiple levels simultaneously: institutional, cultural, interpersonal and individual. Institutional structures, policies and practices interlock with cultural assumptions about who and what matters in order to justify racism. Individuals internalize and enact these assumptions through personal behavior and institutional participation. Woven together, these interactions create and sustain systemic benefits for whites as a group and structure discrimination, oppression, dispossession and exclusion for people from targeted racialized groups. The structures and ideology that justify this system is *white supremacy*.

White supremacy exonerates the nation's history of stolen land from its original inhabitants; the coerced, unpaid labor of enslaved Africans; and colonial war and conquest that extended the American empire in order to valorize a heroic (white) past (Billings, 2016). The system of white supremacy normalizes the interests and perceptions of white individuals, white culture as superior to other racialized groups and white lives as worth more than other lives (Glaude, 2016). Relations of white dominance and subordination of others are reenacted daily through social arrangements in which material resources, policies and institutional norms and practices are overwhelmingly controlled by and for white interests. While overt in white supremacist/nationalist groups, white supremacy is more often unexamined or unconscious. Thus, the best way to challenge racism is to address the outcomes it produces rather than focusing solely on the intentions of those who enact it.

Discussions about racism typically focus on people and groups at the receiving end of discriminatory policies and practices. We cannot talk meaningfully about racism, however, without identifying the advantages that accrue to the white group positioned at the top of the social hierarchy. Whites as a group gain access to valuable social, political and economic resources, including protection from negative pre-judgments based on physical features, language and other cultural factors. White supremacy enables white people, to greater and lesser degrees depending on class and other social locations, to benefit psychologically and materially from accumulated advantage, whether they seek these advantages or not (Croll, 2013; Roithmayr, 2014). (Also see Chapter 6: Classism.)

Racial advantage and disadvantage are two sides of the same coin. The U.S. creed is that our society is a meritocracy in which, despite race or station, anyone willing to work hard can get ahead. Yet research repeatedly shows that segregated schools and neighborhoods, job discrimination and pay inequity, a racialized school-to-prison pipeline and enduring legacies of past discrimination mean that working hard is not enough to overcome institutionalized advantage and disadvantage (Oliver & Shapiro, 2006; Rugh & Massey, 2010; Shapiro, Meschede, & Osoro, 2013). The 2020 COVID pandemic and the racially disproportionate rates of illness and death shed a spotlight on these systemic inequities in which African American, Native American and Latinx people contracted and died of COVID-19 at much greater rates than whites (Golestaneh, Neugarten, Fisher, Billett, Gil, Johns, . . ., & Bellin, 2020).

Ironically, a system that allocates advantage to whites also exacts a price. For example, white racial resentment has been stoked by politicians to undermine support for government policies that would underwrite health care, childcare, well-funded public education and other programs that poor and working-class white people need as desperately as People of Color who share their circumstances (Metzl, 2019). An increasing concentration of wealth at the top is undermining economic opportunity to such an extent that the meritocratic advancement promised in the American Dream ideal may be all but wiped out, even for white people, in this generation (Williams, 2017).

Race and racism intersect with other social identities and systems of oppression to position individuals and groups differently by virtue of gender, class, sexuality, ability, age and other social markers (Crenshaw, 1995; Hill-Collins, 2019). *Intersectionality* operates on both individual and institutional/systemic levels. For example, a woman of color who is poor and disabled experiences racism differently than an upper-class, able-bodied, heterosexual man of color, though racism has negative consequences for both (treatment by police and criminal justice system, for example). Similarly, a poor white or working-class person does not experience the same material advantages of an upper-class white person, though both reap advantages (not being profiled by police). Racism, classism, heterosexism, ableism, sexism and ageism are deeply intertwined systems that sustain inequalities in such institutions as schooling, housing, employment and the criminal justice system to differentially impact poor people, people with disabilities, People of Color, immigrants, elders, youth, women and LGBTQ+ people. In this chapter, we focus on race as central while bearing in mind the ways that race intersects with other social group memberships and isms to shape the particular experiences of differently positioned individuals and groups.

HISTORICAL LEGACIES

Recognizing the historical legacies of racism not only explains how the current racial order came to be but reveals its ongoing reverberations in the present. This history also provides information for how to finally dismantle systemic racism and realize the "more perfect union" invoked in the country's founding documents. In this section we explore some of the threads that extend into the present: the evolution of racial classification and hierarchy, the linking of race to immigration and citizenship rights and the control of the franchise to maintain racial hierarchy and white supremacy.

RACIAL CLASSIFICATION AND HIERARCHY

One of the most pernicious and persistent ideas in U.S. history is belief in the existence of racial categories that mark groups of people as physically and intellectually distinct.

Constructed racial categories were used to establish systems of power that supported white supremacy, in essence granting to whites "the spoils of racial hierarchy" (Bridges, 2019). Initially, religious and class differences were more salient than race. But as wealthy planters embraced a system of chattel slavery and white settlers appropriated Indigenous land, they used race to justify their actions. Then the word "white," rather than "Christian" or "Englishman," began appearing in colonial statutes (Battalora, 2013; Kendi, 2016; Painter, 2010).

Race as a construct was personified in the "one-drop rule" that defined as Black anyone known to have even "one drop" of African ancestry, thus assigning people with mixed heritage to the racial group with the least social status. A one-eighth portion of African ancestry could determine one's status as Black, regardless of a seven-eighths white ancestry. Illustrating the illogic of race, states developed different rules of classification: from one drop in one state to one-quarter in another—so that a person could literally change races by crossing state lines (Roberts, 2011). Blood quantum as an indelible mark of enslavement ensured an ongoing supply of labor once the slave trade was abolished by extending in perpetuity to the offspring of enslaved people, including enslaved women sexually coerced by the men who owned them and the children born of these encounters.

Indigenous people were racialized differently, though no less harmfully. Forced relocation, starvation and disease eliminated scores of tribes. Federal policy terminated reservations and coerced Native people to assimilate, thus annihilating their cultural and social traditions. The Dawes Act (1880s) stripped over 90 million acres of tribal land from Indigenous people and sold it to non-Natives. In contrast to Blacks, who were marked by the tiniest drop of blood, tribes had to prove they had enough blood quantum to be considered Indian and therefore with rights to the land (Dunbar-Ortiz, 2014). This logic was used to drastically reduce the numbers of Indigenous people in order to justify seizure of their land (Deloria, 1982; Wolfe, 2006).

RACE AND CITIZENSHIP

Irrational fear, hostility and hatred toward refugees, immigrants and others deemed foreign, called *xenophobia*, is "a form of racism that has functioned alongside slavery, settler colonialism, conquest, segregation and white supremacy" (Lee, 2020). Xenophobia operated hand in hand with racism to define who was "American" and to restrict citizenship as properly belonging to white Americans. White Protestant settlers even tried to claim for themselves the birthright label of "Native" (i.e. real Americans) in opposition to Indigenous people and "foreign" immigrants (Lee, 2020). The plural term "racisms" underscores that groups were racialized differently (Hall, 1992; Reardon & Tallbear, 2012).

Race was tied to citizenship from the beginning. In 1790, Congress restricted naturalization (the ability to become a citizen) to immigrants who were "free white persons of good character" (Haney-López, 2006). (During the period of indentured servitude, not all whites were free or there would have been no need to add "free" to "white") (Painter, 2010). The Supreme Court Dred Scott Decision (1857) declared that people of African descent, whether slave or free, could *not* be American citizens, while Indigenous people were *only* eligible to become naturalized if they assimilated to white culture. African Americans and Indigenous people were ultimately allowed to become citizens, with the Fourteenth Amendment (1868) and Indian Citizenship Act (1924) respectively, but both groups continued to be barred from full participation in democratic society through Jim Crow segregation, poll taxes and other actions designed to prevent them from voting and partaking meaningfully in civic life. We can see these patterns persisting in present-day attempts to restrict voting and maintain inequalities baked into U.S. institutions and practices.

Mexican people living in the Southwest attained U.S. citizenship automatically at the end of the Mexican-American War when the Treaty of Guadalupe Hidalgo in 1848 ceded the land on which they were living to the U.S. Throughout the 19th and 20th centuries, Mexican Americans experienced Juan Crow segregation and restrictions on their ability to exercise citizenship rights, while U.S. employment practices, such as the Bracero Program, recruited and exploited workers from Mexico only to expel them when they were no longer needed.

Over the course of the 19th century, U.S. law and policy continued to rigidly codify and enforce racial lines in determining who could or could not be a citizen. Immigrants whose applications for citizenship were rejected because they were deemed "not white" took their claims to the courts. Two cases heard by the Supreme Court were *Takao Ozawa v. U.S.* (1922) and *U.S. v Bhagat Singh Thind* (1923). Ozawa had lived in the United States for 20 years when he applied for naturalization, but using the pseudo-scientific claim that he was part of the "Mongoloid race" and therefore not white, the court ruled him ineligible for citizenship (Haney-López, 2006). Using completely opposite logic, the court ruled against Thind, who would have been categorized as Aryan or Caucasian according to the same pseudo-science invoked in Ozawa, and argued that he "would not be considered white in the eyes of the common man."

The Chinese Exclusion Act of 1882, for the first time in U.S. history, barred an entire group based on national origin (Lee & Yung, 2010). Eventually, *all* Chinese residents (not just laborers) were required to have certificates of residence/identity cards, a precursor to "green cards," as proof of their right to live in the country (Lee, 2020). The Exclusion Act was renewed indefinitely, making it impossible for Chinese Americans living in the U.S. to reunite with families in China and prohibiting new Chinese immigrants from entering the country until the mid-20th century. Japanese immigrants who began to arrive in the U.S., mostly in California, were subjected to "alien" land laws that prohibited them from owning property and voting. During World War II, they were interned in camps and their property often confiscated by whites. The designation of Asians as "alien others" continues to affect how new Asian immigrants are treated today.

Descendants of European immigrants considered white today were not always socially accepted, but their economic and social experiences took a much different trajectory from Mexicans, Asians and others. Though granted citizenship, European immigrants at first faced social discrimination ("no Irish need apply") and were viewed as a threat to the social order. Considered less white than the northern European Protestants who preceded them, Irish, Italian and eastern European immigrants did eventually, if grudgingly, attain the advantages of whiteness (Brodkin, 1998; Jacobson, 1998). Religion also impacted the shading process: Catholic, Jewish or Orthodox Christian people were considered less white than their Protestant European predecessors, who came from British, German or Scandinavian stock. Class background likewise played a role (Brodkin, 1998). However, by the second and third generation, Irish, Italians, Greeks, Poles and Jews had gained social and economic mobility and gradually "became" white (Foner, 2005). This change in racial status occurred at the expense of their native languages, cultural traditions and ethnic identities in exchange for embracing mainstream white culture and gaining the advantages of whiteness.

Locking in the racial composition of the U.S. to a time when immigration was dominated by mostly Protestant northern and western Europeans, the Johnson-Reed Act of 1924 limited visas to 2% of the number of people from any given country living in the U.S. as of 1890. The racial intention was overtly stated by President Coolidge when he signed the bill, saying "America must be kept American" (Ngai, 2004). Those most impacted were from southern and eastern Europe and predominantly Jewish, Catholic and Eastern Orthodox, as well as immigrants from Asia. Not until 40 years later was the door to immigration reopened with the Immigration Act of 1965, a result of pressure from the civil rights movement. Arguing for its passage, Senator Fong of Hawaii compared immigration quotas to Jim Crow segregation that contradicted American ideals of equality. The act would make the country much more diverse.

Having an understanding of how and when the doors to immigration have opened and closed, and for which groups, explains current racial demographics and the politics around immigration, race and citizenship that continue today, as seen in recent attempts to ban Muslims and people from Mexico, Central America and Haiti from entering the country. Efforts at exclusion are intimately tied to racialized assumptions of who is "American" and conservative fears of an increasingly diverse racial landscape. People who say, "Slavery is long past and has nothing to do with me" or "I didn't take Indian land" or "My parents immigrated from Ireland or Italy and they worked hard and made it" fail to recognize that systems put in place in the past live on to undergird material and social advantage and disadvantage in the present.

The country is now at a pivotal moment. Estimates are that by 2054, whites will be less than half of the U.S. population. People of Color will increasingly comprise the nation's youth and working-age population, most of the growth in voters and much of the growth in consumers and the tax base. People under 18 are already majority People of Color, and in less than ten years, the majority of those under 30 will be so. An aging white population will increasingly depend on them for their economic contributions to programs like Medicare and Social Security, not to mention for the ideas and commitments to preserving the environment and reducing the impacts of climate change.

These demographics offer a moment to consider the dangers of zero-sum thinking and choices for current public policy. Investing now in quality education and training, health care, safe housing and economic opportunity and reducing poverty and discrimination could be a lifeline to a secure future for all Americans. Eradicating racism and other forms of discrimination could unleash the potential of our diverse youth, including white youth, to thrive, provide support for an aging population and strengthen democracy and the economy. Continuing racial strife, white supremacist agitation, voter suppression and government gridlock, on the other hand, will likely lead to an increasingly dysfunctional government, divided populace and national decline.

REGULATING THE COLOR LINE

Although a biracial and multiracial population has existed from the beginning of the country, it has been concealed by monoracial categories that maintain white dominance (Hamako, 2014). For example, the previously discussed one-drop rule defined as Black those who might now call themselves biracial or multiracial. Multiracial people differ in their experiences and attitudes, depending on the races that make up their background, how they see themselves and how the world sees them (Wijeyesinghe & Jackson, 2012). In 2015, the majority of multiracial adults with a Black background reported that others mostly view them as Black or African American and that their experiences and social interactions led them to align with the Black community. Multiracial and biracial white/Asian adults say they feel more closely connected to whites than to Asians. Among biracial adults who are white and American Indian, only 22% say they have a lot in common with American Indians, whereas 61% say they have a lot in common with whites (Parker, Morin, Horowitz, Lopez and Rohal, 2015). The different racialized experiences and orientations of people who define themselves or are defined by others as multiracial are reflected in tensions within the multiracial movement over how to deal with racism and monoracism (Hamako, 2014).

Monoracism places value on single-race narratives and experiences (Johnston & Nadal, 2010), often deeming multiracial or multiethnic narratives as "inauthentic." Many job and college applications offer the option to select "two or more races" but not to select "multiracial" as a category (Townsend, Marcus, & Bergseiker, 2009). Research that fails to recognize multiracial identities reinforces one-dimensional racial narratives by, for example, not exploring why biracial men and women are victimized by sexual assault more than other intersecting groups of race and gender (Johnston-Guerrero, Wijeyesinghe, & Daniel, 2021). Such oversights contribute to erasing the experiences of the multicultural population and prevent them from receiving recognition and support.

Anti-Black racism is a specific form of racism directed toward Black people, historically and in the present. It includes systematic overt and covert racism experienced by people of African descent as well as the unethical disregard seen in cases of police and civilian brutality against Black bodies that historically included lynching and other forms of targeted violence. Activists argue the need to recognize the specific ways racism affects different communities. More specificity could prevent oversimplification and help tailor actions to challenge racism against Black, Indigenous and other groups of color in different forms and contexts. Acknowledging differing experiences of racism can also support group solidarity.

Some group identities may be racial or ethnic depending on context, or *ethno-race* (Goldberg, 1992). Ethno-race distinguishes racism based on colorism, physical appearance, culture and/or nativism. *Colorism* separates and discriminates based on skin tone, as in the case of police who are more likely to arrest darker- over lighter-skinned suspects (Branigan, Wildeman, Freese, & Kiefe, 2017) or when ethnic and racialized groups differentiate among themselves based on lightness of skin. *Physical appearance* discriminates based on body form, eye shape, hair type, height or facial features, favoring those typical of northern Europeans, as in advertisers and directors who standardize models or actors with such features. Racism based on *culture* is evident when cultures that are not European are portrayed as less evolved or unable to assimilate, as in negative or stereotyped portrayals of African or Indigenous cultures as uncivilized or Asian cultures as inscrutable or alien. *Nativism* is reflected when Asian Americans, Arab Americans and Muslim Americans are portrayed as alien and a subversive threat to "American" identity and cohesion.

Some suggest that the U.S. is moving toward a system that would look more like the racial order in Latin America or the Caribbean where race conflict is buffered by an intermediate group based on class and color gradations (Bonilla-Silva, 2004). In a tri-racial system, intermarriage with whites and economic mobility for some groups of Asians and Latinx people would move them to an honorary white category (a connection that does not hold true in all situations where race and relative economic success are mediated by religion, gender and sexuality, age or disability). The "collective Black" would keep African Americans and dark-skinned Latinx people at the bottom. In these scenarios, the color line and the determination of position and mobility continue to be regulated by the dominant white group to maintain its power.

LEVELS AND TYPES OF RACISM

The historical legacies detailed above provide important information for understanding and changing the racial system that we have inherited and that shapes our world today. In the next section, we examine how racism is reproduced in each generation as people are socialized into the systems that sustain it. We trace the individual and institutional processes through which racism is maintained, reproduced and passed along. Understanding these processes can help us identify effective places to intervene to interrupt racism and move toward racial justice in our individual interactions and institutional patterns.

RACISM IN INDIVIDUAL AND INTERPERSONAL INTERACTIONS

People from all racialized groups in the United States internalize messages about their own group as well as other social groups. This socialization process is reinforced through the major institutions and broader cultural patterns in our society, as well as through individual and interpersonal interactions (see Cycle of Socialization: Racism). When individuals express or act on racist ideas and assumptions, they are exhibiting *individual/interpersonal racism*. Racism tends to be conceptualized as attitudes and behaviors that are intentionally meant to harm individuals or groups of color or treat them as inferior and less entitled to society's benefits. Such attitudes and behaviors are expressions of *overt racism*, such as when People of Color are called racial epithets or when immigrants (or those perceived to be immigrants) are told, "Go back to where you came from." Emails with explicit racist jokes or images, nooses hung on doors or statements that Black and brown people don't deserve government benefits are other examples of overt racism.

In contrast, *covert racism* is hidden and unacknowledged and includes actions by individuals who may honestly believe they are not racist. Because it is typically not conscious, covert racism is frequently more difficult to identify and address. For example, a white person who clutches personal belongings in the presence of Black men, or who expresses amazement that an immigrant from Latin America or Asia speaks "good" English, may be exhibiting covert racism. Covert racism is also described through terms such as *implicit bias*, which describes unconscious associations or stereotypes, such as whites associating criminality with Black men without realizing they are doing so. Though implicit bias is a useful concept for addressing covert racism, we are leery of research that focuses on bias in the brain rather than in our history and social practices (Kahn, 2018).

Actual intent is not necessary to lead to racist outcomes. People from any racial group can end up supporting racism by simply going along with business as usual. For example, when white people go along with racist jokes or put-downs either to fit in or because they fear being ostracized if they speak up, they are supporting racism by doing nothing to interrupt it. When an Asian American person silently endures racist jokes told by a white supervisor or coworkers, or participates in putting down people from their own or other subordinated racial groups, because they fear they could lose status or even their job, they are supporting the ongoing system of racism. In both situations there is a potential cost to intervening and a need for proactive steps if racist patterns and practices are to be undone.

The term *microaggressions* describes daily verbal, behavioral and environmental indignities, intentional or not, that convey hostile, derogatory or negative racial slights and insults toward a targeted individual or group (Sue, 2010). While "micro" may be interpreted as minor or insignificant, it is meant to convey everyday suffering that has been normalized and the tangible ways racism occurs in everyday interactions (Huber & Solórzano, 2015; Solórzano, 2020). Individual microaggressions occur when white people minimize reports of racism by People of Color, with comments such as "I'm sure that isn't what they meant" or "You are reading too much into this," and fail to recognize such experiences are not simply a one-off but occur over and over across a lifetime. Examples include the commonplace experience of Black individuals being ignored by a sales clerk or followed in a store by security guards; Black and Latinx people having to listen to white people say "the most qualified person should get the job," as if affirmative action prevents qualified applicants;

or Latinx and Asian Americans being complimented for speaking "good English" (Sue, Lin, Torino, Capodiluco, & Rivera, 2009).

Marginalization and exclusion occur when People of Color are not invited to social events or into work groups and social clubs or when white people avoid sitting next to them in public places. Questioning a Person of Color's cultural authenticity or "Americanness" is another form of microaggression—for example, when minoritized people are ridiculed for eating foods with spices unfamiliar to those in the dominant group (Waters, 2009) or are assumed to be from somewhere else or less patriotic and not "real" Americans (Xu & Lee, 2013; Tuan, 2001). Indigenous people experience microaggressions when their authenticity is questioned by non-Indigenous people who ask how much "Indian" blood is in their lineage or who romanticize and commodify Native cultural items and practices. Biracial and multiracial people face monoracism and marginalization when their life experiences are not acknowledged in discussions of race and racism or they are forced to choose one racial identity (Johnston & Nadal, 2010). The constant burden microaggressions place on People of Color takes a cumulative, harmful psychological, physiological and academic toll (Solórzano, Ceja, & Yosso, 2000; Kohli & Solórzano, 2012).

Macroaggressions, or microaggressions at institutional or environmental levels, are organization-level arrangements that communicate negative or hostile messages to People of Color (Bridges, 2019). The connection between microaggressions and institutionalized racism is important because they link to large-scale racial stratification and the persistence of racial disparities in education, employment and other areas. Assumptions that someone is less intelligent or more dangerous have material consequences in hiring discrimination and higher incidences of arrest, incarceration and death or injury at the hands of police. Such dangers were evidenced in the uptick of hate crimes against Asians that followed government leaders referring to COVID-19 as the "China flu" (Bardella, 2021).

We all breathe in the racism in our environment, with psychic effects for everyone. For racially minoritized people, the stress of dealing with microaggressions leads to psychological (frustration, shock, anger, anxiety, depression) and physiological (high blood pressure, insomnia) responses, sometimes called *racial battle fatigue* (Smith, Hung & Franklin, 2011). When people from racially minoritized groups consciously or unconsciously believe and/or act on negative stereotypes about themselves and their group, they may be experiencing *internalized racism* (Williams, 2011). For example, an African American woman who is repeatedly passed over for promotion may blame herself for not working harder or downplay her capacities, instead of considering the possibility that an insider white network from which she is excluded may be the cause. A Latinx person who avoids speaking their native language or eating ethnic food to fit in or make white peers more comfortable may be exhibiting internalized racism. Such negative messages can be psychically debilitating and isolating (Joseph & Williams, 2008; Williams, 2011). White people who, consciously or unconsciously, believe or act on assumptions that they and their group are more capable or entitled than People of Color are likely displaying *internalized dominance*. For example, a white man who ignores or speaks over colleagues of color or a white woman who thinks she can "fix" or "help" a community of color without listening to, learning from and collaborating with the people from that community are exhibiting internalized dominance.

RACISM AT CULTURAL AND INSTITUTIONAL LEVELS

Prejudice and discrimination based on the idea that some cultures are superior to others, or that various cultures are fundamentally incompatible, demonstrate *cultural racism*. Cultural racism is reflected in normative assumptions such as defining "professionalism" by white middle-class norms of dress, hair style and communication patterns or assuming that

European philosophies of life, standards of beauty, normality, deviance and perspectives on time are superior. Assertions that Muslims are unassimilable in the U.S. and thus should be banned from entering the country, school and sports policies that prohibit hairstyles such as dreadlocks and non-Native people who claim Native American heritage but know nothing about the specific history and culture and have no present-day interaction with them are other examples of cultural racism.

Another form of cultural racism is *linguicism* or *language domination* (Dardar & Uriarte, 2013). Linguicism reflects dominant attitudes and beliefs about the value and relative ranking of languages, accents and ways of speaking and is also linked to color and class. For example, French and Castilian Spanish (spoken by light-skinned people) are seen as high-status languages, while Spanish spoken by Mexicans, Dominicans and Puerto Ricans and French Creole spoken by Haitians are demeaned. English-only policies that normalize English as "standard" stigmatize other languages and the people who speak them and often link to nativism and anti-immigrant racism. Linguistic profiling, as with visual racial profiling, can have negative consequences for those whose accent or dialect is perceived as undesirable (Baugh, 2003) and is evidenced in cases where applicants who "sound Black" or speak with a Spanish or Asian accent are denied housing or employment (Subtirelu, 2015). Linguistic profiling that takes place over the phone or in written correspondence is often difficult to prosecute because it is subtle; "Not following up by calling back or mailing material is just as malicious as saying, 'I won't give you insurance because you're Black or Mexican'" (Baugh, 2003, p. 160).

Racism is *institutionalized* when policies, laws, rules, norms and customs enacted by organizations and social institutions advantage whites as a group and disadvantage groups of color, whether by design or by effect. For example, a criminal justice system that enacts racially disproportionate stop-and-frisk policies results in higher incarceration rates of Black and brown people (Alexander, 2012) while treating white violations less harshly. Laws that prevent undocumented workers and immigrants from accessing health care or public services for which they pay taxes is another example. More often than not, racially disparate impacts result from institutionalized policies and practices that don't mention race at all, such as the structured inequality of a school funding system based on state property taxes that benefit wealthier (whiter) communities and harm poorer (brown and Black) communities. Violence and discrimination typical of the Jim Crow era—from lynching to legally sanctioned segregation in housing, schooling and transportation—are examples of *overt institutional racism*. Today, overt institutionalized racism can be seen in attempts by state legislatures to pass laws designed to suppress the voting rights of People of Color (Abrams, 2020). *Covert institutional racism* is often disguised with language that downplays clearly racial disproportionate outcomes by invoking "non-racial" explanations that are more acceptable in the broader society (Bonilla-Silva, 2013; Coates, 2008). Examples include job descriptions that discourage diverse candidates from applying, such as requiring that applicants be "native English speakers" and excluding those who speak English as a second language, or rules about "appropriate" hair and dress that are based on white norms.

THE WEB OF RACISM

INTERLOCKING INSTITUTIONS, UNEQUAL OPPORTUNITIES AND OUTCOMES

While racism impacts all institutions, we focus on the particular racial dynamics in seven mutually reinforcing systems: Housing, education, the labor market, the criminal justice system, the media, politics and health care (see Figure 5.1). Racial differences in opportunities and outcomes in these institutions are particularly critical to a person's (and group's) social, economic and political standing in society. Despite civil rights advances and purportedly more liberal attitudes, race serves as a reliable predictor of racially unequal levels of access, participation and success in these institutions. Frye's (1983) birdcage metaphor captures the systemic structure of oppression by shifting our focus beyond a single wire to look at the interlocking apparatus that restricts those trapped within the cage. The diagram in Figure 5.1 illustrates how these systems intersect to create racially unequal opportunities and outcomes in our society.

HOUSING

Where one lives plays a critical role in access to quality education, decent jobs, adequate public transportation, health and economic well-being. Home ownership is the major way that middle-class families accumulate wealth and pass it on to the next generation (Pfeffer & Killewald, 2019). In 2019, the typical white family had eight times the wealth of the typical Black family and five times the wealth of the typical Latinx family (Aladangady & Ford, 2021). This legacy of wealth disparity was underwritten by generations of public policy decisions that supported, justified and enforced segregation and created the racial landscape in which we live today (Williams, 2017). Racial prejudice and discrimination on the part of individuals—politicians, officials, loan officers, developers and individuals who seek to live in homogeneous white communities—also played an important part.

At the systemic/institutional level, racially segregated housing was produced and enforced by discriminatory Federal Housing Administration (FHA) policies and real estate and mortgage lending practices that determined who could live where and in what type of housing. These practices included *redlining* (denying financial and other services to residents of certain areas based on their race or ethnicity in determining eligibility for FHA housing loans), *racial zoning* (ordinances that prevented racial and ethnic minorities from

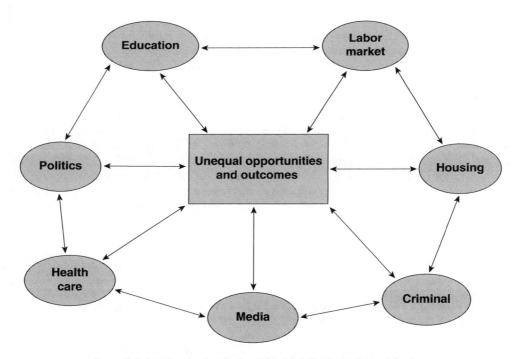

Figure 5.1 Interlocking Institutional/Societal Manifestations of Racism

moving into white neighborhoods) and *restrictive covenants* (that prevented white home-owners from selling to Black families). Realtors deliberately incited white fear of reduced property values if Black families moved into their neighborhoods so that whites would sell low (*blockbusting*). Realtors could then profit by selling high to Black families who were desperate for access to decent housing (Rothstein, 2014).

New Deal housing policies also subsidized white-only suburban development along-side the parallel destruction of Black neighborhoods through *eminent domain*, which enabled confiscation of Black-owned properties for urban renewal projects that benefited white developers. Such practices over the past 70 years excluded People of Color at all socio-economic levels from significant home ownership while benefiting white people by comparison. Disparities in homeownership rates, home equity and neighborhood values contribute substantially to the wealth gap between whites and Black and Latinx people. In addition to inequitable housing practices, African Americans, Indigenous people, Latinx people and poor and working-class people, from Standing Rock to Flint, live in over-polluted and toxic environments most affected by climate change (Johansen, 2020).

Subprime loans were designed to be sold to borrowers with lower credit scores, who were considered to be riskier and so were charged higher interest rates and fees. In the early 1990s, subprime loans were aggressively and deceptively marketed in Black neigh-borhoods, purportedly to enable more families to get into the housing market. All too often these loans were marketed to *existing* homeowners who could have qualified for less expensive loans. By the end of the decade, the share of mortgages that were subprime nearly doubled—to half of the refinance loans in majority Black neighborhoods. Between 2004 and 2008, Black and Latinx homeowners with good credit scores were three times as likely as whites with similar credit scores to have higher-rate mortgages. High fees and deceptive clauses contributed to foreclosures that reduced the wealth of the median Black family by more than two-thirds. While the early victims of predatory lending were dispro-portionately Black, lenders who got away with marketing subprime mortgages to them turned to selling to white homeowners too. In a sense, Black victims were the canary in the coal mine. Ultimately, the subprime mortgage debacle affected the entire country, nearly toppling the economy and causing $19.2 trillion in lost household wealth and eight million lost jobs (McGhee, 2021). Then the government bailed out the banks to prevent further foreclosures but did little for the homeowners who lost their homes.

The COVID pandemic further compounded the loss of generational wealth through rising disparities in housing. Black and Latinx families reported higher eviction rates and foreclosures, mortgage and rent delinquency, unanticipated moves and other forms of hard-ship (Chun & Grinstein-Weiss, 2020). In the midst of rapidly rising housing disparities, the Department of Housing and Urban Development (HUD) curtailed the FHA "disparate impact" policy that combats housing discrimination. The health, racial and economic crises combined to erase gains and return to a disparity between white and Black homeownership comparable to that of 1890 (Ray, Perry, Harshbarger & Elizondo, 2021).

Practical programs and regulatory reforms can begin to address the aforementioned problems. Interventions such as the CARES (Coronavirus Aid Relief and Economic Secu-rity) Act and moratoriums in rents and mortgages as well as student loans offer short-term relief. Longer-term remedies include advocating policies that encourage mixed-income, integrated neighborhoods and enforcing policies that monitor housing discrimination. Federal and state efforts can hold landlords accountable for discriminatory practices such as turning away tenants whose rent is subsidized. Outer-ring suburbs could be required to repeal zoning ordinances that prohibit construction of affordable housing and instead accommodate a "fair share" of low-income populations, as New Jersey has attempted to do (Rothstein, 2017). Stricter enforcement of anti-discrimination laws in housing would increase the ability of People of Color to buy homes in higher-value neighborhoods where they can get the same return on their investment as white homeowners. In a major victory for housing justice, the Supreme Court in June 2015 ruled that policies that segregate minorities in poor neighborhoods, even if they do so unintentionally, violate the Fair Housing Act.

HEALTH-CARE SYSTEM

Racial inequities in access to quality health care also impact participation in education, the labor force and other aspects of public life. Communities of color experience health disparities compared to white communities even when socio-economic status and education levels are controlled. For example, African Americans have the highest cancer rates and deaths from cancer (American Cancer Society, 2021), are twice as likely as whites to suffer from diabetes and represent almost half of HIV-infected persons, with Latinx people representing 86% of children infected with HIV (HIV.gov, 2019). African American women college graduates have a higher infant mortality rate than white women who drop out of high school (Fishman, Hummer, Sierra, Hargrove, Powers, & Rogers, 2020). Recent Latinx immigrants are among the healthiest ethnic groups in the United States, but their health falls to the bottom within five years of immigrating, a phenomenon referred to as the *Latino Paradox* (Campbell, Garcia, Granillo, & Chavez, 2012).

Multiple factors contribute to these disparities. Neighborhoods that are predominantly Latinx and Black have been labeled *food deserts*, with an overabundance of fast-food chains and liquor stores and little access to healthy food. Residents of food deserts are more likely to die at an earlier age due to heart disease and high blood pressure (Dutko, Ver Ploeg, & Farrigan, 2012). *Environmental racism* means that Black and Latinx neighborhoods are less likely to have green space, clean air and recreational facilities where it is safe for children to play and more than twice as likely to have toxic facilities such as sewage plants, dump and disposal sites and transportation depots. Reservations face toxic dumps and reduced life expectancy as well as higher rates for Indigenous people in many categories of preventable illness, including chronic liver disease and cirrhosis, diabetes and chronic lower respiratory diseases (Smith, n.d.).

Health disparities fuel the distrust People of Color have historically held toward the fields of mental health and medicine. For Indigenous people the effects of colonization, forced segregation on reservations and intergenerational trauma from the loss of ancestral ties to land, culture and way of life have a profound impact on health. More than one in five Native Americans report experiencing discrimination in clinical encounters, while 15% avoid seeking health care due to anticipated discrimination (Findling, Casey, Fryberg, Hafner, Blendon, Benson, Sayde, & Miller, 2019). African American distrust of the medical profession results from racialized trauma and a history of egregious medical experiments, distorted diagnoses and overall failure to humanize their experiences (Hoberman, 2012; Menakem, 2017). Undocumented individuals are less likely to seek medical assistance or mental health resources for fear of deportation and are vulnerable to sexual assault and abuse (Ornelas, Yamanis, & Ruiz, 2020).

The COVID pandemic further heightened health disparities for Black, Indigenous and Latinx communities who had higher COVID-19 mortality rates, with Indigenous and Black people more than two and a half times more likely to be infected and almost twice as likely to die than whites (CDC, 2019). Exacerbating disproportionate infection and mortality rates, Black and Latinx people were overrepresented as essential workers, more likely to rely on public transportation that increased their exposure to the virus, more affected by pre-existing health conditions, hit hardest by job loss in industries in which they work and more likely to live in smaller, often intergenerational, living spaces (Gould, Perez, & Wilson, 2020). Finally, historic mistrust of the health-care system led to lower vaccination rates in these populations (Kaiser Family Foundation, 2021).

Race and Health, a collective of activists, artists, academics, policy makers and grass-roots organizations, promotes interventions that challenge racism in health and promote health equity (raceandhealth.org). Improving the capacity and number of providers in underserved communities who understand health disparities and their causes can ensure better responses and earlier interventions. Equally important is expanding health insurance coverage to provide equal access to adequate health care. Educating physicians, nurses and other health-care workers about the history of racism in the profession and training them in anti-bias awareness is another important step. Finally, addressing environmental racism and its impacts is critical for addressing the many negative health outcomes for communities of color. Do Something is an organization of young activists working at the intersection of environmental and racial justice (dosomething.org).

ECONOMIC AND LABOR SYSTEM

The history of the U.S. racialized economic system undergirds material problems experienced today by racially minoritized people and a downward pressure on income for all working-class people. Economically depressed Indigenous communities suffer from dispossession, broken commitments by the federal government, ongoing underinvestment and the highest poverty and unemployment rates and lowest wealth of any group in the country (Muhammed, Tec, & Ramirez, 2019). Despite the major contributions of unpaid, enslaved Black laborers to building the wealth of the country, African American communities never fully recovered from destitution and broken promises of land (40 acres and a mule) that followed Emancipation. White mob violence destroyed wealth created in Black communities such as Tulsa and Rosewood while convict-leasing and sharecropping, 100 years of legal Jim Crow segregation, occupational segregation and exclusion from better-paying jobs stripped wealth away (Weller, 2019). Since the Bracero Program that brought Mexican guest workers to the U.S. for seasonal agricultural work, Latinx workers face xenophobia; discrimination and segregation into seasonal, low-paid farm and construction work; and cyclical unemployment (Zamarippa & Roque, 2021). A racially stratified economic and labor system has also exacted a price from white workers where racial division undermines unions and depresses the pay and working conditions for all (Chui, Prince, & Stewart, 2021).

High levels of poverty in the wealthiest nation on earth is one consequence of a racially stratified system. Black, Latinx and Native Americans are nearly twice as likely to be poor as whites, disparities especially pronounced among children, women, people with disabilities and the elderly (Children's Defense Fund, 2021; Giannarelli, Wheaton, & Shantz, 2021). One of the main causes of poverty is unemployment and underemployment, highest for Black, Latinx, American Indian and Alaska Native workers (U.S. Bureau of Labor Statistics, 2019). The Covid pandemic was devastating for all workers, but racism and economic inequity had particularly negative repercussions for workers of color who were overrepresented as frontline essential workers, less likely to be able to work from home and more likely to suffer job loss, evictions and other financial hardships (Gould, Perez, & Wilson, 2020). Black, Latinx and Asian small businesses were unequally impacted as well (Fairlie, 2020).

Biased hiring practices compound disadvantages for applicants of color (Pedulla, 2020). One study showed that applicants with common Black names on their resumes were 50% less likely to get an interview than applicants with common white names even though the resumes were identical. Another study showed that whites with a criminal history had an equal or better chance of employment than non-criminal Black applicants. Even the most highly educated Black workers are less likely to be employed than their white counterparts and less likely to be in a job consistent with their level of education (Williams & Wilson, 2019).

Racially homogeneous social networks and personal connections disproportionately benefit whites and skew an occupational picture where whites dominate the highest-paying and People of Color the lowest-paying categories. In 2020, whites held over three-quarters of the highest-paying jobs in management, professional and related occupations (U.S. Bureau of Labor Statistics, 2022). Asian men (particularly Asian Indian, Filipino, Taiwanese and Japanese) are more likely to be in high-income professional jobs. By contrast, Black and Latinx workers and some groups of Asian Americans (particularly Hmong, Bangladeshi, Samoan and Thai) were concentrated in low-wage service jobs (Equitable Growth, 2020). Latino men were more represented in agriculture and grounds maintenance and Black men as bus drivers and security guards. Combined racial and gender bias resulted in Latina and Black women predominant as maids and housekeepers, nursing and home health care and Asian women as manicurists, pedicurists and cosmetologists (Pedulla, 2018; Weller, 2019).

Biased hiring and segregated employment have harsh material consequences for workers and their families. The median Black household earned just 61 cents and the median Latinx household 74 cents for every dollar the median white household earned (Wilson, 2020). At all levels, other than doctorate/first-professional, the median income for Black and Latino males was lower than white males, and white females who completed high school, some college or an associate's degree had a higher median income than Black and Latina females with similar education (National Center for Educational Statistics, 2021). Black and Latinx workers are not only paid less but also are more likely to be employed in jobs that do not provide health coverage, paid leave and retirement plans (Demos, 2015). Finally, workers of color are often forced to find affordable housing in segregated communities farther away from job sites and rely on substandard public transportation that makes commuting longer and more costly (Blumenberg & Pierce, 2017).

Access to decent-paying jobs determines whether one can buy a home, accumulate wealth and improve life chances for the next generation. Wealth provides the ability to deal with disruptions to household disposable income (such as unexpected medical expenses or periods of unemployment) as well as access to housing, good public schools and postsecondary education. In 2019, white household income was $76,057 compared to $46,073 Black and $56,113 Latinx households, a racial pay gap that is the largest contributor to the racial wealth gap. Despite civil rights legislation, the wealth gap has not changed in half a century, with white wealth more than ten times that of Black wealth (McIntosh, Moss, Nunn, & Shambaugh, 2020). Illustrating the zero-sum fallacy, the persistent racial wealth gap places a burden on the economic health of society as a whole. Wage stagnation, low-paying jobs and bleak prospects for the future as a result of racism affect the vast majority of income earners, including most white workers (Brown, 2021). One report estimates racism costs between $2,900–$4,300 per person, and closing the racial wealth gap would increase GDP by 4%–6% by 2028 (Noel, Pinder, Stuart, & Wright, 2019).

Enforcement of anti-discrimination laws in hiring, equalizing pay differentials and protecting the rights of immigrant workers would help. A federal jobs program, similar to the New Deal, would provide improved infrastructure, child and elder care and cultural enrichment for all. Raising the minimum wage boosts incomes of lower-paid Black and Latinx workers, as well as white workers. Making it easier to form unions helps all workers, since union membership increases employment benefits such as health coverage and retirement plans (Haney-López, 2019). Tax code reform and increasing taxes on the top 1% would directly decrease the racial wealth disparity by reducing highly concentrated wealth held almost exclusively by whites (Brown, 2021). Exploitative wealth could be tracked to expose businesses and universities built on stolen Indigenous land or profits from enslavement, states that profited from convict leasing and banks that enriched themselves by defrauding Black homeowners (Coates, 2014; Williamson, 2020). Other creative restitution proposals include baby bonds and student loan forgiveness (Darity & Mullen, 2020; Hamilton & Darity, 2010; Ray & Perry, 2020).

EDUCATIONAL SYSTEMS

The COVID pandemic exposed deeply entrenched inequities in education and provided an opportunity to reimagine a system that fails too many. While some K–12 schools made valiant efforts to provide necessary computer, technological and accessibility accommodations for students who needed them, the gap between well-resourced and poorly resourced schools widened even further. There was increased recognition of problems with Wi-Fi accessibility in rural communities and cities overrepresented by People of Color where digital inequities persist, but not nearly enough to rectify these gaps. Alternative approaches in K–16 education, such as eliminating standardized tests from admissions in higher education, showed that necessary reforms are possible (Flaherty, 2020; Galperin, Wyatt, & Le, 2020), but the gaps persist and in many places increased.

Segregated housing preserves a system of educational apartheid that filters educational resources and opportunities to white areas with higher property taxes to pay for good schools, while divesting and marginalizing low-income and poor neighborhood residents where property taxes and financial resources for schools are significantly less. Under-resourced segregated schools force students of color to focus time and energy simply surviving (Love, 2019). Court cases to end racial segregation (*Brown v. Board of Education*), provide bilingual education (*Lau v. Nichols*) and include students with disabilities (Individuals with Disabilities Education Act, or IDEA) had brief periods of success during the 1970s and early 1980s. Since then, backlash to busing, bilingual schooling and integration has rolled back progress. Black students are now six times more likely than white students to attend high-poverty schools, and Latinx students face the triple segregation of race, poverty and language (Ibid). Market-driven "reforms" and charter schools, despite little improvement for students of color, exacerbate segregation and inequality, while segregated neighborhood, school and friendship networks and work settings contribute to white ignorance about People of Color that often leads them to channel resentment toward People of Color rather than systems that are failing most people (Anderson, 2018; Love, 2019; McGhee, 2021; Metzl, 2019).

Students in racially segregated schools also face less rigorous curriculum and access to highly qualified teachers, fewer Advanced Placement courses and inadequate information about financial aid, college opportunities and avenues to well-paying careers. While the student population is increasingly racially and linguistically diverse, the teaching force remains overwhelmingly white and monolingual (Love, 2019). Teachers less knowledgeable about students' families and communities are typically less aware of the challenges of racism their students face. Such social and cultural disconnects often manifest in disciplinary and zero-tolerance policies that treat Black and Latinx students more harshly, contributing to school-to-confinement pathways. While much of pipeline discourse is centered on Black males, the "misogynoir" that characterizes the unique experiences of Black females is often lost (Bailey, 2021). Native American, African American and Latina cisgender and trans females experience surveillance, dress codes and policing of heteronormative culture that lead to higher suspension and detention (Morris, 2012). It is well documented that working-class Latinx, Native American and African American students are overrepresented in special education programs (National Center for Learning Disabilities, 2020). While appropriate support to meet educational needs is essential, students in these populations are too often mislabeled. Immigrants in high-poverty, segregated neighborhoods show declining educational attainment in each succeeding generation, replicating how decades of racism have dampened educational aspirations for African Americans, Native Americans, Puerto Ricans and Mexican Chicano/as (Foner, 2005).

Higher education shows similar disparities. Students from top income brackets with low test scores still have a 71% likelihood of graduating from college and finding employment, compared to 31% for students with the highest scores but lowest income, illustrating the intergenerational reproduction of white privilege (Carnevale, Fasules, Quinn, & Campbell, 2019). Notwithstanding their overall increase in higher education, African Americans show lower persistence rates, are least likely to attend highly selective schools and accrue the highest debt among other racial and ethnic groups. The gender gap is most extreme where Black women represent 62.2% of Black undergraduates and 70.2% of Black graduate students (Espinosa, Turk, Taylor, & Chessman, 2019). Black and Latinx students are overrepresented in community colleges and face poorer odds of successfully transferring and completing a degree at a four-year institution. A larger percentage of white students graduate in five years than Black and Latinx students from predominantly white institutions, even where they have comparable levels of college readiness and test scores (Carnevale & Strohl, 2013). Affirmative programs meant to redress disproportionate college attendance have been challenged in state legislatures and the courts, with nine states legislating anti–affirmative action policies in favor of "race-neutral policies" (DeSilver, 2014). Historically Black colleges and universities (HBCUs) and tribal colleges that serve minority students are severely underfunded (Espinosa, Turk, Taylor, & Chessman, 2019).

The psychological toll from the stresses of racism, microaggressions and stereotyping that face students of color on campuses has been labeled *racial battle fatigue* (Fasching-Varner, Albert, Mitchell, & Allen, 2015). Black, Latinx, Native American and undocumented youth who internalize negative stereotypes and low expectations for academic achievement dampen their performance (Steele, 2010), while Asian-American and Asian youth are often marginalized through a double-edged, "model minority" stereotype that pressures them to perform as super minorities and not seek support when needed (Sakamoto, Takei, & Woo, 2012; Teranishi, 2012; Tuan, 2001). When individual members of one social group embrace "positive" stereotypes of their group in order to avoid negative stereotypes applied to other groups, they may play into racial hierarchy and be used by the dominant white group to discredit claims of injustice by African Americans and others who demand social equality (Kim, 1999).

Faculty of color are underrepresented and often tokenized and expected to carry the double burden of tending to institutional problems around diversity and responding to students of color while having the same academic workload as white peers. They, too, face racial battle fatigue (see Chapter 12: Critical Self-Knowledge). While the racial and ethnic makeup of students in higher education has become more diverse, white college faculty, staff and administrators remain nearly three-quarters of the full-time faculty (AACU, 2019).

The gathering of hate groups at the University of Virginia (UVA) in Charlottesville evoked painful reminders of terror when tiki torches, khakis, polo shirts and unapologetically hoodless white nationalists replaced burning crosses and anonymous white hoods of the past. Media focused on hate groups, but less discussed was the unpaid African labor that helped build the university, an entanglement with slavery that was not unique to UVA.

As this history has come to light, multiracial coalitions of students and faculty mobilized for reparative justice. Brown, Georgetown and Princeton, among others, have acknowledged benefitting from slavery and created policies to provide restitution, such as changing building names, eradicating statues and earmarking scholarships and other tuition-support measures (Harris, 2021).

While educational institutions replicate racism in the larger society, they also provide spaces where students can develop knowledge and skills to understand and challenge racism. In several states, secondary schools that focus on cultural and ethnic empowerment have a proven track record of creating access to college. The National Congress of American Indians works to create counternarratives that combat erasure of Indigenous people and cultures in K–12 education. As places that have historically inspired agitation for social change, schools provide opportunities for students to form cross-racial coalitions to work for equality and inclusion. Academic courses offer valuable frameworks for helping students understand present realities in historical context and identify steps to address them on campus and in the larger society.

CRIMINAL JUSTICE/POLICING SYSTEMS

Racial discrimination, implicit bias and prejudice deeply affect the criminal justice system in areas such as profiling, sentencing, access to adequate legal representation, incarceration and parole (Eberhardt, 2019; Banaji & Greenwald, 2016; The Sentencing Project, 2014). The Equal Justice Initiative has exposed racial injustice within the criminal justice system created through targeted surveillance and disproportionate imprisonment of Black and Latinx people. Federal, state and city policies, such as the war on drugs, three strikes, broken windows and the criminalization of addiction and poverty, disproportionately affect working-class Black and Latinx communities (Alexander, 2012; Hill, 2016). While declining imprisonment rates over the past 30 years for all racial groups are promising, the number of imprisoned Black men is still six times that of white men. Black and Latina females are more likely to be imprisoned than white women (Bureau of Justice, 2019).

In the wake of the police killings of George Floyd, Breonna Taylor, Michael Brown, Andre Hill, Daunte Wright, Sandra Bland, Tony McDade, Philando Castile, Ma'Khia Bryant and too many others, activists and scholars took to the streets, the workplace and classrooms to call attention to the violence of anti-Black racism and the devaluation of Black lives. Black distrust of law enforcement runs deep throughout U.S. history, a result of the trauma they experienced from slave patrols that empowered white civilians to capture and return people who escaped, to Black Codes after slavery ended that allowed whites to arrest Black men on trumped-up charges and send them into forced labor, to Klan members (many with badges) who terrorized Black communities. A white supremacist presence that still exists in many police forces, disparate treatment in the criminal justice system and mass incarceration and its effects have been devastating for Black communities. Black men, from Harvard professors to teenagers in hoodies, have been treated with lethal suspicion. Compounding these injuries, many social scientists then interpreted the number of Black people in jail to mean they were "prone to criminality" (Muhammed, 2010).

Black and Indigenous women, cisgender and transgender, have been murdered by both civilians and police, with few attempts to solve these murders (Finoh & Sankofa, 2019; Neely, 2015; Indian Law Resource Center, n.d.; Urban Indian Health Institute, n.d.). Hate crimes committed on the basis of race/ethnicity, immigration status, national origin and religion have steadily increased since the mid-1980s, spiking after the attacks of September 11, 2001, and again after the COVID pandemic, which right-wing politicians attributed to Asians (Bardella, 2021).

Confidence in the likelihood of fair treatment by law enforcement is low for many groups of color (only 36% of Blacks report confidence in fair treatment compared to 71% of whites; Drake, 2015), while Asian Americans are least likely to report hate incidents in part due to mistrust that justice will be served (Lee & Ramakrishnan, 2021). In turn, police report not being satisfied working in communities that lack trust in them (Baumgartner, Epp, & Shoub, 2018; Morin, Parker, Stepler, & Mercer, 2017). Lack of confidence in the criminal justice system is not only due to interactions with the police. Notwithstanding the constitutional right to a fair and speedy trial by jury, less than 4% of criminal cases and 1% of civil cases are decided by a jury. Plea bargaining is the decisive factor for 95% of cases where there is often pressure to accept a plea even if they didn't do the crime to avoid potentially worse penalties. Racially minoritized people face bias at every stage of litigation, from the counsel that defendants receive (especially those who are poor) to the prosecutorial decisions about which cases to pursue, who to prosecute, what charges to bring and what sentences to seek (including capital punishment) (Sawyer & Wagner, 2020; Thomas, 2016).

Evidence shows that implicit racial bias affects the ability of judges and juries to evaluate guilt and innocence objectively and skews toward guilty judgments in cases with Black defendants regardless of the evidence presented (Stevenson, 2014). Implicit racial bias associates Black Americans as "dangerous," "aggressive," "violent" and "criminal." Implicit bias has been well documented in traffic stops and drug enforcement (Eberhardt, 2019). The vast majority of interactions citizens have with law enforcement are through traffic stops, where Blacks are much more likely than whites to be searched or arrested (Baumgartner, Epp, & Shoub, 2018). Supreme Court decisions expanding the discretion of law enforcement in searches have also had racially disparate impacts that the court has thus far been unwilling to review (Natapoff, 2018). Consequences of imprisonment may include losing the right to vote, receive financial aid and access subsidized housing and a perpetual stigma that carries over into the search for employment.

Juvenile detention rates reveal similarly deep racial disparities. African American children and adolescents are nearly five times more likely to be involved in the justice system than white peers, and Latinx and Native American children and adolescents are between two and three times as likely to be confined (Harris, 2014). As these children move into young adulthood, they are targeted at an even higher rate. Black males ages 18 and 19 are 12 times more likely to be imprisoned than whites (Carson, 2020). Through a school-to-prison pipeline, African American and Latino youth make up 95% of those entering juvenile detention centers, even though they represent only two-thirds of all youth, in New York City (Curtis, 2014; Morris, 2012).

An *immigration industrial complex* expanded under both Democratic and Republican presidents. Under President Clinton, the 1996 Antiterrorism and Effective Death Penalty Act and the Illegal Immigration Reform and Immigrant Responsibility Act sanctioned imprisonment and deportation for border crossing. Under President G. W. Bush, the Department of Homeland Security (DHS) was established to monitor terrorism but has largely been used against undocumented immigrants. Even though President Obama introduced DACA (Deferred Action for Childhood Arrivals) to enable citizenship for children of undocumented immigrants born in the U.S., over 2.5 million migrants were deported during his presidency. President Trump exploited the trope of immigrants as criminals by promising to build a wall to keep out "bad hombres," repealed DACA and banned migrants from a number of Muslim countries from entering the country. The Trump administration also invoked zero-tolerance policies that penalized parents crossing the border, separated them from their children and detained children in cages. The "deportation machine" divides immigrants into categories of "good" and "bad," "deserving and undeserving," as part of a long racist history in immigration policy (Goodman, 2020). Undocumented immigrants are a large revenue source for private prisons. In 2017, two operators of private prisons alone received $4 billion in contracts (Das, 2020). Many employers rely upon undocumented and low-skilled immigrant workers whom they can pay less, prevent from unionizing and let go during economic downturns. The military, when lacking volunteer citizens, relies heavily on immigrants, who enlist in the armed services in exchange for the opportunity to become documented.

When citizens believe they are unfairly treated by the criminal justice system, it erodes trust in democracy (rates of voting are higher for those who perceive the judicial system is fair over those who question its legitimacy; Tyler & Jackson, 2014). Reforms include establishing a national commission to examine racial disparities and make recommendations for systemic reform; scaling back the war on drugs, especially for low-level offenders; eliminating mandatory minimum sentencing; and abolishing capital punishment. Research on traffic stops suggests that focusing on safety (e.g. speeding, running traffic lights), not investigation (seatbelt violations, expired plates), can mitigate implicit bias as well as unreasonable search and seizure protected by the Fourth Amendment (Baumgartner, Epp, & Shoub, 2018). The George Floyd Justice in Policing Act of 2021 (H.R. 1280) aims to create structures for accountability such as minimizing qualified immunity that safeguards police in private civil actions, modifying the criminal intent standard, limiting no-knock warrants and chokeholds and providing education for law enforcement to explore their own bias and learn about structural inequities.

Immigration reform advocates work to change laws that block paths to citizenship. Many seek to help local immigrant rights organizations better represent the needs of their communities and help their members achieve both legal status and democratic participation as citizens and voters. They also build alliances among immigrant communities and native-born, low-income and People of Color groups to promote justice for all (http://www.fairimmigration.org).

MEDIA SYSTEMS

Mass media (newspapers, magazines, social media, books, radio, television, music and movies) affects how society views and responds to people from different racialized groups. Media themes shape public opinion and public policy—how bureaucracies and individual public officials respond—as well as the attitudes and behavior of the public at large. The media can inflame and propagate, as well as shape public aspirations for equity and justice.

The status quo is normalized (or challenged) by who appears in the media, in what roles and in what numbers; which cultures, stories and life experiences are depicted; what kinds of institutional arrangements and possibilities are presented; and what models of community and collaboration are depicted as desirable. Negative representations increase the likelihood that viewers/readers will develop stereotypes about a group (Castañeda, 2018; Ross, 2019). Media that presents Black and Latino men as criminals normalizes racial stereotypes and legitimizes disparate treatment (Bunche Center, 2018). Though Hollywood has increased the number of Black characters and actors, Black men are still often portrayed as scary or angry and Black women as loud and sassy. The token Black character in a movie is likely to be the Black best friend, and when people die in a movie, the Black character is likely to go first. Latinx characters too often represent the spicy Latina or the macho Latin Lover (http://tvtropes.org). The media promotes colorism and white ideals of beauty through disproportionate use of light-skinned models and actors.

Portrayals that equate dark skin with crime, violence, lack of intelligence and poverty also perpetuate colorism. The booming business in skin-bleaching products signifies its enduring legacy.

Who decides what media will be produced; who writes, produces and directs; who hires actors for different roles; and which stories will be told exerts a powerful influence on whether stereotypes and assumptions are reproduced or challenged. The vast majority of producers, writers and actors in Hollywood and television are still white men (Hollywood Diversity Report, 2020). When images of People of Color are in white hands, they are likely to reflect the preferences, stereotypes and misinformation of the dominant group. Ironically, movies and TV shows with fairly diverse casts bring in more at the box office and get higher ratings from audiences; thus it is not only fair but financially profitable to diversify the media (Ibid).

Print and media journalists too are often not prepared to cover racial and social issues effectively. Newsrooms continue to be dominated by white people who look nothing like the demographics of the community they cover (Cobb, 2018). Conventional journalistic practices that rely on anecdotal storytelling tend to overlook societal structures that affect disparate outcomes, leaving readers/audiences with person-blame, individual explanations for unequal outcomes. Lack of awareness of historical and social context and the role of interlocking institutional policies and practices in maintaining racial disparities and privileges contributes to this problem. These problems are exacerbated when journalists fail to reflect on their own biased racial perceptions (Lehrman & Wagner, 2019).

As a virtual public sphere, social media also provides a platform for racism. *Cyber-racism* (Daniels, 2009) includes racial bias on the internet through websites, images, blogs and online comments. The rise in deliberate misinformation and lies, and the weaponizing of digital platforms by white supremacists, has led to increasing racism and hate speech online (Matamoros-Fernández & Farkas, 2021). Facebook has been criticized for not addressing hate speech and lies and for ignoring its own research showing racial bias (Frenkel & Kang, 2021).

Search engines also reflect the biases of those who create them. Noble (2018) describes the *algorithmic bias* created when the monopoly of a relatively small number of search engines uses algorithms that privilege whiteness and discriminate against People of Color, especially women of color. For example, her search for the term "Black girls" yielded pornographic images. Google claimed to be unable to erase such pages because they were not considered unlawful. Noble also exposed *technological redlining*, using data to profile people when, for example, financial institutions look at social networks to make decisions about whom to approve for credit. A 2019 study revealed that mortgage algorithms have been discriminatory in determining creditworthiness of Latinx and African Americans borrowers (Bartlett, Morse, Stanton, & Wallace, 2021).

The Children's Television Project (CTV) has studied content and children's reactions for many years. They note a little progress, mostly due to the efforts of one network, PBS. Racial, ethnic and gender demographics in children's television do not accurately represent the demographics of the population at large; characters of color and female characters are vastly underrepresented. Analysis of the content of TV programming for children finds stereotyping in how heroes and villains are presented, which is important because of the relationship between media portrayals and low self-esteem. Children should see that heroes can be male and female, and from all races, rather than relegating Black characters to the role of side-kick or portraying villains as dark complexioned or having "non-standard" accents.

Protests by Black athletes are not new: iconic boxer Muhammad Ali openly resisted the Vietnam War, and 1968 Olympic gold medalists Tommie Smith and John Carlos raised fists in protest against discrimination. Contemporary players in the NBA, WNBA and NFL in support of Black Lives Matter, #SayHerName and #MeToo effectively use media to call attention to issues of racism and sexism in the broader society.

As more women and People of Color are in the writers' room, behind cameras and in leading roles that are more authentic and reflective of diverse communities, the media can exert a progressive influence. But far more needs to be done to tell the stories of diverse groups in our society, to represent positive community interactions and arrangements and to present alternative possibilities for successful multiracial democracy. Journalism education can provide tools and methods for effectively covering diverse communities (see Lehrman & Wagner, 2019, for example). Organizations such as the National Hispanic Media Coalition, the Media Action Grassroots Network and the Center for Media Justice and Free Press are examples of activist media coalitions that aim to transform media in the 21st century.

SYSTEM OF POLITICAL PARTICIPATION AND REPRESENTATION GOVERNMENT

Congress in 2021 is the most ethnically and racially diverse yet. Still, four out of five members are white males. White Americans account for 77% of voting members in Congress, considerably larger than their 60% share of the U.S. population. This gap hasn't narrowed in the past 40 years (Schaeffer, 2021). More than half of Congress are millionaires, with a median net worth of just over $1 million (Evers-Hillstrom, 2021). Such skewed representation is kept in place by an old-boy network that grooms and promotes people like themselves for political office, gerrymandered districts that often control who can win (with specifically racial outcomes), suppression of voting among young people and People of Color, and big money in politics that favors incumbents—made worse by *Citizens United* (the Supreme Court ruling that corporations and other outside groups can spend unlimited money on elections).

This situation is not new. Despite our nation's heralded claims of democracy, white male property-holders have historically resisted the inclusion of "nonwhites," women and working-class people (as well as prisoners, immigrants deemed "alien" [often Asian] and those deemed "morally and mentally unfit to vote") (Keyssar, 2009). The Supreme Court in 2013 (in a five-to-four split) eliminated Section 4 of the Voting Rights Act, requiring that states with a history of minority voter suppression clear changes to their voting laws with the federal government. This exclusionary cycle continues as right-wing conservatives propose legislation to restrict voting rights through new barriers to voter registration, shorter early voting periods, new requirements for registered voters and trying to rig the Electoral College in some states. Laws put forward in several states expand the power of poll watchers, inviting opportunity for increased voter intimidation and harassment at the polls, and punish local election officials for technical mistakes, including with criminal penalties (Brennan Center, 2021; Daniels, 2020). These exclusionary attempts are driven partly by fear of the potential impact of a growing pool of young voters and voters of color at a time when the proportional white population is declining. Combined with a more liberal youth vote, the collective impact of these groups presents a growing threat to entrenched political power.

The right to vote is more important than ever, especially at state and local levels, where political representation can have the most impact (Abrams, 2020; Anderson, 2018; Berman,

2015; Waldman, 2016). Many coalitions and organizations are working to educate people about the importance of defending voting rights, including the Voting Rights Coalition, Fair Vote and the NAACP Legal Defense Fund. Others, such as Project Vote, work for the restoration of voting rights to former felons and encourage young people to get involved in electoral politics. Rock the Vote, Campus Compact and the National Coalition on Black Civic Participation are other organizations that teach about and foster civic engagement among youth and support more diverse candidates to run for office. As we write in 2021, Congress is debating a federal law to restore and protect voting rights and prevent states from passing laws that undermine elections. The outcome of this struggle will go a long way toward either protecting or further eroding voting rights in this country.

MOVING TOWARD JUSTICE

The justification and institutionalization of white supremacy has never gone unchallenged in this country. Throughout the 19th and 20th centuries, pushback against racist actions and organized efforts toward multiracial democracy were constant, with periods of oscillating progress and retreat. As we discussed manifestations of racism in the interlocking systems, we also provided examples of groups that are working for change. Many others can be found. The workshop design that follows also points to this history of resistance and to current examples of those organizing for a better world that can serve as inspiration for others.

DESIGN FOR TEACHING ABOUT RACISM

The design presented here provides participants with an introductory overview and understanding of racism with the aim of cultivating a racially just society. The design focuses on helping participants develop a historical and conceptual understanding of racism—how it provides benefits for whites and corollary disadvantages for People of Color at individual, institutional and cultural levels. It also focuses on helping participants take action toward racial justice in their personal and institutional lives.

This design, like others in this volume, uses four quadrants to sequence learning goals, key concepts and activities. The quadrants generally follow the sequence: What? So what? Now what? Quadrant 1 focuses on developing a shared language to talk about racism, defining key terms and building a learning community in which participants from diverse racialized groups can honestly examine their own socialization about racism. Quadrant 2 moves to a historical and conceptual understanding of the construction of race and its historical legacies and contemporary manifestations on multiple levels. Quadrant 3 examines the construction and perpetuation of white privilege and advantage in maintaining an unjust status quo. Finally, Quadrant 4 turns to taking accountable action against racism and developing action plans for change. We use the four-quadrant design to keep the learning sequence in focus, and it can be easily adapted to short workshops or semester-long courses.

The quadrant design is immediately followed by learning outcomes and core concepts specific to each of the four quadrants. Actual instructions, facilitation notes and handouts for each of the activities can be found in the racism chapter website that accompanies this volume. The chapter closes with a general discussion of pedagogical, design and facilitation issues central to teaching about racism. Specific considerations of pedagogy, design and facilitation for each of the activities are explained more fully on the website.

OVERVIEW OF RACISM DESIGN QUADRANTS

Quadrant 1: Connecting to Self and Developing Shared Language for Understanding Racism

1. **Welcome, Introductions and Land Acknowledgement**
2. **Developing Community Agreements (3 separate or combined options)**
   A. Community Aspirations for Racial Justice
   B. Hopes and Concerns about Exploring Racism
   C. Liberation Buddies
3. **Racial Social Identity Activities (2 options)**
   A. Racial Justice Artifacts
   B. Mapping Racial Identity
4. **Assumptions Regarding Race**
   A. Racism and Assumptions
5. **Definitions for Racism**
   A. Definitions for Racism Matching Activity
   B. Levels and Types of Racism Mini Lecturette
6. **Racial Socialization Activities (2 options)**
   A. Cycle of Racial Socialization
   B. Earliest Memories of Race Personal Timeline
7. **Closing Activities (2 options)**
   A. Closing Whip
   B. Three Adjectives

Quadrant 2: Historical and Conceptual Understanding of Racism

1. **Opening Activity**
   A. Beads Activity: Intergroup Contact Across Race
2. **History of Racism Activities (4 Options) Racism Timeline links**
   A. Video: The Stories We Tell About Race
   B. Racial Oppression Timeline
   C. The Racial Debt: What Is Owed?
   D. Racism in the U.S. Quiz
3. **Closing Activity**
   A. Sculpting Power Dynamics
4. **Homework (2 options)**
   A. Looking at Racism in Institutions
   B. Tracking Everyday White Privilege

Quadrant 3: Current Manifestations of Racism

1. **Opening Activities**
   A. Race and Privilege Common Ground Activity
   B. Discuss Homework from the Previous Session
2. **Contemporary Manifestations (3 options)**
   A. Construction of White Privilege/Advantage
   B. The Web of Institutional Racism
   C. Five Faces of Oppression
3. **Journal Reflection, Discussion**
   A. Journal Reflection and Sharing
   B. Closing Circle

Quadrant 4: Possibilities for Change and Taking Action

1. **Opening Activities**
   A. Liberation Envisioning Concentric Circle
   B. Check-In and Emotional Timeline
2. **Accountability and Solidarity (2 options)**
   A. Spheres of Influence
   B. Cycle of Liberation
3. **Plans for Taking Action**
   A. Racial Justice Scenarios
   B. Racial Justice: "Solidarity Dividend" Intersections and Collaborations Activity
4. **Closing and Wrap-Up, Support and Next Steps**
   A. Declaration of Commitment
   B. Liberation Pairs or Accountability Buddies

QUADRANT 1: CONNECTING TO SELF AND DEVELOPING SHARED LANGUAGE FOR UNDERSTANDING RACISM

Learning Objectives for Quadrant 1:
- Create a positive learning environment through developing community agreements or guidelines for support and risk taking in exploring racism
- Explore personal learning/experiences about race and racism to begin to develop understanding of the ways that racism is communicated and reinforced at systemic, institutional and cultural levels
- Develop a shared understanding of key terms and ideas

Key Concepts: Group building, personal bias, Cycle of Socialization, assumptions, social location

Activities:
1. **Welcome, Introductions and Land Acknowledgements (20 min.):**
    This process invites participants to reflect on the land they are occupying and recognize that it represents stolen land for Native Americans/Indigenous people (for all options). Introductions invite participants to share the name by which they want to be addressed and the pronouns they use.
2. **Developing Community Agreements (3 separate or combined options):**
    A. Community Aspirations for Racial Justice: Invites participants to collectively develop a set of agreements/aspirations for a positive and effective learning experience that encourages people to take appropriate risks and step out of their comfort zone in order to learn about racism. The activity also acknowledges that participants enter from different social locations and asks them to consider how to create a safe enough space for all.
    B. Hopes and Concerns about Exploring Racism: This activity elicits the hopes and concerns about exploring racism of participants in order to make them explicit to all and lays the groundwork for creating community agreements.
    C. Liberation Buddies for Racial Justice (for all options): Gives participants the opportunity to create self-selected smaller groups, to have a space to connect and check in with each other regarding their learning.
3. **Racial Social Identity Activities (2 options):**
    A. Artifacts Emblematic of Race/Ethnicity and Intersections with Other Identities (60 min): This social identity activity invites participants to share symbols or artifacts that are meaningful for them as a member of various social groups, provides an opportunity to celebrate our multiple identities and examines the intersections of our different identities.
    B. Mapping Identity Activity for Racial Justice (60 min): This social identity activity asks participants to map aspects of their identity of which they are proud and others that they have felt embarrassed or sad about. They compare these aspects with how others may view them and identify stereotypes they have experienced as a result.
4. **Assumptions Activity Regarding Racism (30–45 min):**
    A. Racism and Assumptions: This activity gives participants the opportunity to explore personal assumptions about racism, both implicitly and consciously.
5. **Definitions for Exploring Racism (combined options):**
    A. Definitions for Racism Matching Activity (30 min): Provides the group with a set of terms that helps develop a language to be able to engage in a discussion about racism, as well as creating a foundation for a more in-depth understanding of racism.

B. Defining Race and Racism Levels and Types Mini Lecturette (15 min): Intended to provide the group with an understanding of the different levels that racism is manifested.

6. **Racial Socialization Processes Activities (2 options):**
   A. Racial Cycle of Socialization (35–40 min): Intended to give participants the opportunity to explore their own socialization process through individual, cultural and institutional interactions and norms and how these teach us to accept the system of racism and white privilege/advantage.
   B. Earliest Memories of Race Personal Time Line (60 min) (critical incident activity with guided imagery): Provides participants with the opportunity to examine early memories related to race in order to explore learned (consciously and unconsciously) messages about race, their own racial group and other racial groups. Participants are able to begin to analyze how they are socialized about race and the multiple levels on which racism has affected their lives.

7. **Closing Activities Racism Quadrant 1 (2 options):**
   These closing activities help wrap up the session and give the facilitator and group a sense of what has been learned and how people are responding to the session. This can also help facilitators plan for the next session.
   A. Closing Whip (10–15 min):
      • One thing you learned today that you want to remember?
      • One question that you are still grappling with in regards to the material covered today? Allow individuals to pass if they wish to do so.
   B. Three Adjectives (10 min): Each person (including the facilitators) selects one adjective to describe how they felt when they first arrived today, how they felt at the middle of the session and how they are feeling now. Go around and each person says their three words.

QUADRANT 2: HISTORICAL AND CONCEPTUAL UNDERSTANDING OF RACISM

Learning Objectives for Quadrant 2:
• Understand how racism operates in U.S. history and contemporary life
• Identify and analyze the material consequences of racial construction
• Trace systemic and institutional forms of racism through history and into the present

Key Concepts: Social construction, institutional racism, cumulative racial advantage and disadvantage

Activities:

1. **Opening Activity:**
   A. Beads Activity: Intergroup Contact Across Race (30–45 min): This symbolic activity highlights the impact of racial segregation and encourages participants to examine their own spheres of influence.

2. **History of Racism Activities (4 options): Racism Timeline links** ★
   A. The Stories We Tell About Race: *Race: The Power of an Illusion*, episode 2 (80 min): This episode traces the social construction of race and its consequences for People of Color in the U.S.
   B. Racial Oppression Timeline for Remote Learning via Padlet (30–90 min): Participants are provided with a timeline to identify examples of events that perpetuate racism.

    C. The Racial Debt: What Is Owed? (30–60 min): This activity engages participants in identifying points in U.S. history where disadvantage for Blacks and correlating advantage for whites were constructed and asks participants to look at the consequences for today and discuss what should be done now to remedy injustice.

    D. Racism in the U.S. Quiz (60–90 min): Addresses the needs of content learners and is not administered to be graded or examined by the facilitator. Provides a snapshot of race and racism in the U.S., both historically and contemporarily.

3. **Closing Activity:**

    A. Sculpting Power Dynamics (10–15 min): This activity engages participants in representing the power dynamics discussed prior in a creative and physical way and reinforces what has been learned in the session.

4. **Homework (2 options):**

    A. Homework: Looking at Institutions (5 min): Name an institution you want to know more about; bring one or two examples of how racism operates in this institution to the next class.

    B. Homework: Tracking Everyday White Privilege: Participants will be given a handout that helps them track the number of times in a day they observe or benefit from white privilege.

QUADRANT 3: CURRENT MANIFESTATIONS OF RACISM

Learning Objectives for Quadrant 3:
- Understand the cultural and institutional privileges/advantages attached to "whiteness" in the U.S.
- Recognize examples of how racism operates across different institutions
- Apply Five Faces of Oppression to identify different manifestations of racism

Key Concepts: White privilege/unearned advantage, identifying various manifestations of racism

Activities:

1. **Exploring the Impact of Racism Interpersonally (45 min):** (Deal with homework from the previous session, where appropriate).

    A. Racial Justice Common Ground Activity (30 min): This activity allows participants to experience the impacts of racism and see how these separate people from one another.

2. **Contemporary Manifestations (3 options):**

    A. Construction of White Advantage: *Race: The Power of an Illusion*, episode 3 (45 min): This segment demonstrates how law and public policy create advantages for whites at the expense of other groups in ways that normalize (or make invisible) white advantage.

    B. The Web of Institutional Racism (60–70 min): This activity helps participants make connections about the ways racism operates across different social institutions.

    C. Five Faces of Oppression (30 min): This activity engages participants in identifying the distinctive ways racism operates using five distinct manifestations. Each face can be examined from an intersectional lens that explores how other social groups are systematically oppressed yet varies depending upon the particular historical experiences of each social and racialized group. Participants learn the Five Faces and apply them to examples of contemporary racism.

3. **Journal Reflection, Discussion, Pair Share and Closing Activity (30 min):**
   A. Journal Reflection and Sharing (20 min): Suggested prompts: How does understanding white privilege help you better understand racism and the way that it is maintained and reinforced? How might having an understanding of white privilege help you challenge racism? After 10 minutes, Pair Share: Encourage active listening and purposeful sending.
   B. Closing Circle (10 min): Go around the circle and invite each participant to share one lingering question from the session. Or share a feeling, emotion or thought (one word) based on material engaged with today.

QUADRANT 4: POSSIBILITIES FOR CHANGE AND TAKING ACTION

Learning Objectives for Quadrant 4:
- Plan concrete ways of taking action
- Construct visions of liberatory alternatives and develop actions plans to reach them
- Build coalition and work with others

Key Concepts: Accountability, solidarity, acting as allies, spheres of influence

Activities:
1. **Opening Activities (20–30 min) (2 options):**
   A. Liberation Envisioning Concentric Circle (15 min): This exercise encourages participants to imagine the "ideal world" they would like to live in and to openly reflect upon what they as individuals, as well as others, will need to do for this world to be realized.
   B. Check-In and Emotional Timeline (30 min): Each participant graphs with days or dates of course sessions along the horizontal axis and numbers from 1–5 their least and most impactful, challenging and/or engaging moments in the course. In small groups, participants share as a way to review course and highlight key moments of learning.
2. **Accountability and Solidarity (60 min) (2 options):**
   A. Spheres of Influence (15 min): This activity is intended to give participants the opportunity to 1) gain an understanding that the action an individual can take against oppression can occur in different parts of their life, given that we all are part of different spheres in which we have influence, and 2) identify where in their own spheres of influence they can take action.
   B. Cycle of Liberation (30 to 45 min): This activity is intended to give participants the opportunity to become familiar with the cycle of liberation and to identify their location in the Cycle of Liberation at the moment.
3. **Taking Action Activities (2 options):**
   A. Racial Justice Scenarios (40–60 min): Scenarios provide participants with the opportunity to offer an analysis of how racism occurs individually and institutionally in everyday occurrences. The activity seeks to develop the appropriate skills to disrupt racist attitudes and behaviors and foster the confidence to act.
   B. Racial Justice: "Solidarity Dividend" Intersections and Collaborations Activity (15–20 minutes): This activity focuses on how building coalitions across difference is critical for addressing oppression and challenges participants to see "our" issues as broader, examine inclusion and exclusion in frameworks we use and consider how to can build community across diverse identities and agendas.

4. **Closing and Wrap-Up:**
   A. One-Sentence Declaration or Commitment (15–20 min): This activity enables participants to publicly announce a specific commitment toward eradicating racism.
   B. Liberation Pairs or Accountability Buddies (15–20 min): This activity is designed to add a support system for participants outside of the specified learning community. It encourages participants to be accountable to one another as each works to transform the various levels and types of racism.

PEDAGOGICAL, DESIGN, AND FACILITATION ISSUES IN TEACHING ABOUT RACISM

Teaching about racism in the United States is an intellectually, emotionally and politically challenging undertaking, complicated by the lack of supportive spaces to think and talk about racism in diverse groups and learn about differences in racial experiences. Limited or misinformed knowledge regarding the nation's racial history, the introduction of "alternative facts" to the current discourse and the pervasiveness of race-neutral ideology contribute to this challenge. Like other isms, racism not only operates at different levels (individual, institutional, cultural and societal) but also interconnects with other forms of oppression, adding further complexity and nuance to teaching about it. Furthermore, political tensions and efforts at discrediting racial justice education have generated a span of feelings and experiences, misinformation, confusion and bias about the topic of racism, all of which impact openness to the learning experience and engagement with the topic. Here we discuss some of the typical challenges that arise in teaching about racism and ways that facilitators can respond effectively to these challenges.

DEALING WITH EMOTIONAL CONTENT

Issues of trust and safety are often present for participants in a course on racism. With the aim of civil and informed engagement, it is important to collectively orchestrate community guidelines/agreements to foster a positive learning experience. Working together to develop and *practice* the guidelines is crucial (see Chapter 3: Design and Facilitation). Facilitators should be active role models from the start, willing to acknowledge their own positionality. The concepts of comfort zone and learning edge provide useful tools to help participants monitor their internal reactions and consciously work at staying open to learning, even when feeling challenged emotionally and intellectually.

Participants, particularly white participants, may feel embarrassed or perhaps guilty to share ignorance and misunderstandings of racism or to expose their own racist assumptions and socialization. White participants may be cautious because they are afraid of offending People of Color; People of Color may be apprehensive because they don't feel safe or supported enough to trust white facilitators and/or participants. In some instances, white participants may wait for People of Color to teach them about racism, assuming that they themselves know little about racism and need to hear about it from the "people who have had it done to them." Some People of Color may assume that they know everything there is to know about racism from their own experiences, and they may be skeptical that they will learn anything new. Others may assume the role of "expert" to teach white participants about racism. Facilitators must be attentive to such issues so that participants of color are not asked to be educators or spokespeople for their racial group. Additionally, it is important that participants of color enhance their critical analysis and their understanding of intersecting identities as well as how racism negatively affects all racially minoritized groups beyond their own racialized group.

Activities that examine early experiences might require a trauma-informed approach (Quiros, Varghese, & Vanidestine, 2019) due to the emotional content they can generate. Facilitators are encouraged to acknowledge and be prepared to address these dynamics. For some People of Color, recounting early experiences with racism can revive situations where they or members of their family were targets of prejudice, discrimination or violence, bringing up the emotions felt at an earlier time. For some white people, realizing that parents and others they love and trust have taught them stereotypes about other racial groups and/or engaged in racist behavior may cause discomfort, anger or sadness. It is helpful to note that one of the costs of racism is the emotional pain and dehumanization it causes all people living in a racist system.

Facilitators should create a supportive space where people can express some of those painful emotions while maintaining a productive learning environment (Bell, 2020). It can be useful to remind participants that feelings are neither right nor wrong and invite participants to honor them. Acknowledging feelings is an important step in distinguishing feelings from thoughts and in determining actions based on conscious choice rather than unconscious socialization. For minoritized racial groups, revisiting their experiences with racism may evoke frustration, alienation or feeling misunderstood, powerless, angry or alone. Privileged racial groups often express embarrassment, shame, guilt, defensiveness or ignorance.

While it is important to acknowledge the feelings and emotions of participants, facilitators must make sure that the focus does not end up centering the emotions of white participants at the expense of participants of color. For example, white women are often overwhelmed by emotion when they begin to learn about racism and their own unconscious participation. The challenge for facilitators is to acknowledge the pain of racism while keeping the focus on developing consciousness and action to address racism. People of Color have experienced racism and the emotions of its injustice, and they are more likely to need acknowledgement of their experiences of racism to gain knowledge about how it functions and to learn about actions that can be taken to challenge racism. Otherwise, holding onto emotions without consciously channeling them into action minimizes the agency each of us possess, regardless of our racial identity, to create change.

Affinity groups are one way to address the differing needs of participants from diverse racial groups at different points in the course. White affinity groups provide a space for white participants to express emotions, confusion and lack of awareness or knowledge and get support from white peers. White participants may be more resistant to the idea of meeting separately, may see it as divisive or may not understand the value of affinity groups, so facilitators may need to provide clear explanations. Affinity groups for participants of color likewise provide a space for expressing the aforementioned anger, pain, sadness and confusion while providing the opportunity to receive support from racial peers. In forming affinity groups, facilitators should take into account the demographic makeup of the class. For example, providing options for biracial and multiracial participants of color to meet as a separate caucus group, or for African Americans and Latinx to decide whether to meet as one group or separately, are decisions to be considered. Sometimes white participants may want to focus on other identities (religious, gender) to avoid dealing with whiteness, and facilitators must help them keep the focus on race and racism.

Following the affinity groups, it is important to bring the groups back together to share learning and move forward as a cohesive learning community. Bringing groups back together can be tricky and needs to be well thought out. Facilitators should be aware that there may be different levels of willingness and desire to share in the larger group.

DEALING WITH COMPLEX HISTORICAL INFORMATION

Creating opportunities for participants to talk about and reflect upon their life experiences in the context of accurate historical information can help them understand how their experiences are shaped by systemic patterns of institutional and cultural racism and white privilege/advantage. Learning about our own contributions to the conditions that constrain, oppress and even imprison other people is often quite painful, but it can also generate better understanding of how power functions in society to perpetuate racism (Preskill & Brookfield, 2009). Such knowledge can help participants understand the racial problems we still face today, making it possible to imagine solutions and take steps to address them. It also helps participants move from a perspective of individual blame to one of recognizing the significance of systemic forces. Given the fact that racism is a complex, multifaceted phenomenon, it can be overwhelming, so it is important to encourage inquiry and moving beyond surface analysis without expecting immediate closure or simple answers.

Over the past several years, there has been more public exposure to hate crimes against Asians and police brutality against Blacks and the dehumanizing of Latinx children and families at the U.S. border; however, a critical mass of people are still unaware of the comprehensive history of race and racism in the United States and are likely to assume that society has largely eliminated racism. Facilitators must be able to discuss knowledgeably the historical development of racism in the United States and the myriad ways racism manifests in contemporary times. For example, participants with white immigrant ancestors may be honestly confused about the different trajectories of African Americans, white immigrants and immigrants of color ("If my parents could make it in America, why can't they?"). Without knowledge of the push and pull factors that dictate forced and/or voluntary migration to the states, the various historical barriers to progress and how white advantage has been constructed and perpetuated through government and other institutional policies and practices, participants may not be able to understand the very different experiences of other groups. It is important to acknowledge that while their family members did work hard, they did not face the same barriers African Americans and immigrants of color faced. The use of historical information can help them understand the construction of whiteness as a vehicle to maintain privilege, as well as the costs for white immigrants who gave up language and culture in exchange for the advantages of whiteness. Such information provides a context for seeing that African Americans and numerous immigrants of color are not offered the "choice" to become white or enjoy the privileges that whiteness affords. In general, history matters, and content knowledge puts personal experience in a social and historical context.

The racism history timeline is an effective way to introduce this material, as it lays out how racism has manifested over time in different periods of U.S. history. Using the timeline, participants can track laws and practices that created disadvantages for groups of color and the corollary development of white advantage at different points in our history. This history shows the connection between whiteness and property (Harris, 1993), citizenship rights (Keyssar, 2009) and the accumulation of wealth to pass on to future generations (Oliver & Shapiro, 2006). *Readings for Diversity and Social Justice* (Adams, Blumenfeld, Castaneda, Hackman, Peters, & Zuniga, 2018) provides articles that critically examine the advantages and disadvantages people receive based on racial social group membership.

UNPACKING "RACE-NEUTRAL" TALK

Many people espouse race neutrality by invoking Martin Luther King's dream to assert that they are not racist or practice racism, as in the phrase, "I don't see color, I just see people." In fact, people are socialized to pretend to not notice differences (see Figure 4.2, the Cycle of Socialization), and many incorporate the injunction that to notice or comment on difference is wrong (Bell, 2003). Race-neutral ideology positions race as a taboo topic that cannot be openly discussed and thus makes it more difficult to address the racial problems that persist in our society (Haney-López, 2014).

Participants need information that can help them understand how color-blind ideology actually reproduces racism (Bonilla-Silva, 2015). This requires naming and acknowledging the ways institutional racism shapes life chances and opportunities. It also means acknowledging and appreciating difference as a positive value and understanding positive race-consciousness as a critical step toward imagining and creating racial justice (Bell, 2016).

It is important for facilitators to provide language and tools for thoughtful and open dialogue about race. Our goal is to help participants examine how they have been socialized to ignore race and to help them look at their own racial identities within the broader context of racism. This can be particularly difficult for white participants who are unable or unwilling to tolerate the disequilibrium and stress of facing the realities of racism and white involvement in maintaining the status quo (DiAngelo, 2011). We want to enable students to wrestle with what they have internalized about race and racism, reflect on their social location in relation to other racial groups and consider their own complicity when following business as usual. The Cycle of Socialization helps participants examine their own socialization process and consider points of intervention to go against this socialization.

As a racial ideology, *race neutrality* argues that ending discrimination requires treating everyone the same, without acknowledging racial, cultural or ethnic identities; the very unequal positions from which some start because of past discrimination; and ongoing practices that perpetuate discrimination in the present. Historical information, clear definitions and examples of how racism operates on different levels provide language and tools for discussing cumulative advantage and disadvantage that reveal how "equal" treatment can be inequitable. For example, People of Color who attend underfunded schools in poor neighborhoods face educational, health and economic barriers to attending college that other groups do not. Treating everyone the same will not ameliorate those barriers as much as a fair and equitable society will. Making up for inequities in material resources, knowledge and cultural capital may require different actions to address the unique needs and experiences of different groups. Such targeted actions represent equitable, not equal, treatment.

ACKNOWLEDGING CONFERRED WHITE ADVANTAGE/PRIVILEGE

White privilege defines the unearned advantages granted to white or white-presenting people on the basis of racial group membership. White privilege is normalized in such a way that the majority of whites are unaware of and take for granted the privileges or advantages they receive (McIntosh, 2020). At first, acknowledging the existence of white privilege can be difficult for white individuals who may be resistant to seeing how they have personally benefited from white privilege. Without an understanding of cumulative white privilege throughout history, some may discount examples of cultural or institutional racism as atypical. Others may believe that there is reverse racism in education and employment as a result of affirmative action and other non-discrimination policies. Some may feel that the slight increase in the number of People of Color in positions in government, the media and other professions is an indication of the end of racism. Some resistance to the concept of white privilege might be the result of the salience of other marginalized social identities. For example, a white working-class person might have difficulty accepting the ways in which they benefit from white privilege given their experience with class inequality.

When encountering these challenges, it is important to encourage participants to say more about what they understand the issue to be so that they go beyond a surface analysis to look at the assumptions underlying their position. People often base their positions on taken-for-granted societal norms and beliefs that require deeper reflection. Becoming comfortable with challenges to "common sense" understandings of racial injustice can be difficult for individuals who have never considered such issues before. Helping individuals analyze their own statements and asking open-ended questions rather than arguing with them is more likely to encourage openness to considering alternative information and analysis.

Introducing levels and types of racism provides a useful framework for helping participants examine taken-for-granted understandings. Also important are social science data and analyses about actual representations and outcomes in such areas as education, employment, wealth accumulation and health for different groups in our society. The collaborative quiz located on the website will be helpful for more cerebral, evidence-based learners. Understanding the difference between individual prejudice and the systemic power to oppress is also important, as is the idea that there is no hierarchy of oppression (Lorde, 1983).

An intersectional perspective can also be vital here—keeping the focus on racism while acknowledging the impact of other forms of oppression. Individuals experience manifestations of racism in distinct ways due to the intersection of their social identities. Furthermore, a focus on the complexity of identity helps participants see the diversity that exists within social groups so they don't essentialize all members of a group as the same (Jones & Wijeyesinghe, 2011).

Not all white people benefit in the same way, given other social identities. Yet, instead of shifting the focus off of cumulative white advantage, participants can consider how their other social identities affect their experience of white privilege and how their white privilege affects their experience of their other social identities that may be of advantage or disadvantage. How does my whiteness affect my experience of class? How does my class affect my experience of whiteness and white privilege? Individuals' different social identities must be honored through the content of the curriculum as well as through the process, while keeping race at the forefront of our focus.

DEALING WITH RESISTANCE

Given the complexity of the topic, facilitators may encounter resistance when teaching about racism. Tatum (1992) suggests four strategies that can help address student resistance to learning about racism. These include: 1) creating a safe classroom space through the use of some form of community guidelines or aspirations, 2) creating opportunities for students to generate their own knowledge by assigning hands-on assignments to be completed outside of the class, 3) providing students with a developmental model they can utilize to help understand their own process of emerging awareness about racism, and 4) exploring strategies that empower students as change agents, such as giving students an opportunity to create their own action plans for addressing racism.

Facilitators should assure participants that difficult conversations are part of the learning process about racism and that difficulties that arise can be aired and openly examined together (Brookfield, 2019; Kaplowitz, Griffin, & Seyka, 2019; Miller, Donner, & Fraser, 2004). Readings and activities such as Iris Young's Five Faces of Oppression can help participants gain an understanding of how racism manifests among various racialized groups and also validates other salient marginalized identities they possess.

TRACING LINKS BETWEEN RACISM AND IMMIGRATION

Some participants, including U.S.-born People of Color, may have a hard time seeing how immigrants of color are impacted by racism and may view racism as only a Black/white issue. Misconceptions and misinformation about immigrants can support negative stereotypes about them. For example, some might say that immigrants today are "illegal" and be unaware that there was no such category during earlier waves of "white" immigration. Others may complain that undocumented people don't pay taxes and are "leeches on the system" since they do not know that undocumented people actually pay a lot into a system whose benefits they are unable to access. Additionally, native-born U.S. participants may not be in tune with how xenophobia and sinophobia challenge the experiences of immigrants or minoritized racialized groups that are perceived as immigrants.

It is useful to keep track of the assumptions and misconceptions raised in discussion as well as language used by participants when referring to immigrants so that these terms and assumptions can be analyzed in historical context. It is important to note how patterns of migration have been impacted by larger economic, social and political factors and the ways that immigration policy controls who is included or excluded on the basis of race (and also class, gender, national origin, political affiliation, sexual orientation and disability). Help participants see that migration has been both forced and voluntary, often corresponding to the demand for cheap labor and U.S. political and military intervention that displaced people. They can learn about and trace the patterns of xenophobia and nativism that have occurred throughout history to blame immigrants for problems such as unemployment, crime, overburdened social services and other issues. It is also helpful for participants to see that social justice movements have successfully organized to fight against racism and anti-immigration xenophobia throughout U.S. history.

Teaching and learning about racism are a lifelong learning process. Facilitators who take up this challenge find that it is also rewarding. Helping others understand our racial history and the roots of racism, as well as the role of activists in challenging it across our history, provides clarity for understanding our world today and hope that working for multiracial democracy and racial justice can succeed in making our country live up to its promise for all members of our society.

Note

* We ask that those who cite this work always acknowledge by name all of the authors listed rather than either only citing the first author or using "et al." to indicate co-authors. All collaborated on the conceptualization, development, and writing of this chapter.

References

AACU. (2019). Retrieved from https://www.aacu.org/aacu-news/newsletter/2019/march/facts-figures

Abrams, S. (2020). *Our time is now: Power, purpose and the fight for a fair America.* New York: Picador Press.

Adams, M., Blumenfeld, W., Castaneda, R., Hackman, H., Peters, M., & Zuniga, X. (2018). *Readings for diversity and social justice* (3rd ed.). New York: Routledge.

Aladangady, A., & Forde, A. (Oct, 2021). *Wealth inequality and the racial wealth gap.* https://www.federalreserve.gov/econres/notes/feds-notes/wealth-inequality-and-the-racial-wealth-gap-2021 1022.htm

Alexander, M. (2012). *The new Jim Crow: Mass incarceration in the age of colorblindness.* New York: The New Press.

American Cancer Society. *Cancer facts & figures for African Americans 2019–2021.* Retrieved from https://www.cancer.org/content/dam/cancer-org/research/cancer-facts-and-statistics/cancer-facts-and-figures-for-african-americans/cancer-facts-and-figures-for-african-americans-2019-2021.pdf

Anderson, C. (2018). *One person, no vote; how voter suppression is destroying our democracy.* New York: Bloomsbury Publishing.

Bailey, M. (2021). *Misogynoir transformed.* New York: New York University Press. doi:10.18574/9781479803392

Banaji, M. R., & Greenwald, A. G. (2016). *Blindspot: Hidden biases of good people.* Bantam Books.

Bardella, K. (2021, March 18). 'China virus' redux: For Trump and republicans, it's open season on Asian Americans like me. *USA Today.* Retrieved from https://www.usatoday.com/story/opinion/2021/03/04/covid-racism-asian-americans-trump-provocations-column/6904348002/

Bartlett, R., Morse, A., Stanton, R., & Wallace, N. (2021). Consumer-lending discrimination in the FinTech era. *Journal of Financial Economics.* doi:10.1016/j.jfineco.2021.05.047

Battalora, J. (2013). *Birth of a white nation.* Houston: Strategic Book Publishing Co.

Baugh, J. (2003). Linguistic profiling. In S. Makoni, G. Smitherman, A. F. Ball, & A. K. Spears (Eds.), *Black linguistics: Language, society and politics in Africa and the Americas* (pp. 155–168). New York: Routledge.

Baumgartner, F. R., Epp, D. A., & Shoub, K. (2018). *Suspect citizens what 20 million traffic stops tell us about policing and race.* Cambridge: Cambridge University Press.

Bell, L. A. (2003). Sincere fictions: The pedagogical challenges of preparing white teachers for multicultural classrooms. *Equity and Excellence in Education, 35*(3), 236–245.

Bell, L. A. (2020). *Storytelling for social justice: Connecting narrative and the arts in antiracist teaching, 2nd edition.* New York: Routledge.

Bell, L. A. (2016). Telling on racism: Developing a race-conscious agenda. In H. A. Neville, M. E. Gallardo, & D. W. Sue (Eds.), *The myth of racial color blindness: Manifestations, dynamics, and impact* (pp. 105–122). Washington, DC: American Psychological Association.

Berman, A. (2015). *Give us the ballot: The modern struggle for voting rights in America* (1st ed.). New York: Farrar, Straus and Giroux.

Billings, D. (2016). *Deep denial: The persistence of white supremacy in United States history and life.* Roselle, NJ: Crandall, Dostie & Douglass Books.

Blumenberg, E., & Pierce, G. (2017). The drive to work: The relationship between transportation access, housing assistance, and employment among participants in the welfare to work voucher program. *Journal of Planning Education and Research, 37*(1), 66–82. doi:10.1177/0739456X16633501

Bonilla-Silva, E. (2004). From bi-racial to tri-racial: Towards a new system of racial stratification in the USA. *Ethnic and Racial Studies, 27*(6), 931–950.

Bonilla-Silva, E. (2013). *Racism without racists* (4th ed.). Lanham, MD: Rowman and Littlefield.

Bonilla-Silva, E. (2015). More than prejudice: Restatement, reflections, and new directions in critical race theory. *Sociology of Race and Ethnicity, 1*(1), 73–87.

Branigan, A. R., Wildeman, C., Freese, J., & Kiefe, C. I. (2017). Complicating colorism: Race, skin color, and the likelihood of arrest. *Socius.* doi:10.1177/2378023117725611

Breiding, M. J., Smith, S. G., Basile, K. C., Walters, M. L., Chen, J., & Merrick, M. T. (2014). Prevalence and characteristics of sexual violence, stalking, and intimate partner violence victimization—national intimate partner and sexual violence survey, United States, 2011. *MMWR Surveill, 63*(8), 1–18.

Brennan Center for Justice. (2021). *Voting laws roundup.* Retrieved from https://www.brennancenter.org/our-work/research-reports/voting-laws-roundup-july-2021

Bridges, K. (2019). *Critical race theory: A primer.* St. Paul, MN: Foundation Press.

Brodkin, K. (1998). *How Jews became white folks and what that says about race in America.* New Brunswick, NJ: Rutgers University Press.

Brookfield, S. (2019). *Teaching race: How to help students unmask and challenge racism.* San Francisco, CA: Jossey-Bass.

Brown, D. A. (2021). *The whiteness of wealth: How the tax system impoverishes Black Americans and how we can fix it.* New York: Crown.

Bunche Center (2018). *2018 Hollywood diversity report: Making sense of the disconnect.* Los Angeles: Ralph J. Bunche Center for African American Studies at UCLA. Retrieved from http://www.bunchecenter.ucla.edu/wp-content/uploads/2014/02/2014-Hollywood-Diversity-Report-2–12–14.pdf

Bureau of Justice Statistics. (2010). Retrieved from https://bjs.ojp.gov/library/publications/prisoners-2019

Campbell, K., Garcia, D. M., Granillo, C. V., & Chavez, D. V. (2012). *Exploring the Latino paradox: How economic and citizenship status impact health*. Psychology Faculty Publications. Retrieved from http://journals.sagepub.com/doi/10.1177/0739986312437552

Carnevale, A. P., Fasules, M., Quinn, M., & Campbell, K. (2019). *Born to win, schooled to lose*. Washington, DC: Georgetown Public Policy Institute, Center on Education and the Workforce.

Carnevale, A. P., & Strohl, J. (2013). *Separate & unequal: How higher education reinforces intergenerational reproduction of white privilege*. Washington, DC: Georgetown Public Policy Institute, Center on Education and the Workforce.

Carson, E. A. (2020). *Prisoners in 2019*. U.S. Department of Justice, October 2020, NCJ 255115. Retrieved from https://bjs.ojp.gov/content/pub/pdf/p19.pdf

Castañeda, Mari (2018). The power of (mis)representation: Why racial and ethnic stereotypes in the media matter. In *Challenging inequalities: Readings in race, ethnicity, and immigration* (p. 60). Retrieved from https://scholarworks.umass.edu/communication_faculty_pubs/60

CDC Centers for Disease Control. (2019). *Disparities in COVID-19 deaths*. Retrieved from https://www.cdc.gov/coronavirus/2019-ncov/community/health-equity/racial-ethnic-disparities/disparities-deaths.html

Children's Defense Fund (2021). *The state of America's children: 2021*. Retrieved from https://www.childrensdefense.org/state-of-americas-children/

Chun, Y., & Grinstein-Weiss, M. (2020, December). *Housing inequality gets worse as the COVID-19 pandemic is prolonged*. Washington: The Brookings Institution. Retrieved from https://www.brookings.edu/blog/up-front/2020/12/18/housing-inequality-gets-worse-as-the-covid-19-pandemic-is-prolonged/

Chui, M., Prince, S., & Stewart, S. (2021). *America 2021: The opportunity to advance racial equity*. McKinsey & Co.

Coates, T. (2014). The case for reparations. *The Atlantic*. https://www.theatlantic.com/magazine/archive/2014/06/the-case-for-reparations/361631/

Coates, R. (2008). Covert racism in the USA and globally. *Sociology Compass, 2*(1), 208–231.

Cobb, J. (2018). Missing the story. *Columbia Journalism Review*. Retrieved from https://www.cjr.org/special_report/jelani-cobb-race-and-journalism.php

Crenshaw, K. W. (1995). Mapping the margins: Intersectionality, identity politics, and violence against women of color. In K. Thomas (Ed.), *Critical race theory: The key writings that formed a movement* (pp. 357–383). New York: The New Press.

Croll, P. R. (2013). Explanations for racial disadvantage and racial advantage: Beliefs about both sides of inequality in America. *Ethnic and Racial Studies, 36*(1), 47–74. doi:10.1080/01419870.2011.632426

Curtis, A. J. (2014). Tracing the school-to-prison pipeline from zero-tolerance policies to juvenile justice dispositions. *Georgetown Law Journal, 102*(4), 1251–1277.

Daniels, G. R. (2020). *Uncounted: The crisis of voter suppression in America*. New York: New York University Press.

Daniels, J. (2009). *Cyber racism: White supremacy online and the new attack on civil rights*. Lanham, MD: Rowman & Littlefield.

Dardar, A., & Uriarte, M. (2013). The politics of restrictive language policies: A postcolonial analysis of language and schooling. *Postcolonial Directions in Education, 2*(1), 6–67.

Darity, W. A., & Mullen, K. (2020). *From here to equality: Reparations for Black Americans*. Chapel Hill, NC: University of North Carolina Press.

Das, A. (2020). *No justice in the Shadows: How America criminalizes immigrants*. New York: Bold Type Books.

DiAngelo, R. (2011). White fragility. *International Journal of Critical Pedagogy, 3*(3), 54–70.

Deloria, V (1982). Introduction. In: Lyman, CM (ed.) *The vanishing race and other illusions: Photographs of Indians by Edward S Curtis*. New York: Pantheon Books.

Demos (2015). *The racial wealth gap: Why policy matters*. New York: Demos. Retrieved from http://www.demos.org/publication/racial-wealth-gap-why-policy-matters

DeSilver, D. (2014, April 22). *Supreme Court says states can ban affirmative action; 8 already have*. Washington, DC: Pew Research Center Fact Tank. Retrieved from http://www.pewresearch.org/fact-tank/2014/04/22/supreme-court-says-states-can-ban-affirmative-action-8-already-have/

Drake, Bruce (2015, April 28). *Divide between Blacks and Whites on Police Runs Deep*. Washington, DC: Pew Research Center. Available at http://www.pewresearch.org/ fact- tank/ 2015/ 04/ 28/ Blacks-whites- police/

DuBois, W. E. B. (1935). *Black reconstruction in America*. New York: Harcourt Brace.

Dunbar-Ortiz, R. (2014). *An Indigenous peoples' history of the United States*. Boston: Beacon Press.

Dutko, P., Ver Ploeg, M., & Farrigan, T. (2012, August). *Characteristics and influential factors of food deserts*. Economic Research Report No. 140. Washington, DC: U.S. Dept. of Agriculture, Economic Research Service. Retrieved from http://www.ers.usda.gov/publications/err-economic-research-report/err140.aspx

Eberhardt, J. L. (2019). *Biased: Uncovering the hidden prejudice that shapes what we see, think, and do*. New York: Penguin Books.

Espinosa, L. L., Turk, J. M., Taylor, M., & Chessman, H. M. (2019). *Race and ethnicity in higher education: A status report. Education report*. Washington, DC: American Council on Education.

Equitable Growth. (2020). Retrieved from https://equitablegrowth.org/how-data-disaggregation-matters-for-asian-americans-and-pacific-islanders/

Evers-Hillstrom, K. (2021). Majority of lawmakers in 116th congress are millionaires. *Open Secrets*. Retrieved from https://www.opensecrets.org/news/2020/04/majority-of-lawmakers-millionaires/

Fasching-Varner, K., Albert, K. A., Mitchell, R. W., & Allen, C. (Eds.) (2015). *Racial battle fatigue in higher education: Exposing the myth of post-racial America*. Lanham, MD: Rowman & Littlefield.

Fairlie, R. (2020, December). *COVID-19, small business owners, and racial inequality*. The reporter: No. 4. Retrieved from https://www.nber.org/reporter/2020number4/covid-19-small-business-owners-and-racial-inequality

Findling, M., Casey, L., Fryberg, S. A., Hafner, S., Blendon, R. J., Benson, J. M., Sayde, J., & Miller, C. (2019). *Discrimination in the United States: Experiences of Native Americans*. https://onlinelibrary.wiley.com/doi/pdf/10.1111/1475-6773.13224

Finoh, M., & Sankofa, J. (2019, January). *The legal system has failed black girls, women, and non-binary survivors of violence ACLU human rights watch & ACLU*. Retrieved from https://www.aclu.org/blog/racial-justice/race-and-criminal-justice/legal-system-has-failed-Black-girls-women-and-non

Fishman, S. H., Hummer, R. A., Sierra, G., Hargrove, T., Powers, D. A., & Rogers, R. G. (2020). Race/ethnicity, maternal educational attainment, and infant mortality in the United States. *Biodemography and Social Biology, 66*(1), 1–26. https://doi.org/10.1080/19485565.2020.1793659

Flaherty, C. (2020, May 8). *Reserved: Internet parking, using Wi-Fi ready college parking lots is now a way of life for students with limited or no internet access*. Inside Higher Ed. Retrieved from https://bit.ly/insidehigheredwifi

Foner, N. (2005). *In a new land: A comparative view of immigration*. New York: New York University Press.

Frederickson, G. (2003). *Racism: A short history*. Princeton, NJ: Princeton University Press.

Frenkel, S., & Kang, C. (2021). *An ugly truth: Inside Facebook's battle for domination*. New York: Harper.

Frye, M. (1983). *The politics of reality: Essays in feminist theory*. Crossing Press.

Galperin, H., Wyatt, K., & Le, T. 2020. *COVID-19 and the distance learning gap*. Los Angeles: University of Southern California, Annenberg Research Network on International Communication.

Giannarelli, L., Wheaton, L., & Shantz, K. (2021). *Poverty projections 2021*. Urban Institute. Retrieved from https://www.urban.org/research/publication/2021-poverty-projections

Glaude, E. (2016). *Democracy in Black: How race still enslaves the American soul*. New York: Crown.

Golestaneh, L., Neugarten, J., Fisher, M., Billett, H. H., Gil, M. R., Johns, T., Yunes, M., Mokrzycki, M. H., Coco, M., Norris, K. C., Perez, H. R., Scott, S., Kim, R. S., & Bellin, E. (2020). The association of race and COVID-19 mortality. *EClinicalMedicine, 25*, 100455. https://doi.org/10.1016/j.eclinm.2020.100455

Goldberg, D. T. (1992). The semantics of race. *Ethnic and Racial Studies, 15*(4), 543–569. doi:10.1080/01419870.1992.9993763

Gonzalez, J. (2011). *Harvest of empire: A history of Latinos in America* (revised ed.). New York: Viking.

Goodman, A. (2020). *The deportation machine: America's long history of expelling immigrants*. Princeton, NJ: Princeton University Press. Retrieved from https://www.nationaldisabilityinstitute.org/wp-content/uploads/2019/02/disability-race-poverty-in-america.pdf

Gould, E., Perez, D., & Wilson, V. (2020, August). *Latinx workers—particularly women—face devastating job losses in the COVID-19 recession*. Economic Policy Institute. Retrieved from https://www.epi.org/publication/latinx-workers-covid/

Hall, S. (1992). Race, culture, and communications: Looking backward and forward at cultural studies. *Rethinking Marxism, 5*(1), 10–18. doi:10.1080/08935699208657998

Hamako, E. (2014). *Improving anti-racist education for multiracial students* (Dissertation). UMASS, Amherst.

Hamilton, D., & Darity, W. (2010). Can 'baby bonds' eliminate the racial wealth gap in putative post-racial America? *The Review of Black Political Economy, 37*(3–4), 207–216. doi:10.1007/s12114-010-9063-1

Haney-López, I. (2006). *White by law: The legal construction of race.* New York: New York University Press.

Haney-López, I. F. (2014). *Dog whistle politics: How coded racial appeals have reinvented racism and wrecked the middle class.* New York: Oxford University Press.

Harris, A. (2021). *Affirmative action is ending: What now?* Retrieved from https://www.theatlantic.com/magazine/archive/2021/09/the-end-of-affirmative-action/619488/

Harris, C. I. (1993). Whiteness as property. *Harvard Law Review, 106*(8), 1707–1791.

Harris, Y. R. (2014). Juvenile detention in the US. *Oxford Bibliographies: Childhood Studies, Subject.* doi: 10.1093/obo/9780199791231-0153

Hill, M. L. (2016). *Nobody: Casualties of America's war on the vulnerable from Ferguson to Flint and beyond.* New York: Atria.

Hill-Collins, P. (2019). *Intersectionality as critical social theory.* Durham, NC: Duke University Press.

HIV Gov. (2019). Retrieved from https://www.hiv.gov/hiv-basics/overview/data-and-trends/impact-on-racial-and-ethnic-minorities

Hoberman, J. (2012). *Black and blue: The origins and consequences of medical racism.* Berkeley: University of California Press.

Hollywood Diversity Report. (2020). Retrieved from https://socialsciences.ucla.edu/hollywood-diversity-report-2020/

Huber, L. P., & Solórzano, D. G. (2015). Racial microaggressions as a tool for critical race research. *Race, Ethnicity and Education, 18*(3), 297–320.

Indian Law Resource Center. (n.d.). *Ending violence against native women.* Retrieved from https://indianlaw.org/ending-violence-against-native-women

Jacobson, M. F. (1998). *Whiteness of a different color: European immigrants and the alchemy of race.* Cambridge, MA: Harvard University Press.

Johansen, B. (2020). *Environmental racism in the United States and Canada.* Santa Barbara, CA: Praeger.

Johnston-Guerrero, M. P., & Nadal, K. L. (2010). Multiracial microaggressions: Exposing monoracism in everyday life and clinical practice. In D. W. Sue (Ed.), *Microaggressions and marginality: Manifestation, dynamics, and impact* (pp. 123–144). New York: John Wiley & Sons Inc.

Johnston-Guerrero, M. P., Wijeyesinghe, C., & Daniel, G. R. (2021). *Multiracial experiences in higher education: Contesting knowledge, honoring voice, and innovating practice.* Sterling, VA: Stylus Publishing, LLC.

Jones, S. R., & Wijeyesinghe, C. L. (2011). The promises and challenges of teaching from an intersectional perspective: Core components and applied strategies. *New Directions for Teaching and Learning, 125,* 11–20.

Joseph, V., & Williams, T. O. (2008). "Good niggers": The struggle to find courage, strength, and confidence to fight internalized racism and internalized dominance. *Democracy and Education, 17*(2), 67–73.

Kahn, J. (2018). *Race on the brain: What implicit bias gets wrong about the struggle for racial justice.* New York: Columbia University Press.

Kaiser Family Foundation. (2021, July). *Health coverage of immigrants.* Retrieved from https://www.kff.org/racial-equity-and-health-policy/fact-sheet/health-coverage-of-immigrants/

Kaplowitz, D. R., Griffin, S. R., & Seyka, S. (2019). *Race dialogues: A facilitator's guide to teaching the elephant in the classroom.* New York: Teachers College Press.

Kendi, I. X. (2016). *Stamped from the beginning: The definitive history of racist ideas in America.* New York: Nation Books.

Keyssar, A. (2009). *The right to vote: The contested history of democracy in the United States.* New York: Basic Books.

Kim, C. J. (1999). The racial triangulation of Asian Americans. *Politics and Society, 27*(1), 105–138.

Kohli, R., & Solórzano, D. G. (2012). "Teachers: Please learn our names!" Racial microaggressions and the K-12 classroom. *Race, Ethnicity and Education, 15*(4), 1–22.

Lee, E. (2020). America first, immigrants last: American xenophobia then and now. *The Journal of the Gilded Age and Progressive Era, 19,* 3–18. doi:10.1017/s1537781419000409

Lee, E., & Yung, J. (2010). *Angel Island: Immigrant gateway to America.* New York: Oxford University Press.

Lee, J., & Ramakrishnan, K. (2021). *A rallying cry to stop Asian hate.* AAPI Data. Retrieved from http://aapidata.com/blog/anti-asian-hate-2-million/

Lehrman, S., & Wagner, V. (Eds.) (2019). *Reporting inequality: Tools and methods for Covering race and ethnicity.* New York: Routledge.

Lorde, A. (1983). *There is no hierarchy of oppression, Homophobia and Education*. New York: Council on Interracial Books for Children.

Love, B. L. (2019). *We want to do more than survive: Abolitionist teaching and the pursuit of educational freedom*. Boston: Beacon Press.

Matamoros-Fernández, A., & Farkas, J. (2021). Racism, hate speech, and social media: A systematic review and critique. *Television & New Media, 22*(2), 205–224. doi:10.1177/1527476420982230

McGhee, H. (2021). *The sum of us: What racism costs everyone and how we can prosper together*. New York: Random House.

McIntosh, K., Moss, E., Nunn, R., & Shambaugh, J. (2020). *Examining the black-white wealth gap*. Brookings. Retrieved from https://www.brookings.edu/blog/up-front/2020/02/27/examining-the-Black-white-wealth-gap/

McIntosh, P. (2020). *On privilege, fraudulence, and teaching as learning: Selected essays 1981–2019*. New York, NY: Routledge.

Menakem, R. (2017). *My grandmother's hands: Racialized trauma and the pathway to mending our hearts and Bodies*. Central Recovery Press.

Metzl, J. (2019). *Dying of whiteness: How the politics of racial resentment is killing America's heartland*. New York: Hatchett Books.

Miller, J., Donner, S., & Fraser, E. (2004). Talking when talking is tough: Taking on conversations about race. *Smith College Studies in Social Work, 74*(2), 377–392.

Morin, R., Parker, K., Stepler, R., & Mercer, A. (2017). *Behind the badge-Amid protests and calls for reform, how police view their jobs, key issues and recent fatal encounters between Blacks and police*. Pew Research Center. Retrieved from http://assets.pweresearch.org/wp-content/uploads/sites/3/2017/01/06171402/Police-Report_FINAL_web.pdf

Morris, M. W. (2012). *Race, gender and the school to prison pipeline: Expanding our discussion to include Black girls*. New York: African American Policy Forum.

Muhammed, D., Tec, R., & Ramirez, K. (2019). Retrieved from https://ncrc.org/racial-wealth-snapshot-american-indians-native-americans/

Muhammed, K. G. (2010). *The Condemnation of Blackness: Race, Crime, and the Making of Modern Urban America*. Cambridge, MA: Harvard University Press.

Natapoff, A. (2018). *Punishment without crime: How our massive misdemeanor system traps the innocent and makes America more unequal*. New York: Basic Books.

National Center for Education Statistics. (2021). Annual Earnings by Educational Attainment. Condition of Education. U.S. Department of Education, Institute of Education Sciences. Retrieved from https://nces.ed.gov/programs/coe/indicator/cba

National Center for Learning Disabilities. (2020). *Significant disproportionality in special education: Current trends and actions for impact*. Retrieved from https://www.ncld.org/wp-content/uploads/2020/10/2020-NCLD-Disproportionality_Trends-and-Actions-for-Impact_FINAL-1.pdf

Neely, C. L. (2015). *You're dead—So what?: Media, police, and the invisibility of black women as victims of homicide*. Michigan State University Press. Retrieved from http://www.jstor.org/stable/10.14321/j.ctt16t8z4n

Ngai, M. M. (2004). *Impossible subjects: Illegal aliens and the making of modern America*. Princeton, NJ: Princeton University Press.

Noble, S. U. (2018). *Algorithms of oppression: How search engines reinforce racism*. New York: NYU Press.

Noel, N., Pinder, D., Stuart, S., & Wright, J. (2019). *The economic impact of closing the racial wealth gap*. McKinsey. Retrieved from https://www.mckinsey.com/industries/public-and-social-sector/our-insights/the-economic-impact-of-closing-the-racial-wealth-gap

Oliver, M. L., & Shapiro, T. M. (2006). *Black wealth/white wealth: A new perspective on racial inequality* (2nd ed.). New York: Routledge.

Ornelas, I. J., Yamanis, T. J., & Ruiz, R. (2020). The health of undocumented Latinx immigrants: What we know and future directions. *Annual Review of Public Health*, 289–308. Retrieved from https://www.annualreviews.org/doi/pdf/10.1146/annurev-publhealth-040119-094211

Painter, N. I. (2010). *The history of white people*. New York: W. W. Norton & Company.

Parker, K., Morin, R., Horowitz, J. M., Lopez, M. H., & Rohal, M. (2015). *Multiracial in America: Proud, diverse, and growing in numbers*. Social and Demographic Trends, Pew Research Center. Retrieved from http://ezproxy.cul.columbia.edu/login?url=https://www.proquest.com/books/multiracial-america-proud-diverse-growing-numbers/docview/1735644917/se-2?accountid=10226

Pedulla, D. S. (2018, June). How race and unemployment shape labor market opportunities: Additive, amplified, or muted effects? *Social Forces, 96*(4), 1477–1506. doi:10.1093/sf/soy002

Pedulla, D. S. (2020). *Making the cut*. Princeton, NJ: Princeton University Press.

Pfeffer, F. T., & Killewald, A. (2019, March). Intergenerational wealth mobility and racial inequality. *Socius: Sociological Research for a Dynamic World*, 5, ISSN: 2378-0231. doi:10.1177/2378023119831799

Preskill, S. & Brookfield, S. D. (2009). *Learning as a way of leading: Lessons from the struggle for social justice*. San Francisco: Jossey-Bass.

Quiros, L., Varghese, R., & Vanidestine, T. (2019). Disrupting the single story: Challenging dominant trauma narratives through a critical race lens. *Traumatology*, 26(2), 160. 6/2020, ISSN: 1085–9373 (Advance Online publication).

Ray, R., Perry, A. M., Harshbarger, D., & Elizondo, S. (2021). *Homeownership, racial segregation, and policy solutions to racial wealth equity*. Brookings. Retrieved from https://www.brookings.edu/essay/homeownership-racial-segregation-and-policies-for-racial-wealth-equity/

Ray, R., & Perry, A. M. (2020, April). *Why we need reparations for Black Americans*. Brookings. Retrieved from https://www.brookings.edu/policy2020/bigideas/why-we-need-reparations-for-Black-americans/

Reardon, J., & TallBear, K. (2012). Your DNA is our history: Genomics, anthropology, and the construction of whiteness as property. *Current Anthropology*, 53(S5), S233–S245. doi: 10.1086/662629

Roberts, D. (2011). *Fatal invention*. New York: New Press.

Roithmayr, D. (2014). *Reproducing racism: How everyday choices lock in white advantage*. New York: New York University Press.

Ross, T. (2019). Media and stereotypes. In S. Ratuva (Ed.), *The Palgrave handbook of ethnicity*. Singapore: Palgrave Macmillan. doi:10.1007/978-981-13-0242-8_26-1

Rothstein, R. (2014). *The making of Ferguson: Public policy and the root of its troubles*. Washington, DC: The Economic Policy Institute.

Rothstein, R. (2017). *The color of law: A forgotten history of how government segregated America*. New York: WW Norton.

Rugh, J. S., & Massey, D. S. (2010). Racial segregation and the American foreclosure crisis. *American Sociological Review*, 75(5), 629–651.

Sakamoto, A., Takei, I., & Woo, H. (2012). The myth of the model minority myth. *Sociological Spectrum*, 32(4), 309–321. doi:10.1080/02732173.2012.664042

Sawyer, W., & Wagner, P. (2020, March). *Mass incarceration: The whole pie*. Retrieved from https://www.prisonpolicy.org/reports/pie2020.html

Schaeffer, K. (2021). *Racial, ethnic diversity increases yet again with the 117th Congress*. Retrieved from https://www.pewresearch.org/fact-tank/2021/01/28/racial-ethnic-diversity-increases-yet-again-with-the-117th-congress/

The Sentencing Project. (2014). *The state of sentencing 2014: Developments in policy and practice*. Retrieved from http://sentencingproject.org/doc/publications/sen_State_of_Sentencing_2014.pdf

Shapiro, T., Meschede, T., & Osoro, S. (2013, Feb.). *The roots of the widening racial wealth gap: Explaining the Black-white economic divide* (Research and Policy Brief). Waltham, MA: Institute on Assets & Social Policy, Brandeis University. Retrieved from http://iasp.brandeis.edu/pdfs/Author/shapiro-thomas-m/racialwealthgapbrief.pdf

Smedley, A., & Smedley, B. (2011). *Race in North America: The origin and evolution of a worldview* (4th ed.). New York: Westview Press.

Smith, W. A., Hung, M., & Franklin, J. D. (2011). Racial battle fatigue and the miseducation of black men: Racial microaggressions, sovietal problems and environmental stress. *Journal of Negro Education*, 80(1), 63–82.

Smith, M. (n.d.). *Native Americans: A crisis in health equity*. Americanbar.org. Retrieved from https://www.americanbar.org/groups/crsj/publications/human_rights_magazine_home/the-state-of-healthcare-in-the-united-states/

Solorzano, D. G. (2020). *Racial microaggressions: Using critical race theory to respond to everyday racism*. New York: Teachers College Press.

Solórzano, D. G., Ceja, M., & Yosso, T. (2000). Critical race theory, racial microaggressions, and campus racial climate: The experiences of African American college students. *The Journal of Negro Education*, 69, 60–73.

Steele, C. (2010). *Whistling Vivaldi: And other clues to how stereotypes affect us*. New York: W.W. Norton & Company.

Stevenson, B. (2014). *Just mercy: A story of justice and redemption*. New York: Spiegel & Grau.

Subtirelu, N. C. (2015). "She does have an accent but . . .": Race and language ideology in students' evaluations of mathematics instructors on RateMyProfessors.com. *Language in Society, 44*(1), 35–62.

Sue, D. W. (2010). *Racial microaggressions in everyday life: Race, gender, and sexual orientation.* Hoboken, NJ: John Wiley and Sons.

Sue, D. W., Lin, A. I., Torino, G. C., Capodiluco, C. M., & Rivera, D. P. (2009). Racial microaggressions and difficult dialogues on race in the classroom. *Cultural Diversity and Ethnic Minority Psychology, 15*(2), 183–190.

Tankersley, J. (2020). *The riches of this land: The untold, true story of America's middle class.* New York: Hatchett.

Tatum, B. D. (1992). Talking about race, learning about racism: The application of racial identity development theory in the classroom. *Harvard Educational Review, 62*(1), 1–25.

Teranishi, R. T. (2012). Asian American and Pacific Islander students and the institutions that serve them. *Change: The Magazine of Higher Learning, 44*(2), 16–22.

Thomas, S. A. (2016). *The missing American Jury: Restoring the fundamental constitutional role of the criminal, civil, and grand juries.* Cambridge: Cambridge University Press.

Townsend, S., Marcus, H., & Bergseiker, H. (2009, March). My choice, your categories: The denial of multiracial identities. *Social Issues, 65*(1), 185–204.

Tuan, M. (2001). *Forever foreigners or honorary whites? The Asian ethnic experience today.* New Brunswick, NJ: Rutgers University Press.

Tyler, T. R., & Jackson, J. (2014). Popular legitimacy and the exercise of legal authority: Motivating compliance, cooperation and engagement. *Psychology, Public Policy and Law, 20*(1), 78–95.

U.S. Bureau of Labor Statistics. (2022). Retrieved from https://www.bls.gov/cps/cpsaat11.htm

Waldman, M. (2016). *The fight to vote:* New York: Simon & Schuster.

Waters, M. C. (2009). *Black identities.* Cambridge, MA: Harvard University Press.

Weller, C. (2019). *African Americans face systematic obstacles to getting good jobs.* Center for American Progress. Retrieved from https://www.americanprogress.org/article/african-americans-face-systematic-obstacles-getting-good-jobs/

Wijeyesinghe, C. L., & Jackson, B. J. (2012). *New perspectives on racial identity development: Integrating emerging frameworks* (2nd ed.). New York: New York University Press.

Williamson, V. (2020). *Closing the racial wealth gap requires heavy, progressive taxation of wealth.* https://www.brookings.edu/research/closing-the-racial-wealth-gap-requires-heavy-progressive-taxation-of-wealth/

Wilson, V. (2020). *Racial disparities in income and poverty remain largely unchanged amid strong income growth in 2019.* Retrieved from https://www.epi.org/blog/racial-disparities-in-income-and-poverty-remain-largely-unchanged-amid-strong-income-growth-in-2019/

Williams, J., & Wilson, V. (2019). *Black workers endure persistent racial disparities in employment outcomes.* Retrieved from https://www.epi.org/publication/labor-day-2019-racial-disparities-in-employment/

Williams, R. B. (2017). *The privileges of wealth: Rising inequality and the growing racial divide.* New York: Routledge.

Williams, T. O. (2011, Jan.). *A process of becoming: U.S. born African American and Black women in a process of liberation from internalized racism* (Doctoral dissertation). Available from Proquest, Paper AAI3465244.

Wolfe, P. (2006). Settler colonialism and the elimination of the native. *Journal of Genocide Research, 8*(4), 387–409. doi:10.1080/14623520601056240

Xu, J., & Lee, J. C. (2013). The marginalized "model" minority: An empirical examination of the triangulation of Asian Americans. *Social Forces, 91*(4), 1363–1397.

Zamarippa, R., & Roque, L. (2021, March). *Latinos face disproportionate health and economic impacts.* From COVID-19, Center for American Progress. Retrieved from https://www.americanprogress.org/article/latinos-face-disproportionate-health-economic-impacts-covid-19/

6

Sexism, Heterosexism, and Trans* Oppression

An Integrated Perspective

*Mirangela Buggs, D. Chase J. Catalano, and Rachel Wagner**

INTRODUCTION

Sexism, heterosexism, and trans*[1] oppression are three systems of oppression based on power hierarchies and false binaries of gender and sexuality. Binary and hierarchical constructions of gender (women and men), sex (female and male), and sexuality (heterosexual and homosexual) are pervasive and long-standing and are entangled with hierarchies of race, class, ability, and more. To understand and resist these systems requires not only resisting the hierarchies that privilege some groups while disadvantaging others but also untangling the impacts of binary categorization itself.

In this chapter we call attention to the complexity and pluralities of categories of gender, sex, and sexuality[2] in order to complicate educators' thinking about and beyond binaries and enable them to examine the impact of binarism in cultural perceptions of sex, gender, and sexuality. With the foundation of a critical understanding of binarism, we can better understand and critique how sexism, heterosexism, and trans* oppression operate in their intersection with each other and with other isms.

Our intention is not only to interrupt binary approaches to sexuality and gender and analyze the systems of oppression constituted through such binaries but also to foreground the liberatory movements and world-making that people of minoritized genders and sexualities have created and sustained. We articulate an anti-oppressive, intersectional, and inclusive conceptual landscape rooted in the lived experiences of people across genders and sexualities. We explore tensions and evolutions within feminist movements and particularly draw on the contributions of women-of-color feminisms and trans* feminisms. To effectively challenge sexism and misogyny, heterosexism and homophobia, and trans* oppression and transphobia, we must excavate the fraught historical and contemporary dynamics of gender, race, class, and sexuality and center the experiences and insights of multiply marginalized people who offer liberatory visions for ending these interconnected systems of oppressions.

We begin by explaining the key terms we use while complicating everyday language that people use to talk about sex, gender, and sexuality. Then we provide our rationale for addressing sexism, heterosexism, and trans* oppression together as systems that are intricately linked rather than discrete, singular forms of oppression. The rationale includes presentation of theoretical and conceptual frameworks (always connected to lived experience) necessary for examining historical legacies. We next provide context in the form of the historical legacies and social movements that shaped contemporary views about sex, gender, and sexuality, followed by contemporary examples of sexism, heterosexism, and trans* oppression. Finally, we provide a four-part curriculum design that addresses sexism, heterosexism, and trans* oppression together in the first and fourth quadrants, with options for Quadrants 2 and 3 that focus on sexism, heterosexism, or trans* oppression separately.

DOI: 10.4324/9781003005759-8

We conclude the chapter with pedagogical considerations for the facilitation and design of educational experiences around sexism, heterosexism, and trans* oppression.

OUR APPROACH

We begin by unpacking the language of gender and sexuality to create a common vocabulary and to frame the integration of sexism, heterosexism, and trans* oppression in this chapter. We then present the conceptual frameworks of this chapter—patriarchy, misogyny, feminism, and intersectionality—and use these frames as a critical lens for understanding how to move beyond gender binaries that are embedded in these systems of power. Finally, we explicate how this chapter's integration of sexism, heterosexism, and trans* oppression enables a more critical, historical, and dynamic approach to historical legacies, current manifestations of oppression, and emancipatory movements. By uncovering how genders and sexualities that we assume to be "normal" organizers of social life came and continue to be, we expose how norms predicated on intersecting systems of oppression are anything but inevitable, reasonable, and permanent.

KEY TERMS, CONCEPTS, AND LIVED REALITIES

Sex, gender, and sexuality are concepts that stand in relationship with each other but are not interchangeable. *"Biological" sex* refers to categorization based on characteristics of the body that are typically understood as male and female traits. The idea that sex is binary is not a biological fact but rather an idea asserted and enforced through culture and institutions. This binary notion of sex does not account for the diversity of human experiences. Furthermore, the conflation of binary sex with gender—or the assumption that biological sex determines gender—is inaccurate because gender is a varied and multiple form of identity and expression.

Binary frameworks of thinking about *"biological" sex* rely on the inaccurate assumption that all humans are either *male* or *female*. Either-or notions of sex and gender, perpetuated by medical professionals, categorize *sex* based on physiology. Medical professionals typically rely upon a visual examination of an infant's external genitals to determine sex. Thus, what is often named as *biological sex* is more accurately described as sex *assigned at birth*. Although almost everyone is assigned to a category of male or female, there are myriad of other sex categories and experiences possible beyond the two commonly recognized ones (Fausto-Sterling, 2000).

The criteria for assigned sex "are social decisions for which scientists can offer no absolute guidelines" (Fausto-Sterling, 2000, p. 5). Fausto-Sterling (2000) reminds us that " 'sex' is not a pure physical category" (p. 4). Chromosomes, genitals, and hormones often align to present a version of human development that aligns with presumed binary sex categories, for instance where an infant with XY chromosomes has testes and a penis and produces significant concentration of testosterone to trigger secondary sex characteristics at the onset of puberty. Yet these sex markers do not always align so obviously. The diversity among humans in chromosomes, genitals, and hormones reveals how sex is actually a socially constructed notion, with categorization based on an interpretation of genitals present upon the birth of a human (Butler, 2004; West & Fenstemaker, 1995; West & Zimmerman, 1987). The experience of *intersex* people offers an example of how social and cultural narratives construct so-called biological truths. *Intersex* refers to people with any of a multiplicity of configurations of chromosomes, genitals, and hormones that defy the simplicity of male and female distinctions (Kessler, 1998; Preves, 2003). Put simply, even the biological certainty of sex is false; human bodily realities are diverse and complex.

The common conflation of sex and gender further confuses biological fact with social construction. Mainstream culture confuses body morphology (shapes and parts of bodies), chromosomes, behavior and affect, and other presumed indicators of sex with a person's gender. *Gender* is a constellation of practices that organizes social life; we commonly understand individuals' roles in these practices using categories like woman, man, and trans* and typically use the terms *woman* and *man* as the mainstream social categories of gender. The confounding of sex and gender extends the assumption that individuals are either male or female, with a further assumption that they will conform to the respective categories of boys/men and girls/women in a given culture.

In some cultures, gender rests on a persistent binary of social organization between two presumed opposites, men and women. This idea especially permeates dominant European and Euro-descendant conceptualizations of gender. In cultures dominated by this way of thinking, there is an overwhelming and pervasive assumption that gender categories are mutually constituted; that is, we only understand what it means to be a man in relation to (and often, opposite of) what it means to be a woman. The dynamic of mutually constituting opposites is further reinforced by the norm of heterosexual intimate relationships between people perceived as women and men (Ingraham, 1994). Common cultural perceptions assume that two genders exist to complement and complete one other in kinship networks built around heterosexual intimate and familial relations, in social contexts that often ascribe power and dominance to people gendered as men. *Sexism*, a system of advantage and disadvantage based on perceived gender, rests upon these pervasive gendered cultural dynamics of male/man/masculine dominance and woman/female/feminine subordination.

Sexuality is often used to describe the sexual and/or romantic attraction a person has toward others, usually rooted in assumptions about biological sex. A person's sexuality can signal a romantic and/or sexual attraction toward someone of the same sex ("*homosexual*," *lesbian*, or *gay*), someone of the presumed binary opposite sex (*heterosexual*), both sexes (*bisexual*), or any sex (*pansexual*). Binary distinctions assume that attraction and intimacy (sexual, emotional, and/or romantic) align with assigned sex or body morphology. This narrow focus on sexuality overdetermined by the male/female binary possibly stems from a culture that ties sex with procreation (Hubbard, 1996) and is imposed by societal norms as "compulsory heterosexuality" (Rich, 1980) in which heterosexuality is an overwhelmingly supported social expectation that precludes other forms of intimate partnering. Assumptions about the nature of gender and sexuality mask or conceal a range of other possible organizations of human sexual and/or romantic experience.

Sexuality (as distinct from how "sexual orientation" is usually used) can also include aspects of sexual feelings, experiences, and relationships beyond the gender/s to whom someone is attracted (Ferber, Holcomb, & Wentling, 2009). In this chapter our attention to sexuality allows for the inclusion and consideration of identities and relationships that go beyond sexual orientation to include degrees and kinds of attractions such as, but not limited to, *asexual* (no sexual attraction to others), *aromantic* (no romantic attraction to others), *demisexual* (feeling sexual attraction only in the context of an emotional connection), and *polyamorous* (multiple romantic and/or sexual relationships).

Heterosexism is the system of oppression that upholds heterosexuality as the dominant and valued sexuality and organizer of the familial institution, which has clear connections to dynamics of sexism. *Heteronormativity* reinforces heterosexuality as the assumed default sexuality and the norm through which all other sexualities are viewed and judged. An example of heteronormativity is the mapping of stereotyped heterosexual dynamics onto gay and lesbian couples, as in the question, "Who is the man in this relationship?" This question assumes one can only understand lesbian and gay experience through the lens of heterosexuality, that the only way to understand all romantic/sexual pairings is through an "opposite" sex/gender framework.

We use *queer* as a broad umbrella term that "represents a continuum of possibilities outside of what are considered to be normal sexual or gender identities and behaviors. Affirmation of queerness creates possibility outside the norm" (Carruthers, 2018, Location No. 331). *Queer* is a noun, an adjective, and a verb. As a noun or adjective, *queer* is an identity term with historical roots as both a pejorative slur and a reclamation of power by those outside normative ideas of gender and sexuality (Dilley, 1999). As a verb, *to queer* is to engage in a disruption of normative assumptions, to make something apparent as odd or different, and to transgress boundaries in a way that opens up possibilities or thinking—in this way, to queer expectations about formations of life, work, and relationships (Mayo, 2007).

Queer is not a universal term, as there are still tensions about its use in various communities based on class, race, and nation. We use *queer* in this chapter as a reference to those who do not identify as heterosexual *and/or* those who transgress gender boundaries. The acronym LGBTQ+ (lesbian, gay, bisexual, trans*, queer, plus others) is often used in a similar way, but in spite of the + it evokes a narrowness of identity expectations and is insufficient for inclusion (Driver, 2008). To identify as queer for an individual could be a political, social, or self-identification act (or all three) (Dilley, 1999; Morris, 1998; Shlasko, 2005). The claiming of queerness can be an act of agency and liberation among some who elect to name themselves as such; it can be a recognition of and challenge to oppression based on sexuality and gender.

Complicating Gender

As social markers, we use color, clothing, styles, hair, voice, and many other characteristics to signify gender, which we then link to an assumed assigned sex at birth (woman is female and man is male). These markers have been culturally and socially a part of U.S. norms that frame our ideas about gender (West & Fenstemaker, 1995; West & Zimmerman, 1987). As we discussed, the distinction between sex and gender, when the distinction is made at all, usually relies on a presumption of sex as a biological and gender as a social category. What this means in everyday life is there is an assumption that there are biological "truths" to support the category of sex, while gender is a series of social "doings" understood through interactions between people (West & Zimmerman, 1987; Young, 1994). Time, history, geography, culture, and context also influence these social doings—dress, behaviors, occupations, roles in families and society, etc. (Butler, 2004; Stryker, 2008). For instance, cultural traditions inform whether in each culture robes or skirts are common or acceptable dress for men (e.g., common attire for men in various cultures include Burmese longyi, Scottish kilts, and Bhutanese gho). Additionally, tights or hose were fairly standard among wealthier classes of men in Elizabethan England, yet in contemporary England, men rarely wear them. Thus, geography, time, and culture contextualize social expressions that cue gender.

Gender as a social category also connects to mainstream logics about gender roles and gender expression. For example, a female (sex) is a woman (gender) who cues femininity (expression) and engages in feminized tasks (roles) (Connel, 2002; Feinberg, 1998). Feminine roles and femininity demonstrate the persistent expectations of women as caregivers, mothers, or domestic. Some reasonable working definitions might be: *gender* as the social relationship to assigned sex, *gender identity* as the language an individual uses to define themselves, *gender expression* as the social markers an individual chooses to exhibit to encourage others to see them as they see themself, and *gender roles* as the socially sanctioned behaviors that are associated with one's perceived (binary) gender.

Cisgender people are those who identify with both their sex assigned at birth and assumed gender (e.g., male to boy and man) (Aultman, 2014). For this chapter, to refer to someone who does not conform to their sex and/or gender assigned at birth, we utilize *trans**, recognizing that it is imperfect as an all-encompassing umbrella term. Variations of trans*ness exist from those who do not identify with any gender (*agender*) to gender-nonconforming to nonbinary to transgender or trans*.[3] Trans* identities further complicate the relationship between sex and gender. The gender and sexual binaries are so pervasive as to make it relatively impossible to distinguish between sex and gender in everyday conversation. For example, did I utilize masculine pronouns (he/him/his) for an individual because he is wearing a tie (gender expression) or a mechanic's uniform (gender role), or because he has facial hair (secondary sex characteristic), or because I saw the *M* on his driver's license? Because of assumptions about the fixity of gender to sex, trans*ness and trans* identities challenge the surety of the larger sex/gender structure. "The meaning of sex, then, is socially 'read' through interpretations placed on the visible body. . . . Indeed, recognition of both 'sex' and 'gender' is always already a social act—part of everyday interaction—that occurs simultaneously" (Messerschmidt, 2009, p. 86). In other words, the possibilities raised by trans* identities reveal the tenuous relationship between sex and gender.

CONCEPTUAL FRAMEWORKS: PATRIARCHY, MISOGYNY, FEMINISM, AND INTERSECTIONALITY

Identities and expressions of sex, gender, and sexuality operate within the confines of various systems of power and meaning-making. For instance, *patriarchy* is the ideology that supports systemic *sexism*. Patriarchy is a system of ideas that circulate and elevate presumed masculine characteristics and render feminine-ascribed characteristics as less than. Patriarchal domination is androcentric (Johnson, 2014), centering the experiences of men/masculine people and giving them power and privilege over cisgender women, trans* women, and all people who express what society regards as femininity. Patriarchy devalues all women and expressions of femininities (Rich, 1980; Serano, 2013).

Patriarchy privileges masculinity and maleness and positions cisgender men (and often trans* men) as primary authority figures who occupy positions of power and moral authority, guaranteeing women's subordinate position to them. Patriarchy uses symbols, narratives, stock stories, and cultural artifacts to systematically organize gender relations as two complementary but unequal opposites. It naturalizes masculine aggression, competition, and violence, while reinforcing feminine caretaking, compassion, and cooperation (Johnson, 2014). Societal patterns of patriarchy and sexism exist on a continuum, from seemingly benevolent yet patronizing everyday masculine behaviors to violent *misogyny* (hatred of women and the feminine).

In societies constituted by colonialism and racism, white cisgender men learn to expect they have dominance above all others. Men of color also experience gendered privilege, but due to racism and the racialized constructions of gender, they do not experience masculine dominance in the same way as white men.

Feminist movements over the past several centuries have challenged sexism, patriarchy, and misogyny. Until recently, much of feminist activism did not challenge the conceptualization of sex and gender as binary, implicitly centering cisgender women as those seeking liberation. The feminist analyses of power promulgated by these streams of feminism have revealed patterns and produced knowledge that help us understand sexism, yet they also have significant limitations because as feminist imaginaries of womanhood—in seeking liberation from patriarchal domination—they relied on societal assumptions about gender that centered whiteness (hooks, 1981) and excluded trans* women and nonbinary feminine people (Serano, 2013). Before the interventions of lesbian feminists, women's movements were often historically homophobic and heterosexist (Radicallesbians, 1970; Combahee River Collective, 1977). The full inclusion of the voices and experiences of lesbians was a site of struggle in the mainstream feminist movements, particularly in the U.S. (Jay, 1999). Tensions within and among feminist movements highlight the entwined nature of gender and sexuality with race, class, and nation, pushing feminists to rethink essentialism with respect to liberation of the monolithic category of women (Anzaldúa, 1990; Brown, 1992; Spelman, 1988).

An intersectional and integrative feminist analysis re-centers the experiences of racially oppressed women in experiences of sexism, patriarchy, and misogyny. Additionally, by utilizing intersectional feminism, examinations of gender-based forms of oppression can include an analysis of race, class, sexuality, and nation (Anzaldúa, 1990; Crenshaw, 2008; Davis, 1981; hooks, 1981; Lorde, 1984; Shohat, 1998). The construction and derivation of notions of gender in the United States come from Eurocentric thought, colonialism (Lugones, 2007; Quijano, 2000), and white cultural and political domination. As we work to excavate the overlapping workings of sexism, heterosexism, and trans* oppression, it is important to recognize intersectional feminism as a politics of liberation that impacted the United States and the world (Baca Zinn & Zambrana, 2019; Purkayastha, 2012; Shohat, 1998).

Feminisms that foreground the identities and experiences of Black, Indigenous, and People of Color (BIPOC) profoundly challenge Eurocentrism, both in our understanding of the systems of oppression involving gender and sexuality and in the societal conceptualizations and definitions of gender and sexuality (Anzaldúa & Moraga, 2015). Feminisms that begin with the lived experiences of women of color may pursue different political questions and outcomes than those that center whiteness, such as access to health care, environmental justice, and the ability to exercise the right to vote (not just have the right); moreover, the sociopolitical location of colonized and racialized women lends itself to interrogating binary and heteronormative fictions that buttressed imperialist projects throughout the Southern Hemisphere (referred to as the Global South). Intersectionality is an epistemology and mode of analysis based on the historical realities and structural positionality of Black women in the United States (Crenshaw, 2001, 2008).

Since Black women experience the simultaneous oppressions of race and gender, intersectionality is a framework to explain the multiple forms of oppression that "intersect" in the lives of Black women. In short, intersectionality is a powerful "analytical tool to capture and engage contextual dynamics of power" (Cho et al., 2013, p. 788). An intersectional lens challenges "single-axis frameworks" (Cho et al., 2013) that attempted to "hold still" one form of oppression as universally applicable. As Crenshaw argued in 2001, the adoption of a single-issue framework inherently marginalized Black women whose structural location and lived experiences in patriarchal and racist societies require an interconnected understanding of how social identities and systems function in tandem. In other words, "racism, patriarchy, social class and other systems of oppression simultaneously structure the relative position of these women at any one time" (Mirza, 2009, p. 3). In the present day, the concept of intersectionality "has found a place in the intellectual toolkit of scholars around the world . . . and is used to interrogate problems and policy issues in their national or regional settings" (Bose, 2012, p. 67).

To hold sex, gender, and sexuality in an intersectional frame gives us more to unpack regarding the workings of sexism, heterosexism, and trans* oppression and the multiple dynamics of discrimination and marginalization. Recognizing the plurality and multi-locality of BIPOC histories, cultures, and needs for gender liberation, intersectional feminist thought offers us more potential to move beyond gender binaries, patriarchal constructions, and heteronormativity to contribute to the liberation of people of all genders and sexual orientations (Collins, 2005).

WHY INTEGRATE SEXISM, HETEROSEXISM, AND TRANS* OPPRESSION

In the 21st century, to teach and learn adequately about the workings of sexism, heterosexism, and trans* oppression, we must understand these systems of oppression in relation to each other. An expansive understanding of gender beyond binary conceptions can chart a terrain for more justice-informed, inclusive, and liberatory movements to transform sexism and heterosexism and to support trans* liberation. Sexism, heterosexism, and trans* oppression are systems of oppression that share historical roots and overlap in the current manifestations of oppression. In this chapter, we aim to give educators the conceptual lenses to be able to discern the interconnections and distinctions among sexism, heterosexism, and trans* oppression while holding the facts of their interconnections in teaching/leading groups in dialogue about one or all three forms of oppression.

Sex, gender, and sexuality are all understood in terms of each other, making it difficult to discern where one concept ends and another begins. All three are implicated in systems of sexism, heterosexism, and trans* oppression. For example, articulating and analyzing the impact of sexism reveals that it is not simply about biological or assigned sex but also about perceptions of gender-coded behaviors and aesthetics (gender expression) and romantic/sexual expectations of (hetero or homo)sexuality. Oppressive judgments about women's abilities to lead are based on assumptions about presumed-biological traits (too emotional, lacking physical and/or mental strength), which are reinforced by expectations of feminine appearance, body language, and tone of voice (gender expression). The same elements of feminine gender expression act as signals of heterosexuality, not only in the general sense of attraction to males but more specifically delineated as interest in dating a man who is masculine. To unpack this even more, often our understanding of sexuality relies on assumptions of binary, complimentary opposites in terms of sex (physiological and morphological characteristics), sexual behavior (what those bodies do together), and gendered behavior and expression—as if two chromosomes dictate specific sexual and social behaviors. The relationships that people have with their bodies, desires, behaviors, and identities influence their understanding of other people's bodies, desires, behaviors, and identities.

Movements for liberation around gender and sexuality are likewise entangled. Movements against sexism, heterosexism, and trans* oppression have overlapped, interacted, supported each other, and at times contradicted each other such that it does not make sense to study them separately. As noted prior, feminist activism in the mid-20th century, often called "the women's movement," sought "women's liberation" in a way that flattened and essentialized womanhood and centered white, cisgender, class-privileged, and heterosexual women. Likewise, the contemporaneous movement for "gay liberation" often foregrounded the experiences of white cisgender men and sometimes women but rarely other queer and/or trans* people. Everyone has a part to play in the elimination of sexism, heterosexism, and trans* oppression. To build a movement for gender and sexual justice that truly includes everyone, educators need more accurate understandings of gender and sexuality that are inclusive of people of all genders.

What we offer educators who teach about gender and sexuality is a vision for moving beyond *cisnormativity*—that is, the presumption that all humans are either men or women and that one's assigned sex at birth corresponds with one's gender identity (cisgender)—to an expansive understanding of the systems of sexism, heterosexism, and trans* oppression. The reality of the expansive and multiple categories of gender expression are facts, albeit suppressed, of human history and culture. Binary thinking about gender and sexuality has a relatively short history. Science, prior to the 1800s in the U.S., grappled with defining sex, gender, and sexuality and oversimplified the realities of sex, gender, and sexual diversity to fit within binary frameworks (Fausto-Sterling, 2000). The Western colonial legacy, including the settler colonial legacy of Europe in the Americas and the Pacific, along with the entrenchment of various patriarchal cultures, buried the realities of Indigenous cultures and peoples who did not ascribe to gender and sexual binaries (Lugones, 2007; Rifkin, 2011). Because of the pervasiveness of colonizing projects of Western cultures, forms of resistance to gender-based binaries, particularly in the United States, are a relatively recent dynamic. However, across cultures and histories, humans persistently lived and experienced gendered identities beyond the binary.

Systems of oppression work to bestow power and advantage on some and to silence, disempower, and marginalize others. Sexism (oppression and subordination of cisgender women, trans* women, and others perceived to be feminine), heterosexism (oppression of those who are not heterosexual), and trans* oppression (oppression of transgender, nonbinary, and gender-nonconforming people) are interconnected and also have distinct power dynamics, social constructs, and frameworks embedded in each of them. This chapter focuses on the integration of sexism, heterosexism, and trans* oppression in an overarching framework while also acknowledging their distinctions and the intersections of other forms of oppression that shape interpersonal, institutional, and cultural dynamics. By examining sexism, heterosexism, and trans* oppression together, we acknowledge shared roots in a compulsory, hierarchical binary that the social identities of sex, gender, and sexuality have to each other (Catalano & Griffin, 2016).

HISTORICAL LEGACIES

In the section that follows, we provide context to understand the historical legacies of sexism, heterosexism, and trans* oppression. We utilize a thematic approach to history instead of a linear or chronological one in order to reveal complex dynamics across multiple forms of oppression. We begin with unpacking conceptualizations of gender and feminism that did and did not account for other social identities. Then we trace the impacts of colonization on the categories of gender and sexuality to highlight the impact of dominant whiteness on current notions about bodies, relationships, gender roles, and feminisms. Next, we complicate the histories of queer liberation movements and their intersections with racial, economic, and gender movements. Finally, we utilize the institution of medicine as a site to explore how intersectionality—the overlap of various forms of oppression—functions to oppress marginalized genders and sexualities through ableism.

19TH- AND EARLY 20TH-CENTURY LIBERAL FEMINISMS

In most U.S. K–12 schools, if feminism is mentioned at all, it is usually through stories of liberal struggles for self-determination and equal rights in movements for suffrage, financial autonomy, employment rights, and (less often acknowledged) reproductive rights. Committed to a right or just society, liberalism asserts that individuals must have the right to exercise their autonomy and fulfill themselves. Liberal feminism informed much of the thinking of 19th-century women's rights advocates and the pursuit of the vote by early 20th-century suffragists. Wyoming was the first state to legalize women's right to vote in 1890, but it took 20 years of social movements led by political organizations like the National American Women's Suffrage Association before certain women in the United States won the right to vote in 1920, with the passage of the Nineteenth Amendment to the U.S. Constitution.

The right to vote for women was a limited reform because it excluded women of color groups in numerous ways. Prior to the McCarran Walter Act of 1952, Asian Americans experienced restrictions on citizenship. The passage of the 1924 Snyder Act granted citizenship to Native Americans in the U.S., paving the way for enfranchisement; however, since these voting rights were determined by individual states, there remained significant barriers to voting well beyond 1924. Indigenous citizens in Maine would not achieve the right to vote until 1954. While Black women were technically eligible to vote ostensibly in 1920, a series of legislative and social actions combined to prevent voting access, especially in the South. Poll taxes, literacy tests, and frequent intimidation and violence continued to suppress Black women from enacting their voting rights until the Voting Rights Act of 1965, half a century after the Nineteenth Amendment.

The influx of white women into the paid workforce following the United States' entry into World War II is often heralded as a watershed moment for women in the workplace. While it significantly accelerated and broadened the participation of women in paid employment, it was also a continuation of a longer-term trend in women's employment (Wallace, 2011). Young men leaving jobs to enter the military created critical labor shortages, especially in manufacturing and transportation. Government agencies, instructed by the Secretary of War, targeted employers with instructional pamphlets on employing women and the broader public with propaganda featuring Rosie the Riveter that encouraged women to seek work in factories dedicated to the production of engines, tanks, gas masks, and other war materials. In spite of initial resistance from working men and managers, there was a drastic increase in the number of women employed in male-dominated, "blue-collar" occupations. Factories that had previously employed only white men began recruiting white women, and then men of color, and then women of color (National Park Service, 2021). The first federally funded childcare program, and the beginning of early childhood education as a professional field, came about in order to support mothers' abilities to take jobs in war sectors (Kesselman, 1990; Cohen, 2015).

Although donning a uniform and punching a time clock was new to many middle-class white women, BIPOC women and poor white women had been wage earners (and often exploited as such) since long before World War II, participating in the workforce as teachers, cooks, caretakers, and cleaners as well as working in family businesses and farms (National Park Service, 2021; Cohen, 2015). Indeed, only about a third of the women employed in the war effort were new to paid labor—half had moved from lower-paid positions, and others were returning to the workplace after being unemployed in the pre-war depression years (Wallace, 2011).

After World War II, the propaganda that had urged women into the workforce, along with the support and funding for childcare, dried up (Wallace, 2011; Cohen, 2015). Many women left the workforce or returned to jobs considered more appropriate for women. Although the upheaval in the workforce during that era had lasting impacts on women's employment, many of the specific roles they filled are still overwhelmingly dominated by men (Wallace, 2011). And the lack of quality, affordable childcare remains a major barrier to women's career success, particularly in lower-wage occupations where the cost of childcare may exceed the earnings from a job (Cohen, 2015).

A major political priority of white-led feminist organizations in the 1960s and 1970s was expanding women's access to employment and fighting for "equal rights"—equal, that is, to white men—in the workplace. These efforts achieved some important goals (and there is still a way to go toward workplace equality in wages and promotion) but were often limited in their analysis and impact because they failed to recognize the very different experiences of BIPOC and poor women in the labor force. For BIPOC and poor white women, having "rights" in employment equal to men's sometimes meant being equally vulnerable—or more vulnerable—to exploitation in low-status, low-paid, and physically demanding work. To effectively address the concerns of poor and BIPOC women in employment, as in voting, requires a more robust analytical tool than liberal feminism's focus on equal rights.

DECOLONIZING FEMINISMS

The socio-political locations of Black, Indigenous, and other women of color call for robust theoretical and analytical tools that examine taken-for-granted assumptions about home-making, gender relations, kinship practices, and morality. White domination and settler-colonial nation building in the U.S. had harsh bearings upon the bodies and lives of BIPOC, as colonialism employs practices that are notably ruthless and cruel. European men arrived with a mandate to conquer, subjugate, and enslave human beings and to steal land and resources. These European men colonizers, alongside the European women subjugated by sexism yet privileged as white/colonizers, constructed a complex system of imperial patriarchy that sought to control women's bodies in general, and, in particular, the bodies of the colonized, both in terms of sexuality and labor (Federici, 2004; McClintock, 1995; Stoler, 2002). In colonial contexts, including what would become the United States, "racial distinctions were fundamentally structured in gendered terms" (Stoler, 2002, p. 42). This meant that "colonized women had to negotiate not only the imbalance of their relations with their own men but also the baroque and violent array of hierarchical rules and restrictions that structured their new relations with imperial men and women" (McClintock, 1995, p. 6). White women who conformed to gender identities, expressions, and roles compatible with imperial patriarchy, which required them to embody virtues of purity and domesticity as "appropriate" forms of femininity, engaged in a dynamic of womanhood whereby they received protection from men while accepting a degree of subjugation relative to them (Jones, 1986; Roberts, 1997; Welter, 1966). In contrast, BIPOC of all genders experienced lives of enslavement, displacement, and cultural devastation and were subject to devaluation and exploitation in relation to white people (of all genders) in power. Imperial patriarchy for all of those involved was a profoundly gendered and sexualized system.

Lugones (2007) connects the formation of race with the formation of gender systems and argues that there always was and continues to be a light side/dark side to gender; race is gendered and gender is raced in differential ways for Europeans/whites and colonized/BIPOC peoples. For example, she noted how whiteness protected and infantilized racially dominant (white) women while supporting the exploitation of the labor, land, and reproductive capacity of Black and Indigenous women. Lugones's intersectional feminist work and historical look compel us to further develop a complex lens with respect to the interdependent construction of race with the categories of gender and sexuality and the overarching histories and systems that shaped their formation.

Lugones (2007) asserts that the notion of binary gender is in and of itself a colonial construction. She argues that the colonial establishment of the Americas set into motion a new gender system born out of the imaginaries of European "heterosexualist patriarchy" (Lugones, 2007, p. 187) that overwrote Indigenous and African (specifically Yoruba) pre-colonial, nonbinary gendered systems with binary, Euro-constructed ones. The system of differential treatment and positionality of white women and Black and brown women established a distinctly colonial gendered quagmire where race and gender overlap. The modern/colonial gender system created a complex entangled ideological system that wholly intersected with race and organized how we now construct notions of "women" and "men." Because race was a profound and salient part of the historical construction of gender, the subordination of BIPOC women occurred with different dynamics than the subordination of white women. The racialization of colonized women contributed to the idea that may have positioned them as "without gender," sexually marked as female (in the biological deterministic schema of the binary sex/gender system) but without access to the ascribed characteristics and value of (white) femininity under patriarchy. BIPOC women were excluded from the protections of white femininity while white financial interests exploited their labor and bodies. In effect, colonial society only consistently counted as "women" the white, bourgeois women (Lugones, 2007). Patriarchy and male dominance in colonial-modern societies, like the U.S., have a long, complicated dynamic shaped by race, racism, and white supremacy.

The predicaments of race shape the lives and identities of people of all genders, establishing multiple and conflicting hierarchies and access to power in white-dominant patriarchal worlds. Historian Elsa Barkley Brown (1992) observed that, because of the significance of racialization in U.S. history, "all women do not have the same gender" (p. 300); she noted the contrasting constructions of gender and womanhood attributed to white women were often profoundly different to what was attributed to Black women. bell hooks's pivotal writing in the late 20th century emphasized how Black women "are rarely recognized as a group separate and distinct from black men or as a present part of the larger group 'women' in this culture" (1981, p. 7).

In the United States' racialized systems of domination and rule, there was a "cult of true womanhood" that governed the status of white women and structured a kind of invisibility of Black and other women of color as "women." For white women, this "cult" established "a means to circumscribe, and make dependent, the very women who had the education and resources to wage an effective battle for their rights. The culture reduced them to an image of frailty and mindless femininity" (Giddings, 2006, p. 54). This places in stark contrast the historical construction of womanhood spoken to directly by Sojourner Truth in her famous "Ain't I a Woman?" speech. Truth challenged 19th-century suffrage and abolitionist movements by speaking to her experience, bringing visibility to how enslaved and formerly enslaved women bore the burdens of work and family outside of the bounds of presumed fragile white femininity. Historians who study the period of enslavement wrote about Black women's work alongside Black men under harsh and punishing conditions (Giddings, 2006; Davis, 1981; Lugones, 2007; Roberts, 1997; Welter, 1966).

To effectively teach about sexism, heterosexism, and trans* oppression, educators and facilitators must consider how colonization, racism, and economic exploitation (class-based oppression) construct gender and sexuality and establish dynamics of gendered and sexualized racism and racialized sexism and heterosexism. Social identity groups defined by gender or sexuality are diverse and polyvocal—that is, they contain multiple, sometimes conflicting voices and viewpoints—and "this polyvocality of multiple social locations is historically missing from analyses of oppression and exploitation in traditional feminism" (Brewer, 1993, p. 13). To truly work for the liberation of all gender and sexuality groups, we must excavate fraught historical and contemporary dynamics of gender, race, class, and sexuality. Reframing our understanding of systems of sexism, heterosexism, and trans* oppression by centering the experiences of multiply marginalized people provides for more accurate analysis and more effective action.

Indigenous Understandings of Gender and Sexuality

European conceptualizations of gender were violently introduced and used to destroy Indigenous communities and lifeways in order to justify land theft and labor exploitation (Lugones, 2007). Articulating the realities of pre-contact Indigenous kinship systems actively challenges the erasure of Indigenous knowledge and social organization in service to capitalist domination and settler colonialism. Toward that end, we highlight a few examples of highly contextualized Indigenous renderings of gender, sexuality, and kinship.

While genocide, assimilation projects, and the ongoing violence of settler colonialism (Wolfe, 2006) suppressed and worked to erase pre-contact Indigenous kinship and gender systems, some examples persist in the collective memories of communities and in scholarly records. Among Indigenous communities of what is now North America, there was a recognition of third-gender people (Horswell, 2010; Miranda, 2010). Despite efforts to eradicate Indigenous people and reconfigure Indigenous lifeways as heterosexual patriarchies, multiple Indigenous communities continued to recognize same-gender relationships (Allen, 1992; Rifkin, 2011; Roscoe, 1998). Part of the motivation of the U.S. military action that led to the uprising at Beautiful Mountain in 1913 was a U.S. agent's "discovery" of polyamorous relationships—a practice of consenting sexual and/or intimate relationships among three or more individuals—among the Navajo (Denetdale, 2017). The uprising is an example of resistance strategies employed by Navajo and Hopi people against U.S. settler-colonial heteronormative and monogamous conceptualizations of family, marriage, and sexuality. Learning these histories opens up the often narrowly constructed boundaries of sex, gender, and sexuality that organize contemporary U.S. society while revealing the dispossession and destruction mobilized by settler colonialism's gender order.

CONFLICTING VISIONS OF EQUALITY

While intersectional feminism challenges many assumptions of Western feminist movements and thoughts, white feminisms, including radical feminism, gained much social currency with a particular—and, we argue, limited—vision for gender equality. Additionally, contrasting ideologies between trans* movements and feminism stemmed from trans* people's resistance to gender as a monolithic or unifying category for organizing (Stryker, 2008). While trans* people were pushing back on cisgender normativity, some branches of second wave feminism (now known as trans-exclusionary radical feminism, TERF) chose to draw lines of distinctions between womyn-born-womyn[4] and trans* women (Khayrallah, 2015). The compulsion to determine identity based on biological, physiological, and psychological variables is a method of control and fails to capture the social and cultural influences on human perceptions and interaction with the world (Fausto-Sterling, 2000), dismissing gender identity as irrelevant to what "counts" in being a woman (Finlayson, Jenkins, & Worsdale, 2018). Differentiating biological sex as objective and gender as subjective ignores that science is mediated by the political values that constitute the discourse of biology (Zanghellini, 2020). "Gender-critical" feminists who assert the "unnaturalness" of trans* identities and the immutability of biological realities participate in limiting narratives that categorize and regulate bodies while threatening bodily autonomy. Such practices are part of a long tradition of imperial and colonialist practices that imposed heterosexuality and gender binaries (Hines, 2018; Lewis, 2017, 2019).

The streams of white radical feminism that gained the most traction with the general public in the latter half of the 20th century situated men as the beneficiaries of cultural norms, institutions, and structures that made them dominant. Their focus was often on individual men's behavior as the problem, rather than on institutions and structural arrangements. Morgan (1970) asserted in the Red Stocking Statement that "all men have oppressed women" (p. 533), which in many ways was an analysis that seemed to blame individual men rather than holding a structural and historical analysis about how patriarchy impacts and involves people of all genders (albeit differently). In contrast, the Combahee River Collective—a collective of Black, queer feminists in the 1970s whose work is exemplary of what we now name as intersectional feminism—rejected separatism and the categorical denunciation of men as individuals and as a group and instead worked within activist struggle to upset interlocking forms of oppression. They pointed to the importance of solidarity with progressive Black men and queer non-Black people in the pursuit of liberation and the dismantlement of racism, imperialism, capitalism, and patriarchy. Similarly, the Third World Women's Alliance, rooted in the Black civil rights movement, worked from 1970–1980 to address issues such as sterilization abuse, welfare and wage exploitation, and infant mortality, as well as providing an international analysis of U.S. foreign and military policy on the lives of people in the third world (Romney, 2021).

Many of the prominent women of color feminists of the late 20th century, along with some white feminists, worked to include cisgender men and queer people in their analyses and movements, recognizing the intersectional forms of oppression that shape the lives of Black and Indigenous people and People of Color generally, and argued for politics of liberation that could account for multiple forms of oppression and could involve a range of people across their identities and experiences in struggles for liberation against sexism, racism, classism, homophobia, etc. (Combahee River Collective, 1977; Lorde, 1984; Anzaldúa, 1990).

The specter of radical separatism and casting of men as oppressors by some white feminists had significant resonance within popular rhetoric (Gardiner, 2002). Feminism in the popular imagination treated men as the enemy—an oversimplification of a singular stream of feminist organizing—which justified suspicion of and backlash against feminism. Responses surfaced in both academic and mainstream spaces trumpeting men as victims of feminist rhetoric, encouraging the emergence of a certain brand of men's groups and men's studies that was defensive of men rather posing a challenge to men to support feminist movements and goals (Brod, 1994).

Such positioning of men as victims of feminist ideology was thoroughly challenged by the profeminist men's movement within academia, which foregrounded masculinity as an area of study and urged men to work in solidarity with women for gender equality and liberation (Kimmel, 1996; Stoltenberg, 2000). These scholars focused on masculinity as a social system, referring to the social roles, behaviors, and meaning prescribed for men in a given society at a given time (Kimmel, 1994). (This is distinct from, although not unrelated to, masculinity as an individual affect or expression that may be experienced by people of any gender.) Cultures and structures that shape masculinity often affirm masculine dominance, nuanced by history, geography, life span, and the intersection of multiple social identities. For example, a present-day disabled, Indigenous heterosexual cisgender veteran may experience and express masculinity much differently than a queer white youth. Brod (1994) argued that one reason to focus upon men's standpoints, particularly dominant views of masculinity, is to "identify processes through which men create rituals, reaffirm symbolic difference, establish internal hierarchies, and exclude, belittle, dominate and stigmatize women and non-conforming men" (p. 56). Brod (1994) understood that focusing upon men's standpoints might illuminate stock stories and individual attitudes and behaviors that reinforce misogyny and domination. He further explained that focusing on the functioning of hegemonic masculinity helped reveal both the social construct of gender and the existence of multiple masculinities.

Connell (1995) defined hegemonic masculinity as "the configuration of gendered practices which embodies the currently accepted answer to the problem of the legitimacy of patriarchy" (p. 77). This definition emphasizes how hegemonic masculinity allows for a range of practices, performances, attitudes, and assumptions that constitute gender. The flexibility in the functioning of hegemonic masculinity allows what is masculine to shift in order to accommodate emergent realities while maintaining superiority. While brute strength is valuable in certain economic systems, late-stage capitalism offers advantages to men who are adept at manipulating technologies, so what constitutes authentic masculinity can change to adapt with the times as long as it still secures influence, power, and dominance. While masculinity may adapt to shifts in how power and influence are secured, it may also be susceptible to cultural changes that choose freedom, connection, and reciprocity over domination and oppression. Also, history, culture, race, and class will always shape masculinity.

HISTORICAL MOVEMENTS OF QUEER LIBERATION

In this section, we follow the lead of historian Susan Stryker (2008) in using the word *queer* for a variety of historical people and groups marginalized by gender and/or sexuality, "rather than split hairs about precisely which term would be most accurate at any particular time and place" (p. 24). While many people think of queer identities and politics in terms of sexuality, "from the beginning a vocal minority insisted on the importance of transgender and gender-variant practices for queer politics" (Stryker, 2008, p. 20). Queer is a concise way of referring to a collective group of identities as well as naming that there were various groups working in concert toward gender and sexual liberation (Stryker, 2008). Gender and sexuality liberation movements have deep roots within other social movements. Historians note how the 19th- and 20th-century movement for women's suffrage flowed from the abolitionist movement and that the women's liberation movement of the 1960s and 1970s flowed from the civil rights movement. Disability rights organizers in the 1960s were likewise inspired by the women's movement and the civil rights movement. The gay liberation movement had connections to the women's movement and also overlapped with the disability rights movement, particularly from the early AIDS epidemic onward. Intersectional feminist organizing from the 19th through the 21st centuries connected how women of color saw the convergence of systems of racism, sexism, and heterosexism/homophobia as fundamental structures that organized their lives.

There is richness in the histories of gender and sexuality and the emergence of people's resistances to dominant norms, but whether and how we hear about those stories requires acknowledging that history is not a stable narrative with a fixed point of view. For instance, historian Neil Miller (1995) famously characterized the Stonewall riots as the birth of the gay and lesbian movement, which is an oversimplification and historically inaccurate. To label Stonewall in such a way is an erasure to the numerous trans* women of color, butches, and other gender radicals who led that act of resistance to police brutality at a gay bar in New York City in 1969 and to ignore the systems of race, class, gender, and sexuality that inspired this act of resistance. Queer liberation did not begin at Stonewall; rather, "Stonewall was a phenomenon that was in dialogue with acts of civil disobedience and protest throughout the country" (Ferguson, 2019, p. 22). The pervasive narrative that Stonewall was simply about gay liberation ignores the complexities of the individuals involved and the political work they engaged in throughout their lives (Woo, 2009). "Indeed, the dominant narrative that has come to define gay liberation is one that occludes how Stonewall was a tributary for a variety of social struggles, not just sexuality" (Ferguson, 2019, p. 47). It may be convenient to claim Stonewall as the start of gay and lesbian liberation, but queer and trans* communities, often led by QTPOC (queer and trans* People of Color), engaged in intersectional movement work toward gender and sexual justice for decades prior.

The history of queer and trans* liberation includes acts of resistance to policing tactics and race, class, gender, and sexual discrimination that took place at Cooper's Donuts (1959) in Los Angeles, Dewey's (1965) in Philadelphia, and Compton's Cafeteria (1966) in San Francisco (Stryker, 2008). The Compton's Cafeteria riot marks "the first time . . . direct action in the streets by transgender people resulted in lasting institutional change" (Stryker, 2008, p. 64). The dynamics that led to the Compton's Cafeteria riot were the result of various forms of economic injustice throughout the city of San Francisco, with Black and working-class neighborhoods destroyed through institutionally sanctioned mechanisms of "urban renewal" (Stryker, 2008). The same year saw the founding of Vanguard in San Francisco, "the earliest known queer youth organization in the United States," which was organized by poor and transient queer youth to protect each other from street violence and to protest businesses, including Compton's, that refused to serve them (Stryker, 2008, p. 70). Contextualizing trans* resistance within other forms of injustice allows for a broader understanding that individuals do not lead one-dimensional lives (Ferguson, 2019) and social movements must contend with all aspects of experiences. The intersectional issues that spurred on the Compton's Cafeteria riot reflect conditions that persist today such as "discriminatory policing practices in minority communities, harmful urban land-use policies . . . and political coalition building around the structures of injustices that affect many different communities" (Stryker, 2008, p. 74).

Street Transvestite Action Revolution (STAR) was an organization founded by Sylvia Rivera and Marsha P. Johnson, two trans* women of color, in 1971 (Ferguson, 2019; Lewis, 2017). The formation of the group occurred following a sit-in at New York University that also involved the Gay Liberation Front in response to university administration banning gay functions at the university due to morality questions about homosexuality (Ferguson, 2019). STAR was "the result of an emerging multi-sided understanding of liberation that was shaped by anti-racist and anti-imperialist movements" (Ferguson, 2019, p. 23). STAR's historical connections to social movements beyond sexuality include relationships to the Black Panthers, the Young Lords, Third World Gay Revolution (TWGR, a Black and Latino organization that left the predominantly White Gay Liberation Front), and others (Ferguson, 2019). Not only were queer and trans* movements intertwined, but they were also multi-issue movements seeking to challenge various forms of injustice.

Queer liberation was not a single-issue politic but became focused on single-issue politics (Ferguson, 2019; Vaid, 2012). In fact, Ferguson (2019) asserts that queer politics are intersectional, having roots in "issues of race, colonization, incarceration, and capitalism" (p. 2), but that those issues have been excised from historical recounts of what we broadly describe as queer histories. While it may make telling of histories tidier to consider them through a single lens, we encourage readers to understand how multidimensional queer struggles have always been in their refusal to adhere to normative conceptualizations of sexuality, gender, race, and class (Ferguson, 2019). The oversimplification of queer liberation to exclude issues of race, class, and colonization only serves to conceal "the historical and political complexity of queer liberation itself" (Ferguson, 2019, p. 8) and to isolate queer and trans* politics from each other and from broader political and liberatory possibilities.

The histories of those oppressed by sex, gender, and sexuality are as multi-layered and messy as the terms themselves, although they share historical connections through governmental persecution (Stryker, 2008). Issues of "privacy, censorship, political dissent, minority rights, freedom of expression, and sexual liberation" (Stryker, 2008, p. 52) connect queer and trans* movements. For example, in the 1950s, legal and social definitions of "obscenity" led to the U.S. government monitoring letters, books, and magazines sent through the postal service for sexual content. In the period from 1950 to 1960, there were significant legal, economic, medical, and social consequences if someone were found out to be "homosexual" or "transsexual." At the time queer communities, mostly communities of gay men organized under the term *homophile*, utilized the postal service to send novels, newsletters, and magazines in an effort to connect, build community, and share stories (Cornell University Library, n.d.; Miller, 1995; Stryker, 2008). One of the best-known organizations of the homophile movement was the Mattachine Society, a network that produced "homosexual" content and mailed it across the U.S. "Much of the so-called 'homophile' nonfiction periodical literature from this period, which advocated social tolerance of homosexuals, was deemed obscene" (Stryker, 2008, p. 52). Those found to be sending "obscene" material were sentenced with large fines and years of imprisonment (Stryker, 2008). Similarly, "transsexual" people seeking information about themselves also shared materials via mail. Lack of access to information, resources, and organized trans* communities—particularly outside major cities—meant that trans* people often sought out connection within gay communities and were subject to the same postal laws (Stryker, 2008).

Returning to the historic Stonewall riots, Sylvia Rivera's recount of the events of that night contradicts an often-told narrative of a spontaneous response to police brutality by patrons who could no longer take the surveillance, arrests, and harassment (Ferguson, 2019). Instead, Rivera asserted that Stonewall was a deliberate enactment of resistance by those who were politically active in the women's movement, anti-war movements, and civil rights. Rivera revealed how liberation for queer and trans* people was already tied to "the network of insurrections that was developing all over the US, a network made up of feminists, anti-capitalists, anti-racist, and anti-war movements" (Ferguson, 2019, p. 19).

A detailed look at queer and trans* histories reveals that divisions within LGBTQ+ communities were not inevitable but were manufactured as attempts to curry mainstream political and social acceptance (Ferguson, 2019). As the most well-resourced branches of gay and lesbian activism (made up of mostly white, middle-class people) came to focus increasingly on inclusion into mainstream institutions—particularly advocating for same-sex marriage—the movement became separated from other social justice movements such as those to end homelessness, address health-care disparities, and ensure access to abortion (Bérubé, 2001; Carruthers, 2018; Kendall, 2020). This, in turn, perpetuated a construction of gayness as synonymous with whiteness (Bérubé, 2001). The same-sex marriage movement spotlighted gender-normative gay and lesbian couples who were non-threatening to heterosexuals (monogamous, white, middle-class or wealthy, etc.) to gain acceptance in ways that were and remain inaccessible to many others.

In 2015 the federal government finally recognized same-sex marriage and instituted some limited federal employment protections for LGBT workers. These are tangible strides that gesture toward equality. Yet, as Vaid (2012) notes, "formal equality—and even progress toward greater cultural recognition of one's humanity—can be achieved while leaving larger structural manifestations of inequality and deeper cultural prejudice intact" (p. 9). The change in policies and laws begin to define equality as the norm, but everyday practices and beliefs of homophobia and trans*phobia remain persistent. The popular culture attention on the successful "fight for gay marriage equality" ignores the limitations of legal rights; legal rights only benefit people to the extent that systems enforce those rights and protect people's ability to access them (Spade, 2011, Minter, 2006). Any expectations of such laws' impact must reckon with the foundation of class- and race-based rhetoric and strategy that attempted to distance affluent and white gays and lesbians from other queer and trans* people who are less palatable to those with power and privilege (Minter, 2006).

For many queer and trans* people, to access the promises of these laws requires navigating economic, educational, racial, and institutional barriers (Spade, 2006).

Queer and trans* critiques of the "fight" for same-sex marriage (Conrad, 2009) argued that marriage was not a capacious enough category to include the complexities of genders and sexualities. "The LGBT movement has been coopted by the very institutions it once sought to transform. Heterosexuality, the nuclear family, the monogamous couple-form are our new normal" (Vaid, 2012, p. xiv). Lacking a critical perspective, the public narrative of gay marriage served to create a form of *homonormativity* that reifies heterosexual relationships and principles. As Bornstein (2009) argued, "Seeking to grab oneself a piece of the marriage-rights pie does little if anything at all for the oppression caused by the institution of marriage itself to many more people than sex and gender outlaws" (p. 12). The political and social fights for same-sex marriage ignored how marriage does not rectify persistent economic disparities, especially for those already lacking economic resources. In many ways, the ubiquity of the push to recognize same-sex marriage created a form of erasure of queer histories and flattened out the vibrancy of queerness. Nair (2009) argues that

> the history of gay marriage is now used to overwrite all of queer history as if the gay entrance into that institution were a leap into modernity, as if marriage is all that queers have ever aspired to, as if everything we have ever wrought and seen and known were all towards this one goal.
>
> (p. 4)

Instead of using the fight for same-sex marriage to expose the other inequities that the institution of state-sanctioned marriage upholds, the public rhetorical points focused on assimilationist perspectives. This is not to say that state and federal recognition of deep and abiding relationships is useless; indeed, some families were able to achieve stability, access health care, and stay together because of this recognition. Yet the result of promoting legal recognition of same-sex marriage as a panacea to all of heterosexism and trans* oppression meant that once it was achieved, there was a narrative that the work for equity was complete.

Another notable policy and legal stride that had a similar outcome for queer movements was the repeal of the U.S. military's "Don't Ask, Don't Tell" (DADT) policy. As recently as 2021, the Pentagon, under the direction of President Biden, repealed President Trump's 2018 executive order banning transgender people from the military (Wamsley, 2021). While increasing the general representation and visibility of LGBTQ+ communities in U.S. institutions might be beneficial in some ways, the inclusion of queer and trans* people in institutions like the military (and police) that promote state violence contradicts the intersectional approach of queer liberation movements. Queer anti-war and anti-militarism activists have highlighted that representation cannot be more important than the lives of people lost through military intervention (Conrad, 2009).

HISTORICAL LEGACY: MEDICAL SCIENCE AT THE INTERSECTIONS

The role of medical science to define and pathologize is part of the history of many social identities (e.g., gender, race, sexuality, ability). As we described in the section on key terms, science is not a neutral field. Medical science has a long history of assigning pathology to experiences and identities, leading to social stigma instead of acceptance of human diversity. The pursuit of understanding—a generous description—and control of marginalized communities by medical science led to such abuses as U.S. scientists testing the first birth control pill in the 1930s on Puerto Rican women, often without informed consent. Rather than a neutral scientific endeavor, these experiments were a mechanism of population control, racism, and eugenics (Preciado, 2013). Medical research has also been used to uphold convenient fictions such as the idea that women do not have emotional control due to their uteruses (hysteria) (Scull, 2009). In many ways, science is transnational in its efforts to cure, treat, and protect humans through shared knowledge of diseases, hazards, and medical intervention strategies. This concerted effort gives the work of science the appearance of neutrality and objectivity. However, the sharing of such knowledge also infuses cultural perspectives (and biases) into these same approaches to health, safety, and wellness. Cultural norms and practices influence interpretation of data, aims of research, and practices that follow curative measures.

Early medical and psychological theories about the "cause" of homosexuality were mostly elaborate theories of gender that served to conflate gender and sexuality (Mackenzie, 1994). Fausto-Sterling (2000) in her work on gender politics and sexuality explores

> how—through their daily lives, experiments, and medical practices—scientists create "truths" about sexuality; how our bodies incorporate and confirm these truths; and how these truths, sculpted by the social milieu in which biologists practice their trade, in turn, refashion our cultural environment.
>
> (p. 5)

What Stryker (2008) called the "social power of medicine" (p. 36) provides a conundrum on the help and harm science offers to queer and trans* populations. In defining who is sick or what is a sickness in contrast to what is healthy, science and medicine have enormous power over social, political, and economic systems. The potentiality of science to help, and at times intervene to save lives, also means it has the power to "define and judge" (Stryker, 2008, p. 36). Access to medical care, whether treatments for cancer or biomedical transition for trans* people seeking such interventions, also allow the construction of an "unhealthy other" that connect ableism to sexism, heterosexism and trans* oppression. For example, people with disabilities, cisgender women, and trans* people all must seek permission from medical authorities to access medications (e.g., hormones, anti-anxiety medications) and reasonable accommodations (e.g., extra time on tests for students or leave for childbirth).

Historically, the medical community labeled as transsexuals those who sought to engage in forms of biomedical transition through hormonal and surgical interventions (Meyer et al., 2002). The term *transsexual* might lead one to believe that early medical classification of trans*ness was based on ideas about biological sex, as in the antiquated term *sex change*. However, early medical research about the "transsexual" condition was initially focused on gendered behaviors and sexuality (Meyerowtiz, 2002; Stryker, 2008). Candidates for surgical interventions were evaluated based on their desire and/or presumed compulsion to dress as the "opposite" gender or to change genders in order to validate a queer relationship as heterosexual.

Another example of the medical system's fraught histories around gender and sexuality is its approach to intersex people. *Intersex* describes a range of sex categories for individuals with genital, chromosomal, and/or reproductive variations that do not align with binary sex assignment (Chase, 2012).[5] Intersex people's physiology contradicts the overwhelming societal bias that human bodies must correlate to the cultural notion of a gender/sex binary. Beginning in the 1950s, doctors performed surgeries on intersex children and infants, aiming to "fix" children born with "ambiguous" genitals, not because the surgeries were necessary for the children's health but rather because they assuaged adults' discomfort about the children's bodies (Beh & Diamond, 2000). These procedures were standard practice by

1970. Intersex adults in the 1990s came forward about how physically and psychologically damaging the unnecessary surgeries were and organized to end the practice. The year 2020 was the first time a children's hospital pledged to stop unnecessary surgical procedures to "normalize" the bodies of intersex babies (Knight, 2020) after years of concerted advocacy by intersex youth and adults. The battle over intersex justice continues through the work of many organizations such as interACT: Advocates for Intersex Youth and Human Rights Watch. The lack of widespread knowledge about intersex identities and the experiences of intersex individuals reflect how silence is powerful in service to cultural norms of binary sex and gender.

In the early days of the AIDS epidemic, doctors coined the concept of Gay Related Immuno Deficiency (GRID) to describe what we now know as AIDS. The initial belief that only gay men were at risk (soon joined by injection drug users and Haitian migrants) contributed to intense stigma around HIV/AIDS, neglect by government health authorities, and persistent disinformation about how HIV could be transmitted. In the late 1980s, the organization AIDS Coalition to Unleash Power (ACT UP) used direct action tactics inspired by the civil rights movement—but with a queer twist—to disrupt business as usual and draw attention to the urgent need for treatment options. For first-person accounts that shed light on the work of ACT UP, you can visit their Oral History Project (please see chapter website for link to the full site). ★

The discourse of "neutral" science unrelated to the social world allows medical and psychological literature to focus on individual, supposedly pathological deviations from gender and sexuality norms while ignoring the shared experiences of broad categories of queer and trans* people (Stryker, 2008). When we understand the contradictory role that medicine plays in pathologizing groups of people, connections between queer and trans* oppression and ableism become evident, and there is potential to link social movements to create multidimensional and multi-issue politics toward a change that benefits everyone.

CURRENT MANIFESTATIONS

Despite the emancipatory gains of the liberation movements articulated earlier in this chapter, instances of heterosexism, sexism, and trans* oppression surface in overt and nuanced ways. For instance, in 2021 and continuing into 2022, there were numerous bills in state legislatures to ban or criminalize health-care providers for treating trans* youth, restricting trans* youth access to full school participation (e.g., sports, restrooms), and creating barriers for trans* people to update identification documents to reflect their name and/or gender changes (American Civil Liberties Union, n.d.). At the same time, under attack are reproductive rights, voting rights, and what and how to educate about the roots of racism in U.S. history through attacks on Critical Race Theory. Although these issues may seem specific, what they also reflect is a broader, increasingly politically conservative political agenda that centers white supremacy and reinscribes misogyny, transphobia, and homophobia.

In the following pages, we use specific examples to provide a measure of depth to the specific issues while pulling on the threads of the broader ramifications of current manifestations of sexism, heterosexism, and trans* oppression. While this is far from an exhaustive list of the manifestations of these three interlocking systems, each example highlights shared elements of oppression, including violence, marginalization, discrimination, and exploitation.

INCELS

The rise of young men who identify as and subscribe to the rhetoric of *incel* (short for involuntarily celibate) demonstrates a profoundly patriarchal and misogynistic expectation of entitlement and access to women's bodies, an example that highlights broader political and social dynamics that support the persistence of oppression. Incels are a "subset of straight men . . . [who have] constructed a violent political ideology around the injustice of young, beautiful women refusing to have sex with them" (Tolentino, 2018, para. 6). Incels have a sense of social entitlement to women's bodies (Beauchamp, 2019) and rely on pseudoscience to support their ideology (Lavin, 2020). "What incels want is extremely limited and specific: they want unattractive, uncouth, and unpleasant [cisgender white men] misogynists to be able to have sex on demand with young, beautiful [cisgender] women. They believe that this is a natural right" (Tolentino, 2018, para. 12).

Incel beliefs reject any form of emancipation experienced by women (Beauchamp, 2019) and reveal threads of white supremacy, misogyny, homophobia, and transphobia. Incel forums are filled with homophobia and anti-feminist sentiment (Jaki et al., 2019). The relationship between the extreme misogyny of incels and racism is a complicated one. Lavin (2020) observes a significant amount of white supremacist activity on internet discussion boards for incels. Incels believe that there is a new hierarchy in which conventionally attractive, white (cisgender) men are at the top (Lavin, 2020) and have the most sexual advantages (Kelly et al., 2021). They also use data from dating websites that shows women prefer white men over men of color as evidence that women are racist and thus as justification for the dehumanization of women. At the same time, there are men of color in incel communities online, self-labeling as terms such as "curry-cel" (South Asian incel) or "rice-cel" (East Asian incel) (Kelly et al., 2021). In these online forums, women are faulted for the emasculation of Asian men in the broader society.

Incel rhetoric and actions reflect extreme levels of violence. In online forums, incels have admitted to sexually assaulting women, yelling at women, and catfishing women (using a fake online persona to lure someone into a false relationship) (Beauchamp, 2019). Examples of incel-inspired violence and murder include such incidents as a man killing six and injuring seven in Santa Barbara, California, in 2014 (Abad-Santos, 2014). The perpetrator was fueled by a volatile mixture of patriarchal and misogynist beliefs that were reinforced by his radicalization by internet forums and YouTube propaganda from "men's rights" groups. These acts of violence are valorized on the forums, and users often egg each other on (Beauchamp, 2019).

MISSING AND MURDERED INDIGENOUS WOMEN

The United Nations reports that globally, nearly one in three women (30%) have experienced sexual or physical violence from an intimate partner, family member, or stranger (UN Women, n.d.). Moreover, seven out of ten victims of detected human trafficking are women and girls (UN Women, n.d.). In the U.S., one in four women report experiencing sexual, intimate partner, or physical violence in their lifetime (National Coalition Against Domestic Violence, 2020). Violence against women exercised as an expression of masculine power and dominance is a worldwide problem that reflects the assumption that women are commodities to control, exploit, and be used for the profit or pleasure of men. The risk of violence and assault for women has been especially documented during the COVID-19 pandemic as constituting a "shadow pandemic" (see, for instance, UN Women, 2021). Evidence of women's vulnerabilities in their own homes resulted in 52 countries adding prevention and response items regarding violence against women and girls to their COVID-19 plans. Across every domain of violence against women, women of color and women in low-income communities, regions, and countries are disproportionately affected. While a comprehensive examination of violence against women and girls is beyond the scope of this chapter, the breadth of the problem necessitates centering one particularly vulnerable community: Indigenous women.

In the present day, the colonial legacy of the United States continues to profoundly impact the lives of Indigenous peoples. The gendered violence of settler coloniality informs the reality of violence against Indigenous women and the silence around the loss of Native women. The bodies of women of color are too often devalued, and their realities are often characterized by indifference to their needs for liberation and safety. Native women, along with other women of color, live and navigate the reality of a society formed in and informed by the pervasiveness of violence and the interlocking systems of gender, race, and class that inform their existence.

Over 80% of American Indian and Alaska Native women experienced violence in their lifetime, including sexual violence (56.1%) and physical violence by an intimate partner (55.5%), according to the National Congress of American Indian Policy Research Center (2018). In the wake of a continuing epidemic of violence, the Murdered and Missing Indigenous Women (MMIW) movement seeks to raise public awareness and action. While information-sharing efforts yielded some mainstream news attention (Gray, 2019; Martin, 2020), Indigenous women victims remain a largely overlooked population. In a study of MMIW in urban areas, 95% of the more than 500 cases were never covered by national or international media outlets (Lucchesi & Echo-Hawk, 2018). While violence is consistently under-reported across communities, there are significant impediments to seeking justice within Indigenous communities. For instance, 96% of Indigenous victims of sexual violence report a non-Native perpetrator. Yet, individuals who report face a series of obstacles, including a 1978 Supreme Court decision that ruled that tribes did not have criminal jurisdiction over non-Native perpetrators who commit crimes on community-held lands (Rosay, 2016).

#SAYHERNAME

In 2014, the African American Policy Forum and the Center for Intersectionality and Social Policy Studies, headed by legal scholar and intersectional feminist Kimberle Crenshaw, launched a campaign to bring attention to the killings of Black women by police. Present-day movements mobilizing with the hashtag #BlackLivesMatter brought attention to the disproportionate instances of deadly force by police against Black people. This nationwide and global movement is an important 21st-century force demanding racial justice and an end to racialized violence. Yet, even amid this important activism, there is often less attention paid in the public arena to women and girls who have been lost to police violence. The #SayHerName campaign noted that "Black women are killed by police, too" and affirmed that:

> Black women and girls as young as 7 and as old as 93 have been killed by the police, though we rarely hear their names. Knowing their names is a necessary but not a sufficient condition for lifting up their stories which in turn provides a much clearer view of the wide-ranging circumstances that make Black women's bodies disproportionately subject to police violence.
>
> The African American Policy Forum, #Sayhername

As such, #SayHerName proclaims that "all Black lives matter."

#SayHerName disrupts the pervasive idea that men are the sole victims of police violence; it asserts that Black women also are susceptible to state violence and that activist work around police violence should not only be focused on the lives of men. A present-day manifestation of intersectional feminism, #SayHerName embeds an analysis and practice to make the experiences of Black women visible. In so doing, these activists recognize that, in racially unjust societies, Black people of all genders are targets. This movement insists on the inclusion of women of color's lives and the impact of loss on families and communities—along with acknowledgement of the loss of men to police violence—as an important part of contemporary anti-racist mobilization.

LGBTQ+ YOUTH

Persistent social stigma is a factor that supports heterosexism and trans* oppression. Stigma, for many queer and trans* people, plays out in the home, in what Schulman (2009) calls "familial homophobia." This specific type of homophobia is persistent, pervasive, and largely invisible. The family sphere is private yet shapes the organization of public dynamics and understandings. It is more likely than not for queer and trans* individuals to have heterosexual and/or cisgender family members raise them. Progress in acceptance of queer and trans* people in the larger culture does not necessarily mean families are places of safety for young queer and trans* people. The fear of reactions by family members to "coming out" persists. As Schulman (2009) notes,

> Usually the family is a refuge from the cruelties of the culture. Or, if the family is a source of cruelty, the larger society is a refuge from the family. But when the family and the larger society enact the identical structure of exclusion and diminishment, the individual has no place of escape.
>
> (p. 14)

The lack of a refuge for queer and trans* youth is a national issue, especially with political pressure against the inclusion of queer and trans* youth that leads to diminished resources available to support them.

In their 2019 national survey, the Trevor Project found that over 70% of youth reported experiencing discrimination due to their sexual orientation and/or gender identity and almost 40% of respondents admitted to seriously considering attempting suicide within the past two weeks. Additionally, as the Gay, Lesbian, and Straight Educators Network (GLSEN) reported in their 2017 report on LGBTQ+ youth and U.S. schools (Kosciw et al., 2018), LGBTQ+ youth experience bias, lack of safety, and harassment within the educational setting, both from peers and from adults. Harassment and lack of safety only increase the likelihood of LGBTQ+ absences from school or desire to drop out, which current state policies about classroom content and trans exclusion exacerbate (American Civil Liberties Union, 2022).

REPRODUCTIVE IN/JUSTICE

Reproductive Justice is a vision for justice, an analytic framework, and a movement that goes beyond advocating for the individual right to contraception or abortion and works for "the human right to maintain personal bodily autonomy, have children, not have children, and parent the children we have in safe and sustainable communities" (SisterSong, 2021). Reproductive Justice was developed by Black feminists/scholars in early to mid-1990s, in response to gaps in the analysis and goals of white-led feminist approaches to reproductive rights (Ross, Gutiérrez, Gerber, & Silliman, 2004). Reproductive Justice reframes both reproductive rights and reproductive health as issues of structural power that can only be addressed by changing structures, not by focusing solely on providing services or protecting the legal rights of individuals (Ross & Solinger, 2017; Luna & Luker, 2015).

Patriarchy, heterosexism, and cissexism all manifest in limitations on people's ability to make decisions about conceiving, bearing, and raising children. Access to contraception and abortion has always been a concern of feminist movements, and we currently face vigorous efforts to further restrict access to abortion. At the same time, an intersectional lens reveals how reproductive injustice goes far beyond abortion bans.

Far from making free choices about reproduction, women and other people who can become pregnant make choices constrained by poverty, a woefully inadequate social safety net, entanglement in carceral systems including the criminal legal system and the child welfare system, and more. For people who want an abortion, having the legal right to seek one does not guarantee they'll be able to get one, particularly if they are poor (Matthiesen, 2021). When trying to prevent pregnancy, women still overwhelmingly bear the burden of managing contraception, including negotiating with sometimes-reluctant partners to use condoms and taking on the medical risks and side effects of hormonal contraception and IUDs (intrauterine devices that prevent pregnancy) (Littlejohn, 2021). People who want to parent in the U.S. face the challenge of doing so without the benefit of paid parental leave, quality affordable childcare, prenatal health care, or many other structural supports (Matthiesen, 2021).

Women of color face a long history of having to fight for the right to parent, exemplified by the system of slavery in which white owners could separate parents from their children at any time and by the practice of forcing Indigenous children into boarding schools far from their communities to teach them white cultural norms—a practice that continued through the 1970s. Black motherhood has been so devalued by oppressive institutions in the U.S. that Alexis Pauline Gumbs (2015) suggests Black mothering is "already a queer thing" (para 8)—queer because it contradicts heteronormative expectations because heteronormativity is saturated with white supremacy. While the heteronormative expectations of white women all but require procreation, the same interlocking systems of oppression do everything they can to get in the way of Black women mothering at all.

Among the starkest examples of reproductive injustice toward BIPOC women are forced and coerced sterilizations in the California prison system from the early 20th century through at least 2010 (Lira, 2021; Johnson, 2013) and in immigration detention centers through the present (Amiri, 2020; Hernández & De Los Santos Upon, 2018, 2020). People with disabilities also experience involuntary sterilizations both within and beyond the law (National Council on Disability, 2012), and for trans* people in many U.S. states as well as in some countries, a sterilizing surgical procedure is a requirement to change the gender marks on one's legal ID (Allen, 2019). Although legally sanctioned involuntary sterilization has become less common, it has been replaced in some cases by policies and practices that push poor and BIPOC people to use long-acting contraceptive methods such IUDs, which require a medical professional to remove and so are not directly controlled by the people using them. Some scholars have dubbed this practice "soft sterilization" (Winters & McLaughlin, 2020). Soft sterilization, teen pregnancy prevention programs, and other public health efforts ostensibly intended to help young women of color actually act as instruments of social control. Rather than address the inequalities that affect people's ability to make their own reproductive choices, such programs serve to reveal and reproduce those inequalities (Barcelos, 2020).

The child welfare system is disproportionately used to police families that are poor and/or Black, Latinx, or Indigenous (Roberts, 2021), as well as families with LGBTQ+ parents (Polikoff, 2018) and parents with disabilities (National Council on Disability, 2012). When children are removed from their families even temporarily, parents become enmeshed in a system that scrutinizes their parenting style, financial stability, mental health, and intimate relationships and in some cases pressures them to conform to a particular, narrow view of what a family should look like (e.g. Polikoff, 2018). For a system ostensibly intended to help children, its methods look remarkably similar to those of the "Indian boarding schools" that broke up Indigenous families up to just two generations ago. Hundreds of thousands of children are removed from families and placed in state care every year, costing billions of dollars nationally (Roberts, 2021)—money that is not being used to provide resources like childcare, parental leave, and mental health services that would better enable all families to provide safe and nurturing homes.

COVID-19

The emergence of COVID-19 as a global health threat exacerbated and brought to light glaring pre-existing societal inequities. In an attempt to contain the spread of the highly contagious virus, many businesses, organizations, and governmental agencies were forced to close their doors and send workers to isolate at home. Subsequently, unemployment surged to historic records of nearly 15% overall in April 2020, with the rate high among women at 16.2% and higher yet among Latinas at over 20%. These disparities are partly the result of how heavily service industries rely upon women of color, particularly Black women and Latinas. Women of color are more likely to serve in occupations that require close personal contact such as food preparation, health-care support, personal service, home caregiving services, and retail (Mason et al., 2020), making women of color not only more susceptible to losing their source of income but also to contracting the virus.

Gendered labor disparities under the COVID-19 pandemic took several different avenues. Between February and May of 2020, 11.5 million women lost their jobs in comparison to 9 million men. Such an unprecedented disparity in job losses across gender is significant, compared to how in past recessions and economic downturns there were losses in construction and manufacturing sectors, which overwhelmingly employ men (Hegewisch et al., 2020). Moreover, women account for two-thirds of the workers who make less than $11 an hour, with women of color being overrepresented in these jobs, with the exception of Asian women (Mason et al., 2020). Domestic care workers who provide care for children, elderly, and disabled and chronically ill individuals in the home are overwhelmingly women of color and immigrant women. Similarly, LGBTQ+ workers may be more likely to either lose employment or be at higher risk for exposure to the COVID-19 virus, as one in three LGBTQ+ workers engage in labor impacted by COVID-19, including education, retail, food service, and health care. The Human Rights Campaign (Whittington et al., 2020) reported that LGBTQ+ folks are more susceptible to health and economic crises. One in ten LGBTQ+ adults are unemployed, and one in five live in poverty. Poverty rates are particularly egregious among Black (40%) and Latina (45%) trans* women. Furthermore, trans* women are overrepresented in sectors that do not offer health insurance, like food service, entertainment, and sex work. One in five LGBTQ+ people report that they have not seen a doctor when necessary because they cannot afford it (Whittington et al., 2020). For those who do have health insurance, locating health-care providers who are knowledgeable and capable of affirming health-care practices can be difficult.

LIBERATION VISION AND MOVEMENTS

The social movements that we brought to the fore in the Historical Legacies and Current Manifestations sections have long worked to elucidate and address the persistent and profound need for liberation around gender and sexuality. The legacies of these movements chart important pathways for educators to follow in their desire to enact social justice. To inspire and engage in social, political, and economic movements for justice, we must embrace how movements for gender and sexual justice have not been singular-issue or single-identity movements. Together with movements for racial and economic justice and disability rights and disability justice, social movements for gender and sexual equality have achieved and continue to achieve important gains in the U.S. (and elsewhere) because they are intersectional.

Feminist movements throughout time championed the cause of gender equality; offered important analyses about the workings of patriarchy, misogyny, and masculinity; and advocated for the end of violence, marginalization, and barriers to full participation in society constrained by gender. Gay and lesbian liberation movements exposed the workings of homophobia and heterosexism and affirmed the rights for people to love and exist beyond the bounds of compulsory heterosexuality. Movements for trans* visibility and rights challenged movements working for gender and sexual justice by affirming the lives of trans* people, insisting on nonbinary understandings of gender, and advocating for a more expansive culture that supports multiple experiences of gender identity and expression, thus charting an even more inclusive path for diversity and social justice. Sexism, heterosexism, and trans* oppression are both interlocking and intersectional systems of oppression. Therefore, liberation from them must also be intersectional and multifaceted. For 21st-century education, we encourage teachers and learners to strive to see these interconnections as a part of our ever-growing need as a society for pervasive justice, inclusive movements, and a more robust solidarity.

We have already mentioned several recent and ongoing movements that draw on (and build on) intersectional feminism: reproductive justice, intersex youth advocating for bodily autonomy, some aspects of AIDS activism, #SayHerName, MMIW, and more. Three further contemporary examples are Black Lives Matter (BLM), youth climate justice activism, and disability justice. The Black Lives Matter movement recognizes how Black liberation movements in the past have opened space for mostly Black heterosexual cisgender men. Thus, BLM organizers have made the commitment to place in the center the voices and leadership of Black women and queer and trans* people (http://blacklives matter.com/herstory). Youth activists advocating for climate justice highlight how those most impacted by gender-based violence, poor people, people with disabilities, women and girls living in rural areas, and trans* youth are at higher risk of experiencing the impact of natural disasters and catastrophic effects of climate change. Disability justice organizers center the wisdom of disabled queer and trans* People of Color to advocate for an interdependent approach that goes beyond single-issue disability "rights."

Chandra Talpade Mohanty (2003) envisions a feminism without borders and urges us to "envision change and social justice work across . . . lines of demarcation and division" (p. 2). For educators to begin to embody this vision, we must do our own work to unlearn assumptions of hierarchy and binarism embedded in the current gender system. Educators for diversity and social justice can unlearn some habits and adopt new understandings to join our students in envisioning and acting for gender and sexual justice. As we move through the 21st century, we affirm that:

> Scholars, researchers, and practitioners must stop conflating sex and gender because we are [no longer] studying . . . the impact of assigned sex. This equating of sex with gender only serves to falsely perpetuate sex as dimorphic and gender as a natural phenomenon; assertations that cause the erasure of trans, nonbinary, and intersex people, to say nothing of the rich diversity of how gender operates with/in/through nontrans populations.
>
> (Catalano et al., 2021, p. 8)

Our feminisms and our queer liberation work must take the lessons learned from movements against trans* oppression. The time is now to complicate our thinking and to encourage our students too to move beyond conventional borders to more expansive and liberatory ways of knowing about gender and sexuality.

DESIGN FOR TEACHING ABOUT SEXISM, HETEROSEXISM AND TRANS* OPPRESSION

Most chapters in this volume provide a four-quadrant, 16-hour design. However, since this chapter focuses on three forms of oppression, it is not feasible to adequately address all three and attend to further intersections in that time frame. Therefore, we offer a modular design for teaching about any one of the three systems—sexism, heterosexism, or trans* oppression—in the context of an overarching framework, including goals and guiding assumptions, that understands all three as intimately intertwined. In the design that follows, the first and fourth quadrants address sexism, heterosexism, and trans* oppression together through an integrated approach, while the second and third quadrants focus on one of the three. Specific designs for Quadrants 2 and 3 are on the website.

Following the design outline, we present guiding assumptions and goals for the entire design. Facilitators should refer to the website to identify goals specific to the form of oppression they choose to center in Quadrants 2 and 3. Similar to other chapters in this volume, we understand that educators may adapt these materials to different groups and time frames. Understanding how a particular goal or activity fits into the overall goals and design sequence, facilitators can adapt as needed while meeting each group's needs. Last, we discuss pedagogical and facilitation issues as they uniquely impact settings focusing on sexism, heterosexism, and trans* oppression.

OVERVIEW OF SEXISM, HETEROSEXISM AND TRANS* OPPRESSION DESIGN QUADRANTS

Quadrant 1: Intra- and Interpersonal Awareness
Total Time: 3.5 hours

1. Introductions (15 min.)
2. Agenda and Goals (15 min.)
3. Guiding Assumptions (30 min.)
4. Group Agreements (15 min.)
5. Connecting Activity: Concentric Circles (15 min.)
6. Terms and Definitions (60 min.)
7. Socialization Reflection (60 min.)

Quadrant 2: Intersectional Explorations of Power
Total Time: 3.5 hours

(see website for three design options—one each for sexism, heterosexism, and trans* oppression)

Quadrant 3: Historical Legacies
Total Time: 3.5 hours

(see website for three design options—one each for sexism, heterosexism, and trans* oppression)

Quadrant 4: Liberation and Accountability
Total Time: 3.5 hours

1. Defining Liberation and Action (30 min.)
2. Exploring Social Movements (60 min.)
3. Personal Liberation Reflection (30 min.)
4. Actions and Accountability (60 min.)
5. Closing (30 min.)

Overall Goals

• To engage in critical thinking about sexism, heterosexism, and trans* oppression as interlocking yet distinctive systems of oppression

- To reflect on our socialization (learned behaviors and perspectives) as it informs our thinking about sex, gender, and sexuality
- To engage in multi-level (individual, institutional, and cultural) analysis about how sexism, heterosexism, and trans* oppression impact self-perception, perception of others, and organization of institutions and idea systems
- To examine how sexism, heterosexism, and trans* oppression intersect with all forms of oppression
- To cultivate strategies, tactics, and possibilities for interrupting and dismantling sexism, heterosexism, and trans* oppression

Guiding Assumptions

Guiding assumptions are a list of statements that provide insight about the main tenets that undergird the design. By sharing these guiding assumptions with participants as they begin to approach the topic, facilitators communicate transparency about their approach, key ideas and methods that participants may return to repeatedly throughout their learning, and clear expectations about what is, and what is not, open for discussion.

- There is a still evolving plurality of language to describe sex, gender, and sexual diversity. The potential of changing terms for self-definition reminds us that we seek to find ways to describe ourselves beyond those words imposed on us.
- While sex, gender, and sexuality are socially constructed categories, experiences of those categories are very real to individuals.
- An examination of our relationships to our sex, gender, and sexuality requires considerations of our socialization, including emotions associated with this socialization. By reflecting on individual socialization processes (intrapersonal), we illuminate interpersonal and systemic realities.
- We recognize that naming oneself is an act of agency and respect that everyone is an expert in their own identities; all sexes, genders, and sexualities are valid.
- Fluidity of genders and sexualities is an individual determination, and changes in self-identification do not diminish the validity of a person's assertions.
- To examine sexism, heterosexism, and trans* oppression requires an examination of complex and interrelated systems of gender and sexuality. Dominant assumptions about gender and sexuality influence our understanding of identities, roles, physiology, and psychology.
- In the examination of our socialization, we must consider our intimate relationships with others (i.e., families, friends, and partners) and how those relationships reinforce, challenge, and subvert our self-awareness (intrapersonal) and construction of others' identities (interpersonal).
- While the focus of this design is on sex, gender, and sexuality, our other social identities (race, class, etc.) influence and shape how we understand those identities.
- Paradoxically, gender and sex binaries are harmful and limiting to everyone *and* these binaries can serve as a touchstone for self-awareness.
- The interrelated systems of oppression of sexism, heterosexism, and trans* oppression reflect dynamics of advantage and disadvantage in a U.S. context. Additionally, these systems also operate in nations beyond the U.S., with varying degrees of similarities.
- Systems such as patriarchy, misogyny, and normativity (cis and hetero) manifest through sexism, heterosexism, and trans* oppression. By centering sexism, heterosexism, and trans* oppression, we must also acknowledge how other social identities influence, shape, and engage our perceptions of identities, relationships, and bodies. In this way, sexism, heterosexism, and trans* oppression have connections to all other forms of oppression.

- An intersectional feminist framework provides us with a robust analytical tool to excavate, interrogate, and transform the complex and multifaceted inequities that sexism, heterosexism, and trans* oppression uphold.
- Liberation may look like an individual actively transgressing gender and/or sexual binaries. Liberation may *also* look like an individual seeking alignment with dominant conceptions of these binaries.
- Engaging in liberation as a group, institution, and system is to acknowledge and honor the gender and/or sexuality of how people name their identities and provide opportunities for self-declarations.
- Because aspects of sex, gender, and sexuality are internal to an individual, we cannot know the complexity of an individual's sex, gender, or sexuality by visual or verbal cues alone (i.e., body morphology, couplings, pronouns).
- Understanding sexism, heterosexism, and trans* oppression, as singular forms of oppression and at their intersections, can cause frustration, confusion, and uncertainty. Yet seeking to continuously engage, learn, and reflect are part of the liberation process for everyone.

QUADRANT 1: INTRA- AND INTERPERSONAL AWARENESS

Learning Outcomes:

- Get to know each other and begin to build trust in a learning community
- Explore and examine sex, gender, and sexuality socialization (self and others)
- Build a foundation of common language to support learning about sex, gender, and sexuality

1. Introductions for Sex, Gender, Sexuality Workshop (for example) (15 min.)
   This activity provides an opportunity for participants to identify their name and pronouns, as well as other information that might be helpful to the formation of the learning community, and serves as a way for participants to practice recognizing others in how they name and identify themselves.
2. Agenda and Goals (15 min.)
   Agenda and goal setting is a shared opportunity to help participants anticipate what they will be learning, request areas for learning, and set clear expectations for the duration of the session/workshop.
3. Guiding Assumptions (30 min.)
   Surfacing guiding assumptions makes transparent ideas and understandings that the designers and/or facilitators used to select materials, activities, processes, and facilitation approaches. This activity serves as the foundation for facilitators and an opportunity for participants to seek clarification.
4. Group Agreements (15 min.)
   Choosing a process to explore group agreements makes it possible for learners to set intentions for their learning experience and make requests in service to their own and the group's learning.
5. Connecting Activity: Concentric Circles (15 min.)
   This activity provides participants with an opportunity to learn more about each other while sharing more about themselves. It is a reflection opportunity that allows participants to choose the level of vulnerability to keep it low risk. Concentric circles allow participants to engage with multiple peers to share and learn about each other.

6. Terms and Definitions (60 min.)
   This activity creates opportunities to explore nuances of language used to describe sex, gender, sexuality, and trans* identities.
7. Socialization Reflection (60 min.)
   This activity guides participants through their early memories, current influences, and relationship to social identity groups, centering sex, gender, and sexuality.

QUADRANT 2: INTERSECTIONAL EXPLORATIONS OF POWER

The role of this quadrant is to center one of the three forms of oppression (sexism, heterosexism, or trans* oppression) as a way to identify the complexity of privilege and power. In this quadrant, participants will have the opportunity to explore their own relationship to power, as well as institutional and systemic/cultural dynamics that support existing power structures.

QUADRANT 3: HISTORICAL LEGACIES

Quadrant 3 provides participants the opportunity to delve into the historical legacies that serve as the roots of oppression. Facilitators choose to center a design on the historical legacy of sexism, heterosexism, or trans* oppression.

QUADRANT 4: LIBERATION AND ACCOUNTABILITY

Learning Outcomes:

- Define liberation and social action
- Reflect on personal commitments and capacity to work for liberation around sex, gender, and sexuality
- Explore the conditions that support participation in social change movements
- Identify opportunities for taking action

Quadrant 4 focuses on actions and plans to dismantle systems of oppression.

1. Defining Liberation and Action (30 min.)
   This activity requires participants to define liberation for themselves and reflect on a time when they took action to interrupt and/or stop sexism, heterosexism, and/or trans* oppression or a time when they wanted to take action but did not.
2. Exploring Social Movements (60 min.)
   This activity invites participants to consider what dispositions, action steps, relationships, and conditions support participation in social change movements through the narratives of multiple activists.
3. Personal Liberation Reflection (30 min.)
   In this activity, participants engage in individual action planning to determine ways in their everyday lives they can eliminate sexism, heterosexism, and trans* oppression.
4. Actions and Accountability (45 min.)
   Within this activity, participants will consider opportunities for coalitions and what it means to engage in action within different spheres of their lives (personal, professional, etc.)
5. Closing (30 min.)
   The closing activity allows participants to reflect on their experiences from the entire workshop.

Pedagogical and Facilitation Issues

An integrated approach to teaching about sexism, heterosexism, and trans* oppression requires attention to several aspects of design and facilitation. Facilitators must determine how to focus Quadrants 2 and 3. To determine their approach, they should consider the vastness of content knowledge required to address each individual ism and their interconnections, plus the intersections of other forms of oppression, as addressing sexism, heterosexism, and trans oppression unreasonable to address in one seminar. Thus, facilitators must decide to focus Quadrants 2 and 3 on one specific form of oppression. However, we caution that this decision does not relieve facilitators from doing their own deeper dives into all three forms of oppression to ensure they understand the nuances of how these related forms of oppression interact to affect lived experiences for participants and themselves.

Self-awareness and knowledge expertise are requirements for all those who engage in social justice education. We encourage those with more experience, knowledge, and comfort with sexism, heterosexism, or trans* oppression to engage in intensive research and thinking about the ism(s) in which they feel they need the most growth, as well as how they can connect that learning to the other ism(s). Participants will bring in various levels of awareness and knowledge about these forms of oppression to the sessions, which facilitators should take as an invitation to build from participant knowledge. Many participants might claim familiarity with gender and sexuality because of what appears in mainstream culture, so facilitators should emphasize why participants need to interrogate their assumptions about language, identity, and culture. In the following list, we delineate some common facilitation challenges and offer guidance on how to address them:

1. Because assigned sex at birth, gender, and sexuality are simultaneously shared concepts and private identities, facilitators can anticipate various types of resistance from participants. Resistance might show in the way some participants consider their gender "obvious" and therefore reject utilizing pronouns on their name tags. Facilitators must find opportunities to push back against this resistance by opening up lines of conversation about how assumptions about bodies and identities are a form of harm. Resistance might also appear in the form of declarative statements that their sexuality is not the business of anyone else in the space. Providing opportunities for participants to choose their disclosure levels is paramount to assuage that form of resistance. Facilitators can remind participants that they can choose how much to share about their own identities while also encouraging them to engage in conversations about the broader issues and dynamics of sexuality.

2. Part of the empowerment facilitators offer in this design is the act of self-determination of identities. One of the important learning opportunities for facilitators and participants is to recognize how some language is comfortable and familiar and other language is not. Recognition of identities means understanding that the lack of familiarity with identities and self-identification terms is a form of marginalization. While facilitators want participants to bring their authentic selves and experiences into the space, facilitators must also be aware that participants may use identity language that is problematic. For example, participants could assert "superstraight" as an identity and claim "all identities are valid." Facilitators should explain that this is a political identity, rather than a gender or sexual identity (how is one more heterosexual than heterosexual?), that came into usage specifically to be overtly transphobic and homophobic (e.g., as a mechanism to denounce any queer affects and assert that trans* people cannot identify as heterosexual).

3. Sometimes cisgender participants will state they are comfortable with any pronoun, which might be true. At the same time, the freedom to be open to any pronoun when someone has been consistently recognized as the gender they are may reflect unacknowledged privilege, masked through an attempt at demonstrating openness. It is important for facilitators to consider how to surface the difference between this experience and that of trans* people who face misrecognition and may be disbelieved or disregarded when they communicate their pronouns. Additionally, should any participant not wish to share their pronouns, then facilitators should support that decision and model not using third-person pronouns for that individual (but using only the person's name or speaking directly to the person using "you").

4. Caucus groups, sometimes called affinity groups, are activities where participants meet in a space with others who share a specific identity (gender, sexuality) to discuss their experiences and build rapport. Generally, participants choose the caucus group that suits them best. Forming caucus groups by gender or sexuality should consider the identities of those in the room. For example, gender caucus groups that use three categories of "men," "women," and "other genders" function to literally other the participants who identify in a nonbinary way (e.g., nonbinary, agender, genderqueer). Additionally, some cisgender men or women may question the presence of trans* men or women in their group, which may seem antagonistic and dismissive of trans* and nonbinary people's identities. A similar problem can occur if caucus groups around sexuality are separated into queer and heterosexual caucus, in which case gay and lesbian people who do not identify as queer, as well as some asexual, bisexual, and polyamorous participants who have experiences of both privilege and disadvantage in heterosexism, may feel these are exclusionary groupings. An option to consider is to begin by inviting participants to identify the groupings in which they would like to caucus before naming the groups for them. The first step in facilitating this process is to provide participants reflection and discussion space to surface how they wish to align themselves with identities and/or experiences.

5. An integrated approach destabilizes the dynamics of privilege and oppression because of the multitude of identities and experiences. It is important for facilitators to ensure they give attention to each form of oppression in processing, questions, and discussion throughout all activities in Quadrants 1 and 4. This is particularly important when facilitators recognize they have greater comfort with or knowledge about a specific ism.

6. Because an integrated approach challenges many dominant ideas about sex, gender, and sexuality, it is especially important for facilitators to provide participants time to process and reflect on their confusion and/or resistance. Rather than swiftly moving through activities, facilitators should plan for more time with fewer activities to allow for participants to reflect, question, and make sense of these new frameworks.

7. An integrated approach offers an opportunity for participants to challenge binary thinking. When participants' definitions of man and woman rely on cisgender assumptions, facilitators must address this distinction. When gender includes cisgender and trans*/nonbinary distinctions, this also disrupts how participants think about sexuality because of its roots with assigned sex at birth. This can cause disorientation for some participants, and it is prudent to ensure enough time in the design to make sense of a different way to conceptualize identities, bodies, and relationships.

8. With an integrated approach, it is more likely participants will have opportunities to explore both privilege and disadvantage based on sex assigned at birth, gender, and/or sexuality. This provides opportunities to reveal how almost everyone experiences privilege and oppression and to build a bridge for coalition and connections. For instance,

a participant may hold privilege as a cisgender man and experience oppression as a gay or queer person. This simultaneity of lived experiences provides an opportunity to look at identities from a singular and intersecting lens.

9. Similarly, facilitators must be sensitive to the ways in which they may unintentionally frame privilege and oppression in a binary way when discussing any single issue. Asking participants to think about their assigned sex at birth, gender, and sexuality invites a deeper exploration of lived experiences than asking them to think about only one of the three. This also requires more complicated discussion questions that can lead participants to realize unexplored aspects of their socialization. Facilitators should take time to carefully plan processing questions to draw out complexity.

10. We encourage facilitators to utilize a variety of topics, such as relationship violence, employment discrimination, and access to medical care, as anchor points for discussions about how sexism, heterosexism, and trans* oppression manifest. Utilizing several topics as different windows into the overall functioning of sexism, heterosexism, and trans* oppression provides opportunities to highlight the connections and differential experiences of marginalization and privilege.

CONCLUSION

Gender and sexual identities are multiple and complex, as are the systems that uphold sexism, heterosexism, and trans* oppression. Along with the cultural and historical realities that disrupt binary notions of sex and gender, the important analyses of intersectional feminisms generated by BIPOC thinkers, activists, and educators can untangle and recast mainstream conceptions of gender and sexuality while deepening our understanding simultaneously. For example, to untangle sexism, we must pay attention to the realities of cis women and trans* women, as well as include profeminist work on masculinity in our conceptions. Thus, the traditional gender binary upon which prior understandings of sexism have rested can be refashioned with more inclusive understandings of gender and the various individuals and communities that anti-sexist work can support. The work of intersectional feminism compels us to wrestle with the overlaps and intersections of multiple social identities and the systems that construct identities as they are lived by BIPOC; in this same vein, educators must wrestle with the *intersections of multiple dimensions of gender and sexuality* in our teaching and learning. Teaching and learning about heterosexism can include and extend beyond the realities of gay and lesbian life and disrupt binary notions of gender. The inclusion of trans* people and their lived experiences in work for gender and sexual justice gives us new insights for teaching about oppression and liberation.

Our purpose in this chapter has been to illuminate the interconnections between and among sexism, heterosexism, and transgender oppression; provide updated conceptualizations; and foreground lived realities that help us untangle multiple quagmires of gender in the interest of liberation and justice. The vision of social justice that lives in intersectional feminisms, one with queer-affirmative and trans*-inclusive leanings, encourages us to recast our historical understanding of movements for gender equity between "women" and "men" and movements for "gay and lesbian liberation" to include the existence and realities of trans* people *and* to hold an intersectional analysis while we do this work. As educators for social justice, we can expand beyond the usual imaginaries attributed to societal constructions of gender and be a part of movements for more expansive understandings of gender and more pervasive gender liberation.

Notes

* We ask that those who cite this work always acknowledge by name all of the authors listed rather than either only citing the first author or using "et al." to indicate co-authors. All collaborated on the conceptualization, development, and writing of this chapter.
1 We use an asterisk as an imperfect means to draw attention to the expansiveness of gender identities inclusive of nonbinary and gender-nonconforming folks (Tompkins, 2014). Trans* (with the asterisk) has been used within trans* communities but is less common there than it was a few years ago. The asterisk is still widely used in academic trans* studies by trans* scholars (e.g., Jourian, 2017; Jaekel & Nicolazzo, 2017).
2 The term *sexual orientation* rather than *sexuality* is also common, especially in some educational settings. Sexual orientation usually refers only to the genders to which one experiences attraction (i.e., the same gender, a different gender, or more than one gender), whereas sexuality refers more broadly to feelings, desires, relationships, and behavior. Both are sometimes reduced to a category or label that can serve to affirm identity and community but also oversimplifies the complex experiences of sexuality.
3 Each identity term used to describe variations of trans*ness has an evolving and contested meaning and may mean something different to different people who use it. It is beyond the scope of this chapter to detail these nuances, but working definitions of some gender identity terms are included in the glossary.
4 A term used by trans-exclusionary radical feminists to differentiate between cisgender women who were assigned female at birth and trans* women. It is often used to narrowly define who is allowed into the category of women and to disregard or diminish trans* women as women.
5 *Hermaphrodite* is a term that used to be common in describing intersex people but is now understood to be both offensive and inaccurate.

References

Abad-Santos, A. (2014, May 25). Why #yesallwomen is the most important thing you'll read today. *VOX.* Retrieved from https://www.vox.com/2014/5/25/5749480/why-yesallwomen-is-the-most-important-thing-youll-read-today

Allen, P. G. (1992). *The sacred hoop: Recovering the feminine in American Indian traditions.* Beacon Press.

Allen, S. (2019, March 22). It's not just Japan: Many U.S. states require transgender people get sterilized. *The Daily Beast.* Retrieved from https://www.thedailybeast.com/its-not-just-japan-many-us-states-require-transgender-people-get-sterilized

American Civil Liberties Union (ACLU). (2022, April 8). *Legislation affecting LGBTQ rights across the country.* Retrieved from https://www.aclu.org/legislation-affecting-lgbtq-rights-across-country

American Civil Liberties Union. (n.d.). *Legislation affecting LGBTQ rights across the country 2021.* Retrieved from https://www.aclu.org/legislation-affecting-lgbtq-rights-across-country-2021?redirect=legislation-affecting-lgbt-rights-across-country

Amiri, B. (2020). Reproductive abuse is rampant in the immigration detention system. *ACLU.* Retrieved from https://www.aclu.org/news/immigrants-rights/reproductive-abuse-is-rampant-in-the-immigration-detention-system/

Anzaldúa, G. (1990). La conciencia de la mestiza: Towards a new consciousness. In G. Anzaldúa (Ed.), *Making face, making soul/haciendo caras: Creative and critical perspectives by feminists of color* (pp. 377–389). Aunt Lute.

Anzaldúa, G., & Moraga, C. (Eds.). (2015). *This bridge called my back: Writings by radical women of color* (4th ed.). SUNY Press.

Aultman, B. (2014). Cisgender. *TSQ: Trans*gender Studies Quarterly, 1*(1–2), 61–62.

Baca Zinn, M., & Zambrana, R. E. (2019). Chicanas/Latinas advance intersectional thought and practice. *Gender & Society, 33*(5), 677–701.

Barcelos, C. A. (2020). *Distributing Condoms and Hope.* University of California Press.

Beauchamp, Z. (2019, April 23). Our incel problem. *VOX.* Retrieved from https://www.vox.com/the-highlight/2019/4/16/18287446/incel-definition-reddit

Beh, H. G., & Diamond, M. (2000). An emerging ethical and medical dilemma: Should physicians perform sex assignment surgery on infants with ambiguous genitalia. *Michigan Journal of Gender & Law, 7*(1), 1–64.

Bérubé, A. (2001). How gay stays white and what kind of white it stays. In B. B. Rassmussen, I. J. Nexica, E. Klinenberg, & M. Wray (Eds.), *The making and unmaking of whiteness* (pp. 234–265). Duke University Press.

Black Lives Matter (n.d.). *Herstory*. Retrieved from https://blacklivesmatter.com/herstory/

Bornstein, K. (2009). Open letter to LGBT leaders who are pushing marriage equality. In R. Conrad (Ed.), *Against equality: Queer critiques of gay marriage* (pp. 11–14). Against Equality Press.

Bose, C. E. (2012). Intersectionality and global gender inequality. *Gender & Society*, 26(1), 67–72.

Brewer, R. (1993). Theorizing race, class, and gender: The new scholarship of black feminist intellectuals and black women's labor. In S. M. James & A. P. A. Busia (Eds.), *Theorizing black feminisms: The visionary pragmatism of black women* (pp. 13–30). Routledge.

Brod, G. F. (1994). Premarital agreements and gender justice. *Yale Journal of Law and Feminism*, 6(2), 229–246.

Brown, E. B. (1992). 'What has happened here': The politics of difference in women's history and feminist politics. *Feminist Studies*, 18(2), 295–312.

Butler, J. (2004). *Undoing gender*. Routledge.

Carruthers, C. A. (2018). *Unapologetic: A Black, queer, and feminist mandate for radical movements*. Beacon Press.

Catalano, D. C. J., & Griffin, P. (2016). Sexism, heterosexism, and trans* oppression: An integrated perspective. In *Teaching for diversity and social justice* (pp. 201–230). Routledge.

Catalano, D. C. J., Haslerig, S., Jourian, T. J., & Nicolazzo, Z. (2021). White Paper: An affirmation of trans livelihood in and beyond postsecondary education. *Association for the Study of Higher Education*. Retrieved from https://www.ashe.ws//Files/Position%20Taking/2021.08%20ASHE%20Statement%20on%20the%20Affirmation%20of%20Trans%20Life.pdf

Chase, C. (2012). Hermaphrodites with attitude: Mapping the emergence of intersex political activism. In S. Stryker & S. Whittle (Eds.), *The trans*gender studies reader* (pp. 300–314). Routledge.

Cho, S., Crenshaw, K., & McCall, L. (2013). Toward a field of intersectionality studies: Theory, applications, and praxis. *Signs: Journal of Women in Culture and Society*, 38(4), 785–810.

Cohen, R. (2015, November 18). Who took care of Rosie the Riveter's kids? *The Atlantic*. Retrieved from https://www.theatlantic.com/business/archive/2015/11/daycare-world-war-rosie-riveter/415650/

Collins, P. H. (2005). *Black sexual politics: African-Americans, gender, and the new racism*. Routledge.

Combahee River Collective. (1977). *Combahee River Collective Statement*. Published pamphlet.

Connell, R. W. (1995). *Masculinities*. Polity.

Connell, R. W. (2002). *Gender*. Polity.

Conrad, R. (2009). *Against equality: Queer critiques of gay marriage*. Against Equality Press.

Cornell University Library (n.d.). *25 years of political influence: The records of the Human Rights Campaign*. Retrieved from https://rmc.library.cornell.edu/HRC/exhibition/whatishrc/index.html

Crenshaw, K. (2008). Mapping the margins: Intersectionality, identity politics, and violence against women of color. In A. Bailey & C. Cuomo (Eds.), *The feminist philosophy reader* (pp. 279–309). McGraw-Hill.

Crenshaw, K. W. (2001). The first decade: Critical reflections, or a foot in the closing door. *UCLA Law Review*, 49, 1343–1372.

Davis, A. Y. (1981). *Women, race & class*. New York: Random House.

Denetdale, J. N. (2017). Chairmen, presidents, and princesses: The Navajo Nation, gender, and the politics of tradition. In F. Negrón-muntaner (Ed.), *Sovereign acts: Contesting colonialism across Indigenous nations and Latinx America* (pp. 153–174). University of Arizona Press.

Dilley, P. (1999). Queer theory: Under construction. *International Journal of Qualitative Studies in Education*, 12(5), 457–472. doi:10.1080/095183999235890

Driver, S. (2008). *Queer youth cultures*. SUNY Press.

Fausto-Sterling, A. (2000). *Sexing the body: Gender politics and the construction of sexuality*. Basic Books.

Federici, S. (2004). *Caliban and the witch: Women, the body and primitive accumulation*. Autonomedia.

Feinberg, L. (1998). *Trans* liberation: Beyond pink and blue*. Beacon Press.

Ferber, A. L., Holcomb, K., & Wentling, T. (2009). *Sex, gender, and sexuality reader: The new basics, an anthology*. Oxford University Press.

Ferguson, R. A. (2019). *One-dimensional queer*. Polity.

Finlayson, L., Jenkins, K., & Worsdale, R. (2018). "I'm not transphobic, but . . .": A feminist case against the feminist case against trans inclusivity. Verso Books. Retrieved from https://www.versobooks.com/blogs/4090-i-m-not-transphobic-but-a-feminist-case-against-the-feminist-case-against-trans-inclusivity

Gardiner, J. K. (2002). Theorizing age with gender: Bly's boys, feminism, and maturity masculinity. *Masculinity studies and feminist theory: New directions*, 90–118.

Giddings, P. (2006). *When and where I enter: The impact of black women on race and sex in America*. Amistad/Harper Collins.

Gray, L. A. (2019, March 12). "She was decapitated a block from a police station": Indigenous women are going missing and no one listens. *Independent*. Retrieved from https://www.inde pendent.co.uk/news/long_reads/mmiw-native-american-women-canada-inquiry-savannas-act-missing-murdered-a8803996.html

Gumbs, A. P. (2015). Forget Hallmark: Why mother's day is a queer Black left feminist thing. *Aster (ix): A Journal of Literature, Art, Criticism*. Retrieved from https://asterixjournal.com/forget-hallmark-why-mothers-day-is-a-queer-black-left-feminist-thing-by-alexis-pauline-gumbs/

Hegewisch, A., Barsi, Z., & Hayes, J. (2020). *Dramatic decline in employment hits women even more severely than men*. Institute for Women's Policy Research. https://iwpr.org/wp-content/uploads/2020/05/QF-Breadwinner-Mothers-by-Race-FINAL.pdf

Hernández, L. H., & De Los Santos Upon, S. (2018). *Challenging reproductive control and gendered violence in the Américas: Intersectionality, power, and struggles for rights*. Lexington Books.

Hernandez, L. H., & De Los Santos Upton, S. (2020). Insider/outsiders, reproductive (in)justice, and the U.S.-Mexico border. *Health Communication, 35*(8), 1046–1050. doi:10.1080/10410236.2019.1602819

Hines, S. (2018). Trans and feminist rights have been falsely cast in opposition. *Economist, 13*.

hooks, b. (1981). *Ain't I a woman: Black women and feminism*. South End Press.

Horswell, M. J. (2010). *Decolonizing the Sodomite: Queer tropes of sexuality in colonial Andean culture*. University of Texas Press.

Hubbard, R. (1996). Gender & genitals: Constructions of sex and gender. *Social Text, 14*(46/47), 157–165.

Ingraham, C. (1994). The heterosexual imaginary: Feminist sociology and theories of gender. *Sociological Theory, 12*(2), 203–219.

Jaekel, K., & Nicolazzo, Z. (2017). Teaching trans*: Strategies and tensions of teaching gender in student affairs preparation programs. *Journal for the Study of Postsecondary and Tertiary Education, 2*, 165–179.

Jaki, S., De Smedt, T., Gwóźdź, M., Panchal, R., Rossa, A., & De Pauw, G. (2019). Online hatred of women in the Incels.me forum: Linguistic analysis and automatic detection. *Journal of Language Aggression and Conflict, 7*(2), 240–268.

Jay, K. (1999). *Tales of the lavender menace: A memoir of liberation*. Basic Books.

Johnson, A. (2014). *The gender knot* (3rd ed.). Temple University Press.

Johnson, C. (2013, July 7). Female inmates sterilized in California prisons without approval. *Reveal News*. Retrieved from https://revealnews.org/article/female-inmates-sterilized-in-california-prisons-without-approval/

Jones, J. (1986). *Labor of love, labor of sorrow: Black women, work, and the family from slavery to the present*. Random House.

Jourian, T. J. (2017). Trans*ing constructs: Toward a critical trans* methodology. *Tijdschrift voor Genderstudies, 20*(4), 415–434. doi:10.5117/TVGN2017.4.JOUR

Kendall, M. (2020). *Hood feminism: Notes from the women that a movement forgot*. Penguin/Random House.

Kelly, M., DiBranco, A., & DeCook, J. (2021). Misogynist incels and male supremacism: Overview and recommendations for addressing the threat of male supremacist violence. *New America*. Retrieved from https://d1y8sb8igg2f8e.cloudfront.net/documents/Misogynist_Incels_and_Male_Supremacism.pdf

Kesselman, A. (1990). *Fleeting opportunities: Women shipyard workers*. SUNY Press.

Kessler, S. J. (1998). *Lessons from the intersexed*. Rutgers University Press.

Khayrallah, N. (2015). Born a womyn?: Lisa Vogel's paradigm for transgender exclusion. *The Morningside Review, 11*. Retrieved from https://journals.library.columbia.edu/index.php/TMR/article/view/5420

Kimmel, M. (1994). Masculinity as homophobia: Fear, shame, and silence in the construction of gender identity. In H. Brod & M. Kaufman (Eds.), *Theorizing masculinity* (pp. 119–141). Sage.

Kimmel, M. (1996). *Manhood in America: A cultural history*. Free Press.

Knight, K. (2020, July 30). First U.S. hospital pledges to end intersex surgeries: Historic apology a step toward respect for bodily autonomy. Retrieved from https://www.hrw.org/news/2020/07/30/first-us-hospital-pledges-end-intersex-surgeries

Kosciw, J. G., Greytak, E. A., Zongrone, A. D., Clark, C. M., & Truong, N. L. (2018). *The 2017 National School Climate Survey: The experiences of lesbian, gay, bisexual, transgender, and queer youth in our nation's schools*. GLSEN.

Lavin, T. (2020). Culture warlords: My journey into the dark web of white supremacy. Legacy Lit.

Lewis, A. J. (2017). Trans* history in a moment of danger: Organizing within and beyond "visibility" in the 1970s. In R. Gossett, E. A. Stanley, & J. Burton (Eds.), *Trap door: Trans* cultural production and the politics of visibility*. Massachusetts Institute of Technology.

Lewis, S. (2019). How British feminism became anti-trans. *New York Times*.

Lira, N. (2021). *Laboratory of Deficiency: Sterilization and Confinement in California, 1900–1950s* (Vol. 6). University of California Press.

Littlejohn, K. E. (2021). *Just Get on the Pill: The Uneven Burden of Reproductive Politics* (Vol. 4). University of California Press.

Lorde, Audre. (1984). *Sister outsider*. The Crossing Press.

Lucchesi, A., & Echo-Hawk, A. (2018). *Missing and murdered indigenous women & girls: A snapshot of data from 71 urban cities in the United States*. Urban Indian Health Institute. Retrieved from http://www.uihi.org/wp-content/uploads/2018/11/Missing-and-Murdered-Indigenous-Women-and-Girls-Report.pdf

Lugones, M. (2007). Heterosexualism and the colonial/modern gender system. *Hypatia*, 22(1), 186–209.

Luna, Z., & Luker, K. (2015). Reproductive justice. In *Reproduction and society: Interdisciplinary readings* (Vol. 9, pp. 327–352). Routledge.

Mackenzie, G. (1994). *Transgender nation*. Popular Press.

Martin, N. (2020, January 22). The cyclical crisis of missing and murdered indigenous women. *New Republic*. Retrieved from https://newrepublic.com/article/156263/cyclical-crisis-missing-murdered-indigenous-women

Mason, C. N., Flynn, A., & Sun, S. (2020). Build(ing) the future: Bold policies for a gender-equitable recovery. *Institute for Women's Policy Research*. https://www.jstor.org/stable/resrep34560.6

Matthiesen, S. (2021). *Reproduction Reconceived: Family Making and the Limits of Choice After Roe V. Wade* (Vol. 5). University of California Press.

Mayo, C. (2007). Queering foundations: Queer and lesbian, gay, bisexual, and transgender educational research. *Review of Research in Education*, 31, 78–94. doi:10.3102/0091732X06298013

McClintock, A. (1995). *Imperial leather: Race, gender and sexuality in the colonial conquest*. Routledge.

Messerschmidt, J. W. (2009). Goodby to the sex-gender distinction, hello to embodied gender. In L. Ferber, K. Holcomb, & T. Wentling (Eds.), *Sex, gender and sexuality: The new basics, an anthology* (pp. 71–88). Oxford University Press.

Meyer, III, W., Bockting, W. O., Cohen-Kettenis, P., Coleman, E., DiCeglie, D., Devor, H., . . . Wheeler, C. C. (2002). The Harry Benjamin international gender dysphoria association's standards of care for gender identity disorders, sixth version. *Journal of Psychology & Human Sexuality*, 13(1), 1.

Meyerowitz, J. (2002). *How sex changed: A history of trans*sexuality in the United States*. Harvard University Press.

Miller, N. (1995). *Out of the past: Gay and lesbian history from 1869 to the present*. Vintage.

Minter, S. P. (2006). Do transsexuals dream of gay rights? Getting real about transgender inclusion. In P. Currah, R. M. Juang, & S. P. Minter (Eds.), *Transgender rights* (pp. 141–170). University of Minnesota Press.

Miranda, D. A. (2010). Extermination of the Joyas: Gendercide in Spanish California. *GLQ: A Journal of Lesbian and Gay Studies*, 16(1–2), 253–284. doi:10.1215/10642684-2009-022

Mirza, H. S. (2009). Plotting a history: Black and postcolonial feminisms in 'new times'. *Race Ethnicity and Education*, 12(1), 1–10.

Mohanty, C. T. (2003). *Feminism without borders: Decolonizing theory, practicing solidarity*. Duke University Press.

Morgan, R. (Ed.) (1970). *Sisterhood is powerful: An anthology of writings from the Women's Liberation Movement*. Vintage Books.

Morris, M. (1998). Unresting the curriculum: Queer projects, queer imaginings. In W. Pinar (Ed.), *Queer theory in education* (pp. 275–286). Earlbaum.

Nair, Y. (2009). Against equality, against marriage: An introduction. In R. Conrad (Ed.), *Against equality: Queer critiques of gay marriage* (pp. 1–9). Against Equality Press.

National Coalition Against Domestic Violence. (2020). *Domestic violence*. Retrieved from https://assets.speakcdn.com/assets/2497/domestic_violence-2020080709350855.pdf?1596811079991

National Congress of American Indian Policy Research Center. (2018, February). *Policy update: violence against American Indian and Alaska native women*. Retrieved from https://www.ncai.org/policy-research-center/research-data/prc-publications/VAWA_Data_Brief__FINAL_2_1_2018.pdf

National Council on Disability. (2012). *Rocking the Cradle: Ensuring the Rights of Parents with Disabilities*. Retrieved from https://ncd.gov/publications/2012/Sep272012/

National Park Service. (2021). *The world war II home front*. Website of the Rosie the Riveter World War II Home Front Museum. Retrieved from https://www.nps.gov/rori/learn/historyculture/index.htm

Polikoff, N. D. (2018). Neglected lesbian mothers. *Fam. LQ, 52*, 87.

Preciado, P. B. (2013). *Testo junkie: Sex, drugs, and biopolitics in the pharmacopornographic era* (B. Benderson, Trans.). The Feminist Press at CUNY.

Preves, S. E. (2003). *Intersex and identity: The contested self*. Rutgers University Press.

Purkayastha, B. (2012). Intersectionality in a transnational world. *Gender & Society, 26*(1), 55–66.

Quijano, A. (2000). The coloniality of power, Eurocentrism, and Latin America. *Nepantla: Views from the South, 1*(3), 533–580.

Radicallesbians. (1970). *The woman identified woman*. Know, Inc.

Rich, A. (1980). Compulsory heterosexuality and lesbian existence. *Signs: Journal of Women in Culture and Society, 5*(4), 631–660.

Rifkin, M. (2011). *When did Indians become straight? Kinship, the history of sexuality, and Native sovereignty*. Oxford: Oxford University Press.

Roberts, D. (1997). *Killing the black body: Race, reproduction, and the meaning of liberty*. Pantheon Books.

Roberts, D. (2021). Abolish family policing, too. *Dissent, 68*(3), 67–69.

Romney, P. (2021). *We were there: The third world women's alliance and the second wave of feminism*. Feminist Press.

Rosay, A. B. (2016). *Violence against American Indian and Alaska Native women and men: 2010 Findings from the National Intimate Partner and Sexual Violence Survey*. U.S. Department of Justice, National Institute of Justice. Retrieved from https://www.ojp.gov/pdffiles1/nij/249736.pdf

Roscoe, W. (1998). *Changing ones: Third and fourth genders in Native North America*. St. Martin's Griffin Press.

Ross, L., Gutiérrez, E., Gerber, M., & Silliman, J. (2004). *Undivided Rights: Women of Color Organize for Reproductive Justice*. South End.

Ross, L., & Solinger, R. (2017). *Reproductive justice*. University of California Press.

Schulman, S. (2009). *Ties that bind: Familial homophobia and its consequences*. The New Press.

Scull, A. (2009). *Hysteria: The disturbing history*. Oxford University Press.

Serano, J. (2013). *Excluded: Making feminist and queer movements more inclusive*. Seal Press.

Shlasko, G. D. (2005). Queer (v.) pedagogy. *Equity & Excellence in Education, 38*(2), 123–134.

Shohat, E. (1998). *Talking visions: Multicultural feminism in a transnational age*. MIT Press.

SisterSong. (2021). *Reproductive justice*. Retrieved from https://www.sistersong.net/reproductive-justice/

Spade, D. (2006). Compliance is gendered: Struggling for gender self-determination in a hostile economy. In P. Currah, R. M. Juang, & S. P. Minter (Eds.), *Transgender rights* (pp. 217–241). University of Minnesota Press.

Spade, D. (2011). *Normal life: Administrative violence, critical trans politics, and the limits of law*. South End Press.

Spelman, E. V. (1988). *Inessential woman: Problems of exclusion in feminist thought*. Boston: Beacon Press.

Stoler, A. L. (2002). *Carnal knowledge and imperial power: Race and the intimate in colonial rule*. University of California Press.

Stoltenberg, J. (2000). *Refusing to be a man: Essays on sex and justice, 2nd edition*. Routledge.

Stryker, S. (2008). *Transgender history*. Seal Press.

The African American Policy Forum. (n.d.). #Sayhername. Retrieved from https://www.aapf.org/sayhername

Tolentino, J. (2018, May 15). The rage of the incels. *The New Yorker*. Retrieved from https://www.newyorker.com/culture/cultural-comment/the-rage-of-the-incels

Tompkins, A. (2014). Asterisk. *TSQ: Transgender Studies Quarterly, 1*(1–2), 26–27.

The Trevor Project. (2019). *The Trevor Project national survey on LGBTQ youth mental health 2019*. Retrieved from https://www.thetrevorproject.org/wp-content/uploads/2019/06/The-Trevor-Project-National-Survey-Results-2019.pdf

UN Women. (n.d.). Facts and figures: Ending violence against women. Retrieved from https://www.unwomen.org/en/what-we-do/ending-violence-against-women/facts-and-figures

UN Women. (2021). *Measuring the shadow pandemic: Violence against women during* COVID-19. Retrieved from https://data.unwomen.org/sites/default/files/documents/Publications/Measuring-shadow-pandemic.pdf

Vaid, U. (2012). *Irresistible revolutions: Confronting race, class, and the assumptions of LGBT politics.* Magnus Books.

Wallace, L. (2011, January 11). The complex legacy of Rosie the Riveter. *The Atlantic.* Retrieved from https://www.theatlantic.com/national/archive/2011/01/the-complex-legacy-of-rosie-the-riveter/69268/

Wamsley, L. (2021, March 31). Pentagon releases new policies enabling trans*gender people to serve in the military. *National Public Radio.* Retrieved from https://www.npr.org/2021/03/31/983118029/pentagon-releases-new-policies-enabling-trans*gender-people-to-serve-in-the-milit

Welter, B. (1966). The cult of true womanhood: 1820–1860. Retrieved from http://www.pinzler.com/ushistory/cultwo.html

West, C., & Fenstemaker, S. (1995). Doing difference. *Gender & Society, 9*(1), 8–37.

West, C., & Zimmerman, D. H. (1987). Doing gender. *Gender & Society, 1*(2), 125–151.

Whittington, C., Hadfield, K., & Calderón, C. (2020). *The lives & livelihoods of many in the LGBTQ community are at risk amidst the COVID-19 crisis.* The Human Rights Campaign. Retrieved from https://assets2.hrc.org/files/assets/resources/COVID19-IssueBrief-032020-FINAL.pdf

Winters, D. J., & McLaughlin, A. R. (2020). Soft sterilization: Long-acting reversible contraceptives in the carceral state. *Affilia, 35*(2), 218–230.

Wolfe, P. (2006). Settler colonialism and the elimination of the native. *Journal of Genocide Research, 8*(4), 387–409. doi:10.1080/14623520601056240

Woo, M. (2009). Stonewall was a riot—now we need a revolution. In T. A. Mecca (Ed.), *Smash the church, smash the state! The early years of gay liberation* (pp. 282–294). City Lights.

Young, I. M. (1994). Gender as seriality: Thinking about women as a social collective. *Signs, 19*(3), 713–738.

Zanghellini, A. (2020). Philosophical problems with the gender-critical feminist argument against trans inclusion. *SAGE Open.* doi:10.1177/2158244020927029

Classism

Larissa E. Hopkins, Davey Shlasko, and Marjorie Valdivia*

Classism is too often left out of social justice education. It can be hard to talk about classism because of the widespread assumption that class position is under one's control and so class inequality is only fair. Yet it's getting harder and harder *not* to talk about classism. Over the past twenty years, a series of prominent economic, ecological, and public health crises have focused public attention on classist systems and rhetoric. People increasingly notice the vivid disparities between those whose wealth seems to protect them from everything and those who never have a chance to recover from one crisis before the next is upon them. Now even the middle class experiences greater precarity, and the idea that working hard enough can lead to great wealth, or even to stability, seems ever more out of reach.

In this chapter, we examine classism and its intersections, with particular attention to the historical and continuing intersection of racism and classism in the context of racialized capitalism in the US. As we explore contemporary manifestations of classism, we also highlight ways, both practical and visionary, in which communities resist classism and work toward a more just society. Our analysis of classism informs not only what we teach but also *how* we teach. The chapter concludes with a workshop design and framework for facilitating learning about classism in an anti-classist way that moves toward economic justice.

OUR APPROACH

In order to make sense of the long-term economic inequities in our cultural, social, and political systems, a class analysis must explore not only the economic inequalities that exist but how they came to be, including their interactions with other systems of oppression. Our approach to class and classism is shaped by the core concepts described in Chapter 4: Core Concepts and especially by Young's Five Faces of Oppression (1990). We describe how classism manifests at individual, institutional, and cultural/societal levels through intersectional examples of exploitation, marginalization, powerlessness, cultural imperialism, and violence.

SOCIAL JUSTICE DEFINITIONS FOR TEACHING ABOUT CLASS AND CLASSISM[1]
★

We define *class* as "a relative social ranking based on income, wealth, education, status, and power" and *classism* as "the institutional, cultural, and individual practices and beliefs that assign differential value to people according to their socioeconomic class," in a socioeconomic system characterized by economic inequality and racial stratification (Leondar-Wright & Yeskel, 2007, p. 314; see also Fiske & Markus, 2012; Lareau & Conley, 2008).

Class as "a relative social ranking" is defined by a variety of indicators, many relational rather than quantitative. There is no one number that definitively determines one's class

DOI: 10.4324/9781003005759-9

location. Almost everyone is privileged relative to someone else and at a disadvantage relative to others. Individuals internalize assumptions and stereotypes about different class positions, often based on misinformation about the economic system, and these simplified understandings define their relationships to others within a class hierarchy. Thus, classism implicates all participants in a social system in which class categories are nuanced and opaque and in which relative advantage and disadvantage are reproduced through a complex interaction of social, institutional, cultural, and interpersonal mechanisms.

In addition to examining a variety of class indicators, our approach considers the cultures and identities that form around shared class location. Thus, our understanding of class categories is not simply linear: a person may have higher relative ranking according to one indicator but lower ranking according to another. For example, a woman with greater wealth than another (because she's the owner of a manufacturing company or just won the lottery) may have lower class *status* (because she has less "sophisticated" language or less education). A nuanced view of class also allows us to examine the mechanisms of *class privilege*, by which we mean those advantages and resources accorded to some groups of people and not others (often at the expense of others), based on relative class ranking.

Capitalism

There are different understandings of the relationship between classism and capitalism, including the question (that we do not pursue here) of whether classism can be understood to exist independently from capitalism (as in pre- or non-capitalist agricultural or socialist-industrial societies). Because we focus on the contemporary US, our discussion is limited to the relationship between classism and contemporary manifestations of capitalism.

Capitalism is an economic system based on private ownership of the means of production (agriculture, industry, and technology) in which owners' profit derives from the labor of people who receive fixed wages (rather than a share of profits). Economic growth is driven by competition in the marketplace (thought of as a "free market") in which fairness is assumed to emerge from market forces in the absence of regulation (e.g. by government or unions). In the current capitalist system, there is significant interference in the "free" functioning of markets, primarily by corporate interests that lobby for advantageous laws. Despite government regulations in some countries providing protections like workplace safety and fair banking practices, a capitalist economic system by its nature creates and reproduces class inequality because of the disparity of wealth accumulation between owners and workers. The differences among countries in what, if any, protections are in place provides further opportunities for inequality and exploitation. *Racialized capitalism* is a way of expressing the complete entanglement of capitalism and racism (Kelley, 2017). The Historical Legacies section that follows offers many examples of how our current capitalist system developed hand in hand with racism and remains fundamentally racist.

Conflation of Capitalism With Democracy

One challenge to understanding classism is the conflation of our US *democratic political system*, which assumes political equality (one person, one vote), with the US *capitalist economic system*, which assumes equality of economic opportunity. The democratic myth that every child can grow up to be president has been conflated with the capitalist myth that every child can become rich through hard work and talent.

Democracy is a political system characterized by individual rights and responsibilities and, in the case of the US, a representative (versus direct) system of governance. The conflation of capitalism with democracy has often served as a tool for those with political and economic power to discredit poor and working people's movements (including organized labor and the civil rights movement, among others). When workers organize to protest economic inequities, they have sometimes argued that some version of socialist economic system would be fairer because shared ownership of production would lead to people benefiting more equally from economic growth. People opposed to such a system of distribution have attacked socialism as if it were a political system opposed to democracy, rather than an economic system parallel to capitalism. This confusion of political with economic systems has stifled thoughtful and serious consideration of alternative economic policies and structures in the US.

Additionally, the capitalist assumption that markets are fair supports the psychological investment many people living in the US have in the American Dream—the idea that everyone can achieve prosperity, homeownership, and other markers of a middle-class life if they work hard enough. These assumptions make it difficult to challenge the problems of advanced capitalism, such as continuing racial stratification and the extraordinary influence of large multinational corporations on US democratic institutions.[2]

Wealth and Income

Wealth and *income* are two closely related forms of economic capital that partly define class location. *Wealth* consists of what one owns (money, stocks, real estate) minus what one owes (credit card or school debt, home mortgages). Wealth confers class privilege—advantages and resources available to people with higher wealth that are simply inaccessible to people with less or no wealth. Whereas *wealth* expresses the amount and type of assets one owns, *income* refers to the periodic inflow of resources, whether from investments, salary, hourly wages, government benefits, or any other source. The type or source of income is relevant, as well as the overall amount. For example, families with inherited wealth often have significant income from long-term investments that do not require their ongoing labor to maintain, at a scale that is not possible for those who rely on salary or wages—even those whose salary or wages are very high. The privilege accorded to individuals who have steady high income without needing to work (even if they choose to do so) differs qualitatively and quantitatively from the privilege connected to a high income from working.

The kinds of wealth and income available to families varies across racial lines, and this difference is crucial for explaining the ongoing racial wealth gap in the US. Explicit racism in government policies prevented Black, Indigenous, and other People of Color families from accumulating wealth in the same ways afforded to whites, and these disparities continue to be handed down across generations. For example, local, state, and federal housing policies known as redlining prevented many non-white families from purchasing homes. In the US, wealth is most commonly accumulated through home ownership, and this mandated segregation has perpetuated decades of stagnant inequality.

Class Culture

Class culture describes the norms, values, and ways of life shared by people with a similar class position. Class cultures develop in response to economic realities as well as other dimensions of experience and can be thought of as those aspects of culture that help people survive, thrive, and make sense of their roles in the economic system, whether or not people are consciously aware of that relationship (Shlasko & Kramer, 2011; Williams, 2012).

Class culture is not shaped only by membership in a general class category but also by a more specific location defined by context and other social identities (Matos, 2011; Yosso,

1996). For example, Lamont's (2000) research documents differences in culture among white factory workers, Black factory workers, and white managers. Lamont found that some cultural markers varied across class more than race (i.e. white and Black workers shared a value or norm that differed from that of white managers), and others varied across both class and race (i.e. all three groups were different from each other). Likewise, one could expect to find very different class cultures among new tech industry millionaires than among families with multi-generational wealth.

Even as class culture is intersectional, some aspects of class culture are fairly consistent within class categories even across other differences. Cultural patterns that seem to be strongly correlated with class include parenting beliefs and practices, norms around conflict and politeness, beliefs about morality and values, and linguistic patterns including abstract vs. concrete language and direct vs. indirect communication (Jensen, 2012; Lamont, 2000; Lareau, 2011; Leondar-Wright, 2014; Streib, 2013), all of which intersect with and are inflected by racial and ethnic cultural patterns.

Class culture categories are not binary, however, even though they are often described as pairs of opposites. A study of class cultures in activist groups recognizes at least four class culture categories that people fall into based on their class experiences growing up and current class location: lifelong-working-class, lifelong-professional-range, upwardly mobile, and voluntarily downwardly mobile (Leondar-Wright, 2014). This way of categorizing class cultures recognizes the unique position of class straddlers, including individuals who grew up poor or working class and are the first generation in their family to move into the professional middle class, as well as members who grew up with class privilege and have chosen a lower-income trajectory (Leondar-Wright, 2014). Defining members by either their class of origin or their current class situation would give an incomplete picture. Understanding the unique cultural patterns that emerge with different class trajectories can help groups to collaborate effectively across class culture differences.

Like other kinds of cultures, the patterns of thought and behavior learned from one's class culture often remain unconscious. Because class cultures are rarely talked about, people often fail to notice their own patterns of class culture or ascribe them to another aspect of their identity. Someone who does not "identify with" a class category, or who identifies generically as "middle class" without thinking much about what that means, may nevertheless be steeped in the internalized norms of a working-class or professional middle-class culture that affects how they think, talk, act, and relate to other people and the world.

Class Status

Class *status* conveys the degree of prestige attributed to one's position (Leondar-Wright & Yeskel, 2007), or to a particular cultural marker, by people and institutions with power. Internalizing classism can lead disadvantaged people to buy into the status hierarchy and accept the dominant perspective on who or what is "highly regarded" and who or what may be looked down on or ignored, even at their own expense.

Cultural markers associated with wealth tend to have higher status than others. For example, standard English pronunciation and English spoken with a European accent have higher status than rural regional accents, non-European immigrant accents, and African American English. However, the alignment between wealth and status is not perfect. Professors, clergy, and some artists are examples of occupational groups with relatively high status but, in many cases, relatively low income and wealth. Unexpected alignment between wealth and status also occurs when someone gains or loses wealth. A family that lost some or all of their inherited assets can sometimes retain the culture and status associated with their former wealth. Conversely, someone who grew up working class and recently acquired wealth may continue to think and act from the norms of a working-class culture and may not be highly regarded by other wealthy people.

Cultural Capital and Social Capital

Cultural capital and social capital help explain the relationship among culture, status, and material resources. *Cultural capital* (Bourdieu, 1986) (i.e. knowledge, language, style, way of life, and self-presentation) acts as a personal marker of class and influences economic opportunity as well as quality of life (Lareau & Calarco, 2012; Swartz, 1997).

Class culture becomes *cultural capital*, allowing access to material advantages. For example, students at elite private colleges whose class culture matches the dominant or normalized culture of the institution are likely to "fit in" and benefit from the range of campus resources, while students whose class cultures do not align with the dominant culture of the institution face barriers to accessing such resources (Hopkins, 2014).

Some theorists use *cultural capital* to refer specifically to a person's facility with the cultural markers of the more privileged classes, but in our view, *all* class cultures have their own forms of cultural capital, though these are valued and ranked differently by the broader society. Similarly Tara Yosso, discussing Latinx[3] communities in the US, uses "cultural wealth" to emphasize how the many forms of capital that circulate in these communities—including aspirational capital, familial capital, linguistic capital, resistant capital, and navigational capital—are not *only* valuable in relation to the dominant society but are valued within the specific, marginalized communities that create them (Yosso, 2005). For example, familiarity with the norms of interaction in a working-class community may help a person navigate that social environment successfully and lead to work opportunities, access to aid from the community, and so on. Different groups' cultural capital is not equivalent or interchangeable. In particular, attempting to leverage cultural capital from a lower-status class culture in a context characterized by a higher-status class culture is unlikely to be successful. Further, the cultural capital of high-status groups provides access to material resources on a much larger scale than does that of lower-status groups.

Whereas *cultural capital* refers to "*what* one knows about," *social capital* refers to "*who* one knows"—that is, the social networks one is part of and to which one has ready access. Like cultural capital, *social capital* is sometimes used to describe connections to elite social networks that help people gain access to private schooling, professional advancement, and other forms of class advantage (Allan, Ozga, & Smith, 2009; Mohr & DiMaggio, 1995).

However, all communities' social networks can translate into material benefits, albeit at different scales. Working-class social networks can provide access to referrals for jobs, hand-me-downs from neighbors, and other forms of material aid shared within a class group. Being in close touch with one's family and extended family can be a form of social capital in itself, insofar as it provides access to direct and indirect material support that people with small families, or who are estranged from their families (for example, because of homophobia or transphobia), cannot access. Although social capital can be quantified in terms of *how many* people are in one's network, it is often more useful to consider *who* is in one's network and how that network functions to provide access to resources in a particular context.

Cultural capital and social capital help explain how class differences are reproduced and passed along from one generation to the next (Bourdieu, 1984; Mohr & DiMaggio, 1995). Those with higher wealth and status are likely to have the social connections and cultural capital that assure continued access to material resources, enabling them to replenish or grow their wealth, maintain their status, and pass on all forms of capital to their children (Kozol, 2012; Lareau, 1987, 2011). Their cultural and social capital also provides access to decision makers at organizational and political levels (and opportunities to become a deci-sion maker), allowing them to influence policy to their own advantage. Some individuals with significant class privilege choose to use it for the common good rather than for their own advantage, yet the fact that it is a choice is in itself a privilege.

The cumulative advantages and disadvantages afforded by these class indicators—income, wealth, class culture, status, cultural capital, and social capital—largely deter-mine the degree to which individuals and communities can leverage economic and political power, which may be used to maintain the status quo or create change.

MYTH OF MERITOCRACY

One challenge to understanding classism in the US is the pervasive belief in *meritocracy*—that hard work and talent will always be rewarded by upward economic and social mobil-ity (McNamee & Miller, 2004; Taussig, 2021). This logic assumes poor peoples' status is due to lack of hard work or lack of intelligence, in effect blaming the victim. Meritocratic ideology encourages US citizens, especially the middle or upper class, to believe that they and their children will have equal economic opportunities and that each generation will advance further than their parents.

Among many lower-income communities, it is more common to acknowledge that eco-nomic opportunities are persistently limited by a number of self-perpetuating cycles of race- and/or class-based disadvantage. Since the 2008 recession, the US belief in *meritoc-racy* has been seriously undermined by the failure of the middle class to bounce back to its relative prosperity, despite great gains by the wealthy (Boushey, 2014).

A social justice analysis of class and classism reverses the tendency to blame the victims. Instead, our approach recognizes the underlying forces of global racialized capitalism, cis-normativity, heteronormativity and sexism, ageism and adultism, ableism, and religious oppression that create vast inequalities in wealth, income, and life chances (Collins & Yeskel, 2005; Hacker & Pierson, 2010).

HISTORICAL LEGACIES OF US CLASS AND CLASSISM

The historical legacies of US class and classism offer a stark contrast to the narrative of "the American Dream." The American Dream paints a picture of equal opportunity, meritoc-racy, upward mobility, and national prosperity enjoyed by all Americans, including immi-grants. But the historical record reveals harsher realities. The history that follows covers several broad themes, in roughly chronological order. Many of the themes return later under the Current Manifestations section.

★ RACE/CLASS DISTINCTIONS IN THE COLONIES AND EARLY US[4]

US founding documents articulated egalitarian ideals as part of a rhetorical strategy to legitimize our independence from England. However, the revolution mainly benefitted an emerging US aristocracy, who were well placed to benefit from the spoils of colonization and slavery. Race determined who was allowed to own land and whose land was up for grabs, who was allowed to sell their labor and who could be made to work for free, and who could "own" other people's bodies and labor and who was defined as property. Colo-nial governments stole land from Indigenous people and gave it as land grants to already-wealthy white settlers, who then used their wealth to invest in land, trade, agriculture, industry, or finance. Most white settlers were not wealthy; in fact, many were indentured servants. Those who benefited most from colonial expansion, the slavery economy, and other colonial and early federal policies were those relatively few white settlers who already possessed significant wealth and status before they arrived from Europe (Holton, 2021). The race/class categories in the colonies and early republic included:

- A wealthy white elite who could consolidate local and federal political power for economic benefit;
- A laboring class of mostly white indentured servants and tenant farmers, who owned nothing and had little individual power;
- Unpaid, enslaved Africans whose labor was fundamental to the colonial economy;
- Indigenous people whose land was confiscated and sold to white settlers and whose forced isolation on reservations with few natural resources prevented Indigenous communities from benefiting from the developing economy and often from meeting their basic needs.

Then as now, economic elites used political power to shift government policy in their favor, allowing them to accumulate even more wealth and power at the expense of non-wealthy taxpayers. The political corruption evident in the symbiotic relationships between government and business led historians to conclude that "in industry after industry— . . . businessmen building empires, choking out competition, maintaining high prices, keeping wages low, using government subsidies . . . were the first beneficiaries of the 'welfare state'" (Zinn, 2015, p. 257; see also pp. 253–295). *Welfare state* is a term often used to criticize government spending meant to support poor people's health and well-being, yet history shows that government "handouts" have more often benefited those who need them least.

THE RACIALIZATION OF A TWO-TIER LABORING CLASS

The system of slave labor was enforced through a legal system that segregated Blacks from whites and hindered them from forming common cause, effectively materializing the concept of race in order to prevent mass organizing of poor people across race. "Race laws" outlawed intermarriage and Black literacy and punished collaboration between white and Black workers. Blacks, whether enslaved or free, ranked socially and economically below "free" white men regardless of their skill or capacity. For white men, their presumed racial superiority obscured the realities of their economic exploitation.

Race distinctions *were* class distinctions that officially restricted the ability of Black and Indigenous people to thrive economically. This economic racism was also racialized classism that continued as immigrants of color (including Sikhs, Chinese, and Japanese, and Mexicans after the Treaty of Guadalupe Hidalgo) were shunted into menial labor—for men, farms, factories, mines, and railroads, and for women, domestic work (Steinberg, 1989; Takaki, 1993; Zinn, 2015). Factory and mine owners fueled interracial conflict and discouraged union organizing by exploiting Blacks and Asians as strikebreakers at lower wages than whites.

This racialized class divide played out in late 19th-century US imperialism in the plantations of Hawaii, Standard Oil's control of the global export market, United Fruit's control of the Cuban sugar industry, and the annexation of Puerto Rico and the Philippines (Zinn, 2015). Puerto Rican, Filipino, and South American immigrants soon joined the lower tier of the US racialized labor force.

In sum, the wealth of the US owning class originated in the proceeds of racism: the forced labor system of slavery, the government redistribution of Indigenous land to wealthy investors, and the transatlantic slave trade. A racially tiered labor market created and exacerbated racial tensions among the poor, hindering effective coalitions across race and allowing owners to exploit workers of all races.

As a result of this history, class position remains highly correlated with race. The legacy of this racialized class system continues in a job market that disproportionately keeps Black, Latinx, Indigenous, and immigrant workers stuck in low-paid labor and service roles. Black, Latinx, and Indigenous people are two to three times as likely as whites to have income below the poverty line (Semega, Kollar, Shrider, & Creamer, 2020). Asian Americans have a similar poverty rate to white people overall, but within the category of Asian American, there are large disparities across different ethnic and national identities.

IMMIGRATION

Immigration has been central to the economic and class system in the US. The first immigrants were white, mainly Protestant landowners, financed by European investors, as well as farmers, craftspeople, and indentured workers. They settled the colonies by displacing and killing Indigenous peoples and taking their lands, forming the basis for a landed elite. A second wave of involuntary migration from the mid-17th through early 19th centuries brought millions of African people kidnapped as part of the transatlantic slave trade. They became a racially marked workforce to maintain an agricultural export economy that enriched the white landed elite.

A third wave of immigrants during the mid-19th through early 20th centuries came from diverse racial, ethnic, linguistic, class, and religious backgrounds. The Irish fled famine caused by British colonial policy in the 1840s. Mexicans were absorbed into the southwestern and western US territories through the Treaty of Guadalupe Hidalgo. Millions of southern and eastern Europeans fled poverty, war, and persecution, as did Arabs and Asians from Syria, Lebanon, India, China, and Japan. By 1920, 36 million Americans, more than a third of the population, were immigrants and their children, the majority from southern and eastern Europe with smaller numbers from China, Japan, and India (Daniels, 2002). The European immigrants of this third wave became an ethnically marked working class whose poverty and desperation made them vulnerable to wage exploitation and to being pitted against Black and Mexican workers as well as Asian and Arab immigrant workers (Steinberg, 1989; Takaki, 1993; Zinn, 2015).

Economic competition was racialized, usually to the advantage of white ethnics who got priority and (slightly) higher wages and sometimes to the temporary advantage of Chinese or Black workers who were employed as strikebreakers. White immigrants constituted the "upper" tier of the racialized two-tier working class at the bottom of the overall economic ladder (Brodkin [Sacks], 1998; Guglielmo & Salerno, 2003; Ignatiev, 1995; Roediger, 1991). In subsequent generations, upward mobility was possible for the Irish, Italian, Jewish, and other white ethnic workers that was not available to Blacks, Latinx, Indigenous people, and some Asians and Arabs. The process by which white ethnics moved from the upper rung of the working class into "middle class" status, while most workers of color remained working class, is part of the historical legacy of entangled racism and classism (Foner, 1998; Roediger, 1991).

In the early 1920s, Congress prioritized immigrants from northern and western Europe, restricted immigration from southern Europe, and almost entirely halted immigration from Asia. After 1965, the law changed to prioritize family ties and professional skills rather than particular nationalities, and the number and diversity of immigrants increased drastically. Some were people who had class privilege in their countries of origin and were allowed to immigrate because their technical skills were needed in emerging industries. Others came as students and were able to stay by parlaying their education into skilled jobs. Many others were poor and working-class people who came to join family members who were already here, and some were refugees from wars in Southeast Asia, Central America, Africa, and eastern Europe.

Today, the specter of "illegal" immigration continues a pattern of blaming social ills on the most recent wave of newcomers. Government leaders debate "immigration reform" while blaming immigrants for everything from the decline of manufacturing jobs, to the financial stresses on underfunded public school systems, to drugs and gang violence—all systemic problems traceable to government policies and global financial trends far beyond the reach of poor immigrants. Undocumented immigrants work undesirable jobs in vital industries, without many of the legal protections afforded to citizens and legal residents. They pay taxes but cannot benefit from many of the programs those taxes fund. Politicians debate their status, but they are unable to vote or be represented in government. We might say that undocumented immigrants—many but not all of them from Latin America—have become their own particular tier of the racially tiered working class.

LABOR ORGANIZING AND THE EMERGING WHITE MIDDLE CLASS

Labor movements in the 19th and 20th centuries were the main force that transformed underpaid and exploitative jobs in mining and manufacturing into stable jobs with benefits that could support a middle-class lifestyle. Without unions, many industries were characterized by long hours, dangerous conditions resulting in injuries and deaths, wage theft, and wage cuts during periods of economic downturn. Through organizing, workers sought to leverage collective power to negotiate for fairer wages and working conditions.

Labor unrest accelerated during periods of financial crisis that led to economic depression, high unemployment, and low wages (more than six times between 1837 and 1929), and unions organized to negotiate fairer ways of handling economic downturns. In many cases, unionized workers were met with police and military brutality and private mercenary forces (Zinn, 2015). Examples include the Great Railroad Strike of 1877, the Homestead Strike of 1892, and the Battle of Blair Mountain in 1921 (Zinn, 2015). Companies justified violence against union campaigns by blaming workers, especially immigrant workers, and "foreign influences."

Union organizing was partly inspired by socialist movements in Europe but also by strong US traditions of rebellion against unfair tax and labor practices. Owners leveraged racist, ethnocentric, and antisemitic rhetoric to paint labor organizing as "un-American" and a threat to democracy when it actually threatened owners' financial interests in maintaining unregulated conditions of labor. The ethnocentric and antisemitic legacy of early 19th-century anti-socialism resurfaced during the anti-communist witch hunts of the 1950s and can be seen today in far-right conspiracy theories blaming Jews for the 2008 financial crash and the resurgence of neo-Nazi ideologies masquerading as white populism.

Despite formidable political, corporate, media, and military forces assembled against them, a comparably moderate nationwide federation of labor unions—the American Federation of Labor (AFL)—emerged in 1886. Initially organized as an umbrella organization for craft unions (Nicholson, 2004), it was composed mainly of skilled white ethnic workers. Its success was based in part on its opposition to more radical labor unions and on its exclusion of Black workers. Many Black workers formed their own labor unions, as did Chinese, Japanese, and Mexican workers (Nicholson, 2004; Takaki, 1993; Zinn, 2015).[5]

The unions enabled European immigrants to find employment with stable wages and benefits so that within two generations, their children and grandchildren had become assimilated as "white" middle-class Americans (Brodkin [Sacks], 1998; Guglielmo, 2003; Ignatiev, 1995). Although economic mobility was not universal for white ethnics, enough gained middle-class status to "create a middle-class cushion for class conflict" that obscured vast disparities in wealth and power and created further barriers to class-based organizing (Zinn, 2015, p. 349). As the moderate AFL/CIO membership became more upwardly mobile, they abandoned any egalitarianism of earlier labor unions and took the view that "workers must frankly accept their status as wage earners and seek higher wages" based on "the rigid segmentation of the job market along racial and ethnic lines" (Foner, 1998, p. 135). Thus, the US economy became "more thoroughly racialized at the dawn of the twentieth century than at any other point in American history" (Foner, 1998, p. 135).

★ THE NEW DEAL[6]

After the stock market crash of 1929 brought in the Great Depression, the election of Franklin Delano Roosevelt was taken as a mandate for change and inaugurated regulatory experimentation and job programs such as the National Recovery Act (NRA), Agricultural Adjustment Administration (AAA), and Tennessee Valley Authority (TVA). The National Labor Relations Act of 1935 gave unions legal status, created channels to address some grievances, and channeled union energy into meetings and contract negotiations rather than direct tactics like strikes (Zinn, 2015). However, this law specifically excluded domestic and agricultural workers, who were disproportionately Black and Latinx, an omission that continues to impact workers in these sectors today.

Although the New Deal provided benefits to poor and working-class people, it did not change structural inequalities of wealth and poverty, and it did not address the racialized distribution of wealth. African Americans were initially excluded from most New Deal programs, and, following World War II, Black, Latinx, and Asian veterans did not benefit from the GI Bill that enabled white veterans to attend college, receive affordable home mortgages, and move into the rapidly growing (and racially segregated) middle-class suburban developments (Brodkin [Sacks], 1998; Lipsitz, 1998). White families accumulated wealth through home ownership and gained status and higher earning potential through education. The structural privileges built into the New Deal programs and the GI Bill thus laid the foundation for the racial wealth gap that has persisted to this day (Rothstein, 2017).

In the three decades between the entry of the US into World War I (1917) and the end of World War II (1945), the US emerged as a global power with a form of capitalism that was regulated by banking and workplace protections put in place following the 1929 Depression. Wartime industrialization ended the depression and created an economic "boom" while underwriting post-war global supremacy and a thriving middle class for several decades to come.

THE FREE MARKET AND DEREGULATION

The post-war economic factors that had facilitated middle-class prosperity were undermined by changes in federal policy in the closing decades of the 20th century. These included changes in the tax code to benefit corporate interests, opportunities for corporations to go offshore and avoid US taxes, the movement of factories and jobs to countries with lower pay scales and fewer protections for workers (supported by treaties such as NAFTA), the weakening of regulatory structures of banks and finances, and legal changes making it more difficult for unions to organize and negotiate on behalf of workers (Bartlett & Steele, 1994; Domhoff, 1983; Phillips, 1990). By and large, many of the union jobs whose pay-checks, benefits, and pensions had supported a middle-class lifestyle disappeared, and with them the stability and prosperity of working families who depended on those jobs and networks (Henwood, 2003; Piketty, 2014; Reich, 2007).

Voters were encouraged to trust in "trickle down" economics by which the accumulation of wealth by those already wealthy would somehow benefit everyone else. Political elections and longevity in public office came to depend increasingly on the deep pockets of corporate interests. Intricate tax codes provided loopholes for complex financial arrangements and stock options; unregulated financial interests found ways to garner enormous profits; and companies "too big to fail" were granted federal support not available to individuals.

As industrial jobs became less secure and middle-class income levels decreased, the middle-class lifestyle required the support of two or three jobs per family, supplemented by increased reliance on debt (in the forms of mortgages, car loans, and credit cards). At the same time, changes to welfare policy (such as welfare-to-work programs) and the high cost of healthcare meant that the poorest Americans were less and less able to meet basic needs for food and shelter (Mishel, Bernstein, & Allegretto, 2007).

GROWING GAP BETWEEN RICH AND POOR

The uneven distribution of income and wealth has grown at an ever-increasing pace since the early 1980s. In the 1980s and 1990s, three of the major forces that added to growing income inequality were mass incarceration (largely driven by the "war on drugs"), welfare reform, and consumer debt. The Anti-Drug Abuse Act of 1986 drastically increased the number of drug crimes with mandatory minimum sentences. A 1994 crime bill further created incentives for states to increase both arrests and penalties. These and other "tough on crime" efforts led to an increase in the number of people imprisoned in the US from around 300,000 in 1980 to over 1.6 million at its peak in 2008 (after which it declined slightly)— an increase of over 400% (The Sentencing Project, 2021).[7] Incarceration disproportionately affects communities that are poor, Black, and brown. When people are incarcerated, they're not earning income or supporting their families as they could if they were free. This loss of both financial and human resources drives communities into deeper poverty.

In 1996, Congress passed a sweeping welfare reform law that gave states more latitude to determine how to distribute federally funded aid to the poorest families and established strict limits on how long a family could receive aid. Like earlier generations of the US welfare system, the new way of "helping" the poor aimed as much at controlling their behavior as at alleviating suffering (Roberts, 1999). In particular, many policies took aim at reproductive freedom, tried to deter welfare recipients from becoming pregnant, and changed how financial need was calculated so that children born to a mother already on welfare didn't count (Roberts, 1999). Black women were especially vilified by politicians and the press as "welfare queens," making it all too clear that lawmakers' anxiety about the number of children born to impoverished families was as much a racist anxiety as a classist one.

The welfare system dovetailed with the criminal punishment system in these efforts. Poor mothers charged with minor drug offenses were often offered a "choice" between lengthy prison sentences and parole, with parole available only if they consented to a long-acting contraceptive (Roberts, 1999). While some of the 1990s reforms effectively reduced the number of families receiving welfare, they did not, on average, raise people out of poverty but rather increased the number of families in deep poverty and created new hurdles and hardships (Sherman, 2016; Vallas & Slevin, 2016).

Accelerating class inequities were not necessarily obvious to white, middle-class people during the 1980s and 1990s, even though they also were affected negatively. The reentrance of middle-class women into the workforce and easy access to credit disguised the fall in real value of wages. Some families could maintain a middle-class standard of living but had to rely on two incomes where they used to only need one. Decades of weak and stagnant wage growth made it less feasible for many families to maintain a middle-class lifestyle (Emelech, 2008; Mishel, Bernstein, & Allegretto, 2007; Shierholz & Mishel, 2013). Families borrowed money through second mortgages and accrued increasing credit card debt to send their children to college and pay for day-to-day necessities (Wolff, 2009). The destruction of consumer protection laws allowed banks to prey on consumers by setting high, uncapped credit card interest rates, fees, and penalties (Garcia, Lardner, & Zeldin, 2008), and lower-income workers were vulnerable to exploitative lending by paycheck cashing and loan outlets charging 20%–35% interest (Williams, 2001). In 2010 the Dodd-Frank Wall Street Reform and Consumer Protection Act attempted to address some of the worst abuses but faced many legal challenges (Rappeport & Flitter, 2018). The Economic Growth, Regulatory Relief, and Consumer Protection Act passed in spring of 2018 exempted dozens of US banks from the regulations, and President Trump signed this partial repeal into law.

With the collapse of global financial markets in 2008, the median net worth of US families dropped by 39.4% from pre-recession levels, with Black and Latinx communities hit disproportionately hard (Fry & Kochhar, 2014). The 2011 Census Bureau reported 46.2 million Americans were below the poverty line (including 16.4 million children), and poor Americans became even poorer. Deep poverty rose 44.3%, the highest level in 36 years, with about one in eight Americans and one in four children dependent on government aid (Bishaw, 2013; Tanzi & Saraiva, 2021). While many relatively wealthy people lost large sums of money in the 2008 crash when investments lost value, they bounced back within a few years, while non-wealthy people continued to struggle for financial stability. In only three years (2009–2012), the average growth in family income across all income categories was 6%, but the top 1% saw income growth of 31.4%, compared to only 0.4% for the remaining 99% (Piketty & Saez, 2003, with 2018 updates).[8]

A global movement, largely led by youth and young adults, manifested in protests that literally occupied public spaces in major cities around the world for months—in continuation of the US tradition of class-based activism (Leondar-Wright, 2014). Occupy Wall Street popularized the language of "the 1%" and sought to unify non-wealthy people with the slogan "We are the 99%." By the time the most visible actions dwindled, the Occupy movement had succeeded in shifting public discourse about class, making room for frank discussions of economic inequality in contexts where such discussions had previously been unthinkable. Many groups that began organizing around the Occupy encampments have continued their work around economic inequality in less visible ways (Collins, 2012, 2014; van Gelder, 2011; Korten, 2010).

CURRENT MANIFESTATIONS OF US CLASS AND CLASSISM

The aforementioned historical legacies continue into the present time in the maintenance of an inequitable class structure, in the many manifestations of classism, and in organized movements of resistance. To illustrate the variety and ubiquity of contemporary manifestations of classism, we have organized this section around Iris Marion Young's (1990) Five Faces of Oppression (see Chapter 4: Core Concepts): exploitation, cultural imperialism, violence, powerlessness, and marginalization. According to Young, every system of oppression plays out through some combination of these five categories, and the model can be used to describe how isms play out in similar and different ways (Young, 1990). Within each of the five faces, classism occurs in intersection with other systems of oppression at individual, institutional, and cultural/societal levels (see Chapter 3: Design and Facilitation and Chapter 4: Core Concepts), adding up to a complex and self-reinforcing tangle of oppression.

EXPLOITATION

Exploitation is a form of oppression in which institutional structures, interpersonal behaviors, and social norms collude to transfer the outcomes of the labor of a particular social group to benefit another group (Young, 1990). Exploitation is inherent to capitalism, which systematically transfers the value produced by workers to those few who own the means of production, resulting in ever-increasing concentration of power in the owning class (Young, 1990). Three specific examples we focus on here are domestic labor, farm labor, and globalization of capital and labor.

Paid and Unpaid Domestic Labor

Young (1990) describes unpaid domestic labor as one aspect of gender exploitation, in which women contribute (on average) more than their share of emotional and practical household labor, benefitting the men in their households.[9] In 2020–2021, when many schools closed in an effort to slow the spread of COVID-19, this inequity of gendered household labor was highlighted and exacerbated. Many households with young children had to make a choice about which parent would stay home, and disproportionately women took a break from paid work for the unpaid labor of homeschooling or supervising remote schooling (Ranji, Frederiksen, Salganicoff, & Long, 2021). Upper-class and middle-class women are often able to outsource some emotional labor and housekeeping responsibilities to working-class and poor women who work as housekeepers and childcare providers. Many domestic workers are immigrant women who made the difficult choice of leaving their home countries to financially support their families. For those who are undocumented, their immigration status puts them at risk of even greater exploitation in the form of wage theft and other workplace abuses (Burnham & Theodore, 2012).

The pattern of poor and working-class women fulfilling emotional labor and housekeeping responsibilities for upper-class and middle-class women is part of US history and not solely the result of middle-class women entering the workforce. Historically this work was mainly carried out by Black women, and women of color remain at the front line of the domestic labor industry (Byrd, 2009). There are more than two million domestic workers in the US who work in other people's homes as housekeepers, childcare providers, and health aides (Hilgers, 2019).

As noted prior in the Historical Legacies section, domestic labor is outside many government regulations. Domestic laborers often lack formal labor contracts, health insurance, paid time off, guaranteed breaks, and other standard employment practices (Kaufka, 2003). The lack of regulation of domestic labor at an institutional level, in addition to the fact that it is not valued at a cultural/societal level, creates both financial and emotional incentives for households that can afford it to hire domestic workers, resulting in the increasing commodification of domestic services in the U.S (Kaufka, 2003).

In Young's (1990) definition, domestic labor is always exploitative because it brings more value to the employer than the worker is compensated for. The lack of regulation in the industry creates opportunities for even greater exploitation on top of that, including stolen wages, sexual assault, and human trafficking (Hilgers, 2019; National Domestic Workers Alliance, 2021a).[10] Live-in domestic workers are especially likely to experience abuse and exploitation (Byrd, 2009; Hilgers, 2019). For live-in domestic workers, there are no clear lines between professional and personal life, so it is difficult to find time away from work responsibilities. Many times employers schedule responsibilities in a way that makes it difficult for domestic workers to clock out, and they often end up working beyond their agreed-upon duties. Additionally, employers of live-in domestic workers often provide them with poor living conditions. Many domestic workers are expected to sleep in utility closets, basements, or other inappropriate locations within a home (Byrd, 2009). The majority of domestic workers are paid less than $13 an hour (Hilgers, 2019).

The earnings of domestic workers support many families and are an important part of the American economy, but the significance of the industry goes beyond that. Many domestic workers who are immigrants—almost all of them women—send a portion of their earnings back home to their families overseas as remittances. Thus the US domestic labor industry is an important part of other countries' economies as well, many of them poor developing nations, some of which end up relying on the exportation of women as a labor force and the remittances they send home (Kaufka, 2003). The commodification of domestic workers extends to a global economic level.

Farm Labor

Agriculture is another sector of the workforce in which classism, racism, and immigration are deeply entangled and lead to rampant exploitation. The Fair Labor Standards Act (1938) established basic employment protections including a federal minimum wage and overtime system that, like other employment legislation, did not apply to farmworkers. The law was amended in 1966 to apply some provisions to farmworkers, including the minimum wage but not overtime pay. There are about one million farmworkers employed in the US at any given time (Kandel, 2008). Compared to other workers, farmworkers face challenges including very low wages, substandard housing, occupational safety hazards, and irregular work schedules—for example, being required to work 80 hours a week for several weeks and then having little or no work for several weeks after that (Kandel, 2008).

About half the farmworkers in the US are undocumented, which makes them especially vulnerable to exploitative labor practices including wage theft and overwork. Additionally, about half of farmworkers move from place to place throughout the year to work on different crops as the seasons change (Kandel, 2008). Their mobility can make it difficult to receive benefits for which they may be eligible, such as food stamps or subsidized healthcare, and keeps their children from regular schooling.

Some politicians and media outlets depict farmworkers, especially immigrants, as lazy people mooching off a generous public benefits system, despite the fact that farmworkers perform some of the most demanding labor and have less access to benefits than workers in other industries. These depictions are examples of classism and racism at the cultural/societal level. The structural elements of the agricultural industry that keep farmworkers poor, such as different labor laws than other industries and a heavy reliance on seasonal and often unauthorized workers, are examples of institutional level of classism. At an individual level, one often-unconscious manifestation is the privilege many of us have to remain ignorant of the working conditions of the many people whose labor helps to bring food to our tables.

During the COVID-19 pandemic, farmworkers were considered essential workers, meaning their labor was recognized as imperative even when many industries were temporarily shut down. Farmworkers faced worsening labor conditions when employers failed to provide adequate safety precautions to prevent infection, resulting in the endangerment of the farmworkers' lives through the rapid spread of the virus (Talamo & Hoang, 2020). Other food industry workers, including those in meat-processing plants, faced similar dangers. Farmworkers and other food industry workers engaged in labor strikes for improved conditions, such as the Yakima Valley and Primex strikes in Washington and California (Talamo & Hoang, 2020; Associated Press, 2020).

Globalization of Capital and Labor

Beyond domestic and agricultural labor, globalization in many other industries has also produced complicated networks of capital and people. If we are to understand the international scope and local consequences of global financial interdependency, we need to trace the entanglements of global capital (finance, ownership, and trade) with global resources (cheap labor and raw materials) as well as with educational systems geared to produce a tiered workforce (Apple, 2010; Collins, 2012; Piketty, 2014). The US dependency on oil markets has also affected our diplomatic policy, the outsourcing of clothing manufacture to low-wage workers in South Korea and China to maintain a price advantage within US markets, and the outsourcing of technical jobs to college-trained workers in India and Pakistan. Those who benefit most from such arrangements are the wealthy who own shares in international corporations. Those who lose out are the workers who contribute their labor, the communities where factories and call centers are sited, and consumers who pay nearly as much for a product that costs companies much less to produce.

CULTURAL IMPERIALISM

Cultural imperialism as a form of classism is seen in practices and structures that value some groups' class cultures and cultural capital over others. This hierarchy of cultural value affects access to material and social capital because accessing class-privileged networks and careers is almost always contingent on being able to act "cultured." Since class cultures overlap with racial, ethnic, and national cultures, classist cultural imperialism is often racist at the same time.

For example, the idea of "the culture of poverty" links poor or working-class culture with cognitive deficits, educational failure, and criminal behavior while glossing over the roles of racial and class oppression (Moynihan, 1965; Patterson, 2010; Payne, 1995; Wilson, 2009). The idea of a culture of poverty relies on stereotype and overgeneralization (Ng & Rury, 2006) and blames poor people for the disadvantages they experience while ignoring systemic factors like power, status, and material resources (Gorski, 2005; Gorski & Scherer, 2016; Ladson-Billings, 2017). As part of a social justice approach to classism, class culture needs to be understood within an analysis of the reproduction of power and wealth (Lavelle, 1995; Smith, 2010).

Cultural Imperialism in "Professionalism"

Cultural imperialism shows up in workplaces in the assumptions and expectations about what "everybody knows"—including academic knowledge and conventions of social interaction. Most office workplaces are governed by professional middle-class cultural norms (which are generally aligned with whiteness, Protestantism, masculinity, and hetero-normative gender relations). How people dress, greet each other, interact across levels of hierarchy and resolve disagreements, and what they talk about in the break room, are all circumscribed by what is considered appropriate within that culture. People who can look, sound, and act professional middle-class or owning-class are more likely to be hired, feel included at work, and promoted. Cultural imperialism plays out at the institutional level through workplace policies and at the interpersonal level through the judgments workers make about each other.

Cultural imperialism is also evident in the values implicit in most office workplaces. Professional middle-class cultures tend to value productivity and achievement—doing more, better, faster work and being recognized formally for it. They do not tend to value relational work such as building deep working relationships with colleagues, facilitating group cohesion, helping coworkers build their skills, or doing family labor outside the office. Indeed, such pursuits are often viewed with suspicion, as if you must not be serious about your career if you "waste" your time that way. People from poor and working-class cultures, or whose ethnic cultures are more relational, or who have been socialized as women to value relational ways of being, are less likely to be promoted into leadership and tend to remain at lower salary levels than their counterparts. This is both cultural imperialism and exploitation in that people's labor isn't adequately recognized or compensated.

Higher education has been a route by which some people gain the cultural capital needed to succeed in an office workplace. Many office jobs don't require any of the academic training provided by a liberal arts degree but do require the ability to perform professional middle-class culture. By attending colleges that also normalize professional middle-class culture, people from other class/cultural backgrounds can gain some facility in navigating such environments. Yet this opportunity is not equally useful to all who attend college. Similarly to office workplaces, students who are not already enculturated into these norms are less likely to be admitted, to find a sense of belonging and mentors and champions among the faculty, and to graduate (Jack, 2019).

Fetishization of Poor and Working-Class Cultures

Sometimes privileged groups do seem to value poor or working-class culture. Fashion, music, and art forms created among non-wealthy (and often Black) groups come into style with more class-privileged people. Suburban, professional middle-class kids gravitate to styles of hip hop that glorify a particular image of poor, inner city life. Wealthy college students express radical politics by dressing down in heavy-duty work pants, beat-up boots, and messy-on-purpose hair styles. Although such adoptions of cultural productions across class seem like (and may be) a compliment, they are also often appropriative. Rather than appreciating and honoring an art form in its own context, privileged groups pluck it out of context and create a cleaned-up, depoliticized version of it, sometimes even selling these versions back to the people whose culture inspired it in the first place.

One vivid example can be seen with the hipster aesthetic. Hipsterism is primarily associated with upper-middle-class young gentrifiers, who evade accountability for their actual economic role as gentrifiers because they look and act like "regular folks." They reject the styling of privileged class groups but do not disinvest from the material benefits. In the hipster aesthetic, shopping at thrift stores is a signal of (ironically) up-to-date fashion sense and even virtue. In one sense, the hipster thrifting fad honors the poor and working-class realities of thrifting as a vital tool for physical and spiritual survival, a "queer economy" of pleasure for people who are structurally excluded from mainstream pleasures (Heiliger, 2015). At the same time, it is both cultural imperialism and exploitation in that people gain status by emulating cultures not their own, receiving privilege from a faux-poor presentation that actual poor people do not receive. In earlier generations, commodification of grunge and punk aesthetics followed a similar trajectory. Some hipster trends also use classism as an excuse for casual racism and sexism. Mimicking what they see as authentic working-class bigotry, they simultaneously repeat racist and classist tropes and reinforce classist depictions of poor and working-class white people as prejudiced and unenlightened (Swift, 2014).

Another example comes from observations of activist class cultures. In activist spaces, we often meet people who grew up with class privilege and have chosen to live a less elite lifestyle because they disagree with the economic and perhaps cultural values of the class they grew up in (Leondar-Wright, 2014). Some may genuinely "give up" their class privilege to some extent by giving away inherited wealth. Others give up the appearance but not the realities of privilege. They may go to great lengths to hide their class background, even changing the way they speak or eat so that no one might guess at first that they haven't always occupied the class position they now appear to be in. Such dishonesty can undermine trust and coalition building, especially in cases where a person is still benefiting from material privileges of their class background—for example, if they're able to sustain themselves on a very low income because of inherited wealth they never talk about.

VIOLENCE

As a face of classism, violence includes not only interpersonal violence but also violence enacted by institutions, including education, government, and healthcare. Three examples we highlight here are police violence to suppress political dissent, environmental classism, and the psychological violence inherent in the myth of meritocracy and other cultural/societal manifestations of classism.

Police Violence to Suppress Political Dissent

When people organize to challenge economic inequality and classism, almost always in relation to their intersections with racism, sexism, and other systems of oppression, police violence often follows. In the 2011 Occupy movement, the 2018 strikes in Spain (UNI Global Union, 2018), Chile's 2020 protests challenging the nation's economic inequality, Colombia's 2021 demonstrations against the rising cost of basic necessities (Gonzalez, 2021), and the ongoing demonstrations across the US against racist police violence (which is also often classist and ableist), police attacked protesters with batons, bullets, and chemical weapons (tear gas, pepper spray). As with the periodic waves of protest throughout the 19th and 20th centuries, police tend to protect the property of the wealthy above the lives of the poor (Mitrani, 2015).

Environmental Classism

Another example of violence is environmental classism, which overlaps with environmental racism. Environmental racism/classism refers to the pattern in which poor, Black, and brown communities bear the brunt of environmental degradation created by industries that primarily benefit the rich. For example, most landfills and factories are located in areas populated by poor and working-class people, and industries like hog farming, coal mining, and fracking are concentrated in rural poor communities. Company owners and investors who profit from such operations live far from their dirty realities, while industrial pollution creates health risks in communities with already-inadequate healthcare resources, contributing to cycles of illness, disability, and poverty. On the broader scale of global climate change, we see that the poorest people are least protected from the destructive impacts of shifting weather patterns (such as increasing frequency and severity of floods), while the wealthy who have benefited directly or indirectly from polluting industries are able, at least for now, to protect themselves with expensive renovations, insurance, or living in less impacted areas. When an acute disaster takes place, the wealthy are evacuated to safety, while poor people, disabled people, and disproportionately Black and brown people are left behind (Tomlinson, 2005). (See also Chapter 5: Racism and Chapter 9: Ableism.)

Psychological Violence

Psychological violence plays a significant role in reproducing classism. The shame that's often attached to accepting government assistance, and the invasions of privacy that often accompany it (see prior in Historical Legacies section), can be seen as psychological violence. Policies, individuals, and ubiquitous societal-level discourses continually tell poor people that they are worthless and that their lived experience of being impacted by structures of inequality is not real. Widely held beliefs such as the myth of meritocracy perform a kind of gaslighting, coercing some poor people into disbelieving their own direct experience in favor of believing the stories told by those with power over them. This leads to internalized classism and demands a great deal of emotional labor from people who must not only navigate the financial and practical burdens of economic inequality and classism but also continually remind themselves and each other that the oppression they're experiencing is systemic and not their fault. Consciousness raising, political education, and cross-class dialogue can serve as forms of resistance against the psychological violence of classism.

POWERLESSNESS

Powerlessness, for Young (1990), describes the condition of being unable to exert control over the circumstances of one's life or of having others' decisions dictate the circumstances of one's life. At the most basic level, powerlessness in classism manifests in the reality that poverty restricts one's choices about nearly everything. When someone is in poverty, they can't choose where they'd like to live but must live in the kind of housing they can afford, in a neighborhood they can afford, often sharing with more people than is comfortable. They can't choose what kind of workplace they want to work in but must take whatever job they can get just to get by. They can't choose which healthcare provider to see or what kind of education to pursue but must access whichever resources are subsidized by charity or government funding—when such resources are available at all. Sometimes they must choose between two basic needs, such as buying groceries or filling a prescription (Campbell, 2019). It is not that poor people are unable to make smart choices for themselves but rather that they often lack the power to put those choices into effect.

Although these stark examples of powerlessness mostly impact the poorest groups, people who are not poor but also not wealthy also experience powerlessness. They too can afford to live in some places and not others, to access some kinds of healthcare and not others, to attend some schools and not others regardless of their need or talent. Consumerism sometimes serves to disguise the powerlessness of middle-class people. Advertisements encourage people to feel empowered to choose which latest gadget to buy when, in reality, the most important choices about their lives and futures are outside their control.

Examples that show the impact of powerlessness more deeply include: incarceration, political disenfranchisement, welfare policy, declining union membership, and international economic policy. Incarceration and political disenfranchisement are discussed in Chapter 5: Racism and Chapter 9: Ableism, with additional discussion of the class dimensions of these forms of powerlessness available on the website.

★

Welfare Policy

Many government programs designed to assist people in poverty are premised on the assumption that poor people deserve only the minimum necessary to survive and should be grateful for what they get. (The idea of meritocracy contributes to this framing.) Several of these programs require people to meet unreasonable and sometimes humiliating criteria in order to access any resources at all. For example, single mothers who receive certain welfare benefits are required to disclose the identity of their child's biological father, even if he is abusive and/or absent. Programs ostensibly intended to decrease the impact of class inequality can also serve to take away people's power to form families in ways that work for them. Because of the correlation of race and poverty in the US, along with intentional and unintentional racism from service providers, People of Color are disproportionately affected by these disempowering poverty relief programs. In the case of services aimed at children and their parents, women are disproportionately affected because of the sexist imbalance in child-rearing responsibilities. Programs meant to support poor people with disabilities are sometimes even more restrictive, even affecting people's ability to get married without losing access to life-saving medical resources. (See Chapter 9: Ableism for more examples.)

A more empowering alternative is mutual aid, which includes a variety of practices people use to meet each other's needs while working to transform the systems that create poverty and injustice (Spade, 2020). Dean Spade (2020) distinguishes mutual aid from charity, which often shores up failing systems (like the capitalist housing market and healthcare system) and tends to reproduce discourses of meritocracy that distinguish deserving poor people from the undeserving, contributing to the psychological violence described prior. In contrast, mutual aid occurs in the context of social movement organizing that works to fix and/or re-imagine these systems and contradict classist messages. Mutual aid can protect against the psychological violence of classism because it normalizes interdependence and rejects discourses of shame, meritocracy, and deservingness and decreases powerlessness because it helps people obtain food, shelter, and other basic needs without subjecting them to disempowering and dehumanizing policies and rhetoric.

Declining Union Membership

Unions have been an important way for working-class people to organize for collective political power, as well as to influence the conditions of their labor through negotiations with employers. Union members earn on average 10%–30% higher wages than nonunion workers, and unionized jobs provide better benefits and more favorable workplace policies (McNicholas, Rhinehart, Poydock, Shierholz, and Perez, 2020). Unionizing makes workers less powerless both in relation to their employers and politically through mechanisms like meeting with elected representatives and hiring lobbyists to advocate for workers' interests. Unions can also form Political Action Coalitions to contribute to campaigns, although not at the same scale that corporations and billionaires can.

The percentage of employed workers in the US who are members of a union peaked in 1954 at 28%. The rate has declined steadily since then, and between 1980 and 2013, it fell from around 20% to 11.3% (Bureau of Labor Statistics, 2014). Despite recent and ongoing efforts to unionize agricultural, domestic, and food service workers, and some successful campaigns of teachers' unions to resist funding cuts and unsafe opening plans during the COVID-19 pandemic (Covert, 2021), the decline in union membership has lessened unions' political pull and decreased the number of workers who are politically involved.

Workers and unions continue to organize to push back against the trend of declining union membership, including through new approaches to labor organizing (Mantsios, 1998; Mathews, 2019). An example of current organizing that highlights the intersectionality of class, race, gender, and immigration is the National Domestic Workers Alliance, which supports state- and national-level campaigns to improve working conditions for domestic workers. As noted prior, domestic workers are excluded from most legal worker protections. The alliance works to correct this omission by creating new legislation protecting basic rights of domestic workers, such as the right to sleep uninterrupted, be paid at least minimum wage, and have paid sick days (Burnham & Theodore, 2012). As of 2021 they have succeeded in winning these protections in ten states and two major cities and for some home healthcare workers at the national level (National Domestic Workers Alliance, 2021b).

International Economic Policy

Powerlessness also plays out on a transnational level through neocolonial economic policies like those enacted by the International Monetary Fund (IMF) and the World Bank. Both organizations ostensibly have the mission of protecting poor people by promoting economic stability in poor countries. But many of their programs reproduce colonial power dynamics in which wealthier countries (and corporations) profit at the expense of poor countries while denying poor countries the power to make choices for their own populations, creating both powerlessness and exploitation.

The IMF provides loans to poor countries to help stabilize their economies in moments of crisis to prevent economic collapse—for example, to prevent bankruptcy and defaulting on debts. In exchange the IMF imposes conditions on borrower countries, including austerity measures (decreasing public spending, typically on expenses like education and healthcare), limitations on tax policy (e.g. prohibiting tariffs that allow the country more control over imports from other countries), and privatization (selling off government-owned assets to private corporations). Borrower countries have little say in the conditions of their loans and lose the ability to govern themselves in important ways. Within the IMF, decisions are made by a vote of all member countries, but they don't get equal votes: each country has voting power proportional to its position in the global economy. That means wealthier countries have the power to dictate the economic and social policies of poor countries when their populations are at their most vulnerable (Dreher, 2006).

MARGINALIZATION

When systems of oppression keep some groups of people on the margins of mainstream society, we call it marginalization. Marginalization is both symbolic (who gets to be considered "normal") and literal (exclusion from mainstream institutions). Based on the myth of meritocracy and the principles of capitalism, nearly everyone who is not engaged in economically productive labor is marginalized. We see classist marginalization in the devaluing of individuals and communities who don't or can't participate in paid labor, including youth, elders, disabled people, and the many people, disproportionately women, who do unpaid caregiving labor in their own families. Marginalization also takes the form of more active exclusion from paid work through discrimination (based on race, age, gender, disability, sexual orientation, and more), incarceration (disproportionately of Black and Latina/o/x men and trans women), and occupational segregation whereby people are funneled into different sectors of the labor market based on social identity. This exclusion is not always overt; people access jobs primarily through personal connections, so social capital functions to maintain and magnify patterns of marginalization from the mainstream workforce.

Symbolic marginalization often overlaps with cultural imperialism and shows up in classist language, such as calling poor people's cultural practices unhealthy, uncivilized, or "ghetto" or saying that someone who doesn't prioritize fashion dresses "like a hobo." It also manifests in K–12 schools through bullying of poorer students, in-group/out-group dynamics, stigmatizing public benefits like free lunch, and in the curriculum itself. For example, social studies curricula primarily teach the histories and values of the ruling class, relegating poor, working-class, and even middle-class concerns to a side note if they're included at all. K–12 schooling is also the site of more literal marginalization as poor students, Black and brown students, and students with disabilities are disproportionately suspended, expelled, referred to segregated special education, or otherwise actually removed from the mainstream school setting. Here we'll focus in depth on three examples of marginalization in healthcare, housing, and education.

Healthcare

The US is the only large, wealthy country in the world that does not provide universal healthcare (Tikkanan & Abrams, 2020). Instead, quality healthcare is only available to those who can afford it. People with full-time salaried jobs often receive health insurance through their employers, and the quality of care they can access depends on what they and their colleagues can demand from the employer. When workers are represented by a union, they can leverage collective power to negotiate for better healthcare than non-unionized workers in the same field.

People who don't get health insurance through employers must either purchase it, at costs that most can't afford, or rely on government insurance programs such as Medicaid (for poor people), Medicare (for elderly people and people with disabilities), or VA benefits (for veterans). (The Affordable Care Act expanded access to Medicaid in some states and created a mechanism for people who don't qualify for Medicaid to purchase health insurance through a public marketplace, but the cost is still prohibitive for many.) While government insurance programs can hypothetically provide very good coverage, they only cover certain providers. Someone who uses Medicaid might have to go to a crowded, underfunded public hospital, even though another hospital is closer and/or has more of the services they need. Or they might need to wait for months until a provider who accepts Medicaid has an opening for them, only to find out that provider has rigid cancellation policies and will refuse to reschedule if they miss an appointment.

In effect, this means that people have drastically different access to healthcare institutions based on income, wealth, and status. Those with the most class privilege, who have extensive private wealth and connections with powerful people, can demand the best care whenever they want. Those with the least class privilege, who are homeless, incarcerated, or undocumented, may be refused all but the most dire emergency treatment while ordinary healthcare needs worsen over time from lack of care. Many people have access to quality care only some of the time, such as while enrolled as full-time students or while they have a particular job, and try to squeeze in all their healthcare while they can, knowing they may need to go without for years to come. This results in vast class disparities in diagnosis, treatment efficacy, and life expectancy, in addition to the well-known racial disparities that are correlated with, although not entirely explained by, poverty (see e.g. California Newsreel, 2008).

Housing

Segregation in housing and public space is a literal form of marginalization whereby people with lower class status, especially those who are also People of Color, are kept out of desirable locations and relegated to the spatial margins of the community—far from commercial centers, transit hubs, resources, and services. In public spaces, we see marginalization in the enforcement of so-called "quality of life" laws, which criminalize ordinary activities of poor and homeless people such as sitting on a sidewalk, loitering, sleeping on a bench, or begging for change (Miller, 2007). Police use these laws to justify violence against poor and homeless people, so violence is a tool of marginalization and vice versa. "Hostile architecture"—landscaping features that make it difficult to sit down in a public space—is another way that poor people are forced out of areas where wealthy people and businesses don't want to see them (Jock, 2019). In many city centers, there are few places where people are allowed to spend time without spending money.

Housing segregation has been reinforced by decades of housing policy and financial policy that has dictated who can live where. Beginning in the late 1930s, the Home Owners' Loan Corporation created maps of residential areas, designating which were considered safe investments for mortgage lenders and which were not. An area was considered a good investment if it was populated by white professionals, while banks were warned away from financing mortgages in areas populated primarily by People of Color (even if they were middle class), immigrants, or poor people. The agency issued maps color-coding the least fundable areas in red—literally drawing a red line around areas in which banks simply would not finance home loans. This set up a self-perpetuating cycle where communities that were less resourced were unable to bring resources in or invest in their own neighborhoods. Poor communities and neighborhoods got poorer while wealthy communities accumulated more wealth and mobility between the two—both economic and spatial—was restricted (Nelson & Ayers, n.d.). Although racial discrimination in housing was formally forbidden in the Civil Rights Act of 1968, it still occurs, and housing discrimination based on class has never been illegal.

A related pattern in many US cities is gentrification, a process by which a formerly disinvested neighborhood receives an influx of investment and new residents who have more privilege than existing residents in terms of race, ethnicity, and often occupational status. This raises the desirability of the neighborhood to real estate investors, lenders, and prospective residents with relative class and race privilege. While this can bring some improvements to the neighborhood in terms of services and infrastructure, it also raises the cost of living so that long-time residents are forced out. If rising prices aren't enough to spur out-migration, gentrification often comes with increased police presence, racial profiling, "quality of life" citations, and even pressure to change cultural norms (such as the music played and how yards are decorated) to make the area that's newly "desirable" to those with privilege basically unlivable for the community that had historically made it their home—another example where marginalization overlaps with cultural imperialism.

Redlining and gentrification are powerful intersections of racism and classism. Patterns of segregation that were initially codified primarily by race ended up harming poor whites as well as People of Color. Later investment by wealthy white developers harms those same communities while also pitting poor residents against slightly less poor newcomers, often along racial lines, who don't (or don't want to) recognize that they too will be priced out before long (Chapple & Thomas, 2021).

Marginalization through housing policy is intimately connected with racial wealth disparities overall because home ownership is a major way that middle-class and some working-class families have been able to build financial stability. The impact of the 2008 economic meltdown and foreclosure crisis hit communities of color harder than white communities, reproducing and exacerbating the correlation of class and race (Traub, Reutchlin, Sullivan, Meschede, Dietrich, & Shapiro, 2015). The loss of credit and homeownership disproportionately affected Black and Latinx households, who experienced 53% and 66% losses in wealth respectively, compared to the 16% loss for white families (Kochhar, Fry, & Taylor, 2011). In some cases white families benefited directly from these harms to communities of color when they purchased homes that had been foreclosed on, but the even greater transfer of wealth was to investors—also mostly white—who could hold foreclosed property until a more profitable time to sell. Thus, marginalization and exploitation occur simultaneously, as a transfer of wealth (to the already wealthy) accompanies a transfer of population out of (newly) desirable areas, often breaking up communities and unraveling the community cohesion and cultural resources.

Education

Formal education is a requirement for most jobs that pay a livable wage, and there is a widespread belief that education leads to upward class mobility. In reality, the quality of education one can benefit from is largely determined by class in the first place. Persistent and well-documented disparities in K–12 education mean that students whose families have less class privilege tend to attend schools with relatively low funding per student, experience a lower quality of instruction and materials and higher student-teacher ratios, and have fewer choices and opportunities than students with more class privilege (Barshay, 2020; Kozol, 2012). Classist assumptions and stereotypes lead educators to track low-income students into vocational programs and community colleges and affluent students into elite colleges (Holland, 2019).

Educational inequities also reproduce racial disparities in income and wealth. Inequities in the quality of schooling, differential school funding, and disproportionate penalizing of students of color for breaking rules lead to a higher dropout rate for youth of color (Cookson, 2013; Lui, Robles, Leondar-Wright, Brewer, & Adamson, 2006). Without a high school diploma, they are more likely to enter into a lower tier of the labor market, working in low-wage service jobs with no opportunities for economic advancement.

Tax policies also play a role in the manifestation of exploitation by taking more away from people who have less resources. Public education is funded by a combination of federal, state, and local sources, with about half coming from local property taxes (Biddle & Berliner, 2002). Property values determine the amount of taxes collected and therefore the quality of education schools can provide. Schools in areas with high property values can provide better infrastructure, recruit better teachers, buy newer books and technology, and offer a range of services beyond the classroom, including after-school tutors, school counselors, school psychologists, and extracurricular programming. Funding disparities across districts impact students' academic achievement (Martin, Boser, Benner, & Baffour, 2018) as well as teacher salaries since schools with lower budgets can't attract the most qualified teachers.

Combined with disproportionate policing of communities of color, high dropout rates put poor youth of color at high risk of arrest and incarceration in what some have termed a "school to prison pipeline" (Heitzeg, 2009). Thus, marginalization in K–12 education feeds into marginalization, powerlessness, and exploitation through incarceration.

In higher education, financial access is a major barrier to participation, exacerbated by changes over the past several decades that make higher education increasingly unaffordable. Home foreclosures closed off one source of family collateral for student loans, states decreased their subsidies to public higher education, the cost of college tuition skyrocketed, federal Pell Grants were cut, and many college scholarships became "merit" based rather than need based. Merit-based scholarships do not take into consideration one's economic situation but instead focus on false measures of deservingness such as high SAT scores, impeccable high school records, strong letters of recommendation, and robust extracurricular involvement, which advantage students from financially privileged backgrounds (Espenshade & Radford, 2009; Ehrenberg, Zhang, & Levin, 2006; Hopkins, 2014). Many students have to resort to private loans with high interest rates to finance their education, unwittingly supporting a lucrative new income stream for private banks. Although a postsecondary degree can increase access to better-paying jobs, the benefit is largest for those who already had class privilege before college, while students from poor families get relatively little financial benefit, on average, from their degree (Haycock, Lynch, & Engle, 2010). Thus, economic realities steer many students away from academic programs they might otherwise pursue.

Once enrolled, lower-income students often encounter challenges to their academic and social success in college because the structures of college center those with class privilege (Jack, 2019). Students often struggle to achieve a sense of belonging and to focus on their studies due to ongoing family responsibilities, cultural capital that differs from what is valued by the institution, gaps in academic skills from average or below average K–12 education, or having to work to support themselves or their families (Hopkins, 2014). Some of the "optional" opportunities that have the greatest potential impact on class mobility—such as unpaid internships, study abroad programs, and participation in student leadership—may be out of reach financially or may be unappealing due to class culture mismatch and classist microaggressions. Low-income students may even struggle to access existing campus resources such as tutoring, professors' office hours, counseling, or disability services because their class background doesn't lead them to feel entitled to or confident about using those resources (Hopkins, 2014). All these layers of marginalization can affect students' self-confidence and overall psychological well-being (Hopkins, 2014; Smith & Redington, 2010). Cumulatively marginalization means that class-based inequalities in education and employment are reproduced and reinforced, even while a few students do manage to leverage the system for limited class mobility.

ACTION AGAINST CLASSISM AND FOR ECONOMIC JUSTICE

Among the historical and current manifestations of classism described prior, we mention several ways in which communities resist classism and work for economic justice. For every example of classism, there are and have been people organizing against it in creative, persistent, and often effective ways. As social justice educators, one of the most important actions we can take against classism is to incorporate our understanding of it into our teaching content and practice. The rest of this chapter offers a curriculum for a 16-hour workshop on classism and its intersections, along with notes on pedagogy, design, and facilitation for classism workshops.

DESIGN FOR TEACHING ABOUT CLASSISM

As with any social justice course or workshop, the first step in planning is to articulate the core purpose and from there elaborate concrete goals and learning objectives. The purpose of your course or workshop depends on the setting and the group. In an activist community or political education context, the purpose may be to build the skills and understanding needed for participants to take specific action against classism and/or capitalism. In schools and workplace contexts, the purpose can become entangled and fraught. When we teach people to understand and question classist power structures, they may end up protesting against the very institution in which we are employed to teach them—not only against specific practices within the institution but sometimes also against its fundamental structure or even existence. Depending on our position within an organization, we may risk losing our jobs by encouraging or being perceived as encouraging people to take action to change it. Yet, as social justice educators, we are not neutral. We want participants to do their own critical thinking and make their own choices, and we also want them to leave the course inspired and equipped to take action against classism, even when that's not in the best interest of the institution that hired us.

We find it useful to think about our purpose in any classism course or workshop as aiming to increase solidarity against classism. By solidarity we mean not only ideological support but a sustained commitment, based on common goals, interests, beliefs, and analyses, to collaborative action against classism and its intersections. In a community-based workshop or in a school that draws from a low-income local community, we may focus on solidarity among the participants, building on the relationships and shared community they already have. If our students/participants all come from relative class privilege, our purpose may be to inspire solidarity with communities who are not represented in the room. If our group has a mix of class backgrounds and/or current class situations, solidarity both within and beyond the group may be relevant.

In the design that follows, we assume a group with mixed class positions (although not necessarily very mixed), who are not already in community with each other, and who may or may not realize that they have a shared interest in working against classism. If you are working with a more homogenous group, we encourage you to use what is useful from this design and to adapt it if your group needs something different.

This sample design presupposes familiarity with the core social justice concepts that we consider foundational to any social justice approach that are presented in Chapter 4: Core Concepts. We strongly recommend that instructors and facilitators read Chapter 4 and consider these core concepts fully before applying them in a social justice approach to classism.

The sample design is followed by learning objectives and key concepts specific to each quadrant, as well as brief descriptions of the activities needed to carry out the design. Detailed instructions necessary to carry out the activities can be found on the website. ★

OVERVIEW OF CLASSISM DESIGN QUADRANTS

Quadrant 1
1. Welcome and Introductions
2. Icebreaker (2 options)
   a. Common Ground
   b. Meet and Greet
3. Assumptions, Purpose, Goals, Agenda (2 options)
   a. Class and Classism Assumptions Presentation and Discussion
   b. Assumptions Discussion
4. Group Norms and Guidelines (3 options)
   a. Generating Group Norms and Guidelines
   b. Hopes and Concerns
   c. Don't Do Any Guidelines (see facilitation notes for reasons)
5. Defining Class and Classism (2 options)
   a. Classism Terminology
   b. Defining Class Brainstorm
6. Income and Wealth Distribution (3 options)
   a. Ten Chairs Distribution of Wealth
   b. Distribution of Income Activity—Quintiles
   c. Video Activity/Discussion
7. Transition

Quadrant 3
1. Class Self-Reflection and Sharing about Class Background (2 options)
   a. Class Background Inventory
   b. Cultural Chest
2. Bringing It All Together
   a. Five Faces of Classism
   b. Meritocracy and Workism
   c. Web of Institutional Classism
3. Classism in Your [Insert Context]
   a. Classism in Your (School, Workplace, etc.)
   b. Organizational Classism Assessment

Quadrant 2
1. Class Culture Activity
   a. Class Culture Reading Discussion
   b. Guided Reflection and Class Culture Mismatches
2. Cultural Capital Activity
   a. Cultural Capital Questionnaire
   b. Cultural Capital Brainstorm
3. Social Capital Activity
   a. Exploring Your Social Network
   b. Quantifying Your Social Network
4. History
   a. Historical Gallery and Discussion
   b. Family History in Context

Quadrant 4
1. Moving Toward Action
   a. Identifying Opportunities for Coalition
   b. Panel of Local Organizers
   c. Action Gallery
2. Taking Action
   a. Acting Accountably (4As of Liberatory Consciousness)
   b. Action Continuum and Spheres of Influence
   c. Action Strategy Activity
3. Closing Activity
   a. Closure Using Sentence Stems
   b. Asking and Offering

Learning Outcomes for Quadrant 1:

- Understand this social justice education (SJE) approach to classism
- Understand principles of participating in an SJE learning community
- Explain definitions of *class* and *classism* drawing on multiple class indicators
- Describe key features of the distribution of income and wealth in the US
- Define a set of class categories
- Begin to reflect on personal class backgrounds and connect individual experiences with macro- and meso-level discussions

Key Concepts for Quadrant 1: Class, classism, class indicator, income, wealth, ruling class, owning class, professional middle class, buffer class, working class, poverty class; depending on the workshop's purpose, this quadrant may also include meritocracy, solidarity, and others

Activities and Options for Quadrant 1:

Opening the Session and Introductory Material

The two icebreakers—Option A: Common Ground and Option B: Meet and Greet—are activities through which participants learn something about each other and get a sense of who is in the group. Option A includes a variation for online workshops.

Assumptions, Purpose, Goals, Agenda are brief presentations or activities that establish some parameters for the classism workshop or course (see Chapter 4: Core Concepts). For situations in which participants have completed reading or other homework in advance, we also include an option to generate assumptions and questions through discussion of the homework.

Group Norms and Guidelines
- Option A is a simple group brainstorm to generate guidelines and agreements.
- Option B begins with participants' hopes and concerns and then, through group discussion, creates guidelines to address those hopes and concerns.
- Option C is to use only the most basic guidelines necessary for safety (e.g. confidentiality of personal disclosures) and deliberately *not* develop specific guidelines for behavior in the group but rather note that norms and conflicts may emerge and the group will work through them together. (See "Guidelines for Participation," following.)

Defining Class and Classism
- In Option A the facilitators provide definitions and participants discuss them in small groups before teaching back to the whole group.
- Option B uses an open-ended brainstorm to generate a definition of class based on multiple indicators.

Income and Wealth Distribution
- Distribution of Wealth, Option A: Ten Chairs: A participatory activity that uses a spatial metaphor to demonstrate the distribution of wealth in the US, and to introduce functional definitions of class categories.
- Option B: Distribution of Income: Quintiles: A participatory activity that uses a spatial metaphor to demonstrate changes in the income growth of different class groups (as quintiles) during two recent periods of US history and to begin to make connections with policies that impact income inequality.
- Option C: Video and discussion.

Learning Outcomes for Quadrant 2:
- Explain class culture, cultural capital, and social capital and understand how each is related to the reproduction of power
- Understand historical context for the current class system
- Continue to explore participants' own experiences relative to each class indicator and the historical context they've learned
- Build awareness of intersectionality of other manifestations of oppression with classism

Key Concepts for Quadrant 2: Class culture, cultural capital, social capital, power (and other key words depending on the historical focus)

Activities and Options for Quadrant 2:

Class Culture Activity
- Option A uses cultural texts and discussion to explore some features of class cultures.
- Option B uses guided reflection and discussion to explore participants' experiences of class culture mismatches and discusses implications for cross-class relationships, cross-class situations, and the reproduction of class.

Cultural Capital Activity
- Option A: Cultural Capital Questionnaire helps participants understand how our personal/familial culture and cultural assets intersect with class, class privilege, and class inequality.
- Option B: Cultural Capital Brainstorm helps participants think about the relationship between cultural capital and class cultures.

Social Capital Activity
- Option A: Exploring Your Social Network helps participants identify the people in their social network and who they can go to for certain kinds of connections, resources, and advice.
- Option B: Quantifying Your Social Network helps participants recognize the relationship among cultural capital, material capital, and social capital and how class inequality is perpetuated.

History
- Option A: Historical [Virtual] Gallery and Discussion uses infographics, videos, historical cartoons, etc. to explore highlights and themes in US class history.
- Option B: Family History in Context leads participants through an investigation of their own family history to identify how their families' class experiences were connected with policies, economic trends, social movements, etc.

Learning Outcomes for Quadrant 3
- Further reflect on personal class experiences and relevant intersections, *in the structural and historical context*
- Identify manifestations of classism at different levels and in different forms
- Identify manifestations of classism in familiar contexts (such as participants' own schools, community, or workplace)

Key Concepts for Quadrant 3 (some or all depending on which activity options are used): Individual, institutional, and societal levels of classism; Five Faces of Oppression; solidarity; discourse; meritocracy

Activities and Options for Quadrant 3:

Self-Reflection and Sharing about Class Background
- Option A: Class Background Inventory is a reflection and discussion activity that helps participants begin thinking and talking about the multiple layers of their class background and relevant intersections.
- Option B: Cultural Chest is a less structured option that invites participants to share symbols of their class backgrounds and relevant intersections

Bringing It All Together (classism examples)
- Option A: Five Faces of Classism: An interactive small-group activity that draws out a variety of examples of manifestations of classism and explores some overlaps and interconnections with other systems of oppression.
- Option B: Web of Institutional Classism helps make tangible the connections across different institutions in how classism plays out.
- Option C: Meritocracy and Workism explores the discourse of meritocracy and how it affects individual and shared beliefs, attitudes, and behaviors.

Classism in Your _____
- Option A: Classism in Your _____ (School, Workplace, etc.) helps participants recognize manifestations of classism in their context and begin practicing effective ways to take action against classism in everyday situations.
- Option B: Organizational Classism Assessment helps participants apply concepts and information around classism to their specific organizational context.

Learning Outcomes for Quadrant 4:
- Apply concepts of class and classism to their own behavior as an "ally" to those with less class privilege than them
- Consider elements needed for an effective action plan
- Identify options for different kinds of action to take toward ending classism

Key Concepts for Quadrant 4 (some or all depending on which options are used): Acting as allies, liberatory consciousness, coalition, spheres of influence

Activities and Options for Quadrant 4

Moving Toward Action
- Option A: Identifying opportunities for coalition, a structured problem-solving discussion in small groups that highlights overlaps and intersections between classism and other systems of oppression and begins to transition toward thinking about steps for effective action.
- Option B: Panel of local organizers (e.g. service agencies, union organizers, worker centers, policy makers, donor circles).
- Option C: Action Gallery: Provides opportunity to discuss current and/or local examples of action against classism.

Taking Action
- Acting Accountably (4As of Liberatory Consciousness) introduces a framework for helping participants think about accountable action for liberation.
- Action Continuum and Spheres of Influence uses two simple frameworks to help students identify actions that are within their reach.
- Action Strategy Activity uses an activists' planning tool to get specific about the most effective approach to a particular action campaign.

Closing Activity
- Option A: Sentence Stems: A closing activity for groups that have come together only for this workshop/course.
- Option B: Asking and Offering: A closing activity for intact groups that brings closure to the learning experience and helps the group integrate new learnings into their ordinary work together.

NOTES FOR PEDAGOGY, DESIGN, AND FACILITATION

In classism workshops, as with any other social justice topic, challenges emerge. Some are dilemmas related to the content itself or to design and sequencing decisions, while others are facilitation challenges; many are a combination of two or more of these. Here we present specific issues of pedagogy, design, and facilitation that, in our experience, are important considerations for instructors and facilitators.

CLASS AS CATEGORY AND IDENTITY

The public discourse on class tends to obscure economic realities, sometimes through encouraging nearly everyone to identify as "middle class" and other times through over-simplified categorizations such as "the 1%" and "the 99%." As a result, participants will have different relationships with their own social group memberships regarding class. Some may not "identify with" their class category and may feel that class is a situation they are in and not part of who they are as a person. Others may identify with a class category that does not describe their current or previous class position. Facilitators may be in the awkward position, when teaching about the realities of the class divide, of telling partici-pants what their class identities are, directly or indirectly. In general, it is rude (and unethi-cal, especially when in a position of power as an instructor/facilitator) to tell someone else what their identity is—instead, we practice assuming that "everyone is the expert on their own identity." Yet one of the ways classism is internalized is that people often misunder-stand what their relative class location is.

For participants, being told or realizing during the workshop/course that they have been mistaken about their class can come as a shock. As facilitators, we must balance respecting the ways in which participants have made sense of their experiences with sup-porting them to challenge those understandings with new frameworks and information. It is helpful to distinguish carefully between when we are speaking about class identity per se—meaning the class group with which someone identifies—and when we are speak-ing about class category—one's relative position in more objective or at least describable terms.

The issue of class identification brings up a particularly acute facilitation dilemma around defining class categories. On one hand, participants may be anxious for definitive meanings with which to categorize themselves and others. Yet, since people's implicit defi-nitions of these categories often include value judgments about the desirability of belong-ing to different class categories, participants may also be reluctant to categorize themselves honestly. The process of sorting themselves and their experiences into these categories—as ill defined and emotionally laden as the categories are—can forestall open inquiry into class experiences. In addition, some participants may simply lack awareness about relevant class markers and/or analytic frameworks that would help them make sense of their expe-riences. For example, some participants may not have accurate information about their parents' income.

One way to address this challenge is to postpone defining class categories and first encourage participants to discuss their own class backgrounds and situations with regard to specific class markers rather than general class categories. This approach creates space for important conversations about the range of experience (not just identity categories) in the group and gives participants opportunities to discover and interrogate their own implicit definitions of the categories. However, it can be time consuming. For shorter workshops, especially workshops with a specific goal that isn't served by such conversations, defining the categories at the beginning may be preferable.

Another way that class identification comes up is when participants have internalized beliefs about meritocracy. For example, a middle-class student may insist that their aca-demic success is a result of their own hard work and cannot be attributed to class advan-tage. Or, a working-class student may insist that class barriers won't limit them and that their hard work is going to pay off in financial success, despite well-documented trends to the contrary.

Participants' beliefs about class expressed on a micro level may seem like resistance to acknowledging the realities of classism and may have the effect of distracting from macro-level discussions. At the same time, these beliefs are sometimes deeply ingrained parts of who participants understand themselves to be and may serve important functions for them psychologically. The stories people tell themselves about meritocracy can help them feel worthy and hopeful rather than guilty or hopeless. Rather than engaging with participants' beliefs about themselves as individuals, it is often most helpful for facilitators to distinguish between what may occur at a micro level with any given individual and the macro-systems that create trends, likelihoods, and overall inequity. As participants process learning about macro-systems, their understanding of their own identities and roles will likely evolve as well.

HOW WE TALK ABOUT CLASS PRIVILEGE AND UPWARD MOBILITY

Class is not binary and not straightforwardly categorical—a person may be relatively privileged in terms of some aspects of class (such as cultural capital gained from education) while simultaneously disadvantaged in other aspects (such as wealth and income). Every student/participant we work with will be class privileged relative to someone and less privileged than someone else. "Acknowledging privilege" as part of a classism workshop is not a matter of acknowledging one's membership in a category but rather of identifying specific ways one benefits or does not benefit from the class system.

At the same time, we should be careful not to equate experiences of structural power with experiences of personal or familial difficulty. For example, someone who grew up in a wealthy family may feel that their parents' wealth led them to be distant and unloving. Such a pattern may indeed emerge from some characteristics of wealthy class cultures, such as the focus on individual achievement; on the other hand, the traumatizing experiences of poverty also lead to disruptions in family relationships. It may be easy to romanticize the collectivism that characterizes some poor and working-class cultures; while recognizing it as a strength, we must also understand that it is necessary—and sometimes insufficient—for survival under oppression. We can acknowledge individual difficulties and traumas, including those that are related to an experience of privilege, without minimizing the reality of that privilege.

Discussions of privilege are also complicated by the reality that many participants (and facilitators) are actively trying to increase their class privilege. For some, this contradiction brings up feelings of guilt and shame for wanting to benefit from a system they know is harmful. For others, it raises defensiveness. They may resist engaging with anti-capitalist analysis or even indulge in red-baiting, accusing facilitators or other participants of being "communists" (usually without any clear definition of communism) in order to distract from the difficult considerations of real and desired privilege within a harmful system. In addition to revisiting clear definitions of capitalism and related terms, we find it useful to resist either/or thinking and ideological purity and instead normalize that we all participate in harmful systems (including racism, sexism, etc.) and can resist them at the same time as we try to survive and even thrive within them. For example, if we engage with the idea that "there is no ethical consumption under capitalism," the options are not simply to avoid consumption or be evil; instead, we can try to reduce the harm caused by our consumption—including harm to ourselves, our communities, and others who are less privileged than us.

WHO IS AND WHO IS NOT IN THE ROOM

The class diversity among participants makes a significant difference in the overall experience of the course/workshop, along with diversity of other social identities, generation, family immigration history, and individual experiences. Since some activities are designed to take advantage of the diversity of experiences and viewpoints in the group, it is important that facilitators be aware of the relative diversity or homogeneity of a group and plan accordingly.

In terms of generation, the economic moment in which people experience major milestones like finishing school, getting a first job, and retiring have a large impact on their experience of class. Someone who grew up in a blue-collar family in the 1950s, when many blue-collar workers were unionized and well paid, will have a markedly different experience of being "working class" than someone who grew up in a similar class situation in the 1990s. The difference is not only about their ages now but also about their generations.

Families' immigration histories impact experiences of class both in terms of generations since immigration and in terms of changes in economic context that affect class. For example, some immigrants who are highly trained professionals experience a drop in status and income upon immigrating because their credentials are not valid in the US.

Many class markers vary across regions and urban/suburban/ruralness because of differences in the cost of living and different resources needed to live comfortably in different places. For example, in some major cities, owning a car for each adult in the family is a luxury, while in most rural areas, it is a prerequisite for being able to work outside the home.

To account for these factors, facilitators should learn as much as possible about the group in advance of finalizing design decisions. In some cases a pre-survey may be possible; in other cases facilitators will have to make educated guesses based on the population of the school, organization, or community from which participants are drawn. If some class categories are likely to be very underrepresented or unrepresented, facilitators should explore ways to bring perspectives and issues relevant to those groups into the course/workshop. Facilitators should also be cautious about assumptions or generalizations that may confuse or alienate participants based on differences in region, immigration, generation, and so on.

In some cases, a majority of participants may be within a relatively narrow range of class backgrounds, with a few outliers with far more or far less class privilege. Facilitators should take care to address the needs of outliers and avoid teaching only to the needs of the majority. It is especially important to consider those participants likely to experience themselves as "the only" representative of a particular class group (or other social group). Avoid appointing these participants as "experts" or examples for other participants' learning, yet do consider how the whole group might be served by discussions that seem at first to be mostly for/about the outliers. Often there are larger themes that might be elucidated by dedicating time to the perspectives and experiences of participants who are not in the majority.

In many college contexts (and other groups as well), it is likely that a majority of participants will identify as middle class, whether or not they are middle class according to our definitions. This pattern occurs partly because of the society-wide norm of describing practically everyone as middle class and partly because of the class segregation that shapes student bodies and many workplaces to be relatively class homogenous.

If a participant expressed the opinion that all or most of the participants are middle class, it may be difficult for participants who know they are not middle class to speak up and disrupt that normalized narrative. When someone says, "We are all middle class," facilitators can (1) remind participants that they do not know the experiences of others in the room, (2) initiate discussion of why the group might be as homogenous as it is (what institutional and societal forces lead to some groups not being represented?), and (3) initiate discussion of why people might believe that the group is more homogeneous than it is. If this conversation occurs before more nuanced definitions of class categories are introduced, it can be useful to return to it later, to ask participants to reassess their own class category in light of the new definitions, and to reflect on how that changes their understanding of the range of class experiences in the group.

One specific way "we're all middle class" comes up is when participants assert that being a college student (or a student at a particular college) is such a privilege that it overrides any class differences. This statement often serves to silence discussion of the inequities within the student body and the micro- and meso-level classism that less privileged students face on campus (see Education section prior). Facilitators can address such statements by briefly acknowledging the partial truth they contain and then providing and/or asking for examples of how/why they are not true.

CLASS CULTURE AND CULTURAL CONGRUENCE

It is important to ensure that the course/workshop is culturally relevant for all participants. Instructors/facilitators should give particular attention to known class culture patterns and consider how they might unconsciously bring professional middle-class assumptions to their pedagogy, design, and facilitation. Because professional middle class culture is normalized and privileged in many organizations, this is a risk even if the facilitators/instructors did not grow up professional middle class! Considerations of cultural congruence come up in many ways and are addressed in the following sections focusing on guidelines, risk and taboo, personal vs. academic understandings of class, and action.

GUIDELINES FOR PARTICIPATION

Establishing guidelines or group agreements enables participants to feel more comfortable approaching challenging topics and gives them a sense of ownership of the group process. For classism courses/workshops, it is especially important to set clear guidelines around confidentiality and participation, since participants may be invited to disclose sensitive information about their finances or family situations while participating in group activities. In order to address some participants' need for privacy while still encouraging reflection and participation, one guideline to consider is that when someone chooses not to participate in a particular activity, they should instead reflect on, and if possible share, their reflections and reasons for their choice.

As valuable as guidelines can be, there are arguments against using guidelines in certain situations (Hunter, n.d.; Lakey, 2010). One of the potential pitfalls of guidelines is that they tend to reflect the dominant culture of the group, the facilitators, and/or the organization (see Chapter 3: Design and Facilitation). In a course/workshop about classism, it can be particularly counterproductive to establish guidelines that reflect professional middle-class or owning-class cultural values as if these values are universal. Since most participants and many educators have little practice thinking about class culture, and since those cultural norms are reinforced in many organizations and in college and university settings, this is all too likely to occur, even when the facilitators do not come from middle-class or upper-class backgrounds.

Guidelines addressing how participants should manage conflict are one example. Research suggests that poor and working-class cultures tend to value conflict and express it openly. For some people it may be productive for group members to explicitly express disagreement with another's perspective or actions (Leondar-Wright, 2014; Lakey, 2010). This contrasts with many professional middle-class cultures, which tend to avoid conflict. To many poor and working-class participants, professional middle-class expectations of how to communicate disagreement may feel formulaic, or like "sugar coating." People from poor and working-class backgrounds who participate in majority professional middle-class settings (such as higher education) are already accustomed to having their communication styles stifled, especially around conflict, based on enforced professional middle-class norms. To create a similarly stifling environment in a workshop/course about classism is a contradiction. Instead, we encourage noting the variety of approaches to conflict (and other aspects of group communication) and supporting participants to communicate across differences as relevant, without norming or enforcing any particular communication style over another.

Knowing some of the pitfalls and complications of group guidelines, it is important that facilitators be thoughtful and deliberate in deciding whether to establish guidelines and, if so, how to use and revisit them. These choices have important implications for different expressions of class (and/or ethnic, racial, gender, and other) cultures. When guidelines are not used, the facilitators need another plan for how to keep the course/workshop productive for all participants. For example, they should build in more time for group process and/or for teaching communication and feedback skills that participants can use to help the course/workshop go well. (Of course, communication and feedback skills can also be culturally specific, and facilitators should be careful to frame them as tools to use when they are useful, rather than rules for how people must or should act.)

RISK AND TABOO

In sequencing, we generally encourage facilitators to start with activities that present relatively low emotional risk for participants and progress to higher-risk activities that ask participants to step farther out of their comfort zones. With regard to classism, participants will often have widely varying senses of how risky a particular activity feels because of their class backgrounds and other factors.

To some, describing their class experiences at all may feel like a high-risk activity. Participants at the lower and higher ends of the income and wealth spectrum may be reluctant to disclose out of shame, embarrassment, or guilt or out of fear of judgment from other participants. Many middle-class participants may believe it is inappropriate to talk about family finance, based on the widely held taboo against talking about class differences, especially in quantitative terms.

On the other hand, for some participants from poor and working-class backgrounds, it may feel normal and comfortable to discuss financial struggles in frank and specific terms. These participants may feel impatient with what feels to them like an unnecessarily cautious pace, especially if they see it as accommodating the discomfort expressed by participants with more privilege.

Disclosure about class tends to feel risky in different ways depending on whether participants are an intact group (who already know each other) or a new group (who come together for the course/workshop). With intact groups, participants may feel nervous about disrupting existing assumptions and patterns in their relationships; on the other hand, they may have a foundation of trust that makes disclosure feel like less of a stretch. With new groups, the lack of established trust may make disclosure feel like forced intimacy that participants may not immediately be ready for. When deciding activities and sequencing, we urge facilitators to imagine the range of possible participants and craft a sequence in which all participants are appropriately challenged. Different parts of the workshop may feel risky to different participants, and no group should be in the most vulnerable position for too long.

Additionally, consider initiating a discussion about the taboo itself. Questions to address include what is considered "private" information and why; what purpose shame and guilt play in maintaining the class system; for whom and in what contexts it is taboo to talk about money and for whom and in what contexts it is not taboo; and in what ways does the taboo serve and/or undermine justice.

TENSIONS BETWEEN ACADEMIC AND PERSONAL UNDERSTANDINGS OF CLASSISM

Most participants come into classes/workshops about classism from one of three different perspectives. First, some participants have thought very little about class or classism in any context prior to the course/workshop. Second, some participants may bring significant academic knowledge about class and classism (often gained from courses in economics or sociology) while having limited if any reflection on their own class experiences or role in classism. This group's understanding of class may be highly structured but impersonal, and they may exhibit unconsciously classist behaviors while articulating an anti-classist analysis. Finally, others may come motivated by personal experiences of being *class straddlers* (i.e. people who grew up in one class category and later experienced class mobility) or of being outliers in relation to their peers. Their understandings start from the personal and may be emotional for them and may or may not include some systemic analysis stemming from learning in school or the community.

With participants coming from such different perspectives, the questions arise: Which kinds of knowledge are considered real and valid? Whose views and experiences are given credence? What is the value for the second sort of participant of adding personalized reflection to their understanding of classism, and what is the value for the third sort of participant in adding structured theoretical knowledge to their understanding?

As with all the curricula in this book, we believe a balance of personal and theoretical learning is most effective. Facilitators should appreciate the various kinds of knowledge participants bring to the group, and participants should not be allowed to use any form of knowledge to discount or delegitimize other's perspectives. At the same time, it is important to highlight and interrogate the ways in which academic and impersonal knowledge is privileged over that drawn from personal experience—both because the former is taken more seriously by the power structures and because a level of class privilege is required to have access to it.

Participants with academic understanding about class may need to be reminded that their knowledge does not exempt them from learning about practical, everyday, micro-level impacts of classism; in fact, it may oblige them to approach the learning opportunity with particular openness. Participants with more personal understandings about class may need to be reassured that their lack of academic learning about it (for those for whom that's true) does not take away from their lived knowledge; at the same time, they can be encouraged to explore what they might gain from also learning about classism on a more theoretical level.

FOCUSING ON THE SYSTEMIC/CULTURAL LEVELS TO AVOID THE INDIVIDUAL AND INTERPERSONAL LEVELS OF CLASSISM

A related but slightly different facilitation challenge comes up when some participants focus only on broad-scale structural analysis—the macro level—as a way of avoiding micro-level discussions that would feel too personal. This tendency may let some participants "off the hook" of examining their own experiences of privilege and/or oppression and can silence other participants who could contribute insights based on their micro-level reflections.

Focusing on the macro level is important, but it should not be used to distract from or avoid other issues. If discussion seems to keep drifting back to the macro level while meso- and micro-level topics go unexplored, or if participants say or imply that macro-level issues should take precedence over other parts of the discussion, facilitators should steer the conversation toward a more balanced micro/meso/macro approach. It can be useful to remind participants that classism as a system relies on all three levels; the purpose of the course/workshop is not only to identify classism that happens "out there" in macro trends but also to notice its manifestations "in here"—in our everyday lives, cultures, and institutions—and to seek ways to address it on all three levels.

Similarly, some participants may want to focus on a global context in a way that avoids or masks classism in the US. For example, someone may argue that, relative to people in many other countries, everyone in the US is privileged economically. Such statements contain some truth and can be an important part of the conversation. Yet too often they have the impact of obscuring the reality of classism and inequality within the US. Participants should be encouraged to consider the global context and also to recognize and grapple with the reality of inequality and classism in the US, which is more extreme than they probably realize.

TAKING ACTION

As in any social justice course/workshop, it is important to address how participants can apply the new awareness and knowledge they have gained. In a successful course/workshop, participants' learning will generate a lot of energy and feelings. Reactions may include distress at the injustices they have become aware of, feelings of helplessness at the enormity of the systems they confront, relief at being able to articulate and explain something that they had previously noticed but not understood, and desire to do something to make it better. A well-designed workshop gives participants options and tools with which to channel this energy into useful action.

Too often the question of how to act on new learning is relegated to a short segment at the very end of the course/workshop, but there are many ways to incorporate it throughout. A benefit of starting to think about action earlier in the course/workshop is that participants' learning can be more solution focused, and any helplessness they may feel upon confronting the scale of injustice in the world is likely to be shorter lived. On the other hand, if participants know very little about classism, talking about action too soon can generate resistance from those who are not convinced that classism is a problem. In group action assignments, differences in understanding and analysis among participants can lead to difficulty agreeing on a project, especially in the beginning when participants may not yet have common vocabulary, knowledge, and skills to move their conversation forward. In these cases, introducing an action project in the second half or even toward the end of a longer course may be preferable.

In short one-time workshops, the action segment may be as simple as a closing reflection asking each participant to share one thing they will do next. Allotting even five minutes for reflection on next steps is far preferable to not addressing it at all. However, we urge facilitators to allocate as much time as is feasible to taking action. In the design we devote significant time to action, mostly in the fourth quadrant.

In some contexts, action will be built into every step of the design. For example, training with an intact group may begin with acknowledgement of a specific problem the group is hoping to address through learning about classism. The problem can be revisited at different points throughout the training to make note of how participants' learning adds to their understanding of the problem and possible approaches to solving it, and the training can culminate with a more in-depth problem-solving and action-planning session. Similarly, in a course spanning multiple weeks, an action project may be assigned near the beginning or middle of the course, with periodic touch points and a culminating presentation or report at the end of the course.

INTERSECTIONALITY

An intersectional framework should inform every aspect of a course/workshop, from planning and design to content and facilitation. Before planning a course/workshop on classism, facilitators should consider the possible impacts of doing so in their particular context. Most groups need to learn about classism, but they also need to learn about and address many other systems of oppression. Which voices and conversations are amplified, and which might be talked over or silenced, by offering a course/workshop primarily focused on classism? Are there other topics that should be offered or at least announced simultaneously in order to make the intersectional approach of the project transparent? Whose voices are centered and whose are marginalized in the planning process itself?

We encourage facilitators to introduce intersectionality from the very start. Doing so helps set a tone of inviting complexity and can reassure participants that a focus on classism does not preclude discussion of racism, sexism, or other systems of oppression; on the contrary, a robust exploration of classism *requires* that other systems be considered.

In terms of content and facilitation, many activities in our design include information and opportunities for discussion about classism's intersections with other systems of oppression. Even when intersectionality is not explicit in an activity, facilitators should be alert to opportunities for deepening discussion by giving examples and asking follow-up questions that highlight intersectionality.

For example, on an individual or interpersonal level, if participants are describing their class experiences in one-dimensional terms that only acknowledge class and not other identities/systems, saying things like "as a middle class person, I . . .," facilitators can follow up with questions like: "What other aspects of your identity might contribute to that experience? In what ways in that experience about class, and in what ways might it also be about your race, gender, age, religious background . . .?" Similar responses are appropriate when participants make generalizations about class groups to which they may or may not belong. Intersectionality reminds us of the dangers of saying "*all* poor people experience such-and-such manifestation of classism." Rather, we should be holding as an ongoing question for participants to explore, "*Which* poor people experience such-and-such, how, and why?"

Similarly, on an institutional level, if participants describe examples of institutional classism in one-dimensional terms, a facilitator could ask, "How is racism (and/or another relevant system) also showing up in that example? How does the racism of that institution contribute to its classism and vice versa? What could it look like to examine/address *both* the racism and the classism of that example at the same time?" On a macro level, if participants are discussing broad trends in culture or history in one-dimensional terms, a facilitator can add complexity with questions like, "What else would we learn about that story if we used an intersectional lens? In addition to class, what else is going on there?"

A common and unfortunate pitfall that many participants and facilitators fall into on the way to intersectional analysis is conflating race and class such that discussions hinge on combined categories, as in statements like, "Poor people and People of Color are under-represented in the sciences." The phrase "poor people and People of Color" often comes from a well-intentioned desire to acknowledge both racism and classism and to avoid leaving anyone out. Unfortunately, such statements fail to distinguish between the different mechanisms and impacts of racism and classism; used sloppily, they can imply that classism impacts poor white people identically to how racism impacts People of Color (all of whom are assumed to be poor also). The conversations thus framed tend to focus primarily on those groups that come to mind easily because they represent large numbers of people or highly visible groups or because they match our stereotypes—such as "poor Black urban mothers" and "owning-class white men." Meanwhile many other groups—"poor white rural elders," for example, or "professional middle-class Latinas"—are ignored.

Instead of conflating race and class, we should help participants learn to specify *how* racism and classism each function, how they function together, and how they have similar and different impacts on different groups of people. In addition to offering a more robust analysis and leading to richer conversation, this framework helps ensure that no participant's experience or identity will be invisible in the room because it doesn't match the stereotypical combinations of identities.

SEQUENCING: INDIVIDUAL TO SOCIETAL/CULTURAL LEVELS

One of the key design decisions facilitators make is whether to start with an exploration of personal experiences (micro level) before moving on to institutional (meso level) and societal (macro level) examples or vice versa. There are strengths and liabilities of each approach, which vary depending on the nature of the group. We've found that the micro-to-macro sequencing tends to work best for intact groups that already have a common base of knowledge (whether from reading assignments, previous sessions in an ongoing course, or the group's shared culture that has included talking about class outside of the course/workshop). Macro-to-micro sequencing tends to work best for shorter sessions with new groups in which participants don't know each other, have not completed pre-reading, and/or have little shared experience to draw upon.

BRINGING IT ALL TOGETHER

Whether the course/workshop starts with macro-level analysis or micro-level personal testimonials, there will come a point when the levels come together and participants are asked to generate examples at all levels and/or of various types and to recognize the connections among the different manifestations. Facilitators face pedagogical decisions about how much to rely on the group's own knowledge, how much to insert new information, and how to integrate the two.

Because this social justice approach to classism may present a new framework for many people, some participants may initially be unable to generate examples. It is not that they are unfamiliar with the manifestations of classism but rather that they may be unused to thinking of them *as* classism or unused to thinking of class inequality or devaluation as problematic. It can be helpful for facilitators to seed the discussion with some examples. Examples could be manifestations of classism and/or other systems of oppression. In some cases the latter may be even more generative: when participants see an example that they recognize immediately and obviously as racist, sexist, or heterosexist (for example), it may lead them to think of parallel or related manifestations of classism that would not otherwise have occurred to them.

FACILITATOR PREPARATION

Even with the best design, there is some individual work that every facilitator will need to do in order to facilitate classism effectively. In particular, it is important that facilitators explore their own hot buttons on issues of classism and class as well as their assumptions about their own and participants' class positions. Ideally facilitators should develop this self-awareness in conversation with one or more co-facilitators or colleagues.

Similarly, all our preparation and design cannot keep classism out of the classroom. Even as we articulate and explore the many manifestations of classism, we can count on it manifesting in the course/workshop. At the very least, facilitators should be aware of such manifestations and seek to mitigate their impact on participants. In some contexts, facilitators may choose to draw attention to the classism in the room as a teachable moment, to enrich the discussion with real-life, real-time examples. Such discussions can be challenging to facilitate precisely because they are so "real" and present; for the same reason, they can be among the most powerful learning moments of a workshop/course.

Notes

* We ask that those who cite this work always acknowledge by name all of the authors listed rather than either only citing the first author or using "et al." to indicate co-authors. All collaborated on the conceptualization, development, and writing of this chapter.

1 A glossary of terms is provided on the website. ★

2 The Supreme Court's ruling in *Citizens United v. Federal Election Commission* (2010) directly rolled back longstanding, anti-corruption campaign finance restrictions and has resulted in an undemocratic and disproportionate influence of wealthy donors, special interest groups/Super PACs, and corporations on elections (Callahan & Cha, 2013; Collins & Yeskel, 2005; Hacker & Pierson, 2010; Weiner, 2015).

3 The term *Latinx* moves to end the gendered distinctions embedded within the Spanish language, replacing *Latino* or *Latina* with a singular term to refer to all genders. The term's use is contested and discussed in this volume's preface.

4 A more detailed version of this section is available on the website. ★

5 Organizing for fairer economic and business practices was not only in the cities—a parallel movement of farmers similarly responded to the impacts of economic downturns. See Nineteenth Century Farmer Organizing on the website for some examples. ★

6 A more detailed version of this section is available on the website. ★ ★

7 This figure includes only those serving state or federal prison sentences, not people serving short sentences in local jails or in pretrial detention, immigration detention, juvenile detention, etc. The total figure is around 2.3 million at any one time, with many more incarcerated for short periods during the year (Sawyer & Wagner, 2020).

8 A similar pattern occurred in 2020–2021, when the US's wealthiest around 700 people gained $1.8 trillion dollars over 17 months while millions of other people lost their jobs (Collins, 2021) and spent down any savings they might have had to keep up with living expenses.

9 Although the empirical research on gendered labor is almost always framed in a binary way, we can extend a gendered analysis of household labor to look at how specific gender roles—within and beyond the binary gender system—influence who tends to take on different kinds of care work and whose work tends to be acknowledged within households and communities.

10 Although the word *trafficking* tends to evoke the idea of sex trafficking, domestic workers are the largest group of people trafficked in the U.S. (National Domestic Workers Alliance, 2021a). The rhetoric of sex trafficking has been co-opted by anti-sex-work political interests and applied broadly to further criminalize sex workers.

   Some scholars and activists argue that the term *trafficking* is no longer useful because it lumps together such a wide variety of situations that require different responses (Berlatzky, 2015).

References

Allan, J., Ozga, J., & Smith, G. (Eds.) (2009). *Social capital, professionalism and diversity*. Rotterdam, The Netherlands: Sense Publishers.

Apple, M. W. (Ed.) (2010). *Global crises, social justice, and education*. New York: Routledge.

Associated Press. (2020, June 26). Farm workers strike after they see on TV that dozens of coworkers have coronavirus. Retrieved from https://www.nbclosangeles.com/news/coronavirus/california-farm-workers-coronavirus-strike/2386113/

Barshay, J. (2020, June). *A decade of research on the rich-poor divide in education*. The Hechinger Report. Retrieved from https://hechingerreport.org/a-decade-of-research-on-the-rich-poor-divide-in-education/

Bartlett, D. L., & Steele, J. B. (1994). *America: Who really pays the taxes?* New York: Simon & Schuster.

Berlatzky, N. (2015, October 30). "Human trafficking" has become a meaningless term. *The New Republic*. Retrieved from https://newrepublic.com/article/123302/human-trafficking-has-become-meaningless-term

Biddle, B., & Berliner, D. C. (2002, May). A research synthesis: Unequal school funding in the United States. *Beyond Instructional Leadership, 59*(8), 48–59.

Bishaw, A. (2013, September). *Poverty 2000–2012: American Community Survey Briefs, ACSBR/12–01*. US Census Bureau pdf.

Bourdieu, P. (1984). *Distinction: A social critique of the judgement of taste*. London: Routledge.

Bourdieu, P. (1986). The forms of capital. In J. Richardson (Ed.), *Handbook of theory and research for the sociology of education* (pp. 241–258). New York, NY: Greenwood Press.

Boushey, H. (2014, October 15). Understanding economic inequality and growth at the top of the income ladder. *The Washington Center for Equitable Growth*. Retrieved from http://equitablegrowth.org/research/economic-inequality-growth-top-income-ladder/

Brodkin [Sacks], K. (1998). *How Jews became white folks & what that says about race in America*. New Brunswick, NJ: Rutgers University Press

Bureau of Labor Statistics (BLS). (2014, January 24). *Union membership summary*. Retrieved from http://www.bls.gov/news.release/pdf/union2.pdf

Burnham, L., & Theodore, N. (2012). *Home Economics: The Invisible and Unregulated World of Domestic Work*. New York: National Domestic Workers Alliance.

Byrd, N. Z. (2009). The dirty side of domestic work: An underground economy and the exploitation of undocumented workers. *DePaul J. Soc. Just., 3*, 245.

Callahan, D., & Cha, M. J. (2013). Stacked deck: How the dominance of politics by the affluent & business undermines economic mobility in America. Retrieved from http://www.demos.org

California Newsreel. (2008). *Backgrounders from the unnatural causes health equity database*. Retrieved from https://unnaturalcauses.org/assets/uploads/file/primers.pdf

Campbell, E. (2019, August 7). Poverty speaks: Making tough choices. The Center for Community Solutions. Retrieved from https://www.communitysolutions.com/poverty-speaks-making-tough-choices/

Chapple, K., & Thomas, T. (2021). *Urban displacement project*. Berkeley, CA: UDP.

Ciment, J. (2013). Citizens United V. Federal Election Commission (2010). In R. Chapman, & J. Ciment (Eds.), *Culture wars in America: An encyclopedia of issues, viewpoints, and voices* (2nd ed.). Routledge. Credo Reference: http://ezproxy.cul.columbia.edu/login?qurl=https%3A%2F%2Fsearch.credoreference.com%2Fcontent%2Fentry%2Fsharpecw%2Fcitizens_united_v_federal_election_commission_2010%2F0%3FinstitutionId%3D1878

Collins, C. (2012). *99 to 1: How wealth inequality is wrecking the world and what we can do about it*. San Francisco: Berrett-Koehler Publishers.

Collins, C. (2014, December 15). Echoing in the streets: A growing racial wealth divide. Retrieved from http://www.huffingtonpost.com/chuck-collins/echoing-in-the-streets-a-_b_6319740.html

Collins, C. (2021, August 23). Updates: Billionaire wealth, US job losses, and pandemic profiteers. *Inequality.org*. Retrieved from https://inequality.org/great-divide/updates-billionaire-pandemic/

Collins, C., & Yeskel, F. (2005). *Economic apartheid in America* (2nd ed.). New York: The New Press.

Cookson, P. W. (2013). *Class rules: Exposing inequality in American high schools*. New York: Teacher's College Press.

Covert, B. (2021, May 17). How teachers fought for their safety in the pandemic—and won. *The Nation*. Retrieved from https://www.thenation.com/article/society/teachers-unions-covid-pandemic/

Daniels, R. (2002). *Coming to America: A History of Immigration and Ethnicity in American Life*. Perennial.

Domhoff, G. W. (1983). *Who rules America now? A view for the '80s*. New York: Simon & Schuster.

Dreher, A. (2006). IMF and economic growth: The effects of programs, loans, and compliance with conditionality. *World Development, 34*(5), 769–788.

Ehrenberg, R. G., Zhang, L., & Levin, J. M. (2006). Crafting a class: The trade-off between merit scholarships and enrolling lower-income students. *The Review of Higher Education, 29*(2), 195–211.

Emelech, Y. (2008). *Transmitting inequality: Wealth and the American family*. Lanham, MD: Rowman & Littlefield.

Espenshade, T., & Radford, A. W. (2009). *No longer separate, not yet equal: Race and class in elite college admission and campus life*. Princeton, NJ: Princeton University Press.

Fair Labor Standards Act of 1938 (FLSA). (1938, June 25). 1938, ch. 676, 52 Stat. 1060 (29 U.S.C. 201 et seq.) Short title, see 29 U.S.C.201. Retrieved from http://www.law.cornell.edu/topn/fair_labor_standards_act_of_1938

Fair Labor Standards Act (FLSA) Amendments of 1966. Pub. L. 89–601, Sept. 23, 1966, 80 Stat. 830. Short title, see 29 U.S.C.201 note.

Fiske, S. T., & Markus, H. R. (Eds.). (2012). *Facing social class. How societal rank influences interaction*. New York: Russell Sage Foundation.

Foner, E. (1998). *The story of American freedom*. New York: Norton & Co.

Fry, R., & Kochhar, R. (2014, December 12). *Wealth inequality has widened along racial, ethnic lines since end of Great Recession*. Retrieved from http://www.pewresearch.org/fact-tank/2014/12/12/racial-wealth-gaps-great-recession/

Garcia, J., Lardner, J., & Zeldin, C. (2008). *Up to our eyeballs: How shady lenders and failed economic policies are drowning Americans in debt*. New Press.

Gonzalez, O. (2021, June 9). *Colombia: Egregious police abuses against protesters*. Human Rights Watch. Retrieved from https://www.hrw.org/news/2021/06/09/colombia-egregious-police-abuses-against-protesters#

Gorski, P. C. (2005). Savage unrealities: Uncovering classism in Ruby Payne's framework. EdChange Working Paper. Retrieved from http://www.edchange. org/publications/Savage_Unrealities.pdf

Gorski, P. C., & Scherer, M. (2016). *On poverty and learning: Readings from educational leadership*. ASCD.

Guglielmo, J., & Salerno, S. (2003). *Are Italians White? How race is made in America*. New York: Routledge.

Hacker, J., & Pierson, P. (2010). *Winner-take-all politics: How Washington made the rich richer—and turned its back on the middle class*. New York: Simon & Schuster.

Haycock, K., Lynch, M., & Engle, J. (2010). *Opportunity adrift: Our flagship universities are straying from their public mission*. Education Trust.

Heiliger, E. (2015). Queer economies: Possibilities of queer desire and economic bodies (because 'the economy' is not enough). In N. Dhawan, A. Engel, C. Holzhey, & V. Woltersdorff (Eds.) *Global Justice and Desire: Queering Economy* (pp. 195–212). London: Routledge.

Heitzeg, N. (2009). Education or incarceration: Zero tolerance policies and the school to prison pipeline. *Forum on Public Policy Online: A Journal of the Oxford Round Table, 5*(2), 1–21.

Henwood, D. (2003). *After the new economy*. New York: New Press.

Hilgers, L. (2019). *Out of the Shadows*. The New York Times Magazine. Retrieved from https://www.nytimes.com/interactive/2019/02/21/magazine/national-domestic-workers-alliance.html

Holland, M. M. (2019). *Divergent paths to college*. New Brunswick: Rutgers University Press.

Holton, W. (2021). *Liberty is Sweet: The Forgotten History of the American Revolution*. Simon & Schuster.

Hopkins, L. (2014). *Beyond the Pearly Gates: White, Low-Income Student Experiences at Elite Colleges*. Doctoral Dissertations 2014–current. Paper 96. Retrieved from http://scholarworks.umass.edu/dissertations_2/96

Hunter, D. (n.d.) Break the rules: How ground rules can hurt us. Retrieved from http://www.trainingforchange.org/publications/break-rules-how-ground-rules-can-hurt-us. Philadelphia, PA: Training for Change.

Ignatiev, N. (1995). *How the Irish became White*. New York: Routledge.

Jack, A. A. (2019). *The privileged poor*. Harvard University Press.

Jensen, B. (2012). *Reading classes: On culture and classism in America*. Ithaca, NY: Cornell University Press.

Jock, K. (2019, April 26). The United States has a hostile architecture problem: Is public space becoming private? *INSP News*.

Kandel, W. (2008). Profile of hired farmworkers, a 2008 update (Economic Research Report Number 60) [Electronic version]. Washington, DC: Economic Research Service, United States Department of Agriculture. Retrieved from http://digitalcommons.ilr.cornell.edu/key_workplace/559

Kaufka, K. (2003). The commodification of domestic care: Illegitimacy of care work and the exploitation of migrant workers. *Geo. Immigr. LJ*, *18*, 159.

Kelley, R. D. G. (2017, January 1). What did Cedric Robinson mean by racial capitalism? *Boston Review*. Retrieved from http://bostonreview.net/race/robin-d-g-kelley-what-did-cedric-robinson-mean-racial-capitalism

Kochhar, R., Fry, R., & Taylor, P. (2011, July 26). *Wealth gaps rise to record highs between whites, blacks, Hispanics*. Retrieved from http://www.pewsocialtrends.org/2011/07/26/wealth-gaps-rise-to-record-highs-between-whites-blacks-hispanics/

Korten, D. C. (2010). *Agenda for a new economy from phantom wealth to real wealth*. San Francisco: Berrett-Koehler Publishers.

Kozol, J. (2012). *Savage inequalities: Children in America's schools*. Crown.

Ladson-Billings, G. (2017). "Makes me wanna holler": Refuting the "culture of poverty" discourse in urban schooling. *The ANNALS of the American Academy of Political and Social Science*, *673*(1), 80–90.

Lakey, G. (2010). *Facilitating Group Learning: Strategies for Success with Diverse Adult Learners*. San Francisco, CA: Jossey Bass.

Lamont, M. (2000). *The Dignity of the Working Men: Morality and the Boundaries of Race, Class, and Immigration*. Russell Sage.

Lareau, A. (1987). Social class differences in family-school relationships: The importance of cultural capital. *Sociology of Education*, *60*, 73–85.

Lareau, A. (2011). *Unequal childhoods: Class, race and family life*, 2nd Edition. Los Angeles, CA: University of California Press.

Lareau, A., & Conley, D. (2008). *Social class: How does it work?* New York: Russell Sage Foundation.

Lareau, A., & Calarco, J. M. (2012). Class, cultural capital, and institutions: The case of families and schools. In S. T. Fiske & H. R. Markus (Eds.) (2012). *Facing social class. How societal rank influences interaction*, pp. 61–86. New York: Russell Sage Foundation.

Lavelle, R. (1995). *America's new war on poverty: A reader for action*. San Francisco: Blackside KQED Books & Tapes.

Leondar-Wright, B. (2014). *Missing Class: Strengthening Social Movement Groups by Seeing Class Cultures*. Ithaca, NY: Cornell University Press.

Leondar-Wright, B., & Yeskel, F. (2007). Classism Curriculum Design. In *Teaching for Diversity and Social Justice* (pp. 309–333). New York: Routledge.

Lipsitz, G. (1998). *The possessive investment in Whiteness: How white people profit from identity politics*. Philadelphia: Temple University Press.

Lui, M., Robles, B., Leondar-Wright, B., Brewer, R., & Adamson, R. (2006). *The color of wealth: The story behind the U.S. racial wealth divide*. New York: New Press.

Mantsios, G. (Ed.) (1998). *A new labor movement for the new century*. New York: Monthly Review Press.

Martin, C., Boser, U., Benner, M., & Baffour, P. (2018). *A quality approach to school funding*. Retrieved from https://www.americanprogress.org/issues/education-k-12/reports/2018/11/13/460397/quality-approach-school-funding/

Mathews, D. (2019, August 22). The big new plan to save unions endorsed by Bernie Sanders and Pete Buttigieg, explained. *Vox*. Retrieved from https://www.vox.com/policy-and-politics/2019/8/22/20826642/mary-kay-henry-seiu-sectoral-bargaining

Matos, J. (2011, January 1). *Fulfilling Their Dreams: Latina/o College Student Narratives on the Impact of Parental Involvement on Their Academic Engagement*. Doctoral Dissertations Available from Proquest. Paper AAI3465047.

McNamee, S. J., & Miller, Jr., R. K. (2004). *The meritocracy myth*. New York: Rowman & Littlefield.

McNicholas, C., Rhinehart, M., Poydock, L., Shierholz, H., & Perez, D. (2020). *Why unions are good for workers—especially in a crisis like COVID-19*. Report from Economic Policy Institute. Retrieved from https://files.epi.org/pdf/204014.pdf

Miller, K. (2007). *Designs on the Public: The Private Lives of New York's Public Spaces*. University of Minnesota Press. Retrieved from https://manifold.umn.edu/projects/designs-on-the-public

Mitrani, S. (2015, January 6). The police were created to control working class and poor people, not serve and protect. *In These Times*. Retrieved from https://inthesetimes.com/article/police-and-poor-people

Mishel, L., Bernstein, J., & Allegretto, S. (2007). *The state of working America: 2006/2007*. Ithaca, NY: Cornell University Press.

Mohr, J., & DiMaggio, P. (1995). The intergenerational transmission of cultural capital. *Research in Social Stratification and Mobility*, *14*, 169–200.

Moynihan, D. P. (1965). *The Negro Family: The Case for National Action*, Washington, DC: Office of Policy Planning and Research, US Department of Labor.

National Domestic Workers Alliance (2021a). *Human Trafficking at Home: Labor Trafficking of Domestic Workers*. Retrieved from https://www.domesticworkers.org/wp-content/uploads/2021/05/Human_Trafficking_at_Home_Labor_Trafficking_of_Domestic_Workers.pdf

National Domestic Workers Alliance. (2021b). Retrieved from https://www.domesticworkers.org/programs-and-campaigns/developing-policy-solutions/bill-of-rights

National Labor Relations Act ("NLRA"). *29 U.S.C. §§ 151–169*. (1935, July 5).

Nelson, R., & Ayers, E. (Eds.) (n.d.). *Mapping inequality*. American Panorama. Retrieved from https://dsl.richmond.edu/panorama/redlining/

Ng, J. C., & Rury, J. L. (2006). *Poverty and Education: A critical analysis of the Ruby Payne phenomenon*. Teachers College Record. Retrieved from http://www.tcrecord.org

Nicholson, P. Y. (2004). *Labor's story in the United States*. Philadelphia: Temple University Press.

Patterson, J. T. (2010). *Freedom is not enough: The Moynihan Report and America's struggle over black family life from LBJ to Obama*. New York: Basic Books.

Payne, R. K. (1995). *A Framework for Understanding Poverty*. Baytown, TX: RFT.

Phillips, K. (1990). *The politics of rich and poor: Wealth and the American electorate in the Reagan aftermath*. New York: HarperCollins.

Piketty, T. (2014). *Capital in the twenty-first century*. Cambridge, MA: Harvard University Press.

Piketty, T., & Saez, E. (2003). Income inequality in the United States, 1913–1998. *Quarterly Journal of Economics*, *118*(1), 1–39. Data updated to 2018 in January, 2020. Retrieved from http://eml.berkeley.edu/~saez/

Ranji, U., Frederiksen, B., Salganicoff, A., & Long, M. (2021). Women, work and family during COVID-19: Findings from the KFF Women's Health Survey. Kaiser Family Foundation. Retrieved from https://www.kff.org/womens-health-policy/issue-brief/women-work-and-family-during-covid-19-findings-from-the-kff-womens-health-survey/

Rappeport, A., & Flitter, E. (2018, May 22). Congress Approves First Big Dodd-Frank Rollback. *New York Times*.

Reich, R. B. (2007). *Supercapitalism: The transformation of business, democracy, and everyday life*. New York: Random House.

Roberts, D. E. (1999). *Killing the black body: Race, reproduction, and the meaning of liberty*. Vintage.

Roediger, D. R. (1991). *The wages of Whiteness, revised ed*. London: Verso.

Rothstein, R. (2017). *The color of law: A forgotten history of how our government segregated America*. W.W. Norton & Company.

Sawyer, W., & Wagner, P. (2020, March 24). *Mass Incarceration: The Whole Pie 2020*. Prison Policy Initiative. Retrieved from https://www.prisonpolicy.org/factsheets/pie2020_allimages.pdf

Semega, J., Kollar, M., Shrider, E. A., & Creamer, J. F. (2020). US Census Bureau, Current Population Reports, P60–270, Income and Poverty in the United States: 2019. US Government Publishing Office. Retrieved from https://www.census.gov/content/dam/Census/library/publications/2020/demo/p60-270.pdf

The Sentencing Project. (2021). *Trends in US corrections*. Retrieved from https://www.sentencingproject.org/wp-content/uploads/2021/07/Trends-in-US-Corrections.pdf

Sherman, A. (2016). *After 1996 welfare law, a weaker safety net and more children in deep poverty*. Center on Budget and Policy Priorities. Retrieved from https://www.cbpp.org/research/family-income-support/after-1996-welfare-law-a-weaker-safety-net-and-more-children-in-deep

Shierholz, H., & Mishel, L. (2013, August 21). A decade of flat wages: The key barrier to shared prosperity and a rising middle class. Retrieved from http://www.epi.org/publication/a-decade-of-flat-wages-the-key-barrier-to-shared-prosperity-and-a-rising-middle-class/

Shlasko, D., & Kramer, T. (2011). Class Culture and Classism in Campus and Community Organizing. Presentation at *Pedagogies of Privilege Conference*, University of Denver.

Smith, L. (2010). *Psychology, poverty, and the end of social exclusion: Putting our practice to work*. New York: Teachers College Press.

Smith, L., & Redington, R. (2010). Class dismissed: Making the case for the study of classist microaggressions. In D. W. Sue (Ed.), *Microaggressions and marginality: Manifestations, dynamics, and impact*. Hoboken, NJ: Wiley.

Spade, D. (2020). *Mutual aid: Building solidarity during this crisis (and the next)*. Verso Books.

Steinberg, S. (1989). *The ethnic myth: Race, ethnicity, and class in America*. Boston: Beacon.

Streib, J. (2013). Class origin and college graduates' parenting beliefs. *The Sociological Quarterly*, *54*, 670–693.

Swartz, D. (1997). *Culture and power: The sociology of Pierre Bourdieu*. University of Chicago Press.

Swift, J. (2014, May 31). Hipsters and the co-option of White poverty culture. *Thought Catalog*. Retrieved from https://thoughtcatalog.com/james-swift/2014/05/hipsters-and-the-co-option-of-white-poverty-culture/

Talamo, L., & Hoang, M. (2020). Thursday sees 7th strike by Yakima Valley farmworkers protesting conditions during Covid-19 pandemic. *Yakima Herald*. Retrieved from https://www.yakimaherald.com/special_projects/coronavirus/thursday-sees-7th-strike-by-yakima-valley-farmworkers-protesting-conditions-during-covid-19-pandemic/article_6bcee867–37b0–5ae0-a065-ccfcd594ef9a.html

Takaki, R. (1993). *A different mirror: A history of multicultural America*. Boston: Little Brown.

Tanzi, A., & Saraiva, C. (2021). US suffers sharpest rise in poverty rate in more than 50 years. *Bloomberg News* 2021, January 25. Retrieved from https://www.bloomberg.com/news/articles/2021-01-25/u-s-suffers-sharpest-rise-in-poverty-rate-in-more-than-50-years

Taussig, D. (04/15/2021). *What we mean by the American dream: Stories we tell about meritocracy*. ILR Press.

Tikkanan, R., & Abrams, M. (2020). U.S. Health Care from a Global Perspective, 2019: Higher Spending, Worse Outcomes? *The Commonwealth Fund*. Retrieved from https://www.commonwealthfund.org/publications/issue-briefs/2020/jan/us-health-care-global-perspective-2019

Tomlinson, S. A. (2005). No New Orleanians left behind: An examination of the disparate impact of Hurricane Katrina on minorities. *Conn. L. Rev.*, *38*, 1153.

Traub, A., Reutchlin, C., Sullivan, L., Meschede, T., Dietrich, L., & Shapiro, T. (2015, March 11). *The racial wealth gap: Why policy matters*. Retrieved from http://www.demos.org/sites/default/files/publications/RacialWealthGap_1.pdf

UNI Global Union. (2018, July 18). UNI condemns violence against Spanish Amazon strikers. *UNI Global Union*. Retrieved from https://www.uniglobalunion.org/news/uni-condemns-violence-against-spanish-amazon-strikers

Vallas, R., & Slevin, J. (2016). Everything you wanted to know about the 1996 welfare law but were afraid to ask. *Talk Poverty*. Retrieved from https://talkpoverty.org/2016/08/22/everything-wanted-know-1996-welfare-law-afraid-ask/

Van Gelder, S. (Ed.) (2011). *This changes everything: Occupy Wall Street and the 99% movement*. San Francisco: Berrett-Koehler Publishers.

Weiner, D. (2015, January 15). *Citizens united five years later*. Brennan Center for Justice. Retrieved from https://www.brennancenter.org/our-work/research-reports/citizens-united-five-years-later

Williams, B. (2001). What's debt got to do with it? In J. Goode & J. Maskovsky (Eds.), *The new poverty studies: The ethnography of power, politics, and impoverished people in the United States* (pp. 79–101). New York: New York University Press.

Williams, J. C. (2012). The class culture gap. In S. T. Fiske & H. R. Markus (Eds.), *Facing social class. How societal rank influences interaction*, pp. 39–58. New York: Russell Sage Foundation.

Wilson, W. J. (2009, January). The Moynihan report and research on the black community. *Annals of the American Academy of Political and Social Science*, *621*, 23–36.

Wolff, E. (2009). *Poverty and income distribution*. New York: Wiley Blackwell.

Yosso, T. (1996). Whose culture has capital? A critical race theory discussion of community cultural wealth. In A. Dixson & C. Rousseau (Eds.), *Critical race theory in education: All God's children gotta song*. New York: Routledge.

Yosso, T. J. (2005). Whose culture has capital? A critical race theory discussion of community cultural wealth. *Race Ethnicity and Education*, *8*(1), 69–91.

Young, I. M. (1990). *Justice and the politics of difference*. Princeton: Princeton University Press.

Zinn, H. (2015). *A people's history of the United States: 1492–present*. London: Routledge.

8

Religious Oppression

Maurianne Adams, Marcella Runell Hall, Abdul-Rahman Jaradat, and Hind Mari*

As we finalize this chapter in a time of anxiety and uncertainty created by multiple catastrophes in the U.S. and around the world—pandemic, economic crisis, climate crisis, evictions and foreclosures, uncertainty about democratic institutions holding firm—it is impossible to predict what kind of world our readers will be living in. But it seems fairly certain that U.S. Christian hegemony will have become even more firmly intertwined with U.S. identity and nationalism, unless religious pluralism becomes a stronger part of growing social justice movements. It also appears that the hostility posed by U.S. Christian nationalists to two religions wrongly perceived as opposed to Christianity—Islam and Judaism—might well increase.

The resurgence of overt white nationalism and Christian fundamentalism following the elections of 2016 have stunned many Americans, but it is not surprising to those familiar with the extensive history of U.S. and European antisemitism and Islamophobia. Many people do not understand how deeply the hostility toward Jews and Muslims intertwined with the emergence of a Christian Europe, and how ideas of Christian supremacy were central to colonization of the Americas. An appreciation of this long history helps us understand how religious diversity may feel threatening for those whose faith and politics reject pluralism and seek stability in a (mythic) past of uniformity by which they hope to "make America great again" (Tumulty, 2017).

Recent violence against religiously marginalized communities in the U.S. has targeted not only Jews, Muslims, and Indigenous communities but also appears in vandalism against Hindu temples, murders of Sikhs, and slurs against atheists and agnostics. These attacks lead us to ask: How is it that religious differences impact our sense of national identity? Why do some Americans believe that Hindus, Muslims, and Sikhs pose a threat to the American way of life? Why are atheists and agnostics considered immoral or unpatriotic? To answer these questions, we explore the unending historical debate about U.S. national and religious identity and who is included or excluded from the protections offered by the First Amendment to the Constitution and the "separation of church and state."

In this chapter, we treat the centrality of Christianity to U.S. nationalism as a social justice issue that requires the kind of historical, structural, and cultural analysis we use to understand other forms of advantage and disadvantage. To understand the role of religion in U.S. cultural, social, and political life, we examine how Protestant Christianity initially served the needs of the dominant religious, ethnic, and racialized U.S. majority, thereby ensuring their maintenance of institutional and cultural power. We explore the contradictions that the resulting religious advantage and disadvantage create within U.S. understandings of religious freedom. We examine the historical legacies that survive in current manifestations of Christian hegemony and their intersections with other forms of oppression in the U.S. We then raise some of the key concerns for religious pluralism as a form of social justice, including interfaith organizing as well as the need to provide space for those who identify as agnostic, atheist, non-believers,[1] rationalists, secular humanists, or "nothing in particular."

DOI: 10.4324/9781003005759-10

The chapter concludes with a design for teaching about Christian hegemony and religious oppression, with discussion of pedagogical and facilitation issues. Materials and activities that support the design can be found on the website for this chapter.

★

DEFINITIONS OF KEY CONCEPTS

Religious oppression in the U.S. refers to the systematic subordination of minority religious groups such as agnostics and atheists, Buddhists, Hindus, Jews, Muslims, Sikhs, Indigenous practitioners of their traditional spiritualities, and people with no religious or spiritual affiliation. The subordination of non-Christian beliefs and practices occurs at all levels of society through the actions of individuals, institutional policies and practices, and cultural and societal norms and values that privilege Christianity (Joshi, 2020).

Hegemony generally refers to a society's unacknowledged and unconscious adherence to a dominant worldview through assumed cultural norms and practices whose maintenance depends not on any special effort but on "business as usual." In the U.S., *Christian hegemony* refers to widely held and reinforced Christian norms that are accepted as intrinsic to our national identity, even as a test of patriotism, and valued over the beliefs and practices of non-Christian people, including those belonging to other religions and those who do not believe in or identify with any organized religion. Some key examples of Christian hegemony in the U.S. are the dominance of Christian observances, holy days, and places of worship (Kivel, 2013, pp. 2–36).

Christian privilege refers to the social and cultural advantages held by Christians in the U.S. relative to non-Christians. Having *privilege* with respect to normative Christianity means benefiting from "the assumptions underlying institutional rules and the collective consequences of following those rules" (Young, 1990, p. 41). Christian privilege is generally unacknowledged by those who hold it because it is maintained through pervasive, largely invisible cultural norms (Blumenfeld, 2006; Joshi, 2006, 2020; Schlosser, 2003).

Whereas *Christian privilege* refers mainly to advantages experienced at the individual or institutional level, *Christian normativity* refers to the widely held and enforced norms, traditions, and belief systems that characterize this advantage at the societal level. Throughout this chapter we provide examples of how law and policy, and the norms, traditions, and assumptions behind them, benefit Christians and marginalize, harm, or disadvantage non-Christians.

OUR APPROACH

Our social justice approach examines religious oppression as one of the many ways that people are categorized by the larger society, resulting in group and individual advantage or disadvantage. A social justice approach to religious oppression emphasizes structural and systemic patterns of inequality based on religious group memberships reproduced through interlocking social institutions and culture.

This approach to religious oppression draws upon sociological, legal, and historical lenses. We analyze U.S. history and current manifestations of religious oppression to show the formative role of mainstream Protestant Christian culture in defining U.S. national identity. We use a sociological analysis to describe pervasive religious values, beliefs, and policies within U.S. culture, institutions, and social systems (Fox, 2000; Johnstone, 2004). We explore constitutional protections of religion in light of their mixed history of legal interpretations, which continue to shift today.

It is not our purpose to consider what specific religious beliefs mean to individual believers or to compare different religious beliefs, theologies, or practices. Questions of faith and belief are deeply personal and important for many people, and religious beliefs often do not easily fit into discussions of how social systems function to advantage one group and disadvantage others. Only those beliefs that are part of the fabric of prejudice, discrimination, and oppression toward members of non-dominant religions will be discussed, because maintenance of the religious "other" as "outsider" is one way in which religious oppression operates. In this chapter, we examine religious privilege and oppression at the *individual, institutional, and cultural/societal* levels and explore how these manifestations of *Christian hegemony* have historically reinforced and reproduced each other and how they persist in the present day.

We also pay attention to the intersections of religion with race, sexuality, gender, ethnicity, national origin, and other categories of social difference that are often used to justify inequality. An important aspect of the intersection of religion with race in the U.S. appears in the process of *racialization* or *racial formation* (Omi & Winant, 2014; Zarrugh, 2016). Racialization describes the processes by which ethnic or national groups come to be categorized into racial groups, including the racial categorization of northern European ethnicities (such as British, German, or Scandinavian) as white and peoples of Asian, African, Indigenous, and Arab ethnicities as Black or brown. The *racialization of U.S. religions* relates to minority religions whose members' religious identities are assumed to be connected to their racial identities, such as Hinduism (South Asian), Islam (Arab or "Middle Eastern"),[2] and Sikhism (South Asian). At the same time, the white identity of U.S. European Christian Americans goes unnoticed because it is assumed to be the norm. (The religious segregation of Black Christians and other BIPOC[3] Christian groups are more complex and will be examined later in this chapter.) By this process of dual religious and racial categorization, the racialization of religion reinforces the marginalization of groups that are both non-Christian and non-white (Goldschmidt & McAlister, 2004). As Husain (2017) argues, "Because religion was racialized at the inception of the race concept, our empirical work would do well to track how and to what end religion continues to be racialized today rather than analyzing if it is racialized today" (p. 4).

HISTORICAL LEGACIES OF CHRISTIAN HEGEMONY AND RELIGIOUS OPPRESSION IN THE U.S.

It is difficult to grasp the intensity and longevity of antisemitism and Islamophobia in the U.S. without examining their historical legacies in Europe and in European colonization, including in the Americas. The centuries of religious and racial antagonism of European Christians toward Jews and Muslims formed a dichotomy between believers and unbelievers, civilized and uncivilized, Christians and pagans/heretics. This dichotomy shaped the religious and racial attitudes of a militarily dominant Christian colonizing force upon the Indigenous peoples they encountered in Africa, Asia, and the Americas.

Two formative global historical legacies inform our understanding of contemporary Christian hegemony. The first is rooted in the world of early European Christianity, during which an emerging Christian population and bureaucracy (both in Rome and in the

Byzantine Empire) developed hostility toward the Jews and Muslims living within Europe. The second involves the long-term negative consequences of the Crusades and their outgrowth into violent Christian-justified colonialism in Asia, Africa, and the Americas. Both of these global historical legacies laid the foundations for U.S. hegemonic Christianity. The foundation of U.S. national identity comes largely from European settler colonialism and European (until the 1960s) immigration, and nearly all of these European settlers and immigrants were Christian (whether Protestant or Catholic). The persistence of antisemitic and Islamophobic tropes in the U.S. (as well as in Europe), and the colonial violence against Indigenous people justified by reference to Christianity, can be understood only as a continuation of the hatred, stereotyping, and exploitation of Jews and Muslims (and earlier, pagans) in Europe.

ANTISEMITISM AND ISLAMOPHOBIA IN EUROPE[4]

European Christianity emerged officially in the year 313, when Christianity was legalized by the Roman emperor Constantine. The persecution of Christians ended, and Roman Catholicism competed with the Eastern Church in Constantinople to become the center of the universal church. From the outset, European Catholicism marked Jews and Muslims as enemies of the "one true faith." Jewish people posed an internal theological and psychological threat to Christianity through their refusal to accept the Christian Messiah. They also posed an economic threat through their access to trade. Islam was perceived as a threat due to the competing ambitions of Christian and Muslim nations to consolidate control of regions on the western, eastern, and southern borders of Europe.

On the eastern frontier of Europe, Muslims took control of Jerusalem, Constantinople, and at times parts of eastern Europe such as Hungary and Sicily. Christian Europe responded with a series of military Crusades to retake Jerusalem. The two centuries of Crusades from 1096 until 1271 live on in Christian mythology as grand, heroic, and successful efforts to regain the Holy Lands. In actuality, they were largely unsuccessful and often benefited Christian elites at the expense of common people (Christian, Jewish, and Muslim) pillaged by crusaders along the way (Shepkaru, 2012).

As the Crusades wound down, ruling Christian elites turned their attention to religious heresies within Europe. Martin Luther and protesting (Protestant) groups, fed up with corruption within the Catholic Church, created competing Lutheran and Protestant principalities. These conflicts over several centuries shaped the Catholic and Protestant nation-states of Europe, who shared a Christian European identity, but with important differences of local identity, theology, and religious organization. Yet all inherited what seemed a natural hostility to Jews and Muslims, expressed as vehemently by Martin Luther as it had been by earlier Roman Catholic councils (Fredrickson, 2002; O'Shea, 2006; Reston, 2009; Shaw, 2017).

Antisemitism (hatred of Jews and Jewishness) was preached from both Catholic and Protestant pulpits. It blamed the Jews for the death of Jesus and accused them of poisoning wells, demonizing and dehumanizing them as the antichrist depicted with horns and pig's bodies. European Christians believed that Jews murdered and ate Christian babies (a fiction known as the "blood libel"), desecrated the Holy Sacrament, and caused bubonic plague. The hysteria of the blood libel was carried by European Christian immigrants to the New World, with documented accusations against U.S. Jews into the mid-20th century (Laqueur, 2006; Romero Castello & Macías Kapón, 1994; Weinberg, 1986).

In early Christian Europe, Jews were stigmatized for loaning money at interest, a practice that was forbidden by Christian doctrine as "usury" but was needed to fund Christian ventures such as the Crusades and to bankroll local authorities. In the Middle Ages in

England, Jews were allowed to lend money but prohibited from any other business dealings with Christians (Barzel, 1992), all but requiring them to engage in the very activity for which they were vilified. Jews were blamed for the economic burden of funding the Crusades and later for the economic recessions built into European capitalism.

More dangerous was the widespread belief that Jews were plotting global economic control. As capitalism and socialism became global forces, Christian capitalist power brokers blamed Jews for both. The specter of Jewish world domination was propagated by the fictional *Protocols of the Elders of Zion*, written by Russian antisemites and first published in 1903. The *Protocols* were published as nonfiction in Europe and the U.S. (Bronner, 2000; Laqueur, 2006; Perry & Schweitzer, 2008). A contemporary resurgence can be heard in the chants by white nationalists/racists at Charlottesville, Virginia, in 2017, "Jews will not replace us" (through their presumed control of global labor markets).

Not only were Jews within Christian Europe vilified on religious grounds as Christ killers, and on economic grounds as moneylenders, they were also ostracized on racial grounds as an impure, "mongrel" people. This view of Jewish "racial impurity" grew out of the Jewish diaspora, as Jews intermarried, raised families, and came to resemble the peoples among whom they settled (Fredrickson, 2002; Laqueur, 2006; Parfitt, 2013; Tamarkin, 2020). "Looking Jewish" was not a phenotype but a stereotype that reflected 19th-century pseudoscientific, fixed racial typologies.

Like antisemitism, Islamophobia (hatred of Muslims and Islam) is deeply rooted in Christian religious (and colonialist) assumptions of the superiority of West over East and of Christianity over all other religions. Islamophobia essentializes the diversity of Islamic nationalities, languages, religious sectarian affiliations, ethnicities, and cultures into a single undifferentiated and racialized religious group (Considine, 2017; Rana, 2007).

Christian European presumed superiority is affirmed through racializing religion (Bayoumi, 2015; Joshi, 2006, 2009). The racialization of "semites" (that is, Jews) as a European pseudoscientific racial category was written into law and policy (Haney-López, 2006). Rana (2007) notes that the "Muslim is constructed through a racial logic that crosses the cultural categories of nation, religion, ethnicity, and sexuality" (p. 148), and this can be said of Jews as well (Meer, 2013; Zia-Ebrahimi, 2018).

In the Middle Ages, Jews were driven out of Christian communities or segregated in walled-in neighborhoods called ghettos. In Spain, Jews and Muslims were forced to convert to Christianity or leave, and during the Inquisition, they were subjected to torture if their conversions were thought to be insincere. Kivel (2013) explains, "The Inquisitions were designed to police the boundaries of legitimate thought and behavior within Christian communities and within the psyches of individual Christians" (p. 115). Inquisition practices followed Jews and Muslims to the Americas and are echoed in modern manifestations, including the McCarthy hearings of the 1950s that targeted Jews based on doubts about the sincerity of their loyalty to the (Christian) nation and the more recent Patriot Acts passed by the U.S. Congress after 9/11 that targeted Muslims based on similar assumptions.

"Blood purity" as a test of religious and national identity in 15th-century Spain was an early instance of the intersection of racial, genealogical, and religious identities that later came to characterize race-based antisemitism and other forms of racism (Fredrickson, 2002). It was used to justify the expulsion of Jews and Muslims from the Iberian Peninsula in 1492. Jews who did not hold "certificates of birth" to document their genealogical purity as Christian (Fredrickson, 2002) and all Muslims were killed or driven out in a campaign of ethnic cleansing throughout Europe.

By the 18th and 19th centuries, religious differences were fully racialized by the pseudoscience of racial superiority that classified Aryans (whites) as superior and others (Jews,

Africans, and Asians, including Arabs) as inferior (Laqueur, 2006; Perry & Schweitzer, 2008; Wistrich, 1991). The 19th-century eugenics movements in Europe and the U.S. were vigorously antisemitic as well as anti-Arab and anti-Black (Michael, 2005). The recurrent essentializing of Jewish or Arab/Muslim "differentness" links the religious and economic antisemitism of the Middle Ages to the antisemitic racism behind the Holocaust of the 20th century (Chazan, 2016) and the virulent Islamophobia and antisemitism of today (Jotischky, 2017).

The artistic and cultural richness that emerged from Christian, Jewish, and Muslim collaborations and cross-fertilizations in pre-Inquisition Spain is seen by some scholars as a singular instance that occurred only out of necessity (Akasoy, 2010; Novikoff, 2005). Yet, relations between Muslims and Jews in the Arab world do not follow the same patterns as relations among Christians, Muslims, and Jews in Europe. Muslims and Jews forged trading partnerships across Europe, Asia, and Arabia, enabled by commonly rooted languages (Arabic and Hebrew) that were mutually intelligible. Jews lived in Muslim countries across North Africa, central Asia, and the eastern Mediterranean for 1,400 years as a subordinated, but legally protected, religious minority—not without periods of violence but also not with the unremitting patterns of forced conversion, expulsions, and genocide that characterized European antisemitism (Gilbert, 2003; Sharkey, 2017; Weinberg, 1986).

COLONIALISM, ORIENTALISM, AND EXPLOITATION

Intense competition among European powers to colonize and missionize large parts of Africa, Asia, and the Americas was a long-term consequence of Christian dominance in Europe. The colonial race for power, precious metals, and slave labor created a global racial hierarchy that went well beyond the earlier religious and racial antagonism toward Jews and Muslims. European colonialism became a worldwide enterprise involving the forcible taking of land, minerals, and people from Africa, Asia, the Arabian Peninsula, and the Americas for the enrichment of European nation-states and capitalist enterprises.

As Europeans grabbed land and oppressed people globally, a new variety of racialized religion emerged—*Orientalism*. Because European encounters with the Orient were understood in Europe to be encounters with peoples inferior and antagonistic to European civilization (Said, 1978; see also Said, 1986, 1993), it followed that Europe could exploit these peoples and their resources and appropriate their cultures as something exotic to be monetized. Orientalism was fed by "scientific racism"—the 18th- and 19th-century belief in measurable racial hierarchies. This pseudoscientific belief justified European colonial violence and oppression (Kapila, 2007). The location of "Orientals" in the racial hierarchy (above Negros and below Caucasians, except when Caucasians were seen to be dark-skinned Arabs) intersected with European views of "Oriental" religions such as Buddhism, Hinduism, Islam, and Sikhism (Kapila, 2007).

Racism and religious oppression became mutually reinforcing, virtually indistinguishable tools of colonialism in the Americas, Africa, and Asia, where indigenous peoples were classified as both racially and religiously inferior. Colonialism "in God's name" was implemented through Catholic or Protestant missions, which asserted that uncivilized, so-called heathen peoples would benefit from the imposition of a superior white Christian culture (Rana, 2011; Shohat, 2006). Religious proselytizing served as a euphemism for racial and colonial violence in order to project the illusion that Christian missionaries' hands were clean of the dirty job of military conquest and enslavement. As European explorers and adventurers encountered different "others," race first reinforced and then conveniently replaced religion as a way to establish hierarchies of human value. Some non-Christians also came to the Americas as colonists, but they did so with a precarious relationship to the ruling colonial powers, in many cases as an exploited and oppressed immigrant workforce.

Antagonism between Christian sects was likewise used as a rationale for colonization. Violent settler-colonialism in Ireland, where Irish were starved so that English and Scots-Irish landowners could export Irish food products to Europe, was justified by Protestant/Catholic antagonisms. Protestant/Catholic competition for territory also played out in "the New World" (Spanish Mexico, Florida, the U.S. Southwest, California, and French Louisiana), when the English upper class of New England "racialized" the mid-19th-century Irish immigrants as "white Negroes" (Ignatiev, 2009).

Most of us who have been taught this history likely learned about European, U.S., and global history separately, as if they occurred in totally separate timelines. By looking at the parallel and interrelated events that occurred simultaneously across continents, we can see patterns that illustrate the sweeping impact of policies predicated on the inherent superiority of Western Christianity. The global significance of 1492 is important both for the expulsion of Jews and Arab Muslims from Spain (connected with the expulsion of Arabs from western Europe and of Jews from England 200 years earlier) and because of the simultaneous explosion of European colonialism and the use of Catholic and Protestant missions as "soft" colonization. The oppression toward non-Christian "others" that had been practiced for generations in Europe was exported globally.

Likewise, the persecution, marginalization, and disenfranchisement of Jews in Europe (Middle Ages through 1940s) and Indigenous peoples in the Americas (15th century into the 20th century) were concurrent, and we can understand them better by observing their similarities. Both are accurately described by the historian Raul Hilberg's vivid summary of the long history of antisemitism (see Hilberg, 2003): "Since the fourth century after Christ there have been three anti-Jewish policies: conversion, expulsion, and annihilation" (Hilberg, 1961, p. 3). Hilberg understood that this was a cyclical, historical trend:

> The missionaries of Christianity said in effect: You have no right to live among us as Jews. The secular rulers who followed proclaimed: You have no right to live among us. The German Nazis at last decreed: You have no right to live.
>
> (Hilberg, 1961, pp. 3–4)

The deadly sequence from forced conversion and cultural erasure, to expulsion and relocation, to genocide and extermination was the same for Indigenous peoples in the U.S. as for Jews in Europe: "You can't live among us as Indians" (forced conversions), "You can't live among us" (relocations), and "You can't live" (massacre). Kivel (2013) explains that Christianity was used as a rationale for the subjugation of Indigenous peoples and African Americans as well as for the Nazi extermination of Jews. Hitler was viewed by some of his contemporaries as completing a project promoted by Martin Luther when he called on Germans to confiscate and destroy the property of Jews and kill their rabbis. "The Germans' attempted extermination of the Jews grew from the same history of sacred violence" that shaped colonial genocides (Kivel, 2013, p. 130).

U.S. anti-Muslim stereotypes are similarly rooted in Christian exceptionalism that assumed Christian capacity for democratic self-government but denied such capacity to Muslims (Feldman, 1996; Murray, 2008). Colonizing settlers brought anti-Muslim antagonism from the Old World. Stereotypes of Muslims included the view that Muslims were intrinsically violent, that Shari'a law was barbaric, and that Muslim loyalties to a caliphate undermined their capacity for democratic self-regulation or loyalty to a Christian nation—a view expressed in John Locke's highly influential 1689 "Treatise Concerning Toleration" that the "Mahometan[5] . . . acknowledges himself bound to yield blind obedience to the

Mufti[6] . . . who himself is entirely obedient to the Ottoman Emperor" (quoted in Murray, 2008, p. 91). These views justified the denial of citizenship by the U.S. legal system to Muslims in the 1920s–1960s and also motivate the current-day desecration of mosques; the burning of the Qur'an by self-righteous evangelicals; the attacks on U.S. citizens who "appear Muslim" by virtue of head coverings, beards, or dark skin; and most recently the denial of immigration status to people from countries considered predominantly Muslim (Alvarez & Don, 2011; Hafiz & Raghunathan, 2014; Mamdani, 2004; Rana, 2011).

Considering the historical pathways by which Christianity achieved domination, it can be argued that antisemitism and Islamophobia are the templates by which all other religions are deemed racially and religiously inferior—including BIPOC-specific Christian denominations. Peoples that are non-Christian and/or non-white are considered not "civilized" or worthy of the democratic self-government claimed for U.S. citizens and thus are denied the rights and advantages of white Christians who are considered the norm for the U.S. nation-state.

RELIGIOUS OPPRESSION AND CHRISTIAN HEGEMONY IN U.S. HISTORY

Protestant Hegemony in the U.S.

Protestant dominance in the U.S. resulted from the English victory in the struggle between empires in which Protestant (English) and Catholic (Spanish and French) armies wrestled for control of the colonies. The English colonies established along the Eastern Seaboard were Protestant, although colonists belonged to different Protestant sects from different parts of Europe.

The legal foundation for the U.S., which aspired to be a secular government rather than having an officially established national church like the Church of England, was based upon "an uneasy alliance between Enlightenment rationalists and evangelical Christians" (Jacoby, 2004, p. 31). Although historical accounts generally portray the colonies as religious havens for peoples persecuted elsewhere, most early U.S. religious communities were themselves theocratic and exclusive, with their own church establishments that persecuted members of other faiths and dissenters from within their communities whom they viewed as "heretics" (Ahlstrom, 2004; Fraser, 1999). The Salem witch trials in colonial Massachusetts offer an especially vicious example of religious cleansing, during which citizens accused of heresy were hanged, burned, or drowned. Accusations stemming from neighborhood feuds, class antagonism, and misogyny were pursued under the guise of religious justification and presided over by church-empowered magistrates (Adams, 2008; Boyer & Nissenbaum, 1972; Butler, Wacker, & Balmer, 2003).

U.S. history includes numerous examples of religious persecution in the name of Protestant sectarianism: against Quakers in Plymouth Colony, against Catholic and Jewish immigrants in the late 19th century, and against Mormons and Jehovah's Witnesses (Ahlstrom, 2004; Butler, Wacker, & Balmer, 2003; Wills, 2005). Religious missions to Indigenous peoples, which were supported by federal land grants and funds in violation of constitutional prohibitions against political support for religious institutions, prepared the way for forced relocation and claiming even more land (Echo-Hawk, 2010; Philbrick, 2004). Distrust of non-Protestants (including non-believers) showed up in state law: Massachusetts required that Catholics in public office renounce papal authority, while Pennsylvania allowed Jews but not atheists to hold office. Protestant domination lay behind the 19th-century creation of a nationwide network of Protestant "common [public] schools" to maintain Protestant cultural homogeneity in the face of Catholic and Jewish immigration (Fraser, 1999). For Protestants born in the U.S., other faith traditions seemed incompatible with U.S. citizenship because of their presumed dual loyalties: Catholics to the pope in Rome; Muslims to their imams, muftis, or an Islamic caliphate; and Jews to the Jewish people.

The religious freedom of the early republic was meant for Protestants, which included Congregationalists, Episcopalians, Dutch Reformed, Presbyterians, French Huguenots, Baptists, and Moravian churches as well as Quakers, Amish, and Mennonites. The small Shearith Israel congregation of Sephardic Jews from Spain was tolerated. A narrowly prescribed 18th-century ecumenical toleration left room for the freethought and Enlightenment rationalism associated with the educated elite and their prized traditions of political freedom and freedom of individual conscience—core U.S. values associated with this Protestant consensus. Only later did freethinking become associated with agnostic or atheist beliefs and fall outside the U.S. religious consensus.

Thomas Jefferson, a prominent deist and freethinker, proposed a bill in Virginia "Establishing Religious Freedom" (1779, passed in 1786) that granted complete legal equality "for citizens of all religions, and of no religion" (Jacoby, 2004, p. 18). This bill became the prototype for the religious protection clauses added as the First Amendment to the new U.S. Constitution. The text of the Constitution itself was explicit about religion only in its assertion that no religious test be required for holding public office, a clear break from English precedent (Jacoby, 2004).

Racialization of Religion

English, French, and Spanish colonizers became "white" in the same cultural and ideological process by which colonizers understood Indigenous peoples to be racialized as "red," or African peoples as "black," although explicit and legalized racial segregation and inequality took a century or more to formalize (Lipsitz, 2006; Roediger, 1991). The foundational Protestant communities along the Eastern Seaboard were understood to be *white* communities. Relocations of Indigenous people as well as enslavement of Africans were justified by presumed religious as well as racial superiority—a superiority that was sanctioned by the Christian God (Harvey, 2003; Loewen, 1995; Wills, 2005).

White Christian thought leveraged its own narrow understanding of other religions to create and preserve "those very social boundaries that we call 'races' and ethnicities'" (Prentiss, 2003, p. 1). The presumed religious and racial inferiority of Indigenous peoples became intersecting and mutually supportive justifications for massacre throughout the Americas as Christian European settler-colonists moved westward and for their expulsion from their ancestral lands and forcible removal of their children (Ballantine & Ballantine, 2001; Chavers, 2009; Grinde, 2004). With the immigration of Arabs and Asians, religion and race became conflated and interchangeable markers of the religious, racial, and, more often than not, economically exploited "other" (Maira, 2004).

U.S. Protestant churches were racially segregated, not only in terms of who worshiped with whom but theologically, culturally, and politically as well (Jacobson & Wadsworth, 2012; Jones & Sheffield, 2009). Mainstream white Protestant congregations split over religious and ethical questions posed by slavery and racial segregation in both the North and South and developed biblical interpretations and theological arguments that either rationalized or excoriated race-based bondage and segregation. Bitter denominational and sectarian disputes within white churches stimulated the growth of a separate Black church. Black churches provided refuge, community, solidarity, and support for formerly enslaved people and Black sharecroppers and fostered Black political leadership, economic development, and education. Black churches were centers for organized protest during the 19th and 20th centuries, including and beyond the civil rights movement (Fulop & Raboteau,

1997; Lincoln & Mamiya, 1990; Morris, 1986). Chinese, Korean, and Latino/a evangelical and Catholic religious communities have also provided similar cultural/ethnic/linguistic solidarity (Carnes & Yang, 2004; Chen & Jeung, 2012; Espinosa, 2014; Garces-Foley & Jeung, 2013; Min & Kim, 2001).

The 19th-century U.S. eugenics movement further entrenched the merging of race and religion. Centered among the elite at Harvard and elsewhere, eugenics identified Jews, among other immigrants, as racial "mongrels" who were "not quite white" (Diner, 2004; Takaki, 1991). Designating "Mexican" as a racial category, in part based on Mexico's Catholicism, was used to justify the 19th-century appropriation of Spanish and Mexican lands into the new states of California and the "anglo" (a term that conflates language with race and religion) Southwest (Menchaca, 2001; Takaki, 2008). The racialization of religion provided the basis for vehement opposition to immigrants, such as the Chinese, Japanese, Arab, and South Asian Sikhs, Muslims, and Hindus; Irish, Italian, and Polish Catholics; and eastern European Jews. The notion of citizenship itself was racially and religiously charged (Eck, 2001; Jacobson, 1998).

Religion, Race, and Immigration

Prior to the Civil War, an estimated half of the U.S. population and 85% of Protestants were evangelical (Emerson & Smith, 2000), forging a white, Protestant evangelical national identity. This remained largely unquestioned until the late 19th century, when significant increases in immigration of non-Protestant peoples poked holes in a previously homogeneous, racialized, mainly Protestant American sense of nationhood. Total immigration rose from 143,000 during the 1820s, when most immigrants were northern Europeans, to 8,800,000 during the first decade of the 20th century, when most immigrants were from southern or eastern Europe or Arab and Asian countries (Office of Immigration Statistics, 2006).

In the potato famine, 1.5 million Irish laborers fled starvation to migrate to the cities of the U.S. East Coast and Midwest. (As noted prior, the famine was itself caused by Protestant English colonial policies in Ireland.) Italian Catholics and Jews fled European revolution, poverty, and pogroms, settling mainly in urban centers. Wherever they settled, Irish, Italian, Polish, and Latino/a Catholics established separate parishes where they could worship in their languages of origin. In 1860, the foreign-born U.S. population was over 4 million, with more than 1.5 million from Catholic Ireland (Jacobson, 1998).

By 1920, more than a third of the total population included immigrants and their children, the majority of them Roman Catholic, Greek Orthodox, and Jewish, with significant numbers of Buddhists, Hindus, Muslims, and Sikhs from China and India (Daniels, 2002). Asian immigration (first Filipino and Chinese, followed by Japanese and South Asian) and Arab immigration (initially Syrian, including Lebanese Maronite Christians and Palestinian Christians)[7] brought Buddhist, Confucian, Hindu, Muslim, and Sikh beliefs and practices, as well as Orthodox Christian practice, to the U.S. (Bald, 2013; GhaneaBassiri, 2010; Haddad, 2002; Jensen, 1988; Takaki, 1998).

Irish, German, Italian, and Polish Catholics (Guglielmo, 2003; Ignatiev, 2009), perceived as a challenge to the white Anglo-Saxon Protestant way of life, often faced violent backlash. At the turn of the 20th century, intense anti-Catholicism, antisemitism, and opposition to Asians and Arabs, generically painted as "not like us," were enforced through intimidation by white "nativist" groups, who feared their brand of Protestant Americanism was under assault by foreign religions and ethnicities. Nativist activism resulted in the Immigration Act of 1917, specifically eliminating Asian immigration and excluding almost all adherents of Buddhism, Confucianism, Hinduism, Islam, or Sikhism. The 1924 National Origins

Act limited the number of immigrants from any country to 2% of the number of people from that country who were living in the U.S. as of the 1890 census. Together, these laws excluded all Asians, including Arabs, and drastically restricted southern and eastern European immigration, effectively barring most non-Protestant immigrants. These targeted and restrictive laws were part of a widespread xenophobia characterized at its extreme by the Ku Klux Klan and other Christian identity groups, whose anti-Catholicism and antisemitism seamlessly melded with anti-Black racism (Daniels, 2002; Lee, 2004).

Because of restrictions in place after 1924, Jewish Holocaust refugees were refused immigration status during the 1930s and 1940s, despite strenuous rescue efforts (Wyman, 2007). During the period from 1924–1965, many Jews and Catholics whose ancestors immigrated before 1924, and who had assimilated into mainstream (Protestant) American culture, became white—or at least "almost" if "not quite" white. At the same time, religious observance became increasingly private, with religious education taking place in separate parochial, homeschooling, or weekend classes ("Sunday school").

Following World War II, educational, residential, and professional barriers to upward mobility were slowly dismantled for white ethnic communities. The beneficiaries were mainly white Ashkenazi Jews and white Catholics (Italians and Irish), but not Black or brown Catholics or Protestants (African Americans, Afro-Caribbeans, Puerto Ricans, Chicanos/as and Mexican Americans, and South or Central Americans) (Brodkin, 1998; Guglielmo & Salerno, 2003; Ignatiev, 2009; Roediger, 1991) or Muslim or Orthodox Christian Arabs. European immigrants who had been seen as "ethnic" assimilated by giving up the languages and accents of their home communities, cooking and dressing "American," surgically altering stereotyped features with "nose jobs," and moving to the "integrated" (interreligious, but not interracial) suburbs.

Not until 1965 did a new immigration act reopen the door to immigration that was religiously non-Christian and racially non-white, opening the way for a renewal of the earlier religious, racial, and ethnic diversity. By 2010, immigrants numbered over 40 million and together with second-generation Americans (immigrants' children) totaled nearly 72 million. Many migrated as family units within strong religious community networks (Grieco, Trevelyan, Larsen, Acosta, Gambino, de la Cruz, Gryn, & Walters, 2012). A major outcome of the 1965 Immigration Act has been the growing number of Hindu, Muslim, and Sikh religious, cultural, and ethnic communities in the U.S. as well as major increases in Asian, African, and Latino/a Christian communities (Chen & Jeung, 2012; Ecklund & Park, 2005; Haddad, 2011; Joshi, 2006, 2020; Kurien, 2014; Min, 2010).

Naturalization and Citizenship

Religion also intersected with race when courts considered cases about naturalization and citizenship (Bayoumi, 2015; Haney-López, 2006; Joshi, 2020). The Naturalization Law of 1790 had restricted citizenship to "free white men," thereby excluding all women, Blacks (until passage of the fourteenth Amendment in 1868), Indigenous Americans, and other men of non-white racial ancestry. Citizenship was not fully available to Indigenous Americans until the 1968 Indian Civil Rights Act, which extended citizenship to Indigenous peoples living on reservations, providing them with legal standing and the ability to file claims for religious protection (Adams, 2012; Witte & Nichols, 2016). (See also Chapter 5: Racism.)

Chinese, Filipino, Hawaiian, Indian, Japanese, Mexican, Syrian (Arab), and Turkish immigrants turned to the courts, using a range of arguments to buttress their claims for naturalization, with contradictory results that often involved the intersection of religious and racial identities. These applicants were racially ambiguous: Not Black, but also not white, and marked by the perception that their non-Christian religions were unassimilable and "fundamentally at odds" with American culture and democratic self-government (Ngai, 2004).

In cases involving Syrians (Arabs), the intersection of religious identity (Muslim) and skin color became determinative, as in the 1909 case of the light-skinned Costa Najour, who was granted citizenship by a court that identified Syrians as members of the "white race" but also registered their concern that Najour, as a "subject of the Muslim Ottoman Sultan,[8] was incapable of understanding American institutions and government" (Gualtieri, 2001, pp. 34, 37). By contrast, in 1942, the dark-skinned Yemeni Arab Ahmed Hassan was denied citizenship on the religious grounds that "a wide gulf separates [Mohammedan] culture from that of the predominantly Christian peoples of Europe" (Gualtieri, 2001, p. 81; Bayoumi, 2015). Even Syrian Christians who were deemed white and granted citizenship faced discrimination, harassment, and violence from the Ku Klux Klan (Gualtieri, 2001).

Two pivotal Supreme Court decisions, *Takao Ozawa v. U.S.* and *U.S. v. Bhagat Singh Thind*, illustrate the haphazard, jumbled conflations of religion and race in Supreme Court naturalization cases. Takao Ozawa was a Japanese-born, California-educated, and English-speaking Christian church member who had lived in the U.S. for 20 years when he applied in 1914 for naturalization. To the courts, Ozawa was not "white" because the court accepted the pseudoscientific classification of Japanese as "Mongoloid" (Haney-López, 2006). Following this racial logic, Bhagat Singh Thind, an Indian Sikh, petitioned for citizenship as a white man, arguing that South Asian Indians were classified racially as Aryans/Caucasians and therefore white. The Supreme Court reversed its logic from the Ozawa case, arguing that while Singh might be classified as white, "the average man knows perfectly well that there are unmistakable and profound differences" between "the blond Scandinavian and the brown Hindu" despite their shared Caucasian ancestry. The court further argued that "Hindus could not be assimilated into a 'civilization of white men,'" confusing Sikh with Hindu identity based on Thind's Indian roots (quoted in Haney-López, 2006, p. 63; Snow, 2004, p. 268). The twisted and contradictory logics of Supreme Court naturalization litigation tied religious to race-based rationales against citizenship to argue that racialized religious minorities were not eligible for U.S. citizenship.

Discrimination Against White Religious Minority Groups

Racial exclusion of Christian communities of color from white churches occurred alongside religious exclusion of minority white religious sects from U.S. political life. Violence was directed against minority white religious sects who broke from denominational Protestantism to form the Church of Jesus Christ of Latter-day Saints (the Mormons), the Seventh-day Adventists, and the Jehovah's Witnesses, triggered by outrage over their rejection of establishment Protestantism and their repudiation of federal, state, and local political authority that was closely interwoven with Protestant Christianity (Butler, Wacker, & Balmer, 2003; Mazur & McCarthy, 2001; Prentiss, 2003; Witte & Nichols, 2016). The clashes of police and armed mobs against Mormons and Jehovah's Witnesses led these groups to withdraw into their own relatively autonomous geographical spaces and to relinquish their sectarian claims to political autonomy (Mazur, 1999).

Although Mormons, Jehovah's Witnesses, and Seventh-day Adventists have been at times considered denominations within Christianity, their theological claims, political separatism, and aspirations toward autonomy alienated them from Protestant Christianity. The 19th-century violence against Mormons, Jehovah's Witnesses, and Seventh-day Adventists was similar to the colonial expulsions and executions of so-called heretics who threatened the religious/political status quo in the early northeastern colonies. The antagonism toward Mormons broke into the political and constitutional arena when Congress prohibited polygamy in 1862 and the Supreme Court rejected Mormon claims to maintain multiple marriages under the Free Exercise Clause of the First Amendment (*Reynolds v. United States*, 1879). In this precedent-setting case, the defendant argued that the anti-polygamy statute violated his free religious exercise as a Mormon. The Supreme Court reasoned that polygamy constituted an "action," not a "belief," and not only was not constitutionally protected but should be restricted for the good of society (Feldman, 1996).

The distinction between "action" and "belief" gave the Supreme Court considerable latitude in its interpretation of "free religious exercise" for Christian or non-Christian religious and worship practices. From the *Reynolds* case on, one cannot find a clear, bright line between "belief" and "action"; the Supreme Court's interpretive line zigs and zags according to the court's willingness to accept that a practice is required by sincerely held religious belief. Two issues came to be at stake here: (1) whether the court sees a religious practice as opposed to the public good, and (2) whether the court accepts the religious practice as authentic. Both issues are tethered to traditional U.S. Protestant norms.

Discrimination Against Agnostics and Atheists

Many of the framers of the Constitution, such as Jefferson and Madison, were freethinkers and deists, and the founding documents of the early republic reflect their secular views. Until 1914, there was a vigorous freethought movement in the U.S. that linked secular beliefs to an "absolute separation of church and state" (Green, 2012; Jacoby, 2004, p. 153). Christian distrust of freethinkers, agnostics, and atheists hardened once the evangelizing fervor of 19th-century revivalist and evangelical Protestantism overwhelmed the rationalist freethought traditions of an earlier period.

The traditions of freethought and secularism, as well as atheism and agnosticism, collided with powerful religious organizations that emerged and forged political bonds between immigrant Catholic institutions and U.S.-born evangelical Protestants. Religious opposition to secularism and atheism became political, as the perceived threat of "foreign" socialism, anarchism, and radicalism among immigrant activists gained visibility in the 19th century. Irish union organizers, Italian radicals, and Jewish socialists were targeted by politicians and the media as dangers to U.S. business and commerce. Socialists were opposed on religious as well as political grounds, partly because some immigrant activists were Jewish socialists or Irish Catholic unionizers and partly because a socialist worldview promoted a path to human progress that could be achieved without divine intervention or sanction.

By the mid-20th century, the global threat of "godless communism" to U.S. capitalism had discredited U.S. atheism and agnosticism and cemented the association of atheism with communism and socialism. The Palmer raids on union organizers following the Red Scare of 1919 equated religion with political unorthodoxy, and atheism with socialism, so that earlier proud intellectual traditions of freethought, agnosticism, atheism, and secularism were tarred with the brush of bolshevism.[9] All were positioned as potent political heresies that could undermine the powerful Christian-identified nation-state that the U.S. considered itself to be, focused on capitalism and global finance and "exceptional" through divine sanction (Kruse, 2015).

The McCarthyism of the 1950s, largely a repeat of the Red Scare of 1919, used theological grounds to purge the godless on behalf of the body politic. It was during the McCarthy era that the phrase "under God" was added to the Pledge of Allegiance as a religious reference that would differentiate the god-fearing U.S. from the godless Soviets. A successful 2003 lawsuit brought by an atheist, who argued that the phrase "under God" violated the establishment clause of the First Amendment, led to hate mail against the plaintiff and furor in the media (Jacoby, 2004).

Atheists of color have been critical of racism they see playing out in white atheist organizing and call for more intersectional approaches (Hutchinson, 2020). Hutchinson notes that advocacy efforts of white atheists often miss opportunities to address issues that impact communities of color at the intersections of racism, sexism, heterosexism, and religious oppression:

> Progressive secularists of color argue that you cannot fight for economic justice in communities of color without advocating for reproductive justice, unrestricted abortion rights, and access to universal health care. You cannot preach "gender equality" without redressing the heterosexist erasure of queer and trans people of color in K–12 curricula. You cannot advocate for LGBTQI enfranchisement without confronting all of the mechanisms that criminalize queer and trans youth of color and place them at greater risk for being incarcerated, being placed in foster care, and/or becoming homeless.
>
> (p. 62)

The Separation of Church and State

Most U.S. citizens assume that freedom of religious practice has been definitively assured by the First Amendment to the U.S. Constitution, but this assumption is contradicted by more than a century of Supreme Court rulings that differentiate "belief" from "expression" or "practice." In large measure, the court has ruled against plaintiffs whose religious *practices* do not accord with the court's understandings of traditional U.S. Christian practices (Adams, 2012; Echo-Hawk, 2010; Feldman, 1996; Mazur & McCarthy, 2001; Witte & Nichols, 2016).

The two religious protection clauses of the First Amendment (adopted 1791) stipulate that "Congress shall make no law respecting an establishment of religion, or prohibiting the free exercise thereof." These clauses (the Establishment Clause and the Free Exercise Clause) were created to provide mutual assurance among the Protestant denominations of the original 13 colonies that there would be no federally subsidized church supported by taxes such as they had rebelled against while governed by England (Fraser, 1999; Mazur, 1999). These clauses, however, have had very different histories in case law.

The question of whether religious freedom extended only to Protestants across denominations, or to Catholics, Jews, and all other religions outside Protestantism, has haunted discussions of these religious protection clauses ever since. On one hand, the language of the constitutional religion clauses declined to name the protected religions, reflecting the more inclusive language of Jefferson's 1779 Act for Establishing Religious Freedom for Virginia "that all men shall be free to profess, and by argument to maintain, their opinions in matters of religion, and that the same shall in nowise diminish, enlarge, or affect their civil capacities" (quoted in Feldman, 1996, p. 151). But some early U.S. leaders feared that the First Amendment became "a door opened for the Jews, Turks, and Heathens to enter in public office" and an "invitation for Jews and pagans of every kind to come" to the U.S. (quoted in Feldman, 1996, pp. 162–163).

The well-known phrase "separation of church and state" comes not from the Constitution itself but from an 1802 letter from Jefferson to assure a Baptist congregation that the two clauses of the First Amendment had built "a wall of separation between Church and State" (Butler, Wacker, & Balmer, 2003, pp. 155–160; Fraser, 1999, pp. 18–21). This "wall of separation" between government and religion is still referred to as "the separation of *church* and state," though it is now understood to refer to all religions, even though non-Christian religions don't call their places of worship churches.

Two centuries later, the court ruled initially for the Jeffersonian perspective of religious inclusion:

> Perhaps in the early days of the republic these words were understood to protect only the diversity within Christianity, but today they are recognized as guaranteeing religious liberty and equality to the infidel, the atheist, or the adherent of non-Christian faith such as Islam or Judaism. . . . The anti-discrimination principle inherent in the Establishment Clause necessarily means that would-be discriminators on the basis of religion cannot prevail.
>
> (*County of Allegheny v. American Civil Liberties Union*, 1989)

In resolving legal questions brought under the religious protection clauses, the Supreme Court has rarely used a strict "wall of separation." Instead, most decisions have used "accommodation" or "non-preference" to avoid tilting advantage to one religion over another. For example, in applying the Establishment Clause, the Supreme Court found that students might be released from K–12 classes to receive religious instruction outside public school premises but did not allow public reimbursement to parochial schools for expenses incurred in teaching secular subjects inside the school premises (*Lemon v. Kurtzman*, 1971). In reaching these decisions, the court posed questions such as: What is the secular purpose of any legislation in question? Is its primary effect to advance or inhibit religion? Will a legal decision avoid "excessive government entanglement with religion" (Maddigan, 1993, p. 299)?

The Free Exercise Clause has generally been interpreted by the courts to affirm free religious belief but not to affirm religious practices or behaviors that conflict with neutral-seeming legal norms. Freedom of religious belief has generally not been challenged because it is so closely linked with freedom of speech (also a First Amendment right). But religious worship, practice, behavior, expression, or action have been challenged if they conflict with traditional U.S. social norms.

Claiming "free exercise" rights has proven daunting for non-Christians. For example, in a free exercise claim brought by an Orthodox Jew in the military who argued that he was required by religion to maintain head covering at all times, the court deferred to the military code. The court argued that wearing the yarmulke was a personal preference, not a requirement of his religion, and that military regulations were reasonable and did not violate the Free Exercise Clause (*Goldman v. Weinberger*, 1986). On the other hand, the court had no difficulty affirming the "religious requirements" in cases brought by the Amish, Jehovah's Witnesses, and Seventh-day Adventists (Witte & Nichols, 2016).

Similarly, Indigenous free exercise claims from 1980 on were unsuccessful and were evaluated by shifting, unfavorable criteria (Feldman, 1996; Long, 2000). The court found that Cherokee and Navajo plaintiffs were not justified in claiming "free exercise" with regard to performing their religious practice on sacred sites that had been designated as federal parks or other public uses. The court also sided with the government to allow a road built through a sacred ground used by three tribes for hundreds of years (Witte & Nichols, 2016). In contrast to earlier findings for the Amish and Seventh-day Adventists, the court did not recognize that Indigenous peoples, too, practiced ancient, recognized religions and held their beliefs sincerely (Beaman, 2003; Echo-Hawk, 2010).

The pattern in Supreme Court findings related to religious freedom appears to be that the cases rejected by the courts were those in which the free exercise claims were not based upon norms of religious worship familiar to them. It did not occur to the court that standardized uniforms "will almost always mirror the values and practices of the dominant majority—namely Christians. Put bluntly, the U.S. military is unlikely to require everyone to wear a yarmulke as part of the standard uniform" (Feldman, 1996, p. 247). The court did not consider that in Orthodox Judaism (as in other orthodox religions), head-covering is required at all times. In numerous Indigenous cases, "free exercise" claims were subordinated to the federal government's authority in controlling what had become federal lands, with no regard for the ways in which such land had been acquired (Linge, 2000, p. 314).

At the same time, the Supreme Court upheld the use of politically sanctioned religious speech, ritual, and symbols derived from Christian texts and traditions, which they ratio- nalized as a "civil religion" (Bellah, 1967; Jones & Richey, 1974). For example, the phrase "In God We Trust" was added to the U.S. currency in 1864, and Congress made Christmas a national holiday in 1865 (during the Civil War). The phrase "In God We Trust" uses the Christian norm of naming the deity as if it refers to a universal deity. Yet it clearly refers to the Christian God because many non-Christian religions would never talk about their god or gods in that way. "In God We Trust" also excludes agnostics and atheists from the hegemonic Christian national identity ("we") assumed by this phrase. Supreme Court deci- sions between 1890 and 1930 included statements that the U.S. "is one of the 'Christian countries,'" a "Christian nation," and a "Christian people," although in 1952 the phras- ing became more ecumenical: "We are a religious people whose institutions presuppose a Supreme Being" (Feldman, 1996).

Religion and Public Schooling

Religion has been central to U.S. education, from the colonial period, when it was a fam- ily responsibility to educate one's young, into the 19th century, when it became a prior- ity for the state. The common schools of the 19th century shared Protestant religious texts, prayers, and values as a nationalizing glue for a newly established system of primary schooling. The need for a public educational system had become evident following the Civil War, when immigrants as well as U.S.-born settlers migrated into western territories, all needing to ensure literacy and practical education for their children. There was also the perceived need to "Americanize" the children of Irish and German Catholic immigrants at mid-century and the many other immigrants that followed (Ignatiev, 2009). To meet these needs, Protestant leaders established a "non-denominational" network of schools that were racially segregated and whose common curriculum forged the values for a shared national identity (Fraser, 1999).

The common schools formed the precursor for today's public school system. They delivered a core curriculum upon which the major Protestant denominations could agree. They could be considered non-denominational only in the sense of bridging sectarian dif- ferences within a Protestant framework. Amish, Mennonites, and Quakers more often maintained their own schools. Catholic immigrant communities likewise established their own parish-based (parochial) school system, designed to maintain Catholic education by using the Douay Bible and Roman Catholic catechism, rather than the King James Bible and Protestant Book of Common Prayer used in the common schools.

The emergence of two major educational networks, each with explicit religious affili- ations, led to political, financial, legal, and at times violent conflicts between the public schools and the parochial schools. This conflict only intensified as the political leverage generated by Jewish, Catholic, and other non-Christian populations increased. Prayer and Bible readings in public schools came under scrutiny in establishment cases of the 1950s and 1960s (Jacobsen & Jacobsen, 2012).

Two such cases went to the U.S. Supreme Court and continue to impact the dialogue about religion and public schools today. In *Engel v. Vitale* (1962), Jewish families in Long Island protested the daily prayer that had been mandated by state legislation in 1951. The Supreme Court agreed with the plaintiffs that prayer in public schools violated the Establishment Clause. Then, in *Abington Township School District v. Schempp*, 1963, the U.S. Supreme Court ruled against Bible reading and recitation of the Lord's Prayer in public schools but commented that study *about* religions (as distinct from *religious study*) in the nation's public schools is both legal and desirable. The justices stated that a student's education is not complete without instruction concerning religious influences on history, culture, and literature (Muñoz, 2013; Murray, 2008).

Further cases brought to the courts concerning religion and public schools have addressed issues ranging from prayer in schools or at school events, to the celebration of Christian holidays in public spaces, to curricular decisions concerning evolution or creationism in biology classes, to the appropriate garb for public school students. School boards and religious communities across the country continue to debate whether public schools should be religion-free zones or whether teaching *about* religion should be included in public school curricula (Prothero, 2009). An example in recent years is a Christian student and her parents who sued her high school about a history lesson that included a worksheet on Islam. The case took years to resolve, and the court ruled against the family in early 2019 (Marimow, 2019).

In this chapter, we take the position that to truly understand our own neighbors and to participate effectively in a diverse citizenry and global society, we will need to do a much better job of understanding each other's religions, beliefs, and traditions of worship, as well as the salience of religion in our different cultures (Ennis, 2017).

DEMOGRAPHICS OF CURRENT U.S. RELIGIOUS DIVERSITY

Data on religious identity in the U.S. is collected by a variety of governmental and non-governmental agencies, using different methods that make them difficult to compare (Pew, 2018). The numbers in Table 8.1 are gathered from composite sources to provide an estimate of religious demographics.

Of the 2.2–3.6 million Buddhists, about 33% are of Asian ancestry (Pew Research Center, 2014), primarily from Japan, China, Tibet, Thailand, and Cambodia. The other two-thirds are primarily converts of all races. Most Sikhs are of Indian origin, from Punjab.

Table 8.1 U.S. Religious Demographics

Religion	Numbers	Sources
Buddhist	2.2–3.6 million	Pew Research Center (Lipka, 2014) *Dharma World Magazine* (Tanaka, 2011)
Christian	248 million	Pew Research Center (Diamant, 2019)
Hindu	2.3–3 million	Association of Religion Data Archives (Melton & Jones, 2011) U.S. Census Bureau's American Community Survey (Hinduism Today, 2008)
Jewish	4.2–6.8 million	Pew Research Center (Lipka, 2013) Brandeis University's Steinhardt Social Research Institute (Tighe, Saxe, Magidin de Kramer, & Parmer, 2013)
Muslim	1.8–7 million	Pew Research Center (Mohamed, 2018), Pew Research Forum (Pew Research Center, 2011a) *The American Mosque* (Bagby, 2011)
Sikh	200,000–700,000	Sikh American Legal Defense & Education Fund (SALDEF, 2014)

Islam is a pan-ethnic religion, with adherents in the U.S. from all parts of Asia, the Arab World, and Africa. There are also African American and European American (mainly Albanian) Muslims. African Americans, Arabs, and South Asians make up more than three-quarters of all Muslims in the United States. South Asians are the fastest growing Muslim immigrant population. Around 60% of U.S.-born Muslims are African Americans (Pew Research Center, 2011a). As noted prior in the "Demographics of Current U.S. Religious Diversity" section, many European Jewish families immigrated to the U.S. in the late 19th and early 20th centuries. A much smaller wave came from Europe and Arab countries after World War II, and the 1990s saw a wave of Soviet Jewish immigration. Although the U.S. Jewish population is predominantly white, it also includes Jews of color who are Sephardi and Mizrahi, as well as mixed-race families of Ashkenazi (European) heritage.

The overall Christian share of the U.S. population dropped from 78% in 2007 to 70% in 2014 and to 65% in phone surveys conducted in 2018 and 2019, with the loss mainly to mainstream Protestants and Catholics, accompanied by increases in those who self-identified as "unaffiliated" or non-Christian (Pew Research Center, 2015, 2019). Inter-religious marriages increased, from 19% prior to 1960 to 39% in 2010 (Pew Research Center, 2015, p. 5). Pew reported that "the religiously unaffiliated share of the population, consisting of people who describe their religious identity as atheist, agnostic or 'nothing in particular,' now stands at 26%, up from 17% in 2009" (Pew Research Center, 2019). In the same time period, the populations of Catholics and evangelical Protestants of color grew. In broad brushstrokes, however, the U.S. has more Christians than other countries globally: 65%–70% of the people in the U.S. identify with some branch of Christianity. This percentage includes all those who identified as Christians, regardless of the level of their belief or religious practice (Pew, 2018).

CONTEMPORARY MANIFESTATIONS OF CHRISTIAN HEGEMONY

CHRISTIAN NORMATIVITY AND PRIVILEGE

Many of the historical legacies noted prior persist today in examples of Christian normativity, including practices that carry Christian culture into the public sphere yet are widely accepted as "normal," such as the lighting of a Christmas tree at the White House, community Easter egg hunts, and the presumptively non-denominational prayer at the start of a city council meeting. These public rituals are based in Christianity and repackaged as a U.S. "civil religion," supposed as generically "American" traditions (Steinberg & Kincheloe, 2009). Thus, Christianity becomes the national religion by default and acts as a marker of U.S. national identity and an indicator of patriotism. The term "civil religion" ignores the specifically Christian nature of these rituals and downplays the role of Christianity in the American way of life (Feldman, 1996; Murray, 2008).

Many people consider such public Christian practices to be normal, appropriate, and joyous activities. Yet it is important to think seriously about the ways in which U.S. Christianity has institutionalized its own values and practices while marginalizing and subordinating those of other religions. The normalization of public Christian ritual—not just *in* public but *on behalf of* the entire public—privileges Christians while contributing to the marginalization and invisibility of non-Christian faiths and of atheists and agnostics. Christianity is a visible ingredient of U.S. patriotism in wartime, such as during the Cold War of the 1950s when popular discourses portrayed atheists and Jews as "un-American" and of dubious loyalty and today with the unwarranted suspicion of Muslims. This conflation of Christianity with Americanness and distrust of non-Christians emerged in questions of President Obama's religious convictions, even to rumors about whether he took the oath of office holding a Bible or the Qur'an.

Christian norms also shape assumptions about how other religions must work, such as where and how to worship: In recognizable religious buildings (churches) but not in geographic sacred sites, with hands clasped in prayer but not stretched forward on the floor from a kneeling position. The respect shown to core Christian beliefs (the virgin birth, the resurrection, the Second Coming) is not accorded to the religious or spiritual beliefs of Indigenous peoples. Prophet Mohammed's midnight flight to heaven (Islam) or Lord Vishnu's periodic visitations under different guises (Hinduism) are mocked and/or reduced to the status of myths or folkways. These views devalue their religious meaning through an implicit comparison with Christian beliefs (Joshi, 2006).

Because Christianity is culturally normative, non-Christians may be asked, "What is 'your' Bible?" and "When is 'your' Christmas?" Such questions assume that other religions have equivalent versions of Christianity's one sacred text and one or two major holidays. By contrast, Hinduism has more than one sacred text, as does Judaism.

The idea of *Christian hegemony* conveys the societal power inherent in these cumulative normative markers of Christianity (Kivel, 2013). The patriotism conveyed by "one nation under God" or the usual valedictory of the U.S. presidents and government officials, "God bless America," often affirms identification with a Christian God. Beyond the cultural insult, hegemonic Christianity has real economic consequences for those whose religious practices conflict with the Christian calendar—Jews who worship and rest from Friday sundown through Saturday, Muslims who have weekly congregational prayer obligations on Fridays (Juma'h prayer) and fast during the month of Ramadan, and Hindus, Sikhs, and others whose major holidays may not coincide with the seven-day week at all. Across the U.S., historically and today, state laws and local ordinances, including strict regulations against work, shopping, and other activities, have been used to ensure that Sunday would be treated as the "Sabbath" (the day of rest).

Christian hegemony at the institutional level and Christian norms at the cultural and societal level intertwine and result in Christian ideas and practices being ingrained in U.S. culture, law, and policy. This results in Christian privilege, a circumstance where Christians enjoy advantages that are denied to non-Christians. Some of these advantages are also shared by people who do not identify as Christian but who were raised Christian and feel comfortable and connected with Christian practice.

At the interpersonal and individual level, there are many examples of Christian privilege in everyday life (Joshi, 2020, Killermann, 2012; Schlosser, 2003). Americans who are Christian can:

- Easily find Christmas cards, Easter baskets, or other items and food for holiday observances;
- Wear a religious symbol (such as a cross) without being afraid of being attacked;
- Travel to any part of the country and know their religion will be accepted and they will have access to religious spaces to practice their faith;
- Fundraise to support congregations of their faith without being investigated or having their fundraising considered terrorist behavior;
- Have politicians responsible for their governance who overwhelmingly share their faith;
- Run for office without their religion becoming an issue;
- Participate in protest without their patriotism getting questioned.

RELIGIOUS OPPRESSION: DISADVANTAGE, MARGINALIZATION, AND DISCRIMINATION

Religious oppression refers to the cultural marginalization and societal subordination of non-Christian religious groups including but not limited to Buddhists, Hindus, Jews, Muslims, practitioners of Native American and other Indigenous spiritualities, Sikhs, and those who identify as atheists, agnostics, or freethinkers. Religious oppression is present in individual biases and prejudices, in institutional policies and practices, and in the cultural norms and societal hegemony of Christianity.

Many examples of bias, prejudice, and ignorance at the individual level have already been mentioned in the preceding section, such as Christian prayer at sports practices, which excludes non-Christians, and disrespectful questions about one's practices posed in language framed by Christian norms. Other examples include stereotypes such as that Jews are cheap or that Muslims are violent terrorists, as well as expecting a member of a non-Christian religion to speak as a representative of their entire religious group.

Non-Christians, including adherents of other religious traditions as well as agnostics and atheists, are subject to the proselytizing encouraged in evangelical Christian practice. Christians who believe they are doing the right thing by carrying the "good news" to non-Christians might be shocked to know that such proselytizing can be experienced as microaggressions—that, when repeated, can build up to the point of bullying and harassment. The recent proselytizing claim "that all Hindus should open their eyes and find Jesus" (Hafiz & Raghunathan, 2014, p. 13) sounds much the same note as the obviously prejudiced article in a Butte, Montana, newspaper (1870) that stated "the Chinaman's life is not our life, his religion is not our religion" (Eck, 2001, p. 166).

Finally, there is always the possibility of personal violence. Many Hindus, Jews, Muslims, and Sikhs feel vulnerable on the basis of both the dark-skinned physiognomy and religious attire that mark their outsider religious status, confounded with and multiplied by racial, ethnic, and linguistic markers. They have bricks thrown through windows and hear vicious slurs from passersby. Sikhs who wear turbans are attacked; Hindu women wearing a bindi or forehead dot are harassed and insulted. Hate crimes against Jews have increased at synagogues and Jewish community centers. Muslim women who wear the hijab are harassed and have their scarves pulled off their heads. As numerous studies have shown, such violence is regrettably neither rare nor a phenomenon of the past (Eck, 2001; Mohamed, 2021).

At the institutional level in the workplace, individuals whose religious identities are visible may not be considered appropriate for customer service positions and have been denied employment or moved to less visible positions. In these situations, grooming and dress policies reproduce mainstream cultural norms that clash with the kippa (yarmulke), turban, long hair, beard, or hijab that are required of or practiced by observant Jewish, Sikh, or Muslim men and women. For example, a U.S. Supreme Court decision in 2015 revealed that clothier Abercrombie & Fitch had refused to hire a Muslim girl as one of its sales staff because she wore the traditional Muslim headscarf, or hijab. When non-Christian religious groups have attempted to erect a house of worship in some towns and cities across the country, city councils and neighborhood groups created legal roadblocks and in many cases prevented the construction or poisoned the cultural atmosphere so that religious minorities chose to go elsewhere (Eck, 2001; Esposito & Kalin, 2011; Singh, 2003). Attitudes toward other religions have been translated into violent acts of vandalizing, bombing, or burning mosques (Beydoun, 2018) and attacking and killing Sikh or Jewish worshippers (SPLC, 2019).

The cultural devaluation of non-Christian religions is also expressed at the institutional level in the marketplace, where popular dress fads commodify and trivialize markers of marginalized religions. Sales in gift shops of dream catchers inspired by Hopi tradition (distinct from Indigenous artists who make and sell work inspired by their own traditions and whose proceeds support Indigenous artists and communities) are one example of religious misappropriation. Another is the popularity of Hindu god and goddess images on candles, perfume, and clothing with secular purposes in the U.S. On the mass-production market, these deities become fetishized, portrayed as cartoonish, despite their religious seriousness to believers as manifestations of the divine.

Our overarching vision of social justice is one where the current privileges held by Christians in the U.S. become considered rights that are protected for everyone, regardless of religious or non-religious affiliation. For social justice to take place, U.S. Christians will need to become far more aware of their privilege and of the cumulative and powerful normative influence of Christianity in everyday life.

CONTEMPORARY RACIALIZATION OF RELIGION

Particularly since 9/11, brown-skinned, bearded Arab Americans and South Asian Americans, as well as some Latino/a and multiracial people, are assumed to be Muslim on the basis of their racial appearance. Muslims are now among the most demonized members of U.S. society as a result of overgeneralized associations with extremism and violence.

The trope of the "Muslim terrorist" had been powerfully etched in the minds of many Americans since before 9/11. This stereotype is too often the first assumption of the press and the police when violence occurs, as demonstrated at the time of the bombing of the Oklahoma City Federal Building in 1995 (carried out by a white right-wing extremist) (Beydoun, 2018). While every example of violence by a Muslim is taken as evidence of the violence of Islam generally, we don't tend to overgeneralize in the same way about Christian violence. Threats and arson against medical clinics that provide abortion services, murders of Jews, and the execution-style massacre of Black worshippers at a South Carolina prayer service were all conducted by white Christian ideological extremists who were not described as "Christian terrorists" (Singh, 2013). Instead, their fanaticism and violence were attributed to unique individual psychological or ideological factors (Beydoun, 2018). Indeed, "Muslim" or "Islamic" and "terrorists" seem a single, hyphenated term in media coverage (Alsultany, 2008; Rana, 2011).

Islamophobia in the U.S. is not just a post-9/11 phenomenon, as noted in the earlier section on historical legacies. There has been clear acceleration in the religious and racial stereotyping of Muslims—a "phobia" toward adherents of Islam (*Islamophobia*)—as if all were violent extremists. These assumptions have been reinforced in political rhetoric in response to the oil crisis of 1973; the Gulf Wars of the 1980s, 1990s, and 2010s; the attacks of September 11, 2001; and the bombings in London, Madrid, Brussels, and Paris. Most recently, the stereotyping in the media builds on stories of Western-born young Muslims joining ISIS and accelerates fears of a geopolitical threat brought back to Europe and the U.S. by ISIS-trained jihadists.

Media representations essentialize Muslims as if all were intrinsically violent, destructive, and incapable of self-regulation or democracy, whether on the basis of theology or genetics (Esposito & Kalin, 2011; Jamal & Naber, 2008). Remarks from political leaders and the news media reinforce caricatures that are filmmakers' or cartoonists' stock-in-trade (Alsultany, 2008; Bayoumi, 2015; Shaheen, 2001, 2008). These negative images echo the antisemitic cartoons at the height of antisemitism in pre–World War II Europe and the U.S.

The widespread use of the term "Muslim terrorist" not only perpetuates fallacious and harmful stereotypes but erases the complexity of religious traditions that are encapsulated within Islam, a religion as complex and multifaceted as Buddhism, Christianity, Hinduism, and Judaism. All, like Islam, contain a wide spectrum of beliefs that range from literal ultra-orthodoxy (at times marked by fanaticism) to progressive liberalism (at times verging on secularism). In a variation of the well-known phrase "driving while Black," referring to the racial profiling of African Americans, Singh (2013) notes the new racial designation "apparently Muslim" to capture the daily experience of Arab Americans when traveling, interacting with police, applying for jobs, and receiving poor service in restaurants.

GLOBAL RELIGIOUS AND POLITICAL VIOLENCE

While the focus of this chapter is on religious oppression in the U.S., the dynamics we describe occur globally. Most nation-states have one dominant religion that is hegemonic and shapes national identity, thereby marginalizing or subordinating religious minorities in ways that intersect with class or caste, race, and ethnicity.

Some countries, such as Australia, Canada, France, India, South Africa, and the U.S., have religious protections built into their constitutions. Others maintain formal religious establishments as part of the political framework, such as Anglicanism in Great Britain, Islam as an official state religion in Pakistan and Saudi Arabia, and Judaism in Israel. In either situation, countries share the dilemma of protecting the human rights of all peoples, including religious minorities, despite political decisions driven by majoritarian electoral politics.

Many nations have experienced violent upheavals that reflect dynamics of religious hegemony and marginalization, such as the Hindu/Muslim conflicts in India and Muslim/Christian violence in Pakistan. Religious rationales for conflict are complicated by ethnicity, class, or caste; historical and geographic competition for resources; and national identity as in Bosnia, Croatia, and Serbia, as well as Israel and Palestine (Armstrong, 2014; Fox, 2000, 2002). The role of religion can be seen in the British-Irish conflict over the island of Ireland, where religious difference as a mechanism of colonial rule embeds political and economic privilege based on religion and colonial loyalties (Adams, 2005). The framing of conflicts such as these as based merely on religion can mask the centrality of colonization and homogenize a variety of historical and contemporary conflicts that include religion as a component. Similarly, framings of what is going on in Israel/Palestine often generalize the issue as a conflict between Jews and Muslims, which oversimplifies the complexities of competing nationalisms and territorial claims (Jacobsen & Jacobsen, 2012).

In the case of Israel/Palestine, the oversimplification has direct implications for Jews and Muslims in the U.S., including on college campuses. There are widespread assumptions, amplified by well-funded pro-Israel lobbying groups, that all Jews are (or should be) aligned with the Israeli government's policies toward Palestinians. These groups seek to suppress thoughtful critiques of Israeli policies and nationalism by claiming that such critiques are necessarily antisemitic. Ironically, this approach feeds the antisemitic misperception that all Jews are at fault for Israeli military and colonial policies in the Palestinian land that is occupied by Israel, such as the building and expansion of settlements that are illegal under international law. It also reinforces stereotyped, Islamophobic depictions of all Muslims as fundamentalists and terrorists. Race further complicates the debate, as these arguments tend to rely on the assumption that all Jews and Israelis are white (most but not all U.S. Jews are white, and many Israeli Jews are Arab) and all Muslims are Arab and brown (there are Muslims of all races, throughout and beyond the Arab World).

Such arguments leave no space for Jews who critique Israeli politics but also need to identify as Jewish (Karpf, Klug, Rose, & Rosenbaum, 2008; Kushner & Solomon, 2003). This applies to individuals as well as groups such as Jewish Voice for Peace (JVP) (JVP website, 2020) and also to Muslims who oppose radical Islamic groups but identify (sometimes visibly) as Muslim. Muslim and Jewish identity are hypervisible in these campus debates, while the role of Christian Zionism in funding Israeli settlements goes largely unmentioned.

The Palestinian/Israeli issue seriously impacts the relations between Jews and Muslims in the U.S., whatever their convictions about the politics of that region of the world (Shavit, 2013; Tolan, 2006). Muslim/Jewish relations play out in complex ways that negatively affect campus Jews and Muslims (Kosmin & Keysar, 2015; Berlak, 2014). The Trinity College Anti-Semitism Report found alarmingly high reports of antisemitic incidents, mainly one-on-one, sometimes in groups or classrooms, and that generally were ignored or downplayed by campus administrations (Kosmin & Keysar, 2015). A similar pattern of administrators ignoring reports of Islamophobia is also found in grade school throughout the U.S. In a 2017 survey, 42% of Muslim students reported being bullied; bullying by teachers and administrators accounted for 25% of reported incidents (Mogahed & Chouhoud, 2017). The essentializing inherent to antisemitism and Islamophobia disrupts efforts to build bridges and coalitions within educational settings, at a time when young people may be most open to cross-religious dialogue, friendships, collaboration, and interfaith activism—potentially including activism that would challenge Christian hegemony and privilege.

INTERSECTIONS OF RELIGIOUS HEGEMONY AND OPPRESSION WITH OTHER ISMS

While we particularly highlight the intersection of religion and race, Christian hegemony and religious oppression intersect with other social identities and forms of oppression as well. Two Supreme Court split decisions in 2014 and 2015 placed religious freedom claims in opposition to the right to have an abortion and the right of same-sex couples to marry. In *Burwell v. Hobby Lobby* (2014), a narrow conservative majority found that family-owned companies could be exempted from providing health insurance meeting the minimum standards for contraception coverage on the basis of their religious opposition to contraception (LoGiurato, 2014). The court's finding was based on a new interpretation of the Religious Freedom Restoration Act (RFRA, 1993), which had been originally crafted by Congress to protect marginalized religions such as those of Indigenous peoples. This new reasoning on RFRA would protect the religious exercise of individuals and companies whose religious convictions oppose the rights of groups marginalized on the basis of sex, gender, and sexual orientation.

In 2015, a liberal narrow majority in the court found marriage equality to be a constitutionally protected right. In nearly simultaneous protest, state legislatures passed local versions of RFRA protecting businesses (such as florists and bakeries) who denied services to same-sex couples based on the owners' religious objection to marriage equality. Civil rights groups responded by pointing out that the denial of service to legally protected minorities is the very definition of discrimination. The resulting political firestorm over "religious protection" legislation in opposition to anti-discrimination laws shows no sign of abating and is likely to be a hotly contested issue in the future (Cole, 2015; Eckholm, 2015).

Many global issues may wear a religious veneer, but below the surface one finds long-simmering conflicts among social classes, racial or ethnic groups, and the suppression of women's rights to their bodies and to education. Conflicts that have been framed as religious require closer analysis of economic inequality (land, jobs, education), sexist abuse and subordination, violence toward sexual and gender diversity, and competing nationalisms that have been subsumed by the religious dimensions that seem most visible (Little, 2007). Similarly, the sexual victimization of women and gender-nonconforming people in African countries, China, India, and Pakistan, or efforts to prevent their education (as in

Afghanistan), may reflect ethnic authoritarian enforcement of religious patriarchy within families, reinforced by police or other authorities.

An intersectional approach to religious oppression explores the "co-constitutive relationships" (Goldschmidt & McAlister, 2004, p. 6) between religion and other social categories—race, ethnicity, economic class, gender, and sexuality—to which we must add nationality. The intersection of religion with nationalism accounts for many of the most vicious attacks on members of "outsider" religious groups historically (such as pogroms against Jews in Russia) and currently (such as attacks on Sikhs in the U.S. and Christians in Pakistan). In such cases, it is extraordinarily difficult to try to hold in place one strand—religion—while also understanding that it is not truly a single strand but involves a "simultaneity of systems." Issues we call race, ethnicity, culture, class, caste, or religion are interactive rather than unitary, "constructed in and through each other, and through other categories of difference" (Goldschmidt & McAlister, 2004, p. 7).

If one attempts merely to isolate religion from the complex web that includes cultural, ethnic, racial, class, and gender-based rationales for oppression, one risks adding religion as yet another category of analysis within systems of domination and oppression, without making any new sense of these systems. The primary reason for this chapter's focus on religious oppression is to better understand how religious oppression functions together with other systems of oppression, particularly how religious justifications are used in tandem with other rationales, to dehumanize the "other," dismiss minority religions, relocate or restrict their living spaces, and eradicate their cultures.

MOVING TOWARD JUSTICE

Promoting religious pluralism means to provide space for people of all religions, as well as for non-believers who may identify in various ways—as agnostic, atheist, non-believer, rationalist, secular humanist, or "nothing in particular." Agnostics and atheists have become more outspoken and openly challenge the beliefs and traditions of formal religion (Andrews, 2013; Christina, 2012; Hitchens, 2007). One way for our society to be more inclusive is to not use religion as a rationale or excuse for discrimination against groups that may seem outsider to one's own faith tradition. For example, religious beliefs, individually and institutionally, have been used to perpetuate homophobia. The renewed attention on the free exercise of religion demonstrates the need for greater clarity and understanding about what can and cannot be done to express or suppress religion in the public arena, as in the cases of denial of public services on the basis of religious objections to gays, lesbians, and trans and gender-nonconforming people.

In the case of Christian public celebrations, public officials need to consider how to be authentically inclusive and pluralistic as distinct from "additive" when it comes to celebrating religious traditions that are not Christians. For example, during the Christmas season, some public officials incorporate celebrations of Hanukkah and Kwanzaa. The first is a minor holiday that got elevated due to Christian normativity and its convenient proximity to Christmas in the calendar, and the latter is a cultural holiday rather than a religious holiday. Public officials' acknowledgements of them sometimes come across as lip service demonstrating their ignorance rather than promoting true inclusion. Likewise, it is important to question the hegemonic assumption that authorities should invoke a specific deity for guidance in public matters. While officials might look for guidance in their private moments, it can be argued that a public meeting should not presume agreement among participants as to the nature or the role of divine guidance (Jacobsen & Jacobsen, 2012).

The interfaith arena offers some opportunities for mutual understanding and respect, if not agreement, including but not limited to interreligious dialogue (Forward, 2001; McCarthy, 2007; Patel, 2012; Smock, 2002). Interfaith councils have in recent decades included representatives of many religious traditions. Some interfaith groups focus on learning and understanding through dialogue; others address common social concerns; still others revolve around campus environments or public spaces such as hospitals or prisons (McCarthy, 2007; Patel & Scorer, 2012). Despite their different approaches, interfaith groups share the unifying belief in intentional relationship-building to resolve intergroup conflict.

Interfaith groups have provided support to specific religious communities in times of crisis, as in the case of members of Jewish communities who were victims of white supremacist hate crimes in Billings, Montana (NIOT, 1995/1996). In the aftermath of 9/11, church members reached out to local Muslim organizations and mosques to ensure their fellow neighbors could pray peacefully and without fear of violence. Protestant ministers came together in 2002 in New Jersey to advance dialogues among different religious communities (Niebuhr, 2008). After the massacre at the Oak Creek Gurdwara in Wisconsin, Sikhs and non-Sikhs alike made their way to *gurdwaras* in record numbers to show their support while the Sikh community emphasized that their doors had been and would continue to be open. The massacre at the Tree of Life Synagogue in 2018 in Pittsburgh brought many interfaith groups together to support and fundraise for the victims. These were especially egregious acts of domestic terrorism committed by white nationalists and sparked interfaith engagement worldwide. Interfaith efforts continue to focus on opportunities for members of each group to learn more about the others by meeting in different places of worship and sharing meals to create bonds and communities.

At the same time, interfaith dialogues draw criticism for several reasons. One reason is that these dialogues are often among people who come from conflict areas where religion is used as an excuse for violence and oppression but is not the real cause of that conflict. In these cases the dialogue programs may be guilty of ignoring or even masking power dynamics and systems of oppression by focusing solely on religion. Participating in such dialogues can improve relationships among some individual participants but will not lead to a meaningful change in the conflict. Some critics go so far as considering these dialogues part of Christian hegemony, particularly in situations where they are promoted and hosted by Christian churches and where Christianity is still centered while members of other religions are only invited in. While such dialogue may build interpersonal understanding, it does not seek to challenge Christian hegemony.

Beyond interfaith coalitions, the vigorous theological, as well as moral and pragmatic, demands for economic justice by Pope Francis have reached a broad and enthusiastic public, with considerable media attention. Pope Francis's public apology for the participation of the Roman Catholic Church in colonial-era violence against Indigenous peoples throughout the Americas offered a dramatic instance of the church's willingness to acknowledge its share of responsibility for the horrors of Spanish colonialism. Pope Francis places responsibility for global poverty and economic injustice on the inequities of capitalism, with a critique that goes well beyond traditional Catholic social teachings and recalls the efforts of liberation theology, whose spirit this pope now embraces.

As we hope for a future that includes religious justice, we must not only look to our religious and secular social movements but also look for clarity about the role of religion in the public education curriculum. Educators have come to understand that modernization calls for pluralism, not secularization, among its "diversity" concerns (Patel, 2015), although secularists or non-aligned non-believers must also be included in such religious pluralism (Prothero, 2009; Jacobsen & Jacobsen, 2012; Ennis, 2017). Such pluralism must take an intersectional approach and make sure to take into account the needs of atheists and humanists of color (Hutchinson, 2020).

Teaching about religion in public education has been hampered because of anxiety and misunderstanding about the applicability of the religion clauses of the First Amendment to public schooling. The constitutional prohibition against devotional reading or sectarian prayer in schools has frightened policy-makers into choosing "non-religious" secularism over religious pluralism in efforts to maintain "total separation" between religion and public education. This approach misrepresents the constitutional mandate, which does not require that public schools provide a "religion-free zone." The Supreme Court has encouraged that religion be made part of the school curriculum so long as the distinction between "teaching" and "preaching" is respected. The court has made clear that schools may, and should, promote awareness of religion and expose students of all ages to the diversity of religious worldviews but may not endorse or denigrate any particular religion or belief (Jacobsen & Jacobsen, 2012).

The court on several occasions argued that the First Amendment calls for political neutrality, but not exclusion, with regard to religion by describing the constitutional requirement for "the state to be neutral in its relations with groups of religious believers and non-believers. . . . State power is no more to be used so as to handicap religions than it is to favor them" (*Everson v. Board of Education*, 1947). In a subsequent decision (*Abington v. Schempp*, 1963), the court suggested a path forward—namely, a renewed commitment to teaching about religious traditions (not the teaching of any one specific religion) as part of the regular curriculum. Writing with the majority, Justice Tom Clark said:

> It might well be said that one's education is not complete without a study of comparative religion or the history of religion and its relationship to the advancement of civilization. It certainly may be said that the Bible is worthy of study for its literary and historical qualities. Nothing we have said here indicated that such study of the Bible or of religion, when presented objectively as part of a secular program of education, may not be affected consistently with the First Amendment.
>
> (*Abington v. Schempp*, 1963)

Understanding religious differences and the role of religion in the contemporary world—and in our students' lives—supports personal growth and development, exposes religious prejudice, and helps build classroom communities where students develop the trust, knowledge, and skills to become thoughtful global citizens. Educators and nonprofit organizations like Tanenbaum (Tanenbaum, 2021) have prepared guides to support these efforts in K–12 schooling as well as in higher education (Anderson, 2007; Haynes, Chaltain, Ferguson, Hudson, & Thomas, 2003; Haynes & Thomas, 2001; Jones & Sheffield, 2009; Moore, 2007; Murray, 2008; Nash, 2001).

In classrooms, community groups, and religious organizations, members of different religious communities—and those who do not identify with any religion—can explore the Christian hegemony and religious discrimination that characterize our historical past and present and consider how to foster religious pluralism and social justice in the future. We aim for something greater than merely to reduce religious discrimination against non-Christians, although that is surely an important intermediary step (Ennis, 2017). Our aim is a genuinely pluralistic society that is socially just and in which religious and nonreligious communities are visible but without privileges accorded to some and disadvantages placed on others (Joshi, 2020). As we imagine ways of moving from "here" to "there," we focus upon how to challenge Christian hegemony in the public square and in educational settings so that, in the words of an earlier Supreme Court, "The anti-discrimination principle inherent in the

Establishment Clause necessarily means that would-be discriminators on the basis of religion cannot prevail" (*County of Allegheny v. American Civil Liberties Union*, 1989).

DESIGN FOR TEACHING ABOUT CHRISTIAN HEGEMONY AND RELIGIOUS OPPRESSION

The following curriculum design uses a social justice approach to Christian hegemony and religious oppression, drawing upon themes and information presented in this chapter. This design does not teach about religion or focus on the differences among religions, but rather specifically on oppressive power dynamics related to religious affiliation. However, we recognize religious literacy is an important component in a pluralistic society and refer to organizations such as the Tanenbaum Center for Interreligious Understanding and programs such as Faith Zone (Ennis, 2017) for information and resources for teaching religious literacy. This design focuses on historical and contemporary manifestations of religious oppression as it plays out in the U.S. through pervasive Christian hegemony.

The sample design offered here, organized into four quadrants, is followed by an explanation of the learning objectives and core concepts for each quadrant as well as brief descriptions of the activities in the design. We close with a discussion of pedagogical, design, and facilitation issues specific to teaching about religious oppression. Instructions and facilitation notes for each activity can be found on the website that accompanies this volume.

This design presupposes familiarity with the core social justice concepts that we consider foundational to any social justice approach (presented in Chapter 4: Core Concepts). We assume that instructors and facilitators will have read Chapter 4 and will have considered these core concepts prior to applying them to religious oppression.

OVERVIEW OF RELIGIOUS OPPRESSION DESIGN QUADRANTS

Quadrant 1: Personal Awareness of Religious Identity and Religious Difference in the U.S. (approx. 3.5 hr.)

1. Welcome and Overview (30 min.)
2. Community Building (30 min.)
3. Group Norms and Guidelines (20 min.)
4. Who's in the Room (20 min.)
5. Personal Awareness and Reflection Activity: Religion and Stereotypes (25–40 min.)
6. Understanding Religious Oppression as a Social Justice Issue (20 min.)
7. Social Justice Approaches to Religious Oppression (30–45 min.)
8. Understanding Christian Privilege (30–45 min.)
9. Closing Activity (5–10 min.)

Quadrant 2: Historical and Conceptual Understanding of Religious Oppression in the U.S. (3 hr. 20 min.)

1. Check-in (10 min.)
2. Timeline: History of Religious Oppression and Christian Normativity in the U.S. (45–90 min.)
3. Processing of Historical Legacies (30–60 min.)
4. Intersections with Other Isms, New Insights, New Questions, and Takeaways (15–30 min.)
5. Closing Activity (10 min.)

Quadrant 3: Recognizing Examples of Christian Hegemony and Religious Oppression in the U.S. Today (3 hr.)

1. Opening Activity (15 min.)
2. Examining Institutional Religious Oppression (30–90 min.)
3. Examples of Everyday Christian Normativity and Religious Oppression (25–40 min.)
4. Closure Activity: New Insights, New Questions, and Takeaways from the Quadrant (30 min.)

Quadrant 4: Recognition of Manifestations of Religious Oppression, Steps toward Change, and Action Plans (3–4 hr.)

1. Opening Activity (30 min.)
2. Moving Forward (45 min.)
3. Personal Considerations Prior to Action Planning (30–45 min.)
4. Action Planning (45 min.)
5. Next Steps (30 min.)
6. Closing Circle

QUADRANT 1: PERSONAL AWARENESS OF RELIGIOUS IDENTITY AND RELIGIOUS DIFFERENCE IN THE U.S.

Learning Objectives for Quadrant 1:

- Understand the social justice education (SJE) approach to Christian hegemony and religious oppression
- Understand the ingredients needed for an SJE learning community
- Recognize the impact of stereotypes and experiences of subordinated religious communities in U.S. history and contemporary life
- Explore personal implications of one's own religious/non-religious experiences and perspectives in relation to those of the extended family and cultural context
- Understand the concept of privilege and disadvantage in relation to U.S. Christianity

Key Concepts for Quadrant 1: Religious oppression; social justice education; Christian hegemony, normativity, privilege; stereotypes; personal and institutional manifestations of religious oppression; personal bias; Christian advantage and non-Christian disadvantage

Activities and Options for Quadrant 1:

1. **Welcome and Overview (30 min.):** This activity identifies goals and learning objectives for the course/workshop and presents our assumptions for an SJE approach to religious oppression.
2. **Community Building (30 min.)**
   Option A: Introductions: The instructor and participants introduce themselves by presenting the meanings of their own names in the context of their families' religious (or non-religious) history.
   Option B: Introductions: The instructor and participants introduce themselves by presenting information relevant to the classroom or workshop context.
3. **Group Norms and Guidelines (20 min.)**
   Option A: Creation of Group Norms and Guidelines. The group collaborates to decide on guidelines for participation in the workshop.
   Option B: Hopes and Concerns. Participants identify and name the hopes and concerns they bring into the class through an active group process. These hopes and concerns become the basis for group guidelines.
4. **Who's in the Room (20 min.)**
   Option A: Common Ground: The questions posed in this activity about religious identity, background, and modes of worship help participants see who is in the group and make personal connections while engaging with the different life experiences that participants bring to this subject.
   Option B: Treasure Hunt: The participants mingle to find classmates with a variety of religious experiences or identities described on a handout.
5. **Personal Awareness and Reflection Activity: Religion and Stereotypes (25–40 min.):** A short presentation on stereotypes is followed by an activity in which small groups brainstorm stereotypes of marginalized religious groups, share their examples, and discuss the sources and common themes in the information generated.
6. **Understanding Religious Oppression as a Social Justice Issue (20 min.):** This presentation emphasizes the structural and sociological analysis of institutional manifestations and historical legacies of religious oppression.

7. **Social Justice Approaches to Religious Oppression (15–30 min.)**
   Option A: Levels of Christian Advantage (15 min.): This activity offers examples of Christian advantage at the personal, institutional, and societal levels.
   Option B: Overview of Five Faces of Oppression (30 min.): This activity provides examples of religious advantage and disadvantage using Young's "Five Faces" framework.
8. **Understanding Christian Privilege (30–45 min.):** This activity enables participants to identify and "unpack" the unconscious Christian privileges that enable Christians to navigate in everyday life.
9. **Closing Activity (5–10 min.)**
   Option A: Take the Temperature (10 min.): Participants are invited to offer a brief comment about how they are feeling at the end of this first segment.
   Option B: Geometric Shape Check-in (5 min.): Participants reflect individually and submit a handout with their new learnings and remaining questions.

QUADRANT 2: HISTORICAL AND CONCEPTUAL UNDERSTANDING OF RELIGIOUS OPPRESSION IN THE U.S.

Learning Objectives for Quadrant 2:
- Understand the historical legacies of Christian hegemony and the pervasive Christian norms that result in advantages for U.S. Christians and disadvantages for U.S. marginalized religious groups
- Understand the emergence of Christianity in early European history and the patterns of antisemitism and anti-Islam built into early Christianity
- Understand the Protestant policies and norms of U.S. Christianity until the mid-20th century
- Identify examples of how Christian hegemony results in unexamined norms at the institutional, societal, and individual levels
- Understand the role of religion in national identity and nationalism
- Explore intersections of religion with other forms of identity at the individual, institutional, and societal/cultural levels

Key Concepts for Quadrant 2: Christian normativity; religious hegemony; historical legacies and contemporary manifestations; social/cultural (macro), institutional (meso), and personal (micro) manifestations; antisemitism, Islamophobia or anti-Islam; Protestantism, Catholicism; national identity, nationalism; intersections

Activities and Options for Quadrant 2:
1. **Check-in (10 min.):** Check-in at the start and close of a quadrant is an important ingredient of maintaining a learning community.
2. **Timeline: History of Religious Oppression and Christian Normativity in the U.S. (45–90 min.):** This activity allows participants to identify, explore, and discuss events that perpetuate Christian normativity and hegemony and the historical religious oppression against non-Protestant faiths and atheists in the U.S.
3. **Processing of Historical Legacies (15–45 min.)**
   Option A: Social/Cultural, Institutional, and Personal Manifestations of Christian (Protestant) Hegemony and Marginalization of the Religious Other (30 min.): Participants use worksheets for small-group discussions.

Option B: "Five Faces" of Christian (Protestant) Hegemony and Marginalization of the Religious Other (30 min.): Participants use worksheets for small-group discussions. They should include "intersections" or "reinforcers" from other forms of social advantage or disadvantage where they can.

4. **Intersections with Other Isms, New Insights, New Questions, and Takeaways (15–30 min.):** Participants use a worksheet to process while the information is being presented. The worksheet focuses on identifying intersections of religious oppression with other forms of advantage and disadvantage.

5. **Closing Activity**
   Option A: Take the Temperature (10 min.): Participants are invited to offer a brief comment about how they are feeling at the end of this first segment.
   Option B: Geometric Shape Check-in (5 min.): Participants reflect individually and submit a handout with their new learnings and remaining questions.

QUADRANT 3: RECOGNIZING EXAMPLES OF CHRISTIAN HEGEMONY AND RELIGIOUS OPPRESSION IN THE U.S. TODAY

Learning Objectives for Quadrant 3:
- Understand the historical context for adding the religious protection clauses as part of the First Amendment to the U.S. Constitution
- Understand the issues raised by historical and contemporary cases brought under the religious protection clauses
- Identify major topics in reading assignments
- Continue reflection within a learning community that respects different perspectives and personal experiences

Key Concepts for Quadrant 3: Historical context and legacies; "separation of church and state"; constitutional religious protection clauses; Christian hegemony in U.S. legal decisions; intersections among forms of religious oppression and other forms of oppression

Activities and Options in Quadrant 3:
1. **Check-in (5–15 min.):** Ask whether some of the questions participants brought into the session have now been addressed, and take note of those that have not yet been addressed.
2. **Examining Institutional Religious Oppression (30–90 min.)**
   Option A: U.S. Constitutional Protections: "You Be the Judge" (90 min.): Participants explore the constitutional protection of religion clauses by trying to guess the outcome of real legal cases dealing with religious oppression.
   Option B: Guided Discussion Groups (30–75 min.): Participants draw on assigned readings and on content previously presented by instructors to explore themes, insights, and connections related to historical and contemporary religious oppression. We used readings from the Religious Oppression chapter of *Readings for Diversity and Social Justice, 4th edition* (Adams, Blumenfeld, Catalano, DeJong, Hackman, Hopkins, Love, Peters, Shlasko, & Zúñiga, 2018).
3. **Examples of Christian Normativity and Religious Oppression (25–40 min.)**
   Option A: Recognizing Everyday Christian Hegemony and Religious Oppression (40 min.): This three-part activity has participants identify current U.S. Christian hegemonic norms and the ways in which they become oppressive, exclusive, and discriminatory to non-Christians. The second part asks participants to identify

"intersections" or "reinforcers" for examples of Christian hegemony and religious oppression from other forms of advantage and disadvantage. The third part of the activity visualizes the ways in which these norms or exclusions operate as a societal and cultural "web" of religious oppression.

Option B: Everyday Scenarios (25 min.): Participants analyze everyday situations to see how Christian normativity and religious oppression are present in schools and workplaces.

4. Closure Activity: New Insights, New Questions, and Takeaways from the Quadrant (5–10 min.)

Option A: Take the Temperature (10 min.): Participants are invited to offer a brief comment about how they are feeling at the end of this first segment.

Option B: Geometric Shape Check-in (5 min.): Participants reflect individually and submit a handout with their new learnings and remaining questions.

QUADRANT 4: RECOGNITION OF MANIFESTATIONS OF RELIGIOUS OPPRESSION, STEPS TOWARD CHANGE, AND ACTION PLANS

Learning Objectives for Quadrant 4:

- Apply recognition of current examples of religious oppression at all three levels to support action planning
- Consider personal and organizational factors that impact action planning
- Collaborate in groups or coalitions to plan action

Key Concepts for Quadrant 4: Cycle of Liberation and openings for change; spheres of influence, risk levels, building coalitions, advocacy, and action planning

Activities and Options for Quadrant 4:

1. Opening Activity (30 min.)

Option A: Interfaith Four Squares (30 min.): Participants assess their own individual and group knowledge about religions in the U.S. This activity can support strategizing about teaching about religion in U.S. public schools, as one kind of action.

Option B: Action Continuum—Room-Stations Activity (30 min.): Participants explore the range of action and inaction and identify where they are and where they want to be on the Action Continuum.

2. Moving Forward (45 min.)

Option A: Walking the Line in Public Schools (45 min.): Presentation and discussion about the legal and policy considerations concerning what can be done to teach about religion and/or change policy regarding religion in public schools.

Option B: What's Possible in Professional, Organizational, or Community Settings (45 min.): Participants identify situations in which religion can be addressed in settings other than public schools.

3. Personal Considerations Prior to Action Planning (30–45 min.)

Option A: This option provides a structured approach to self-assessment of the personal factors that should be considered prior to creating an action plan.

Option B: Participants tell personal stories about earlier experiences in which they were an advocate or change agent and what those experiences taught them about becoming an advocate for action and change concerning Christian hegemony and religious oppression.

4. **Action Planning (45 min.)**

    Option A: Planning for Action in Schools: Participants re-think a particular school district's calendar and work toward creating a calendar that is more equitable.

    Option B: Developing Your Own Plan for Workplace, Organizational, Professional, School, Community, or Other Settings: Participants pick up where they left off in the "Personal Considerations" from Options 3A or 3B listed prior to create a plan to take the action or change the policy or practices they identified in the earlier activity.

5. **Next Steps (30 min.):** Participants discuss their "takeaways" from the preceding two segments.

6. **Closing Circle:** The closing activity can take place in a circle with participants using stems ("One thing I learned," "One thing I'm willing to do," "One thing I want you to know") or some other closing phrase that is appropriate to the group.

PEDAGOGICAL, DESIGN, AND FACILITATION ISSUES TO CONSIDER WHEN TEACHING ABOUT RELIGIOUS OPPRESSION

The classroom or workshop is one of many settings where the merest reference to religion may elicit feelings of defensiveness, embarrassment, vulnerability, anxiety, appreciation, anger, and curiosity. These feelings may be heightened when the word "religion" is linked with the word "oppression." Because some consider religion to be a private matter, it is not always easy to talk about Christians having advantages in our society or to identify intersections of religion with other forms of structural privilege and disadvantage. This is especially complex when using an intersectional lens, because "the religious choices of individuals and collectivities are differently constrained by larger societal structures of power and inequality" (Yukich & Edgell, 2020, p. 7). For example, the intersection of race and religion complicates Christian privilege for Black Christians. Black Christian leaders have played important roles in the civil rights movement and in motivating their congregations to vote, and it may be hard to reconcile this anti-oppressive function of the Black church with the idea of Christian privilege. At the same time, the same churches that have been a source of empowerment for some of their Black members have not been as welcoming to the LGBTQ+[10] members of their community, leaving many LGBTQ+ Black Christians with conflicted relationships with the Black church and Christianity in general.

For many participants, it may be easier to focus on the bias, prejudice, and discrimination experienced by marginalized religions, rather than on the cultural and systemic privilege that go along with Christianity in the U.S. or on how some groups within the Christian faith are oppressed in their own churches. Often in these discussions, participants who are religiously observant and for whom religion is a highly salient identity may feel especially visible and uncomfortable. This is especially true of Christians who may become defensive, even angry, when the terms "Christian hegemony" or "Christian normativity" become part of the workshop vocabulary.

If participants stray too far from the course or workshop design to discuss specific religious or theological beliefs, facilitators should acknowledge these remarks but not allow the discussion of advantage and disadvantage to get sidetracked by ideological or theological issues. Instructors need to remind the group that this class focuses on the ways in which the dominant religion has shaped the culture for all members of the society and the historical legacies that contribute to religious advantage and disadvantage in the U.S. It can be useful to have resources available for participants who want, in another setting, to explore their religious beliefs or learn more about other religions.

Some participants will self-identify as non-religious, non-affiliated, non-believers, agnostics, atheists, spiritual but not religious, secular or humanists, or "nothing in particular." It is important to keep space open for those positions, even if no one in the class explicitly owns such a position. The cultural bias in the U.S. against atheists or those who do not have religious beliefs is very strong and needs to be acknowledged and addressed in the context of Christian hegemony. At the same time, some people in these categories who were raised Christian may benefit in limited ways from Christian privilege, at the same time as they are also disadvantaged.

Religiously conservative Christians (and other religious groups) may also feel vulnerable in social justice spaces where being religious is not always accepted. Instructors need to ensure that all participants are respected. Because feelings can arise unexpectedly in this (as in any other) course or workshop, we have some suggestions for instructor or facilitator preparation.

INSTRUCTOR/FACILITATOR SELF-AWARENESS AND KNOWLEDGE

Because religious identity is not always thought of as a source of social advantage or disadvantage, it is important for instructors and facilitators to reflect upon their own religious upbringing, experiences, beliefs, assumptions, and values as they prepare for the course or workshop. If they are atheists or do not believe in organized religion, this too is an important subject for self-reflection concerning the steps that have led to that identity and commitment. For facilitators to be effective in helping participants manage these conversations, they need to have thought in advance about their own religious position vis-à-vis specific religions as well as religion more generally, and they need to understand issues that might provoke emotional reactions for them in such discussions.

They also need to have reflected in advance on how their own religious identities and experiences have shaped or intersected with their other identities such as gender, sexual orientation, class, ethnicity, and race. They will need to have examples and anecdotes prepared in advance to illustrate various points and to encourage participant self-reflection. Finally, facilitators should consider their positionality as group leaders in relation to religious identity and in relation to campus or professional or community religious norms.

This course/workshop does not call for expertise on U.S. or world religions or religion and the law. But it does call for advance preparation on the topics in the design and anticipating how to facilitate discussions where disagreement, withdrawal, silence, or avoidance can occur. Instructors and facilitators should use the information in this chapter and the website materials that support our sample design as they prepare themselves to lead participants through a deep exploration of a social justice approach to religious oppression and Christian hegemony.

ESTABLISHING AN INCLUSIVE AND SUPPORTIVE LEARNING COMMUNITY FOR PARTICIPANTS

As with all social justice topics, the learning community is the context for support and challenge that encourage new learning. Participants will bring varying degrees of comfort and knowledge to the course/workshop. Developing group guidelines is a crucial ingredient for establishing trust and commitment to the learning community from all group members. Here are some potential guidelines for the group that may be helpful:

- Respect what participants say about their religious identification and experiences.
- Be aware of your own ignorance and bias about various faith traditions and about those who do not believe in any religion.

- Name and acknowledge difficulties of discussing religion and religious oppression in a setting with people from different religious backgrounds and experiences.
- Acknowledge the difficulty of discussing religious beliefs that people experience as oppressive, such as sexist, homophobic, or classist.
- Do not expect members of marginalized faith communities to speak for other members of that community.
- Speak from your experience and do not claim to represent or speak on behalf of a religious community.
- Participate in the discussion even if you are fearful of making mistakes.

Constitutional Questions

Religious oppression seems so fundamentally to contradict a core U.S. belief in freedom of religion, and this seeming contradiction is important to explore. Participants may assume that the First Amendment assures the free exercise of religion (as distinct from freedom of religious belief). It can be helpful to consider the difference between "beliefs" or conscience on the one hand, and "action" or practice on the other, and to illustrate some of the contradictions in Supreme Court cases dealing with religious freedom.

There is a related constitutional question that facilitators might want to anticipate—namely, the role of the First and Fourteenth Amendments in protecting minority rights and the role of majority rule in a democracy. How do participants believe we should balance the protection of free religious exercise and the constitutional protection of marginalized social groups, including religious groups?

Sometimes individuals are fearful about crossing the line that "separates" the public arena from religion or saying something that could result in pushback or taking offense or even in litigation. This fear can become an excuse for silence and avoidance. There are many resources to help teachers and others in public service understand what the law prohibits, what it allows, and where the gray areas might be.

CONTEMPORARY U.S. AND GLOBAL EXAMPLES

As local or global religious conflicts appear in the media, topics related to those conflicts may become especially salient and may need to be addressed even if facilitators hadn't planned to do so. When issues come up that the facilitators have not prepared to cover and do not have expertise in, it can be useful to ask what questions you would need to answer and where you would find answers to these questions before bringing discussion back to the planned topics. In a class or workshop that extends over many days, it is possible to set up assignments to prepare participants for informed discussions of current events using a social justice approach.

When issues regarding global religious conflicts arise, remind the class that our main focus is on systems of advantage and disadvantage in the U.S. At the same time, it is valuable to consider whether or how the core concepts apply to global religious conflicts. Conceptually, the social justice approach is applicable in every nation-state that has either a state religion or an "unofficial" state religion, like the U.S. However, unless the instructor/facilitator has planned to devote time to geopolitical conflicts that involve religion along with nationalist and colonialist dynamics, it is wise to deflect such discussions—or to anticipate the likelihood it will come up, based on current events, and prepare accordingly.

COMPLEXITIES OF CHRISTIAN PRIVILEGE

It is often difficult for participants who have Christian privilege to recognize and acknowledge that fact. Some may feel targeted and think of themselves as discriminated against because of being observant, and they may be so focused on not feeling accepted that they are unable to recognize the ways in which they benefit from Christian privilege. Some may be in the middle of difficult journeys away from a Christian family background and may find it hard to see the privilege in the midst of their pain. Some may be Christians of color for whom the intersections with racial, ethnic, linguistic, class, or gender identities complicate the relationship to Christian privilege. Some may be questioning or confirmed disbelievers from Christian backgrounds; they are disadvantaged in their agnostic or atheist identity even as they may benefit in some limited ways from Christian privilege and may feel they have more in common with non-believers from Jewish or Muslim or other traditions than with religious Christians.

Although moving toward social justice requires recognizing Christian privilege, it is important to hear what participants describe as their experiences and to explore the presence or absence of religious advantage or disadvantage. Often such discussions surface intersections or other factors that add nuance to the reality of Christian privilege, rather than contradicting it, and may make it easier for some participants to recognize their privilege. It is helpful to hold a "both/and" approach, affirming participants' feelings and understandings of being disadvantaged in some ways while encouraging them to recognize ways in which they simultaneously benefit.

ADDITIONAL FACILITATION CONCERNS AND TIPS

- It is helpful to know, in advance, the religious affiliation or non-affiliation of the participants in the group in order to include examples and activities that enable participants to see themselves reflected. Several of the activities in Quadrant 1 will enable the instructor/facilitator and the participants to place themselves and each other in religious contexts and to feel seen. Other activities throughout the design can be modified to encourage further disclosure and sharing among participants.
- A question worth asking throughout the workshop or class is, "How can you get the information you might need, in the future, to understand the background and components of religious oppression in the U.S. or elsewhere?" Participants can help each other identify resources for continued exploration and learning.
- The role of religion in public life, and the ways that communities experience religious homogeneity or diversity, playsout in different ways in various geographical regions of the U.S. For some communities, religion may be interfused with public life. In others, it may be considered private or taboo. It may be challenging for participants to separate their own regional and family experiences from the larger U.S. context in order to talk about the role of religion in national culture.
- Participants may lack knowledge or have misinformation about their own religion as well as the religion of others. Knowledge about the strong and dramatic sectarian differences within religions may seem confusing. It is helpful to give examples that illustrate the broad continuum—from orthodox, fundamentalist, and observant to liberal or reformist—within all religions. It helps also to understand that religions are "alive" and that they grow and change, that different religious communities emerge within a given religious belief system—and may then break off to form a new religion. There is as much variability (theological, cultural, geographical) within religions as there is between them.

- Religious conflict is a painful subject, especially the indisputable evidence of violence in the name of a religion. The fact that all religions have, at some time, justified violence provides an important perspective on this challenging issue from which no major religious group is immune.

- Participants may feel cynical or disillusioned by the contradictions between the high ideals of religions (peace, justice, love, caring for the stranger) and the behaviors of many peoples who claim those religions. Facilitators may need to point out other locations of contradiction—in politics, in organizational life, in families—to suggest that the contradictions may feel more dramatic in religion because the bar is often higher and the ideals may be more visible.

- Participants may feel estranged and excluded by their religious communities because of gender or sexual identity or other forms of nonconformity with their religion's norms. They may express anger and disillusionment with their religious community. This is an opportunity to note the intersections of forms of oppression and the ways in which advantaged as well as disadvantaged religious communities perpetuate those norms. It is also an opportunity to note that while homophobia happens in secular spaces as well, religious homophobia gets denigrated as "backward" when it occurs within a religious community that is not Christian.

- Participants may feel daunted by the complexities of religious conflicts globally as well as domestically and may feel hopeless about achieving understanding of the issues or perspectives. It is worth the time to unpack the complexity of specific U.S. contemporary or historical examples of religious oppression. Here, again, the question, "Where can you go to find the information you will need to unpack this situation?" is a valuable question to ask to reinforce participants' responsibilities for their lifelong learning.

- Sometimes, when people try to become more inclusive, greater respect seems to be shown to members of minority religions (Jews, Hindus, Muslims, non-believers) than to observant Christians. As a result, observant Christians may feel singled out, blamed, and defensive about the historical and systemic approach taken to their own faith. Some participants from Christian families or legacies may want the group to know that they themselves are personally not Christians, while other participants may want participants to know that they are deeply believing Christians. It is important to maintain space for both kinds of identity and affiliation while emphasizing that the purpose of this class is not to share personal religious beliefs but to understand the historical legacy and systemic power of hegemonic Christianity that is experienced by everyone in the U.S.

CLOSURE

This chapter and design represent a brief overview of the historical and contemporary context in which we are currently operating and a set of pedagogical tools designed to examine the complexity of the subject matter. We acknowledge it is not possible to "complete" an exploration of religious oppression generally or of Christian hegemony in the U.S. Nonetheless, classes and workshops need to come to closure by openly naming their new insights or remaining questions, sharing resources for further study, or establishing networks, study groups, or informal connections to continue their conversations or action plans.

The common element in these experiences is that the journey started within the course or workshop and is intended to be a lifelong journey. The class or workshop should end with plans and attention to future action and continued learning, with support nets established among participants or plans to build support nets as part of personal or collective action plans.

Notes

* We ask that those who cite this work always acknowledge by name all of the authors listed rather than either only citing the first author or using "et al." to indicate co-authors. All collaborated on the conceptualization, development, and writing of this chapter.

1 Atheists are those who believe that there is no god, agnostics are those who do not know whether there is a god, and non-believers are those who do not think there is a god.

2 Throughout the chapter, we use the terms "West Asia" or "Arab World" as more accurate than "Middle East" (Arab America Website, 2020; Khalidi, 1998). The term "Middle East" was adopted by the British Empire, which referred to regions under its colonial control as Near East, Middle East, and Far East. Since this region falls in the western part of the Asian continent, the more accurate name would be West Asia and North Africa or Arab World. The current use of "Middle East" includes several non-Arab countries, and it is sometimes confusing as to which countries are included in the term.

3 BIPOC stands for Black, Indigenous, and other People of Color. It includes all people racialized as non-white while bringing to the fore Black and Indigenous groups to acknowledge the specificity of their relationships to systems of coloniality and racism. This volume's preface discusses the emergence and uses of the term BIPOC and debates surrounding it.

4 An expanded version of this section is available on the website as an additional resource.

5 "Mahometan" is an old term that refers to Muslims as the followers of the prophet Mohammed.

6 A mufti is a Muslim scholar who makes fatwa, a religious ruling on an Islamic matter or an Islamic law enacted by a religious authority figure.

7 In 1922, colonial Britain and France divided Greater Syria into four different countries—what are now known as Syria, Lebanon, Palestine, and Jordan.

8 The Ottoman Empire ruled Greater Syria until the end of World War I.

9 Bolshevism is a specific form of communist government characterized by strong central control and associated with the Bolshevik ruling party in Soviet Russia and later the Soviet Union.

10 LGBTQ+ stands for lesbian, gay, bisexual, transgender, queer, and others whose gender and/or sexual identities are considered to be outside of dominant societal norms. See Chapter 6: Gender and Sexuality Oppressions.

References

Abington v. Schempp (1963, June 17). *School District of Abington Township, Pennsylvania, v. Schempp*. 374 U.S. 203.

Adams, G. A. (2005). *A farther shore: Ireland's long road to peace*. New York: Random House.

Adams, G. A. (2008). *The specter of Salem: Remembering the witch trials in nineteenth-century America*. Chicago: University of Chicago Press.

Adams, M. (2012). Separation of church and state. In J. A. Banks (Ed.), *Encyclopedia of diversity in education*. New York: Sage.

Adams, M., Blumenfeld, W., Catalano, C. J. C., DeJong, K., Hackman, H., Hopkins, L., Love, B., Peters, M., Shlasko, D. & Zúñiga, X. (Eds.). (2018). *Readings for diversity and social justice* (4th ed.). New York: Routledge.

Ahlstrom, S. E. (2004). *A religious history of the American people*. New Haven, CT: Yale University Press.

Akasoy, A. (2010). Review Article: Convivencia and its discontents: Interfaith life in Al-Andalus. *International Journal of Middle East Studies*, 42(3), 489–499. Retrieved from http://www.jstor.org/stable/40784829

Alsultany, E. (2008). The prime time plight of the Arab Muslim American after 9/11. In A. Jamal & N. Naber (Eds.), *Race and Arab Americans before and after 9/11: From invisible citizens to visible subjects* (pp. 204–228). Syracuse, NY: Syracuse University Press.

Alvarez, L., & Don, V. N., Jr. (2011, Apr. 1). Pastor who burned Koran demands retribution. *The New York Times*. Retrieved from http://www.nytimes.com/2011/04/02/us/politics/02burn.html

Anderson, R. D. (2007). *Religion and teaching: Reflective teaching and the social conditions of schooling; A series for prospective and practicing teachers*. New York: Routledge.

Andrews, S. (2013). *Deconverted: A journey from religion to reason*. Denver: Outskirts Press.

Arab America Website. (2020). Retrieved from https://www.arabamerica.com/renaming-the-middle-east/

Armstrong, K. (2014). *Fields of blood: Religion and the history of violence*. New York: Knopf.

Bagby, I. (2011). *The American mosque: Basic characteristics of the American mosque attitudes of mosque leaders*. Council on American-Islamic Relations (CAIR). Retrieved from http://www.cair.com/images/pdf/The-American-Mosque-2011-part-1.pdf

Bald, V. (2013). *Bengali Harlem and the lost histories of South Asian America*. Cambridge, MA: Harvard University Press.

Ballantine, B., & Ballantine, I. (Eds.). (2001). *The Native Americans: An illustrated history*. East Bridgewater, MA: JG Press.

Barzel, Y. (1992). Confiscation by the Ruler: The Rise and Fall of Jewish Lending in the Middle Ages. *The Journal of Law & Economics, 35*(1), 1–13. Retrieved from http://www.jstor.org/stable/725552

Bayoumi, M., (2015). *This Muslim American life: Dispatches from the War on Terror*. New York: New York University Press.

Beaman, L. G. (2003). The myth of pluralism, diversity, and vigor: The constitutional privilege of Protestantism in the United States and Canada. *Journal for the Scientific Study of Religion, 42*(3), 311–325.

Bellah, R. N. (1967). Civil religion in America. *Daedalus, Journal of the American Academy of Arts & Sciences, 96*(1), 1–21.

Berlak, C. (2014). *Constructing campus conflict: Antisemitism and islamophobia on U.S. college campuses, 2007–2011*. Somerville, MA: Political Research Associates.

Beydoun, K. A. (2018). *American Islamophobia: Understanding the roots and rise of fear*. Oakland, California: University of California Press. Retrieved from http://www.jstor.org/stable/10.1525/j.ctv1wxs79

Blumenfeld, W. J. (2006). Christian privilege and the promotion of "secular" and not-so "secular" mainline Christianity in public schooling and in the larger society. *Equity & Excellence, 39*(3), 195–210.

Boyer, P. S., & Nissenbaum, S. (Eds.). (1972). *Salem-Village witchcraft: A documentary record of local conflict in Colonial New England*. Boston: Northeastern University Press.

Brodkin, K. (1998). *How Jews became white folks and what that says about race in America*. New Brunswick, NJ: Rutgers University Press.

Bronner, S. E. (2000). *A rumor about the Jews: Reflections on antisemitism and "the protocols of the learned elders of Zion."* New York: St. Martin's Press.

Burwell v. Hobby Lobby Stores, Inc. (2014) 573 U.S. 682. Retrieved from https://supreme.justia.com/cases/federal/us/573/682/

Butler, J., Wacker, G., & Balmer, R. (2003). *Religion in American life: A short history*. Oxford, UK: Oxford University Press.

Carnes, T., & Yang, F. (2004). *Asian American religions: The making and remaking of borders and boundaries*. New York: New York University Press.

Chavers, D. (2009). *Racism in Indian country*. Bern, Switzerland: Peter Lang.

Chazan, R. (2016). *From anti-Judaism to anti-Semitism: Ancient and Medieval Christian constructions of Jewish history*. Cambridge University Press.

Chen, C., & Jeung, R. M. (Eds.). (2012). *Sustaining faith traditions: Race, ethnicity, and religion among the Latin and Asian American second generation*. New York: New York University Press.

Christina, G. (2012). *Why are you Atheists so angry? 99 things that piss off the godless*. Charlottesville, VA: Pitchstone.

Cole, D. (2015, May 7). The angry new frontier: Gay rights vs. religious liberty. *The New York Review of Books*. Retrieved from http://www.nybooks.com/articles/archives/2015/may/07/angry-new-frontier-gay-rights-vs-religious-liberty/

Considine, C. (2017). The Racialization of Islam in the United States: Islamophobia, Hate Crimes, and "Flying while Brown." *Religions, 8*(9), 165. MDPI AG. Retrieved from http://dx.doi.org/10.3390/rel8090165

County of Allegheny v. American Civil Liberties Union (1989, July 3). 492 U.S. 573.

Daniels, R. (2002). *Coming to America: A history of immigration and ethnicity in American life* (2nd ed.). New York: Harper Perennial.

Diamant, J. (2019 April, 1). *The countries with the 10 largest Christian populations and the 10 largest Muslim populations.* Pew Research Center. Retrieved from https://www.pewresearch.org/fact-tank/2019/04/01/the-countries-with-the-10-largest-christian-populations-and-the-10-largest-muslim-populations/

Diner, H. R. (2004). *The Jews of the United States.* Berkeley, CA: University of California Press.

Echo-Hawk, W. R. (2010). *In the courts of the conqueror: The 10 worst Indian law cases ever decided.* Golden, CO: Fulcrum.

Eck, D. (2001). *A new religious America: How a "Christian country" has become the world's most religiously diverse nation.* San Francisco: Harper One.

Eckholm, E. (2015, March 31). Eroding in the name of freedom. *The New York Times.* Retrieved from http://www.nytimes.com/2015/03/31/us/politics/religious-protection-laws-once-called-shields-are-now-seen-as-cudgels.html

Ecklund, E. H., & Park, J. Z. (2005). Asian American community participation and religion: Civic model minorities? *Journal of Asian American Studies, 8*(1), 1–22.

Emerson, M. O., & Smith, C. (2000). *Divided by faith: Evangelical religion and the problem of race in America.* New York: Oxford University Press.

Engel v. Vitale. (1962) 370 U.S. 421.

Ennis, A. (2017). *Teaching religious literacy: A guide to spiritual diversity in higher education.* New York, NY: Routledge.

Espinosa, G. (2014). *Latino Pentecostals in America: Faith and politics in action.* Cambridge, MA: Harvard University Press.

Esposito, J. L., & Kalin, I. (2011). *Islamophobia: The challenge of pluralism in the 21st century.* Oxford, UK: Oxford University Press.

Everson v. Board of Education. (1947). 330 U.S. 1, decided February 10, 1947.

Feldman, S. M. (Ed.). (1996). *Please don't wish me a merry Christmas: A critical history of the separation of church and state.* New York: New York University Press.

Forward, M. (2001). *Inter-religious dialogue: A short introduction.* London, UK: Oneworld Publications.

Fox, J. (2000). Religious causes of discrimination against ethno-religious minorities. *International Studies Quarterly, 44*(3), 423–450.

Fox, J. (2002). *Ethnoreligious conflict in the late 20th century: A general theory.* Lanham, MD: Lexington Books.

Fraser, J. W. (1999). *Between church and state: Religion and public education in a multicultural America.* New York: St. Martin's Press.

Fredrickson, G. M. (2002). *Racism: A short history.* Princeton, NJ: Princeton University Press.

Fulop, T. E., & Raboteau, A. J. (Eds.). (1997). *African-American religion: Interpretive essays in history and culture.* New York: Routledge.

Garces-Foley, K., & Jeung, R. (2013). Asian American Evangelicals in multicultural church ministry. *Religions, 4*(2), 190–208.

GhaneaBassiri, K. (2010). *A history of Islam in America: From the new world to the new world order.* Cambridge, UK: Cambridge University Press.

Gilbert, M. (2003). *The Routledge atlas of Jewish history* (6th ed.). New York: Routledge.

Goldschmidt, H., & McAlister, E. A. (Eds.). (2004). *Race, nation, and religion in the Americas.* Oxford, UK: Oxford University Press.

Goldman v. Weinberger. (1986) 475 U.S. 503. Retrieved from https://supreme.justia.com/cases/federal/us/475/503/

Green, S. K. (2012). *The Bible, the school, and the Constitution: The clash that shaped modern church-state doctrine.* Oxford, UK: Oxford University Press.

Grieco, E. M., Trevelyan, E., Larsen, L., Acosta, Y. D., Gambino, C., de la Cruz, P., Gryn, T., & Walters, N. (2012, Oct.). *The size, place of birth, and geographic distribution of the foreign-born population in the United States: 1960 to 2010* (Population Division Working Paper, 96). Population Division, U.S. Census Bureau. Retrieved from https://www.census.gov/population/foreign/files/WorkingPaper96.pdf

Grinde, D. A. (2004). Taking the Indian out of the Indian: U.S. policies of ethnocide through education. *Wicazo Sa Review, 19*(2), 25–32.

Gualtieri, S. (2001). Becoming "white": Race, religion and the foundations of Syrian/Lebanese ethnicity in the United States. *Journal of American Ethnic History, 20*(4), 29–58.

Guglielmo, T. A. (2003). *White on arrival: Italians, race, color, and power in Chicago, 1890–1945*. Oxford, UK: Oxford University Press.

Guglielmo, T. A., & Salerno, S. (2003). *Are Italians white? How race is made in America*. New York: Routledge.

Haddad, Y. Y. (2002). *Muslims in the West: From sojourners to citizens*. Oxford, UK: Oxford University Press.

Haddad, Y. Y. (2011). *Becoming American? The forging of Arab and Muslim identity in pluralist America*. Waco, TX: Baylor University Press.

Hafiz, S., & Raghunathan, S. (2014). *Under suspicion, under attack: Xenophobic political rhetoric and hate violence against South Asian, Muslim, Sikh, Hindu, Middle Eastern, and Arab communities in the United States*. South Asian Americans Leading Together (SAALT). Retrieved from http://saalt.org/wp-content/uploads/2014/09/SAALT_report_full_links.pdf

Haney-López, I. F. (2006). *White by law: The legal construction of race*. New York: New York University Press.

Harvey, P. (2003). "A servant of servants shall he be": The construction of race in American religious mythologies. In C. R. Prentiss (Ed.), *Religion and the creation of race and ethnicity* (pp. 13–27). New York: New York University Press.

Haynes, C. C., Chaltain, S., Ferguson, J., Hudson, D. L., Jr., & Thomas, O. (2003). *The First Amendment in schools: A guide from the First Amendment Center*. Alexandria, VA: Association for Supervision & Curriculum.

Haynes, C. C., & Thomas, O. (2001). *Finding common ground: A guide to religious liberty in public schools*. Nashville, TN: The First Amendment Center.

Hilberg, R. (1961). *The destruction of the European Jews*. New York: Harper & Row.

Hilberg, R. (2003). *The destruction of the European Jews* (3rd ed.), 3 volumes. New Haven: Yale University Press.

Hinduism Today (2008, January–March). So, how many Hindus are there in the U.S.? U.S. Census Bureau's American community survey provides the best answer. *Hinduism Today*. Retrieved from http://www.hafsite.org/sites/default/files/HT_Census_USA_Jan08.pdf

Hitchens, C. (Ed.). (2007). *The portable Atheist: Essential readings for the nonbeliever*. Boston: Da Capo Press.

Husain, A. (2017). Retrieving the religion in racialization: A critical review. *Sociology Compass, 11*, e12507. doi:10.1111/soc4.12507

Hutchinson, S. (2020). Intersectional Politics among Atheists and Humanists of Color. In Yukich G., & Edgell P. (Eds.), *Religion Is Raced: Understanding American Religion in the Twenty-First Century* (pp. 58–73). New York: NYU Press. Retrieved from http://www.jstor.org/stable/j.ctv1sjwnt5.6

Ignatiev, N. (2009). *How the Irish became white*. New York: Routledge.

Jacobsen, D., & Jacobsen, R. H. (2012). *No longer invisible: Religion in university education*. Oxford, England: Oxford University Press.

Jacobson, M. F. (1998). *Whiteness of a different color: European immigrants and the alchemy of race*. Cambridge, MA: Harvard University Press.

Jacobson, R. D., & Wadsworth, N. D. (2012). *Faith and race in American political life*. Charlottesville, VA: University of Virginia Press.

Jacoby, S. (2004). *Freethinkers: A history of American Secularism*. New York: Holt.

Jamal, A., & Naber, N. (Eds.). (2008). *Race and Arab Americans before and after 9/11: From invisible citizens to visible subjects*. Syracuse, NY: Syracuse University Press.

Jensen, J. M. (1988). *Passage from India: Asian Indian immigrants in North America*. New Haven, CT: Yale University Press.

Jewish Voice for Peace. (2020). Retrieved from https://jewishvoiceforpeace.org/

Johnstone, R. L. (2004). *Religion in society: A sociology of religion*. Upper Saddle River, NJ: Pearson/Prentice Hall.

Jones, D. G., & Richey, R. E. (1974). The civil religion debate. In D. G. Jones & R. E. Richey (Eds.), *American civil religion* (pp. 3–18). New York: Harper & Row.

Jones, S. P., & Sheffield, E. C. (Eds.). (2009). *The role of religion in 21st century public schools*. Bern, Switzerland: Peter Lang.

Joshi, K. Y. (2006). *New roots in America's sacred ground: Religion, race, and ethnicity in Indian America*. New Brunswick, NJ: Rutgers University Press.

Joshi, K. Y. (2009). The racialization of religion in the United States. In W. J. Blumenfeld, K. Y. Joshi, & E. K. Fairchild (Eds.), *Investigating Christian privilege and religious oppression in the United States* (pp. 37–56). Rotterdam/Taipei: Sense Publishers.

Joshi, K. Y. (2020). *White Christian privilege: The illusion of religious equality in America*. New York, NY: New York University Press.

Jotischky, A. (2017). Ethnic and religious categories in the treatment of Jews and Muslims in the crusade states. In J. Renton & B. Gidley (Eds.), *Antisemitism and Islamophobia in Europe: A shared story?* (pp. 25–49). Palgrave Macmillan. Retrieved from http://ndl.ethernet.edu.et/bitstream/123456789/24335/1/59.pdf

Kapila, S. (2007). Race matters: Orientalism and religion, India and beyond. *Modern Asian Studies, 41*(3), 471–513.

Karpf, A., Klug, B., Rose, J., & Rosenbaum, B. (Eds.). (2008). *A time to speak out: Independent Jewish voices on Israel, Zionism and Jewish identity*. New York: Verso.

Khalidi, R. (1998). The "Middle East" as a framework of analysis: Re-mapping a region in the era of globalization. Comparative Studies of South Asia, Africa and the Middle East (formerly South Asia Bulletin), Vol. XVIII (1), 74–80. Retrieved from https://novact.org/wp-content/uploads/2012/09/The-%E2%80%98Middle-East%E2%80%99-as-a-framework-for-analysis-Remapping-a-region-in-the-era-of-Globalization-Rashid-Khalidi.pdf

Killermann, S. (2012). *30+ examples of Christian privilege*. Project Humanities, Arizona State University. Retrieved from https://humanities.asu.edu/christian-privilege-checklist

Kivel, P. (2013). *Living in the shadow of the cross: Understanding and resisting the power and privilege of Christian hegemony*. Vancouver, BC, Canada: New Society Publishers.

Kosmin, B. A., & Keysar, A. (2015, Feb.). *National demographic survey of American Jewish college students 2014: Anti-semitism report*. The Louis D. Brandeis Center for Human Rights Under Law, Trinity College. Retrieved from http://www.trincoll.edu/NewsEvents/NewsArticles/Documents/Anti-SemitismReportFinal.pdf

Kruse, K. (2015). *One nation under God: How corporate America invented Christian America*. New York: Basic Books.

Kurien, P. (2014). Immigration, community formation, political incorporation, and why religion matters: Migration and settlement patterns of the Indian diaspora. *Sociology of Religion, 75*(4), 524–536.

Kushner, T., & Solomon, A. (Eds.). (2003). *Wrestling with Zion: Progressive Jewish-American responses to the Israeli-Palestinian conflict*. New York: Grove Press.

Laqueur, W. (2006). *The changing face of anti-Semitism: From ancient times to the present day*. Oxford, UK: Oxford University Press.

Lee, D. B. (2004). Religion and the construction of White America. In H. Goldschmidt & E. McAlister (Eds.), *Race, nation, and religion in the Americas* (pp. 85–110). Oxford, UK: Oxford University Press.

Lemon v. Kurtzman. (1971) 403 U.S. 602. Retrieved from https://supreme.justia.com/cases/federal/us/403/602/

Lincoln, C. E., & Mamiya, L. H. (1990). *The Black church in the African American experience*. Durham, NC: Duke University Press.

Linge, G. (2000). Ensuring the full freedom of religion on public lands: Devils Tower and the protection of Indian sacred sites. *Boston College Environmental Affairs Law Review, 27*(2), 307–339.

Lipka, M. (2013, October 2). *How many Jews are there in the United States?* Pew Research Center. Retrieved from http://www.pewresearch.org/fact-tank/2013/10/02/how-many-jews-are-there-in-the-united-states/

Lipka, M. (2014, July 17). *How many people of different faiths do you know?* Pew Research Center. Retrieved from http://www.pewresearch.org/fact-tank/2014/07/17/how-many-people-of-different-faiths-do-you-know/

Lipsitz, G. (2006). *The possessive investment in whiteness: How white people profit from identity politics* (rev. & expanded ed.). Philadelphia: Temple University Press.

Little, D. (2007). *Peacemakers in action: Profiles of religion in conflict resolution*. Cambridge, UK: Cambridge University Press.

Loewen, J. W. (1995). *Lies my teachers told me: Everything your American history textbook got wrong*. New York: The New Press.

LoGiurato, B. (2014, July 3). Female justices issue scathing dissent in the first post-Hobby Lobby birth control exemption. *Business Insider*. Retrieved from http://www.businessinsider.com/sotomayor-ginsburg-kagan-dissent-wheaton-college-decision-supreme-court-2014-7

Long, C. N. (2000). *Religious freedom and Indian rights: The case of Oregon v. Smith*. Lawrence, KS: University Press of Kansas.

Maddigan, M. M. (1993). The establishment clause, civil religion, and the public church. *California Law Review, 81*(1), 293–349.

Maira, S. (2004). Youth culture, citizenship and globalization: South Asian Muslim youth in the United States after September 11th. Comparative Studies of South Asia, Africa and the Middle East. 24(1), 219–231. Retrieved from https://www.muse.jhe.edu/article/181213

Mamdani, M. (2004). *Good Muslim, bad Muslim: America, the Cold War, and the roots of terror*. New York: Harmony Books.

Marimow, A. E. (2019, February 13). Christian student challenged a school history lesson on Islam and lost in court. *The Washington Post*. Retrieved from https://www.washingtonpost.com/local/legal-issues/christian-student-challenged-a-school-history-lesson-on-islam-and-lost-in-court/2019/02/12/2a7d78fa-2ee4–11e9–813a-0ab2f17e305b_story.html

Mazur, E. M. (1999). *The Americanization of religious minorities: Confronting the Constitutional order*. Baltimore: Johns Hopkins University Press.

Mazur, E. M., & McCarthy, K. (Eds.). (2001). *God in the details: American religion in popular culture*. New York: Routledge.

McCarthy, K. (2007). *Interfaith encounters in America*. New Brunswick, NJ: Rutgers University Press.

Meer, N. (2013). Racialization and religion: Race, culture and difference in the study of antisemitism and Islamophobia. *Ethnic and Racial Studies, 36*(3), 385–398, DOI:10.1080/01419870.2013.734392

Melton, J. G., & Jones, C. A. (2011). *Reflections on Hindu demographics in America: An initial report on the first American Hindu census*. Retrieved from http://www.thearda.com/asrec/archive/papers/Melton_Hindu_Demographics.pdf

Menchaca, M. (2001). *Recovering history, constructing race: The Indian, black, and white roots of Mexican Americans*. Austin, TX: University of Texas Press.

Michael, R. (2005). *A concise history of American antisemitism*. Lanham, MD: Rowman & Littlefield.

Min, P. G. (2010). *Preserving ethnicity through religion in America: Korean Protestants and Indian Hindus across generations*. New York: New York University Press.

Min, P. G., & Kim, J. H. (Eds.). (2001). *Religions in Asian America: Building faith communities*. Walnut Creek, CA: AltaMira Press.

Mogahed, D., & Chouhoud, Y. (2017). *American Muslim Poll 2017: Muslims at the Crossroads*. Institute for Social Policy and Understanding. Retrieved from https://www.ispu.org/american-muslim-poll-2017/

Mohamed, B. (2018, January 3). *New estimates show U.S. Muslim population continues to grow*. Pew Research Center. Retrieved from https://www.pewresearch.org/fact-tank/2018/01/03/new-estimates-show-u-s-muslim-population-continues-to-grow/

Mohamed, B. (2021, September 1). *Muslims are a growing presence in U.S., but still face negative views from the public*. Pew Research Center. Retrieved from https://www.pewresearch.org/fact-tank/2021/09/01/muslims-are-a-growing-presence-in- u-s-but-still-face-negative-views-from-the-public/

Moore, D. L. (2007). *Overcoming religious illiteracy: A cultural studies approach to the study of religion in secondary education*. London, UK: Palgrave Macmillan.

Morris, A. D. (1986). *Origins of the civil rights movements*. New York: Free Press.

Muñoz, V. P. (2013). *Religious liberty and the American Supreme Court: The essential cases and documents*. ProQuest Ebook Central https://ebookcentral.proquest.com

Murray, B. T. (2008). *Religious liberty in America: The First Amendment in historical and contemporary perspective*. Amherst, MA: University of Massachusetts Press.

Nash, R. J. (2001). *Religious pluralism in the academy: Opening the dialogue*. Bern, Switzerland: Peter Lang.

Ngai, M. M. (2004). *Impossible subjects: Illegal aliens and the making of modern America*. Princeton, NJ: Princeton University Press.

Niebuhr, G. (2008). *Beyond tolerance: Searching for interfaith understanding in America*. New York: Viking Press.

Not In Our Town (NIOT). (1995, 1996). *Information*. Retrieved from https://www.niot.org/

Novikoff, A. (2005). Between tolerance and intolerance in Medieval Spain: An histographic enigma. *Medieval Encounters: Jewish, Christian and Muslim Culture in Confluence and Dialogue, 11*(1–2), 7–36. Retrieved from https://doi-org.silk.library.umass.edu/10.1163/157006705775032834

Office of Immigration Statistics (2006, January). *2004 yearbook of immigration statistics*. U.S. Department of Homeland Security (DHS). Retrieved from http://www.dhs.gov/xlibrary/assets/statistics/yearbook/2004/Yearbook2004.pdf

Omi, M., & Winant, H. (2014). *Racial formation in the United States*. New York: Routledge.

O'Shea, S. (2006). *Sea of faith: Islam and Christianity in the medieval Mediterranean world*. London, UK: Walker & Company.

Parfitt, T. (2013). *Black Jews in Africa and the Americas*. ProQuest Ebook Central. Retrieved from https://ebookcentral.proquest.com

Patel, E. (2012). *Sacred ground: Pluralism, prejudice, and the promise of America*. Boston: Beacon Press.

Patel, E. (2015, March 11). In promoting campus diversity, don't dismiss religion. *The Chronicle of Higher Education*. Retrieved from http://chronicle.com/article/In-Promoting-Campus-Diversity/228427/

Patel, E., & Scorer, T. (2012). *Embracing interfaith cooperation: Eboo Patel on coming together to change the world*. New York: Morehouse Education Resources.

Perry, M., & Schweitzer, F. M. (Eds.). (2008). *Antisemitic myths: A historical and contemporary anthology*. Bloomington, IN: Indiana University Press.

Pew Research Center (2011a, January 27). *The future of the global Muslim population*. Retrieved from http://www.pewforum.org/2011/01/27/the-future-of-the-global-muslim-population/

Pew Research Center. (2014). *Religious landscape study*. Retrieved from https://www.pewforum.org/religious-landscape-study/

Pew Research Center (2015, May 12). *America's changing religious landscape: Christians decline sharply as share of population; unaffiliated and other faiths continue to grow*. Retrieved from http://www.pewforum.org/2015/05/12/americas-changing-religious-landscape/

Pew Research Center. (2018, July 5). *How does Pew Research center measure the religious composition of the U.S.? Answers to frequently asked questions*. Retrieved from https://www.pewforum.org/2018/07/05/how-does-pew-research-center-measure-the-religious-composition-of-the-u-s-answers-to-frequently-asked-questions/

Pew Research Center. (2019, October 17). *In U.S., decline of Christianity continues at rapid pace: An update on America's changing religious landscape*. Retrieved from https://www.pewforum.org/2019/10/17/in-u-s-decline-of-christianity-continues-at-rapid-pace/

Philbrick, N. (2004). *Sea of glory: America's voyage of discovery, The U.S. exploring expedition, 1838–1842*. London, UK: Penguin Books.

Prentiss, C. R. (Ed.). (2003). *Religion and the creation of race and ethnicity: An introduction*. New York: New York University Press.

Prothero, S. (2009). *Religious Literacy: What Every American Needs to Know-And Doesn't*. Reprint edition. New York: Harper One.

Rana, J. (2007). The story of Islamophobia. *Souls: A Critical Journal of Black Politics, Culture, and Society*, 9(2), 148–161.

Rana, J. (2011). *Terrifying Muslims: Race and labor in the South Asian diaspora*. Durham, NC: Duke University Press.

Reston, J. (2009). *Defenders of the faith: Christianity and Islam battle for the soul of Europe, 1520–1536*. London, UK: Penguin Books.

Roediger, D. R. (1991). *The wages of whiteness: Race and the making of the American working class*. New York: Verso.

Romero Castello, E., & Macías Kapón, U. (1994). *The Jews and Europe: 2,000 years of history*. New York: Holt.

Said, E. W. (1978). *Orientalism*. New York: Vintage Books.

Said, E. W. (1986). Orientalism reconsidered. In F. Barker, P. Hulme, M. Iversen, & D. Loxley (Eds.), *Literature, politics, and theory* (pp. 210–229). London: Metheun & Co.

Said, E. W. (1993). *Culture and imperialism*. New York: Vintage Books.

Schlosser, L. Z. (2003). Christian privilege: Breaking a sacred taboo. *Journal of Multicultural Counseling & Development*, 31(1), 44–51.

Shaheen, J. G. (2001). *Reel bad Arabs: How Hollywood vilifies a people*. Northampton, MA: Olive Branch Press.

Shaheen, J. G. (2008). *Guilty: Hollywood's verdict on Arabs after 9/11*. Brooklyn, NY: Olive Branch Press.

Sharkey, H. J. (2017). *A history of Muslims, Christians, and Jews in the Middle East*. Cambridge, UK: Cambridge University Press.

Shavit, A. (2013). *My promised land: The triumph and tragedy of Israel*. New York: Spiegel & Grau.

Shaw, W. M. (2017). Theology of religions in Martin Luther. *Perspectives on Theology of Religions, HTS Theological Studies/Teologiese Studies*, 73(6, suppl. 12), a4839. doi:10.4102/hts.v73i6.4839

Shepkaru, S. (2012). The preaching of the first crusade and the persecutions of the Jews. *Medieval Encounters*, 18(1), 93–135. Retrieved from https://doi.org.silk.library.umass.edu/10.1163/157006712X634576

Shohat, E. (2006). *Taboo memories, diasporic voices*. Durham, NC: Duke University Press.

Sikh American Legal Defense & Education Fund (SALDEF). (2014). *Who are Sikh Americans*. Retrieved from http://saldef.org/who-are-sikh-americans/#.VfnQdnBVhBc

Singh, J. (2003). The racialization of minoritized religious identity: Constructing sacred sites at the intersection of white and Christian supremacy. In J. N. Iwamura & P. Spickard (Eds.), *Revealing the sacred in Asian and Pacific America* (pp. 87–106). New York: Routledge.

Singh, J. (2013). A new American apartheid: Racialized, religious minorities in the post-9/11 era. *Sikh Formations: Religion, Culture, Theory, 9*(2), 115–144.

Smock, D. R. (Ed.). (2002). *Interfaith dialogue and peacebuilding*. Washington, DC: United States Institute of Peace.

Snow, J. (2004). The civilization of white men: The race of the Hindu in United States v. Bhagat Singh Thind. In H. Goldschmidt & E. McAlister (Eds.), *Race, nation, and religion in the Americas* (pp. 259–280). Oxford, UK: Oxford University Press.

Southern Poverty Law Center (SPLC) (2019, March 16). Weekend Read: A horrifying pattern of white supremacist attacks. Retrieved from https://www.splcenter.org/news/2019/03/16/weekend-read-horrifying-pattern-white-supremacist-attacks

Steinberg, S. R., & Kincheloe, J. L. (Eds.). (2009). *Christotainment: Selling Jesus through popular culture*. Boulder, CO: Westview Press.

Takaki, R. (1991). Between "two endless days": The continuous journey to the Promised Land. In *A different mirror: A history of multicultural America* (pp. 277–310). Boston: Little, Brown & Co.

Takaki, R. (1998). *Strangers from a different shore: A history of Asian Americans* (updated & rev. ed.). Boston: Little, Brown & Co.

Takaki, R. (2008). *A different mirror: A history of multicultural America* (rev. ed.). Little, Brown & Co.

Tamarkin, N. (2020). *Genetic Afterlives: Black Jewish Indigeneity in South Africa*. Durham; London: Duke University Press. doi:10.2307/j.ctv16qjzh0

Tanaka, K. (2011, July-Sept.). Dramatic growth of American Buddhism: An Overview. *Dharma World: For Living Buddhism & Interfaith Dialogue*. Retrieved from http://www.kosei-shuppan.co.jp/english/text/mag/2011/11_789_2.html

Tanenbaum. (2021, September 1). *Tanenbaum education*. Tanenbaum. Retrieved from http://www.tanenbaum.org

Tighe, E., Saxe, L., Magidin de Kramer, R., & Parmer, D. (2013, Sept.). *American Jewish population estimates: 2012*. Steinhardt Social Research Institute, Brandeis University. Retrieved from http://www.brandeis.edu/ssri/noteworthy/amjewishpop.html

Tolan, S. (2006). *The lemon tree: An Arab, a Jew, and the heart of the Middle East*. New York: Bloomsbury.

Tumulty, K. (2017, January 18). How Donald Trump came up with 'Make America great again'. *The Washington Post*. Retrieved from https://www.washingtonpost.com/

Reynolds v. United States. (1879) 98 U.S. 145. Retrieved from https://www.loc.gov/item/usrep098145/

Weinberg, M. (1986). *Because they were Jews: A history of antisemitism*. New York: Greenwood Press.

Wills, D. W. (2005). *Christianity in the United States: A historical survey and interpretation*. Notre Dame, IN: University of Notre Dame Press.

Wistrich, R. S. (1991). *Antisemitism: The longest hatred*. New York: Pantheon Books.

Witte, J. J., & Nichols, J. A. (2016). *Religion and the American constitutional experiment*. ProQuest Ebook Central. Retrieved from https://ebookcentral.proquest.com

Wyman, D. S. (2007). *The abandonment of the Jews: America and the Holocaust 1941–1945*. New York: The New Press.

Young, I. M. (1990). *Justice and the politics of difference*. Princeton, NJ: Princeton University Press.

Yukich, G., & Edgell, P. (2020). Introduction: Recognizing Raced Religion. In Yukich G. & Edgell P. (Eds.), *Religion Is Raced: Understanding American Religion in the Twenty-First Century* (pp. 1–16). New York: NYU Press. Retrieved from http://www.jstor.org/stable/j.ctv1sjwnt5.3

Zarrugh, A. (2016). Racialized political shock: Arab American racial formation and the impact of political events. *Ethnic and Racial Studies, 39*(15), 2722–2739, DOI: 10.1080/01419870.2016.1171368

Zia-Ebrahimi, R. (2018). When the Elders of Zion relocated to Eurabia: Conspiratorial racialization in antisemitism and Islamophobia. *Patterns of Prejudice, 52*(4), 314–337, DOI: 10.1080/0031322X.2018.1493876

9

Ableism and Disability Justice

Hillary Montague-Asp, Leah Lakshmi Piepzna-Samarasinha,
Davey Shlasko, and Lilith Logan Siegel*

In summer of 2019, PG&E, the monopoly electricity provider for much of California, conducted a series of planned power shut-offs in order to prevent wildfires. For many residents losing electricity was an inconvenience, but for some disabled people,[1] it became a life-threatening emergency (Ho, 2019). People who rely on medical equipment like oxygen concentrators, ventilators, or power wheelchairs were suddenly scrambling to find workarounds to meet their most basic physical needs.

Some disabled people contacted PG&E, but the company had no plans in place to help customers with medical needs (Ho, 2019). Others reached out to their local governments for assistance and were told to "use their own resources to get out" of the power outage zones—which most people could not do (Orenstein, 2019). Some local governments eventually activated emergency plans to support disabled people in their communities, but these programs only reached a small minority of disabled residents.

The most effective response to the crisis came from the disability community. In Oakland and Berkeley, disability activists quickly created a simple mutual aid system—a shared document where disabled people could communicate about their needs and help each other with transportation, emergency housing, refrigeration for medications, and more. Oakland's Disability Justice Culture Club raised money to purchase a generator so that it could provide an accessible safehouse the next time there are power outages (Ho, 2019).

North of Oakland in El Dorado County, at least one person died while trying to get to his backup, battery-operated breathing machine minutes after losing power in the middle of the night. A coroner determined that the cause of death was the person's medical conditions and not his life-sustaining medical equipment suddenly turning off (Sullivan & Bolag, 2019). For his family and for many disabled people, this determination is devastating evidence of the lethal impacts of ableism.

In this chapter we offer a framework to help readers understand situations like the 2019 electrical outages. How is it that disabled people were so invisible to those who made decisions about emergency planning? What historical legacies led up to a moment where the default approach to keeping "the public" safe considered only non-disabled members of the public? How do disability communities leverage unique strengths and practices to survive and thrive in the face of such injustice? And how can we as educators support transformative learning about ableism and disability justice while practicing disability justice in our learning communities?

This story mirrors the ways in which other, current crises both reveal and reproduce structural inequalities. The uneven response to the global public health crisis of COVID-19 has highlighted and magnified inequalities in healthcare access along lines of race, class, disability, and more. As mass movements of protest against police murders of Black people ripple across the US and beyond, we are reminded again and again that the US has always considered some lives expendable. Mutual aid projects blossom in the face of failing social safety nets, with neighbors and strangers sharing resources in ways unfamiliar to many. Shifting seasons and weather patterns (including California's increasingly catastrophic fire

DOI: 10.4324/9781003005759-11

seasons), brought about by human effects on the global climate, continue to have the hardest impact on communities that were already the most marginalized. Disability communities are not always part of the story that the media tell about this moment. But ableism has long been integral to the functioning of oppressive systems, and disabled wisdom has a lot to teach us all about survival, resistance, and liberation.

The COVID-19 pandemic has forced many people to reexamine how they think about illness, vulnerability, mortality, and care work, as well as access practices. As disabled and chronically ill people, we watch our abled friends bemoan how hard it is to be isolated from community, to face delays in accessing services, or to confront the potential of long-term health difficulties—challenges we have been dealing with since long before this pandemic. Responses to the pandemic show that accommodations disabled people had requested for years—remote meetings, schooling, and work; guaranteed income (in the form of expanded unemployment payments); freezes on evictions and student loan payments; robust mutual aid networks; and more—are all more than possible when the need is taken seriously. In the midst of the terrible loss and grief of the pandemic, many disabled people reported feeling less isolated, not more, as mass accommodations were put in place for everyone. Access to online classes, captions, and ASL (American Sign Language) interpretation in remote meetings, as well as online dance parties and performances, all enabled a sense of community and connection. Meanwhile, access in other arenas is even harder than before—for example, with IEPs (individualized education plans) all but abandoned in school systems stretched thin by an abrupt transition to online learning.

However, through challenging times, disability communities continue to get stronger and more organized. A growing intersectional disability justice (DJ) movement challenges the sidelining of disability as peripheral to other social justice struggles (See list of current disability organizing on website). Emerging disability identity communities, such as the Autistic Self Advocacy Network and the Disability Justice Culture Club, work to destigmatize diverse ways of thinking, feeling, and interacting with the world. BIPOC[2] women and queer and trans people are in the forefront of much of this work and bring powerful intersectional approaches. These movements to reclaim neurodivergence and disability can have profound impacts on how we understand education, learning, and human relations, while organizing around disabling chronic illness expands how we think about aging and caregiving.

This chapter's approach to teaching about ableism and disability justice is informed by the disability justice movement, emerging disability identity communities, and our lived experiences as chronically ill and disabled activists, writers, cultural workers, and educators. We also draw on recent scholarship in critical disability studies and social justice education (SJE) and on the wealth of community-based wisdom in these fields that has always existed alongside their more academic counterparts.

First we outline our approach, including key terminology and frameworks. Then we trace some historical legacies of ableism and its intersections with other systems of oppression. The Current Manifestations section presents contemporary examples of ableism along with examples of organizing for change. As in the other chapters, we offer a curriculum design for a 16-hour weekend workshop, which can be adapted to other formats. The final section offers reflections on pedagogy and facilitation for workshops on ableism and disability justice.

OUR APPROACH

Ableism, or disability oppression, is the pervasive system that oppresses *people with disabilities/disabled people* while privileging people who are *abled*. It is intimately entangled with other systems of oppression, particularly with racism, in the ways it values some bodies over others (Lewis, 2022).[3] Like other systems of oppression, ableism operates through institutional policy and practice, cultural norms and representations, and individual beliefs and behaviors.

One of the functions of ableism—as with many other isms—is to produce confusion and misconceptions about what disability and ableism are. Ableist narratives portray disability as natural and obvious—as if everyone just knows what does or doesn't "count" as a "normal" body—obscuring the social forces that construct and maintain ableist categories and definitions. This chapter aims to demystify disability and ableism, lay bare its mechanisms, and offer tools to resist ableism and move toward disability justice in social justice education settings and beyond.

DEFINING DISABILITY

We understand *disability* as a socially constructed category whose definition is necessarily political. One widely used definition is that of the Americans with Disabilities Act (ADA): "a physical or mental *impairment* that substantially limits one or more major life activity" (Americans with Disabilities Act, 1990). Life activities include tasks like eating, breathing, walking, talking, interacting with others, reading, thinking, getting dressed, using common tools like a pen or scissors, and other tasks necessary to care for oneself. The ADA prohibits discrimination not only against people who have a disability but also against people who have a history of disability even if they're no longer disabled and people who may be regarded by others as having a disability.[4]

The ADA's definition includes a very wide range of disabilities, including:

- Chronic illnesses such as epilepsy and other neurological conditions; multiple sclerosis, rheumatoid arthritis, lupus, and other autoimmune diseases; cancer; chronic fatigue syndrome; chronic Lyme disease; fibromyalgia; and any chronic condition that limits one or more life activities even if it doesn't have a definitive cause or diagnosis.
- Developmental and intellectual disabilities like Down syndrome, autism, and many other conditions in which people think and process information differently than average.
- Learning disabilities such as dyslexia, auditory processing disorder, and attention deficit disorder.
- Mental health disabilities such as depression, anxiety, schizophrenia, and post-traumatic stress disorder.
- Physical disabilities such as cerebral palsy, spinal cord injury, paralysis of one or more limbs, amputation, having body parts that look different from the norm, having a facial difference, or being a *little person* (the term of self-identity used by many people with dwarfism).
- Sensory limitations like blindness and other visual impairment or deafness[5] and other hearing impairment.[6]

Within each category and condition, people's specific abilities and limitations can vary widely. Some conditions are not disabling for everyone who has them. Many disabilities do not cause pain, limitation, or suffering in and of themselves but are just different ways for bodies and minds to function. Many people have more than one disability. People's experiences of disability can change throughout their lifetime, and people can become disabled at any point in life.

Our understanding of disability largely aligns with the ADA's definition, except that we understand not only disability but also impairment to be socially constructed. What "counts as" an impairment is determined by social norms and structures as much as by the realities of an individual's body/mind. We are also interested in how someone chooses to identify as disabled or to be part of a disability community and the extent to which individuals are free to make that choice. As with other social identities, someone's self-identification, how others identify them, and the supposed basis for identification (i.e., bodily/cognitive/psychological realities) do not always align, and they all matter in different ways. For some kinds of disabilities, getting official recognition or diagnosis can require a lot of resources and privilege; in a social justice approach, a formal diagnosis is not required for someone to be considered, or to consider themself, disabled.

The complexities of disability identity show up in the language promoted by different facets of the disability community to describe themselves. Some disability communities promote a strict guideline of always using *person-first language*—for example, saying "people with disabilities" rather than "disabled people" and "a person who uses a wheelchair" rather than "a paraplegic." This language was introduced by independent living advocates in the 1960s as an intervention against a dominant assumption that people's disabilities define them entirely and overshadow everything else about their personhood. Other disability communities have highlighted some downsides of person-first language and argue that person-first language distances the person from the disability, as if disability were shameful or incompatible with personhood (Brown, 2011; Ladau, 2015). Another downside of person-first language is that it sometimes minimizes disability in a manner somewhat akin to so-called color-blind racism (see Chapter 5: Racism), implying that the speaker doesn't notice a person's disability. Although well intentioned, the attitude of "I don't see you as disabled" is both untrue and unhelpful. Because of these downsides, some disability communities use *identity-first language*, often in an explicitly reclaimed way, turning pejorative words into markers of pride. For example, people may talk about being "autistic" (rather than "a person with autism") or "a Ceep" (rather than "a person with cerebral palsy") or "a Crip" (as in cripple). In this chapter we don't take a stance on which language is better but rather urge readers to use words thoughtfully and consider their sometimes contradictory implications. We default to identity-first language except when talking about a person or group that we know prefers person-first language.

MODELS OF DISABILITY

Our primary framework for this chapter is disability justice (DJ), which aligns with, and in some ways goes beyond, a typical SJE approach. DJ is a framework and movement led by those most impacted by ableism, particularly disabled people who are BIPOC, poor, queer, and/or trans. DJ's core principles include centering the most marginalized, focusing on intersectionality, celebrating all bodies/minds, and interdependent collaboration for justice. The DJ movement has gained traction in the years since our previous edition and offers a powerful model for drawing on the power and brilliance of disabled people to move toward justice. Before we elaborate on that approach, it's important to understand some other frameworks that are common in the dominant culture. These frameworks have real consequences for disabled people and may influence the ideas and experiences that students/participants bring to an ableism training.

★ A table available on the chapter website summarizes some characteristics of the frameworks that we describe in the following. We focus on a few frameworks that have significant power in today's society; there are and have been other models, some of which we discuss in the Historical Legacies section. While the table is a useful reference for identifying key features of each framework, in the real world, the models overlap and coexist a lot more than the table would imply. In any given situation, several frameworks may be competing to define disability and disabled people and to determine what should happen. Moving toward disability justice sometimes requires untangling these competing meanings in order to better recognize unspoken assumptions that may be at play.

The Medical Model

The *medical model* is one of the most dominant frameworks for understanding and addressing disability in contemporary societies. The medical model defines disability as an individual flaw or abnormality that is inherently negative. It seeks to prevent or cure disabilities when possible and to assimilate disabled people into non-disabled mainstream institutions (schools, workplaces, etc.) through medical treatments that make them as similar to non-disabled people as possible. When cure and assimilation are impossible, the medical model has often been used to segregate disabled people from mainstream society in separate special education programs, sheltered workshops, and long-term residential facilities (see section Historical Legacies of Ableism).

The medical model provides important resources for some disabled people, but it has caused great harm as well. Prostheses, pain treatments, and sensory aids (like eyeglasses and hearing aids) all come from the medical model and improve the lives of many disabled people. However, in the medical model, the *only* role a disabled person has is that of patient. Disabled people are expected to defer to medical experts rather than define their own priorities and wishes for their bodies/minds. When a disabled person disagrees with the medical model's approach to their condition, medical professionals often label them as "non-compliant" and immature. Non-compliance becomes a reason to blame the person for their disability and may be used as further evidence that they're incapable of making their own decisions. In the case of people who are categorized as mentally ill, disagreeing with the medical providers' diagnosis or treatment plan can be labeled a symptom of the illness, creating a catch-22 that can make it all but impossible for a patient to exercise choice and agency in how their body/mind is treated.

The Social Model

The *social model* came about as a direct response to the harmful aspects of the medical model. It differentiates *impairment*—an individual difference that limits functioning—from *disability*, which is a result of a mismatch between an individual's abilities and the expectations of the built and social environment. For example, in this model paraplegia is considered a disability not because it limits the ability to walk but because the ability to walk is demanded by the built environment (e.g., stairs) and the social environment (it's the default expectation). Paralysis itself is an impairment; the way the impairment interacts with societal expectations makes it a disability. The ADA definition of disability draws on the social model, particularly in the "regarded as" aspect of the definition, which implicitly acknowledges it is not only an impairment that makes a disability but also how others understand that impairment.

The social model defines impairment as not necessarily negative but as a neutral difference. It does not seek to cure impairments but rather to make social changes to increase access to participation in spite of impairments. The social model is associated with the *Independent Living Movement* and the activism that created curb cuts, accessible bus systems, and government agencies that help disabled people access employment (Fleischer & Zames, 2012). Rather than passive patients, disabled people are seen as empowered individual consumers of services, and the goal of the model is for disabled people to live independently in mainstream communities. Where the medical model aims for disabled people to assimilate as if they were non-disabled, the social model and Independent Living Movement want them to be able to participate in society as they are, taking pride in their independence as people with disabilities.

The social model enables significant movement toward justice for many disabled people but falls short in some ways. One critique of the social model is that in defining disability as a positive identity and discouraging a focus on cure, it fails to account for disabilities that are painful and for which people do want a cure—not out of internalized shame about their disability but because all the accessibility features in the world won't address their needs. Another critique is that the independent living model—the social model's primary tool for improving disabled people's lives—works best for those who hold many privileged identities apart from their disability. For disabled people who would have been marginalized and disempowered even without their disability—BIPOC, queer and trans people, immigrants, and so on—creating technical access to mainstream institutions does not make it possible for them to participate as equals in those institutions, and it does not make those institutions positive forces for marginalized communities. Finally, and relatedly, the social model's focus on individual independence ignores the *inter*dependence that actually sustains communities, especially marginalized communities that cannot count on mainstream institutions to meet their needs.

At its best, the social model can begin to address the intersections of ableism with other systems of oppression in its attention to "the built and social environment." The "built environment" includes architectural features like curbs, stairs, and sidewalks but can also be understood to include societal structures like housing segregation (by race and class) that lead to access features being unavailable to multiply marginalized people in their own neighborhoods. The "social environment" includes social norms like the expectation that people can walk, talk, and read at a particular pace but also patterns like race and gender pay disparities, capitalist expectations of productivity in paid work, and age-normed standardized testing. When understood this broadly, the social model of disability approaches the more radical approach of the disability justice model.

The Disability Justice Model

The disability justice or DJ model is an intersectional social justice approach to disability. Whereas the social model posits that some people have impairments, DJ assumes that *all* people have limitations and all people have strengths. It points out that where we draw the line between disabled and non-disabled is not natural or obvious and is usually tied up in other systems of oppression. DJ is intersectional both in centering the experiences and wisdom of disabled people who are also BIPOC, queer, and otherwise marginalized and in highlighting how ableism is often mobilized in service of other isms (Berne, 2015; Mingus, 2011).

Unlike the social model, DJ questions the possibility and desirability of individual independence and instead emphasizes how all people are *interdependent* and rely on each other in community to meet our human needs. Rather than minimizing disabled people's dependence on others, DJ seeks to create and sustain interdependent networks where all people's needs can be met with dignity and all people's strengths can be appreciated and honored.

The DJ model highlights how the meanings and limits of disability are socially constructed rather than natural or inevitable and how, at the same time, disability is very real and material. Disability is both the social experience of being defined as disabled by societal norms and expectations and the embodied experience of having a mind and/or body with a particular set of limitations that may be inconvenient, inconsistent, unexpected, or painful. Since we are social beings, the material and social aspects of disability can't always be disentangled.

The DJ model can be summarized in the following ten principles (Sins Invalid, 2019). Here the authors of this chapter summarize how we understand each of the principles in relation to the work of this volume. We also elaborate upon them in the Pedagogical, Design and Facilitation Considerations section.

1. Intersectionality: Both our analysis and our actions for change must account for multiple, interlocking identities and systems of oppression.
2. Leadership of those most impacted: The people most impacted by a problem know best what is needed, and others should support their leadership.
3. Anti-capitalist politics: Capitalism requires competition, encourages standardization, and tends to value people only for their economic productivity (see Chapter 7: Classism); DJ promotes cooperation rather than competition, creativity and flexibility in how people work and live, and valuing all people as people.
4. Cross-movement solidarity: DJ aligns itself with racial justice, economic justice, reproductive justice, queer and trans liberation, and other social justice movements; this includes confronting racism, heterosexism, and other forms of oppression in disability communities as well as confronting ableism in other movements.
5. Recognizing wholeness: Disabled people are whole people who do not need to be completed or fixed.
6. Sustainability: DJ resists artificial urgency and paces its work to be sustainable in the long term.
7. Commitment to cross-disability solidarity: People with different types of disabilities bring different perspectives and strengths to the movement; DJ aims to break down boundaries between these communities.
8. Interdependence: We work to meet each other's needs in community.
9. Collective access: Creating accessibility for all is a community responsibility.
10. Collective liberation: Liberation for anyone requires liberation for everyone.

DISABILITY IDENTITY AND DISABILITY COMMUNITY

Disability identity is complicated. Some people proudly identify as disabled or as a person with a disability. Others may not identify with the idea of disability in general but do identify strongly with people who share their particular disability. Some people are categorized as disabled in systems that govern access to services and resources (such as Social Security Disability Insurance [SSDI], special education, etc.) while not identifying as disabled. Ableism targets all of these groups, in similar and different ways.

There are many reasons that someone who has a disabling condition might not identify as disabled, including internalized ableism and strategy for surviving in ableism. The stigma of diagnostic categories (Clare, 2017), the patronizing and coercive nature of many disability services, and widespread violence against disabled people sometimes makes it safer to pass as non-disabled, even to oneself. Many disabled people are bombarded with ableist messages growing up, and even if someone doesn't believe those messages, they may learn to minimize or hide their disability in order to be respected and included.

Another reason someone may not identify as disabled is because of the entanglement of ableism with racism, sexism, and other systems. For example, racist discourses define Black bodies/minds as inferior to white bodies/minds. For a Black person who is resisting that message about race, to call oneself disabled can feel like giving in to a racist lie. Likewise, sexist, heterosexist, and transphobic discourses portray women as "too emotional" and lesbian, gay, bisexual, queer and trans (LGBTQ+) people as emotionally "damaged" or "crazy." For women and LGBTQ+ people who have a mental health disability, identifying with that disability might feel like admitting that those harmful discourses are true.

Even when a multiply marginalized person resists the devaluing of disabled bodies/minds, identifying publicly as disabled opens the door to having other people and organizations using the disability as an excuse to discriminate. A hiring manager might say, "Of course we didn't discriminate against her for being a Black woman—but she mentioned hearing voices, and we can't have someone that unstable working here." In this example, stereotypes of people with mental illness as volatile or unreliable conveniently align with stereotypes of women as emotionally unstable and of Black women as dangerous. Mia Mingus writes,

> Over and over I meet disabled women of color who do not identify as disabled, even though they have the lived reality of being disabled. . . . It can be very dangerous to identify as disabled when your survival depends on you denying it.
>
> (Mingus, 2011)

Mingus (2011) also distinguishes between "descriptively disabled," meaning someone who lives with the medical and/or social realities of disability regardless of their identity, and "politically disabled," meaning someone who claims a positive disability identity as part of an anti-ableist politics. Through a politically disabled identity, people can begin to build community. Disability community can be a place to counteract shame, understand one's experiences and bodies as ordinary (Clare, 2007) rather than monstrous or pitiful, share practical problem-solving wisdom, and find a sense of belonging.

ABLEISM AS A SYSTEM OF OPPRESSION

Simply put, ableism is the system of oppression that privileges abled people at the expense of disabled people and the system of meaning-making that defines which bodies and minds are considered "normal" enough to count as non-disabled. TL Lewis (2022) offers a more nuanced conceptualization of ableism as

> A system assigning value to people's bodies and minds based on societally constructed ideas of normalcy, productivity, desirability, intelligence, excellence, and fitness. These constructed ideas are deeply rooted in eugenics, anti-Blackness, misogyny, colonialism, imperialism, and capitalism. This systemic oppression leads to people and society determining people's value based on their culture, age, language, appearance, religion, birth or living place, "health/wellness", and/or their ability to satisfactorily re/produce, "excel" and "behave." You do not have to be disabled to experience ableism.
>
> (Lewis, 2022)

As Lewis's definition brings to the fore, many of the ideas that construct disability are inextricably linked with other systems of oppression. In the US, the categorization of good and bad bodies and minds through a conglomeration of ableism, racism, classism, sexism, and heterosexism has been a central tool in capitalist and colonialist nation-building. One striking example comes from the eugenics movement of the early 1900s, which argued that some groups were "unfit" to reproduce. Those designated as unfit included many BIPOC people, poor people, sex workers, women who got pregnant outside of marriage, non-heterosexual people, illiterate people, and disabled people. By defining these groups as outside the category of normal citizens, the eugenics movement sought to solidify a national identity that was white, fit, able, wealthy, patriarchal, and committed to the status quo.

Interlocking systems of oppression continue to determine the boundaries of which people "count" as fully human, who should be protected from violence, and who should be allowed to reproduce and under what circumstances. Ableism, racism, and other isms mutually reinforce each other and harm everyone who is targeted by any of these systems. As TL Lewis (2022) points out, and the ADA definition of disability makes clear as well, people who are not directly targeted as disabled per se can still be harmed by ableism.

HISTORICAL LEGACIES OF ABLEISM

In this section, we trace major themes in the history of disability and ableism, including how different frameworks emerge and interact. Rather than attempting to be comprehensive, we focus on a few important themes so that educators and students may better understand how these historical legacies shape the present day.

ABLEISM AND COLONIZATION

The conditions that we now understand as disabilities have not always been understood that way. Pre-colonial societies have had a wide range of approaches to disability.

Prior to European colonization, many Indigenous communities had neutral or positive views of disability, some of which are still evident in contemporary Indigenous communities. For example, the people of the Iroquois Confederacy historically understood bodily and mental differences in terms of imbalance and assumed, like the DJ model, that all people have both strengths and weaknesses (Nielsen, 2012). In many Indigenous cultures through the present, personhood is defined by relationships more than by occupation or productivity (Nielsen, 2012). Across many North American Indigenous nations, community responsibility for meeting each other's needs makes access and accommodation a fluid and reciprocal process (Lovern, 2008). Looking beyond the U.S., the Anangu in Western Australia, the Māori in New Zealand, and Indigenous people in Mexico embrace and celebrate the naturally occurring diversity of bodies and minds rather than using Western concepts of impairment, deficiency, and disability to classify individuals (Velarde, 2018). In these communities and others, Indigenous views of disability were not entirely suppressed by colonization; there are now efforts to reclaim and build on traditional conceptions of disability as a community strength (Velarde, 2018; Lovern, 2008).

Processes of colonization disrupted many Indigenous communities such that they weren't able to support community members in the ways they were used to. Violence, forced migration, and impoverishment caused many preventable disabilities (Nielsen, 2012). Colonizers enforced and normalized their own worldviews, including their understandings of disability, and used ableist discourses to devalue Indigenous people as subhuman. Ableism served as a tool of colonization and racism against Indigenous people, and likewise, racism served to reinforce some core assumptions of ableism.

DISABILITY AND SLAVERY

Concurrent with the colonization of the Americas, a particular form of racialized capitalism arose, exemplified by the transatlantic slave trade and the system of chattel slavery. Erevelles (2011) helps us think about "the processes by which the body becomes a commodity of exchange in a transnational economic context, and how this becoming proliferates a multiplicity of discourses of disability, race, class, gender, and sexuality" (p. 28). That is to say, much of the global economy in a colonial and post-colonial context is constructed on a racist and ableist model that understands the human body as a material good to be bought, sold, traded, and exchanged, based on its ability to work.

In this model, the worth of enslaved Africans was equated with their physical strength and their capacity to reproduce. The system of slavery placed economic value on enslaved people's non-disabled bodies while also ironically defining those bodies as "unfit" in comparison to white bodies and creating impairment when bodies were damaged through violence and overwork. Disability discourses were leveraged by both proponents and opponents of slavery, with abolitionists noting the immense physical and emotional toll of forced labor, which was itself disabling, while proponents used the purported physical and emotional inferiority of slaves as a paternalistic justification for the continuation of the institution (Boster, 2013).

INDUSTRIALIZATION AND CAPITALISM

Racialized capitalism has changed form since slavery was abolished, but it remains entangled with ableism. In industrial capitalism, job expectations are standardized, and personhood is defined in large part by profession. A wage labor system demands consistency in pace, quality, and method of production. A worker whose abilities are not close enough to average may be forced out of the workforce. Charities or "special" programs must be set up to care for people who are excluded from the mainstream economy based on disability.

EUGENICS AND THE IDEAL CITIZEN

Beginning in the 14th century, and escalating in the 17th century, laws against vagrancy were enforced against people with disabilities in Europe. The dominant model of disability was a religious model in which disabilities, especially those that couldn't be explained by a visible injury, were seen as a punishment for sin. People with mental illnesses, limb differences, and other unexplained disabilities were ejected from charity shelters because they were seen as dangerous and undeserving of the community's support. Instead, they were forced to beg in the streets for sustenance and could be arrested for begging without a license (Pelka, 2012).

Similar laws were passed throughout the United States in the late 19th and early 20th centuries and remained on the books as late as the 1970s. Called "unsightly beggar ordinances" and later dubbed "ugly laws" by disability scholars (Schweik, 2009), these laws prohibited many disabled people from showing themselves in public. They particularly targeted women, as well as cross-dressers and other gender-nonconforming people, as "indecent" or "unseemly" (Schweik, 2009; Sears, 2008). At the same time, they used professed concern for healthy white women to rationalize the restrictions on the grounds that the disturbing sight of a "deformed" or otherwise "unsightly" person would be too much for their delicate nerves (Schweik, 2009).

Beginning in the 17th century, a scientific approach to social ills, rather than a religious approach, gradually gained momentum—a momentum that continued into the 20th century. Where disabled people had been considered morally suspicious, now some were depicted as innocent, if inferior, victims of nature. The moral discourse continued to have immense power but was increasingly masked by the language of logic and science.

The late 19th and early 20th century saw the development of the pseudoscience of eugenics. The goal of eugenics is to "improve the quality of the human race" (Garland-Thomson, 2015, p. 74), based on assumptions about the desirability of certain physical, mental, and moral traits. Eugenics was mainstream medical science throughout the early 20th century, and doctors promoted selective breeding, sterilization, and euthanasia as tools to achieve an "ideal" human form and a more orderly society. A 1927 Supreme Court case known as *Buck v. Bell* enshrined the right of states to sterilize disabled people and to terminate their parental rights. The decision famously stated,

> It is better for all the world if, instead of waiting to execute degenerate offspring for crime, or to let them starve for their imbecility, society can prevent those who are manifestly unfit from continuing their kind. . . . Three generations of imbeciles are enough.
>
> (*Buck v. Bell*, 1927)

Eugenics was central to pseudoscientific racism and defined as naturally inferior not only people with physical and mental disabilities but also Black, Indigenous, and Asian people, as well as people categorized as "mongrel" or mixed-race (see also Chapter 8: Religious Oppression). It also became a tool of classism, sexism, and heterosexism, defining as "unfit" everyone from homeless people, to gay and lesbian people, to women who had sex outside of marriage. The desire to "perfect the race" was deeply grounded in the demands of industrial capitalism and a desire to eliminate those who would purportedly be a burden to the state. This desire for a perfect citizenry shaped the development of the United States' immigration laws: The Immigration Act of 1882 barred from entering the United States any "lunatic, idiot, or any person unable to take care of himself or herself without becoming a public charge" (Nielsen, 2012, p. 103). In 1891, the law was revised to bar anyone "likely to become a public charge," and in 1903, the category "feebleminded" was added to the law and operated as a sort of catch-all for anyone who immigration officials saw as socially undesirable. These categories were grounded not in a particular medical diagnosis but in eugenic norms of social desirability that could also be policed along race and class lines (Nielsen, 2012).

Eugenics also shaped popular culture. People with disabilities were seen as freaks, monsters, and less than human. Societal curiosity about people with severe disabilities made freak shows very popular. Paradoxically, freak shows became one of the few viable ways for people with disabilities to earn a living (Pelka, 2012), along with cross-dressers and other gender-nonconforming people (Sears, 2008).

THE RISE OF INSTITUTIONALIZATION

Eugenic science formed the foundation for the medical model of disability and for the mass institutionalization of people with disabilities. From the 18th century through the 1960s, many people with intellectual disabilities and mobility impairments were confined to asylums and state hospitals. While some of these institutions purported to provide medical care, they also explicitly aimed to remove disabled people from the community because they were seen as dangerous to the social order (Pelka, 2012). Physicians convinced many families that they could not or should not care for their loved ones at home and encouraged them to send them to institutions instead (Pelka, 2012). These same physicians often had a financial interest in filling beds in those institutions (Hornick, 2012). There were hundreds of such institutions throughout the United States and around the world.

As with other eugenicist approaches, institutionalization affected many people based on not only disability but also race, class, gender, and sexuality. Beggars, unwed mothers, and women who accused powerful men of sexual assault could all be institutionalized to get them out of the way. As Nielsen (2012) notes, institutionalization became a tool of social control: "The warehousing of those considered deviant in one way or another, combined with the threat of sterilization, policed behaviors and literally controlled the reproduction of social norms (p. 119).

Institutions operated without external oversight, and overcrowding and understaffing were common. In some institutions, people with mobility impairments were rarely moved from their beds while other residents went naked because attendants did not have time to change their clothes. Doctors performed unnecessary medical procedures in order to make attendants' jobs easier, such as removing healthy teeth to make it easier for staff to feed patients. Some patients were subjected to experimental treatments that we would now call torture. The supposedly scientific belief that disabled people were less than fully human gave doctors a rationale to research cures or ways to control patients through techniques like dunking in cold water, electric shock, insulin shock, and lobotomy (removal of part of the brain) (Pelka, 2012; Russell, 1998).

THE "GOOD CRIPPLES" AND REHABILITATION

Returning from World War I, newly disabled veterans wanted to work. The surge in demand for rehabilitative services spurred advances in medical technology such as pros-thetics, as well as increasing acceptance that disabled people could work. Programs to help disabled veterans return to civilian life saw them as the "good cripples," contrasted with "peace-time cripples" who didn't have the excuse of being war heroes (Nielsen, 2012). The *rehabilitation approach* to disability began to gain traction based on the idea that anyone who could work, even with modification, should work. At the same time as some disabled people were still being institutionalized, others who could be rehabilitated enough to meet the demands of available jobs had other options.

Polio epidemics also produced a generation of "good cripples." Polio is an infectious disease that, for some people, leads to long-term effects including paralysis. From 1916 until a vaccine was developed in 1955, the US saw at least one major outbreak per year. Long-stay hospitals specializing in polio proliferated, providing both treatment and reha-bilitation. Children impacted by post-polio syndrome, along with their parents, advocated for some of the first efforts to make schools and colleges accessible for people using wheel-chairs (Nielsen, 2012). As with the returning war veterans, the benefits of these reforms were not evenly distributed. Many polio treatment and rehabilitation centers were racially segregated, and others served only the wealthy.

As we write this chapter in 2021, the history of polio raises questions about the future of COVID-19. Will people impacted by lasting symptoms from the infection inspire a new wave of access reforms? Or will they be painted as the "good cripples," while people who have similar limitations for other reasons continue to be marginalized?

DEINSTITUTIONALIZATION

In the early 20th century, there was a desire to reform institutions but not to abolish them entirely (Appleman, 2018). Parents of institutionalized children began to organize, drawing attention to the lack of educational, work, and living opportunities for their dis-abled children as well as the conditions inside institutions (Nielsen, 2012). Their refusal to keep their children hidden and shrouded in shame served as a particularly potent response to the eugenicist claim that cognitive disability was hereditary or otherwise the result of familial flaws. Parent-activists emphasized that disability existed in families and communities of all kinds (Nielsen, 2012). Parent groups, largely staffed by mothers, merged to form the National Association of Retarded Children (today known as ARC). This organization filed wide-reaching lawsuits, leveraging the language of *Brown v. Board of Education* to challenge the educational exclusion of young people living in institutions (Pelka, 2012).

In addition to the legal efforts undertaken by parents, a number of high-profile families, including the Kennedys, began to speak publicly about their experiences with disabled family members. The 1950s saw the introduction of new medications to treat mental illness, which, along with the rise of the idea that a positive living environment could aid in the treatment of those with mental illnesses, made community-based living seem more viable (Appleman, 2018). Legislative advances created early infrastructure for community-based living, including the Community Mental Health Act (1963) and the adoption of Medicaid (1965).

Efforts towards *deinstitutionalization* were aided by journalism that informed the public about heinous conditions at state hospitals, such as Willowbrook. The Willowbrook State School in New York was the subject of a scathing 1965 speech by Senator Robert Kennedy, demonstrations by parents and staff members, and several local newspaper stories. In 1972 it finally gained national attention when a young television journalist snuck in with a camera. The conditions at Willowbrook were much like those in earlier asylums: residents received little care or education, often went unclothed, and were subjected to physical and sexual abuse as well as unethical medical experiments. A class action lawsuit filed by parents of the children housed there led to gradually improved conditions and the facility's eventual closure (Reiman, 2017).

Yet the struggle against unnecessary institutionalization was far from over. In 1995, two women sued the Georgia Department of Human Resources in a case that eventually went to Supreme Court and became known as the Olmstead decision. The case rested on the fact that the two women, Lois Curtis and Elaine Wilson, were stuck in a state psychiatric hospital in spite of being cleared by mental health professionals to go home because the services they would need to successfully live at home weren't available. On June 22, 1999, the United States Supreme Court ruled in *Olmstead v. L.C.* that unjustified segregation of persons with disabilities constitutes discrimination in violation of Title II of the Americans with Disabilities Act. The court held that public entities must provide community-based services to persons with disabilities. Although there are still some limitations, the Olmstead decision has opened up options for many disabled people, which we explore in the Current Manifestations section.

INDEPENDENT LIVING MOVEMENT

In the 1960s and 1970s, a cross-disability social movement among people with disabilities and allies began to emerge that became known as the Independent Living Movement. Inspired by other civil rights and justice movements of the era, disability activists drew on an individual rights framework to organize around a common social identity as people with disabilities and to advocate for needed changes. They began to refer to people with disabilities as "consumers" who make choices about accessing services. Slogans like "nothing about us without us" (borrowed from the disability rights movement in South Africa) emphasized the importance of people with disabilities participating in policy decisions, as well as in decisions that affected their lives.

In contrast to the medical model and its institutionalization and rehabilitation approaches, the Independent Living Movement identified the "problem" of disability as primarily social rather than biological, manifesting in the cultural and institutional patterns that forced people with disabilities to be dependent on medical professionals, family, and charities to meet their needs. Activists advocated for and created services by and for people with disabilities, emphasizing mutual support and self-help and using collective political action to remove barriers to independent living. The first independent living center (ILC) opened in Berkeley, California, in 1972 (Fleischer & Zames, 2012), and there are now hundreds of ILCs in the U.S. alone.

A key goal of the Independent Living Movement was to establish community-based services and support systems such that people with disabilities could live as independently as possible, integrated into communities rather than isolated in institutions. The Independent Living Movement contributed to a shift from institutionalization as the default for people with severe disabilities to the majority of people with severe disabilities living in communities. Often referred to as deinstitutionalization, this shift has had both positive and negative consequences, which we explore in the following under Current Manifestations.

The Independent Living Movement was instrumental in spurring the passage of Section 504 of the Rehabilitation Act in 1973 and the ADA in 1990—both significant federal policy victories that protect the rights of people with disabilities in areas including transportation, communication, and employment.

CROSS-MOVEMENT SOLIDARITY AND THE IMPLEMENTATION OF 504

The disability movement depended on solidarity with movements for human rights, racial justice, and LGBTQ+ rights. These bonds are not always acknowledged in mainstream disability organizing today, and some white-led disability rights organizations have faced scrutiny for failing to include issues of racism in their work.[7] The connections with other movements were essential in allowing the Independent Living Movement to meet its objectives, never more so than in the direct action required to push for the implementation of the non-discrimination provisions of Section 504 of the Rehabilitation Act of 1973.

A little-known provision, Section 504 prohibited federally funded organizations from discriminating against any "otherwise qualified handicapped individual" (Schweik, 2013). When the Reagan administration refused to sign the regulations needed to implement Section 504, disabled activists engaged in direct actions, culminating in 1977 with the occupation of the federal Health, Education, and Welfare building in San Francisco for around 26 days—the longest ever occupation of a federal building.[8] The activists won. Less than a month after the sit-in started, Section 504 implementation began. The protection from discrimination afforded by 504 increased disabled people's access to education, employment, and public participation and laid the foundation for the eventual passage of the Americans with Disabilities Act.

In undertaking that sit-in, disabled activists explicitly leveraged the strategies of the civil rights movement and depended on cross-movement solidarity for strategic and logistical support. The Black Panthers and the Chicano group Mission Rebels provided meals to the activists inside the federal building, and a gay community defense group known as "Butterfly Brigade" smuggled walkie-talkies in to them. The occupiers also received support from local and national labor organizations, as well as several grassroots organizations run by and for poor people, drug users, and formerly incarcerated people (Schweik, 2013; Johnson, 1983).

AMERICANS WITH DISABILITIES ACT

The Americans with Disabilities Act was originally passed in 1990 and, like Section 504, was based partly on the Civil Rights Act. The ADA prohibited discrimination against people with disabilities and established a uniform basis for government definitions of disability.

The ADA is a powerful yet imperfect tool for disability rights advocacy. Reflecting the social model of disability, the ADA defines disability not merely as a characteristic of an individual but as an interaction between a person and the social and built environment (Scotch, 2014). For example, in terms of employment discrimination, the ADA defines a qualified person with a disability in terms of their ability to perform the essential functions of a job. This gives the ADA potential to address a wide range of inequities for people with disabilities yet also makes it confusing and difficult to implement uniformly. As with rehabilitative services, the protections offered by the ADA are likely to be most helpful to individuals who have the most privilege. Furthermore, because of ongoing stigma, the ADA is underutilized: Many people who could qualify as having a disability under the law do not identify as disabled, and many more are unaware of their rights.

CURRENT MANIFESTATIONS

Many of the historical legacies of ableism continue through the present day, and new forms of ableism have emerged with changes in technology, culture, and the physical and environmental landscapes of society. Disability communities continue to work for justice, building on the foundations laid by disability movements discussed earlier. In this section, we discuss some current examples of ableism and ways disabled people are organizing and resisting it. All the examples described here include overlapping manifestations at various levels of analysis (individual, institutional, and systemic).

CONTINUING SHORTCOMINGS OF THE MEDICAL MODEL

The medical model remains the primary framework shaping public understanding of disability. Advances in diagnostic and treatment technologies mean more people receive effective medical interventions than ever before, yet there remain downsides to medicalization. Some disabilities are over-medicalized, meaning that doctors are unreasonably seen as experts on every aspect of the disability, including issues beyond their expertise, such as what job duties someone is capable of performing. In many legal interactions (such as requesting *accommodations* or applying for disability-related financial assistance), a doctor's confirmation is required to "prove" a disability, even though in most cases disabled people themselves or non-medical professionals (such as ergonomics experts and educators) could much more accurately describe someone's capacities and needs. Ableism manifests not only in individual doctors' attitudes and behaviors but also in the policies (institutional level) and widely held beliefs and norms (societal level) that give them such power over disabled people's lives.

The medical model's imperative to "fix" disabilities conflicts with other community perspectives. For example, the development of cochlear implants (CIs) has made it possible for some deaf people to gain access to sound. But people who are culturally Deaf define themselves not only through the condition of not hearing but also through a shared culture and language (ASL). Some Deaf individuals and communities resent the pressure from the medical community to get CIs because the drive to "cure" deafness implies that Deaf culture and ASL are not as valuable as hearing culture and spoken languages. Deaf advocates argue that making CIs a default treatment is tantamount to cultural genocide (Christiansen, Leigh, Spencer, & Lucker, 2001).

For disabled people, as for others, the benefits and risks of being a patient in the medical system are uneven across race, class, gender, and other axes of identity and oppression. In the US and many other parts of the world, access to medical and rehabilitation care is directly related to class status. The systems that are supposed to help fund such care for poor and disabled people are full of contradictions and inequities (National Council on Disability, 2009).

In some cases the medical system itself can be disabling. For example, many studies have documented that Black people with diabetes in the US are less likely to be given the standard recommended treatments than white people and tend to receive treatment after their disease has become more severe, reflecting both individual and institutional bias (e.g., Sequist, Fitzmaurice, Marshall, Shaykevich, Safran, & Ayanian, 2008). Without proper treatment, diabetes can lead to impairments including loss of vision and amputation of feet or legs. Additionally, some disabled people find themselves used in the medical system as objects of curiosity and as teaching tools for the providers (e.g., Bluth, 2018). Outside of particular specialties like palliative care, many healthcare providers have a hard time reconciling their medical training with a DJ model that values all bodies as they are (Engelman, Valderama-Wallace, & Nouredini, 2019).

A rehabilitation approach also remains predominant and is implemented in the U.S. in part through state Departments of Rehabilitation that provide services for disabled people who want to have a job. One critique of the rehabilitation approach is that its emphasis on employment prioritizes economic participation as central to someone's value as a person. The rehabilitation approach assumes that people with disabilities who *can* work *should* work, no matter how difficult it is. The push for disabled people to work is further fueled by the inadequacy of financial assistance available to those who can't or shouldn't work and by cultural biases that lead people to feel strongly about not being a "burden." Some disability activists have challenged the assumption that people with disabilities should work if at all possible and instead argue for the right *not* to work (Taylor, 2004). They argue that people's value should not be based on their economic contributions alone and that the idea of "independence" should be broader than mere economic self-sufficiency.

EMPLOYMENT

For those who can and want to work, disabled people continue to face discrimination in employment. In 2019, the U.S. Bureau of Labor Statistics reported that 19.3% of persons with a disability were employed—compared to 66.3% of those without a disability. Many disabled people find that they receive job interviews and offers as long as they do not disclose their disability or accommodation requests (Ameri, Schur, Adya, Bentley, McKay, & Kruse, 2018). It is common in disability communities for people to advise each other to wait to ask for accommodations until they've been hired and to choose photographs for LinkedIn or other professional profiles that do not show their access equipment.

The ADA mandates that employers provide *reasonable accommodations*, which it defines as "any modification or adjustment to a job or the work environment that will enable an applicant or employee with a disability to participate in the application process or to perform essential job functions" (Americans with Disabilities Act, 1990). However, enforcement of this provision is minimal and is usually only available after someone has been discriminated against, not preventatively. It is not uncommon for employees to bend or break the law or simply drag their feet on making access changes. Furthermore, the ADA only applies to larger employers. Ableism manifests in the bias of hiring managers (individual level), in hiring processes designed without disabled people in mind (institutional level), and in the economic system that treats workers as interchangeable commodities (societal level). Even a hiring manager with a keen disability justice lens would have a hard time eliminating ableism entirely from their hiring process.

If someone receives Supplemental Security Income (SSI), SSDI, or other state disability income plans, there are strict guidelines in place that can prevent them from working. To be eligible for Social Security Disability benefits in 2019, a person needed to make $1,220 or less per month. Many people in these systems are subject to "clawbacks," where every dollar they make is deducted from their SSI or SSDI check. While in some ways serving as a safety net, these systems keep many disabled people far below the poverty level.

State guidelines also affect the ability of people with development and intellectual disabilities to make a living. In many states, it is still legal to pay disabled people a subminimum wage. This is especially true for work that can be considered "occupational therapy" and for "sheltered workshops," including large-scale nonprofit businesses like Goodwill, which promote themselves for the good deed of employing developmentally/intellectually disabled people and sometimes pay as little as a dollar an hour (Heumann & Hill, 2019; United States Commission on Civil Rights, 2020).

Many disabled people figure out creative ways to make money and advocate for our accommodations and access needs. There are many disabled and neurodivergent people doing sex work, selling drugs, and doing other street-economy or under-the-table work, which is often more accessible than a mainstream job. Many disabled people are also self-employed.

ACCESS TO PLEASURE, SEXUALITY, AND FAMILY MAKING

The medical model in all its approaches (institutionalization, rehabilitation, treatment, and cure) fails to address many important aspects of disabled life. Pleasure, sexuality, and family making are issues where the medical model falls woefully short.

In residential institutions, disabled people receive basic food and shelter but often do not have choices about their treatment, food, activities, or goals. The implicit assumption that disabled people are only entitled to the bare minimum, combined with the ableist and eugenic terror of disabled people creating more people like themselves, inspires strict regulation of sexuality and relationships. Many institutions forbid sexual and intimate relations among residents, assuming disabled people to be incapable of consent. Meanwhile, sexual abuse of disabled people by staff is extraordinarily high. People with intellectual disabilities are seven times more likely than other people to be sexually assaulted—and more likely to be assaulted by someone they know, in the daytime—including in residential facilities and day programs (Shapiro, 2018). This pattern of abuse is another way that institutions, and the individuals who work within them, maintain dehumanizing control over disabled people's sexuality; it's a catch-22 wherein disabled people are not allowed to say yes and are not empowered to say no.

The ability to live outside of institutions is crucial for bodily autonomy. But deinstitutionalization and rehabilitation are not enough, and disabled people still face barriers to making free choices about our lives. For example, for many people who receive state benefits like SSI and SSDI, marriage or domestic partnership means losing one's benefits (because the eligibility calculation includes the partner's income). This forces disabled people to choose between legal recognition of their partnerships and retaining access to the income and health benefits we need to survive. For many disabled people, being kept from accessing marriage or domestic partnership is a denial of the human right to love, partner, and create family and has the effect of infantilizing us (Pulrang, 2020).

In states without Medicaid expansion, many disabled adults live with their parents. Activist Stacey Milbern Park wrote frequently about the importance of other options. Living in a state without Medicaid expansion, Stacey relied on her parents for assistance with her home healthcare and personal care needs. Although they lovingly provided the care, she could see that it was a lot for them. To complicate things further, Stacey wasn't out to her parents as queer. Although preferable to living in an institution, living with her parents still left her trapped and unable to participate in community as an independent person. Stacey moved to California specifically because of the ability to get care providers from outside her family and make her own choices about her social, professional, and political life. She said,

> Though I work and have robust insurance coverage through my company, private insurance does not cover the services I need. I am able to access these services by purchasing Medicaid through a California program for working people with disabilities. . . . Community-based services became available because advocates argued that people with disabilities should not have to live in an institution to receive services that could be provided at home or in other community-based settings. . . . The quality of life for people with disabilities greatly decreases when our only options are to rely on support from our families and friends or to go into an institution like a nursing home.
>
> (Milbern, 2017)

Stacey's story speaks to the deep desires disabled people have for community, pleasure, autonomy, and freedom of choice. Some disability organizing has focused on increasing disabled people's access to information about sexuality and relationships. (See list of current disability organizing on website.)

★

CONTINUING LEGACY OF EUGENICS

Eugenic ideology and practice continue to play out around race, poverty, and immigration status as well as disability. *Buck v. Bell* has never been struck down, and several states still have eugenics or forced sterilization laws on the books. Forced or coerced sterilization of disabled people continues to happen both within and beyond the letter of the law (National Council on Disability, 2012). The 2020 film *Belly of the Beast* documents similar abuses against women incarcerated in California state prisons (Cohn, 2020); since incarcerated people are disproportionately disabled, this is an example of racist, classist, and ableist eugenics. The example also demonstrates the bizarre, self-reinforcing logics of eugenics: people who are poor, People of Color, and/or disabled are all considered unfit to reproduce, so the government intentionally (further) disabled women who are primarily low-income People of Color by taking away their ability to reproduce.

In spite of the forces arrayed against them, millions of disabled people become parents. Ableism shapes their ability to parent with autonomy and dignity as well as how they are treated in child welfare and legal systems. Disabled parents are disproportionately likely to lose custody of their children even in the absence of abuse or neglect (National Council on Disability, 2012). Disabled parents who use personal care attendant services face a specific challenge because these services usually may not be used to support parenting activities, even though they can be used for all other activities of daily living (National Council on Disability, 2012). A number of disability rights organizations are working to improve conditions for disabled parents, among them the Center for the Rights of Parents with Disabilities, the National Research Center for Parents with Disabilities, and the National Council on Disability. (See list of current disability justice organizing on website.)

★

Right to Die/Right to Live

The idea of the "right to die"—or chosen, voluntary euthanasia—has been fought for by a number of people asking for the right to end their life when faced with terminal or painful conditions. Unfortunately, some of the rhetoric that comes out of "right to die" advocacy conflates conditions that are imminently terminal with conditions that cause impairment. Abled people may imagine they would "never want to live like that" based on ableist assumptions about the quality of disabled lives. Public conversation about the "right to die" often ignores the voices of disabled people who are living with some of the same conditions that others imagine as unlivable (Griego, 2019). Disability rights activists have brought up concerns that right to die laws could be used by the state, medical practitioners, or families/guardians against vulnerable disabled people, especially those living in institutions or with family members. The disability rights group Not Dead Yet took its name from these struggles and specifically fights against right to die laws by advocating for the right to live for disabled people.

Genetic Technology

The availability of routine genetic testing during pregnancy raises ethical dilemmas around selective abortion. Between 50%–85% of fetuses found to have Down syndrome are aborted in the US (Natoli, Ackerman, McDermott, & Edwards, 2012). Many disability rights activists who support access to abortion in general nevertheless have deep concerns about the pattern of selective abortions based on a fetus's predicted disability. To some, selective abortion implies an assumption that it would be better not to be born than to be born with a disability, which ignores the meaning, value, and joy that one can derive from disability (see, e.g., Roberts & Jesudason, 2013). Nevertheless, most disability activists don't see bans on selective abortion as the solution. As Toscano and Doyle (2019) put it, "Beyond undermining women's autonomy unfairly, bans on selective abortion also worsen the stigma against people with disabilities—while doing nothing to address the practical issues they and their families face" (para. 5).

Ongoing research into CRSPR gene editing techniques promises a future in which genes thought to hold disabilities can be "edited out" of fetuses. Companies that research CRSPR applications tout its potential to cure conditions including sickle cell disease, some forms of blindness, and muscular dystrophy. Disability scholars warn against the allure of such technology. On one hand, it could potentially reduce suffering and benefit many disabled people. On the other hand, the technology is embedded in an ableist, racist, and capitalist context that devalues disabled existence and in which even well-intentioned interventions can all too easily be turned toward eugenicist ends (Obasogie, 2017). Eli Clare's concept of "brilliant imperfection" (2017) highlights another downside of technologies that promise an end to disability. Brilliant imperfection refers to the beauty, power, skills, and unique outcomes that can only come from disabled bodies and minds, which is lost when eugenics eliminates disabled people from the world. He gives examples as varied as Whoopi Goldberg's comedic genius emerging in part from her experiences with dyslexia and his own experiences as an adaptive long-distance tricycle racer allowing him to encounter wildlife he would not have seen if he was riding a traditional bicycle.

Decisions About Triage and Prioritization of Medical Resources in COVID-19

From the beginning of the COVID-19 pandemic, disability justice and rights activists have been fighting under the banner of #NoBodyIsDisposable, organizing against what we call "ICUgenics." ICUgenics refers to the likelihood that if faced with shortages of ventilators or other medical equipment, healthcare workers will prioritize abled people requiring these resources over disabled people. An example of ICUgenics is the death of Michael Hickson, who was hospitalized in Austin, Texas, after contracting COVID-19 in June 2020. Hickson was quadriplegic and was moved from the ICU to hospice after hospital staff determined that his disabilities left him with a low quality of life and made the decision to deny him lifesaving medical treatment (Shapiro, 2020).

There is an entire branch of medical ethics addressing how scarce medical resources should be distributed during a crisis (e.g., Chen & McNamara, 2020; Bagenstos, 2020). This scholarship often focuses on individual solutions, framed in false binaries, (e.g., should we use a lottery or first-come, first-served model to decide who gets a ventilator during COVID? Should young disabled people be prioritized before or after those who are abled but elderly?) to a systemic problem (i.e., a healthcare system that is designed to work well only for wealthy, white, abled people). Instead, we encourage considering systemic solutions to systemic problems. For example, we might ask, "Why is there a shortage of ventilators and other medical supplies? Why is healthcare so expensive? How could there be enough for everybody?"

INSTITUTIONALIZATION AND DEINSTITUTIONALIZATION

The struggle to live outside of institutions has been one of the most fundamental struggles for disabled people. Although structured very differently than in the past, institutionalization is still a major feature of ableism.

The institutions that are most similar to the asylums of the past are state psychiatric hospitals, which house about 40,000 people on any given day (SAMHSA, 2019). Over half of those residents are "forensic" patients (usually those who have been charged with a crime or who have committed violence for which they could be charged with a crime), and another third are involuntarily admitted for other reasons, leaving only around 10% who enter these facilities voluntarily. Forensic patients are sometimes stuck for years in an institution where treatment is aimed not at enabling the person to live independently but at stabilizing them enough to return to jail or prison (Wik, Hollen, & Fisher, 2020; SAMHSA, 2019; MacCourt, 2005).

Even in less restrictive institutions such as group homes, conditions can be quite poor. Residents are often vulnerable to violence from staff and each other (Disability Justice, 2021; Weiser & Hakim, 2019) and to neglect from understaffed or underfunded facilities. The civil rights of residents can also be restricted by legal mechanisms like conservatorship.

Olmstead and After

As a result of the Olmstead case, referenced in the Historical Legacies section, many thousands of people have been able to move out of hospitals and nursing facilities to live in a home supported by community-based and in-home services. Yet many disabled people still face hurdles and have to advocate for themselves to receive the community-based services they need. Numerous court cases have been argued since the original decision to ensure states are implementing it effectively. Some of the barriers are created by long-standing funding structures and slow-moving bureaucracies. For example, many states'

Medicaid programs have a structural bias toward institutional services (which all Medicaid programs must cover for everyone who needs them) over community-based services (which some states consider extra and provide to a limited number of people each year). In the decades since the Olmstead decision, states have gradually shifted to make it easier to fund community-based services. The Affordable Care Act provided further resources and incentives for this shift (AAPD, 2016).

Deinstitutionalization has also had an unfortunate side effect. The drastic decrease in available beds for in-patient or residential mental health treatment is a very good sign that fewer people are being institutionalized unnecessarily, but it has also meant that some people who need and want 24-hour care for mental health reasons can't find it. Waiting lists for residential programs (which provide intensive but non-emergency care) are months or years long. People in immediate crisis are held in emergency rooms or released even when they aren't safe because a bed can't be found for them. Many times, people with serious mental illness who can't access care they need end up becoming homeless and/or getting arrested and incarcerated. The police and prison system therefore becomes another facet of ableist institutionalization.

Community Responses to the Limits of Deinstitutionalization

The legal framework that enables deinstitutionalization leaves some gaps. In almost any community in the U.S, a search for wheelchair-accessible housing will turn up limited results. While newer public housing is generally mandated to be accessible, the waiting lists are often decades long. Further, the accessibility requirements these facilities must follow don't actually make them accessible to everyone. For most homeowners, the expense of renovating for accessibility is a private responsibility, and renters often aren't allowed to make such changes at all (DREDF, 2021).

Disability justice organizers have been writing and organizing around *collective access*— the idea that access can be a collective responsibility, where communities come together to create accessibility. Collective access includes disabled people organizing access for themselves on the principle that they know best what they need. Collective access holds relationship building, respect for disabled people, and love as its core tenants. As Korean queer disability justice writer and organizer Stacey Park Milbern wrote, "Disabled people are so much more than our access needs; we can't have a movement without safety and access, and yet there is so much more still waiting for us collectively once we build this skillset of negotiating access needs with each other" (as cited in Piepzna-Samarasinha, 2018, p. 131). For Milbern, interdependence makes visible the potential of disabled community beyond navigating inaccessibility.

POLICE VIOLENCE

Researchers estimate that between 33% and 50% of the times police use physical force against a person, the person is disabled (Perry & Carter-Long, 2016). Disability advocates point out that the true number is likely much higher because many disabled people who are poor and/or People of Color don't have access to a diagnosis (Harriet Tubman Collective, 2018). Disabled poor people and People of Color are caught in a messy intersection in which ableism, racism, and classism collude to treat them as less than human, as if their lives don't matter.

Many police encounters with a disabled person go badly when police officers don't understand a disabled person's behavior or communication. For example, many deaf and hard-of-hearing people are injured by police because they can't hear what the officers are telling them to do. Even when someone tries to tell an officer that they can't hear, officers sometimes ignore or disbelieve them. Similarly, some people with intellectual disabilities are unable to understand or respond to verbal instructions. Some autistic people who manage overstimulation by flapping their hands (*stimming*), as well as people with neurological conditions that affect their muscle control, are assumed to be intoxicated or their movements are interpreted as physically threatening. Too often, police respond to these situations with violence (Lewis, 2014). The failure of police officers and others to recognize body movements that don't align with their expectations as inconsequential, ordinary behavior points to the extent to which disabled people are understood to be outside the realm of normal human experience.

Laws against "disorderly conduct" often come into play when police justify their interventions with disabled people in public. Jamelia Morgan (2020) describes how these laws enforce ableist norms, as well as racist and gendered norms, and are a direct continuation of historical "ugly laws" and vagrancy laws that served similar purposes. Disorderly conduct can include a variety of behaviors such as using obscene language, yelling, sitting or lying down on a sidewalk, and failing to obey a police officer's instructions. People with psychiatric disabilities can be arrested for behavior that stems directly from their disability, such as pacing, talking to themselves, or laughing or crying uncontrollably, merely because the behavior is not seen as desirable in a public space (Morgan, 2020; Abdelhadi, 2013).

Media coverage of police violence often uses a victim's disabilities as justification for the violence against them. After an officer killed Eric Garner in 2014 by strangling him with a chokehold, *New York Times* coverage (Goldstein & Schweber, 2014) emphasized Garner's disabling *chronic illnesses* (asthma, sleep apnea, and diabetes). The reporters questioned whether the chokehold was even the cause of death, implying that perhaps Garner died as a result of his disabilities at the very moment when a police officer just happened to be strangling him. The brief article mentions Garner's large size (weight and height) no less than seven times. The logics of ableism, *sizeism*, and racism—specifically anti-Blackness—converge to depict Garner as dangerous and untrustworthy, making it almost impossible for some people to see him as innocent.

DISPROPORTIONATE INCARCERATION

Even when there is no "use of force," encounters with police can lead to disabled people becoming entangled in a criminal justice system that is itself disabling. There is no evidence that disabled people are more likely to commit crimes than others, but there is extensive evidence that they're more likely to be victims of crimes (Harrell, 2017). Yet disabled people are often disbelieved when they try to report a crime (e.g. Shapiro, 2018), and reporting systems are often inaccessible.

In courts, the situation is no better. Whether a defendant, a victim, or a lawyer, disabled people may find courts lacking in even the most basic accommodations. For example, deaf people are routinely denied interpreter's services in court hearings (Vallas, 2016; Morgan, 2017; Oberholtzer, 2017), making it extraordinarily difficult for them to advocate for themselves. When a public defender is overwhelmed with a caseload of hundreds, a client who requires slower-than-average communication or faces greater-than-average barriers to participating in their own defense is likely to fall through the cracks.

Official estimates are that 32% of those incarcerated in prisons and 40% of those incarcerated in jails have at least one disability (Bronson, Maruschak, & Berzofsky, 2015). Given the complexities of self-identification and diagnosis, we can reasonably assume that the actual proportion of prisoners who are impacted by disability is much higher. Although prisoners are legally entitled to reasonable accommodations, the reality is that prisoners are often denied access to adequate healthcare, assistive technologies, and resources to maintain their health (like a nutritional diet) (Morgan, 2017; Oberholtzer, 2017; Vallas, 2016).

Many facilities isolate disabled prisoners in solitary confinement not because of any disruptive behavior but simply because they don't know where else to put them. Segregation of disabled prisoners in solitary confinement can exacerbate existing disabilities and lead to devastating psychological harm. It also denies them access to programs that other prisoners can use to demonstrate good behavior, shorten the amount of time they serve, and prepare for release (Guy, 2016; Morgan, 2017). Additionally, disabled prisoners are subject to disproportionate violence from staff and fellow inmates (Vallas, 2016).

ABLEISM IN K–12 EDUCATION

Subini Annamma, in her book *Pedagogy of Pathologization*, points out a central irony of disabled students in K–12 schools: "Students in special education have traditionally been imagined as a protected class in schools, but, in fact, have rarely been protected from the deleterious effects of disproportionate discipline, poor curriculum, and problematic pedagogy" (Annamma, 2018, p. 39). Similarly, Erevelles and Minear explain that "special education, instead of being used to individualize education programs to meet the special needs of students, is instead used to segregate students who disrupt the 'normal' functioning of the schools," consistent with "Jim Crow and eugenic ideologies" that kept US schools formally racially segregated for so long (Erevelles & Minear, 2010, p. 142).

Inadequate educational services combine with disproportionate discipline to put students with disabilities (across race), Black students (with and without disabilities), and some other students of color in what some have termed a "school to prison pipeline" (Heitzeg, 2009). Many schools are policed by "school resource officers," and disabled students face all the same barriers when interacting with them as disabled adults do when interacting with police (Merkwae, 2015): Difficulty hearing and understanding instructions, having body movements misinterpreted, and so on. School resource officers often have enormous leeway in how they search, question, and detain students, yet as educational officials, they are not always held to the standards outlined for police (Merkwae, 2015).

Disabled students, especially those who are BIPOC, queer, and/or trans, are subjected to harsher discipline than their abled peers. Disabled students of all races are more likely to receive disciplinary action and about twice as likely to be referred to law enforcement as the average student (U.S. Department of Education Office for Civil Rights, 2014). These rates are similar to those of Black students with or without disabilities (U.S. Department of Education Office for Civil Rights, 2014).

Those disabled students who evade the unfair disciplinary structures are often segregated (or "tracked"), along with Black and brown students both disabled and abled, into courses of study with low expectations and scarce resources. All disabled children are not tracked equally—those with specific learning disabilities that are less stigmatized and considered more treatable, and are disproportionately diagnosed in white children, can receive accommodations and other services to help them succeed in classes that prepare them for college (Connor, 2006). Meanwhile, students who are categorized with vaguer diagnoses, including "retarded"[9] and "emotionally disturbed," are disproportionately Black and brown students (Donovan & Cross, 2002; Franklin, 1992; Rogers & Mancini, 2010; Duhaney, 2000) and disproportionately assigned to special education programs (Harry & Klinger, 2006; Shepherd, Linn, & Brown, 2005). These classes are designed more to control than to teach or nurture and do not prepare students for further education or for any but the most low-status work. The tracking system is an example of how the scientific rhetoric of the medical model continues to be used in the service of racism, classism, and ableism.

There are several foundational assumptions of most contemporary education systems that are inherently ableist. The idea of age norming—that certain skills and knowledge "should" be acquired by specific ages—normalizes a single developmental path and pathologizes students who have different needs or gain skills at different times than their average peers. If education were viewed as a cooperative or creative enterprise rather than a competitive one, this interpretation of fairness would be irrelevant (see Chapter 2: Pedagogical Foundations). An education system built on a disability justice model would start from the premise that every student deserves access to the different resources and supports they need to achieve their highest potential according to their own goals.

ABLEISM IN HIGHER EDUCATION

As with K–12 education, the basic widely shared beliefs that form the foundation of many college and university systems are inherently ableist. Beliefs about the nature of rationality, about what it means to think and speak well, about student participation and faculty productivity, all "intersect problematically with mental disability" (Price, 2011, p. 5). Staff and faculty with learning disabilities or mental health challenges, or who might identify as mad, neurodivergent, or autistic, confront an odd contradiction: The university is required to provide reasonable accommodations, and usually has an office dedicated to coordinating accommodation services, yet everything else about the institution devalues and dehumanizes them. Even for people whose disabilities do not affect their ability to learn or demonstrate learning, the legacy of eugenic thought in the dominant culture—and specifically in science and academia—may create a similarly hostile environment.

Disabled students face significant barriers and stigma in higher education, beginning with the process of choosing which colleges to apply to and attend. Navigating a complex process that is known for rewarding students with relative privilege (Bergerson, 2009), disabled students have often enjoyed fewer opportunities to acquire the knowledge and connections necessary for making skillful and informed decisions about postsecondary education (Hitchings, Retish, & Horvath, 2005), partly because of lower expectations placed on them in K–12 settings (Grigal, Hart, & Migliore, 2011; Hitchings, Retish, & Horvath, 2005; Masino & Hodapp, 1996). Because of the intersections of classism and ableism, many disabled students forgo college due to concerns about the cost and their ability to repay student loans (Cheatham & Elliott, 2013; Cheatham, Smith, Elliott, & Friedline, 2013).

Once enrolled, students must decide how and whether to disclose their disabilities and seek accommodations. In the US K–12 system, schools are responsible for assessing and accommodating students' disabilities, but in college, the onus is on students to disclose their disability, provide supporting documentation, and advocate for the accommodations they need (Hamblet, 2009). Stigma and inequities are built into the qualifying procedures at most institutions (Brabazon, 2015; Loewen & Pollard, 2010). Due to disability stigma and resulting desires to "fit in," as well as the difficulty of navigating an unfamiliar bureaucracy, many choose not to enroll with disability support services at all.

Underlying the processes for requesting accommodations is an implicit assumption that students may seek to exploit the system to obtain "unfair advantage." Jung's (2002) research shows how many women with disabling chronic illnesses are met with suspicion and resistance to their accommodation requests. Faculty members who support disability inclusion in general may dispute specific requests for accommodations based on their own, uninformed judgments of which needs seem legitimate.

While disabled people outside academia have formed community and shared culture around the Independent Living Movement and later around DJ, university approaches to disability continue to be based on a rehabilitation model. They operate as a service provider with disabled students as their clients. Only a few universities have opened disability cultural centers, where disabled students can build community and foster a positive disability identity. These centers can serve as an important counterbalance to the institutional and rhetorical ableism so ubiquitous in academia and as incubators for new disability scholarship and organizing (Elmore, Saia, & Thomson, 2018).

MEDIA AND CULTURAL REPRESENTATION

Media representation has a huge impact on how disabled people are thought of—or not thought of—and how we can imagine disabled people and disability. Some of the most common tropes related to ableism are that of disabled people as monsters or villains whose disabilities are a sign of their evil (think of Bain from *Batman*, Captain Hook, various characters in *American Horror Story*, and Buffalo Bill in *Silence of the Lambs*) and, on the other hand, that of disabled people as "noble cripples" who are tragically doomed to die young or kill themselves (Beth in *Little Women*, Jackson Mane in *A Star Is Born*, and the protagonist of *Me Before You*).

There is also the trope of the inspirational disabled person. Disabled Australian activist Stella King popularized the term *inspiration porn* to describe media that portrays disabled people as inspirational just for doing ordinary things that most people do—eating, tying their shoes, going on a date. Some examples of inspiration porn can be found in images and memes showing a disabled child or adult going for a walk, swimming, etc., with phrases like "The only disability is a bad attitude" or "What's your excuse?" It's sometimes hard to criticize inspiration porn; it's common for people to be confused and wonder why people would resist something "positive" (Young, 2012). But inspiration porn plays into Eli Clare's idea of the "supercrip" as the only kind of disabled person ableism can admire; the amputee marathon runner and the person with Down syndrome who goes on a date are seen as "exceptional" and thus "unlike the other depressing disabled people" who might call attention to the limitations placed on them by ableism (Clare, 2015).

Disabled people fight back through creating media and culture that reflects their experiences, sense of humor, gifts, and voices. Although commonly viewed as exploitative, many disabled people during the Great Depression found working in circuses a place where they could live freely from institutions, have community, and make a living (Clare, 2019). Disability rights activists in the 1960s and beyond created performance art; poetry; magazines like the *Disability Rag*, the *Ragged Edge*, *Phoenix Rising*, and *Not Dead Yet*; and long-running radio stations, as well as books and films about our lives. Groundbreaking disability justice collective Sins Invalid began in 2005 as a performance art collective creating full-scale performances about sex and disability, making people examine their beliefs about whose bodies are desired and whose are not, weaving in histories of ableism, racism, and eugenics along the way. Leroy Moore's Krip Hop has been amplifying the voices of disabled hip hop artists globally since the 1990s.

Disabled people are incredibly active on Twitter, Instagram, TikTok, and other media, where hashtags like #DisabledAndCute, #ActuallyAutistic, #TheAbledsAreAtItAgain, and #BlackASL host huge community conversations, creative outpourings, hilarious inside jokes, and sharings of resources. Campaigns such as #CripTheVote have been credited with shifting policy and elections.

Many disabled writers and creatives, like Keah Brown, Jillian Mercado, Lateef McCloud, Imani Barbarin, Porochista Khakpour, Alice Sheppard, and more, are fueling a disabled publishing, dance, film, and arts boom. Clothing makers like Rebirth Garments and their "radical visibility" aesthetic challenge mainstream conceptions of accessible clothing and medical equipment as ugly, dull, and made to blend in. Instead, they make beautiful metallic and jewel-toned wheelchair-accessible and sensory-friendly clothing and access equipment. This is one example of how disability communities build opportunities for disabled joy—a radical notion in a world where disability is seen as a deficit and tragedy. Keah Brown writes,

> Unfortunately, we live in a society that assumes joy is impossible for disabled people, associating disability only with sadness and shame. So my joy—the joy of professional and personal wins, of pop culture and books, of expressing platonic love out loud—is revolutionary in a body like mine.
>
> (Brown, 2020)

CLIMATE CRISIS

Disabled people often talk about being the "canaries in the coal mine" of the climate crisis (Berne & Raditz, 2019). People with environmental illness, autoimmune disease, and other disabilities recognize how environmental changes often affect us first and most severely. Extreme heat and cold, wildfire smoke, floods, and possible increases in the frequency of novel virus pandemics due to climate change all have a disproportionate impact on disabled people. Further, many emergency rescue services are unprepared to work with disabled people. We hear ableist rhetoric about the supposed necessity of "leaving older and disabled people to die," backed up in reality when people are abandoned in nursing homes, shelters, and homes they have not evacuated from because of accessibility issues. For example, one study estimates that people over 60 years old were five times as likely as younger people to die in Hurricane Katrina, mostly because they had disabilities that made them more vulnerable; younger people with disabilities were also more likely to die in the hurricane and resulting floods than their abled peers (Friedan, 2006). Here ableism intersects with environmental racism and classism, which often put poor, Black, and brown people in the way of the most severe consequences of human impact on the natural environment (see Chapter 7: Classism).

Many of the popular campaigns to fight pollution and climate change on a consumer level—such as the banning of straws, plastic water bottles, and plastic bags—ignore the impact of these products on disabled people. For example, straws were originally created as medical equipment for disabled people who cannot drink by holding a cup with their hands. Many disabled people have protested "straw bans" and similar campaigns, asking why larger-scale polluters weren't targeted instead.

DESIGN FOR TEACHING ABOUT ABLEISM AND DISABILITY JUSTICE

The design that follows seeks to inform, equip, and inspire people to incorporate disability justice into their work in the world and feel themselves connected to communities and movements of disabled people. In this design we aim to practice disability justice, while teaching about it, through collective access practices, celebrating disabled wisdom and culture, and honoring the contradictory experiences of disability as sometimes painful, frustrating, and full of grief yet also joyfully ordinary and full of possibility.

OVERVIEW OF ABLEISM DESIGN QUADRANTS

Quadrant 1: Establishing a Disability Justice Approach; Exploring Models of Disability

1. Welcome and Framing
2. Icebreaker
   - Option A: Abstract Shapes Icebreaker for Ableism and DJ Workshop
   - Option B: Scavenger Hunt Icebreaker
3. Access Check-in
4. Community Agreements
   - Option A: Collectively Developed
   - Option B: Facilitator Developed
5. Comparing and Contrasting Models of Disability
   - Option A: Models of Disability Table
   - Option B: Using Vignettes to Illustrate Models of Disability
6. Exit Tickets

Quadrant 2: Reflecting on Personal Connections and Historical Legacies

1. Personal Reflections on Ableism
   - Option A: Early Learnings
   - Option B: Reading Discussion
   - Option C: Reflection Homework
2. Exploring Disability History
   - Option A: Timeline of Ableism and Disability Justice
   - Option B: Film Discussion on History of Ableism and Disability Justice
3. Closing Circle

Quadrant 3: Identifying Current Manifestations of Ableism

1. Revisit Community Agreements and Access Needs
2. Exploring Current Manifestations of Ableism
   - Option A: Current Events and Disability History
   - Option B: Identifying Ableism in Your School/Workplace/Community
3. Current Manifestations of Ableism and Disability Justice Film Discussion
4. Exit Tickets

Quadrant 4: Moving Toward Disability Justice

1. Energizer
2. Imagining Disability Justice
   - Option A: Sculpting Ableism and Disability Justice
   - Option B: Exploring Current Disability Organizing
   - Option C: Sins Invalid Film
3. Doing Disability Justice
   - Option A: Mapping Disability Justice in Your Context
   - Option B: Mapping Disability Justice Here
   - Option C: Scenarios for Taking Action against Ableism
4. Action Planning
   - Option A: 4As for Self-Assessment and Action Planning
   - Option B: Backward Planning and Goal Setting
5. Closing Circle

Learning Objectives for Quadrant 1:
- Understand this social justice approach to ableism and disability justice
- Compare and contrast the medical, social, and disability justice models
- Establish shared expectations for a positive learning community, including meeting each other's access needs

Key Concepts for Quadrant 1: Access needs, disability, ableism, medical model of disability, social model of disability, disability justice, Universal Design for Learning

Activities and Options for Quadrant 1
1. Welcome and Framing (15–20 min): Facilitators introduce themselves and discuss the relevance of the workshop to the context of the group, and participants introduce themselves briefly.
2. Icebreaker (10–20 min)
   - Option A: Abstract Shapes Icebreaker for Ableism and Disability Justice Workshop (10–15 min): Participants brainstorm creatively in response to abstract shapes, getting to know each other while practicing a style of thinking not typically valued in academia.

- Option B: Scavenger Hunt Icebreaker for Ableism and Disability Justice Workshop (15–20 min): Participants and facilitators share meaningful objects representing how they're doing, what brings them joy, and their identities and/or communities.

3. Entry Points and Access Needs for Ableism and Disability Justice Workshop (30–40 min): Facilitators and participants introduce themselves in terms of their relationships to the topic and their access needs for this workshop.

4. Community Agreements for Ableism and Disability Justice Workshop
    - Option A: Community Agreements for Ableism and Disability Justice Workshop, Collectively Developed (10–25 min): Participants collectively develop community agreements for the workshop, with attention to the previously shared access needs.
    - Option B: Community Agreements for Ableism and Disability Justice Workshop, Facilitator Developed (5–10 min): Facilitators propose a few community agreements and get feedback from participants while also discussing the limitations of community agreements.

5. Comparing and Contrasting Models of Disability
    - Option A: Models of Disability Table (30 min): Matching game in which participants match statements about disability to which model of disability they align with.
    - Option B: Using Vignettes to Illustrate Models of Disability (45 min): Participants use scenarios to explore how models of disability show up in everyday experiences.

6. Exit Tickets (5 min): Participants write down brief reflections on their experience of the course/workshop so far.

Learning Objectives for Quadrant 2:
- Identify common beliefs and assumptions about disability, and reflect on how they come up in participants' own socialization and everyday life
- Gain familiarity with some themes and events in disability history

Key Concepts for Quadrant 2: Socialization, stereotypes, eugenics, Independent Living Movement, levels of oppression, religious model of disability, colonization, deinstitutionalization, access features, accommodation

Activities and Options for Quadrant 2
1. Personal Reflection on Ableism: Choose one *or more* depending on the group's learning needs and scheduling constraints.
    - Option A: Early Learnings about Ableism and Disability Justice (45–60+ min): Participants reflect and share about their earliest learnings about ableism and disability; develop a shared understanding of common beliefs, norms, and stereotypes related to disability; and explore how these messages play out in their current thinking and behavior.
    - Option B: Reading Discussion on Ableism and Disability Justice (30–60 min): Participants reflect on and discuss examples of ableism and disability justice that emerge from assigned readings (and/or other media) and make connections to their own experiences and thinking.
    - Option C: Reflection Homework on Ableism and Disability Justice (30–60 min as homework +30 min during facilitated session). This homework activity, followed by discussion when the group convenes, encourages participants to notice

ableism in their day-to-day lives and to begin to understand how people navigate ableism.

2. Exploring Disability History: Choose one *or more* depending on the group's learning needs and scheduling constraints.
    - Option A: Timeline of Ableism and Disability Justice (75+ min): Participants interact with a timeline of disability-related themes and events, along with other historical touchpoints, and share reactions. They make connections with stereotypes and beliefs discussed earlier and with the histories of other social justice movements.
    - Option B: Film Discussion on History of Ableism and Disability Justice (2.5 hours): Using the 2020 film *Crip Camp*, participants discuss themes in the history of ableism and disability activism. They make connections with stereotypes and beliefs discussed earlier and with the histories of other social justice movements.
3. Closing Circle for midway through Ableism and Disability Justice Workshop (15 min): Participants reflect on their learning so far.

Learning Objectives for Quadrant 3:
- Explore contemporary manifestations of ableism
- Begin to identify positive practices for disability liberation and justice

Key Concepts for Quadrant 3: Levels of oppression, others depending on activity choices

Activities and Options for Quadrant 3
1. Revisit Community Agreements and Access Needs for Ableism and DJ workshop (15 min): Participants review the previously documented agreements, amend them if needed, and have the opportunity to update each other about their present access needs.
2. Exploring Current Manifestations of Ableism: Choose one *or more* depending on group's learning needs and scheduling constraints.
    - Option A: Current Events and Disability History (75 min): Using examples drawn from current news and social media, participants draw connections between current manifestations of ableism and themes from disability history. Participants then use the same examples to describe how the interpersonal, institutional, and societal levels of ableism reinforce each other.
    - Option B: Identifying Ableism in Your School/Workplace/Community (60 min): Beginning with a framework of ableism at the interpersonal, institutional, and societal levels, participants identify and analyze examples from their own contexts.
3. Current Manifestations of Ableism and Disability Justice Film Discussion (variable): Discuss contemporary manifestations of ableism and disability organizing, using any of a number of documentaries as a starting point.
5. Exit ticket (5 min): Participants write down brief reflections on their experience of the course/workshop so far.

Learning Objectives for Quadrant 4:
- Practice imagining disability justice as a process and an outcome
- Identify examples of current disability organizing
- Begin to make plans for bringing disability justice into participants' work/schools/lives

Key Concepts for Quadrant 4: Disability justice, accessibility, accommodation, universal design, elements of liberatory consciousness

Activities and Options for Quadrant 4

1. Energizer (varies): An accessible energizer gets participants excited for the last quadrant of the workshop.
2. Imagining Disability Justice: Choose one *or both* depending on the group's learning needs and scheduling constraints.
   - Option A: Sculpting Ableism and Disability Justice (60+ min): Participants use collaborative embodied practice to represent course ideas spatially and verbally, learning to feel and do disability justice.
   - Option B: Exploring Current Disability Organizing (75+ min, less if introduced as homework): Participants research current disability organizing and draw inspiration for actions they might take in their contexts.
3. Doing Disability Justice: Choose one *or both* depending on the group's learning needs and scheduling constraints.
   - Option A: Mapping Disability Justice in Your Context (60 min): Participants collaboratively create a visual representation of what disability justice would be like in their own school, workplace, or community.
   - Option B: Mapping Disability Here (60 min): Participants explore the location of the workshop (including the physical place and the social/institutional setting) with an access and disability justice lens.
   - Option C: Scenarios for Taking Action against Ableism (60 min): Participants use scenarios to identify and practice responses to ableist situations.
4. Action Planning: Choose one *or both* depending on the group's learning needs and scheduling constraints.
   - Option A: 4As for Self-Assessment and Action Planning (30 min): Participants use Barbara Love's "Elements of a Liberatory Consciousness" to explore how to become more prepared to take effective, accountable action.
   - Option B: Backward Planning and Goal Setting (45 min): Participants identify stakeholders, barriers, resources, and steps to pursue more complex actions.
5. Closing Circle (20 min): Participants reflect on their experiences and transition out of the workshop space.

PEDAGOGICAL, DESIGN, AND FACILITATION CONSIDERATIONS

Ableism and disability justice workshops should be designed and facilitated using a disability justice lens. We want to *do* disability justice when teaching about disability justice and support our students or participants to do the same. Here we use the ten principles of disability justice (Sins Invalid, 2019) to outline some key considerations for pedagogy, design, and facilitation of ableism workshops before turning to specific concerns related to working in ableist contexts, ableism as an intersectional system, and the roles of participants and facilitators in an ableism and disability justice workshop.

KEY CONSIDERATIONS BASED ON THE TEN PRINCIPLES OF DISABILITY JUSTICE

1. Intersectionality: An intersectional framework should inform every aspect of a course/workshop, from planning to design to content to facilitation. We encourage facilitators to ask themselves at each stage: Who has been left out? How can we re-center the

voices of those who are marginalized in multiple ways? While this (content, activity, facilitation question, or whatever) is obviously about ableism, how might it also be about racism, classism, sexism, heterosexism, etc.?

2. Leadership of those most impacted: The voices of disabled people—especially those who are also marginalized in terms of race, class, sexuality, etc.—should be centered in discussions of disability justice. Yet we must be careful to avoid tokenization. Ideally one or both facilitators will bring personal experience as a disabled person, but their personal experience should not be the only disabled experience that is centered. No matter who the facilitators are, they can work to follow the lead of multiply marginalized disability scholars/activists. This may require drawing on non-academic sources such as blogs, videos, journalistic articles, and documents produced by community organizations. We must also avoid relying on personal or published narratives of disability that overly focus on experiences of individual hardships; instead, facilitators should seek out a variety of disabled voices that address systemic ableism and disability justice.

3. Anti-capitalist politics: Capitalism inscribes ableism in standards of productivity that determine what is required of individuals in order to be considered valuable members of society. In education, this plays out in the kinds and amount of academic performance required of students. Facilitators can practice this DJ principle by allowing flexibility and creativity in assignments, participation, and deadlines. Rather than assuming all students should achieve the same thresholds of academic performance, it can be helpful to ask: What is the overall goal of this assignment, attendance policy, or deadline? How broadly can I imagine ways in which students can reach that goal?

4. Commitment to cross-movement organizing: Intersectionality should infuse not only the content and analysis that we teach but also explorations of action for justice. Facilitators should pay attention to current movements or mobilizations that may not define themselves in terms of disability justice but that are or should be in coalition with disability justice organizers. If a local union is on strike, we might have participants explore how workers' rights are part of disability justice. If student activists are working on policing issues, we can make the connection between disability justice and disproportionate policing.

5. Recognizing wholeness: No one can be reduced to their disability. Disabled people, like everyone, have thoughts, experiences, emotions, and histories that make up who we are and how we navigate the world. Facilitators should look for opportunities in design and facilitation to recognize the wholeness of students, facilitators, and disabled people who are discussed.

6. Sustainability: The right pace for disability justice work is the pace that people can do. Facilitators can ask themselves: Is the pace and density of the workshop sustainable for participants' concentration and energy? Are we asking them to "show up" in ways that will deplete them and take away from their ability to show up for their work/school the next day or for their family that evening? Have we built in adequate breaks, and how will we be flexible if participants need more rest than we anticipated?

7. Commitment to cross-disability solidarity: Facilitators should be wary of designs or activities that may inadvertently claim a single truth for all disabled people. We can ask ourselves: Have we universalized disability in a way that may serve some disability communities more than others? Are some disability communities over-emphasized in our examples? If we choose to focus on particular disabilities for part or all of a session, have we articulated a clear rationale for that decision and helped participants avoid overgeneralizing the content?

8. Interdependence: Learning, like other life activities, does not need to be individual to be worthwhile. How much are we expecting participants to do "by themselves"? How could the work of learning be made more collaborative? How can we normalize relying on each other? To the extent that students with lived experience of disability are doing the work of educating other students and instructors, we urge facilitators to find ways to acknowledge and compensate that labor so that there is mutuality in the exchange.

9. Collective access: Since universal design is never universal, we must use creativity and collective responsibility to maximize access for everyone. Rather than putting the onus on individual students to request accommodations, we can be proactive in anticipating and asking about access needs and finding ways to meet them. Facilitators should make room for the messiness of problem-solving for access, beyond the general access practices or individual accommodations that are required by our institutions.

10. Collective liberation: It can be too easy to focus on low-bar goals, like increasing access to buildings and bathrooms. Those issues are important, but at the same time, we can hold a bold vision that goes beyond access to existing institutions and enacts belonging, community, and liberation for all people.

WORKING IN AN ABLEIST CONTEXT

In order to do disability justice while teaching about ableism and disability justice, we first must acknowledge and understand the ways that the contexts and systems we are working within are ableist. This understanding can allow us to conceptualize and prioritize access for all participants and to shift our practices toward disability justice.

We encourage facilitators to get creative and think outside of current systems and norms around attendance, assignments, and participation. For example, in an academic context, there is a strong norm that students must all meet the same requirements to complete a course. Instead, what if we acknowledge that students learn in different ways and that homogeneity in learning is unfair and ableist? If we need students to demonstrate their learning through an assignment, instead of requiring a formal paper with a certain number of words/pages, we can provide a variety of options for responding to assignment prompts. Options could include writing a paper, recording a video/audio file, scheduling time for a conversation with one of the facilitators to discuss the prompt, posting to social media about their learning, or submitting an original poem/song/piece of art along with a written or recorded artist's statement identifying how the art relates to the prompt. Students will not have done "the same" work, and may not put in the same amount of time, but part of disability justice is recognizing that such sameness isn't possible or desirable.

In a weekend workshop format, facilitators should consider the sustainability of participation; 16 hours of transformational learning in one weekend is not feasible for most people. Rather than being beholden to rules about classroom time, it may be beneficial to offer both asynchronous and synchronous learning activities, thus shortening the consecutive hours spent in the classroom and offering flexibility for participants to meet their own needs. Facilitators should provide estimates of the amount of time needed to complete asynchronous activities so that participants can plan their out-of-class time around doctor's appointments, work, medication schedules, childcare, naps, caregiving, etc.

Universal Design for Learning, Accommodations, and Collective Access

Universal Design for Learning, or UDL (sometimes called Universal Instructional Design, UID), is an approach to curriculum design that aims to make a course as accessible as possible for the widest range of people possible and reduce the need for individual accommodation. For example, rather than wait until we learn that a participant will need captions on any video content, we can assume that captions benefit many people and provide them as a default. Chapter 3: Design and Facilitation provides further discussion of UDL. The activities in the four-quadrant design have been designed with a UDL lens. Still, facilitators should be aware of students' potential needs and be ready to make adaptations. Some basic practices that can help make sessions accessible are provided in the Universal Design for Social Justice Education handout on the website, which provides a valuable ★ checklist for planning.

Access Check-ins

As a part of the opening and introductions each day, facilitators should ask about access needs participants may have. While students' documented accommodations through Disability Services offices or similar entities must be met, access check-ins are about more than that. Access check-ins create space for participants and facilitators to communicate what they need from each other, from the physical or virtual space, and from themselves in order to participate as fully as possible. Sometimes participants and/or facilitators may have conflicting access needs. When this happens, facilitators must get creative! For example, when preparing to facilitate this workshop a couple of years ago, we learned that overhead fluorescent lighting was a barrier to learning for multiple students. In order to make our space more accessible, we brought a couple of small clamp lights. During our opening access check-in, a student named the need for additional lighting. Because we prepared ahead of time, we were able to leave the fluorescent lights off *and* provide ample light for the individual who needed it by attaching a clamp light to the table.

Facilitators should participate in the access check-in and share their own access needs, both to model appropriate vulnerability and to ensure their needs are met. Likewise, co-facilitators should discuss access needs in advance, both so that they can be met and so that co-facilitators can be strategic about what makes sense to share. Some access needs may need to be communicated well in advance so that the whole group can prepare to help meet them—severe food allergies and chemical sensitivities are two examples.

Pre-training Assessments

Another tool to support access in an ableist context is to include access needs in a pre-training survey, with replies requested at least two weeks in advance to provide ample time to acquire access tools and solve problems. Because participants may not be used to having their needs met in such a context, it can be helpful to offer examples of available access tools. For in-person sessions these may include cushions, stim toys, lighting options, snacks, attention to a wide variety of learning styles, seating options, and a variety of ways to demonstrate learning. In an online session, they may include simultaneous captions, frequent breaks, the option to have cameras on or off, various ways to communicate (e.g., by voice and/or text chat), allowance for interruptions for self-care needs, opportunities to share pets and emotional support animals on screen (it makes everyone feel better!), options to wear comfortable/informal clothes, freedom of location (i.e., people may call in from their bed, couch, desk, outside, in a car, etc.), and position (lying down, sitting in chair, standing).

FOCUS ON ABLEISM AS AN INTERSECTIONAL SYSTEM

Without sufficient attention to the systemic nature of ableism, education about disability issues can inadvertently reinforce problematic, individualist representations of disability.

For example, many participants enter an ableism course/workshop with a tendency to focus on what disabled people can't do rather than on what a person would need to do those tasks. Facilitators may need to remind participants more than once to reframe in terms of access needs rather than inability. Such reframing prompts participants and facilitators to shift our perspectives from a focus on individual deficits to an exploration of the supports, accommodations, and access practices that are or should be available through institutions. In other words, it reminds us to seek understanding through a social model rather than only a medical model of disability. This reframing also creates opportunities for intersectional analysis. For example, two people may have the same disability and the same access needs but may have very different resources with which to meet those needs based on their positions in systems of racism, classism, etc.

Throughout a course/workshop, facilitators should make room for systemic and intersectional analysis through the examples they give and the questions they ask. It is helpful to have many, varied examples about ableism and its intersections ready to use as needed. When providing an example of an individual experiencing the impacts of ableism, facilitators should note how the person's other identities might impact their experience and explicitly name the systemic forces that structure the experience and its meaning. Facilitators can draw out ideas about intersectionality with questions like, "What might play out differently in that situation depending on the person's race [or class, gender, sexual orientation, age, etc.], *and why?*"

Many students may be more familiar with other isms than with ableism, so an instructive parallel is sometimes useful. However, facilitators should be careful to avoid making parallels that seem to claim that ableism is "just like" another system of oppression. Even when the systems operate similarly, the differences matter. Highlighting both parallels and differences among systems of oppression, as well as the ways in which ableism may be deployed in support of another system of oppression, can lead to more complex understanding.

Sequencing and Systemic Analysis

Chapter 3: Design and Facilitation outlines some of the considerations in developing a sequence of activities to scaffold student learning. These include sequencing in terms of the subjective risk of an activity (beginning with low risk and moving toward higher risk) and in terms of level of analysis (often beginning with individual level and moving toward systemic level or sometimes vice versa). With ableism, it is frequently the case that participants have no previous understanding of ableism as a system, and many have very little previous knowledge of disability in any framework. The pervasive ignorance about ableism and disability presents both challenges and opportunities: On one hand, facilitators may find themselves spending a lot of time covering basic information, limiting the time available for systemic analysis and action planning. On the other hand, participants tend to come into ableism courses with an awareness of their own ignorance, eager to learn, with little of the defensiveness or privilege guilt often encountered when teaching other isms. Because of the relative lack of privilege guilt, activities that highlight some participants' privilege may be experienced as low to medium risk, even if a parallel activity about a different ism would be higher risk. Yet that does not mean that activities focused on privilege should necessarily come early in an ableism sequence. If participants have not yet internalized an understanding of the systemic nature of ableism, discussions of privilege can lead them to focus on how hard they imagine it must be to have a disability, rather than on how ableism constructs disability and marginalizes disabled people, and on feelings of pity and impulses toward charity, rather than feelings of solidarity and impulses toward collective action. Later in the sequence, after participants have developed a strong systemic lens, discussions of privilege can help participants understand disability as an issue that affects everyone and ableism as a system they are part of and can help dismantle.

A Counterexample: Disability Simulations

Disability simulation activities are a popular educational intervention in many schools and workplaces, in which participants are assigned a disability to "live with" for a period of time. After the simulation, participants discuss the difficulty of performing daily activities with their disability. *We strongly advise against using disability simulations.* They tend to reinforce an understanding of disability as individual deficiency and an attitude of paternalism. A participant who is asked to role-play blindness will likely remember their fear and incompetence all too clearly and may leave the training still unaware of the tools, skills, and resources that blind people use to live independent and interdependent lives. Rather than disability simulation exercises, we urge facilitators to use activities that highlight the interaction of individuals' needs and capacities with the demands of the built and social environment, as well as the systems that structure those demands. The Reflection Homework on Ableism and Disability Justice is one such activity. ★

Intersectional Facilitation Challenges

Sometimes the intersection of ableism and other systems of oppression can manifest during a workshop in ways that may be counterintuitive and challenging to facilitate. On an individual level, we sometimes notice intersectionality in terms of who feels entitled to accommodations. For example, individuals who are privileged in terms of several salient identities and become disabled as adults often come across as very assertive and are relatively successful in getting their access needs met. Individuals who have had a disability their whole lives and/or who are members of other subordinated groups may tend to be more patient with delays in accommodation or may assume that some needs just won't be met. If such a pattern emerges within a workshop, such as during an access check-in, facilitators should name what they observe without implying that any student is "wrong" in what they are or are not asking for. The observation can become an opportunity to encourage reflection about different ways in which we have all been socialized to get our needs met, to "make do" when our needs are not met, to persevere, and/or to accept disappointment.

On a systemic level, intersectionality of ableism and other systems can come up in the ableist rhetoric sometimes employed in social justice movements. Even though ableism so often operates as a tool for justifying or legitimizing other systems of oppression, people may also call on ableist assumptions when attempting to *de*legitimize or resist another system of oppression. For example, someone who is passionate about transgender liberation may argue against the categorization of gender dysphoria as a psychiatric diagnosis, using language like, "Trans people aren't sick or crazy. Gender diversity is healthy and normal." Their intention is to support gender justice by disrupting the oppressive pathologization of trans people, and they may not realize that, at the same time, their arguments implicitly support ableist tropes of people with mental illness as unpredictable, unreasonable, and broadly unwell or incapable and of illness generally as being outside the range of "normal" human experience.

If such a claim comes up in a workshop, it is not enough to address the ableism in the statement; facilitators must engage with the intersectional complexities in all their messiness. In the prior example, "calling out" the participant's use of ableist language without addressing the content of their statement about gender diversity could have the side effect of silencing an important discussion about the pathologization of trans people—which is very much related to the pathologization of disabled people in the medical model. Instead of trying to delineate which parts of a statement are "right" and "wrong," we encourage facilitators to dig into underlying issues, such as: How does pathologization work? How does it benefit and/or harm individuals and populations? What is the political impact when ableist language is used in support of and/or in opposition to other systems of oppression? How could an intersectional lens help gender justice advocates and disability justice advocates work together to disrupt the harmful impacts of pathologizing discourses on everyone?

WHAT STUDENTS BRING

Facilitators should be aware of and sensitive to the range of experience, awareness, and knowledge about disability that participants may bring so as to facilitate a meaningful experience for all participants/students. Some disabled participants may come to a workshop with extensive knowledge and analysis about ableism. Many others may not be knowledgeable about or sensitive to the needs of people with disabilities different from theirs. Some participants may have experience with friends or family members who are disabled, yet this does not guarantee that they will have an understanding of systemic ableism.

Participants who are disabled or who have experience with disability in their families will vary in their desire to discuss those experiences. People with non-apparent disabilities may or may not choose to disclose their disabilities. Others may not think of themselves as disabled when they begin an ableism course but may come to understand their experiences differently as a result of learning new frameworks and definitions. We recommend creating opportunities for participants to disclose disabilities or experiences with disability throughout the sequence of the course/workshop. Disclosure should always be voluntary, and the group should be reminded to keep such information confidential and to respect individuals' boundaries regarding whether/how they discuss their own disabilities.

Most people will know someone who has a disability at some point, but the dominant culture teaches people without disabilities not to think of disability as something relevant to their lives. All participants can benefit from an opportunity to explore their feelings about disability, including fears about their own fragility, loss of control, and mortality. In such discussions, participants may recognize patterns around privilege, including how fears cause them to avoid people with disabilities or feel anger toward people with disabilities for reminding them of these realities of life.

The characteristics of the group, as well as each participant's previous experience with disability, affect how specific activities or topics may be experienced as more or less "risky." For example, in our experience, participants without disabilities do not seem to be embarrassed or uncomfortable talking about disabilities in front of people with disabilities. However, they may avoid talking about the specific disability that someone in the room has disclosed (or that is apparent). Facilitators can address this simply by making sure to bring up that disability as an example among others so that it is not conspicuous in its absence from the conversation. In some situations, it may also be useful to create an opportunity for participants to bring up topics or ask questions anonymously.

Another common dynamic is participants with disabilities falling into the role of expert with regard to their own disability or disability in general. Facilitators should remind participants that those with apparent or disclosed disabilities are not responsible for educating their classmates and that disabled participants may also have plenty to learn about ableism.

FACILITATORS' ROLE

Power and Expertise

Chapter 2: Pedagogical Foundation discusses the role of power and expertise in an educational environment and the importance of social justice educators considering how they will navigate power dynamics related to their role as well as to their identities. Expertise is also a key mechanism of ableism. When facilitating a session on ableism and disability justice, it's important to consider what kinds of expertise we claim and how that may inadvertently play into models of disability and manifestations of ableism.

For example, we discuss prior how the rehabilitation approach assigns expertise to professionals such as case workers, occupational therapists, or special ed teachers, denying many disabled people the power to define their own experiences and make decisions about their lives. Facilitators who bring professional expertise from working in such roles (including in a university office of disability services) can and should bring that expertise into the workshop but should avoid claiming "expert" status *over* disabled people themselves. We encourage facilitators to be transparent about these tensions and to discuss the complexities of their roles advocating for disability justice from within an institution and profession steeped in ableist legacies.

Likewise, facilitators who have disabilities and/or identify as disabled should consider in advance whether and how to use the "expertise of experience." For facilitators with non-apparent disabilities, the decision of whether, when, and how to disclose can be an important pedagogical one. In our experience, participants are usually eager to work with a facilitator who has a disability and to trust them as an "expert." On the other hand, participants may hesitate to ask questions that they fear may be offensive. Facilitators should consider how personally vulnerable they want to be as a facilitator and prepare themselves to hold clear and compassionate boundaries with regard to personal questions participants may ask. Facilitators should also be prepared to speak from their particular locations in terms of ableism and other systems; for example, a white disabled facilitator should model acknowledging the impact of white privilege on their experience of disability.

Like with most social justice education, it is helpful if co-facilitators bring different experiences and identities than each other, in terms of both disability and intersecting identities. This does not always mean there must be a non-disabled facilitator; sometimes two facilitators with different kinds of disabilities, or with similar disabilities but different experiences of race, class, gender, etc., can bring a diversity of perspectives that is supportive for the group's learning.

Preparation and Parallel Processes

As with all social justice education, facilitators must prepare themselves not only to teach content but also to recognize and attend to the ways ableism has impacted their own thinking. Completing the activities that participants will go through is one way to raise one's awareness about ableism. The co-facilitation relationship is another opportunity for a parallel process: We encourage co-facilitation teams to check in about their own access needs (whether related to a disability or not) and use creativity and a "collective access" approach to collaborate in ways that account for everybody's unique strengths and needs.

Notes

* We ask that those who cite this work always acknowledge by name all of the authors listed rather than either only citing the first author or using "et al." to indicate co-authors. All collaborated on the conceptualization, development, and writing of this chapter.

1 Within disability communities, some people strongly prefer person-first language (e.g., "people with disabilities," "people with mobility impairments") while others feel as strongly about identity-first language (e.g., "disabled people," "autistic people"). Both ways of naming disability come from disability activism, and we explore their histories under the Our Approach section. In this chapter, when we are writing about a specific person, we use the language that person prefers as far as we know. Otherwise, we primarily use identity-first language because it is what we use for ourselves and what is most common in our disability activism communities.

2 BIPOC stands for Black, Indigenous, and other People of Color. It includes all people racialized as non-white while bringing to the fore Black and Indigenous groups to acknowledge the specificity of their relationships to systems of coloniality and racism. This volume's preface discusses the emergence and uses of the term BIPOC and debates surrounding it.

3 In the Historical Legacies section that follows, we trace the overlap of ableism and racism in eugenics.

4 It's important to note that this definition is only used to prohibit discrimination but not to determine who qualifies for government-funded disability services. Most people who "count" as disabled under the ADA do *not* qualify for Social Security Disability benefits, for example.

5 Many Deaf people (who are culturally Deaf and use ASL) do not consider themselves disabled but rather part of a linguistic minority. We're including deafness in this list because Deaf people are targeted by ableism similarly to those who are deaf (but not necessarily culturally Deaf) who do consider it a disability, as well as to people with other characteristics that are widely considered to be disabilities.

6 These categories are not the only way to organize types of disability. We've organized them this way here in order to be as broad and comprehensive as possible to counteract the dominant culture's tendency to represent disability narrowly as including only significant mobility and sensory limitations. Another approach categorizes most mental, intellectual, and learning disabilities all as forms of *neurodivergence*. The term *neurodivergent* was coined by longtime autistic activist and writer Kassiane Asasumasu to refer to the state of having a brain, nervous system, or both that operate differently from the typical (Alexis, 2020). Neurodivergence is a broad framework that encompasses everything from autism to ADHD, multiplicity/plurality, schizophrenia, traumatic brain injury, cerebral palsy, dementia, and more (Walker, 2014). One strength of the neurodivergence framework is that it interrupts assumptions and value judgments about which forms of neurodivergence are more or less legitimate, severe, acceptable, etc.

7 For example, in 2017 the Harriet Tubman Collective, a group of "Black Deaf and Disabled community builders and activists," publicly criticized the organization Respect Ability for repeated racist, classist, and ableist statements by its president and other representatives; see https://www.facebook.com/HTCollective/posts/1658826824414755.

8 The sit-in is depicted in the 2020 film *Crip Camp*.

9 Diagnoses of retardation were removed from the DSM-V (a US-based system for categorizing psychiatric diagnoses) in 2013 and the ICD-11 (an international system for classifying all diagnosis) in 2022 and replaced with terms like "disorders of intellectual development."

References

Abdelhadi, A. (2013). Addressing the criminalization of disability from a disability justice framework: Centring the experiences of disabled queer trans indigenous and people of colour. *The Feminist Wire*. Retrieved from https://thefeministwire.com/2013/11/addressing-the-criminalization-of-disability-from-a-disability-justice-framework-centring-the-experiences-of-disabled-queer-trans-indigenous-and-people-of-colour/

Alexis, D. (2020). *What is neurodivergence?* Retrieved from https://danialexis.net/2020/01/09/what-is-neurodivergence/

Ameri, M., Schur, L., Adya, M., Bentley, F. S., McKay, P., & Kruse, D. (2018). The disability employment puzzle: A field experiment on employer hiring behavior. *ILR Review, 71*(2), 329–364.

American Association of People with Disabilities (AAPD). (2016). *Support Americans with disabilities in their homes and communities*. Retrieved from https://www.aapd.com/wp-content/uploads/2016/03/aapd-hcbs-medicaid-fact-sheet.pdf

Americans With Disabilities Act of 1990, 42 U.S.C. § 12101 *et seq.* (1990). Retrieved from https://www.ada.gov/pubs/adastatute08.htm

Annamma, S. A. (2018). *The pedagogy of pathologization: Dis/abled girls of color in the school-prison nexus*. London: Routledge.

Appleman, L. I. (2018). Deviancy, dependency, and disability: The forgotten history of eugenics and mass incarceration. *Duke LJ, 68*, 417.

Bagenstos, S. R. (2020, March 24). May hospitals withhold ventilators from COVID-19 patients with pre-existing disabilities? Notes on the law and ethics of disability-based medical rationing. *Notes on the Law and Ethics of Disability-Based Medical Rationing, 130*, 20–007.

Bergerson, A. A. (2009). College choice and access to college: Moving policy, research and practice to the 21st century. *ASHE Higher Education Report, 35*(4).

Berne, P. (2015, June 10). Disability justice: A working draft by Patty Berne. Sins Invalid. Retrieved from https://www.sinsinvalid.org/blog/disability-justice-a-working-draft-by-patty-berne

Berne, P., & Raditz, V. (2019, July 31). To survive climate catastrophe, look to queer and disabled folks. *Yes!* Retrieved from https://www.yesmagazine.org/opinion/2019/07/31/climate-change-queer-disabled-organizers

Bluth, R. (2018, October 28). For the disabled, a doctor's visit can be literally an obstacle course—and the laws can't help. *Washington Post*. Retrieved from https://www.washingtonpost.com/national/health-science/for-the-disabled-a-doctors-visit-can-be-literally-an-obstacle-course—and-the-laws-cant-help/2018/10/26/1917e04c-d628–11e8-aeb7-ddcad4a0a54e_story.html

Boster, D. (2013). *African American slavery and disability: Bodies, property and power in the antebellum South, 1800–1860*. London: Routledge.

Brabazon, T. (2015). *Enabling university: Impairment, (dis)ability and social justice in higher education* (e-book). New York: Springer, 2015.

Bronson, J., Maruschak, L., & Berzofsky, M. (2015). *Disabilities among prison and jail inmates, 2011–12*. Bureau of Justice Statistics. Retrieved from https://www.bjs.gov/index.cfm?ty=pbdetail&iid=5500

Brown, K. (2020, June 30). My joy is my freedom. *Elle*. Retrieved from https://www.elle.com/culture/books/a32983436/my-joy-is-my-freedom-keah-brown-essay/

Brown, L. (2011). The Significance of Semantics: Person-First Language: Why It Matters. Retrieved from https://www.autistichoya.com/2011/08/significance-of-semantics-person-first.html

Buck v. Bell, 274 U.S. 200 (1927).

Cheatham, G. A., & Elliott, W. (2013). The effects of family college savings on postsecondary school enrollment rates of students with disabilities. *Economics of Education Review, 33*, 95–111. doi:10.1016/j.econedurev.2012.09.011

Cheatham, G. A., Smith, S. J., Elliott, W., & Friedline, T. (2013). Family assets, postsecondary education, and students with disabilities: Building on progress and overcoming challenges. *Children and Youth Services Review, 35*(7), 1078–1086. doi:10.1016/j.childyouth.2013.04.019

Chen, B., & McNamara, D. M. (2020). Disability discrimination, medical rationing, and COVID-19. *Asian Bioethics Review, 12*(4), 511–518.

Christiansen, J. B., Leigh, I. W., Spencer, P. E., & Lucker, J. R. (2001). *Cochlear implants in children: Ethics and choices* ([Online-Ausg.] ed.). Washington, D.C.: Gallaudet University Press. pp. 304–305.

Clare, E. (2007). Body shame, body pride: Lessons from the disability rights movement. In Stryker, Susan & Aizura, Aren. *The Transgender Studies Reader 2* (261–265). London: Routledge.

Clare, E. (2015). *Exile and pride*. Duke University Press.

Clare, Eli. (2017). *Brilliant Imperfection: Grappling with Cure*. Duke University Press.

Clare, Eli. (2019). "Listening to the Freaks: A History of Circus Tents, Dime Museums, and Everyday Gawking." Talk at Western Washington University, Bellingham, WA.

Cohn, E. (2020). *Belly of the beast*. Film. Retrieved from https://www.bellyofthebeastfilm.com/

Connor, D. J. (2006). Michael's story: "I get into so much trouble just by walking": Narrative knowing and life at the intersections of learning disability, race, and class. *Equity and Excellence in Education, 39*(2), 154–165.

Disability Justice. (2021). *Abuse and exploitation of people with developmental disabilities*. Retrieved from https://disabilityjustice.org/justice-denied/abuse-and-exploitation/

Disability Rights Education & Defense Fund (DREDF). (2021). *Know your disability rights in California & COVID-19*. Retrieved from https://dredf.org/wp-content/uploads/2021/02/Know-Your-Disability-Rights-in-California-COVID-19-and-Rental-Housing.pdf

Donovan, M. S., & Cross, C. T. (Eds.). (2002). *Minority students in special and gifted education*. Washington, DC: National Academy Press.

Duhaney, L. G. (2000). Culturally sensitive strategies for violence prevention. *Multicultural Education, 7*(4), 9–17.

Elmore, K., Saia, T., & Thomson, E. A. (2018). Special feature: An introduction to disability cultural centers in U.S. Higher Education, Part I. *AHEAD: Association on Higher Education and Disability*.

Retrieved from https://www.ahead.org/professional-resources/publications/hub/hub-nov-2018/hub-nov-2018-special-feature-disability-cultural-centers

Engelman, A., Valderama-Wallace, C., & Nouredini, S. (2019). State of the profession: The landscape of disability justice, health inequities, and access for patients with disabilities. *Advances in Nursing Science*, 42(3), 231–242.

Erevelles, N. (2011). *Disability and difference in global contexts: Enabling a transformative body politic.* New York, NY: Palgrave MacMillan.

Erevelles, N., & Minear, A. (2010). Unspeakable offenses: Untangling race and disability in discourses of intersectionality. *Journal of Literary and Cultural Disability Studies*, 4(2), 127–145.

Fleischer, D., & Zames, F. D. (2012). *The disability rights movement: From charity to confrontation* (Updated edition). Temple University Press.

Friedan, Lex. (2006). "The Impact of Hurricanes Katrina and Rita on People with Disabilities: A Look Back and Remaining Challenges." *National Council on Disability.* Retrieved from https://ncd.gov/publications/2006/aug072006

Franklin, M. (1992). Culturally sensitive practices for African American learners with disabilities. *Exceptional Children*, 59(2), 115–122.

Garland-Thomson, R. (2015). 23. Eugenics. In *Keywords for Disability Studies* (pp. 74–79). New York University Press.

Goldstein, J., & Schweber, N. (2014, July 18). Man's death after chokehold raises old issue for the police. *New York Times.* Retrieved from https://www.nytimes.com/2014/07/19/nyregion/staten-island-man-dies-after-he-is-put-in-chokehold-during-arrest

Griego, T. (2019, February 24). Pioneering disability rights attorney Carrie Ann Lucas dies. *The Colorado Independent.* Retrieved from https://www.coloradoindependent.com/2019/02/24/griego-carrie-ann-lucas-disability-rights/

Grigal, M., Hart, D., & Migliore, A. (2011). Comparing the transition planning, postsecondary education, and employment outcomes of students with intellectual and other disabilities. *Career Development for Exceptional Individuals*, 34(1), 4–17.

Guy, Anna. (2016). Locked Up and Locked Down: Segregation of Inmates with Mental Illness. Amplifying Voices of Inmates with Disabilities Prison Project. Retrieved from http://www.avidprisonproject.org/

Hamblet, E. C. (2009). Helping your students with disabilities during their college search. *Journal of College Admission*, 205, 6–15.

Harrell, E. (2017). *Crime against persons with disabilities, 2009–2015 – statistical tables.* Bureau of Justice Statistics, US Department of Justice. Retrieved from https://www.bjs.gov/content/pub/pdf/capd0915st.pdf

Harriet Tubman Collective (2018). Accountable Reporting on Disability, Race, & Police Violence: A Community Response to the "Ruderman White Paper on the Media Coverage of Use of Force and Disability." https://harriettubmancollective.tumblr.com/post/174479075753/accountable-reporting-on-disability-race-and

Harry, B., & Klinger, J. (2006). *Why are so many minority students in special education? Understanding race and disability in schools.* New York: Teachers College Press.

Heitzeg, N. A. (2009). Education or Incarceration: Zero tolerance policies and the school to prison pipeline. In *Forum on public policy online* (Vol. 2009, No. 2). Urbana, IL: Oxford Round Table.

Heumann, J., & Hill, E. (2019). Building coalitions and the disability rights movement. *Geo. J. on Poverty L. & Pol'y*, 27, 199.

Hitchings, W. E., Retish, P., & Horvath, M. (2005). Academic preparation of adolescents with disabilities for postsecondary education. *Career Development for Exceptional Individuals*, 28(1), 26–35. doi:10.1177/08857288050280010501

Ho, Vivianne. (2019, October 11). California power shutoff: How PG&E's actions hit the medically vulnerable the hardest. The Guardian. Retrieved from https://www.theguardian.com/us-news/2019/oct/11/california-pge-utility-power-shutoff-disabled

Hornick, R. (2012). *The girls and boys of Belchertown: A social history of the Belchertown State School for the Feeble-Minded.* Boston: UMASS Press.

Johnson, Roberta Ann. (1983). "Mobilizing the Disabled," in Jo Freeman, ed. *Social Movements of the Sixties and Seventies,* p. 95. Longman.

Jung, K. E. (2002). Chronic illness and educational equity: The politics of visibility. *NWSA Journal*, 178–200.

Ladau, E. (2015, July 15). *Why Person-First Language Doesn't Always Put The Person First.* Retrieved May 1, 2017, from Think Inclusive. Retrieved from https://www.thinkinclusive.us/why-person-first-language-doesnt-always-put-the-person-first/

Lewis, T. L. (2022). *Working definition of Ableism—January 2022 update.* Retrieved from https://www.talilalewis.com/blog

Lewis, T. A. (2014). Police brutality and deaf people. *American Civil Liberties Union, 21.*

Loewen, G., & Pollard, W. (2010). The social justice perspective. *Journal of Postsecondary Education and Disability, 23*(1), 5–18.

Lovern, Lavonna (2008). "Native American Worldview and the Discourse on Disability," Essays in Philosophy: Vol. 9: Iss. 1, Article 14. Available at http://commons.pacificu.edu/eip/vol9/iss1/14

MacCourt, D. (2005). Caught in Limbo between law and psychiatry. *Psychiatric Times, 22*(7), 1.

Masino, L. L., & Hodapp, R. M. (1996). Parental educational expectations for adolescents with disabilities. *Exceptional Children, 62*(6), 515–523.

Merkwae, A. (2015). Schooling the police: Race, disability, and the conduct of school resource officers. *Michigan Journal of Race & Law, 21,* 147–181.

Milbern, S. (2017, July 13). A life of my own terms, thanks to Medicaid. *ACLU Blog.* Retrieved from https://www.aclu.org/blog/disability-rights/integration-and-autonomy-people-disabilities/life-my-own-terms-thanks

Mingus, M. (2011). Retrieved from https://leavingevidence.wordpress.com/2011/08/22/moving-toward-the-ugly-a-politic-beyond-desirability/

Morgan, J. (2017). *Prisoners with physical disabilities are forgotten and neglected in America.* ACLU blog. Retrieved from https://www.aclu.org/blog/prisoners-rights/solitary-confinement/prisoners-physical-disabilities-are-forgotten-and

Morgan, J. N. (2020). Policing marginality in public space. *Ohio St. LJ, 81,* 1045.

National Council on Disability. (2009). *The current state of healthcare for people with disabilities.* Retrieved from https://www.ncd.gov/publications/2009/Sept302009

National Council on Disability. (2012). *Rocking the Cradle: Ensuring the Rights of Parents with Disabilities.* Retrieved from https://ncd.gov/publications/2012/Sep272012/

Natoli, J. L., Ackerman, D. L., McDermott, S., & Edwards, J. G. (2012). Prenatal diagnosis of down syndrome: A systematic review of termination rates (1995–2011). *Prenatal Diagnosis, 32*(2), 142–153.

Nielsen, K. (2012). *A Disability History of the United States.* Boston: Beacon Press.

Obasogie, O. (2017, November 1). Revisiting Gattaca in the era of Trump. *Scientific American.* Retrieved from https://blogs.scientificamerican.com/observations/revisiting-gattaca-in-the-era-of-trump/

Oberholtzer, E. (2017). Police, courts, jails and prisons all fail disabled people. *Prison Policy Initiative.* Retrieved from https://www.prisonpolicy.org/blog/2017/08/23/disability/

Olmstead v. L.C., 527 U.S. 581. (1999). Retrieved from https://www.loc.gov/item/usrep527581/

Orenstein, N. (2019, November 5). Berkeley residents with disabilities say their needs 'not built into' PG&E shutoff policy. *Berkeleyside.* Retrieved from https://www.berkeleyside.org/2019/11/05/berkeley-residents-with-disabilities-say-their-needs-not-built-into-pge-shutoff-policy

Pelka, F. (2012). *What we have done: An oral history of the disability rights movement.* Amherst, MA: University of Massachusetts Press.

Perry, D., & Carter-Long, L. (2016). *The Ruderman white paper on media coverage of law enforcement use of force and disability.* Retrieved from https://rudermanfoundation.org/wp-content/uploads/2017/08/MediaStudy-PoliceDisability_final-final.pdf

Piepzna-Samarasinha, L. L. (2018). *Care work: Dreaming disability justice.* Vancouver, BC: Arsenal Pulp Press.

Price, M. (2011). *Mad at School: Rhetorics of mental disability and academic life.* University of Michigan Press.

Pulrang, A. (2020, August 31). A simple fix for one of disabled people's most persistent, pointless injustices. *Forbes Magazine.* Retrieved from https://www.forbes.com/sites/andrewpulrang/2020/08/31/a-simple-fix-for-one-of-disabled-peoples-most-persistent-pointless-injustices/?sh=70c09b266b71

Reiman, M. (2017, June 15). Willowbrook, the institution that shocked a nation into changing its laws. *Timeline.* Retrieved from https://timeline.com/willowbrook-the-institution-that-shocked-a-nation-into-changing-its-laws-c847acb44e0d

Roberts, D., & Jesudason, S. (2013). Movement intersectionality: The case of race, gender, disability, and genetic technologies. *Du Bois Review, 10*(2), 313–328.

Rogers, R., & Mancini, M. (2010). "Requires medication to progress academically": The discursive pathways of ADHD. In C. Dudley-Marling & A. Gurn (Eds.), *The myth of the normal curve* (pp. 87–101). New York: Peter Lang.

Russell, M. (1998). *Beyond ramps: Disability at the end of the social contract—A warning from an uppity crip.* Monroe, ME: Common Courage Press.

Schweik, S. (2013). Lomax's matrix: Disability, solidarity, and the Black power of 504. In *Foundations of Disability Studies* (pp. 105–123). New York: Palgrave Macmillan.

Schweik, S. M. (2009). *The ugly laws: Disability in public* (Vol. 3). NYU Press.

Scotch, R. K. (2014, April). Models of disability and the Americans with disabilities act. *Berkeley Journal of Employment & Labor Law, 21*(1), Article 7. Retrieved from http://scholarship.law.berkeley.edu/cgi/viewcontent.cgi?article = 1279&context=bjell

Sears, Clare. (2008). Electric brilliance: Cross-dressing laws and freak show displays in Nineteenth-century San Francisco. *WSQ: Women's Studies Quarterly, 36*(3–4), 170–187.

Sequist, T. D., Fitzmaurice, G. M., Marshall, R., Shaykevich, S., Safran, D. G., & Ayanian, J. Z. (2008). Physician performance and racial disparities in diabetes mellitus care. *Archives of Internal Medicine, 168*(11), 1145–1151.

Shapiro, Joseph. (2020). One Man's COVID-19 Death Raises The Worst Fears Of Many People With Disabilities. National Public Radio. Retrieved from https://www.npr.org/2020/07/31/896882268/one-mans-covid-19-death-raises-the-worst-fears-of-many-people-with-disabilities

Shapiro, Joseph. (2018). The sexual assault epidemic no one talks about. Report for NPR's special series *Abused and Betrayed*. National Public Radio. Retrieved from https://www.npr.org/series/575502633/abused-and-betrayed

Shepherd, T. L., Linn, D., & Brown, R. D. (2005). The disproportionate representation of English language learners for special education services along the border. *Journal of Social and Ecological Boundaries, 1*(1), 104–116.

Sins Invalid. (2019). *Skin, Tooth, and Bone: The Basis of Movement is Our People* (2nd ed.). [Digital version]. Retrieved from sinsinvalid.org.

Substance Abuse and Mental Health Services Administration (SAMHSA). (2019). National Mental Health Services Survey (N-MHSS): 2018. Data on Mental Health Treatment Facilities. Rockville, MD: Substance Abuse and Mental Health Services Administration.

Sullivan, Molly & Bolag, Sophia. (2019, October 11). Autopsy says Northern California man's death wasn't caused by PG&E power shutoff. *The Sacramento Bee*. Retrieved from https://www.sacbee.com/news/local/crime/article236043743.html

Taylor, S. (2004). The right not to work: Power and disability. *Monthly Review, 55*(10). Retrieved from http://monthlyreview.org/2004/03/01/the-right-not-to-work-power-and-disability/

Toscano, Pasquale & Doyle, Alexis. (2019, June 19). Legal Abortion Isn't the Problem to Be Solved. *The Atlantic*. Retrieved from https://www.theatlantic.com/ideas/archive/2019/06/selective-abortion-bans-treat-disability-tragedy/592000/

United States Commission on Civil Rights. (2020). Impacts on the Civil Rights of People with Disabilities. Retrieved from https://www.usccr.gov/files/2020-09-17-Subminimum-Wages-Report.pdf

U.S. Department of Education Office for Civil Rights. (2014, March 21). Civil Rights Data Collection: Data Snapshot (School Discipline). Retrieved from https://www2.ed.gov/about/offices/list/ocr/docs/crdc-discipline-snapshot.pdf

Vallas, Rebecca. (2016). *Disabled Behind Bars The Mass Incarceration of People With Disabilities in America's Jails and Prisons*. Center for American Progress.

Velarde, M. R. (2018). Indigenous perspectives of disability. *Disability Studies Quarterly, 38*(4).

Walker, Nick. (2014). Neurodiversity: Some basic terms and definitions. Retrieved from https://neuroqueer.com/neurodiversity-terms-and-definitions/

Weiser, B., & Hakim, D. (2019, June 9). Residents Cowered While Workers at a Group Home Smacked and Pushed Them. *New York Times*. Retrieved from https://www.nytimes.com/2019/06/09/nyregion/new-york-group-home-abuse.html

Wik, A., Hollen, V., & Fisher, W. (2020). Forensic patients in state psychiatric hospitals: 1999–2016. *CNS Spectrums, 25*(2), 196–206. doi:10.1017/S1092852919001044

Young, S. (2012). We're not here for your inspiration. *The Drum, 3*.

10

Youth and Elder Oppression

Barbara J. Love, Keri "Safire" DeJong, and Valerie D. Jiggetts*

INTRODUCTION

Around the globe, youth are rising up and demanding change. Not content to be seen but not heard, Sudanese students demanded the removal of what they experienced as a corrupt regime (Rashwan, 2019). Native American youth in the US marched to protect water (Richards, 2018). In Chiapas, Mexico, 11-year-old Xóchitl Guadalupe Cruz López created a solar-powered water heater so that young people can take a warm bath (Hambleton, 2021; Beatriz, 2020). Youth in Hong Kong protested for "five demands, not one less" related to national autonomy and democracy (Barron, 2020). Young people in Ponce, Puerto Rico, broke into a warehouse in January 2020 and distributed supplies that had been stored unused since Hurricane Maria in 2017 (Giusti, 2020; Time for Kids, 2020). Youth in Chile claim that "it wasn't a depression, it was just capitalism" that resulted in economic difficulties facing their country. Lebanese youth called the situation in their country "electile dysfunction" (Time for Kids, 2020, p. 48). Youth from many parts of the world marched in the 2019 New York City Climate Summit, declaring, "There is no Planet B" (Weston & Riotta, 2019, September 21).

Youth are concerned about corruption and bad government, genocide, gun control, health care, poverty, immigration laws, the lives of refugees, inequality, and whether or not there will be a livable earth for their future. Meanwhile, in the United States, federal judges declared that "the U.S. government may be harming the nation's youth through its fossil fuel-based energy policy, but that courts cannot stop that harm" (Drugman, 2020, para 1). The judges ruled that youth have no legal standing from which to sue their government in an effort to hold it accountable for the harm done (Alter, 2020).

"You are failing us, but the young people [of the world] are starting to understand your betrayal. The eyes of all future generations are upon you" (Rosenblatt, 2019, para 9). Challenging world leaders at the 2019 United Nations Climate Action Summit, teen climate crisis activist Greta Thunberg voiced the views of millions of young people around the globe who admonish world leaders and hold them accountable for their failure to adequately address the global climate crisis. From their point of view, the mistreatment of young people includes not only "all types of physical and/or emotional ill-treatment, sexual mistreatment, neglect, negligence and commercial or other exploitation, which results in actual or potential harm to the child's health, survival, development or dignity," as described by the World Health Organization (2014, para 1), but also failure to take the steps necessary to make the world habitable for future generations.

Though initially viewed as the least vulnerable population for COVID-19, by fall 2020, young people became a fast growing population of hospitalizations and deaths from coronavirus (Leatherby & Jones, 2020). Required to return to schools where limited provisions for their safety were in place, young people faced potentially life-threatening circumstances with little decision-making input.

On the other end of the age continuum, elders in the United States, a population predicted to nearly double by 2050 to almost 84 million, are pushing back against the punitive

DOI: 10.4324/9781003005759-12

attitudes, pejorative language, and restrictive policies and procedures directed toward them (Karpf, 2015). Maggie Kuhn, founder of the Gray Panthers, an elder advocacy organization, argued that "instead of making a fetish of independence, we should value the idea of interdependence between generations" (Phillipson, Bernard, & Strang, 1986). The COVID-19 pandemic made more visible the widespread neglect and mistreatment of elders, who immediately became members of the most vulnerable category around the world (Barnes, 2020). Many elders were confined to nursing homes already under scrutiny for failure to adequately care for them. Clustering in nursing homes made them more immediately susceptible to a virus that, for its first nine months, had no known vaccine or cure. During this worldwide crisis, elders in hospitals were likely to be triaged into the expendable category when health-care professionals and facilities faced shortages of testing kits, ventilators, hospital beds, and professional care. It was widely assumed that elders would forego treatment to make it available to younger people (Heid & Pruchno, 2021).

In this chapter, we discuss the widespread mistreatment of youth and elders, our rationale for naming this mistreatment as oppression, and the assumptions and frameworks we use to situate youth oppression and elder oppression as social justice issues. We provide context for youth and elder oppression through the examination of four key historical legacies. Individual, institutional, and cultural manifestations of youth oppression and elder oppression globally and in the US are discussed, along with an intersectional description of these systemic inequities, with examples of both resistance and liberation work. We also discuss how youth and elder oppression is internalized. A sample design for facilitating learning experiences on youth oppression and elder oppression in different locations, formats, and time frames is included, with recommendations for sequencing activities in classes, workshops, and remote learning experiences. Lectures and activities are more fully described in the accompanying website.

OUR APPROACH

RATIONALE, DEFINITIONS, AND ASSUMPTIONS UNDERLYING THIS CHAPTER

Our analysis that the mistreatment of young people and elders is oppression rather than a simple case of mistreatment is rooted in core concepts of social justice education (see Chapter 1: Theoretical Foundations and Chapter 4: Core Concepts). These core concepts include an understanding of oppression as the manifestation of systemic inequalities organized around relationships of domination and subordination, the role of social identity categories as rationales for the creation and maintenance of relationships of inequality, and the normalization and unquestioned acceptance of relationships of domination and subordination based on social identities.

We define *youth oppression* and *elder oppression* as the systematic subordination and mistreatment of young people and elders based on age through the restriction and denial of opportunities to exercise social, economic, and political power. Youth and elder oppression includes restricted access to goods, services, and privileges, along with loss of voice and decision-making and limited access to participation in society. The subordination of young people and elders is supported by institutional structures and practices; networks of laws, rules, policies, and procedures; and the attitudes, values, and actions of individuals that combine to ensure the subordinated status of members of these socially constructed identity groups. Young people and elders are marginalized and excluded by practices that give middle-aged adults the power to act on and for them, often without their agreement or consent (Bell, 2010; Butler, 1969; Cannella, 1997; DeJong & Love, 2013; Jenks, 1996).

Though youth and elder oppression are based on age as a social identity and share certain similarities, there are some key differences. In particular, we describe youth as the social location in which oppression is first experienced and through which the mechanics of oppression are learned. Youth oppression serves as the template for learning and enacting other forms of oppression. Elder oppression ensues at the end of a lifetime of practicing and enacting other forms of oppression, including youth and elder oppression. While young people are new to the experience of oppression and must learn its tenets through the socialization process, elders have already participated in normalizing the oppression of elders before growing older and assuming the identity of elder. By the time they come to the receiving end, the oppression is already normalized and embedded in their expectations for their own treatment as elders. Young people are born into the identity of youth, whereas people growing older may actively seek to delay assumption of the identity of elder. Another key difference between these two age-based identities is in access to power and rights of participation. While class and other identities might mediate how an individual young person experiences being young, across the board young people experience absence of power and rights of participation. Many elders, however, retain positions of power into old age, serving as leaders of government, business and industry, financial, educational, and many other institutions.

Based on these and other social justice education core concepts, this chapter proceeds from the assumption that ageism (elder oppression) and adultism (youth oppression) exist as cultural norms that both inform and are reproduced by institutional policies and practices and by individual relationships. We assume that youth oppression and elder oppression characterize US society as well as societies around the globe, similar to the ways in which racism, classism, sexism, heterosexism, ableism, and other social identities shape our social systems and play out at societal, institutional, and individual levels. This means that the marginalization and disadvantage experienced by youth and elders in most societies, both in the US and around the globe, are structural and institutionally and culturally embedded. Frameworks of intersectionality and social constructionism inform our understanding of the normalization of the mistreatment of young people and elders.

INTERSECTIONALITY

Collins's (1990) discussion of intersectionality provides a key framework for examining how the experiences of both youth and elders are mediated by other social identities. Young people and elders have different and unique standpoints depending on their race, class, sex, gender, religion, and other social identities (Collins, 1990; Smith, 1987). Young people and elders are devalued, excluded, exploited, marginalized, and mistreated on the basis of age as well as multiple combinations of racism, sexism, heterosexism, classism, ableism, transgender oppression, religious oppression, linguicism, and xenophobia. In addition to the social identities discussed by Collins (1990), Smith (1987), and others, we extend our discussion of intersectionality to include geography as a factor, acknowledging that, like race, class, sex, gender, and sexuality, the life experiences of young people and elders are deeply affected by where in the world they live.

Not only does geographic location mediate the effect of oppression globally, but it can result in profound differences in the experience of young people and elders within a single nation. In the US, for instance, the life experiences of Native American elders and young people of all class groups who live on reservations tend to be different from the life experiences of elders and young people of all groups residing outside the reservation. The life experiences of Southern elders and young people of all social identity groups can be very different from the life experiences of elders and young people residing outside the South. For example, an owning-class white elder in Boston may be less likely to experience neglect in a nursing home than a working-class African-heritage elder living in Boston. Both are likely to receive better health care than a poor elder of any race living in Appalachia. Poor elders of any race or class will be less likely to receive life-saving and life-extending services in Appalachia than they are in another location in the US, such as Boston or California. Clearly, geographic location influences the experiences of elders and young people, independent of their other intersecting social identities.

Similar to the experience of elders, social class, race, sexuality, and other social identities intersect to differentiate the life experiences of young people. Within the US, owning-class and middle-class white children are less likely to be followed in stores and may be less likely to face teacher assumptions about limitations of their intelligence than working-class and poor children. White middle-class and upper-class students are more likely to attend schools with less security, more resources, and more flexibility in disciplinary practices and are less likely to face the "school to prison pipeline" than working-class and raised-poor students of color. According to data released by the US Department of Education, "nationally black girls were suspended *six times* more than white girls, while black boys were suspended three times as often as white boys" (Crenshaw, Ocen, & Nanda, 2015, p. 2). Race mediates the experience of boys, influencing which boys are likely to be perceived as aggressive and which are likely to be shot by police (Camero, 2020). According to the Equal Justice Initiative, the percentage of Black boys who will not live to see adulthood as a result of police killings is grossly disproportionate to the percentage of white boys who face a similar fate. Black children are six times more likely to be shot to death by police (Equal Justice Initiative, 2020).

While bias and discrimination affect all lesbian, gay, bisexual, trans, queer and questioning (LGBTQ+) persons, it affects youth and elders in particular ways. Alabama, Florida, Texas, Utah and other states have passed anti-LGBTQ+ legislation, specifically targeting young people, focusing on access to health care, public bathrooms, participation in schooling activities such as sports, and in some cases, prohibiting talking about LGBTQ+ issues in schools (Jones, & Franklin, 2022). According to NBC news, nearly 240 anti-LGBTQ bills have been filed by legislators in the first four months of 2022 (Lavietes & Ramos, 2022). Most of the legislative proposals aiming to restrict trans* rights in the US are directed at young people, who are the primary advocates of trans* rights (Loffman, 2021, n.p.).

LGBTQ+ elders often grow old alone, without many benefits that heterosexual couples take for granted—the community and family sanctioned and approved companionship of a lifelong partnership, access to a partners' retirement benefits, and the freedom to openly support their partner as they age. The authority to attend to partners, or to make significant life decisions, such as medical treatment options and life-extending procedures, are often not available to LGBTQ+ couples.

In addition to understanding the ways that class, race, religion, and other social identities intersect with heterosexism to mediate the targeting of LGBTQ+ youth and elders, it is important to understand the ways youth oppression itself is used to disempower both elder and youth LGBTQ+ experiences. Youth who identify as trans* and/or queer may be seen as simply going through a phase that they will outgrow and may not be taken seriously. Heteronormative marriage is a signifier of adulthood in most societies. LGBTQ+ relationships are often not recognized in the same way as heteronormative relationships and are treated differently.

The concept of intersectionality helps us understand that while all these experiences are faced by some young people and elders, differing social identities and geographic locations will determine which of these experiences a given young person or elder is likely to face (Collins, 2019). While intersecting social identities and geographic locations mediate the experience of oppression, they can also provide an insulating function. White, able-bodied, Protestant, owning-class, heterosexual boys and men outside the mental health system in the US share a measure of protection from the worst of the ravages of youth and elder oppression (see Storytelling and Listening Activity and Liberation for All Ages).   ★

SOCIAL CONSTRUCTION, NOT BIOLOGY

While humans experience developmental commonalities across the lifespan, conceptions of role, place, behavior appropriate to age group, conceptions of what power they can exercise, and the nature of their participation in the social, political, and economic life of society are socially constructed. These socially constructed roles and expectations for age-based groups vary within societies across time and across societies within the same time period, based in part on the needs of that society. Western contemporary societies need to have children in school and not in a largely mechanized workplace, while societies in other parts of the world extensively employ child labor in their factories (Dinopoulos & Zhao, 2007). Western societies that currently prohibit child labor formerly welcomed child labor at the beginning of the industrial revolution (Bengtsen, 2018).

There are different biological ages across the life cycle, from infancy to old age. There are "transformations in the organization of intellectual abilities and their underlying cognitive processes across the lifespan" (Li, Lindenberger, Hommel, Aschersleben, Prinz, & Baltes, 2004, p. 5). Learning to color inside the box, drive a car, or process higher-order questions occurs at different periods of development. While each age period has its own developmental tasks, according to developmental psychologists, "children show variations in intellectual abilities at different ages and some adults remain cognitively fit into old age while others show cognitive decline" (Baltes, 1997, p. 27). Abilities shown by people at different ages across the lifespan may differ across societies. Expectations for performance also differ across societies. Rogoff (2003) describes tasks performed by children in some societies that are considered inappropriate or prohibited to people their age in other societies. Four-year-old Kaware'ae children in Oceania, for instance, skillfully cut fruit with a machete. Three-year-old Efa children in Zaire take care of younger siblings. These tasks would be considered inappropriate in some societies, and the parents of these children would be criminalized in others (Rogoff, 2003). Elders remain in charge of the extended household in some societies, have a more marginalized role in some, and are practically excluded in others.

Being young and growing old are biological realities that exist in our physical world. The mistreatment and denial of opportunities to young people and elders on the basis of age are a product of our cultural, social, economic, and political world (Schieffelin & Ochs, 1986). Being young and growing old do not constitute biological or developmental justifications for exclusion, devaluation, powerlessness, or limitation of participation in society (see Chapter 9: Ableism).

NORMALIZATION OF MISTREATMENT OF YOUNG PEOPLE AND ELDERS

The oppression of young people and elders is normalized and rendered invisible by the everydayness of their mistreatment. Jokes, humor, and ridicule of young people and elders, commonly communicated by comedians and social media, not only normalize negative perceptions about and mistreatment of young people and elders but make them a laughing matter (see Assessing Youth & Elder Oppression in the Media). Rather than focus on an individual's knowledge, skills, or competence, many laws, policies, and procedures rely on age as the sole criterion to determine what rights a person can exercise, what resources they can have access to, and what relationships they can enter. Age is used to determine when a person can vote, drive, and hold public office as well as when one is required to retire and become eligible to receive a retirement pension. These laws normalize allocating participation in society solely on the basis of age, rather than on some combination of individual circumstance, such as the requirements of a task, community support and needs, or individual capacities and talents (see Attitudes, Assumptions, and Beliefs).

The ethics of age-based rationing of medical care (Dey & Fraser, 2000), including life-saving services, such as whether to resuscitate or not, whether to provide oxygen or transfusions, or extending medical care, such as organ transplants and dialysis, has been the focus of debate in the medical community (Debolt, 2010; Teutsch & Rechel, 2012). This debate seems to have achieved deeper traction during the COVID-19 pandemic, during which communities developed protocols for triaging elders into the last category to receive life-saving treatment and equipment, after adults and young people. Indeed, internalized ageism has resulted in elderly people foregoing treatment for COVID-19, instructing doctors to "save it for younger patients" (Kumar, 2020, para 3). In their discussion of "principles for allocation of scarce medical interventions," Persad, Wertheimer, and Emanuel (2009) recommend what they call the "complete lives system—which prioritizes younger people" (p. 2). Though such a system meets the ethics of these theorists, their principles help normalize the idea that the lives of elders are of less value than the lives of others. These principles help rationalize the act of withholding or extending medical care and ultimately access to life itself on the basis of age alone.

We note here that the triaging of health-care services for elders is an example of the ways that elder oppression keeps us from focusing our attention on the vastly unequal distribution of wealth. Rather than addressing an under-resourced health-care system, elder oppression puts our focus on trying to manage a perceived scarcity of resources. (See Chapter 7: Classism.)

YOUTH: WHERE OPPRESSION IS FIRST EXPERIENCED AND INTERNALIZED

Humans first observe and experience oppression as young people. They are born into societies where "all the mechanics, assumptions, rules, roles, and structures of oppression are already in place and functioning" (Harro, 2013, p. 47). In most societies, part of the experience of being a young person is to have one's group—young people—socially located as subordinate and a target of oppression (see note at end of chapter regarding the use of the term *subordinant*).

Oppression is characterized by relationships of domination and subordination. Dominants occupy an independent status with greater access to power, resources, and decision-making. Subordinants occupy the status of dependent with limited access to power, resources, and decision-making. In most societies, the physical location of youth is synonymous with the social location of subordinant. Through this lived experience, youth internalize how to enact appropriate "roles" in relationships of domination and subordination with limited access to power. Socialization into society is one of the primary life tasks of young people and one of the key mechanisms through which they learn the roles of dominant and subordinant, which are defining features of all manifestations of oppression. "Through the socialization process, every member of society learns the attitudes, language, behavior and skills that are necessary to function effectively in the existing society" (Love, 2018, p. 610). Learning how to function successfully in contemporary society means learning how to enact roles of dominant and subordinant.

No human is born with attitudes and behavior patterns that reproduce and maintain systems of mistreatment on the basis of social identity (Harro, 2013; Love, 2018). These are learned through the socialization process. At the same time, few young people have the information, resources, power, or tools of analysis to contest, challenge, or resist racism, religious oppression, heterosexism, sexism, classism, ageism, trans* oppression, ableism, or other manifestations of oppression that are encountered, witnessed, or experienced when they are young.

This process of socialization into systems of oppression as young people coincides seamlessly with their subordinant, dependent status, is made to seem natural and unavoidable, and their dependence on adults for well-being is used to justify their subordinant status. For example, adults want to keep young people safe, and this is important and necessary. However, rules designed by adults that are intended to keep young people safe without the active participation of young people in that decision-making model for young people who gets to define, determine, and enforce over others (dominant) and who is required to comply (subordinant). In the end, dependence does not justify oppression.

When we apply this analysis of youth oppression, we see that sometimes rules aimed at keeping young people safe end up maintaining adults in power. The Society for Women's Health Research recently found that strictly enforced rules around bathroom privileges in schools are detrimental to the physical and psychological well-being of young people (Wong, 2019). This includes threats to bladder health, increased potential for impacting the ability to focus, and the potential for social stress if a student has an accident. In this instance, young people, located in a subordinant role, must rely on adults for permission, changing policies, and advocating on their behalf.

Youth oppression is used to justify collusion with intersecting oppressions. For instance, adults sometimes deny that young children can know that they are trans* or nonbinary. Adults then use this denial as a rationale to avoid supporting and celebrating students' gender identities in the classroom. Trans* students who identify as nonbinary in first grade sometimes have a classroom experience of teachers who say, "I don't believe in that—in trans* identity." In such cases, that teacher is not likely to encourage the class to use the appropriate pronouns for that student. Colluding with stereotypes and dangerous biases about Black children not feeling pain results in adults' failure to intervene and interrupt physical and emotional bullying at school. These types of experiences train young people to effectively participate in the maintenance of other forms of oppression.

CONCEPTUAL FRAMEWORKS

We frame our examination of youth and elder oppression with Memmi's (2000) criteria for oppression, Young's (1990) Five Faces of Oppression, and Hardiman, Jackson, and Griffin's (2010) discussion of levels and types of oppression. We use Love's (2018) Developing a Liberatory Consciousness as a framework for evolving strategies for ending oppression and the development of liberation movements (see website for Defining Key Concepts and Terms).

★

MEMMI'S CRITERIA FOR OPPRESSION

Memmi (2000, p. xvii) describes four criteria that characterize oppression: (1) an "insistence on a difference, real or imaginary," (2) imposing a "negative valuation" on those differences, (3) generalizing the negatively valued differences to the entire group, and (4) using the generalized negative valuations to justify and legitimize hostility and aggression against members of that group. Youth oppression and elder oppression share each of these four criteria.

Developmental theorists agree that humans differ, in physical as well as in mental and emotional development, across the lifespan (Li, Lindenberger, Hommel, Aschersleben, Prinz, & Baltes, 2004). These developmental differences are considered natural and normal. Here we examine the "negative valuations" imposed by society on youth and old age and the way those negative valuations are generalized to the entire group and then used to rationalize and justify disadvantaged status for members of these two groups. Negative assumptions and valuations about the physical and mental capacities of young people (DeJong, 2014) and elders (Palmore, Branch, & Harris, 2005), assumptions about their inadequate knowledge and limited or diminished intelligence (Calasanti & Slevin, 2001; Nelson, 2002), and assumptions about their capacity to make decisions regarding their own lives are generalized to the group as a whole and used to rationalize mistreatment and subordinant, disadvantaged status.

For example, we noted earlier the variations in intellectual abilities demonstrated by children, adults, and elders (Baltes, 1997). The cognitive decline of some elders has been generalized to the entire group in some countries and has become the basis for mandatory retirement laws that interrupt viable and gainful employment for all elders based on age rather than on an individual elder's ability to continue work. The massive increase in Equal Employment Opportunity Commission (EEOC) cases on age discrimination in the US workplace reflects the growing impact of negative attitudes about elders' capacity for effective workplace participation (Winerip, 2013). The direction to doctors in Italy to abandon treatment for elders during the COVID-19 pandemic is another example of the way that age rather than individual attributes became the factor determining access to potentially life-saving medical treatment.

"Must be 18" policies that restrict the entry and unsupervised participation of young people at shopping malls across the United States (Russell, 2005, p. A1) are another illustration of Memmi's criteria for oppression. According to the mall manager at the Ingleside Mall in Holyoke, Massachusetts:

> Just the fact that they're young people they are perceived by some people [adults] as intimidating [imposing a negative valuation on that difference]. It might cause you [adults] to leave [generalizing to the group to legitimate hostility toward the group], or not shop in stores you [adults] want to shop in.
>
> (Russell, 2005, p. A1)

"Just the fact that they're young people" highlights Memmi's criteria of "insistence on a difference" as the rationale for differential treatment. Some young people have undoubtedly behaved inappropriately in a mall, as have some adults. Generalizing the inappropriate behavior of some young people to the entire group and creating policies based on that generalization is one example of the effect of negative assumptions and valuations on young people (Males, 2004).

YOUNG'S FIVE FACES OF OPPRESSION

Young (1990) names five conditions that characterize oppression, including: (1) exploitation, (2) marginalization, (3) powerlessness, (4) cultural imperialism, and (5) violence. We use these five conditions to illustrate the ways that mistreatment of young people and elders constitutes oppression (see website Five Faces of Youth & Elder Oppression).   ★

EXPLOITATION

Young (1990) uses the term *exploitation* to describe a "structural relation between social groups" (p. 14) that involves a relationship of domination and subordination. In addition to our relationships as children, parents, grandparents, siblings, and friends, exploitation occurs because oppression establishes a structured relationship of domination and subordination between us as members of social groups. Exploitation includes "systematic and unreciprocated transfer of power from one group to the other" (p. 15). Though many elders occupy positions of power and decision-making, young people as a social group are fairly thoroughly excluded from participation in decision-making, both in the public arena and in the private sphere of the family.

Young (1990) refers to a description of exploitation to mean "a seriously unequal distribution of wealth, income, and other resources that is group based and structurally persistent" (p. 17). Exploitation is the act of using people's labor to produce profit while not compensating them fairly. Young people are routinely compensated at lower rates than adults. Many low wage jobs, such as in the fast-food industry, are seen as the province of young people. Elders might have independent wealth, but their control over that wealth can be challenged and removed at any time. Financial exploitation of elders through misappropriation of their assets is a common form of exploitation. Both elders and young people can be excluded from work solely on the basis of age. Poor and working-class elders who are dependent on social security find a greatly restricted standard of living and are frequently forced to make choices between food and medicine or other necessities.

Owning-class young people might have access to wealth but seldom have independent control of their resources. Working-class and poor young people in the US have limited to zero access to wealth. Working-class and poor youth have limited access to wage-earning work outside the agricultural sector and fast-food industry. Child labor is still common in many parts of the world, including the agricultural sector in the US. The income from child laborers, however, is seldom placed in their hands or under their control. While the US and many western countries have child labor laws, presumably designed to protect young people from exploitation, these laws generally exempt the agricultural sector, where most child laborers are employed. According to the International Labor Organization (Goodweave, 2010, p. 5), "over 215 million children between the ages of 5–17 are involved in child labor." In India, 12% of children are estimated to be involved in child labor: "Some children are forced to weave up to 18 hours a day, often never leaving the confines of the factory or loom shed" (Goodweave, 2010, p. 6). Clearly, they do not control the income produced by their labor. Child trafficking, a huge global problem, is compounded by the reality that "children trafficked into one form of labor may be later sold into another, as with girls from rural Nepal who are recruited to work in carpet factories but are then trafficked into the sex industry over the border in India" (Goodweave, 2010, p. 7). Individuals who traffic children, sweat shops that employ them, and people who buy the goods and services resulting from the exploitation of young people are all complicit in and contribute to societal acceptance of the mistreatment of young people.

In addition to contributing to "inequality of status, power and wealth," exploitation involves exclusion of members of subordinant groups from participation in privileged activities (Young, 1990, p. 15). Additional exclusions affect the participation of young people, such as the ability to drive on public roads, get married without permission of adults, purchase alcoholic beverages, sign legal documents, leave school without permission of adults, purchase real estate, run for public office, or engage in sex. On the other hand, as noted earlier, elders, especially white men, are often key decision-makers in public life. Class, race, religion, sex, gender, and other social identities often mediate elder access to power and decision-making.

MARGINALIZATION

Young (1990) describes marginalization as being "expelled from useful participation in social life and thus potentially subjected to severe material deprivation and even extermination" (p. 18). Marginalization involves depriving members of certain groups of the opportunity for participation in "organized social cooperation" and in the "cultural, practical, and institutional life of society" (p. 19). Young describes injustices of marginality to include a sense of "uselessness, boredom, and lack of self-respect" (p. 20). Invisibility, isolation, loss of status and place, and limited access to power characterize the marginalization of elders and young people in most societies.

The marginalization of elders can have devastating consequences, especially in emergency situations. Evacuations of dogs and cats occurred within 24 hours after the September 11, 2001, attack on the World Trade Center in New York City, while elders and people with disabilities were abandoned in their apartments "for up to seven days before ad hoc medical teams arrived to rescue them" (Acierno, Hernandez, Amstadter, Resnick, Steve, Muzzy, & Kilpatrick, 2010). During COVID-19, elders in New York, Massachusetts, Texas, California, and other states in the US were literally moved out of their nursing homes to make space for COVID patients when local hospitals ran out of beds (Jaffe, 2020). Elders found that all their rights, including the right to a 30-day notice of intent to transfer and the right to an appeal, were waived by the federal government.

Health-care providers and others who direct questions about an elder's life and health to another person instead of to the elder contribute to the *marginalization* of elders (Geber, 2019, Nov 25). Media addressed to "those who have an older loved one" reinforce this sense of marginalization. When the travel and dining-out junk mail is replaced by ads for hearing aids and funerals, many elders receive the message that they are no longer sought after for active participation in mainstream society (Barnhart & Peñaloza, 2013).

Invisibility and refusal to appreciate and celebrate aging characterizes the experience of most elders. Aging is referred to in advertising as what everyone (especially women) is supposed to fear. According to advertising and other media, aging should be avoided at all costs. People, especially women, should do everything possible to "reverse" it when any signs of aging appear. Constant media advertisements urging everyone to fight back against aging are indicators of macro-level negative societal attitudes toward aging (Heid & Pruchno, 2021). If historical common lore can be believed, a campaign of genocide and the deaths of millions of Native people in the Americas, was sparked by the search for a fountain of youth.

Marginalization of young people and elders is illustrated through their exclusion from participation in decision-making about policies and programs, particularly those affecting their own lives. Greta Thunberg, the Swedish teen who spoke to the United Nations about the climate crisis, was mocked by the US president (Smith, 2019). Leah Namugerwa, a 14-year-old Ugandan climate activist who is leading the fight for "greater action on climate change [and] plastic pollution," is largely ignored by her government and the world press (Obonyo, 2019, para 4).

POWERLESSNESS

According to Young (1990), "The enactment of power occurs mostly through one group of people mediating the decisions of others (p. 22)." Limited access to power marks the experience of most young people and elders. The situation for elders is mixed, given that elders often occupy the most powerful positions in the world, though mediated by race, class, sex, and other social identities.

Both elders and youth are excluded from decision-making about day-to-day living arrangements and housing, medical care, and decisions about their own financial affairs. Few young people are involved in selection of school personnel, curricular standards, or their own daily schedule. Few young people are involved in family decision-making about significant family affairs. Some states in the US allow young people to state a parental custodial preference in divorce cases, but most do not. In some states, the law stipulates, "When a child is under the age of 14, the court must first determine whether or not it is in the child's best interest to listen to him or her" (Farzad, 2013, para 3). In other words, young people are excluded from being heard and expressing their own preferences.

One key consequence of systematic powerlessness is the internalization of the oppression by members of the subordinant group. Internalized oppression of elders and young people results in them accepting that their exclusion from involvement in decision-making about their own lives is correct, legitimate, and normal. A second consequence is the development of what Freire describes as a culture of silence (Freire, 1970). Discussion of their oppression is prevented, either because it is prohibited or because young people and elders have become silent. Their experience of powerlessness is so complete that they feel that discussion of it will be pointless.

CULTURAL IMPERIALISM

"Cultural imperialism is the universalization of one group's experience and culture over all others, and its establishment as the norm" (Young, 1990, p. 285). Cultural imperialism results in the values, belief systems, spiritual practices, language, standards of beauty, music, dress, and ways of being of the dominant culture being regarded as the norm, while other ways of being and cultural practices are devalued, ignored, and marked as illegal, inappropriate, or wrong. Cultural imperialism often results in efforts to eliminate or exterminate cultural practices that are not produced by the dominant group. At the very least, the effort is made to stamp them as inferior, deviant, and "marked out as other" (p. 285). Cultural imperialism results in the cultural expressions of non-dominant groups only being mentioned or referred to "in stereotyped or marginalized ways" (p. 286).

In his foundational work on ageism, Butler (1969) described a range of societal attitudes and beliefs about old people that reflect widespread cultural imperialism. According to

Butler, elders are categorized as "rigid in thought and manner, and old fashioned in morality and skills." They are described as:

> boring, stingy, cranky, demanding, avaricious, bossy, ugly, dirty, and useless. . . . Old men become geezers, old goats, gaffers, fogies, coots, gerries, fossils, and codgers, and old women are gophers, and geese. A crone, hag or witch is a withered old woman.
>
> (p. 243)

These stereotypes and myths reflect societal attitudes of dislike, disdain, and disrespect and result in "scorn, subtle avoidance, and discriminatory practices in housing, employment, pension arrangements, health care, and other services" (Butler, 1969, p. 244). Talk show hosts and people in public life who might never intentionally tell a racist or sexist joke think nothing of telling disparaging jokes about elders and young people. From greeting cards to cartoons to social media, elder oppression is a taken-for-granted fact of US culture. According to Barnhart and Peñaloza (2013), "Almost every stereotype we associate with being elderly is something negative" (p. 1136). When elders look or behave in ways that do not fit the stereotype, they are treated as "not old."

Cultural imperialism results in the dismissal and marginalization of the cultural forms of young people. Rap music, b-boy dress, graffiti art, and other forms of youth culture (Dyson, 2007) were systematically disparaged by adults until it became financially lucrative to pay attention (Wyner, 2014). Economic appropriation of the cultural practices of young people is another way that cultural imperialism is manifested, though many adults continue to express ignorance of and disdain for hip hop, rap, and other genres of music that constitute the culture of young people. Baggy clothes, a distinctive style of dress adopted by young people, was so thoroughly disapproved of by adults that some cities passed laws criminalizing sagging pants (Demby, 2014). Clothing manufacturers, however, discovered enormous profit in selling baggy pants to young people as well as to adults. While baggy clothes were not adopted by mainstream culture, economic opportunity interacted with adult taboos to mediate the impact of cultural imperialism on this cultural form (Larson, 2020). Cultural imperialism focuses on young people as a market for consumerism of both goods and services as well as political and social ideas and norms. Anti trans legislation passed by several states in the US, which withholds medical services and denies participation to trans youth, is being done in the guise of protecting young people.

Cultural imperialism toward young people in any society is about controlling their behavior and forcing compliance with the wishes and desires of adults. When young people in the US claimed to have successfully used social media (especially TikTok) to disrupt activities of one of the major political parties, the president of the US signed an executive order banning that media (Nickelsburg, 2020). Though the ban did not stick, it is worth noting that the Office of the President of the United States was used in an effort to ban a social media platform that is actively used by young people to communicate with other young people throughout the world, to express their individuality, to explore questions and ideas about themselves and the world, and to create new forms of employment. One young person who used TikTok to create a paying career declared that the platform had "given me my entire life" (Lerman, 2020, para 20). Other, larger social media platforms, such as Facebook, Twitter, Twitch, and more, have been credibly implicated in foreign manipulation of the US presidential election and continue to serve as platforms for hate groups, conspiracy theorists, and neo-Nazi groups that have been influential in the growth and spread of white nationalism. These white nationalist groups actively target young people with propaganda, enlisting their participation to start a "race war" in the US. No presidential or other action has been taken toward those platforms.

VIOLENCE

Young (1990) writes that "many groups suffer the oppression of systematic and 'legitimate' violence. The members of some groups live with the knowledge that they must fear random, unprovoked attacks on their persons or property, which have no motive but to damage, humiliate, or destroy the person" (p. 287). Young describes "legitimate violence as "the sense that most people regard it as unsurprising and it usually goes unpunished" (p. 287). Violence can be physical, mental, psychological, and emotional. In addition to the enactment of violence, the threat of violence has a limiting effect on members of marginalized groups. Violence and the threat of violence serve to keep young people and elders in the subordinant status reserved for them by society. The reality that violence against elders and young people goes unacknowledged, unremarked, and unpunished emphasizes their devalued status, a devaluation that is underscored and emphasized by the often random, unprovoked nature of attacks against them.

Violence toward elders in the form of physical abuse is tolerated, and few systems are in place to prevent it (Acierno, Hernandez, Amstadter, Resnick, Steve, Muzzy, & Kilpatrick, 2010; U.S. Department of Health and Human Services, n.d.). The first study of elder abuse in the US in 1988 (Pillemer & Finkelhor, 1988), found that abuse toward elders was occurring at a rate of 32 per 1,000. A 2011 study found that "7.6%–10% of study participants experienced abuse in the prior year" (Lachs & Berman, 2011). More recently, the Centers for Disease Control found that the rate of violence toward elders was on the rise and that few strategies to prevent violence toward elders are available (Kassraie, 2019).

US Senate hearings on abuse of elders in nursing homes noted, "Seniors in nursing homes are among the people most vulnerable to the life-threatening consequences of abuse and neglect" (Adler, 2019, para 2). They further noted, "Across this country, that vulnerability is being exploited in unimaginably cruel ways" (Adler, 2019, para 2). While some federal agencies have sought to impose regulations on nursing homes, attacks on Medicare and Medicaid reflect societal indifference to violence toward elders. The American Association of Retired Persons noted that "any weakening of federal nursing home regulations will negatively impact the approximately 1.3 million Americans across the country who are currently receiving care at these facilities" (Adler, 2019, para 11).

The United Nations Convention on the Rights of the Child (1989) includes a specific article stipulating the right to be "protected from all forms of physical or mental violence" (Human Rights Watch, 2020; Kidswatch Changemaker, n.d.). Yet violence toward young people is catastrophic on a global level and assumes multiple forms. The World Health Organization (2020a, para 1) defines violence against young people as "all forms of violence against people under 18 years old, whether perpetrated by parents or other caregivers, peers, partners, or strangers." It can include sexual abuse, emotional and psychological abuse, bullying, human trafficking, war, armed conflict, terrorism, refugee experiences, exposure to substance abuse, child neglect and abandonment, exploitation of young people in factories, child trafficking, child brides, selling young people to pay the debt of parents, and malnutrition and hunger (Dyson, 2014; IRIN News, 2020; Human Trafficking Search, 2017). These forms of violence toward young people have been noted in all parts of the world (KidsRights Changemakers, n.d.).

In the US, violence against young people in the form of corporal punishment in the home is lawful in all states (Global Initiative, n.d.), and only 11 states have banned corporal punishment in schools (Gershoff & Font, 2018). School shootings, another form of violence against young people, are on the rise in the US (Gershoff & Font, 2018). A CNN study revealed that in the ten-year period between 2009 and 2019, there were 180 school shootings with 365 victims (Walker, 2019). Yet there is no national database on school shootings, no national strategy to address school shootings, and no national consensus on gun control. A 2018 commission on school safety rejected calls for gun control (Malin & Flaherty, 2018). Young people who advocate for gun control have been mocked by public figures as well as elected officials. Some school administrators threatened suspension for any student taking part in gun control demonstrations during school hours (Smith, 2018). This failure to address the growing crisis of violence against young people in schools highlights violence as a tool and manifestation of oppression.

The COVID pandemic further contributed to violence against children. A 2020 World Health Organization report on global child abuse noted:

> Schools were closed to 1.5 billion children worldwide because of the pandemic, and their parents face heightened stress and anxiety from lost income, social isolation, and potential crowding in the home. . . . Additionally, more time online may expose children to an increased risk of online sexual exploitation or bullying.
>
> (World Health Organization, 2020a)

Health officials reported an increase in the number of children being treated for physical injuries since the beginning of the pandemic even as several states have seen child abuse reports fall by double digits (World Health Organization, 2020b). "These reductions do not reflect decreased incidences of child maltreatment, but unfortunately are a direct result of the precipitous decrease in contact between children, educational personnel, and other community youth programmes" (Thomas, Anurudran, Robb, & Burke, 2020). Even worse is the situation for children in refugee locations, war zones, and areas of armed conflict; homeless children; and children already suffering from hunger and malnutrition who find their conditions grossly exacerbated by the pandemic. Lack of a concerted worldwide effort to address violence against children underscores youth oppression as violence (Convention on the Rights of the Child, n.d.).

HISTORICAL CONTEXTS AND LEGACIES

The average age for a first marriage in colonial America was 12–14 years for a girl and 16–18 years for a boy. According to Taylor (2002), a girl who reached her 20s unmarried in colonial America was considered a social pariah. A 2015 online column titled "The Childbearing Years" suggested that while teenagers are biologically capable of becoming pregnant, they are not "emotionally or mentally capable of caring for a baby" (Loop, 2015). These differing views of maturity, too old at 20 and too young at 20, reflect changing conceptions of childhood over time within one society. Similarly, notions of old age have ranged from old at 25 during the Roman Empire (Rosenberg, 2014), to old at 30 at the turn of the last century in the US (Taylor, 2002), to a 21st-century worldwide average life expectancy of 72.81 (Macrotrends, 2021). Changing biological realities of age across the lifespan in addition to changing sociological realities and conditions within societies helped transform societal conceptions of youth and old age.

In this section, we explore four historical contexts and legacies that have influenced current conceptions of what constitutes *young people* and *old people* and their role and place in contemporary society. Connections between modern European colonialism and current constructions of childhood (Cannella & Viruru, 2004; DeJong, 2014), the industrial revolution (Hendricks, 2004), the printing press, and the advent of modern, mandatory public schooling (Rogoff, 2003) are explored. These contexts and legacies helped shape present-day manifestations of youth and elder oppression (see website for Mini-Lecture on Historical Context and Legacies).

★

EUROPEAN COLONIALISM AND CURRENT CONSTRUCTIONS OF CHILDHOOD

When European colonizers proclaimed that "the sun never set" on their flag, they gave testament to the imposition of European culture worldwide. The globalization of capitalism combined with European colonization to reinforce the effects of European cultural imperialism on societies in all parts of the world. While many communities retain their ancestral forms, including communities within western societies, such as the Roma in Europe and Indigenous, Asian American, and African American communities in North America, many of the impacts of European cultural imperialism can still be observed in those societies as well. Current constructions of childhood and youth oppression is one of those observable effects.

While noting that youth oppression and elder oppression are not solely products of contemporary western society, in this discussion, we examine the globalization of western cultural imperialism and its effects on constructions of childhood throughout the world. This includes the work of scholars who examined parallels between concepts of modern European colonialism and contemporary constructions of childhood (Burman, 2007; Cannella & Viruru, 2004; Nandy, 1983). Evidence that principles of colonialism both borrowed from and contributed to principles of human development, including current constructions of childhood, broadens our understanding of contemporary manifestations of youth oppression and elder oppression.

The period of western European colonial exploration and expansion—between the 16th and 19th centuries—was also a period during which westerners conceptualized *"youth"* as dependent, uncivilized, and savage, along with colonized people who were conceptualized to be dependent, uncivilized, and savage (Cannella & Viruru, 2004). They conceptualized western societies to mean advanced and civilized, and adult to mean independent and civilized. This conceptual parallel of youth who were savage, uncivilized, and dependent on families, and colonized people who were savage, uncivilized, and dependent on colonizers, provided conceptual justification for familial and colonial relationships of domination and subordination (Cannella & Viruru, 2004). The literature suggests that these two conceptualizations, like the proverbial chicken and egg, developed simultaneously and borrowed generously from each other (Burman, 2007).

Along with rationalizations rooted in Christianity, colonization borrowed notions of biological development and the language of infantilization to justify hierarchical relationships of domination and subordination, evident in both colonialism and contemporary constructions of childhood (Burman, 2007; Cannella & Viruru, 2004; Nandy, 1983). Science was used to justify notions of the inferiority of colonized people to European colonizers and the inferiority of young people to adults. Notions of dependency rationalized conceptions of young people as biologically incapable of making decisions about their lives. This conceptualization of adult superiority holds that adults can think better and make better decisions simply because of their age, rather than because they also have access to more information and more years of experience on which to base their thinking and decisions. Adult superiority was used to justify removing young people from useful participation in the work of the family and the life of the community.

This notion of adult superiority coincided with 17th- and 18th-century European colonial discourses describing Africans, Indigenous people, and some groups of Asians (Indonesians, Indians, Filipinos) as childlike. Conceptualizing Africans, Asians, and Native Americans as childlike, infantile, savage, uncivilized, and primitive was used to justify removing them from their land, usurping their resources, and establishing European domination over them (Lakota People's Law Project, 2013; Swain, 2009). Being cast as childlike was used to justify colonial management and control and being cast as savage to justify cultural and physical genocide. Native Americans were subjected to genocide or placed in the restricted environments of reservations controlled by the US government. On the basis of their presumed childlikeness, Africans were subjected to genocide, sold into slavery, denied the right to self-government, and their territories were turned into colonies.

The construct of infantilization established European imperial powers as the mature adult with authority to dominate the economic, social, political, health, and educational policies and directions of subordinated nations—called dependencies—and peoples. Colonial discourse established *childlike* as a pejorative term, indicating lacking sensibility or the capacity for rational thinking. Colonial discourse helped to firmly establish *youth* as a subordinated group in need of direction and control (Burman, 2007). Until colonial discourse established that young people are mentally and emotionally incompetent for such responsibilities, 14-year-olds had been considered competent to marry and run a household.

This same infantilization and judgment as childlike is used to restrict self-determination and self-control for elders. Researchers have documented the propensity of adults to use baby-talk, including exaggerated tone, simplified speech, and high pitch, when speaking to elders. Physicians have been shown to condescend to and patronize older patients by providing oversimplified information or speaking to the family instead of the older patient (Austin, 2013). This infantilization and rendering of elders as "childlike" is used to justify their subordinant status.

Current constructions of youth and elders as subordinant groups clearly did not develop in a vacuum and overlaps historically with the colonizing project of European nations. The language of infantilization is so embedded in western culture that in contemporary discourse, people, projects, ideas, and whole nations can be minimized, marginalized, and dismissed by being labeled as childlike. Contemporary discussions of relationships between former European colonial powers and formerly colonized nations continue to use the language of infantilization.

THE WESTERN INDUSTRIAL REVOLUTION

The western industrial revolution had a profound effect on our understanding of the role and place of young people and elders in society. While we focus on youth and elders in western society, we recognize that one consequence of the European colonial project is that western conceptions of young people and elders have been forcibly exported and consequently influence people and societies in all parts of the world.

The western industrial revolution forced a transition from a rural, agrarian society to an urban, manufacturing society and from skilled artisans and family commerce to machine production in factories and the large-scale commercial marketplace. This had a profound effect on the role and place of young people and elders in contemporary western society. Work now took place in the factory instead of the home and community. Young people moved from work in the home and community to work in the new factories of the industrial revolution, where they were exploited (Thompson, 1968) and eventually excluded from wage-earning work (Freudenberger, Francis, & Clark, 1984; Hutchins & Harrison, 1911). Elders similarly moved from work as skilled artisans, who supervised the apprenticeship of others and passed on their knowledge and skills to apprentices and young people, to marginalized participation in the workplace. This resulted in the complete economic dependence of young people and nearly complete dependence of elders on wage-earning adults for their livelihood.

Child labor laws that resulted in the exclusion of young people from productive participation in the life of the community, and particularly from participation in the paid labor force, both removed some children from horrific, often dangerous conditions in factories and at the same time excluded them from earning a wage that might grant a measure of economic independence. Though creating safe working conditions in the industrial workplace was not the focus of child-labor laws, they did remove many young people from unsafe working conditions. Child labor laws only addressed some children and some work locations. Young people were not excluded from farm work. As recently as 2012, the US Department of Labor withdrew proposed regulations that would have protected "child farmworkers from the most dangerous tasks" (Human Rights Watch, 2012). Many of those child farmworkers are immigrants from Mexico and South America. Excluded from the protections of child labor laws, these child workers perform the same labor as adults, like children in many parts of the world (Dinopoulos & Zhao, 2007).

Elders in western societies experienced both restricted participation in the industrial workforce and diminution of their significance in society as a result of the western industrial revolution. The institutionalization and specialization of jobs requiring manual labor in factories replaced the role of skilled artisan once played by elders. Specialized knowledge accumulated over a lifetime and often passed down from one generation of artisans to the next was no longer central to the economic life of the community. Workers learned routinized, specialized skills on the job, rather than from venerated elders. Quantity or products growing from routinized specialization required workers who could excel at monotonized tasks, often at lower rates of pay. Elders were now often overlooked in favor of workers who could presumably more easily adapt to assembly-line production. This meant that elders were now often excluded from both productive economic employment as well as from a valued social role in families and in the community.

IMPACT OF THE PRINTING PRESS AND MODERN MANDATORY PUBLIC SCHOOLING

The invention of the printing press had profound effects on role and place for both young people and elders in contemporary western society. Prior to the invention of the printing press, elders were often treasured for the "knowledge they have acquired from their ancestors, through social learning" and the "key role [they played] in the evolution of [the] social species" (Coe & Palmer, 2009, p. 5). Many societies depended on elders for the preservation and transmission of their oral traditions, which served as the record of the culture and history of the group. In addition to serving as the depositories of the culture, history, and traditions of the group, elders were valued contributors to the preservation of the knowledge, understandings, and skills accumulated by the group. Elders carried knowledge of traditional medicines, food production, preservation, and preparation. They taught apprentices the art and skills accumulated over the history of the group. Elders were depositories of knowledge that was critical to the survival and well-being of the group.

The invention of the printing press meant that the history, culture, and traditions of a society could be recorded in books and read by any literate person. The knowledge and skills required for future employment could be learned from reading a book (Branco & Williamson, 1982). Most of what people needed to know could now be included in books and presumably learned in school. Literate societies were no longer dependent on the presence of an elder or their oral traditions for records of the traditions, culture, and history of the group or to learn the skills needed for wage-earning work.

The industrial revolution and the invention of factories as the primary location of work for the majority of the adult community members made schools necessary. The exclusion of young people from factories made public schooling mandatory (Rogoff, 2007). Excluded from active participation in the workforce, modern society had the problem of finding a holding place for young people until they could enter the workplace from which they had been excluded. The invention of the printing press made modern public schooling possible as the availability of textbooks supported teachers in following a particular sequence of lessons that taught reading and writing (Rubinstein, 1999).

Schools serve a variety of social, civic, and economic functions. They are primary agencies of socialization, teaching young people what they need to know to participate effectively and appropriately in modern society. They learn the attitudes, understandings, and behavior patterns necessary to preserve the existing society.

In 1647, the Massachusetts Bay Colony commanded that towns of 50 families have elementary schools and towns of 100 families have Latin schools. The purpose of this mandate was to teach children to read the Bible and to instruct them on the basics of their Calvinistic faith. Employers quickly saw public schools as a means to create better laborers. Therefore, the most crucial elements of school to them were punctuality, following directions, the ability to tolerate long hours of work, and the ability to read and write. National leaders and reformers also saw opportunities in schooling children to cultivate patriotism, teach moral lessons, and create academic scholars in Latin and mathematics. As a result, schooling became a mix of agendas of what adults thought children ought to learn (Bogle, 2018, para 14).

This discussion does not examine the myth of schooling as the great equalizer, except to acknowledge that the existing class society has not been greatly disrupted by the advent of schooling. By and large, the children of working-class adults grow up to be working-class adults, while the owning-class children grow up to be owning-class adults. We acknowledge that in some cases, schools teach young people knowledge and skills that prepare them for future employment. Our concern is the role that schools play as a societally approved placement and holding ground for young people while adults earn wages at work (Rogoff, 2007, pp. 8–9). The site of learning and the transmission of the culture was relocated from extended intergenerational families to the school. The COVID-19 pandemic highlighted the dependence of contemporary western economies on schooling. The closing of schools or moving to remote learning models in communities around the world created a crisis for employers when workers, including health-care and other frontline workers classified as essential employees, now had to create individual plans for the care and instruction of their children and find someplace for their children to be while they went to work.

The invention of the printing press gave rise to modern schooling as the center of learning. The industrial revolution gave rise to factories as the center of work. Factories as the primary location of wage-earning work gave rise to the nuclear family (Nelson, 1982; Stearns, 1986). Though there were many notable exceptions (African American, LatinX, and Indigenous communities in the United States and immigrant communities in Europe), families became increasingly nuclear and were no longer the center of learning or production. Elders were increasingly relocated to residential homes and isolated from active participation in families, community, and society (Nelson, 1982; Stearns, 1986).

MANIFESTATIONS OF YOUTH OPPRESSION AND ELDER OPPRESSION

In this section, we discuss manifestations of youth and elder oppression, illustrating how they play out on institutional/systemic, cultural/societal, and individual levels as well as in US and global contexts (see website: Undesigning Youth & Elder Oppression with Jenga-Style Blocks).

We refer to institutional/systemic youth and elder oppression as the ways that policies and practices within and across institutions of society, including economic, political, social, health, educational, and other systems, combine to maintain and reproduce advantage and dominant status for adults and corollary disadvantage and subordinant status for young people and elders. The hegemonic, or business-as-usual, dimensions of youth and elder oppression persist over time and are made to seem natural and normal, whether intentional or unintentional, overt or covert. Cultural/societal youth and elder oppression includes cultural representations, popular stereotypes, images, frames, and narratives that are reinforced by media, language, and other forms of mass communication and "common sense." Though cultural representations can be positive or negative, they have the overall effect of allowing unfair treatment to seem fair and/or "natural." Individual oppression includes attitudes (bias, prejudice, or hate), beliefs, and behaviors about young people and elders that are rooted in adult supremacy and reflect or result in a disadvantaged and subordinant status for young people. While we describe three broad levels of oppression, institutional/systemic, cultural/societal, and individual levels, for elder and for youth oppression, we note that most manifestations of oppression do not fit neatly into one category or another, often spanning all three.

MANIFESTATIONS OF ELDER OPPRESSION

The consistent experience of inferior health care (Acierno, Hernandez, Amstadter, Resnick, Steve, Muzzy, & Kilpatrick, 2010; National Center on Elder Abuse, 2017) is a major manifestation of individual, institutional, and societal elder oppression. The withholding of life-supporting and life-extending medical procedures, including organ transplants, from elders represents decisions made by individual health-care providers, institutional decisions that triage health care, and societal undervaluing of the lives of elders. For example, "guidelines from the International Society for Heart and Lung Transplantation caution against lung transplants for those over 65" (Span, 2013, para 5). We noted earlier that public health officials in many parts of the world discussed withholding ventilators and other potentially life-saving medical services from elders during the COVID pandemic (Kirkpatrick, Hull, Fedso, Mullen, & Goodlin, 2020). "Do not attempt resuscitation," policies along with decisions regarding withholding medical treatment from elders during COVID-19 clearly revealed compromised access to health care for elders (Kirkpatrick, Hull, Fedso, Mullen, & Goodlin, 2020, para 1). In some globally celebrated cases, elders refused access to ventilators, advising that the resource should be given to a younger person (Slisco, 2020). Global media celebration of these cases communicated the widely accepted idea that the lives of younger persons should be valued differently than the lives of elders. According to the World Health Organization (2014), health care for the elderly is limited or missing altogether in many parts of the world.

Elders experience financial abuse as well as physical and emotional abuse. Individual manifestations of financial abuse of elders includes cashing checks and withdrawing from the accounts of an elderly person without their knowledge or consent, unauthorized transfer of their property, identity theft in which a person opens credit cards fraudulently in the name of an elder, as well as Medicaid scams (Bush, 2013). Institutional manifestations of financial abuse of elders are reflected in financial targeting schemes, including predatory lending practices, questionable investment plans, insurance policies, and disproportionate targeting of elders for reverse mortgage schemes that prey on elders' fears about financial viability in their final years.

Cultural/societal manifestations of elder oppression are reflected in the denial of aging in western society. According to Lamb and Gentry (2013), "research has shown that Western culture holds predominantly negative views about aging into old age" (p. 36). The greeting card industry, jokes, and advertising broadly reflect society's negative attitudes and values toward elderly people.

Mistreatment of elders is so pervasive across so many societies that the International Network for the Prevention of Elder Abuse and the World Health Organization established World Elder Abuse Awareness Day at the United Nations to "promote better understanding of abuse and neglect of older persons" in communities around the world (National Center on Elder Abuse, 2017, para 2). Cultural acceptance of the mistreatment of elders means that services and agencies designed to protect elders from abuse exist in some societies and not in most others. The Affordable Care Act was the first piece of federal legislation in the US to authorize a specific source of funds to address elder "abuse, neglect and exploitation" (National Center on Elder Abuse, 2017). The US Administration on Aging was designed to address and ameliorate abuse of elders in the US (Administration on Aging, n.d.). The Older Americans Act Reauthorization in 2016 resulted in the creation of a number of agencies and programs designed to provide social services to elders (National Center on Elder Abuse, 2017).

MANIFESTATIONS OF YOUTH OPPRESSION

Schooling is one site where young people experience the various levels of oppression. The disruption of schooling during the COVID pandemic revealed the ways in which young people are excluded from decisions that impact their lives. In the US, school systems were closed, reopened, and then closed again without including young people (or sometimes even teachers) in the planning process. There were reported instances where young people were punished for sharing photos of packed hallways with unmasked students, relaying information about how their schools were handling reopening during the virus (Jones, 2020). Institutional policies combined with individual decision-making of school officials to enact the oppression of young people throughout this crisis.

On an individual level, a range of teacher decision-making affected the schooling experience of young people who had to learn remotely during the pandemic. Some teachers punished students for failure to turn on a camera in a home in which there was little room for privacy. Reports of teachers who threatened young people because of minor infractions, such as turning away from the screen to connect their device to a power source, are one example reflecting the impact of individual actions on the oppression of young people.

The *school-to-prison pipeline* provides another representation of institutional oppression combined with widespread negative societal attitudes toward young people as a group and toward young People of Color in particular (*Rethinking Schools*, 2011). School architecture, particularly those schools attended by poor, working-class, and young People of Color, resemble prisons with no windows (Hadi-Tabassum, 2015). Poor and working-class students, students with disabilities, queer and trans* students, and students of color are often treated as criminals or potential criminals, reflecting the societal attitude that their behavior must be watched, controlled, and regulated.

Schools in lower-income areas with a majority of students of color are often characterized by zero-tolerance policies and procedures, school-based arrests, exclusions and expulsions, locker searches, unregulated interrogation, metal detectors, and entryway screening devices. At one Chicago high school, large numbers of students were arrested following massive locker searches. Most of those teens were arrested for possession of phones (Mitchell & Leachman, 2014). In the instances where zero-tolerance policies exist in higher-income areas or predominantly white schools, the research shows race-based disproportionalities in suspensions and expulsions (McIntoshm Girvan, Horner, & Smolkowski, 2014).

Health and health care are another context where youth oppression manifests. According to the World Health Organization, one third of the young people of the world are poisoned by lead (Buechner, 2020). Within the United States, race and income are strong determinants of who may or may not be exposed to lead poisoning. According to the Centers for Disease Control and Prevention, being Black or brown and living in a low-income area are among the leading risk factors for lead poisoning among children (2019). In Flint, Michigan, a decision by government leaders to save money by switching water sources resulted in contaminated drinking water, and poisoning, for more than 12,000 children (The Associated Press, 2021, para 9). In the case of Flint, a panel appointed by the governor of Michigan concluded that "the state of Michigan is 'fundamentally accountable'" (The Associated Press, 2021, para 9). Both neglect and deliberate decisions made by policymakers, such as lack of funding for infrastructure, led to these results (Almendrala, 2019).

Young people, who are among the most at risk for experiencing adverse effects of lead poisoning, lack access to political processes that influence the decisions that impact their lives. While elders do have access to the political process, as stated earlier in this chapter, they are subject to subordinant treatment in the medical system. The adverse health impact from situations, like Flint, places them at the mercy of a medical system that deems them low priority and disposable.

The 2021 US legal case of brain damage to children caused by the use of the pesticide chlorpyrifos is another example of multi-level manifestations of youth oppression. The research showing the connection between chlorpyrifos and lower birth weight, brain damage, and learning disabilities in children is over a decade old. According to the Natural Resource Defense Council, the EPA "completely abandoned any commitment to protecting children from this extremely toxic chemical" (Friedman, 2020, para 7). Ultimately, the 2021 actions of another individual, Judge Rakoff of the Ninth Circuit Court, interrupted this oppression by ordering the EPA to "either demonstrate that chlorpyrifos does not harm children or to legally end its use on food crops" (Davenport, 2021, para 20).

Whether the oppression of young people and elders shows up in individual, institutional, or societal and cultural manifestations, they form an interlocking network of hegemony that maintains a position of disadvantage and subordination for young people and elders in most societies throughout the world.

INTERNALIZED YOUTH AND ELDER OPPRESSION

Messages developed by the dominant group to justify oppression are often internalized by members of groups targeted by oppression (Friere, 1970). Oppressive systems work because people internalize messages of domination and subordination that are necessary for them to play their part in the maintenance of the oppressive system (Love, 2018). Friere (1970), Memmi (2000), and others have discussed the process and the consequences of that internalization (see website Internalized Youth & Elder Oppression Triads).   ★

Young people and elders internalize negative societal attitudes of ageism and adultism directed toward them and come to regard those negative messages as normal. Laws regulating age instead of competency requirements for voting, holding office, receiving an education, testifying in court, when and under what circumstances young people or elders can establish an independent domicile, who can receive mortgages and loans, and who can otherwise fully participate in the civil, social, economic, and political life of society are seen as normal and even necessary once youth and elder oppression are internalized. Both young people and elders internalize assumptions about the rightness of those who are midlife adults to have more power and resources and to make decisions about other's lives. Elders and young people act on the basis of these assumptions in their relationships with each other as well as in their relationships with members of the dominant group.

A key element of internalized oppression is identification with the dominant group. Just as women often identify with men and People of Color often identify with white people, young people and elders often identify with middle-aged adults as the superior group. Encouraged and rewarded for enforcing youth oppression on other young people, young people act to keep each other in line:

> [Many young people] spend their entire childhood identifying with the perspective of adults . . . [and] feel that . . . other young people . . . actually deserve to be treated with disrespect. . . . [Youth employ a variety of strategies] to dissociate themselves from other young people, trying to shed the negative status of childhood.
>
> (Bonnichsen, 2003, p. 2)

Similar to Black people who express greater respect and deference to other Black people who look, speak, and act more like white people, many young people accord respect on an age scale and act out oppression on anyone perceived to be weaker, possessing fewer resources, smaller, or younger than themselves (DeJong & Love, 2013). Older young people can give orders to younger people, who in turn can give orders to those younger and so on down the age-based scale.

Identification with the dominant group leads to collusion through behaviors that support the superiority of the dominant group. Elders, for example, are rewarded for efforts to hold on to the appearance of middle age as long as they can. A multi-billion-dollar beautification/youth restoration industry supports them in this process. From hair dyes, which may be harmful to their health, to age-defying serums, youth-restoration spas, and the age-old search for the fountain of youth, elders enact and display their internalization of society's contempt for aging and fear of getting old. Internalized oppression among elders often shows up as feelings of resignation and isolation. Elders may suffer depression stemming from internalized feelings of "loss of value, being a bother, worthlessness, feeling that they are unworthy of the caretaking of others, and the fear that they will one day be unable to take care of themselves" (DeJong & Love, 2013, p. 536). Both elders and young people internalize attitudes and behaviors of powerlessness and learn to not trust their own thinking, to give up their own voice, to allow others to speak for them, and to allow others to make decisions on their behalf.

For young people, like members of any other targeted group, the quality of their survival depends on learning both sides of the oppression. Young people who learn to show appropriate deference and submission to parents, teachers, school administrators, police, and other authority figures, all of whom are adults, have a less troublesome experience than young people who don't mind their manners.

Once the oppression is internalized, the perpetuation of the oppression is assured, for the subordinated groups will join with the dominant group to enforce and maintain the oppression. Internalizing the attitudes, beliefs, and behaviors associated with the roles of subordinant and dominant prepares young people for participation in those roles for the remainder of their lives. Whether called on to play the role of agent or the role of target, childhood socialization helps people internalize the attitudes, beliefs, and behaviors required for effective participation in an oppressive society (Love, 2018).

LOVE'S LIBERATORY CONSCIOUSNESS

Liberatory consciousness (Love, 2018) is presented here as a framework within which movements to end the oppression of young people and elders can be envisioned, formulated, enacted, and continually reframed with the collaboration of allies. Liberatory consciousness is a mindset that enables humans to live their lives in oppressive systems, with awareness of and intentionality to change that oppression. This mindset replaces the patterns of thought and behavior learned through the socialization process that lead to collusion with oppressive systems. Liberatory consciousness enables individuals to maintain awareness of the pervasiveness of oppression without succumbing to hopelessness, helplessness, and despair. Liberatory consciousness is a mindset that holds awareness of the role played by each individual in the maintenance of oppressive systems without blaming them for the roles they play. It is based on a vision of a society that works well for all members and a mission of movement with intentionality toward liberation. Liberatory consciousness includes the idea that examining and understanding oppression is a first step in envisioning how to dismantle it and create liberatory structures, institutions, communities, and relationships (see website Icebreaker: Envisioning Liberation for All Ages; Liberation for All Ages; and Closing: Liberation Commitments). ★

Five dimensions of liberatory consciousness identified by Love (2018) include: awareness, analysis, action, allyship, and accountability. Developing *awareness* about the attitudes, beliefs, behaviors, and processes through which the oppression of young people and elders function is a necessary first step. This includes awareness of the historical contexts within which the oppression of young people and elders was constructed and the contemporary justifications that are provided for youth and elder oppression.

Analysis of the norms, policies, institutional structures, behaviors, and practices that maintain youth and elder oppression proceeds from this awareness. Analysis provides an informed basis for determining appropriate *actions* to challenge and transform youth and elder oppression. Allyship occurs within the understanding that youth and elders must stand at the center of any strategies and efforts to end the oppression. While there are key roles for allies to play, that role must occur within the context of backing and supporting young people and elders, not taking over the thinking, planning, and leading of youth and elder liberation movements. Liberatory consciousness shapes thinking about how to build better and more *accountable allyship* with young people and elders for liberation movements. Accountability to a vision of a society characterized by liberatory principles helps to shape allyship for ending oppression and working toward transformation and liberation.

LIBERATION MOVEMENTS FOR ELDERS AND YOUNG PEOPLE

From Joan of Arc, 15th-century teen peasant girl turned warrior, to the 21st-century Black Lives Matter movement, along with the Gray Panther movement and the Elders Action Network, young people and elders have been at the forefront of movements for liberation for centuries (History.com, 2020). In many societies across the globe, young people, elders, and their allies are actively challenging oppressive cultural attitudes and beliefs as well as individual and institutional policies and practices that maintain the oppression of young people and elders. They are developing policies, programs, and practices that enable young people and elders to contribute to their community and have real power in controlling their lives. There are many examples of young people and elders collaborating on liberation work (see website Ending Youth and Elder Oppression Movement Research & Presentations).

Elders on the Navajo Reservation in the United States raised funds to secure a generator to lessen the brunt of the ravages of COVID-19 on reservation residents. Young people and elders work together with other members of the community as water protectors and in the fight against climate change. Elders in Japan are speaking up and talking about how the bombing of Hiroshima and Nagasaki affected their lives (Moakley & Rothman, n.d.). No longer content to be silent and/or have others speak on their behalf, they are making visible the human toll of suffering from atomic bombs. Elder and youth activists are working on immigration, asylum, and incarceration. Though the American Association of Retired People does not claim a liberation agenda, their efforts are focused on improving conditions in the lives of retired people, who are most often elders.

The Institute for Democratic Education and Culture supports a movement for young people to come together and dialogue about racial justice and a radical reimagination of a post-COVID world, in which young people support and empower each other to address societal inequities (Institute for Democratic Education in America, 2020). Young people in Honduras have become reporters for U-Report to help get accurate and timely information to other young people and their families about COVID-19 (UNICEF, 2020). Black and Latina teen girls are "leading movements marching against gun violence and for Black lives, leading the push to get police out of schools, and raising awareness of the threat posed by climate change" (Teen Vogue, 2020, para 1). Canadian water protector Autumn Peltier, the indigenous-led Guardians of the Forest, and Zero Hour's Zeena Abdulkarim are helping lead the youth climate movement (Janfaza, 2020).

William Kamkwamba, the Malawi teenager who harnessed the wind to help his village survive extreme famine, is one of a number of teens in many parts of the world who noticed the challenges and difficulties in their communities and in the world around them and develop initiatives and actions to address the problem and create change (Kamkwamba, 2009). Teen immigrant rights activists are organizing to protect DACA (Deferred Action for Childhood Arrivals) recipients in the United States. Black trans* and queer young feminists are fighting for disability justice, reproductive justice, and an end to all gender-based violence. In Mauritius, young people fight against the oil spill polluting the ocean (Ball, 2020; BBC My World, 2020). The Black Lives Matter movement, led by young Black activists, is a cross-generational movement connecting with people from all over the world in its commitment to defend all Black lives and create Black political will and power (M4BL, 2020).

Indigenous youth in the United States are working to confront racism and settler colonialism on reservations and in urban settings. Youthbuild-USA is one example of youth-centered organizing to support young people's liberation. FIERCE, a membership-based organization in New York City, is committed to building the leadership and power of LGBTQ+ youth.

There are organizations working to make it easier for youth under 18 to serve on boards of directors, especially of youth-serving agencies. Part of the work is teaching adults some non-adultist strategies for interacting with young people, including making space for their voices, listening to their ideas, respecting them as colleagues, respecting their judgment, backing their leadership, and sharing resources. This is a relatively accessible step that many people can enact in their organizations. Instead of publishing their thinking for them, allies could collaborate with a young person and listen to them, record their thinking, transcribe the recording, assist the young person in editing the transcript, and then encourage editors to publish the writing of that young person. This collaboration will take time and energy but, in the end, will result in the voice of young people becoming a part of the literature on young people's liberation. The same process can be repeated for elders.

Young people organizing liberation movements face a few challenges. Young people are taught to accept their mistreatment as a rite of passage or as something that is natural and normal. To move from embodying to challenging this perspective is a huge step. Some adult researchers and activists work with young people to create space and organize resources for young people to identify problems in their community, develop their own leadership, take action to transform problems, and reflect on this work to develop a vision for how their communities can thrive (Cammarota & Fine, 2008; Duncan-Andrade & Morrell, 2008; Tuck & Yang, 2013). The Center of Racial Justice and Youth Engaged Research (CRJ) "centers Black, Indigenous, and People of Color (BIPOC) in the work of fighting for antiracism and educational justice with youth, communities, educators, and schools through enduring reciprocal relationships" (CRJ, 2021, para 1).

Young people often need the support of adult allies to organize resistance to adult mistreatment. Young people rarely have their own transportation or their own money, and they can't legally take out loans without an adult co-signer. They must be a certain age to have access to social media and electronic communication, which is a key organizing tool for young people (Protalinski, 2011).

Youth-based liberation movements necessarily suffer transiency in leadership. Young people grow older and are no longer members of this social identity group. Their attention turns to the challenges of being an adult. This precludes their continued involvement in youth liberation activities. When they choose to focus on youth liberation, they must do so as an ally. Unlike other movements that can develop leadership over time, youth-based liberation movements often have a very short leadership trajectory.

Elder liberation too suffers a number of age-based challenges. Elder liberation movements often lack the long-term leadership development available to some other liberation movements. With limited open discussion of elder oppression and the mistreatment of elders generally accepted as normal, by the time many people accept the reality of their elderhood and come to the realization that their mistreatment constitutes oppression, the time and energy to fight against it are often already limited. Intersectionality of other oppressions, particularly race and class, often interfere with the availability of broad intersectional participation in elder liberation work. The elders who have survived, the elders who have good health, and the elders with resources to participate in elder liberation work often represent a narrow spectrum of elderhood. A call to elder activism on behalf of climate change seems appropriate and timely:

> It would be entirely fitting if the angry troublemakers came from the ranks of those of us who are older. For one thing, we're the ones who caused the problem. If someone has to sit down on the tracks of the coal train and get arrested it should be the grandparents who have been pouring carbon into the atmosphere for half a century. . . . But there's something else, too: the greatest moments in the lives of the baby boomers were precisely the times when they raised their voices, when they declared their selfless

devotion to peace or civil rights. . . . Now is the boomer's chance to reclaim their better natures and to end their run as they began.

(McKibben, 2008, p. 352)

This call to activism on behalf of the climate crisis could be extended to activism on behalf of elder liberation. Having fought for civil rights, gay rights, women's rights, and immigrant rights, it would be fitting and proper for elders to also fight for elder rights.

The centrality of the voices and thinking of young people and elders from various social identity groups has broadened and enlarged our vision of a liberatory society. They contribute to our vision of a world without youth and elder oppression as well as a world without racism, sexism, classism, heterosexism, transgender oppression, ableism, religious oppression, linguicism, and xenophobia. Intergenerational organizing and learning, where middle-aged people, elders, and young people share reflections and experiences about the impact of youth and elder oppression, can help shape the direction and scope of all liberation movements. Such centrality and cross-generational listening and collaboration are necessary for success in ending youth oppression and elder oppression—and, indeed, in creating a world without oppression.

CONCLUSION

Our goal in studying youth and elder oppression is to help develop the knowledge base, competencies, and understandings that enable effective movement toward the elimination of youth and elder oppression. Movement forward will depend on mediating the impact of the youth empowerment and elder protection industries, where middle-aged adults receive a salary to tell young people how to be empowered and elders how to be protected. Youth liberation and elder liberation movements will be enhanced when young people and elders are paid for their intellectual labor in the same way that middle-aged adults expect compensation for their contributions. When middle-aged adults, elders, and young people work together to develop ways for young people and elders to be equal participants in every aspect of liberation movements, and when adults learn to follow the leadership of young people and elders, liberation movements for youth and elders will blossom. Globally, we can work together toward a liberatory society.

DESIGN FOR TEACHING YOUTH AND ELDER OPPRESSION

PEDAGOGICAL SEQUENCE AND FACILITATION ISSUES

The Ending Youth and Elder Oppression design is organized into four quadrants. The workshop begins by envisioning a non-oppressive society in Quadrant 1, introducing basic concepts and examining individual and institutional/social/cultural manifestations of the oppression in Quadrants 2 and 3, and envisioning transformation and liberation in Quadrant 4. Considerations of liberation and transformation are presented at the beginning of the design and included in each quadrant. Quadrant 4 brings together visioning and reflections completed in the first three quadrants to develop action strategies focused on social justice movements and personal movement toward liberation.

OVERVIEW OF YOUTH AND ELDER OPPRESSION DESIGN QUADRANTS

Quadrant 1

1. Icebreaker: Envisioning Liberation for All Ages (10 minutes)
2. Welcome, Introduction, & Course Overview (15 minutes)
3. Culture of Care (30 minutes)
4. Attitudes, Assumptions, and Beliefs about Young People and Elders (30 minutes)
5. Break (5 minutes)
6. Mini-Lecture on Historical Context and Legacies with 2 Options (55 minutes)
7. Internalized Youth and Elder Oppression Triads (25 minutes)
8. Lunch (1 hour)

Quadrant 2

1. Warm-Up & Welcome Back (10 minutes)
2. Defining Key Concepts and Terms (45 minutes)
3. Storytelling and Listening Activity Chapter (80 minutes)
4. Break (10 minutes)
5. Five Faces of Youth and Elder Oppression (40 minutes)
6. Movements to End Youth & Elder Oppression *or* Assessing Media for Youth & Elder Oppression (30 minutes)
7. Closing (25 minutes)

Quadrant 3

1. Welcome (15 minutes)
2. Assessing Youth and Elder Oppression in the Media: Homework Report-Out (20 minutes)
3. Undesigning Youth and Elder Oppression with Jenga-Style Blocks with 2 Options (1 hour 45 minutes)
4. Break (10 minutes during the prior activity)
5. Lunch (1 hour)

Quadrant 4

1. Liberation for All Ages with 2 Options (50 minutes)
2. Ending Youth and Elder Oppression Movement Research and Presentations with 2 Options (2 hours)
3. Closing: Liberation Commitments (20 minutes)
4. Closing Logistics (10 minutes)

SEQUENCING AND LEVEL OF RISK

The sequencing begins with low-risk activities for participant disclosure or personal investment in learning outcomes. This is followed by high-risk activities, and the final quadrant returns to low-risk activities. We recommend that this risk sequence be followed in all designs, whether a weekend workshop or a shorter, ongoing course. We do not generally recommend beginning or ending a workshop or class with high-risk activities. The beginning of a class or workshop has not allowed enough participant relationship-building for high-risk activities to be successful. The end of a class or workshop does not allow time to adequately process high-risk activities and enable participants to return to equilibrium.

Activities focus on *task* and *relationship* as well as *content* and *climate*. Activities, including introductions, goal setting, guidelines, and listening exercises that focus on relationship-building, are designed to help participants develop a sense of connection to other learners. A learning community characterized by safety and learner inclusion helps create the conditions for learner buy-in. Altogether, these activities work to *create a learning community* in which participants feel comfortable acknowledging the edges of their current comfort zone and knowledge level. Participants can test their level of awareness about youth oppression and the oppression of elders and feel encouraged and supported to push beyond those limits. Activities are designed to interrupt the *culture of perfection* that grows out of typical schooling socialization and a focus on getting the right answer. Climate-setting and relationship-building activities are designed to support participant exploration of unfamiliar ideas and concepts. While important for all learners, activities that create connections among learners are especially important for young people, young adults, and elders. Such activities help interrupt the isolation inherent in internalized adultism and internalized ageism induced by schooling, socialization, and the push to get the right answer.

This design is learner centered in that participants are able to relax as their prior knowledge is activated and made available for analysis. A group research project and creative presentations provide the opportunity to focus on a social justice movement that addresses problems relevant to participants' own lives and makes their learning visible.

DESIGN AND SCHEDULE OF ACTIVITIES

The sequence of activities presented in this design can be organized into a variety of formats. They are presented here as the basis for a two-day workshop that includes around 16 hours of instruction. Each activity includes goals, procedure, and instructions. This allows for decisions about where each might fit in a weekend workshop, three-hour class, or other format. Instructors can select activities based on the specific goals, objectives, and time frame for their instructional activity.

For instructors who teach in a weekly seminar format, activities can be adapted to a series of three-hour class meetings. A semester-long course that meets weekly or twice weekly will have different closure and summary needs than a weekend workshop format. The level of risk for most of the activities included are low to moderate. We would not recommend including a high-risk activity in a weekly design due to lack of time to adequately process and debrief.

Each activity presented in this design has been successfully tested. Each can be used for in-person learning as well as for synchronous remote learning using a video-conferencing platform that can support breakout groups. When different materials are required for in-person or remote learning, those are noted in the activity descriptions. When possible, we have added example materials (e.g., a Google Jamboard activity template) that can be copied and edited.

DEVELOPING SHARED MEANING OF TERMS AND CONCEPTS

Misinformation, intentional and unintentional, about many social justice-related concepts, terms, and theoretical frameworks are prevalent on the internet. To develop a shared starting point, key concepts and definitions are included in each module and for all core concepts on the website. We are quite specific to use the terms *youth oppression* and *elder oppression* to distinguish these two specific manifestations of oppression while acknowledging that they are both focused on age-based identity groups (see website Defining Key Concepts and Terms).

We use the term *charades of empowerment* (DeJong, 2014, p. 229) to describe practices by adults that give the appearance of empowerment to young people while retaining power and decision-making in the hands of adults. Such activities are often designed to make young people "feel" that they are included in decision-making that typically falls short of "actual" sharing of power with young people. We use the term *liberation* to describe both an individual state and a condition of society. We use the term *transformation* to describe the process of engagement that leads to the creation of a society characterized by liberation.

We begin and end the design with a focus on liberation and transformation (see Icebreaker). We study oppression as a basis for learning about liberation and transformation, not for the sake of knowing about oppression. Our goal is for participants to use liberation and transformation as a framework for entering the learning process and using the content and activities to assist the overall goal of liberation and transformation.

FACILITATION ISSUES

Here, we share some common dynamics and ideas for how to work with them when facilitating learning about youth oppression and elder oppression. As social justice education facilitators, we ask people to consider information and perspectives that often challenge a particular worldview and prior knowledge. We dispute false equivalencies and deny "equal-space" for ideas that support the maintenance of oppression. We know that learning about liberation and oppression necessarily involves unlearning previously held ideas. Participants do not show up as empty vessels. Shunning a "banking model" of education, we encourage "facilitation" focused on creating conditions in which participants can unlearn what they already know in order to encounter something different. This work requires the skill and patience to address *unlearning*. Relationships built on respect can hold discomfort that arises from unlearning what we think we already know. Thoughtful planning for how to work through resistance that is a natural part of learning is important.

WELCOMING, MEDIATING, AND TRANSFORMING RESISTANCE

Different forms of resistance can occur when facilitating these topics. We encounter resistance to the idea that mistreatment of youth and elders constitutes a legitimate social justice issue. Some resistance is rooted in the idea that society's current treatment of youth is appropriate based on the developmental levels of young people. Many think it appropriate to deny elders and young people the opportunity to participate in decision-making or exclude them from participation in the economic life of society. Many adults, annoyed by the behavior of some young people or elders, feel it is appropriate to ban them from spaces such as malls, community centers, or even the workplace. Some adults believe that as long as young people are under their [the adult's] roof, they must abide by their rules, or that being obligated to take care of older people gives them the right to make decisions for them. They resist the notion that such beliefs constitute oppression.

A second form of resistance sometimes occurs among participants who resist being taught or led by young people and elders. We suggest that young people and elders be included in the development of the design of a workshop or class. This practice constitutes a powerful contradiction to youth and elder oppression as both a content and a pedagogical strategy. Including young people and elders in design and facilitation provides a visual and experiential affirmation of their capacities and significance. It elevates the story of youth and elder liberation from a theoretical discussion to a practical reality, where young people and elders are not simply discussed but are included in and perhaps lead discussions of the oppression that affects their lives.

One strategy for transforming resistance to being taught by young persons or elders is to remind participants that this is an opportunity to consider new ideas and information while they retain the right to determine what they choose to believe. We can also remind them that every manifestation of oppression was once held as true, correct, and appropriate by a majority of society. For instance, it was once commonly believed, including by many women, that women and children were the property of men who had the right to do as they wished to and with women and children, including punish and beat them. Female infanticide was a commonly accepted belief in some societies. Some people, including entire societies, still hold such beliefs. In the United States, some still wish to enact legislation preserving the right of men to regulate the lives and bodies of women. The Constitution of the United States once included a clause counting African-heritage people as three-fifths of a person, and many societies sanctioned slavery. Remind participants that whether a majority of people approve of a specific attitude, belief, or practice is not a useful test of whether it constitutes oppression. Encourage participants to apply the philosophical and conceptual frameworks of Young (1990) or Memmi (2000) to analyze ideas, beliefs, or practices to determine whether they meet the criteria for oppression.

Adult resistance to learning about youth oppression and elder oppression often arises after being asked to reflect on their own experiences as young people. Many of the memories of experiences with youth oppression are painful and involve loved ones in our lives. It can feel threatening or overwhelming to bring a critical lens to these memories in order to understand youth oppression. For some, it can seem as though they are being asked to be critical of beloved parents and caretakers whom they have viewed as paragons. It can likewise be disorienting to examine interactions with elders through a lens of oppression. This work can change the way we see our families. We suggest naming these examples. Facilitators can use pace, time to process content and emotions, and breaks to engage in self-care. Inviting participants to organize follow-up listening/reflection time with each other after the workshop can create additional support.

COVID-19 sensitivity and awareness: This chapter includes many references and examples of the many ways people have been affected by the COVID pandemic as one of the defining experiences of this era. Millions of people have died worldwide, and many have lost homes, communities, jobs, and family members. As of July 2021, at least two million children have lost a parent or grandparent caregiver to COVID. It is quite possible that one or more participants will have been impacted. It will be important for the instructor to prepare a sensitive way to address what might come up as participants are asked to reflect on experiences with family members during the class.

MANAGING POWER DYNAMICS

When the participant group is mixed across ages, it is important to pay attention to the power dynamics in the group. The power dynamics reflected in differential use of airtime that often occurs across gender, class, and race/ethnic identity groups will also occur across age. In a group of adults and young people, adults will often fail to notice that they speak first, more often, and use the majority of airtime. They may fail to observe that young people might feel reluctant to speak first, share opinions, or disagree with adults. Similarly, elders may expect to be excluded, ignored, or belittled and therefore may stay quiet. The facilitator can draw attention to the use of airtime, how the group responds to participant input across age ranges, and seating patterns in the group. Just as men sometimes appropriate ideas shared by women and present them as their own, middle-aged adults may appropriate the ideas shared by young people and elders. Facilitators can interrupt the tendency to respond to young people's ideas only after they have been claimed and repeated by an adult.

Notes

* We ask that those who cite this work always acknowledge by name all of the authors listed rather than either only citing the first author or using "et al." to indicate co-authors. All collaborated on the conceptualization, development, and writing of this chapter.
* We prefer *subordinant* rather than *subordinate* to refer to young people and elders as members of the disadvantaged group. *Subordinant* parallels the term *dominant*, commonly used in discussions of oppression. Just as we do not use the term *dominate* to refer to those in the dominant role, we avoid using *subordinate* to refer to those in the disadvantaged role. The use of the term *subordinate*, which is a modifying adjective, to refer to members of the disadvantaged group seems to exacerbate the reduction and objectification of members of that group.

References

Acierno, R., Hernandez, M. A., Amstadter, A. B., Resnick, H. S., Steve, K., Muzzy, W., & Kilpatrick, D. G. (2010). Prevalence and correlates of emotional, physical, sexual, and financial abuse and potential neglect in the United States: The national elder mistreatment study. *American Journal of Public Health, 100*(2), 292–297. doi:10.2105/AJPH.2009.163089

Adler, S. E. (2019, March 6). *Senators ramp up outrage over nursing home abuse.* AARP. Retrieved from https://www.aarp.org/politics-society/advocacy/info-2019/senate-hearing-nursing-homes.htm

Administration on Aging (n.d.). Retrieved from http://www.aoa.gov/AoA_programs/elder_rights/EA_prevention/whatisEA.aspx

Almendrala, Anna, (2019, June 26). *Poisoned by their homes: How the U.S. is failing children exposed to lead.* Retrieved from https://www.theguardian.com/us-news/2019/jun/26/lead-exposure-us-childrens-blood-as-detectors

Alter, C. (2020, January 1). Youthquake: How the world will change when a new generation leads. *Time*, Single Issue, 1–46.

The Associated Press. (2021, January 12). Retrieved from https://apnews.com/article/us-news-health-michigan-rick-snyder-flint-7295d05da09d7d5b1184b0e349545897

Austin, K. (2013, February 16). *Elderspeak: Babaytalk directed at older adults.* ChangingAging. Retrieved from https://changingaging.org/elderhood/elderspeak-babytalk-directed-at-older-adults/

Ball, S. (2020, August 11). *Mauritius oil spill: Volunteer army races to contain environmental disaster.* France 24. Retrieved from https://www.france24.com/en/20200811-mauritius-oil-spill-volunteer-army-races-to-contain-environmental-disaster

Baltes, P. B. (1997). On the incomplete architecture of human ontogeny: Selection, optimization, and compensation as foundation of developmental theory. *American Psychologist, 52*(3), 366–380.

Barnes, P. (2020, March 13). *Did the response to COVID-19 lag due to age discrimination? Forbes.* Retrieved from https://www.forbes.com/sites/patriciagbarnes/2020/03/13/did-us-response-to-covid-19-lag-due-to-age-discrimination/#114d6fc1784a

Barnhart, M., & Peñaloza, L. (2013). Who are you calling old? Negotiating old age identity in the elderly consumption ensemble. *Journal of Consumer Research, 39*(6), 1133–1153.

Barron, L. (2020, January 23). I absolutely will not back down: Meet the young people at the heart of Hong Kong's rebellion. *Time Magazine.* Retrieved from http://www.time.com

BBC My World. (2020, August 21). *Fighting the oil spill in Mauritius.* YouTube. https://www.youtube.com/watch?v=dBHwIW6DS7k

Beatriz, H. (2020, September 16). *Meet Mexico's tiniest inventor.* LATV.com. Retrieved from https://latv.com/meet-mexicos-tiniest-inventor/#:~:text=X%C3%B3chitl%20Guadalupe%20Cruz%20L%C3%B3pez%20is,talked%20about%20inventor%20in%20Mexico

Bell, L. A. (2010). Theoretical foundations. In M. Adams, W. J. Blumenfeld, R. Castañeda, H. Hackman, M. Peters, & X. Zúñiga (Eds.), *Readings for diversity and social justice* (2nd ed., pp. 20–25). London: Routledge.

Bengtsen, P. (2018, March 21). China's forced labor problem. *The Diplomat.* Retrieved from https://thediplomat.com/2018/03/chinas-forced-labor-problem/

Bogle. (2018, May 26). The revealing origins of US public education. *Medium.* Retrieved from https://medium.com/@benjaminbogle/the-revealing-origins-of-us-public-education-a316f29e3ba8

Bonnichsen, S. (2003). *Objections to calling adultism an oppression* (p. 2). [blog]. Retrieved from http://www.youthlib.conynotepad/archives/2003/12/objections_to_c.html

Branco, K. J., & Williamson, J. B. (1982). Stereotyping and the life cycle: Views of aging and the aged. In A. G. Miller (Ed.), *In the eye of the beholder: Contemporary issues in stereotyping* (pp. 364–410). New York: Praeger.

Buechner, M.M. (2020). *1 in 3 of the world's children poisoned by lead.* Retrieved from https://www.forbes.com/sites/unicefusa/2020/08/05/1-in-3-of-the-worlds-children-poisoned-by-lead/#27db632f352e

Burman, S. (2007). *Developments: Child, image, nation.* London: Routledge.

Bush, M. (2013, May 8). *Financial exploitation of the elderly difficult to detect.* WAMU 88.5 American University Radio. Retrieved from http://wamu.org/news/13/05/08/financial_exploitation_of_elderly_difficult_to_detect

Butler, R. N. (1969). Ageism: Another form of bigotry. *Gerontologist, 9,* 243–246.

Calasanti, T. M., & Slevin, K. F. (2001). *Gender, social inequalities and aging.* Lanham, MD: AltaMira Press.

Camero, K. (2020, November). *Black kids 6 times more likely to be shot to death by police than white kids.* Retrieved from https://www.miamiherald.com/news/nation-world/national/article247407480.html

Cammarota, J., & Fine, M. (2008). Youth participatory action research: A pedagogy for transformational resistance. In J. Cammarota & M. Fine (Eds.), *Revolutionizing education: Youth in participatory action research in motion* (pp. 1–12). London: Routledge.

Cannella, G. S. (1997). *Deconstructing early childhood education: Social justice & revolution.* New York: Lang.

Cannella, G. S., & Viruru, R. (2004). *Childhood and postcolonization: Power, education, and contemporary practice.* London: Routledge.

Centers for Disease Control and Prevention. (2019, July 30). *Healthy people objectives.* Centers for Disease Control and Prevention. Retrieved from https://www.cdc.gov/nceh/lead/data/healthy-people-objectives.htm

Center For Racial Justice and Youth Engaged Research. (2021). Retrieved from https://www.umass.edu/education/center/racial-justice

Coe, K., & Palmer, C. T. (2009). How elders guided the evolution of the modern human brain, social behavior, and culture. *American Indian Culture and Research Journal, 33*(3), 5–21.

Collins, P. H. (1990). *Black feminist thought: Knowledge, consciousness and the politics of empowerment.* London: Routledge.

Collins, P. H. (2019). *Intersectionality as critical social theory.* Durham, NC: Duke University Press.

Convention on the Rights of the Child. (1989, November 20). Retrieved from https://www.ohchr.org/en/instruments-mechanisms/instruments/convention-rights-child

Crenshaw, K. W., Ocen, P., & Nanda, J. (2015). *Black girls matter: Pushed out, overpoliced and underprotected.* African American Policy Forum and Columbia Law School's Center for Intersectionality and Social Policy Studies. Retrieved from http://portside.org/2015–02–04/black-girls-matter-pushed-out-overpoliced-and-underprotected

Davenport, C. (2021). *E.P.A. to block pesticide tied to neurological harm in children.* Retrieved from https://www.nytimes.com/2020/09/23/climate/epa-pesticide-chlorpyrifos-children.html

DeBolt, K. (2010). What will happen to Granny? Ageism in America: Allocation of healthcare to the elderly & reform through alternative avenues. *California Western Law Review, 47*(1), 127–172.

DeJong, K. (2014). *On being and becoming: An exploration of young people's perspectives of status and power* (Dissertation). UMass Amherst.

DeJong, K., & Love, B. (2013). Ageism & adultism. In M. Adams, W. J. Blumenfeld, R. Castañeda, H. Hackman, M. Peters & X. Zúñiga (Eds.) *Readings for diversity and social justice: Third edition* (pp. 470–474). New York: Routledge.

Demby, G. (2014, September 11). *Sagging pants and the long history of 'Dangerous' street fashion. Code Switch.* Retrieved from https://www.npr.org/sections/codeswitch/2014/09/11/347143588/sagging-pants-and-the-long-history-of-dangerous-street-fashion

Dey, I., & Fraser, N. (2000). Age-based rationing in allocation of health care. *Journal of Aging and Health, 12*(511), 511–537.

Dinopoulos, E., & Zhao, L. (2007). Child labor and globalization. *Journal of Labor Economics.* Retrieved from https://www.poverties.org/blog/child-labour-in-china

Drugman, D. (2020, January 27). Judges point dismissed youth climate plaintiffs to political system corrupted by fossil fuel cash. *Nation of Change.* Retrieved from https://www.nationofchange.org/2020/01/27/judges-point-dismissed-youth-climate-plaintiffs-to-political-system-corrupted-by-fossil-fuel-cash/

Duncan-Andrade, J. M. R., & Morrell, E. (2008). *Art of critical pedagogy possibilities for moving from theory to practice in urban school.* New York: Peter Lang.

Dyson, M. E. (2007). *Know what I mean? Reflections on hip-hop.* New York: Basic Civitas Books.

Dyson, M. E. (2014, September 17). Punishment or child abuse? *The New York Times.* Retrieved from http://www.nytimes.com/2014/09/18/opinion/punishment-or-child-abuse.html?_r=0

Equal Justice Initiative. (2020, December 02). Retrieved from https://eji.org/news/black-children-are-six-times-more-likely-to-be-shot-to-death-by-police/

Farzad, B. R. (2013). How is a child's preference and choice in custody determined. *Farzad Family Law.* Retrieved from http://farzadlaw.com/california-child-custody/childs-preference-custody-how-when-choose/

Freire, P. (1970). *Pedagogy of the oppressed.* New York: Seabury.

Freudenberger, H., Francis, J. M., & Clark, N. (1984). A new look at the early factory labour force. *Journal of Economic History, 44.*

Friedman, L., (2020). *E.P.A. rejects its own findings that a pesticide harms children's brains.* Retrieved from https://www.nytimes.com/2020/09/23/climate/epa-pesticide-chlorpyrifos-children.html

Geber, S. Z. (2019, Nov 25). *How not to talk to an older adult*. Retrieved from https://www.forbes.com/sites/sarazeffgeber/2019/11/25/how-not-to-talk-to-an-older-adult/?sh=6bea8c2b1f3d

Gershoff, E., & Font, S. (2018, January 12). *Corporal punishment in U.S. public schools: Prevalence, disparities in use, and status in state and federal policy. Social policy report*. HHS Public Access. Retrieved from https://www.ncbi.nlm.nih.gov/pmc/articles/PMC5766273/#:~:text=Nineteen%20U.S.%20states%20currently%20allow,%2C%20Louisiana%2C%20Missouri%2C%20Mississippi%2C

Giusti, C. (2020, January 20). In Puerto Rico, demonstrators demand governor's resignation. *NBCNews.com*. Retrieved from https://www.nbcnews.com/news/latino/puerto-rico-demonstrators-demand-governor-s-resignation-n1118931

Global Initiative to End All Corporal Punishment. (n.d.) Homepage. Retrieved from https://endcorporalpunishment.org/

Goodweave. (2010). *International Labor Organization: Accelerating action against child labor*. Retrieved from http://www.goodweave.org/child_labor_campaign/facts.

Hadi-Tabassum, S. (2015). Why do some schools feel like prisons? *Education Week*. Retrieved from http://www.edweek.org/ew/articles/2015/01/28/why-do-some-schools-feel-like-prisons.html

Hambleton, J. (2021, July 26). 8-year-old Mexican girl wins nuclear sciences prize for her invention. *The Premier Daily*. Retrieved from https://thepremierdaily.com/8-year-old-girl-invents-solar-powered-water-heater-and-wins-nuclear-sciences-prize/

Hardiman, R., Jackson, B., & Griffin, P. (2010). Conceptual foundations for social justice. In M. Adams, L. Bell, & P. Griffin (Eds.), *Teaching for diversity and social justice*. London: Routledge.

Harro, B. (2013). The cycle of socialization. In M. Adams, W. J. Blumenfeld, C. Castaneda, H. W. Hackman, M. L. Peters, & X. Zuniga (Eds.), *Readings for diversity and social justice* (3rd ed., pp. 45–52). London: Routledge.

Heid, A. R., & Pruchno, R. (2021, February). Challenges experienced by older people during the initial months of the COVID-19 pandemic. *The Gerontologist, 61*(1), 48–58. doi:10.1093/geront/gnaa138

Hendricks, J. (2004). Public policies and age old identities. *Journal of Aging Studies, 18*(3), 6, 245–260.

History.com. (2020, March 10). *Joan of Arc*. History.com https://www.history.com/topics/middle-ages/saint-joan-of-arc

Human Rights Watch. (2012 April 27). *US Labor Department abandons child farmworkers*. Human Rights Watch. Retrieved from https://www.hrw.org/news/2012/04/27/us-labor-department-abandons-child-farmworkers

Human Rights Watch. (2014, Feb. 4). *Afghanistan: Reject new law protecting abusers of women*. Human Rights Watch. Retrieved from http://www.hrw.org/news/2014/02/04/afghanistan-reject-new-law-protecting-abusers-women

Human Rights Watch. (2020, October 28). *25th anniversary of the convention on the rights of the child*. Human Rights Watch. Retrieved from https://www.hrw.org/news/2014/11/17/25th-anniversary-convention-rights-child?gclid=Cj0KCQjwgMqSBhDCARIsAIIVN1WsXsLbGfqdJukmVSSRXeLljRimst635snxrX4z4wwPTbRv6q4kGuwaAlc8EALw_wcB#

Human Trafficking Search. (2017). *Child marriage in the United States*. Human Trafficking Search. Retrieved from https://humantraffickingsearch.org/201766child-marriage-in-the-united-states/?gclid=Cj0KCQiAzsz-BRCCARIsANotFgPw_bZrGeI-zH1zaVa644UzhKnEgV3MiEkeccqH7PlX7Qsl7bfypMoaAuB8EALw_wcB

Hutchins, B. L., & Harrison, A. (1911). *A history of factory legislation*. London: P. S. King & Son.

Institute for Democratic Education in America (IDEA). (2021, November 30). Retrieved from http://www.democraticeducation.org/

IRIN News. (2020). *IRIN News*. Retrieved from https://www.thenewhumanitarian.org/feature/2011/06/06/selling-children-pay-debt

Jaffe, I. (2020, April 4). *Nursing home residents moved out to make way for COVID-19 patients*. NPR. Retrieved from https://www.npr.org/sections/coronavirus-live-updates/2020/08/04/897239846/nursing-home-residents-moved-out-to-make-way-for-covid-19-patients

Janfaza, R. (2020, January 3). 9 Climate activists of color you should know. *Teen Vogue*. Retrieved from https://www.teenvogue.com/story/youth-climate-activists-of-color

Jenks, C. (1996). *Childhood*. London: Routledge.

Jones, T. (2020, August 6). Paulding Co. principal threatens punishment for students who share school pics on social media. *WSBTV.com*. Retrieved from https://www.wsbtv.com/news/local/paulding-co-superintendent-threatens-punishment-students-who-share-school-pics-social-media/MJ2QI7ND5BFBJOW35BYNLZYLRQ/

Jones, D., & Franklin, J. (2022, April 10). *Not just Florida. More than a dozen states propose so-called 'don't say gay' bills.* NPR. Retrieved from https://www.npr.org/2022/04/10/1091543359/15-states-dont-say-gay-anti-transgender-bills

Kamkwamba, W. (2009). *The boy who harnessed the wind.* New York: Harper Perennial.

Karpf, A. (2015, January 3). The liberation of growing old. *The New York Times.* Retrieved from https://www.nytimes.com/2015/01/04/opinion/sunday/the-liberation-of-growing-old.html

Kassraie, A. (2019, April 5). *Physical abuse against older adults on the rise.* Retrieved from https://www.aarp.org/politics-society/advocacy/info-2019/violence-against-older-adults.html#:~:text=The%20report%20estimates%20that%20the,to%202016%2C%20the%20CDC%20

KidsRights Foundation. (n.d.). *Violence.* KidsRights. Retrieved from https://www.thekidsrightschangemakers.org/en/your-rights/violence

Kirkpatrick, J., Hull, S., Fedso, S., Mullen, B., & Goodlin, S. (2020). Scarce-resource allocation and patient triage during the COVID-19 pandemic: JACC review topic of the week. *Journal of the American College of Cardiology, 76*(1), 85–92. doi:10.1016/j.jacc.2020.05.006

Kumar, V. (2020, April 3). *Coronavirus dying woman refuses to use ventilator, says "I had a good life, save it for younger patients."* Retrieved from https://www.india.com/viral/coronavirus-dying-woman-refuses-to-use-ventilator-says-i-had-a-good-life-save-it-for-younger-patients-3989072/

Lachs, M., & Berman, J. (2011). (rep.). Under the Radar: New York State Elder Abuse Prevalence Study. *New York State Office of Children and Family Services, William B. Hoyt Memorial New York State Children and Family Trust Fund.* Retrieved from https://ocfs.ny.gov/reports/aps/Under-the-Radar-2011May12.pdf

Lakota People's Law Project. (2013). *Lakota child rescue project.* Retrieved from http://lakotalaw.org/lakota-child-rescue-project

Lamb, E., & Gentry, J. (2013). The denial of aging in American advertising: Empowering or disempowering? *The International Journal of Aging and Society, 2*(4), 35–47.

Larson, E. (2020). Baggy clothing is the next big trend. *Drake Magazine.* Retrieved from https://drakemagazine.com/fashion-beauty/baggy-clothing/#:~:text=Baggy%2C%20loose%2C%20and%20oversized%20clothing,is%20coming%20back%20into%20style.&text=Because%20anyone%20can%20wear%20baggy,of%20nonchalance%20accompanies%20every%20outfit

Lavietes, M., & Ramos, E. (2022, March 20). Nearly 240 anti-LGBTQ bills filed in 2022 so far, most of them targeting trans people. *NBCNews.com.* Retrieved from https://www.nbcnews.com/nbc-out/out-politics-and-policy/nearly-240-anti-lgbtq-bills-filed-2022-far-targeting-trans-people-rcna20418

Leatherby, L., & Jones Waanen, L. (2020, August 31). U.S. Coronavirus Rates are Rising Fast Among Children. *The New York Times* https://www.nytimes.com/interactive/2020/08/31/us/coronavirus-cases-children.html?action=click&module=Top%20Stories&pgtype=Homepage

Lerman, R. (2020, August 17).'45 days of ambiguity': What a U.S. TikTok ban could mean for users and employees. *The Washington Post.* Retrieved from https://www.washingtonpost.com/technology/2020/08/17/tiktok-ban-us-faq/

Li, S.-C., Lindenberger, U., Hommel, B., Aschersleben, G., Prinz, W., & Baltes, P. B. (2004). Transformations in the couplings among intellectual abilities and constituent cognitive processes across the life span. *Psychological Science, 15*(3), 155–163. https://doi.org/10.1111/j.0956-7976.2004.01503003.x

List of countries by infant and under-five mortality rates. (2020, December 4). In *Wikipedia.* Retrieved from https://en.wikipedia.org/wiki/List_of_countries_by_infant_and_under-five_mortality_rates

Loffman, M. (2021, April 16). New poll shows Americans overwhelmingly oppose anti-transgender laws. *PBS.* Retrieved from https://www.pbs.org/newshour/politics/new-poll-shows-americans-overwhelmingly-oppose-anti-transgender-laws

Loop, E. (2015). *What are the childbearing years?* Retrieved from http://www.ehow.com/info_8105014_childbearing-years.html

Love, B. (2018). Developing a liberatory consciousness. In M. Adams, W. Blumenfeld, D. Catalano, K. DeJong, H. Hackman, L. Hopkins, B. Love, M. Peters, D. Shlasko, X. Zúñiga (Eds.), *Readings for diversity and social justice* (pp. 610–615). London: Routledge.

M4BL. (2020). *The preamble.* Retrieved from https://m4bl.org/policy-platforms/the-preamble/

Macrotrends. (2021). *World life expectancy 1950–2022.* Retrieved from https://www.macrotrends.net/countries/WLD/world/life-expectancy#:~:text=The%20life%20expectancy%20for%20World,a%200.24%25%20increase%20from%202018

Males, M. (2004, February). Coming of age in America. *Youth Today.*

Malin, A., & Flaherty, A. (2018, December 18). After Parkland shooting, Trump safety commission rejects calls for gun control, sticks with suggestions that schools arm themselves.*ABC News.* Retrieved from https://abcnews.go.com/Politics/trump-administration-releases-school-safety-report-demands-parkland/story?id=59883062

McIntosh, K., Girvan, E., Horner, R., & Smolkowski, K. (2014) Education not incarceration: A conceptual model for reducing racial and ethnic disproportionality in school discipline. *Journal of Applied Research on Children: Informing Policy for Children at Risk, 5*(2), Article 4. Retrieved from https://digitalcommons.library.tmc.edu/childrenatrisk/vol5/iss2/4

McKibben, B., (2008). *The last best chance for baby boomers. The Bill McKibben reader: Pieces from an active life.* New York: St. Martinsburg Publishing Group.

Memmi, A. (2000). *Racism.* Minneapolis, MN: University of Minnesota Press.

Mitchell, M., & Leachman, M. (2014). *Changing priorities: State criminal justice reforms and investments in education.* Center on Budget and Policy Priorities. Retrieved from http://www.cbpp.org/cms/?fa=view&id=4220

Moakley, P., & Rothman, L. (n.d.) After the bomb: Survivors of the atomic blasts in Hiroshima and Nagasaki share their stories. *Time.* Retrieved from https://time.com/after-the-bomb/

Nandy, A. (1983). *The intimate enemy: Loss and recovery of self under colonialism.* Oxford: Oxford University Press India.

National Center on Elder Abuse. (2017, June 15). *World elder abuse awareness day.* Administration for Community Living. Retrieved from https://acl.gov/news-and-events/events-and-observances/world-elder-abuse-awareness-day

Nelson, G. (1982). Social class and public policy for the elderly. *Social Service Review, 56*(1), 2, 85–107.

Nelson, T. E. (Ed.). (2002). *Ageism: Stereotyping and prejudice against older persons.* Cambridge, MA: The MIT Press.

Nickelsburg, M. (2020, August 6). Trump issues executive order banning transactions with TikTok parent ByteDance in 45 days. *GeekWire.* Retrieved from https://www.geekwire.com/2020/trump-issues-executive-order-banning-transactions-tiktok-parent-bytedance-sept-20/

Obonyo, R. (2019, December). Youth key in fight against climate change. *Kenyan Digest.* Retrieved from https://kenyandigest.com/youth-key-in-fight-against-climate-change/

Palmore, E. B., Branch, L., & Harris, D. K. (Eds.). (2005). *Encyclopedia of ageism* (p. 2). New York: The Haworth Press.

Persad, G., Wertheimer, A., & Emanuel, E. J. (2009). Principles for allocation of scarce medical interventions. *The Lancet, 373*(9661), 423–431. Retrieved from http://www.thelancet.com/journals/lancet/article/PIIS0140-6736%2809%2960137-9/

Phillipson, C., Bernard, M., & Strang, P. (1986). *Dependency and interdependency in old age-theoretical perspectives and policy alternatives.* Centre for Policy on Ageing. Retrieved from http://www.cpa.org.uk/ageinfo/records/Ageinfo930425001.html

Pillemer, K., & Finkelhor, D. (1988). The prevalence of elder abuse: A random sample survey. *Gerontologist, 28*(1), 51–57.

Protalinski, E. (2011, May 20). Mark Zuckerberg: Facebook minimum age limit should be removed. *ZDNet.* Retrieved from http://www.zdnet.com/blog/facebook/mark-zuckerberg-facebook-minimum-age-limit-should-be-removed/1506

Rashwan, N. (2019, July 30). Killing of student protesters in Sudan sets off new unrest, and worry. *The New York Times.* Retrieved from https://www.nytimes.com/2019/07/30/world/africa/sudan-protest-killing.html

Rethinking Schools. (2011). Stop the school to prison pipeline. *Rethinking Schools, 26*(2). Retrieved from https://rethinkingschools.org/articles/editorial-stop-the-school-to-prison-pipeline/

Richards, R. (2018, April 11). 13-year-old Native water protector addresses United Nations. *Native Sun News Today.* Retrieved from https://www.indianz.com/News/2018/04/11/native-sun-news-today-13yearold-native-w.asp

Rogoff, B. (2003). *The cultural nature of human development.* Oxford: Oxford University Press.

Rosenberg, M. (2014). Overview of life expectancy. *Thought Co.* Retrieved from http://geography.about.com/od/populationgeography/a/lifeexpectancy.htm

Rosenblatt, K. (2019, September 24). Teen climate activist Greta Thunberg delivers scathing speech at U.N. *NBC News.* Retrieved from https://www.nbcnews.com/news/world/teen-climate-activist-greta-thunberg-delivers-scathing-speech-u-n-n1057621

Rubinstein, G. (1999). *Printing: History and development. Jones International and Jones Digital Century.* Retrieved from http://karmak.org/archive/2002/08/history_of_print.html

Russell, J. (2005, September 11). At regional malls, a teen test. *Boston Globe,* A1. Retrieved from http://archive.boston.com/news/local/articles/2005/09/11/at_regional_malls_a_teen_test/

Schieffelin, B. B., & Ochs, E. (Eds.). (1986). *Language socialization across cultures.* Cambridge: Cambridge University Press.

Slisco, A. (2020, March 24). Priest who gave up ventilator to younger patient dies of Coronavirus. *News-Week*. Retrieved from https://www.msn.com/en-us/news/world/priest-who-gave-up-ventilator-to-younger-patient-dies-of-coronavirus/ar-BB11C0uI

Smith, A. (2019, December). *Trump mocks Greta Thunberg after she wins Times person of the year*. Retrieved from https://www.nbcnews.com/politics/donald-trump/trump-mocks-greta-thun berg-after-she-wins-time-person-year-n1100531

Smith, D. E. (1987). *The everyday world as problematic: A feminist sociology*. Boston: Northeastern University Press.

Smith, T. (2018, March 1). Students get mixed messages on whether protesting will get them in trouble. *NPR*. Retrieved from https://www.npr.org/2018/03/01/590022636/colleges-say-suspensions-for-gun-control-protests-wont-hurt-applicants

Span, P. (2013, January 8). Who should receive organ transplants? *New York Times*. Retrieved from http://newoldage.blogs.nytimes.com/2013/01/08/who-should-receive-organ-transplants/?_r=0

Stearns, P. J. (1986). Old age family conflict: The perspective of the past. In K. A. Pillemer & R. S. Wolf (Eds.), *Elder abuse: Conflict in the family* (pp. 3–24). Boston: Auburn House Publishing.

Swain, S. (2009). Sweet childhood lost: Idealized images of childhood in the British child rescue literature. *The Journal of the History of Childhood and Youth, 2*(2), 198–214.

Taylor, D. (2002). *The writer's guide to everyday life in colonial America, 1607–1783*. New York: Penguin Publishing.

Teen Vogue Staff. (2020, August 4). *Girls leadership report finds black and Latinx girls are ready to lead*. Retrieved from https://www.teenvogue.com/story/girls-leadership-report-black-latinx-girls

Teutsch, S., & Rechel, B. (2012). Ethics of resource allocation and rationing medical care in a time of fiscal restraint—US and Europe. *Public Health Reviews, 34*(1), 1–10.

Thomas, E. Y., Anurudran, A., Robb, K., & Burke, T. F. (2020). Spotlight on child abuse and neglect response in the time of COVID-19. *The Lancet: Public health, 5*(7), e371. doi:10.1016/S2468-2667(20)30143-2

Thompson, E. P. (1968). *The making of the English working class, effect of the industrial revolution. modern world history textbook* (pp. 366–367). Penguin. Retrieved from http://webs.bcp.org/sites/vcleary/ModernWorldHistoryTextbook/IndustrialRevolution/IREffects.html

Time for Kids. (2020). 7 young inventors who see a better way. *Time*. Retrieved from https://time.com/collection/davos-2020/5765632/young-inventors-changing-the-world/

Tuck, E., & Yang, K. W. (2013). Introduction to youth resistance research and theories of change. In E. Tuck & K. W. Yang (Eds.), *Youth resistance research and theories of change* (pp. 1–24). London: Routledge.

UNICEF. (2020, June 4). COVID-19: *One third of youth in Latin America and the Caribbean believe they are not at risk from disease, new UNICEF poll shows*. UNICEF. Retrieved from https://www.unicef.org/lac/en/press-releases/covid-19-one-third-youth-in-LAC-believe-they-are-not-risk

U.S. Department of Health and Human Services, Administration for Community Living. (n.d.). *Current Federal Elder Justice Laws*. National Center on Elder Abuse. Retrieved from https://ncea.acl.gov/What-We-Do/Policy/Federal-Laws.aspx

Walker, C. (2019). 10 years. 180 school shootings. 356 victims. *CNN*. Retrieved from https://www.cnn.com/interactive/2019/07/us/ten-years-of-school-shootings-trnd/

Weston, P., & Riotta, C. (2019, September 21). *There is no Planet B: Millions take to the streets to in what could be the largest environmental protest ever*. Retrieved from https://www.independent.co.uk/environment/global-climate-strike-greta-thunberg-protests-fossil-fuels-crisis-a9113856.html

Winerip, M. (2013, July 22). Three men, three ages. Which do you like? *The New York Times*. Retrieved from http://www.nytimes.com/2013/07/23/booming/three-men-three-ages-who-do-you-like.html?_r=0

Wong, A. (2019, February 26). When schools tell kids they can't use the bathroom. *The Atlantic*. Retrieved from https://www.theatlantic.com/education/archive/2019/02/the-tyranny-of-school-bathrooms/583660/

World Health Organization. (2014). *World health statistics 2014: A wealth of information on global public health*. World Health Organization. Retrieved from https://apps.who.int/iris/handle/10665/112739

World Health Organization. (2020a). *Global status report on preventing violence against children*. UNICEF. Retrieved from https://www.unicef.org/media/70731/file/Global-status-report-on-preven ting-violence-against-children-2020.pdf

World Health Organization. (2020b). *Child maltreatment*. Retrieved from https://www.who.int/news-room/fact-sheets/detail/child-maltreatment

Wyner, A. (2014, April 29). How hip-hop flourished in America. *The Harvard Crimson*. Retrieved from http://www.thecrimson.com/column/the-gospel-of-rap/article/2014/4/29/gospel-of-rap-how-hip-hop-flourished/

Xu, J., Murphy, B. S., Kochanek, K., & Arias, E. (2020, January). *Mortality in the United States*. NCHS Data Brief No. 355. Retrieved from https://www.cdc.gov/nchs/data/databriefs/db355-h.pdf

Young, I. M. (1990). *Five faces of oppression*. Princeton: Princeton University Press.

11

Social Justice Education Online

Rachel R. Briggs and Mathew L. Ouellett*

INTRODUCTION

In this chapter, our goal is to guide readers in how to conceptualize, design, implement, and assess teaching social justice in an online environment. We do this by pointing toward emerging theoretical and practice-based frameworks and principles that shape our approach to this work. We highlight the evolving nature and exciting opportunities (pedagogical and technological) afforded by teaching and learning in an online environment, as well as the challenges for social justice education (SJE) practice. There are a number of widely available resources for learning how to effectively teach online (Darby & Lang, 2019; Johnson, 2013; Miller; 2014; Stavredes, 2011; Boettcher & Conrad, 2016). That said, our focus is less on the mechanics of running an online course and more on how to design a course that reflects our social justice values and principles. Our goal is that readers will understand a process-based approach and then be able to apply it to their own context with the tools and resources available to them.

When we began conceptualizing and writing this chapter, we had no idea how seismically the landscape of teaching and learning was about to change. As it is, this chapter emerges at a particular moment in history and in the context of three major societal issues: COVID-19, racism and economic disparities, and climate change. Additionally, there is the hotly contested presidential election cycle, insurrectionists at the Capitol, and a renewed call for responsibility and transparency in media literacy. The contemporary political context in which we began working on this chapter has changed tremendously from the beginning to now and is sure to change again.

Another huge change is the scale and scope of instructors and students who have now had substantial experiences in online teaching and learning, albeit by necessity. Schools, instructors, students, and families (as well as workplaces) all pivoted to online environments across the country in unprecedented numbers. As schools progressed from emergency remote teaching to implementing a mix of blended, hyflex, fully online, or some variation in 2021, it is clear that we are all still in a process of reflecting on and learning about how to design, implement, and assess learning opportunities in the online environment. Workplaces and community organizations have also shifted to online training programs. While these experiences appear to be leading to increasingly positive changes in students' and instructors' views about the value and rigor of online learning (Askeroth & Richardson, 2019), much is yet to be gleaned. Here we will focus on how to provide quality social justice education online, not the broader questions and implications of fully remote schooling or workplaces or the pros and cons of online learning, though both can either support or undermine social justice principles and require careful choices, as in any other learning format.

This chapter begins by highlighting our process-based approach to designing workshops and courses for teaching social justice online. We track the historical emergence of online education and examine the current interdisciplinary context of online learning and the broader politics affecting teaching online for social justice. The next section details the

DOI: 10.4324/9781003005759-13

pedagogical and facilitation issues specific to teaching social justice online. Both Chapter 2: Pedagogical Foundations and Chapter 3: Design and Facilitation offer a more in-depth examination of broader issues, and our focus here is on what specifically makes teaching social justice online unique. Finally, we offer a list of example activities for online SJE. Each activity has an accompanying web resource that details the objectives of the activity and how educational technologies and pedagogical strategies can be used to adapt the activity to the online learning environment. We conclude by pointing readers toward emerging trends and issues in online learning, educational technology, and emerging political consequences of online technologies for social justice.

OUR APPROACH

A core challenge to learning to teach online is the rapid changes in technologies and platforms. We anticipate that this remarkable pace of change will hold true in the future. Consequently, it is beyond the scope of this chapter to offer operational training on specific technologies. Therefore, we focus on pedagogical principles first and only secondarily on specific platforms, applications, or software, highlighting the ways that the specific technologies we describe meet various pedagogical goals for SJE.

As in any endeavor, becoming a fluent online instructor or facilitator takes time and experimentation. We assume readers will come from a range of prior online course design experiences, including technological skill sets, access to tools, and professional development support. Here we assume readers have some basic knowledge of tools for teaching online. For readers who don't yet have this foundational knowledge, we've provided a resource list that includes several resources for general good practices for online teaching. We recognize that facilitators will have access to different tools, technologies, and applications depending on their organization, experience levels, the availability of free or affordable technologies, and other factors.

In this chapter, we offer a set of online course design principles and pedagogical practices grounded in social justice and an explanation of how to match learning outcome goals with a range of pedagogical strategies that can be utilized in an online environment. In the activities section, we then highlight specific examples of activities that utilize collaborative technologies and offer an explanation of how they can be utilized for teaching social justice online. In the website resources, the focus is on the rationales for our pedagogical choices and how the choices meet the learning goals of SJE. This way, readers can take this decision-making process and apply it to their specific context, organization, and resources available to them, even as technologies continue to change at an accelerated pace.

HISTORICAL CONTEXT: EMERGENCE OF ONLINE EDUCATION

Distance education has a long history, and online teaching emerged out of this educational tradition. Distance education has been an option for adult and continuing education learners for decades to improve professional and technical skills, achieve certifications, and improve career opportunities. Mail correspondence courses became popular in the 1800s, although the earliest known distance lessons were available in the 1700s (Kentnor, 2015). Throughout history, the emergence of new media was also incorporated into distance learning, including the use of radio, phonograph, and then television (Kaplan & Haenlein, 2016; Kentnor, 2015). In the 1870s, the first academic institution offered a distance learning degree program (Kentnor, 2015).

The emergence of the internet and household computers with internet access as a more common household resource shifted distance education to using the internet as the primary mode of content delivery (Kentnor, 2015). There was subsequent rapid growth of online degree programs in the late 1990s and early 2000s, including programs and organizations with online-only education (Kentnor, 2015). Many of these online-only startups ultimately failed; however, online education became a pedagogical field of study in its own right, and many academic institutions began offering online courses, certificates, and programs. The massive open online course movement began with the aspiration to radically transform education (Altbach, 2014), utilize technological innovations to make higher education free, and attract a diverse group of learners for whom higher education was not previously attainable (Baker, Passmore, & Mulligan, 2018).

More recently, there has been significant growth for institutions specializing in fully online programs leading to credentialed degrees at every level. These institutions are invested in serving adult learners who may be balancing careers, families, military service, and other considerations (e.g., living in remote locations) to provide wider and better educational opportunities for more people. Before the COVID pandemic, the proliferation of online education was already growing at a steady rate (Palvia, Aeron, Gupta, Mahapatra, Parida, Rosner, & Sindhi, 2018), and markers indicate that it will continue to grow both in the US and globally. The need for more research and practice-based literature related to teaching online is more urgent than ever before.

CURRENT CONTEXT

INTERDISCIPLINARY CONNECTIONS

There is an increasingly robust set of resources, both discipline specific (Byrne, 2020; Dalton & Hudgings, 2020; Bolter, Tayloe, Gomez, Eliason, Van Olphen, & Veri, 2021) and interdisciplinary (Bandy, Harbin, & Thurber, 2021), for incorporating equity content in online learning using anti-racist and inclusive pedagogical strategies. Research in social work has examined the importance and limitations of online learning in a context of increasing digital communication and telehealth work (Goldingay & Boddy, 2017). Online education offers possibilities for urban education and pedagogies that resist oppression (Turpin, 2007) and offers potential in the field of service-learning (Guthrie & McCracken, 2010). Feminist pedagogy, in particular, has examined the structural inequalities of online teaching and learning and how educators can challenge hierarchical power structures in online teaching (Bailey, 2017). Online learning and distance education provide opportunities that positively impact the lives of women and provide access to college courses for a broader range of students (Herman & Kirkup, 2017). Literature on feminist pedagogies has also examined affect theory and embodiment online (Boler, 2015), positionality and lack of visibility of identities online (Bailey, 2017), and ways instructors can deepen meaning and interactions in the online learning community (Bailey, 2017).

MASSIVE ONLINE OPEN COURSES (MOOCS)

The growing popularity of massive online open courses has influenced online learning in higher education, as well. Instructor perceptions of quality are improving rapidly, and students report that MOOCs offer a more flexible learning design accommodating a wide variety of participants' personal and situational factors and learning goals (Askeroth & Richardson, 2019). MOOCs have contributed to focusing faculty, academic leaders, students, and staff on what matters most in learning (Kim & Maloney, 2020), and these discussions often lead to innovation on campuses and the exploration and implementation of proven active-learning pedagogies (Olson & Riordan, 2012) and new educational technology strategies in learning and teaching (Bruff, 2019). MOOCs have the possibility to transform accessibility and inclusion, both goals of social justice education, by offering free and flexible learning beyond the traditional brick-and-mortar campuses (Baker, Passmore, & Mulligan, 2018). There are drawbacks of MOOCs, though. Altbach points out the socio-centric nature of current efforts: "The majority of MOOC courses that have been offered are presented in English, have American instructors, western content and pedagogical approaches, and are placed within course management systems developed and supported by major American universities, thus reinforcing the dominant academic culture of the west" (Altbach, 2014, p. 117).

CRITICAL DIGITAL PEDAGOGY

Critical digital pedagogy offers a theoretical and praxis-based framework for understanding online teaching and learning and puts the focus on building empowering relationships with students and constructing content that supports educational goals. Stommel, Friend, and Morris (2020) offer a definition of critical digital pedagogy as "an approach to teaching and learning predicated on fostering agency and empowering learners (thus implicitly and explicitly critiquing oppressive power structures)" (p. 2). Critical digital pedagogy brings together the intersection of critical theories, media and digital literacies, and activism and defines digital literacy as "the ability to use digital tools to critically read online texts in different modes, interpret online media, interrogate, problem-solve, and create" (Amgott, 2018, p. 333). Critical digital pedagogy argues that technologies mirror the values, implicit biases, and modes of relationships of the dominant culture and that critical digital pedagogy is activism and a field practice as much as it is a theory (Stommel, Friend, & Morris, 2020).

OPEN EDUCATIONAL PRACTICES

Beyond specific courses in the disciplines, examples are emerging of approaches to consciously including social justice education content as part of specific pedagogical strategies such as open educational practices and service-learning. Bali, Cronin, and Jhangian (2020) offer a critical analysis of the social justice implications of how Open Educational Practices (OEP) such as but not limited to Open Educational Resources (OER) can support change along cultural, economic, and political dimensions. They offer a framework for assessing the social justice and pedagogical impacts of OEP as: "transformative (addresses systemic/structural roots of injustice), ameliorative (addresses surface injustice), neutral (having no social justice impact), or negative (reproducing or even exacerbating injustice)" (Bali, Cronin, & Jhangian, 2020, p. 3).

BEST PRACTICES IN ONLINE TEACHING FOR INCLUSION AND SOCIAL JUSTICE

A small but growing body of research in higher education addresses best practices of online teaching for inclusion and social justice. The literature highlights the importance of finding ways to teach that are not teacher centered and encouraging collaboration among students (Barber, 2020). Researchers have looked at best practices in culturally responsive teaching online (Woodley, Hernandez, Parra, & Negash, 2017), multicultural education online (Chen, Basma, Ju, & Ng, 2020; Tharp, 2017; Merryfield, 2001), and the emerging evidence for best practices for teaching social justice online (Ukpokodu, 2008; Montelongo & Eaton, 2019). A key to online teaching is the cultivation of connections and communication among the learners. Thus, online learning can be compatible with the type of community-building practices essential to goals of inclusion and social justice (Askeroth & Richardson, 2019; Guthrie & McCracken, 2010; Bondy, Hambacher, Murphy, Wolkenhauer, & Krell, 2015). Montelongo and Eaton (2019) found that discussion boards, videos, video conferencing, and synchronous opportunities influence learner engagement and accelerate learning. Other researchers have focused on how language use affects online education (Funes & Mackness, 2018), how online learning communities and their communication can be inclusive (Hughes, 2007), and how the use of counternarratives can promote social justice (Woodley, Mucundanyi, & Lockard, 2017).

Researchers investigate how to make online education more equitable and able to reach nontraditional students to provide inclusive learning opportunities (Reyes & Segal, 2019). Reyes and Segal (2019) argue that online education should be a public good and warn against using transactional models where online education is a commodity available only to those who already have resources to access them. If used thoughtfully, digital tools offer the opportunity to support social justice goals. Digital activism coupled with concrete actions can lead to tangible and generative gains in social justice, such as the ways that the Black Lives Matter and #MeToo movements use these tools to communicate to a broader public and organize action (Amgott, 2018).

IMPACTS OF ONLINE LEARNING

Research is starting to emerge that suggests online learning outcomes are generally comparable to face-to-face (F2F) learning outcomes and that online diversity education can have similar outcomes to F2F (Behm-Morawitz & Villamil, 2019; Nguyen, 2015), including asynchronous online learning (Bell & Lie, 2015). Comparable outcomes have been highlighted in undergraduate diversity courses (Kernahan & Davis, 2007; Cole, Case, Rios, & Curtin, 2011), multicultural psychology courses (Alvarez & Domenech Rodríguez, 2020), and social justice courses (Merryfield, 2001; Ukpokodu, 2008; Montelongo & Eaton, 2019). Online settings can help learners analyze and address real-world problems through critical dialogue and promote personal insight and growth (Guthrie & McCracken, 2019).

FUTURE RESEARCH

Faculty and student attitudes are becoming more positive as more have successful experiences in online environments (from hybrid to fully online) and online education is fast becoming an integrated part of higher education (Kim & Maloney, 2020). The unparalleled number of instructors and students participating in online learning during the pandemic has left students and faculty with more positive attitudes toward online learning (McKenzie, 2021). While current popular discourse right now suggests that many students have had negative experiences with remote learning during the pandemic, overall, the emerging evidence indicates that the significant downsides were caused by the stress of a global crisis, such as the negative emotional impacts of social isolation or the lack of preparedness during an emergency move to remote learning in terms of technologies, reliable Wi-Fi, or appropriate quiet spaces needed for successful online learning (Gonzalez-Ramirez, Mulqueen,

Zealand, Silverstein, Reina, Bushell, & Ladda, 2021; Lemay, Bazelais, & Doleck, 2021). When students have appropriate amounts of time to prepare for online learning and have agency in choosing online learning as an option, online teaching is able to accomplish the same goals as F2F learning. Research on student learning and perceptions of online education during the pandemic shows comparable outcomes for students and comparable student perceptions of online learning experiences (Hilton, Moos, & Barnes, 2020; Lemay, Bazelais, & Doleck, 2021). Many institutions are still returning to remote learning for periods of time during the ongoing pandemic, and research on the impacts of these shifts to and from F2F and online will continue to shed light on students' experiences.

An unanticipated outcome of these times has been an elevated interest in the potential of online learning and an explosion of interest from those seeking resources, models, examples, and guidance. As we social justice educators and our participants explore the possibilities for social justice online, it will be important to theorize the relationships among technology, pedagogy, content, and student learning (Montelongo & Easton, 2019) and continue to examine best practices and impacts of online learning for social justice. The need for research and practice-based literature about teaching social justice online is greater than ever before.

DESIGN AND PEDAGOGY ONLINE

This section looks at the design and pedagogical issues of teaching social justice education online. First, we address general course design considerations and the myriad issues of using educational technologies for social justice. The second part takes the five elements for teaching social justice education presented in Chapter 2: Pedagogical Foundations, applying and extending them to online teaching and learning for social justice.

A key challenge for online instructors/facilitators is to find authentic ways to bring the best attributes of face-to-face learning (e.g., student-centered active learning, care for the whole student, experiential learning, and inclusive curriculum and pedagogies) to the online environment while avoiding the worst aspects (e.g., emphasis on overly prescriptive approaches, discounting students' experiences, and instructor-centric practices) (Morris & Stommel, 2018; Darby, 2020). We support using backward design as a useful way to create a student-centered learning environment that can meet curricular and process social justice goals. Backward design starts with determining the goals for learning and the students and their learning needs in order to meet those needs flexibly and compassionately when teaching online. Technologies are secondary and are chosen based on the context, the objectives of the workshop or course, and the needs of the students/participants.

COURSE DESIGN CONSIDERATIONS

Unique Time Constraints of Online Teaching

In this section we highlight the unique time constraints of teaching online. We recognize that such courses require a lot of preparatory work, and in our experience, it takes significantly longer to prepare, edit, make accessible, and post materials/activities for the online teaching environment. Unlike F2F environments where facilitators may organically build the course together with students over time, for students (and instructors) to be successful, online learning requires a much greater degree of pre-planning and preparation. Much needs to be in place before a workshop begins, including writing and recording course materials and making the course materials accessible, an issue of equity that is time consuming. Facilitators must deal with the tension between being responsive to students and doing the up-front work of preparing an online course. This is not to say that *everything* must be completed prior to an online workshop, but much of the work of online course design needs to be completed before class starts, as opposed to face-to-face courses where it might emerge more organically. Another aspect of online design that takes up time is teaching students the technologies and applications that will be used. Instructors should test run everything beforehand and provide low-risk opportunities for students to test platforms (like submitting papers/projects) before high-stakes assignments are due.

Aspects of a F2F teaching setting need to be structured in, such as informal moments of communication and connections among participants and with the facilitators. Online design must explicitly build in low-stakes, team-building opportunities that happen more organically and naturally in F2F settings through informal chats before and after workshops or during in-class transitions.

Online learning is time consuming for participants as well. Students need to be explicitly taught how to be successful in an online environment, what kinds of time demands are expected, and how best to use their time. One of the impacts of moving so many courses online during the COVID pandemic was that students were dismayed by the amount of work assigned for different online courses, perceiving the total demand as much higher than in typical F2F courses. Whether true or not, it demonstrates that time management for online learning can *feel* different for students, and it is difficult for instructors and students alike to estimate their time allocation and account for differences in cognitive load that online activities require. Instructors should be clear and explicit about the purpose of assignments, provide students with an estimate of how much time they should allocate to an assignment or activity, and consider putting time limits on some activities. For example, for different types of writing assignments, instructors can suggest a time limit and clarify when students should worry about grammar/punctuation/spelling/etc. and when they should just focus on ideas. Then, students can adjust their expectations and spend an appropriate amount of time on an activity. Finally, instructors should regularly seek feedback from participants on the "costs" (time, effort, bandwidth) of different learning activities and assignments. Faculty can also utilize a workload estimator (e.g., https://cat.wfu.edu/resources/tools/estimator2/) so they can make adjustments to their online designs.

UDL: Universal Design for Learning

Chapter 2: Pedagogical Foundations and Chapter 3: Design and Facilitation address general considerations of Universal Design for Learning (UDL), and here we address the application of UDL in the online space. The following are some general tips for UDL in the online environment:

- Implement all required accommodations in the online classroom, and incorporate ADA (Americans with Disabilities Act) compliant design as much as you can.
- Ask students what they know about their access and learning needs without needing official documentation of accommodations from the institution.
- Clearly organize and consistently name activities in your Learning Management System (LMS) as a key accessibility feature. Write descriptive labels and links in your LMS.
- Choose technology tools and applications that are accessible. For example, an application should be compatible with assistive technology that the students might use, such as a screen reader.

- When choosing materials, work to choose accessible content: readings that are screen-reader friendly, include text descriptions of images, closed captioning (CC) on all videos/films used, transcripts of audio or video materials used (students use CC and transcripts differently, and the more information you can provide in the most formats available, the more accessible your course materials will be to all students).
- Make sure digital text is readable when magnified.
- Make the course website design readable:
  - Dark or black text on a white or light-colored background helps readers with disabilities.
  - Avoid putting text over images, which can be difficult to read.
  - Avoid using color as meaning—for example, making readings one color, assignments another, discussion boards another color. Color-blind students or students who print a lot of materials (most things get printed in black and white) will not have access to these meanings.
  - Assign volunteer note takers for synchronous sessions, and give all students access to notes.
- Make any slides used in lecture videos or during synchronous sessions available to students on your LMS.

Overall, we advocate for multimodality and a range of ways to engage with materials as a way to make online SJE workshops as accessible as possible. We think it best to avoid deterministic "must haves" when it comes to technology because mandating certain technological tools makes inclusivity an afterthought (Stommel, Friend, & Morris, 2020). Discuss accessible use of technologies as part of creating community guidelines and norms. For example, allow students alternative activities if they aren't able to video record themselves and upload the recording. From a course design perspective, beginning with multimodalities is a good foundation for centering UDL for SJE online.

Course Materials

The organization and clarity of materials provided to participants is also an issue of accessibility. When building an online course, be consistent in naming assignments, activities, readings, videos, and all course materials. Everything should be named exactly the same across multimodalities: verbally, on the syllabus, in the LMS, when mentioned in emails, etc. Such efforts are crucial in trying to ameliorate uncertainty for students and provide clarity. Poor organization can make it more difficult for students with processing issues to follow the threads of the course. Be as clear and explicit as possible in your instructions. The asynchronous online environment may not allow for organic moments in which students ask questions and get clarity on assignments from hearing answers to everyone else's questions. Students will benefit from examples and models from prior participants, as well. Being explicit and clear up front will also prevent extra labor on the part of the instructor in fielding multiple questions about the materials.

The syllabus is an essential document in online teaching and learning as it serves as a readily available touchstone and common point of reference throughout the course. The use of course design signals, such as inclusive images and diversity statements, can cue students who are looking for courses and may help welcome more participants from marginalized groups in digital learning environments. We also recommend including an inclusion/diversity statement in your syllabus or course orientation materials as a way to signal to students the philosophy of the course. A diversity/inclusion statement can be personalized to reflect the instructor's own voice and transparent values. The statement should be specific to the course or workshop and connected to the syllabus and other workshop materials.

Synchronous and Asynchronous Considerations

This section addresses the possibilities and drawbacks of synchronous and asynchronous activities. A synchronous activity is any activity in which participants and/or facilitators are working together, in the same "space," at the same time. Asynchronous activities do not occur at the same place or the same time, and participants are able to engage the materials and work on their own schedule. Overall, designs should include various types of course activities and opportunities for student engagement, and the types of activities should support the process and content goals of the course. The standard for making learning the most accessible to the largest number of students is that asynchronous learning prioritizes equity for the greatest number of students. The expectation that students can and should engage in synchronous online learning is based on multiple assumptions about students' and participants' resources. This section addresses the possibilities of asynchronous learning, the hurdles of synchronous learning, and how to make synchronous learning more accessible.

Asynchronous learning makes courses and workshops the most accessible to the largest number of students. Beyond this, asynchronous designs open doorways to expand the multimodal nature of courses and give students more flexibility in how, where, and when they engage with materials. Effective asynchronous activities are able to structure dialogues among participants and facilitators, including allowing students more time to be reflective (Bondy, Hambacher, Murphy, Wolkenhauer, & Krell, 2015). Online activities can provide the extra space and time for participants who take longer to process and find it challenging to speak up in F2F large-group discussions. Online discussions also offer all participants the opportunity to participate without the time constraints of a F2F discussion session. As in F2F designs, the choices of activities should meet the process and content goals of the session.

During the COVID pandemic, many online or remote courses were taught with the expectation that students were available during the scheduled class time. Hurdles for synchronous engagement may include differing time zones, levels of technological fluency, widely varying personal or work schedules, and other family or community obligations. The following are access and equity issues that may affect which students are able to join synchronous sessions:

- Not all students have reliable and fast internet access to join a video conferencing session, either because they are in a geographical area where it is not available or because they cannot afford to pay for internet services or internet-ready devices.
- Some participants are sharing a living space in which internet speed is slowed by multiple users.
- Participants may not have access to or be able to afford a device that can be available to them and can be assured to be working.
- Not all participants have a reasonably distraction free environment in which to join a video conferencing session.
- Not all participants want to share their physical space or want to be seen in a video conferencing session with video.
- Some participants may have safety issues related to disclosure and discussions of topics that their families may not know about or participants' families might not feel comfortable that their child is taking these courses. For example, participants might be asked to share preferred names and pronouns, but they may not be out to their family yet.

We don't want to imply that synchronous sessions are inherently negative, but they come with a myriad of equity issues. This list should give readers a sense of some of the issues at hand.

Synchronous sessions are not limited to Zoom or other video conferencing apps. Working together at the same time on a Google Doc during a planned time frame is also synchronous. Other synchronous activities include: scheduled text-based chat sessions, instant messaging, conference calls via phone, or viewing a lecture or film together at the same time. Zoom sessions have, in some ways, become synonymous with synchronous learning during the COVID pandemic. Video sessions are a tool that many facilitators and participants are now familiar with, and these types of sessions can be useful to build community, facilitate large- and small-group discussion, promote collaboration, and create active learning opportunities for participants. Zoom sessions may also warm up the classroom as students see instructors more fully as people (e.g., children and pets may make cameo appearances).

With the proliferation of Zoom and other video conferencing apps being used for synchronous online learning, we find it important to reiterate that video conferencing sessions are not the same as a classroom. Zoom is perhaps the best-known platform for meetings and small-group work. Not everybody experiences the Zoom space as a classroom or a way to feel connected. That being said, video conferencing is a powerful technology tool for synchronous online education, and video sessions can lead to many participants feeling more connected to a learning community. In particular, Zoom and other video conferencing apps can be utilized to create small-group discussions in breakout rooms. Such opportunities can promote building student-to-student relationships and a sense of belongingness, promote peer learning, and allow participants to work together on complex activities.

Here we provide some general guidelines for making synchronous learning opportunities more active and accessible and thus more reflective of social justice pedagogy:

- Be clear in your design about the goals that your synchronous Zoom session is supposed to meet.
- Provide any slides, notes, or links that are important to the session.
- Utilize breakout rooms for small-group work, and visit the breakout rooms.
- Utilize Google Docs, Google Slides, or other technologies for small-group reporting back to the large group.
- Create structures for taking turns, such as alphabetical by first name or having participants choose who speaks next in a round-robin fashion.
- Utilize the chat function so students have more opportunities to be actively engaged.
- Ask students to engage in nonverbal ways (such as nodding to signify understanding or using emojis to indicate completion of a task), practice these often, and offer participants positive feedback for engaging in these ways.
- Encourage the personalizing and ragged edges of online teaching, such as normalizing interruptions from family members or seeing pets on the screen. Avoid creating a new professional standard that is inaccessible to some participants.
- Offer flexibility in scheduling synchronous sessions. For example, disseminate a questionnaire that finds out when students are available or create multiple meeting times and ask participants to sign up for a certain number of them.
- If there are required synchronous sessions, create other ways to participate as well. For example, sessions can be recorded, viewed at a later time, and participants can then submit brief reflections to engage with the synchronous content they've later viewed.

- As a learning community, create guidelines about when cameras are on or off, and be explicit about the reasoning.
- Remember that students have physical bodies, and encourage them to move, take breaks, and take care of themselves in similar ways to F2F sessions.

TECHNOLOGY AND MEDIA CONSIDERATIONS

Technology is developed out of and reflects the social and political systems in which it is created and at times amplifies the biases and cultural values of people who design the technology (Gutherie & McCraken, 2010). Media technology is a prime example of this amplification, given the massive amounts of misinformation and the media saturation in our lives. Media is value laden and works as a mechanism of socialization, perpetuating stereotypes and inequity. Critical media literacy seeks to interrogate the politics of representation, critique the structures in which media emerges, make informed decisions about media consumption, and explore how media can potentially empower communities and be used for social justice and change. Critical media literacy also examines media in its contexts. The theoretical foundations of social justice education can help us understand these broader contexts and also how different people experience the same piece of media differently and how this is often connected to the multiple social identities people inhabit.

Technology and Inequality

As social justice educators facilitating online, consideration of the political implications of technology as it relates to our social justice values is important. A range of technologies have been critiqued for promoting inequities. Facial recognition technologies encode racism in the inability to distinguish between faces of Black people and Asian people, a new iteration and perpetuation of the myth and stereotype that all Black or Asian people look the same (Stommel, Friend, & Morris, 2020). The algorithms of search engines reinforce unequal social relationships and perpetuate the technology users' biases through racial profiling (Noble, 2018). Predictive policing models perpetuate racism in the criminal justice system (Heaven, 2020), and big data holds the potential to perpetuate discrimination—for example, leading to ethnic profiling in housing or the exclusion of racial minorities from economic opportunities (Favaretto, De Clercq, & Elger, 2019). Anna Lauren Hoffman (2018) coined the phrase "data violence" to describe the impacts that harmful technologies and usage of algorithms have on already vulnerable communities. The critiques of and research about inequalities embedded in technologies and media continues to grow. These critiques have implications for how social justice educators design and facilitate classes and workshops online.

Educational technologies are also embedded in power relations and have the potential to perpetuate inequalities. As educational platforms continue to be monetized, they risk further commodifying education and can make education less democratic. Some educational technology companies profited greatly during the COVID pandemic and the move of schooling to remote learning (Williamson, Eynon, & Potter, 2020). During the pandemic, digital inequalities that existed prior to COVID were greatly exacerbated (Williamson, Eynon, & Potter, 2020). Economic disparities were glaringly evident in student access to resources to continue their education at home, access to high-speed Wi-Fi, adequate space and resources to complete assignments, the quiet necessary to focus, educational technologies like iPads and laptop computers, and the loss of social interactions and community support systems. Instead of focusing on these systemic inequities, too many educational technology companies promoted plagiarism detection software and exam surveillance technologies during the pandemic. Some companies strip-mine students' work for content and data, using it for their own profit (Morris & Stommel, 2018). On a pedagogical level, cheating is not a problem to be fixed through technology, but it is social in nature and begs questions about the pedagogical imperatives an educator prioritizes (Stommel, Friend, & Morris, 2020).

This is not to imply that technology is evil but rather that it's an ever-evolving field that necessitates social justice educators to be abreast of changes and think critically about the choices we make about technologies in our pedagogy. Technologies can potentially re-entrench inequities but can also be used in transformative ways (Stommel, Friend, & Morris, 2020, p. 98) and can support culturally relevant teaching to promote student learning (Shelton, 2021).

Making Choices

The needs of the participants should be central to making choices about technology in social justice design. Researchers advocate that educators "look for technologies that are designed for learning" (Bruff, 2019, p. 26) and be student focused when choosing digital technologies (Hood, 2018). For example, consider socio-economic class and how much devices, internet, and applications cost; whether the technologies are accessible to participants with different disabilities; and whether the technology needs high-speed internet that not every participant can access. Avoid thinking of technologies as a way to deliver information, which models a banking approach to education. Rather, technologies should be seen as tools for students to create knowledge together, in community.

Learning technologies can offer key affordances such as interactivity, adaptivity, feedback from multiple sources, choice (what to learn, when, and how to learn it), nonlinear access, open-ended input, and communication with other people. They can empower learners as producers and creators of content beyond simple acts of consumption. However, such benefits are predicated on the alignment of goals for learning, available support for instructors and learners, and equitable access (National Academies of Science, Engineering, and Medicine, 2018, p. 196). To support educators in making decisions about technologies, we include on the website a rubric for critically evaluating digital tools (Stommel, Friend, & Morris, 2020).

While making these choices, it is important for instructors to take stock of their own resources and experiences with learning technologies. First, find out what resources your institution or organization offers. For example, some universities and organizations have instructional designers or instructional technologists to offer support. Many organizations provide an LMS and sometimes a range of technologies. Second, assess your own experiences with and knowledge of technology and its applications. All educational technology and apps have a learning curve for both the facilitator and the students, and it takes time to learn new technologies. Learning one new technology each semester or period of a workshop is a reasonable amount of work, and after a few years of facilitating online, these experiences add up to facility with multiple technological tools. It is reasonable to begin with the resources available and that facilitators have knowledge or training on. A good guideline for beginners is to choose one technological tool that has a lot of flexibility and is free. For example, Google Docs provides a flexible space for students to work both synchronously and asynchronously, allows a group to have access to the document together, and is a fairly straightforward and easy application to learn. Though it is a popular app, it is important to teach the students about how to use Google Docs and any other applications and technologies utilized in the design. Be willing to create backup plans if someone cannot access a particular technology or application that is part of the curriculum.

An LMS can offer structure for the course and participants. We do not advocate any particular LMS but recognize that LMSs often reflect needs of administrators who are concerned with course enrollment numbers, scheduling, and traditional grading policies (Kim & Maloney, 2020, p. 32) and not necessarily prioritizing student learning and engagement. LMSs tend to be instructor centered whereas SJE pedagogy is student centered. Furthermore, once students complete a course or graduate, they may lose access to digital material posted on the LMS course website, and instructors may lose access to all the work they have done to develop their LMS course sites if they leave the institution. Some LMS systems are now actively working on inclusivity on their platforms. Blackboard's Ally is an application that makes digital content more accessible. Online communities have begun to develop around LMS, as well. For example, Canvas has an active online community that discusses issues of online education. These are all considerations for facilitators to take into account when using an LMS.

PEDAGOGICAL CONSIDERATIONS FOR SJE ONLINE

In this section, we take as a structure the five pedagogical elements central to social justice education that are presented in Chapter 2: Pedagogical Foundations and apply them to SJE in the online learning environment.

Element 1: Consider the Roles of Facilitators and Participants in the Learning Community

In the online environment, as in the F2F context, SJE is concerned with disrupting the traditional teacher-student dynamics of banking education (Freire, 1970) that treat students as empty vessels in which information is to be deposited by the instructors. This section highlights how to avoid a banking approach in the online environment and what facilitators should consider about the roles of facilitators and participants in an online learning community.

Knowing Our Participants

As in the F2F classroom, facilitators need to meet students where they are. When online, this also includes participants' access to Wi-Fi and reliable devices; their general experiences with learning online; and their experiences using the apps and technological tools that facilitators plan to use. To make courses as accessible as possible, a goal of SJE, knowing student technology access needs will assist instructors in designing courses that are accessible to the most students. This information helps avoid the assumption that all participants have a working, dependable laptop with updated software and Wi-Fi. Using a pre-assessment tool to find out what previous experience students have learning online allows teachers to gauge how much support students will need to fully participate in the online class or workshop. Facilitators should set aside sufficient time to teach the skills needed to successfully use the apps that will be used in the course. Also, facilitators may be able to identify leaders in the group who can support/mentor other students who haven't had as much experience with tech and/or learning online. When choosing which technologies and/or applications to utilize in a design, keep in mind that some apps demand a faster and more consistent Wi-Fi connection than some participants might have. We encourage instructors to make choices that are the most accessible given your own resources as an educator and the needs of your participants.

Accept and plan for technology problems. Inevitably, during a session/course, someone's device/computer crashes or breaks or an application doesn't work properly. Consider ways that flexibility can be built in for when these inevitable tech problems occur. It is also helpful to explicitly state in the syllabus or other such document that students are encouraged to communicate about technological problems as soon as they arise so that the facilitator and participant can work together to make sure everyone can be included in the learning community.

Knowing Ourselves as Facilitators

In addition to knowing ourselves as SJE facilitators in the ways addressed in Chapter 2: Pedagogical Foundations and Chapter 12: Critical Self-Knowledge, there are considerations specific to teaching online. Seasoned facilitators should reflect on their strengths in the F2F classroom and examine how they could apply these assets to the online context. In the F2F environment, many facilitators may be successful in creating engaging learning environments for participants, informally assessing learning, supporting relationship-building, and debriefing and other classroom processes. A good place to start as an online educator is to take stock of your own strengths and make connections to the online environment, explicitly developing strategies that utilize your skills.

Reflecting on our own online teaching and learning preferences can help us be aware of our own biases in terms of types of activities we might prefer over others. We can consider how our own levels of comfort and competence with various technologies and our own personal experiences with educational technology might affect decision-making when designing a workshop or course. Be aware that communication style preferences come across differently in the online space, and make intentional decisions about how to communicate with participants. For example, sarcasm via the written word is often difficult for people to decode. Reflect on and solicit feedback about how your own communication style is being interpreted online.

Element 2: Foster an Inclusive Learning Community

In online SJE, like in F2F, it is essential that participants get to know each other and build relationships to foster a learning community. In an online context, we have to work in a different way to build relationships among participants and between participants and facilitators, and we must be intentional about how this occurs. This section focuses on the importance of understanding embodiment in the online space, how to set the tone for the community, specific online concerns when developing norms in the online community, and, finally, several strategies to meet a variety of needs in the learning community.

Embodiment and Presence in the Online Community

There are parts of F2F education that are lost in the online space but are essential to building community. For example, chatting before and after class, down time in small groups/pairs where people connect, and talk that happens during transitional times. To successfully navigate an online environment, these social practices and informal processes need to be built into the design (Davidson, 2020). To address this, facilitators should emphasize the importance of developing a learning community, connecting with participants, and finding ways for them to connect with each other. Here is a brief list of strategies to support these types of informal communication as part of team building:

- Utilize some of the F2F techniques in synchronous video conference sessions (e.g., Zoom), such as pair share interviews, practicing names each session, and building in time for participants to get to know each other and potentially exchange contact information in small groups.

- Give participants the opportunity to connect outside of class away from the facilitator. Participants can create Snapchat groups, Slack groups, or Discord servers, for example.
- Utilize asynchronous small-group work.
- Emphasize names, such as on discussion boards, or ask students to reiterate names when responding in discussion boards or in reflective writing.
- Have participants make introductory videos to share.
- Have participants upload a photo to their profile if using an LMS (or a representational picture, such as a landscape, pics of a beloved pet, cartoon renditions of the self, or a drawing a participant completed themselves).
- Have participants share something about their physical spaces with each other.
- Have participants create web biographies and read each other's biographies.
- Explicitly have participants reflect on contributions that other participants have made during activities—both synchronous and asynchronous.
- Create a chart in which participants share relevant interests and/or something they want to connect over, along with their contact info.

These opportunities for informal and low-stakes communication are important for participants to feel like they are part of a community (Beins, 2016).

Social justice in an online environment is also just as likely to evoke emotional and kinesthetic as well as cognitive responses for participants as the F2F environment. Students and instructors bring their whole beings into the online classroom—their bodies, lived experiences, emotions, and stories. Be careful to acknowledge the bodies of participants and include attention to physical selves when creating a social justice education design. For example, when people spend copious amounts of time online, as many have during the pandemic, they often need reminders to take care of themselves in physical ways. For example, Rachel found herself designing synchronous sessions in which students were implicitly expected to stay in one place the entire session, which would never be a F2F expectation. Explicitly build in acknowledgements of bodies and body movements in structured activities. The following are some suggestions for how to do this online:

- Integrate stretch breaks or meditation breaks into a synchronous session or in recorded videos.
- Incorporate embodiment by asking participants to move during a synchronous session or talk out loud or record themselves as part of an asynchronous activity.
- Allow participants to turn off cameras during synchronous sessions when needed and when appropriate.
- Offer some breathing exercises to help participants process feelings, get present, and feel more grounded.
- Include icebreaker activities where students notice sensory details about their personal space.

Acknowledging bodies also means addressing ability and disability, as not all bodies are able to sit in front of a screen for long periods of time or are able to engage their bodies in the same way. It helps to explicitly state that students should do what works for their own bodies and learning experience.

Getting Started

In F2F social justice education, facilitators think about the space, how students enter the room, and how we engage. Similarly, facilitators need to consider how these operate in the online space and how to set the tone for the workshop or course. For example, reflect on what the first communication will be with your participants, in what format you plan to do the introduction, and which content it will include. If the design is asynchronous, consider what medium will make students feel connected, such as a personalized video of the facilitator where the participants can hear your voice, see you, and get a sense of what you will be like as a facilitator. In a synchronous session, consider how you will greet students and introduce the course, such as playing music, greeting students by name as they join, offering an engaging question, or displaying an interesting picture students can respond to in the chat. All introductory activities, both asynchronous and synchronous, should be intentionally structured to set the tone for your workshop or course.

Explicitly Creating Norms

An online learning community needs to establish group norms and guidelines; this can, at times, be more intense than in F2F spaces since there are few norms around the online classroom. At this point, many participants have had some sort of online learning experience. These experiences, though, have varied in context and quality. The broader norms around online learning are still beginning to develop. Riggs and Linder (2016) discuss the architecture of a classroom and how this shapes how a group of people interact. For example, in the setup of a classroom or lecture hall, most students will know to find a seat, turn their attention to any information on a whiteboard or a projected slide, and take out a notebook and pen or laptop. In the online context, though, even the very structure of the course varies. The very foundations of online learning vary from course to course and workshop to workshop. Riggs and Linder (2016) recommend that a syllabus outline communication policies. For a social justice education design, a course orientation video or activity can orient participants to all these structural aspects of the course, such as how and where to communicate with facilitators and each other, where information can be accessed, how it will be accessed, any time expectations or due dates, how activities will be submitted, and how often participants should check the LMS or website. Including some participant self-reflection into this orientation can also support participants in examining their own expectations and biases around interacting with others online, such as reflection questions that address previous online learning experiences, attitudes about online communications in social media, and understandings of norms around text-based online communication, such as usage of punctuation or complete sentences.

Communication norms, specifically, are pertinent to address when developing norms for online learning. Facilitators can craft a document, such as a *netiquette*, that lays out these types of expectations. Consider how to keep conversations about these norms open and collaborative. For example, make the crafting of norms participatory by using a collaborative tool, such as Google Jamboard or an LMS discussion board, for group brainstorming. Be careful not to spend too much time on group norms, as an unintentional consequence of spending too much of the design's time on guidelines is that participants feel "locked in" to a set of guidelines. Limiting initial time on norms and then returning to the guidelines throughout the course or workshop to review and revise these norms is a helpful practice.

Use of technologies should also be part of creating community guidelines in which facilitators and participants come to a consensus about how the learning community wants to use various devices and/or technologies. For example, in synchronous video sessions, such as with Zoom, whether or not cameras should be on or off should be negotiated as a guideline, and these guidelines will vary from group to group and in different contexts, as well. For example, workshop participants in a professional office setting might already have a community culture in which everyone keeps cameras on.

In another setting, groups members might want to allow each participant to choose for themself whether to turn on the camera as a way to participate. This allows participants to consider their own circumstance—for example, their personal space, Wi-Fi connection, or whether they feel "camera-ready"—and exercise agency over how they choose to participate. A group may even develop more specific guidelines that center visual connections in which they might agree to something such as cameras on during the first and last 10 minutes as a form of connection or during smaller breakout rooms, with the flexibility to turn off cameras for other reasons as needed. Similar group processes can be used to develop guidelines around uses of cell phones, other devices, and digital technologies in F2F and online settings.

Meeting a Variety of Needs

Overall, a best practice for social justice education online is to use multiple modalities to meet the different needs of participants and the various process goals. If a facilitator is contemplating which technologies to learn and incorporate, learning an application or technology that allows you to include a new modality in your design is helpful. A perhaps less labor-intensive way to include more modalities is to curate multimedia content to use as discussion starters. Using multimedia, such as documentaries, videos, or podcasts, also gives facilitators the space to include a diversity of voices and points of view, de-centering the facilitator as sole knowledge holder.

Students who are successful in an online environment tend to be self-regulating learners, self-motivated and good at time management (Ballen, Wieman, Salehi, Searle, & Zamudio, 2017; National Academies of Sciences, Engineering, and Medicine, 2018). The successful completion rate for participants in online courses improves significantly when taking the course with friends (Kizilcec & Schneider, 2015). Facilitators can support students in multiple ways by helping them assess their readiness for SJE online learning and providing them with tips/suggestions for successful online learning.

Element 3: Center an Analysis of Systems of Oppression and How They Operate in Society and in the Classroom

All Education Is Political

In a previous section, we addressed some of the social justice impacts of educational technologies and how systemic oppression shapes our experiences online. As previously highlighted, online platforms can lend themselves to administration needs, rather than students' needs. Moreover, some technologies lend themselves to banking methods of education, such as lecture videos, copious amounts of written text, or examination platforms, in which the student is passively viewing or simply regurgitating information while being surveilled. This isn't to imply that these are always negative educational technologies but that many of them have been built around the assumption that the students will be engaging in forms of passive learning. As facilitators, then, we must critically analyze our choices and bring the social justice content of technology into the design and discuss these choices with our participants.

Connecting Personal Experience with Understandings of Systems

SJE online can connect personal experiences with understandings of systems by explicitly examining participant and facilitator experiences with technology and reflecting on how these relate to multiple identities. Activities can examine which skills participants have, how and where technology experience was gained, and access to technology participants have had or not during their lives. Participants can examine their assumptions about what access and experience they think other participants have had, self-reflect on their own position, and bring light to issues such as socio-economic class or geographic differences that have influenced our experience with and around technology.

Finally, our understanding of the impact of our identities and their visibility/invisibility in the online environment is evolving at a swift pace. During synchronous video sessions, students physically get to see and potentially make assumptions about markers of some visible identities, such as race and gender. If a course or workshop is completely asynchronous and video is not used, this may not be the case. Names of participants may flag some identities and may lead to assumptions made about others in the class. To bring this important social justice content to the forefront, facilitators should incorporate opportunities to discuss these issues and, if appropriate, should center these issues in activities and discussion as part of the design content to address the biases that emerge based on these assumptions.

Element 4: Define Goals, Learning Objectives, and Evaluation Mechanisms for SJE

When adapting SJE designs for the online context, content goals can remain the same as F2F, and process and action goals can be expanded to include considerations of online learning. Process goals should take into consideration the technologies and applications the participants will use. This means both accounting for the extra time needed for participants to learn a new technology and considering how technologies can potentially support process goals of the design. For example, using a collaborative application where participants work together to create content can support team-building goals.

Some of the action and skill-building goals of F2F SJE can remain similar to SJE online, such as objectives that focus on what participants will be able to do beyond the classroom setting. Action/skills goals sometimes include communication skills that are practiced in the F2F classroom setting. In an online setting, action/skills goals can focus on skill building around online communication and usage of technologies or can be expanded to include activities in which students are given a task to complete in their own in-real-life context in which they practice a skill, such as active listening, with a trusted person in their life.

Additionally, Chapter 2: Pedagogical Foundations critiques mainstream evaluation methods of learning. In social justice education online, the technologies we use likewise can reinforce and emulate banking education and mainstream evaluation models. Many applications designed for "evaluation" rely on traditional types of tests (T/F, multiple choice) that are easily graded by machine, are surveilled to prevent plagiarism, and use a banking education model of learning in which students regurgitate information to earn a passing grade.

Evaluation and assessment strategies should center participants, reflect multiple learning styles, and support diverse learning community members to meet their goals. Online SJE designs should include both low- and high-stakes assessment, and the intent of each type should be clearly articulated to the participants. Some participants, especially students in academic settings, interpret all submitted work as high stakes, particularly when it's text based. Clarify expectations so participants can understand the purpose of each activity. Low-stakes assessments might focus on participant engagement with ideas, participants' learning process, or an application of topics to participant experiences—*not* emulating the facilitator's point of view or the reading, which is often a banking education expectation. For example, having participants submit low-stakes journal writing, especially writing that reflects on their own ideas, learning, and experiences, can be a helpful way to gauge what participants are learning. When an activity or assignment is higher stakes, especially in an academic setting where grades are mandatory, participants should be made aware of this and given clear criteria that will be used for grading. Facilitators should not rely solely on text-based assessments that favor some learning styles and not others. A variety of assessment strategies is more likely to access a range of learning styles and preferences. The following are strategies for assessment of learning and engagement. Instructors can note:

- The number of comments participants make
- How often participants engage with each other in various modalities
- Who participants engage with most often and least often
- The number of video views and duration, if your LMS or technology allows
- Specific instances in activities where participant content reflects negotiating meaning of workshop topics
- Participants communicating connections with different areas of knowledge
- Participants communicating new perspectives learned from the diverse learning community or from readings

Whenever they are to be evaluated formally for an organization or class, participants should be made aware. Also, many of these strategies address participation, and this can look different for different participants. For example, some participants may prefer text-based activities. Others may prefer creating and posting videos. And yet others may enjoy a new educational technology that is being utilized by the learning community. To account for various learning styles, include multimodalities in your assessments and evaluations. These assessment strategies also highlight the importance of facilitators being online regularly to have a sense of how things are going for participants.

Element 5: Utilize Collaborative and Active Learning

A key aspect of SJE is engaging learners in active and collaborative learning. While this may seem more challenging online, this section highlights strategies for including more active learning in the online context and how to promote collaboration among the participants.

Active Learning

As previously noted, many educational technologies are developed using banking education models or models that promote passive learning from participants. Especially in academic settings, the tools provided by an organization can lend themselves to rote learning and memorization, emulating instructor-centered teaching models, such as lecture capture technologies, online quizzes and exams, activities that demand a right or wrong answer, or traditional hand raising and turn taking. For example, having all students post on a discussion board the answer to the same question leads to rote answers that center the instructor's questions rather than the participant's knowledge. Avoid solely doing rote-style, text-based work in which students complete readings and post to a text discussion board for all the course content. This type of activity can be used occasionally, but it should meet content and process goals of a session.

When designing SJE online, utilize multimodality and various technologies to make activities as interactive and active as possible. Offer multiple ways for participants to engage each other and the facilitators—for example, having students post videos, offering participants recorded audio or video feedback, or giving participants the opportunity to offer each other recorded audio or video feedback. In both synchronous and asynchronous settings, give participants opportunities to share contact information and to form communication connections among each other separate from the class. Video conference sessions can be used similar to in-person discussion processes, such as small groups to generate content and ideas, pair shares to generate or clarify ideas, go-arounds to hear all voices, time doing individual reflections or journaling, or large-group discussions. Discussion questions that are posed in discussion boards should involve the flexibility for participants to focus on what is important to them. In discussion boards, consider utilizing group posts, giving participants choices among topics, crafting specific discussion questions that lead students to apply topics to experience, or asking participants to share experiences or tell personal stories.

Consider doing simple activities with text or video instructions that include creativity or body movements. Participants can create sketches or collages and share them via photo or video. Finding and sharing photos and videos from the internet can make participants more active in shaping course content, and sharing can occur in a free and fairly easy to use application, such as Google Docs. Participants can learn a fun technology, such as a meme generator, and create memes to reflect their learning around a topic. Sharing a gallery of memes made by participants can also be a great discussion starter. Finally, including body movement in instructions is a straightforward way to make online learning more physically active (ensuring it is adaptable to different bodies and abilities) and to have participants do something other than sitting and looking at a screen. For example, a recorded lecture can include a guided meditation or other contemplative activities. Check-ins, including asynchronous check-ins, can ask students to reflect on taking care of their bodies when engaging with online content and can ask them to be intentional about it.

Another useful consideration is reflecting on how to adapt specific F2F activities from the various chapter designs in this book to the online space. For example, Common Ground can potentially be a Zoom activity in which all participants turn off their cameras, the facilitator asks a question, and in lieu of stepping in the center of a circle, participants turn on their camera to answer a question. Google Slides or other such presentation applications can become a gallery walk. A fishbowl can be a video recording of a small group of participants having a conversation about a relevant topic and then other students watch and reflect on it. Google Jamboard can be used like newsprint is used in classrooms. And some technologies emulate specific activities, such as timeline applications, where participants can cooperate to create timelines on topics. There is no perfect technology, but some lend themselves to collaboration, and we can utilize them in collaborative ways.

Collaborative Learning

In SJE, participants have mutual responsibility for each other's learning and work together to generate content for the workshops. Technology tools can be utilized to meet this collaborative goal of content generation and can offer a multitude of modalities for collaboration, such as working on Google Docs or Google Slides together, annotating workshop readings in small groups, participating in discussion boards, or creating a topical wiki as a group. These are just a few current examples of technologies that can be used for collaborative goals. When deciding which technologies to implement or what new technology to learn, this can be a good place to use your time when choosing a new tool.

Collaborative learning also happens through working in small groups and reflecting on the process of this small-group work. In a synchronous setting, this can be as straightforward as utilizing breakout rooms in Zoom (or another video conference app) and a debriefing process in a large-group discussion. For asynchronous learning, participants can utilize technologies for collaboration and then be asked to debrief by reflecting on their experience of the collaborative process, the different technologies used for collaboration, and the specific contributions of their fellow participants. These types of reflections can be shared via a discussion board or another collaborative app to emulate a large-group discussion process, or it can be low-stakes reflections, such as journaling, where participants make connections to their own experiences and identities. It's particularly important in an asynchronous setting to frequently circle back and ask participants specifically about the contributions of their fellow learners. Reflecting on other students' contributions takes seriously the input of other participants and emphasizes the importance of mutual responsibility for learning in an SJE learning community. This circling back also helps students feel more connected to the community and, in an asynchronous setting, especially, feel less like they are completing a list of tasks. Facilitators can support this type of collaboration and reflection by referring to specific participant contributions and thanking students regularly for their engagement. This works to de-center the facilitator and the course materials as authoritative knowledge and instead models the importance of participants as knowledge and content creators in the SJE learning community.

Preparing for Online Teaching

We acknowledge that choosing the most suitable learning activities is dependent on a number of important variables:

1. Who your participants are and the range of their tech knowledge/comfort
2. Context (synchronous/asynchronous)
3. Group size
4. Availability of no- or low-cost options
5. Your confidence with platforms/applications you will ask participants to use
6. The availability of tech support in your organization
7. Many platforms may be used both synchronously and asynchronously, depending on the learning outcome goals of the activity
8. Allow ample time for students to work on asynchronous activities, be aware of the time also needed for students to read through the texts and artifacts that other groups have created, and include time for students to reflect on their experiences; these types of reiterative processes are often more time consuming for participants than in F2F environments

Pre-assessments
*   Participants can be asked to complete a pre-workshop survey on their prior experiences related to content, online learning, access to technologies, and comfort levels with the specific platforms you anticipate using ★
    *   Possible applications: Survey Monkey, Qualtrics, Google Forms, survey/questionnaire in your organization's LMS

Establishing Instructor and Participant Presence

Being visible and available to participants and supporting them to be visible to each other helps create a learning community and "warms up" the learning environment.

*   Have a video presence as a facilitator, particularly in asynchronous settings
*   Regularly give low-stakes feedback on activities
*   Be an active participant in technologies, such as discussion boards and Google Docs
*   Have participants do low-stakes reflections in an ongoing journal in which you interact with them regularly
*   Have facilitators and students upload a photo (a picture of themselves or a representational image such as a landscape or drawing)

Communicating with Students

In an online environment, making yourself available and approachable through establishing clear channels for regular communication is essential.

- Encourage students to come to you early and often to troubleshoot technology problems
- Structure ways for them to be in communication with each other
  - Possible apps: Slack, Discord
- Reach out to students if they seem to fade or "disappear"
- Provide individual options for students who are nervous asking questions or posting comments to the whole group, such as anonymous posting or emailing the facilitator
- Invite participants to reach out to you offline (sometimes a brief phone call can be enormously powerful) to share feelings they may not feel comfortable putting in writing

ADAPTING SOCIAL JUSTICE ACTIVITIES FOR ONLINE LEARNING

This section offers recommendations for preparing for online teaching and facilitation, strategies for creating online presence and communicating remotely, and a list of asynchronous and synchronous activities for SJE online. The activity list contains brief descriptions of the activity, and a detailed handout for each is available on the website. The first list contains asynchronous activities and the second contains synchronous activities, though most asynchronous activities can be utilized in a synchronous setting, as well. These activities were chosen because they are frequently used in many or all of the workshop designs, save for the Course Orientation Video, which we recommend all online courses include. The handouts for the activities detail the process goals for each activity and utilize a breadth of technologies to meet these goals. This demonstrates how to take a specific activity from an SJE design and adapt it for the online environment using available technologies. For beginners, the plethora of technologies mentioned may be overwhelming, and learning new technologies is time consuming. A strategy for beginners is to choose one technology and use this one technology for active learning and collaboration purposes. One such tool is Google Docs—it's free, widely accessible to most people, and can be used on different types of devices, including smartphones. Like the text of the chapter, the purpose of these activities and the detailed handouts is to demonstrate a backward design process that you can apply to your own courses in your own context and use the resources available to you and your participants.

Asynchronous Activities

1. Course Orientation Video
   Content recommendations and general tips for recording a short course orientation video for participants.
2. Group Guidelines
   Asynchronous, online options for using technology to collaboratively create group guidelines for the learning community.
3. Icebreaker/Introductions/Closings
   Includes a list of options for online icebreakers, brief introductory activities, and closing activities.
4. Interactive Lecture
   Guidance for creating recorded lectures that include active learning components.

5. Self-Reflective Learning through Digital Storytelling

Uses digital storytelling as a creative, multimodal tool for participant self-reflection and for facilitator evaluation of participant learning.

6. Historical Timeline

Uses a currently available technology to collaborate on constructing a historical timeline of an ism and for participants to connect personal experiences to the visual representation of history.

7. Spheres of Influence

Demonstrates how to adapt the Spheres of Influence activity to the online space as a collaborative activity.

8. Cycle of Socialization

Demonstrates how to adapt the Cycle of Socialization activity to the online space as a collaborative activity.

Synchronous Activities

1. Icebreakers/Introductions/Closings

Synchronous, online options for using technology to collaboratively create group guidelines for the learning community.

2. Common Ground

Creatively adapts the Common Ground activity for use on Zoom or other video conferencing application.

3. Annotation Activity for Readings

Utilizes currently available technology for participants to collaboratively learn from assigned readings.

4. Web of Oppression

Demonstrates how to adapt the Web of Oppression activity by utilizing various aspects of Zoom technology.

CONCLUSION

The contemporary economic, political, and social context in which we began working on this chapter has already changed tremendously from the conceptualization to our current thinking and is sure to change again before the publication due to emerging social justice issues and changing technologies. In conclusion, we point readers to future considerations of teaching online and educational technologies that have implications for social justice education. The ongoing privacy issues of social media platforms, such as Twitter and Facebook, remain relevant and unsolved. Researchers are beginning to grapple with racism and bias in artificial intelligence and the racist applications of big data. In newer technologies of virtual reality, the "meta" space, and the use of avatars, issue of social identity will inevitably emerge as users make decisions how to represent themselves in these online environments, and it's not yet clear how systems of oppression will shape this and how we can address them as they emerge. Finally, with the perpetuation of misinformation through social media and mass media, some have a newfound interest in or understanding of media literacy and the importance it holds for teaching social justice. Educational technologies, in particular, will continue to be developed and utilized as online learning continues to proliferate. It remains to be seen how many instructors will continue to teach online after the pandemic, but online learning will continue to be a big part of the future, and SJE online can and should be a part of this future in ways that effect change for social justice.

Note

* We ask that those who cite this work always acknowledge by name all of the authors listed rather than either only citing the first author or using "et al." to indicate co-authors. All collaborated on the conceptualization, development, and writing of this chapter.

References

Altbach, P. G. (2014). MOOCs as neocolonialism: Who controls knowledge? *International Higher Education*, 75(7), 5–7. doi:10.6017/ihe.2014.75.5426

Alvarez, M. de la C., & Domenech Rodríguez, M. M. (2020). Cultural competence shifts in multicultural psychology: Online versus face-to-face. *Translational Issues in Psychological Science*, 6(2), 160–174. Retrieved from https://doi-org.silk.library.umass.edu/10.1037/tps0000229

Amgott, N. (2018). Critical literacy in #DigitalActivism. *The International Journal of Information and Learning Technology*, 35(5), 329–341. doi:10.1108/IJILT-05-2018-0060

Askeroth, J. H., & Richardson, J. C. (2019). Instructor perceptions of quality learning in MOOCs they teach. *Online Learning*, 23(4), 135–159. doi:10.24059/olj.v23i4.2043

Bailey, C. (2017). Online feminist pedagogy: A new doorway into our brick-and-mortar classrooms? *Feminist Teacher*, 27(2–3), 253–266. Retrieved from https://doi-org.silk.library.umass.edu/10.5406/femteacher.27.2-3.0253

Baker, R., Passmore, D. L., & Mulligan, B. M. (2018). Inclusivity instead of exclusivity: The role of MOOCs for college credit. *Enhancing education through open degree programs and prior learning assessment*, 109–127.

Bali, M., Cronin, C., & Jhangian, R. S. (2020). Framing open educational practices from a social justice perspective. *Journal of Interactive Media in Education*, 1, 1–12. doi:10.5334/jime.565

Ballen, C. J., Wieman, C., Salehi, S., Searle, J. B., & Zamudio, K. R. (2017). Enhancing diversity in undergraduate science: Self-efficacy drives performance gains with active learning. *CBE-Life Sciences Education*, 16(4), ar56.

Bandy, J. M., Harbin, B., & Thurber, A. (2021). Teaching race and racial justice: Developing students' cognitive and affective understanding. *Teaching & Learning Inquiry: The ISSOTL Journal*, 9(1). https://doi.org/10.20343/teachlearninqu.9.1.10

Barber, W. (2020). Building creative critical online learning communities through digital moments. *Electronic Journal of e-Learning*, 18(5), 387–396.

Behm-Morawitz, E., & Villamil, A. (2019). The roles of ingroup identification and implicit bias in assessing the effectiveness of an online diversity education program. *Journal of Applied Communication Research*, 47(5), 505–526. doi:10.1080/00909882.2019.1678761

Beins, A. (2016). Small talk and chit chat : Using informal communication to build a learning community online. *Transformations*, 26(2), 157–175. https://doi-org.silk.library.umass.edu/10.5325/trajincschped.26.2.0157

Bell, P. E., & Lie, L. (2015). Social justice reasoning of education undergraduates: Effect of instruction in moral development theory and dilemma discussion in the asynchronous online classroom. *International Journal of Technology in Teaching and Learning*, 11(1), 60–75.

Boettcher, J. V., & Conrad, R.-M. (2016). *The online teaching survival guide: Simple and practical pedagogical tips* (2nd ed.). Jossey-Bass.

Boler, M. (2015). Feminist politics of emotions and critical digital pedagogies: A call to action. *PMLA*, 130(5), 1489–1496.

Bolter, N. D., Tayloe, S. D., Gomez, D. H., Eliason, M., Van Olphen, J. E., & Veri, M. J. (2021). Transforming undergraduate research methods courses using social justice pedagogy: A pre-post analysis. *Journal on Excellence in College Teaching*, 32(1), 47–66.

Bondy, E., Hambacher, E., Murphy, A. S., Wolkenhauer, R., & Krell, D. (2015). Developing critical social justice literacy in an online seminar. *Equity & Excellence in Education*, 48(2), 227–248. doi:10.1080/10665684.2015.1025652

Bruff, D. (2019). *Active learning in hybrid and physically distanced classrooms*. Retrieved from https://cft.vanderbilt.edu/2020/06/active-learning-in-hybrid-and-socially-distanced-classrooms/

Byrne, A. M. (2020, April). Using esports to teach bystander leadership and collaboration for students in STEM. *About Campus*, 25(1), 24–27.

Chen, S. Y., Basma, D., Ju, J., & Ng, K.-M. (2020). Opportunities and challenges of multicultural and international online education. *The Professional Counselor*, 10(1), 120. Retrieved from https://doi-org.silk.library.umass.edu/10.15241/syc.10.1.120

Cole, E. R., Case, K. A., Rios, D., & Curtin, N. (2011). Understanding what students bring to the classroom: Moderators of the effects of diversity courses on student attitudes. *Cultural Diversity and Ethnic Minority Psychology*, 17(4), 397–405. doi:10.1037/a0025433

Dalton, C., & Hudgings, J. (2020). Integrating equity: Curricular development and student experiences in an intermediate-level college physics major course. *The Physics Teacher*, 58, 545–551. doi:10.1119/10.0002374

Darby, F. (2020). How to be a better online teacher: Advice guide. *The Chronicle of Higher Education*, 1–38.

Darby, F., & Lang, J. M. (2019). *Small teaching online*. Jossey-Bass.

Davidson, C. (2020). Why start with pedagogy: Four good reasons and four good strategies. In *Critical digital pedagogy: A collection* (pp. 75–82). Hybrid Pedagogy Inc.

Favaretto, M., De Clercq, E., & Elger, B. S. (2019). Big Data and discrimination: Perils, promises and solutions. A systematic review. *Journal of Big Data*, 6(12), 1–27. https://doi.org/10.1186/s40537-019-0177-4

Freire, P. (1970). *Pedagogy of the oppressed*. Herder and Herder.

Funes, M., & Mackness, J. (2018). When inclusion excludes: A counter narrative of open online education. *Learning, Media and Technology*, 43(2), 119–138. doi:10.1080/17439884.2018.1444638

Goldingay, S., & Boddy, J. (2017). Preparing social work graduates for digital practice: Ethical pedagogies for effective learning. *Australian Social Work*, 70(2), 209–220. doi:10.1080/0312407X.2016.1257036

Gonzalez-Ramirez, J., Mulqueen, K., Zealand, R., Silverstein, S., Reina, C., Bushell, S., & Ladda, S. (2021). Emergency online learning: College students' perceptions during the Covid-19 crisis. *College Student Journal*, 55(1), 29–46.

Guthrie, K. L., & McCracken, H. (2010). Teaching and learning social justice through online service-learning courses. *International Review of Research in Open and Distributed Learning*, 11(3), 78–94. doi:10.19173/irrodl.v11i3.894

Heaven, W. D. (2020). *Predictive policing algorithms are racist: They need to be dismantled*. MIT Technology Review.

Herman, C., & Kirkup, G. (2017). Combining feminist pedagogy and transactional distance to create gender-sensitive technology-enhanced learning. *Gender & Education*, 29(6), 781–795. Retrieved from https://doi-org.silk.library.umass.edu/10.1080/09540253.2016.1187263

Hilton, R., Moos, C., & Barnes, C. (2020). A comparative analysis of students' perceptions of learning in online versus traditional courses. *E-Journal of Business Education & Scholarship of Teaching*, 14(3), 2–11.

Hoffman, A. L. (2018, April 30). Data violence and how bad engineering choices can damage society. *Medium*. Retrieved from https://medium.com/s/story/data-violence-and-how-bad-engineering-choices-can-damage-society-39e44150e1d4

Hood, N. (2018). Re-imagining the nature of (student-focused) learning through digital technology. *Policy Futures in Education*, 16(3), 321–326.

Hughes, G. (2007). Diversity, Identity and Belonging in E-Learning Communities: Some Theories and Paradoxes. *Teaching in Higher Education*, 12(5–6), 709–720.

Johnson, A. (2013). Excellent! Online teaching: Effective strategies for a successful semester online. Aaron Johnson. Retrieved from http://www.excellentonlineteaching.com

Kaplan, A. M., & Haenlein, M. (2016). Higher education and the digital revolution: About MOOCs, SPOCs, social media, and the Cookie Monster. *Business Horizons*, 59(4), 441–450. https://doi-org.silk.library.umass.edu/10.1016/j.bushor.2016.03.008

Kentnor, H. E. (2015). Distance education and the evolution of online learning in the United States. *Curriculum and Teaching Dialogue*, 17(1–2), 21–34.

Kernahan, C., & Davis, T. (2007). Changing perspective: How learning about racism influences student awareness and emotion. *Teaching of Psychology*, 34(1), 49–52. doi:10.1080/00986280709336651

Kim, J., & Maloney, E. J. (2020). *Learning innovation and the future of higher education*. JHU Press.

Kizilcec, R. F., & Schneider, E. (2015). Motivation as a lens to understand online learners: Toward data-driven design with the OLEI scale. *ACM Transactions on Computer-Human Interaction (TOCHI)*, 22(2), 1–24.

Lemay, D. J., Bazelais, P., & Doleck, T. (2021). Transition to online learning during the COVID-19 pandemic. *Computers in Human Behavior Reports*, 4. Retrieved from https://doi-org.silk.library.umass.edu/10.1016/j.chbr.2021.100130

McKenzie, L. (2021, April 27). Students want online learning options post-pandemic. *Inside Higher Ed*.

Merryfield, M. M. (2001). The paradoxes of teaching a multicultural education course online. *Journal of Teacher Education*, 52(4), 283–299. Retrieved from http://pascal-francis.inist.fr/vibad/index.php?action=search&terms=1164970

Miller, M. D. (2014). *Minds online: teaching effectively with technology*. Harvard University Press.

Montelongo, R., & Eaton, P. W. (2019). Online learning for social justice and inclusion: The role of technological tools in graduate student learning. *International Journal of Information and Learning Technology*, 37(1–2), 33–45. doi:10.1108/IJILT-11-2018-0135

Morris, S. M., & Stommel, J. (2018). *An urgency of teachers: The work of critical digital pedagogy*. Hybrid Pedagogy Inc.

National Academies of Sciences, Engineering, and Medicine. (2018). *How people learn II: Learners, contexts, and cultures*. The National Academies Press. doi:10.17226/24783

Noble, S. U. (2018). *Algorithms of oppression: How search engines reinforce racism*. New York University Press.

Nguyen, T. (2015). The effectiveness of online learning: Beyond no significant difference and future horizons. *Journal of Online Learning & Teaching*, 11(2), 309–319.

Olson, S., & Riordan, D. G. (2012). *Engage to excel: Producing one million additional college graduates with degrees in science, technology, engineering, and mathematics*. [Report to the President]. Executive Office of the President.

Palvia, S., Aeron, P., Gupta, P., Mahapatra, D., Parida, R., Rosner, R., & Sindhi, S. (2018). Online education: Worldwide status, challenges, trends, and implications. *Journal of Global Information Technology Management*, 21(4), 233–241. doi:10.1080/1097198X.2018.1542262

Reyes, M., & Segal, E. A. (2019). Globalization or colonization in online education: Opportunity or oppression? *Journal of Teaching in Social Work*, 39(4–5), 374–386. doi:10.1080/08841233.2019.1637991

Riggs, S. A., Linder, K. E., & IDEA Center. (2016). *Actively engaging students in asynchronous online classes*. IDEA Paper #64. Geneva: IDEA Center, Inc.

Shelton, K. (2021). "Techquity": Going from digital poverty to digital empowerment. *Educational Leadership*, 79(1), 39–42.

Stavredes, T. (2011). *Effective online teaching: Foundations and strategies for student success*. Jossey-Bass.

Stommel, J., Friend, C., & Morris, S. M. (2020). *Critical pedagogy: A collection*. Hybrid Pedagogy Inc. Retrieved from https://hybridpedagogy.org/critical-digital-pedagogy/

Tharp, S. D. (2017). Imagining flipped workshops: Considerations for designing online modules for social justice education workshops. *Multicultural Perspectives*, 19(3), 178–184. doi:10.1080/15210960.2017.1335081

Turpin, C. A. (2007). Feminist praxis, online teaching, and the urban campus. *Feminist Praxis*, 18(1), 9–27.

Ukpokodu, O. N. (2008). Teachers' reflections on pedagogies that enhance learning in an online course on teaching for equity and social justice. *Journal of Interactive Online Learning*, 7(3), 227–255. Retrieved from http://www.ncolr.org/jiol

Williamson, B., Eynon, R., & Potter, J. (2020). Pandemic politics, pedagogies and practices: Digital technologies and distance education during the coronavirus emergency. *Learning, Media and Technology*, 45(2), 107–114.

Woodley, X., Hernandez, C., Parra, J., & Negash, B. (2017). Celebrating difference: Best practices in culturally responsive teaching online. *TechTrends: For Leaders in Education & Training*, 61(5), 470. Retrieved from https://doi-org.silk.library.umass.edu/10.1007/s11528-017-0207-z

Woodley, X., Mucundanyi, G., & Lockard, M. (2017). Designing counter-narratives: Constructing culturally responsive curriculum online. *International Journal of Online Pedagogy and Course Design*, 7(1), 43–56.

12

Critical Self-Knowledge for Social Justice Educators

Lee Anne Bell, Diane J. Goodman, and Rani Varghese *

INTRODUCTION

What do we need to know about ourselves in order to teach about social justice issues and interact thoughtfully, sensitively, and effectively with participants and the broader communities and institutions in which we teach? Chapter 3: Design and Facilitation introduces instructors[1] to six dimensions in the design and facilitation of social justice courses and workshops: students/participants, instructors/facilitators, curriculum/content, pedagogy, classroom/workshop climate and group dynamics, and the broader context. In this chapter, we focus on who we are as instructors/facilitators as central to social justice education. We explore how our own social identities and dominant and subordinate statuses affect the way we engage with learners and the critical self-knowledge we need to be effective social justice educators.

While the focus of this chapter is on face-to-face learning, we recognize that remote teaching and facilitation offer both similar and unique opportunities and challenges. Facilitators need self-knowledge in both situations, yet the different contexts may affect how students see us and how we engage with them. (Chapter 11: SJE Online explores such online teaching issues in depth.)

SITUATING OURSELVES

Our particular and unique personalities, family backgrounds, life histories, and educational training (to name a few) impact both *who we are* and *how we appear* in a classroom or workshop. To understand what we need to know about ourselves to be more effective social justice educators, we consider how we are situated in the classroom and broader society, using the lenses of social identities, positionalities, and related privileges and disadvantages. While our approaches as educators cannot be reduced to these factors, they play a significant and complex role in shaping our sense of self and our experiences and responses in workshops and classrooms.

INTERSECTING SOCIAL IDENTITIES AND POSITIONALITY

Our social identities based on race, ethnicity, gender, sexuality, class, religion, age, nationality, (dis)ability, and primary language(s), along with socialization in our families and communities, shape our cultural orientations, perspectives, and behaviors and position us in particular ways in relation to social justice content and pedagogical processes.

DOI: 10.4324/9781003005759-14

PERSONAL EXPERIENCE OF SOCIAL IDENTITIES

In conventional classrooms or training spaces, where content or pedagogy may not take into account social justice principles, the facilitator's constellation of social and cultural identities often remains in the background. In the social justice classroom, social identity is central to the content, and who we are often is more in the foreground. We may be more or less aware of different aspects of our identity and how they affect our capacity to be effective social justice educators. We can reflect on the following:

- What aspects of my social identities are most/least important to me?
- Which of my social identities are most/least salient in different contexts?
- How are my social identities "read" and reacted to by others?
- With which social identities am I most/least comfortable?
- How do my different social identities affect and interact with each other? Where are the alignments or tensions among my different social identities in different contexts?

Our social identities do not operate in isolation from each other. Nor do we live as individuals removed from our social group memberships and our positioning within the social, historical, and political landscape in relation to other social groups. Although the three authors of this chapter identify similarly in terms of gender, we are positioned differently based on other aspects of our identities, underscoring that we embody our intersecting social identities simultaneously (Collins, 2008; Crenshaw, 1989, 1993).

As a white, middle-aged, full professor, I am more likely to be treated as an expert in my field. When I initially asked my undergraduates to call me by my first name, instead of the title "Professor" typical at my new institution, only the white male undergraduates felt comfortable doing so.

(Lee)

Even though I am white, upper-middle-class, and got good academic preparation, it has only been as I've gotten older with many years of experience that I have felt more confident and more respected by others.

(Diane)

As a South Asian woman who gets "read" as younger than my actual age, I find myself at the beginning of the semester listing my degrees, the schools I've attended, and my years of experience in order to get students to buy into the course and the topics that I am teaching.

(Rani)

The following examples from the book authors and other colleagues further illustrate how our racial or ethnic groups, class status, gender identity, religious affiliation, disabilities, and age are linked and impact how we show up in the classroom and how students see and interact with us.

In classes, I am always aware that I am a Muslim woman. When I bring up my religion, I become aware of the stereotypes people have. For example, assumptions that I'm oppressed or have always worn a hijab (I've never worn one). Or, questions like, "How is her husband allowing her to work?"

(Hind)

I'm multiracial, Carmel Indigenous, and white. Being white-passing, I have lots of stuff that comes up around, "When do I identify as white or multiracial or not," "How early do I cue it?" When I do land acknowledgements, I anticipate that how people will read me is also very place based—in AZ or FL I am rarely read as white, but in New England and Iowa, I am absolutely read as white. In training/teaching, racial fluidity is incredibly challenging for participants.

(Rachel W.)

As a chronically ill person teaching an ableism workshop, I disclosed being trans at the beginning. At the end, when I asked, "What stood out for you?" one student said: "This is the first time I ever met a trans adult." And I'm thinking, "This whole time that's what you've been thinking, that's what stands out for you? What did you learn about ableism?" I realized I need to be clear about my focus and how to mention being trans without making it the most salient.

(Davey)

IMPACT OF SOCIAL IDENTITIES AND POSITIONALITY ON OUR COMPETENCE AS SOCIAL JUSTICE EDUCATORS

Understanding who we are also means acknowledging our positionality in relation to systems of domination/subordination. How do our dominant and marginalized identities affect what and how we teach or facilitate?

Each of us has varying levels of *self-awareness*, *knowledge*, and *critical consciousness* about different forms of oppression. Awareness of our social identities and positionality vis-à-vis the experiences of others and our knowledge of systems of oppression and social justice content are important to consider. We will likely have explored some social justice topics deeply, while others we may understand more superficially. We may have relationships with and insight into the lives of individuals from some social identity groups but have had little exposure to the realities of other groups. We may have worked hard on rooting out our stereotypes and assumptions about people from certain social/cultural groups but still carry unconscious biases about others. Questions to consider include:

- With which issues of oppression do I feel most/least knowledgeable?
- Which topics or isms do I feel most/least comfortable teaching?
- Which individuals from which social groups do I feel I educate most/least effectively?

By asking such questions, we can recognize how our positions of advantage and disadvantage across different forms of oppression may enhance and impede our efforts and can identify areas where we need to do more work. Social identity development theory is one helpful way to reflect on our self-knowledge since where we are in our identity development influences how we intellectually understand and emotionally respond to particular social topics and interpersonal dynamics in the classroom (Hardiman & Jackson, 1992; Helms, 2020; Sue, Sue, Neville, & Smith, 2019).

Instructors who are early in their process of social identity development may not be ready to teach about social justice issues where they lack in-depth knowledge of the subject, have not gained awareness of their internalized assumptions or ability to critique dominant narratives that support a particular form of oppression, or lack the confidence to be teaching the material. Consider these examples:

- A cisgender instructor, new to transgender issues, is tentative about addressing transgender concerns and stumbles as they try to find the right language.

- A white facilitator's self-consciousness about her racial identity and authority to speak on racial issues makes her reluctant to question an inaccurate statement about race made by a participant of color.
- A secular Jew who has given little thought to their Jewish identity is unprepared to address the questions and challenges Jewish students raise about the intersections of antisemitism, racism, and white privilege.

Some instructors at early points in their process may find it especially challenging to manage feelings such as anger, guilt, or frustration and may be more likely to react emotionally to participant comments or behaviors and lack the patience or compassion to work with them empathically and effectively. This dynamic can occur whether we are in the dominant or subordinated group or working with people from our own or different social identity groups.

Early in my teaching about racism, when I was still grappling with guilt about being white, I sometimes found myself feeling disdainful and judgmental towards other white participants, in ways that interfered with my effectiveness. As I became clearer about my own white identity and my responsibility to educate other white people about racism, I was able to be more empathic about their struggles and more effective in helping them engage with the issues.

(Lee)

When I first started teaching about sexism, I found myself being activated by women in the class who were adamant that sexism was not an issue for "their generation." Over time, I was able to ask these women questions about why they didn't think sexism was relevant for them rather than bombard them with endless examples to try to get them to change their mind.

(Rani)

As we gain greater awareness and progress through our own social identity development around different issues, we can be more conscious and purposeful in addressing participants who are at various stages in their own learning. Often the intensity of our reactions diminishes and we can more skillfully address situations that arise.

Certain identities may be more salient depending on where we are in our development *across* forms of oppression. Sometimes when we are deeply involved with one identity or inequality, it can be more difficult to attend to other social identities or forms of oppression. As one instructor shared, "I know it's really important that I'm white, but right now I'm dealing with coming out as a lesbian!" Often we are not even aware that we are overlooking the significance of our other social identities.

Reflecting on our process of social identity development can help us relate to the feelings and challenges students/participants may be facing as they move through their own social identity development with different issues of oppression. We can share how we have dealt with oppressive conditioning at different stages so as to continue to grow. When educators model self-awareness about our identities, gaps in knowledge and consciousness, and ongoing commitment to learning, we are more likely to garner trust and respect from students. Transparency is especially critical for educators from advantaged groups working with individuals from disadvantaged groups who may withhold trust until they see evidence that the facilitator is aware of their own social location(s) vis-à-vis what marginalized groups experience. As we become more comfortable with our own development across the range of identities, we can be more authentic and teach with greater clarity, empathy, and effectiveness.

Members of dominant groups are generally less conscious of our privileges and of the disadvantages and oppression experienced by members of marginalized groups since dominant identities and experiences are so normalized they can be harder to recognize. The culture of higher education and most organizations in the US tends to take for granted white, Western, heterosexual, middle- and upper-class norms that may or may not match the cultural styles and social experiences of participants. Our familiarity and comfort with these norms may vary depending on the mix of our social identities and dominant/subordinated statuses. Examples of how we can reinforce norms that marginalize participants include:

- A cisgender and able-bodied facilitator does not consider the location of gender-neutral or accessible bathrooms that may be needed by trans or disabled participants.
- An upper-middle-class, able-bodied instructor assigns expensive textbooks and requires students to attend a local theater performance or museum exhibit without considering accessible transportation for those with disabilities or the impact of book, transportation, and ticket costs on those with limited means.
- A heterosexual instructor uses only heteronormative examples or assumes all participants are in heterosexual romantic relationships.

After reviewing active listening skills, including eye contact (with the caveat that this varies for different ethnic/cultural groups), a student on the autism spectrum told me he experienced that as an ableist norm that does not consider how eye contact may be difficult and uncomfortable for people who are neurodivergent.

(Diane)

I am aware of universal design and the need for audio and closed captions in Zoom. Yet, students still have to remind me of their needs. Often I just get so busy I take able-bodied norms for granted.

(James)

Instructors from dominant groups are also often less informed about the history and lived experiences of people from marginalized groups. Such lack of knowledge can lead to limited perspectives or leaving out information and views that are central to a social justice curriculum. It is not surprising that people from marginalized groups more often notice omissions and push to have their experiences and voices included:

- People of Color have to fight for their histories and realities to be recognized as important and accurately reflected, especially in courses that are not exclusively about race.
- LGBTQ+ (lesbian, gay, bisexual, transgender, queer, plus others) students have been the ones to spearhead efforts to have their experiences and oppression included in diversity and social justice courses and workshops.
- Discussions of sexism, patriarchy, and reproductive justice may not acknowledge the experiences of trans and nonbinary people.

During a workshop, a Deaf participant objected to having deafness considered a disability because for her deafness is a culture. This was an important perspective for me and the class to learn about.

(Diane)

In teaching about race, I often share my experience as a Black man but find myself sometimes buying into the Black/white binary. After one class, an Indigenous student sent me an email naming the microaggressions they experienced across their graduate studies and resources for how to integrate issues of colonialism into the curriculum.

(Mike)

Sometimes, our marginalized statuses can make us more aware of and sensitive to issues faced by others from our social group.

As someone who grew up working class and is a first-generation academic, I am intentional about discussing graduate school with undergraduates I teach. Many of them are first generation, so I want to dispel the idea that this is not a route for them and to explicitly encourage graduate school as a possibility they can consider for themselves.

(Rani)

As a first-gen, immigrant, working-class student and then parent, I felt lost at times and have a lot of empathy and compassion for my students. I realize not all students have support to just focus on their studies and may have many other responsibilities. I want them to be transparent and honest with me so I can be flexible.

(Romina)

While facilitators from marginalized groups have some first-hand knowledge of oppression, none of us is an expert on everything there is to know about our own social group(s). Even when well informed about a form of oppression we experience, if we are not also knowledgeable about other forms of oppression, we cannot effectively see and address how these issues intersect.

As an African American facilitator who is male and cisgender, I may not be aware of or account for Black trans, working-class, or differently abled participants and assume that "the Black experience" is the same for all.

(Mike)

While it can be helpful to focus on one social identity at a time when we are in the process of learning, we ideally want to become aware of our role in all forms of oppression. To be most effective, we need to understand how our intersecting identities and positionalities affect our social identity development process. Undoubtedly, we will have varying degrees of awareness of different identities and will need to continue increasing our self-awareness and critical consciousness across all forms of inequality as we grow over time.

I share with students that I didn't have to confront the ways in which I was privileged as a Christian until later in college because most people assume I am Hindu or Muslim. I use this example to illustrate my awareness about the complexity of identity, that I can simultaneously get "read" ethnically and religiously in a subordinate way but experience privilege because of my affinity to Christianity. Some of my students who don't feel "privileged," but are part of dominant social identity groups, can relate to this example.

(Rani)

As a Black, Christian, heterosexual cisgender woman, an important part of my own learning has been to recognize the ways I have internalized oppression and how it permeates my consciousness without my awareness. For example, learning to confront the homophobia at the heart of my own religious tradition has been vital to being able to support students who are seeking to learn about heterosexism and homophobia while remaining loyal to their own religious beliefs.

(Barbara)

RECOGNIZING OUR BIASES AND STEREOTYPES

We all have biases, both recognized and unrecognized. Like our students, we have internalized assumptions and stereotypes about our own and other social groups through our societal conditioning. As facilitators, we need to recognize that our perspectives are inevitably partial and shaped by our social locations and that none of us stand outside or above the systems about which we teach.

Implicit or unconscious bias can be insidious, affecting perceptions of behavior, expectations for achievement, evaluation, and likelihood to mete out punishment (Eberhardt, 2019; Chugh, 2018; Banaji & Greenwald, 2013). Microaggressions (the commonplace, persistent, and often unintentional negative slights toward people from marginalized groups) are another way biases reveal themselves and can harm others in profound ways (Huber & Solórzano, 2015; Torino, Rivera, Capodilupo, Nadal, & Sue, 2019; Solórzano, Ceja, & Yosso, 2000; Sue & Spanierman, 2020). To ensure we do not unwittingly perpetuate or allow microaggressions and bias in our classes or workshops, we must consciously examine our own assumptions and recognize how they may shape interactions with participants in damaging ways we may not consciously intend.

During a fishbowl activity where different ethnic/racial groups talked about their specific experiences of race and racism, the Native American affinity group was listed to go last, resulting in those students having the least amount of time to talk, literally enacting structural racism, where Indigenous voices and perspectives are silenced or made invisible. In my next class, it was critical that I named what my co-instructor and I had unconsciously done and the ways we, as a white woman and South Asian woman, could still engage in oppressive behaviors after having taught about race and racism for years.

(Rani)

Whenever someone tells me they are very religious, I always want to know where they are coming from. It brings up negative feelings I have about religious fanatics—that they are narrow minded and think they are right and everyone else is wrong. I always have to check myself, remind myself of amazing people who go to synagogue, church, or mosque every week and who aren't fanatics.

(Hind)

In one class I thought a young man of color was disengaged and said to him, "That's not appropriate." Later I thought (as a white woman), "Why did I say that to him? Maybe he had a bad night. Why did I feel I had to employ my authority at that moment?" Then I wondered, "What kind of experiences has he had with authority figures?" Ever since, I have taken the stance of "Hey are you okay . . . what's going on with you?" It opens doors for those who do have something going on, or even for those who are zoning out for a moment. I have used that to check my assumptions about who is disengaged.

(Rachel B.)

There are innumerable ways prejudices, stereotypes, and assumptions can show up. An instructor may treat students as "experts" or representative of their whole group rather than as individuals who enact their experiences as members of that group in a range of ways. For example:

- Expecting a student from Colombia or Ecuador to know about the Mexican holiday Cinco de Mayo, not recognizing the variety of national, cultural, and historical experiences among people who are defined as Latina/o/x in the US;
- Requesting that a Jewish participant explain a particular Jewish holiday, assuming all Jews are knowledgeable about Judaism.

Facilitators may also unconsciously act on the pervasive societal messages about the superiority of dominant groups and inferiority of subordinated groups. For example:

- A facilitator pays more attention to male participants or gives more credence to their comments;
- An instructor takes a paternalistic stance that discourages independence and risk-taking by a student with a disability;
- A faculty member exhibits lower academic or intellectual expectations, such as being surprised or dubious when a working-class student hands in a particularly well-written paper.

While it can be unnerving to have our prejudices or unconscious biases revealed, we can learn to appreciate such missteps as important learning opportunities.

> *When I mixed up the names of two Black women in a class, one of them said she felt it was a racist microaggression. I had to resist the urge to explain why I made that mistake. Instead, I took a breath and apologized, saying I understood why she was offended and would commit to not do that again.*
>
> *(Diane)*

> *As a Black Latina immigrant from Venezuela who lived in the Northeast, when I started teaching in New Mexico, I assumed anyone who spoke Spanish and appeared to me as Latinx would identify as Mexican or Chicana. Some students would correct me and tell me that they proudly identified as Hispanic (with relatives from Spain) or as Spanish. I realized my arrogance and lack of curiosity about learning the history of the place.*
>
> *(Romina)*

We know that recognizing and rooting out deeply socialized prejudices and practices is a difficult and long-term learning process. When we demonstrate willingness to acknowledge, get feedback, reflect on our assumptions and biases (intentional or not), and make efforts to correct them, we model for students that they, too, can be open to constructive feedback, will survive being challenged, and, with practice and persistence, will develop more thoughtful and socially just ways to respond. Research suggests that effective ways to mitigate unconscious bias include: expanding knowledge of and contact with different groups, monitoring thoughts and biases, engaging in perspective-taking, and building empathy (Staat, 2013). This is important ongoing work since acting on unconscious bias only undermines our educational effectiveness and efforts for social justice.

INTERPERSONAL AND GROUP DYNAMICS

Self-knowledge of our interpersonal and communication styles is essential for understanding interactions with participants and how we interpret and respond to group dynamics.

INTERPERSONAL AND COMMUNICATION STYLES

Our socialization and cultural norms influence our interpersonal and communication style. Some social/cultural groups view it as improper and inappropriate to share or solicit personal information, while in others such sharing is considered appropriate and valued. Some facilitators (and participants) are more comfortable with a more personal, fluid, and experiential approach that draws on storytelling, sharing feelings and experiences, and using imagery and metaphors, while others prefer a formal, linear approach to teaching/learning that focuses on facts and figures. Such cultural norms can influence how an instructor teaches, interacts with, and is perceived by participants.

> *I have found that my sarcastic sense of humor and direct communication style, a product of my New York area Jewish upbringing, can be perceived as harsh to those unaccustomed to that style.*
>
> *(Diane)*

- A fast-talking trainer may make it difficult for a hearing-impaired participant who is reading lips or using an interpreter or for people for whom English is a second language.
- An instructor who requests eye contact from students may be perceived as intrusive or insensitive by those raised in cultures where eye contact, especially with authority figures, is considered inappropriate or disrespectful.

The constellation of a facilitator's dominant and subordinated status may also affect how the same behavior gets read differently.

- A soft-spoken man may be viewed positively as gentle and approachable, while a soft-spoken woman may be seen as unassertive and weak.
- A white woman who speaks strongly may be seen as confident and authoritative, while a Black woman may be seen as angry and strident.

As we gain greater awareness of our social identities and related interpersonal styles and orientations, we can better appreciate how we may be perceived or misperceived by participants, adjust accordingly, and be prepared to deal with their reactions more skillfully.

HOW WE NOTICE AND RESPOND TO GROUP DYNAMICS

The *content* of social justice education provides information about enduring historical injustice and inequitable patterns and practices that are normalized in mainstream society. It also includes information about struggles for justice and possibilities for change. The *process* of social justice education involves managing the individual, interpersonal, and group dynamics that arise as we and our participants, with divergent levels of awareness, knowledge, and experience, grapple with social justice issues. Engagement with information that affirms or challenges what individuals have thought to be true generates feelings of anger, shock, guilt, disbelief, sadness, and powerlessness as they confront the enormity and pervasiveness of oppression. While group dynamics are important in any learning situation, in the social justice classroom/workshop, they take on added weight. Group members must deal with emotional reactions and negotiate asymmetric power relations and historically and culturally embedded patterns of interaction—whether tacit or explicit, acknowledged or not. Thus, social justice education requires attention to *both* content and process.

Facilitators who have spent time exploring how to respond to process-level issues will be better prepared to address rather than be taken off guard or unable to handle them when they arise. For example, what do we do when a participant makes an offensive comment and all eyes turn to us to see how we will respond? The more we have reflected on our automatic feelings and reactions in such situations (fright, exposure, inadequacy, shutting down, freezing), the more able we will be to respond in thoughtful and appropriate ways, rather than ineffectively avoiding and moving past the moment.

I was facilitating a fishbowl discussion on the film Race: The Power of an Illusion *when an African American woman tearfully shared her deep sadness at realizing the structural barriers she had always taken as personal. When a white participant interrupted to say it was the same for her as a working-class white person and thus not about race, I could feel the air leave the room. I paused the conversation to examine the dynamics of what had just happened. We were able to listen more carefully to each speaker and unpack relations of dominance and subordination reflected in the interaction. Had the conversation continued without fully discussing the dynamics involved, we would have reproduced the very dynamics of racism we were trying to challenge.*

(Lee)

I do a guided meditation of a world without gender. A young trans woman sat me down after and said, "For me and some of the other trans folks, it was traumatizing." As a cisgender person, I recognized that the activity was recreating oppressive experiences trans people have, so I redid the intro to highlight that the issue is with structures of cisgender normativity and not with gender per se. Later, for my dissertation, I interviewed that student. One of my standard questions was, "Have you ever had a conflict with a professor in a gender studies class?" and she said no. The student had totally forgotten about it, but it had stayed with me. She then said, "I don't remember the actual incident. What I remember is I could sit down with you and talk about it."

(Rachel B.)

What we notice and how we respond to interpersonal dynamics are to a large extent shaped by our families and communities of origin and the early injunctions we internalized about what is and is not appropriate. Families and communities have different norms around eye contact, touch, speaking patterns, expression of humor and emotion, and degree of directness and indirectness in conversation and gestures (DuPraw & Axner, 1997; Sue & Sue, 2013). These messages affect how we respond to both verbal and nonverbal behavior. Those raised with familial or cultural norms that deem it inappropriate to comment on others' interactions or conduct may have a difficult time doing so in the classroom. For example:

- When a participant makes a rude face while another participant is speaking, a facilitator raised to ignore nonverbal cues may fail to address facial expressions and other nonverbal behaviors that impact relationships in the group in ways that interfere with learning.

- A trainer who was taught not to notice race or was "shushed" when noticing people with disabilities may be uncomfortable discussing differences and may prefer to highlight similarities among people, thus avoiding important conversations about difference and discrimination.
- A female instructor raised to be "polite" and not interrupt may find it challenging to intervene when a participant is dominating or derailing the discussion.

Our ability to notice and respond to interpersonal dynamics is also affected by our various social group identities and relative positions of dominance and subordination. For example:

- White people are socialized to view the world from a white normative frame and thus may not notice the racial dynamics when a white participant interrupts or minimizes comments by peers of color.
- Native English speakers may ignore or resist calling on participants for whom English is a second language, further marginalizing them in class discussions.

Facilitators who have not examined our own socialization may find it difficult to openly and effectively address racial, gender, sexuality, class, and other dynamics in ways that facilitate rather than impede learning. Examining our own social identities and cultural conditioning can help us be more conscious and willing to notice and name interactions we have been taught to ignore, even when we feel uncomfortable doing so. We can learn to address group dynamics directly, whether naming what is going on, asking clarifying questions, providing time for people to reflect silently on the situation, or opening up a discussion about the impact of language and behavior and how people are feeling. (See Chapter 2: Pedagogical Foundations and Chapter 3: Design and Facilitation for additional strategies.) Greater awareness of our socialization will help us facilitate group dynamics in ways that effectively interrupt oppressive interactions and promote learning.

HOW WE RESPOND TO EMOTIONAL INTENSITY

Strong emotions are inevitably generated when we explore issues of social injustice, encounter information that challenges deeply held views and convictions, and discuss historical and contemporary examples that restimulate frustration and anger at painful experiences of subordination or our implication in others' oppression. We have been shaped by the same damaging, misinformed view of the world as our participants, and, like them, we respond to learning about injustice emotionally as well as cognitively.

For those of us socialized to show expertise and convey confidence and certainty in what we know, acknowledging the affective (emotional) parts of learning may be challenging. Many of us have not been prepared to deal with emotionally laden content. Moreover, confronting the often fraught emotions raised by issues of injustice, and acknowledging that we don't have all the answers, challenges how many of us have been groomed, especially in the academy. How we personally handle emotional intensity affects our ability to allow and handle emotion in the classroom or workshop in constructive ways. We can prepare ourselves by examining and reflecting on those emotions with which we feel most and least comfortable and how we came to these:

I grew up in a household with immigrant parents where I was taught to "keep to myself" and avoid conflict. Thus, in social justice classrooms where constructive conflict is encouraged and may be a part of dialogue, I've had to re-examine my comfort or discomfort with conflict.

(Rani)

I grew up in a family where I remember elders yelling at each other in good fun as they discussed the issues of the day. I now realize that I am not unnerved by conflict or strong voices and emotions.

(Diane)

I have had to examine how anger and other intense emotions were handled in my household to get a better understanding of my current response to emotions in the classroom. Quite apart from my professional training to be carefully neutral and suppress any display of emotion, I was raised in a household where feelings were denied until they erupted. My response has been to deny feelings any place in discussions, and especially to disallow loud voices. Learning to listen to loud voices and to encourage others to be receptive to them has been important for my ability to facilitate authentic discussions. Reminding learners that loud voices sometimes indicate that a person cares a lot about an issue can provide a context that allows "heated" discussions to take place.

(Barbara)

Being raised in a family or culture where feelings are not openly expressed further reinforces professional training to be "neutral" and suppress the display of emotions—responses that are usually counterproductive to facilitating authentic discussion. For example, a facilitator who is uncomfortable with tears may refocus discussion when a student starts crying while speaking passionately, rather than accept the tears and tune into what the person is saying. On the other hand, being raised in a familial or cultural context where feelings are stated bluntly and directly may clash with participant beliefs that such directness is rude or improper. Those socialized to read strong emotions as hostile or to be feared may withdraw or shut down in the face of such emotions. Even instructors/facilitators who are comfortable with emotion may not always know how to effectively work with it in a class or workshop.

Self-reflection becomes a critical tool for understanding our reactions and developing the ability to respond to emotions honestly and constructively rather than avoid them. We can become more conscious of feelings we find hardest to address, especially those we tend to avoid, distort, or fear. We can learn to moderate automatic first reactions or interpretations and consider how emotional expressiveness can be a reflection of cultural and familial styles of expression that differ from ours. For example, white people may read People of Color as "angry" when they are simply expressing strong feelings. White facilitators who are aware of this pattern can be more conscious and open to participants who express themselves in this way. Men often read women as "irrational" when they are expressing emotion directly. Male facilitators who have examined their own response to emotional expressiveness can be more respectful and empathic of other styles of response.

Emotional reactions may also be affected by dominant/subordinated status. It is common for those in the dominant group to take a more intellectualized stance in discussions of injustices we have been taught to ignore or accept as normal. In fact, one of the ways privilege works is through insulating people in dominant groups from the stress of dealing with the uncomfortable topics of oppression. It is much harder for someone who is directly targeted by oppression to have a dispassionate view. Acknowledging one's own feelings of outrage at injustices our group faces can help a facilitator be more empathic and understanding of participants from other groups who react strongly. We can proactively help those from dominant groups understand and respect the intensity their peers from subordinated groups feel. Learning to recognize different patterns of expression can provide a frame for developing more comfort with emotional or "heated" discussions and can help us respond in ways that support learning from such encounters.

I actually don't really try to control emotions, but I do try to manage outlets for expressing them through dyads or journals, for example. If people are upset, I say, "Be upset! Be angry, whatever, and we'll just notice it." I just acknowledge that it's part of the process.

(Sharon)

IDENTIFYING AND DEALING WITH "HOT BUTTONS"

Dealing with comments and behaviors that "push our buttons" or that instantly spark emotion in us is a common concern for social justice educators. Being emotionally charged happens when we get "hooked" or have an unexpected, intense reaction to a situation or person (Obear, 2013, 2016). When we feel a rush of emotion, it can become harder to pay attention to what is going on in the moment while we are caught up with our own internal thoughts, feelings, and physical sensations.

People from marginalized communities usually have a long history with and heightened sensitivity to negative cues (language as well as verbal and nonverbal behaviors) that signal oppressive attitudes. They have been subjected to, suffered from, discussed, and thought about such cues throughout the course of their lives and so are highly tuned to note them in the behavior and language used by members of the dominant group. Such cues add to the traumatic load from intergenerational and current experiences with oppression that people from marginalized communities encounter on an ongoing basis (Menakem, 2017). Dominant group members, on the other hand, are often oblivious to the effects of their verbal and nonverbal communication on people from subordinated groups. Information that contradicts their normative assumptions or feedback that exposes the impact of their behavior on others often activates strong emotional reactions. Thus, the potential for breakdown in communication, hurt feelings, defensiveness, and recrimination can be high.

Since we as facilitators are not immune to such reactions, we need to recognize the comments and signals to which we are most susceptible. As noted previously, where we are in the process of our own social identity development around different forms of oppression can affect how likely we are to be emotionally charged in particular situations. Facilitators who are members of a marginalized group may understandably find it difficult to listen to hurtful stereotypes and attitudes they have been confronted with all their lives.

I was doing a pre-planned role-play about addressing a homophobic comment. When we were done, my co-presenter, a lesbian, who was supposed to lead the discussion, sat there immobilized. She later explained that she was unexpectedly overwhelmed with emotion watching that interaction.

(Kathy)

I teach social justice education from a position of hope and belief that our efforts can make a difference in the elimination of oppression. I was co-teaching an antisemitism course with a Jewish colleague who said she did not think antisemitism would ever be entirely eliminated and that other Holocausts were and are possible. Before I could catch them, tears coursed down my face as I felt the enormity of the task before me and the challenge to my own optimism. Several students later told me this was a powerful learning moment for them.

(Barbara)

Other situations where emotional charges may arise include:

- A facilitator who grew up in poverty may want to lash out when participants talk about a fancy vacation or second home, oblivious to the privilege of those experiences.
- A facilitator with a disability may bristle at listening to participants express pity and condescension toward people with disabilities after encountering these sentiments over and over in their own life.
- A well of deep sadness may overcome the Native American facilitator when non-Native students assert that there are no Native communities outside of reservations.

Facilitators from dominant groups also can be emotionally charged by situations in the classroom or workshop. Questions/reactions from students may activate their own fears of being seen as ignorant, incompetent, or prejudiced; stimulate unresolved issues in their own identity development; or reveal their lack of awareness of the privileges they receive as members of the dominant group:

- A white facilitator may feel panic when challenged by a participant of color about a racial issue, feeling ignorant and exposed.
- A professor who is a straight white man may react angrily when women students frame him as the "oppressor," feeling invalidated for all the work he has done on feminist issues.
- An instructor who grew up wealthy but has been committed to addressing income inequality may feel embarrassment and disdain when upper-class students express classist sentiments, reminding her of her own struggles.

I know that I am emotionally charged by participants who dominate conversation and seem unable to accurately hear what others are saying. I think this comes from my own experiences as a child feeling unheard or misinterpreted by the adults around me and helpless to change the situation. The more I have thought about this issue, the better able I have been to acknowledge when I am feeling these emotions and to respond in a way that is constructive rather than defensive and emotionally loaded.

(Lee)

We can notice and respond to emotional charges on several levels: We can reflect on our own reactions to what is occurring in the moment: "Why am I having such a strong response to this person or comment? What feelings does it stimulate for me?" On another level, we can consider how the individual who stimulated our emotional reaction might be thinking or feeling and shift the frame to figure it out. Questions such as, "What prompted this behavior?" "What's really going on for this individual?" and "How can I help them try out a new perspective?" may help us respond more productively. Last, if we are feeling emotionally charged, others may be as well, so we also need to consider the effect on other members of the group. Not only do we need to try to gain clarity and composure about our own reaction and consider how to respond to the person whose behavior or words stimulated charged feelings, but we need to assess what is happening for others in the group.

In a discussion about sexual assault, when victim-blaming comments were made, I felt overwhelmed. How could I engage those specific students effectively, as well as deal with the likelihood that others in the room were survivors of gender-based violence and might be retraumatized by those comments?

(Rani)

As a Black facilitator of a People of Color dialogue on racism, I had to confront two Black students who were mimicking speaking in an Asian language while an Asian student was talking. I had to overcome my feelings of shock that it was Black students who were actively participating in racist behaviors.

(Mike)

In situations where we experience a rush of charged feelings, there are numerous options we can take. We can pause, draw a deep breath, and try to refocus our attention on the situation at hand. We can utilize self-talk to help us regain composure and shift our reaction. We can acknowledge the tensions of the moment and suggest a short break or have people sit, reflect, and free-write for a few minutes and then come back and share their thoughts with a partner or with the group as a whole. We can pose questions to the group that help participants to process the situation in a reflective and thoughtful way. (Also see Chapter 3: Design and Facilitation for suggestions.)

Developing a support system of peers with whom we can discuss issues, share feelings, and get support can be extremely helpful. For example, meeting regularly with a colleague to debrief, and/or keeping a journal to note and analyze our feelings and reactions to certain statements or actions that push our buttons, can provide outlets for ongoing self-reflection. Analyzing how we typically react, and thinking through other possible responses ahead of time, provides more options for responding in thoughtful ways in the moment when our buttons are pushed.

In the beginning, I had strong emotional reactions (anger, frustration, fear/panic) but less and less after 17–18 years of doing my own work. A colleague and I have had hours of conversations about class issues. That was practice that translated into the classroom. Obviously we need to do reading and keep up with how things are changing, but it's an embodied practice talking to other people in our lives about the emotional challenges we experience.

(Rachel B.)

It's impossible to do this work alone; it's not meant to be done alone. We need people to process with and get support from. I tell people, "Don't sign a contract unless there are two or three people you trust, respect and can be in the trenches with."

(Mike)

The more we stay open to our own internal process, the more insight we can gain into our feelings and reactions. Knowledge of what stimulates emotional charges in us helps us anticipate and even plan for them. This awareness allows us to get less hooked by particular actions and gives us more options for how to address various situations. An appreciation for the process we all go through in developing awareness about oppression can remind us to be patient when dealing with our frustrations and feelings toward participants and more present to what may be going on for our students so that we can respond to them with compassion and understanding.

NAVIGATING ISSUES OF COMPETENCY AND AUTHORITY IN INSTITUTIONS AND COMMUNITIES

Competency encompasses our knowledge of the content we teach and our ability to effectively convey relevant theories and concepts, as well as our ability to manage group dynamics and relationships with participants in ways that promote learning. Authority includes our ability to establish ourselves as credible and to use our position in strategic and effective ways to accomplish curricular goals. Our social identities and social locations affect both our felt and perceived competence and authority, and greater self-knowledge can help us deal with both internal and external challenges to our sense of efficacy as social justice educators. These dynamics can include navigating organizational cultures, norms, and rules as well as managing interactions with other members of the institution (colleagues, faculty, staff, administrators, students, or clients) and the larger community.

SELF AND OTHER PERCEPTION OF COMPETENCY AND AUTHORITY

Our social identities and social locations affect both how we experience ourselves as capable and authoritative, as well as how our competence and authority are viewed by others. Faculty of color, women, LGBTQ+ faculty, and other faculty from subordinated groups are often perceived as less authoritative, may experience resistance to course content, and face questions about their competency and authority in ways that members of the dominant group(s), whose competence and authority are assumed, do not (Amos, 2014; Jean-Marie, Grant, & Irby, 2014; Messner, 2000; Gutierrez y Muhs, Niemann, Gonzalez, & Harris, 2012; Niemann, Gutierrez y Muhs, & González, 2020; Tuitt, Hanna, Martinez, Salazar, & Griffin, 2009).

> As a faculty member of color, I have had to ask students to call me "Dr." or "Professor," refer explicitly to my educational training, and dress in a more formal manner to project authority even though the culture of the institutions where I've worked is one where faculty are called by their first names and the style of dress is much less formal.
>
> (Rani)

At times, being in the dominant group can work to our advantage:

> In an effort to be a strong ally to the LGBTQ+ community, I often talk about my heterosexual privilege and use examples of heterosexism. One student complained that I "talk about gays all the time" and asked to be moved to a different section. I faced no consequences but wonder if heterosexual privilege played a part—people knew I was married to a man. I wonder if it would have been different if I was LGBTQ+.
>
> (Romina)

Questions about our competency and authority are heightened when the course or training includes social justice content and pedagogy. Moving away from hierarchical, banking models and facilitating an interactive process that invites engagement, exploration, and critical analysis represents a different definition of competency and authority than the traditional one of content mastery and expertise (Brookfield, 2012; hooks, 1994; Maher & Tetreault, 2001). Utilizing social justice education pedagogy may raise additional concerns for instructors from marginalized groups. For example, a new young instructor may feel obligated to rely on PowerPoint in order to assert her authority rather than use interactive, learner-centered approaches that she believes are more effective for particular learning goals. Given these issues, it is important to think through and be able to articulate and support with confidence the philosophies that undergird our pedagogical decisions.

The interplay of race, class, gender, sexual orientation, age, ability, and other subordinated identities can impact how comfortable instructors feel acknowledging mistakes or gaps in knowledge when they often already get constructed as less competent. For example:

* An older instructor may find it difficult to acknowledge when he says something inaccurate because of fears that displaying uncertainty will be attributed to his age.
* A gay or lesbian instructor who has to weigh the risks of self-disclosure may not invite the further scrutiny that personal sharing may bring.
* An immigrant instructor who speaks with an accent may not want to reveal lack of knowledge of an issue for fear of being further invalidated.

Issues of authority become especially complicated for those with multiple subordinated identities. For example:

* An Asian American woman instructor in a class on race and racism may not be seen as having legitimate knowledge about the material or authority to speak on the subject matter because she's not Black.
* A gay Latino may be perceived as politicizing course content when he teaches about heterosexism and linguicism.
* A working-class African American teaching about race and racism in a predominantly white classroom may be perceived by students as dealing with his "personal problem" or "agenda."
* A woman instructor who uses a wheelchair may be patronized by students who fail to recognize her scholarly strengths and pedagogical skills.

Through the process of socialization, women are bombarded with messages about deferring to male authority, being "nice," and not seeing themselves as those with power and voice. Women who ultimately achieve positions of power may be pressured to embody a "male" style of leadership or distance themselves from other women. Students may evaluate and judge women faculty according to gender stereotypes.

> *I once co-taught with a woman professor who used examples of her experiences raising her daughter to illustrate sexism. She received feedback in her end-of-semester evaluations that the course was not theoretically grounded and too focused on personal narratives.*
>
> *(Rani)*

Or students may expect a woman faculty member to fulfill stereotypes, such as being more nurturing, and may push back when she does not.

> *A Latina faculty member at my institution was read by students as cold and distant because she resisted taking on a nurturing role and demanded hard work from her students.*
>
> *(Lee)*

Many times students are unaware of the stereotypes they project onto us, so we need to anticipate and work with both conscious and unconscious projections that are at play in the group. We especially need to be aware of how participants' projections can stimulate our vulnerabilities about competency and authority and our own internalized oppression (i.e., internalized racism, sexism, classism, etc.). Facilitators from subordinated groups may internalize the dominant group's ideology and accept their subordinated status as deserved, natural, or inevitable (Joseph & Williams, 2008; Niemann, 2012; Tappan, 2006). As a result, they may underestimate their abilities or second-guess their pedagogy and struggle with the "imposter phenomenon" (Collins, Price, Hanson, & Neaves, 2020; Edwards, 2019; Muradoglu, Horne, Hammond, Leslie, & Cimpian, 2021; Parkman, 2016). Instructors from dominant groups may question their right and legitimacy to speak about social justice issues. Facilitators from both dominant and subordinated positions need to continually try to distinguish between what is true about themselves and what are participant assumptions and projections.

> *I have colleagues who earned an advanced degree, who are from low-income backgrounds and the first in their families to go to college. They are particularly vulnerable to self-doubts about being smart enough or belonging in academia when they get critical feedback on a manuscript or a class that didn't go well.*
>
> *(Kathy)*

Many courses that address social justice content are seen as less rigorous and often characterized as "soft science" (DiAngelo & Sensoy, 2014). Instructors who teach social justice–related courses note that students often have the misconception that the course will be "easy." Students who feel entitled to an "easy A" may challenge the instructor's authority if they don't not receive the expected grade. Faculty who hold subordinated identities may be challenged more than faculty who hold privileged identities.

Being aware how we are constructed in the classroom, institution, and community can prepare us for some of the dynamics and challenges to our competency and authority. Self-knowledge about our own vulnerabilities and how we typically react to these challenges can enable us to develop ways to respond more skillfully and confidently and be more self-affirming. We should recognize that we do not have to be all-knowing or perfect and do not operate independent of the contexts in which we work. Projections and judgments are inevitable, and we need and deserve a network of people who can help us sort through the feedback we receive, discern what is useful, and support our ongoing growth and development as facilitators.

INSTITUTIONAL AND COMMUNITY CHALLENGES AND SUPPORT

One of the concerns about teaching from a social justice perspective is the institutional response when we depart from traditional formats and content. As we engage with social justice issues and experiential pedagogy, we often come into conflict with institutional norms of professed objectivity, authority, and professorial distance in ways that can undermine our confidence and in some cases jeopardize our positions. Instructors who are female and instructors of color often receive lower evaluations in courses, and those who teach courses about social justice often receive lower ratings than those who teach mainstream courses (Lazos, 2012; Messner, 2000; Pittman, 2010; Tusmith & Reddy, 2002). Faculty who choose to and/or are asked to teach social justice courses are frequently from underrepresented groups and often untenured. Thus, the most vulnerable groups take on the most difficult and institutionally risky teaching. Instructors from marginalized groups often face heightened challenges and frequently receive less institutional support than colleagues from dominant groups, especially in higher education.

> *A student's mother complained to the dean that her daughter's Latina professor (my colleague) was a bad teacher and that if she did not get the grade she "deserved" the mother would take it up the chain of command. What was powerful about this example was that while the dean was ultimately supportive, the faculty member felt interrogated and that she had to "prove" herself in ways not expected of white colleagues.*
>
> *(Lee)*

> *On campus I can't call it the LGBTQ+ Center, we have to call it the "Community Center" because of the homophobia in the Board of Directors. We also can't use "race" in titles of classes, we must use "multicultural."*
>
> *(Rachel W.)*

> *The invisible and emotional labor of Black faculty has been coined as the "Black tax." Because these conversations about social justice are not integral to the department or program, the same people do all the heavy lifting. When George Floyd happened, no one else would write a statement, so I had to write something. Who will talk to students . . . who is going to support these students? This additional work doesn't show up in contract or tenure reviews. More lip service to social justice happens than actually integrating these issues into their disciplines.*
>
> *(Mike)*

> *As a newly minted economics Ph.D., my first tenure track job was at a small liberal arts college. The school was very white, and there was much ado about hiring a Black Latina in the Economics Department. My office was next to the faculty kitchen. One day before classes started, one of the male faculty stopped by my open door to say hello and ask how I was doing. I said I was preparing and working hard. He proceeded to say, "You know Cruz, the kitchen is so clean . . . the kitchen has never been this clean. Are you cleaning the kitchen for us?" I responded, "I don't know what you are talking about . . . I don't even clean my own apartment with the workload I have here. I pay someone to clean at my place and I pay well because as a feminist economist I value reproductive labor." I took his comments to mean that he would never see me as his colleague or equal, that Black Latinas like me are house cleaners, nannies, sex workers, meant to serve "us, whites," not as professors, and that's where I existed in his racial imaginary. He knew I was a Ph.D. economist and a new assistant professor, and this is how he put me in "my place" or where he thought my place was, and he sat on the Tenure and Promotion Committee. My experience in academia hasn't changed much in the eight years since I finished my dissertation.*
>
> *(Cruz)*

Such institutional dynamics and risks are not limited to academe. In other contexts, such as human services, nonprofit, and community or business organizations, People of Color are often expected to formally or informally shoulder the Diversity, Equity, and Inclusion (DEI) work and the education of their colleagues, without additional compensation or training. Leaders of social justice training also can be invalidated as "too touchy feely" or "too political." Experiential approaches may be devalued as inappropriate or not serious, and the judgment and expertise of the facilitator may be questioned, especially when the facilitator is from a marginalized group. Facilitators who do not have traditional credentials or organizational status, or come from a lower socio-economic group than others in the organization, may be discounted as having "only personal experience" to offer.

Beyond the classroom or organization, instructors may have experiences within the community that further challenge their legitimacy. Ferrari (2020) writes of her experience of being mistaken for a "prostitute" and asked to leave when waiting in the lobby of a hotel where she was interviewing for a faculty position. She mentions how that experience followed her: "As an untenured Black woman, I am constantly reminded of the ways I don't fit, whether it's a colleague questioning my academic training or always being the 'voice of diversity' in a faculty meeting." Another Black faculty member shared on Twitter that she had been asked by campus security to show her campus ID as proof of residence after knocking on the door of her university housing. As only one of seven Black faculty in a college of arts and science that had a Black student body population of only 2%, she reports that her experience is consistent with other Black students and faculty who feel harassed by the police (Morgan, 2020).

How do instructors manage the burden of knowing that they are perceived first by their race, skin color, and gender expression rather than their talents, credentials, and the valuable contributions they can make? What are the vulnerabilities they navigate as they decide whether to share their stories publicly with peers and students? Naming systemic inequities when they occur and honoring what is true about ourselves is critical in order to cope and thrive. All people, but especially those from marginalized groups, need supportive friends and colleagues as well as mentors who can help them navigate such institutional challenges.

CO-FACILITATION ISSUES

Our self-awareness also affects how effectively we collaborate with another instructor/facilitator, especially when we represent different identity groups and dominant/marginalized statuses. *How we interact* as co-facilitators is at least as important as what we *say*. Our self-awareness affects how well we can model for participants equitable and respectful dynamics with our co-facilitator.

As we plan with a co-trainer, we can stay mindful of the impact of our personal and cultural styles, social locations, and preferred pedagogical approach to ensure that each person is having equitable input into developing the course or workshop. In the design process, we can watch for how we may be playing out power dynamics related to our social identities. We can assess if the design reflects and balances each other's styles, perspectives, and strengths and limitations (Kaplowitz, Griffin, & Seyka, 2019, ch. 7; Maxwell, Nagda, & Thompson, 2011; Ouellett & Fraser, 2005; Zúñiga, Nagda, Chesler, & Cytron-Walker, 2007). When co-facilitating with people who have different dominant and marginalized/subordinated identities, we can pay attention to how we may be enacting internalized dominance and internalized oppression (DiAngelo & Flynn, 2010). For example, people with dominant group identities may jump in unnecessarily, interrupt their co-facilitator, or take more time for their parts than was planned. Or they may overcompensate for their identities by "playing small."

I co-facilitated with a white man around the topic of sexism on campus where I felt like I was an impatient and overbearing facilitator. In checking in with my co-facilitator about what was going on, he realized that his fear of being seen as dominant was getting in his way of being authentic and speaking up.

(Rani)

Co-facilitation is the place that surfaces my biases the most. I witness all the ways anti-Blackness comes running at my Black co-facilitator and how much privilege and entitle-ment comes to me; the same with cisnormativity. It is the richest place to surface my uninterrogated assumptions and biases. Only because of the quality of the relationship can these missteps happen and not result in violent harm. Having space for missteps I make, I am able to take accountability. My co-facilitator knows that I will learn and do better.

(Rachel W.)

People with marginalized identities may hold back due to lack of confidence or back off from handling more challenging moments and let the other facilitator routinely take the lead. Given that facilitators have an intersectional mix of privileged and marginal-ized identities and may be addressing more than one form of oppression, these dynamics are not necessarily simple. We also need to be aware of when we may be colluding with participants' biases—for instance, by not addressing situations where students are talking to the man and ignoring the woman in a male/female team or when participants accept information from the white person but challenge the information presented by the Person of Color in a mixed-race team.

In training, my female Muslim partner typically starts first so as not to reinforce stereo-types of male domination in Arab culture. I also deflect questions to her to underscore that we are equal since males often want to talk to me. Once, watching a video of a workshop we did together on racism, we noticed how much more space she took. So in the ensuing workshop she held back, but participants then thought it was because of gender. The next day we openly discussed the racial and gender dynamics with the group.

(Abdul-Rahman)

Negotiating the various power dynamics can be complex. As a white, Jewish, straight woman, I have co-facilitated with Christian, gay, men of color and we both were trying to be mindful of how we were engaging with each other given our various social identi-ties and positionalities.

(Diane)

Our internalized sense of competence and authority, and how we are seen by students, colleagues, and the institution, affects the risks that different facilitators may be willing to take in terms of content shared, personal disclosure, and challenging students.

As a younger, less experienced Latina, I felt somewhat institutionally protected by regu-larly co-facilitating with a high-status, older white male faculty. The trust and knowl-edge built by our ongoing co-teaching relationship also allowed us to address and work through our interpersonal dynamics.

(Ana)

Knowing oneself and knowing one's co-facilitator allows for mutual support and the ability to model respectful and equitable dynamics. Moreover, when we know each other's hot buttons, we can be prepared to support each other in handling tension-filled moments when they arise.

CONCLUSION

Knowing ourselves as instructors and facilitators in social justice education is an ongoing process of exploration, challenge, new insights, and personal and professional growth. Self-examination about the effects of our socialization and experiences within systems of inequality ensures that we never take for granted the challenges of understanding systems of oppression and keeps us tuned into the struggles our participants may be facing. We are continually reminded that we all have areas of limited awareness, particularly where we are members of the advantaged group(s) and where we have not yet explored how our intersecting identities position us vis-à-vis other groups and contexts. We need to be vigilant and engage in self-reflection to challenge internalized oppression and discern what is true about ourselves. Networks of support and mentoring relationships help guide and sustain us in this process. When we can stay open to ongoing learning and accept the inevitable mistakes as we uncover new areas for growth, we show our students that they can do so as well. Most crucially, self-reflection and self-awareness help us take the long view needed to sustain our commitments over a lifetime and not retreat from this difficult but essential lifelong work.

Notes

* We ask that those who cite this work always acknowledge by name all of the authors listed rather than either only citing the first author or using "et al." to indicate co-authors. All collaborated on the conceptualization, development, and writing of this chapter.
1 We use the terms "participants"/"students" and "faculty"/"instructors"/"facilitators" interchangeably because our work is used in a variety of contexts.

References

Amos, Y. T. (2014). To lose is to win: The effects of student evaluations in a multicultural education class on a Japanese faculty with a non-native English Accent. *Understanding and Dismantling Privilege, 4*(2). Retrieved from http://www.wpcjournal.com/article/view/12220

Banaji, M., & Greenwald, A. (2013). *Blind spot: The hidden biases of good people*. New York: Random House Publishing.

Brookfield, S. (2012). *Teaching for critical thinking: Tools and techniques to help students question their assumptions*. San Francisco: Jossey-Bass.

Chugh, D. (2018). *The person you mean to be: How good people fight bias*. New York, NY: Harper Collins.

Collins, P. (2008). *Black feminist thought: Knowledge, consciousness and the politics of empowerment*. New York: Routledge.

Collins, K. H., Price, E. F., Hanson, L., & Neaves, D. (2020). Consequences of stereotype threat and imposter syndrome: The personal journey from STEM-practitioner to STEM-educator for four women of color. *Taboo, 19*(4), 161–180. Retrieved from http://ezproxy.cul.columbia.edu/login?url=https://www-proquest-com.ezproxy.cul.columbia.edu/scholarly-journals/consequences-stereotype-threat-imposter-syndrome/docview/2456177611/se-2?accountid=10226

Crenshaw, K. (1989). Demarginalizing the intersection of race and sex: A black feminist critique of antidiscrimination doctrine, feminist theory and antiracist politics. In *University of Chicago Legal Forum 1989: Feminisms in the law, theory and practice* (pp. 139–167). Chicago: University of Chicago Legal Forum.

Crenshaw, K. (1993). Mapping the margins: Intersectionality, identity politics, and violence against women of color. *Stanford Law Review, 43*(6), 1241–1279.

DiAngelo, R., & Flynn, D. (2010, August). Showing what we tell: Facilitating anti-racism education in cross-race teams. *Understanding and Dismantling Privilege, 1*(1).

DiAngelo, R., & Sensoy, O. (2014, Winter). Leaning in: A student's guide to engaging constructively with social justice content. *Radical Pedagogy, 11* (1). Retrieved from http://www.radicalpedagogy. org/radicalpedagogy.org/Leaning_In__A_Students_Guide_To_Engaging_Constructively_With_Social_Justice_Content.html

DuPraw, M., & Axner, P. (1997). *Working on common cross-cultural communication challenges.* Retrieved from http://www.pbs.org/ampu/crosscult.html

Eberhardt, J. (2019). *Biased: Uncovering the Hidden Prejudice that Shapes What We See, Think and Do.* New York: Viking.

Edwards, C. W. (2019). Overcoming imposter syndrome and stereotype threat: Reconceptualizing the definition of a scholar. *Taboo, 18*(1), 18–34. Retrieved from http://ezproxy.cul.colum bia.edu/login?url=https://www-proquest-com.ezproxy.cul.columbia.edu/scholarly-journals/overcoming-imposter-syndrome-stereotype-threat/docview/2307370579/se-2?accountid=10226

Ferrari, C. (2020). You need to leave now ma'am. *Chronicle of Higher Education.* Retrieved from https://www.chronicle.com/article/you-need-to-leave-now-maam

Gutierrez y Muhs, G., Niemann, Y. F., Gonzalez, C. G., & Harris, A. P. (Eds.). (2012). *Presumed incompetent: The intersections of race and class for women in academia.* Boulder, CO: University Press of Colorado and Utah State University Press.

Hardiman, R., & Jackson, B. (1992). *Racial identity development: Understanding racial dynamics in college classrooms and on campus. New Directions for Teaching and Learning* (no. 52, pp. 21–37). San Francisco, CA: Jossey-Bass.

Helms, J. E. (2020). *A race is a nice thing to have: A guide to being a white person or understanding the white persons in your life* (3rd ed.). San Diego, CA: Cognella Academic Publishing.

hooks, bell (1994). *Teaching to transgress: Education as the practice of freedom.* New York: Routledge.

Huber, L. P., & Solórzano, D. G. (2015). Racial microaggressions as a tool for critical race research. *Race, Ethnicity and Education, 18*(3), 297–320.

Jean-Marie, G., Grant, C. M., & Irby, B. (2014). *The duality of women scholars of color: Transforming and being transformed in the academy.* Charlotte, NC: Information Age Publishing.

Kaplowitz, D., Griffin, S., & Seyka, S. (2019). *Race Dialogues: A Facilitator's Guide to Tackling the Elephant in the Classroom.* New York: Teachers College Press. (ch. 7 co-facilitation.)

Joseph, V., & Williams, T. O. (2008). "Good niggers": The struggle to find courage, strength, and confidence to fight internalized racism and internalized dominance. *Democracy and Education, 17*(2), 67–73.

Lazos, S. R. (2012). Are student teaching evaluations holding back women and minorities? The perils of "doing" gender and race in the classroom. In G. Gutierrez y Muhs, Y. F. Niemann, C. G. Gonzalez, & A. P. Harris (Eds.), *Presumed incompetent: The intersections of race and class for women in academia* (pp. 164–185). Boulder, CO: University Press of Colorado, Utah State University Press.

Maher, F. A., & Tetreault, M. K. (2001). *The feminist classroom: Dynamics of gender, race and privilege.* Lanham, MD: Rowman and Littlefield.

Maxwell, K. E., Nagda, B., & Thompson, M. C. (2011). *Facilitating intergroup dialogues: Bridging differences, catalyzing change.* Sterling, VA: Stylus Publishing.

Menakem, R. (2017). *My Grandmother's Hands: Racialized trauma and the pathway to mending our hearts and bodies.* San Francisco: Central Recovery Press.

Messner, M. A. (2000). White guy habitus in the classroom: Challenging the reproduction of privilege. *Men and Masculinities, 2*(4), 457–469.

Morgan, D. [@mosdaf]. (2020, August 22). SANTA CLARA UNIVERSITY SECURITY. [Tweet]. Twitter. Retrieved from https://twitter.com/mos_daf/status/1297231369353834496

Muradoglu, M., Horne, Z., Hammond, M. D., Leslie, S.-J., & Cimpian, A. (2021). Women—particularly underrepresented minority women—and early-career academics feel like impostors in fields that value brilliance. *Journal of Educational Psychology.* Advance online publication. doi:10.1037/edu0000669

Niemann, Y. F. (2012). The making of a token: A case study of stereotype threat, stigma, racism, and tokenism in academe. In G. Gutierrez y Muhs, Y. F. Niemann, C. G. Gonzalez, & A. P. Harris (Eds.), *Presumed incompetent: The intersections of race and class for women in academia* (pp. 336–355). Boulder, CO: University Press of Colorado and Utah State University Press.

Niemann, Y. F., Gutierrez y Muhs, G., & González, C. G. (2020). *Presumed Incompetent II: Race, class, power, and resistance of women in academia.* Louisville, CO: University Press of Colorado and Utah State University Press.

Obear, K. (2013). Navigating triggering events: Critical competencies for social justice educators. In L. M. Landreman (Ed.), *The art of effective facilitation: Reflections from social justice educators.* Sterling, VA: Stylus Publishing.

Obear, K. (2016). *Turning the tide.* Difference Press.

Ouellett, M. L., & Fraser, E. C. (2005). Teaching together: Interracial teams. In M. L. Ouellett (Ed.), *Teaching inclusively: Resources for course, department and institutional change in higher education.* Stillwater, OK: New Forums Press.

Parkman, A. (2016). The imposter phenomenon in higher education: Incidence and impact. *Journal of Higher Education Theory and Practice, 16*(1), 51–60.

Pittman, C. T. (2010). Race and gender oppression in the classroom: The experiences of women faculty of color with white male students. *Teaching Sociology, 38*(3), 183–196.

Solórzano, D., Ceja, M., & Yosso, T. (2000). Critical race theory, racial microaggressions, and campus racial climate: The experiences of African American college students. *The Journal of Negro Education, 69,* 60–73.

Sue, D. W., & Spanierman, L. (2020). *Microaggressions in everyday life* (2nd ed.). Hoboken, NJ: John Wiley & Sons.

Sue, D. W., & Sue, D. (2013). *Counseling the culturally diverse* (6th ed.). Hoboken, NJ: John Wiley & Sons.

Sue, D. W., Sue, D., Neville, H., & Smith, L. (2019). *Counseling the Culturally Diverse: Theory and Practice.* Hoboken, NJ: John Wiley & Sons.

Tappan, M. B. (2006). Reframing internalized oppression and internalized domination: From the psychological to the sociocultural. *Teachers College Record, 108*(10), 2115–2144.

Torino, G., Rivera, D., Capodilupo, C., Nadal, K., & Sue, D. W. (2019). *Microaggression Theory: Influence and Implications.* Hoboken, NJ: John Wiley & Sons, Inc.

Tuitt, F., Hanna, M., Martinez, L. M., Salazar, M., & Griffin, R. (2009). Teaching in the line of fire: Faculty of color in the academy. *The NEA Higher Education Journal: Thought & Action, 25,* 65–74. Retrieved from http://www.nea.org/assets/docs/HE/TA09LineofFire.pdf

Tusmith, B., & Reddy, M. T. (2002). *Race in the college classroom: Pedagogy and politics.* Rutgers, NJ: Rutgers University Press.

Zúñiga, X., Nagda, B. A., Chesler, M., & Cytron-Walker, A. (2007). *Intergroup dialogues in higher education: Meaningful learning about social justice.* ASHE-ERIC Report Series. San Francisco: Jossey-Bass.

Contributors

Maurianne Adams was one of the pioneers in social justice education at UMass Amherst. Arriving at the university in 1973 as Coordinator of Academic Affairs for Project 10, the experimental residential education program in the Southwest Residential Area, she developed an elective curriculum focused on racism, sexism, heterosexism, classism, and ableism. When that project was ended in 1982, she took her ideas to the School of Education, where she became the Director for Social Issues and Instructional Development for Residential Academic Programs (RAP). Over the next several years, she and her colleagues developed one of the first general education diversity courses, and she became part of the founding faculty for the graduate program in Social Justice Education. Since her retirement in 2015, she has remained active in promoting social justice activities, working with the Coalition of Amherst Neighborhoods (CAN) and the Amherst Community Land Trust, which provides opportunities for affordable homeownership.

Lee Anne Bell is Professor Emerita, Barnard College, Columbia University. Her innovative Storytelling Project, created in collaboration with artists and educators, provides a model for designing anti-racist and social justice curriculum. This model is described in her book *Storytelling for Social Justice: Connecting Narrative and the Arts in Anti-racist Teaching* (Routledge, 2020). See interview about the project at https://organizingengagement.org/interview/lee-anne-bell/. Bell's documentary, *40 Years Later: Now Can We Talk?*, telling the stories of the first class of African Americans to desegregate the white high school in their Mississippi Delta town in the years 1967–1969, received the 2013 Media Award from the National Association for Multicultural Education and the 2014 Charles and Margaret Witten Award for Distinguished Documentary Film in Education.

Rachel R. Briggs, Ph.D., is a learning and development expert with experience in a wide range of contexts with over 20 years of experience addressing issues of social justice and equity. She is a multimedia artist who creates equity and inclusion-focused videos and webinars. Rachel has seven years of experience on the editorial staff of *Equity & Excellence in Education* (EEE), an SJE-focused, peer-reviewed education journal, and was co-editor with Maurianne Adams of the special-themed issue of *EEE*: Engaging Praxis in Social Justice Education: Continuity and Change in Social Justice Education Theory/Pedagogy/Research.

Mirangela Buggs, Ed.D., has been a leader for diversity, equity, inclusion, and social justice education in nationally and internationally known K–12 independent college prep schools for nearly 14 years. Her diversity, equity, and inclusion (DEI) leadership in schools involves her in faculty-staff professional development, student leadership for diversity and social justice, curriculum development and instructional support, policy, program and school culture, recruitment and hiring, and work with parents and Boards of Trustees. Mirangela also sometimes works as an adjunct professor and as a consultant providing introductory, intermediate, and advanced training with schools and organizations. When inspired, she writes. In addition to her collaborative work on the chapter in this volume, Mirangela has published pieces in *Independent School* and *Chronicles of Quaker Education* and is the co-author with Agustín Lao-Montes of "The Translocal Space of Afro-Latinidad: Critical Feminist Visions for Diasporic Bridge-Building" in *Translocalities/Translocalidades: Feminist Politics of Translation in Latin/a Americas* (Duke University Press, 2014).

D. Chase J. Catalano is an assistant professor of Higher Education at Virginia Tech. He served as an assistant professor for four years at Western Illinois University in the College Student Personnel Program. Chase's career in higher education began in student affairs and spanned numerous functional areas, with his most recent role as Director of the LGBT Resources Center at Syracuse University. As a trans scholar, his research and scholarship address topics of trans(*)ness, social justice, queerness, and masculinities within the context of higher education. He is a co-editor of *Readings for Diversity and Social Justice*, 4th ed. (Routledge, 2018). Beyond his various book chapters, he published articles in *Equity & Excellence in Education*, *Transgender Studies Quarterly* (TSQ), and *Journal for Diversity in Higher Education*. He co-edited *Advising & Supporting in Student Affairs* (Charles C. Thomas Publisher, 2021) with Rachel Wagner.

Keri "Safire" DeJong, Ed.D., is Social Justice and Equity Specialist at the Collaborative for Education Services. Safire provides social justice-focused consulting and professional development for PK–12 schools with an array of talented and experienced co-facilitators. She works with an amazing team of colleagues to support public school leaders, educators, caregivers, and students to think proactively and act strategically toward building resilient, joyful, and liberatory school communities that keep young people's experience, interest, and voice at the center of education. Safire holds a doctorate in Social Justice Education from UMass Amherst (2014), where her research focused on legacies of colonialism within constructions of childhood and young people's experiences with status and power.

Michael S. Funk, Ph.D., is Clinical Associate Professor for the Steinhardt School of Culture, Education, and Human Development and Director of the Higher Education and Student Affairs program at New York University. In addition to working as a faculty member, he has two decades worth of experience working in higher education within various capacities, including Academic Affairs, Student Affairs, Academic Advising Services, and Residence Life. Michael's scholarship primarily focuses on issues of equity, diversity, and how to operationalize social justice frames works within the classroom setting and co-curricular across student affairs.

Diane J. Goodman, Ed.D., has been addressing issues of diversity, inclusion, equity, and social justice for over three decades. As a trainer, facilitator, consultant, and coach, she has worked with range of organizations, community groups, schools, and universities. Diane has been a professor at several universities in the areas of education, psychology, social work, and women's studies. She regularly presents at national and international conferences and is the author of *Promoting Diversity and Social Justice: Educating People from Privileged Groups*, 2nd ed. and co-editor and contributor to *Teaching for Diversity and Social Justice*, 3rd and 4th ed. and other publications. Her website is http://www.dianegood man.com.

Marcella Runell Hall is Vice President for Student Life and Dean of Students and Lecturer in Religion at Mount Holyoke College. Hall has authored numerous books, articles, and curriculum on topics of popular culture, friendship, race, spirituality, and critical pedagogy. Hall was a founding co-director for the Of Many Institute for Multifaith Leadership at New York University and served as an education fellow at the Tanenbaum Center for Interreligious Understanding. Hall was also recognized with a NASPA award for the design of the NYU Faith Zone training and curriculum. Hall also holds a Doctorate in Education from the University of Massachusetts Amherst, a Master of Arts in higher education administration from New York University, and a Bachelor's Degree in Social Work from Ramapo College of New Jersey.

Larissa E. Hopkins is an experienced Student Affairs professional with 18+ years supporting student success and strategically developing inclusive, holistic departments and programs. Larissa has served in various Assistant Director/Director and Assistant Dean/Associate Dean roles with an emphasis on student advising, accessibility, first-generation student support, and student health and well-being. Larissa received her B.A. from Hamilton College and her M.Ed. and Ed.D. in Social Justice Education from the University of Massachusetts Amherst.

Abdul-Rahman Jaradat earned his Ph.D. in Social Justice Education at the University of Massachusetts Amherst. His dissertation focused on factors that shape Arab American college student identity. Abed's research and presentations have been on topics related to Arab and Muslim American college students, as well as international and study-abroad students. He has been a presenter on these topics as well as an active member of ACPA since 1998 and has been a Residential Life Educator at UMass for many years.

Valerie D. Jiggetts believes in the power of people. She is a social justice educational practitioner and effective people experience professional. With a passion for supporting young adults and early career professionals, Valerie utilizes human-centered approaches to create conditions for individuals to thrive and achieve their goals. Valerie utilizes empathy and data to build equitable and inclusive environments.

Barbara J. Love, Professor of Education Emerita, Social Justice Education Concentration, College of Education at UMass Amherst, is a speaker, consultant, coach, and writer on Justice, Equity, Diversity, and Inclusion issues related to liberation and individual and societal transformation. Her research and publications appear in a variety of journals and anthologies and focus on personal, organizational, and societal transformation and strategies for liberation. She has authored and co-authored chapters on knowing ourselves as instructors, racism, youth and elder oppression and liberation, developing liberatory consciousness, and self-awareness for liberation workers.

Love is recognized globally for her work with a broad range of organizations, including business and industry, government, civic, and education. Her recent focus includes work with climate change organizations addressing issues of social justice in the climate movement, working to build the broad-based coalitions needed to effectively address climate change. She facilitated conversations between environmental justice advocates and national environmental organizations to create the Equitable and Just National Climate Platform. She is a member of the Advisory Board for Citizens Climate Lobby.

Hind Mari came to the University of Massachusetts Amherst upon receiving a Fulbright for her master's studies, where she also earned her doctorate in Education with a focus on gender equity. Working with college students at the Women of Color Leadership Network at the Center for Women and Community–UMass affords Hind the ability to work daily on multiple social justice and equity issues while centering race and gender. Previously, Hind worked with international students and scholars and taught refugee students at UN schools. A transcript of an interview by NEPR (now NEPM) appears in *Words in Transit: Stories of Immigrants*, 2016 (https://www.umasspress.com/9781625342195/words-in-transit/).

Hillary Montague-Asp is a white, upper-class, queer, fat, cisgender femme with a chronic illness (Multiple Sclerosis) that is sometimes disabling. She is a doctoral candidate in Social Justice Education at UMass Amherst, where she has taught courses on social justice and the U.S. education system, ableism and disability justice, and intergroup dialogue. Hillary has worked at the UMass Stonewall Center for the past ten years, supporting and advocating for/with queer and trans students. She also works with UMass' Center of Racial Justice and Youth Engaged Research as a member of the white Co-Conspirator team. Outside of UMass, Hillary works with educators to best support LGBTQ+ students in K–12 schools and does racial justice work with LGBTQ+ middle and high school students. Hillary's dissertation research focuses on the possibilities that exist for higher education if student affairs graduate programs use radical approaches, social justice-based skills, and critical theory to educate soon-to-be student affairs practitioners.

Matt L. Ouellett is the founding executive director of Cornell University's Center for Teaching Innovation. Matt offers well-received courses on social justice, higher education, and the implications of race and racism for social work practice, most recently co-teaching Teaching and Learning in the Diverse Classroom as a MOOC on edX. Matt has regularly been the recipient of internal and external research support, acting as primary or co-primary investigator on three National Science Foundation–funded grants. He is a regular contributor to the literature, most recently with Christine Stanley (*Friendship in Educational Development: Reflections on Intersectional Identities and Inclusive Professional Practices*). Matt was honored with the Robert Pierleoni Spirit of POD Award for outstanding lifetime achievement and leadership in the enhancement of teaching, learning, and faculty development in 2012.

Romina Pacheco, Ph.D., is Director of Diversity, Equity, Inclusion, and Belonging at The Windward School. During her undergraduate college years in her home country of Venezuela, Romina became a teacher of English as a Foreign Language and developed a passion for teaching. It was during this time that Romina became conscious of the importance for educators to contribute to the transformation of our society to be more equitable and inclusive. She has extensive experience supporting institutions in their equity journey, both in K–12 and postsecondary education. When she is not envisioning schools as joyful spaces for everyone, you can find her learning about the latest trends from Asha, her 13-year-old child, or playing with Pierre Aristides, her 4-year-old son.

Leah Lakshmi Piepzna-Samarasinha is a nonbinary femme disabled writer and disability and transformative justice movement worker of Burgher and Tamil Sri Lankan, Irish, and Galician descent. They are the author or co-editor of nine books, including (with Ejeris Dixon) *Beyond Survival: Strategies and Stories from the Transformative Justice Movement, Tonguebreaker, Care Work: Dreaming Disability Justice*, and *Bodymap*. A Lambda Award winner who has been shortlisted for the Publishing Triangle five times, they are the 2020 Jean Cordova Award winner "honoring a lifetime of work documenting the complexities of queer experience" and are a 2020 Disability Futures Fellow. Since 2009, they have been a lead performer with disability justice performance collective Sins Invalid. They co-founded the performance collectives Mangos With Chili and Performance/Disability/Art (with Syrus Marcus Ware). Raised in rustbelt central Massachusetts and shaped by T'karonto and Oakland, they currently make home in South Seattle, Duwamish territories. Their new book, *The Future Is Disabled: Prophecies, Love Notes and Mourning Songs* is forthcoming October 2022. Their website is http://brownstargirl.org.

Davey Shlasko is the founder and director of Think Again Training & Consulting, a collaborative consulting group that supports organizations and communities to integrate social justice principles into their structures and practices. For over 20 years, Shlasko has been facilitating adult learning to support organizational and systemic change using creative expression, popular education, and practical skills building. In addition to contributing to several editions of *Teaching for Diversity and Social Justice* and *Reading for Diversity and Social Justice*, Shlasko is author of *Trans Allyship Workbook* and teaches as Adjunct Associate Professor in social theory and trans studies at Smith College School for Social Work. More about Shlasko's work can be found at http://www.thinkagaintraining.com.

Lilith Logan Siegel is a disabled and queer judicial law clerk and lawyer. She received her B.A. in Government from Smith College and her J.D. from Berkeley Law, where she studied the intersection of disability, race, and educational equity. She is the co-editor of a forthcoming edition of the *Journal of Legal Education* covering disability in law school.

Marjorie Valdivia serves as Action Planning Coordinator and Facilitator at Smith College. She received a B.A. in Women Studies and Social Thought and Political Economy from the University of Massachusetts Amherst and her M.Ed. in Social Justice Education from the University of Massachusetts Amherst. She is currently finishing her doctorate in the field of social justice education.

Rani Varghese, Ph.D., is Associate Professor in the School of Social Work at Adelphi University. She was trained in the fields of Social Justice Education, Social Work and Women, and Gender and Sexuality Studies. Her clinical experience has been in the context of colleges and universities supporting survivors of gender-based violence, and she now brings those skills to supporting organizations around DEI. Her scholarship examines social work education through a social justice framework and an interdisciplinary lens and explores the impact of intergroup dialogue.

Rachel Wagner, Ed.D., is Assistant Professor in Higher Education and Student Affairs in the department of Educational and Organizational Leadership at Clemson University. The goal of her research is to understand how postsecondary environments can support human flourishing. Specifically, her scholarship centers critical and emancipatory perspectives of equity and social justice in higher education through two primary areas of inquiry: (1) gender aware and expansive practice in higher education, and (2) social justice approaches to student affairs practice. She received the Harry Cannon Outstanding Professional Award (2014) and the Outstanding Research Award (2015) from ACPA's Coalition on Men and Masculinities. In 2020 ACPA named her an Emerging Scholar Designee. She lives, works, plays, and prays on the ancestral homelands of the Eastern Band of Cherokee and the Cherokee Nation, which were seized through diplomatic and military incursions by the United States.

Ximena Zúñiga, Ph.D., Professor, Department of Student Development—Social Justice Education concentration—University of Massachusetts Amherst, is a national leader in social justice education and critical approaches to dialogue across differences in higher education. She is co-editor of *Multicultural Teaching in the University* (Praeger, 1993) and *Readings for Diversity and Social Justice* (Routledge, 2001; 2010; 2013; 2018) and co-author of *Intergroup Dialogue in Higher Education: Meaningful Learning about Social Justice* (2007), *Dialogues across Differences* (Russell Sage, 2013), and *Engaging Identity, Difference and Social Justice* (Routledge, 2014). She teaches theory and practice courses in social justice education for graduate students and a multi-section interracial/ethnic dialogue undergraduate course: http://people.umass.edu/educ202-xzuniga/index.html. Her research and teaching centers on social justice education praxis, particularly in graduate training and in higher education. She co-led the Five College Faculty and Staff Intergroup Dialogue initiative and the Transformative Racial Justice Initiative at UMass Amherst. She consults regularly with colleges and universities interested in fostering inclusive pedagogies and intergroup dialogue practices in college campuses.

Index

Note: Page numbers in *italics* indicate a figure on the corresponding page.